ADO

Programmer's Reference

Dave Sussman

ADO Programmer's Reference

ISBN: 1-59059-342-1

Printed and bound in the United States of America 12345678910

Technical Reviewers: Clive Browning, Robert Chang, James Conard, Mark Horner, Ron Landers, Kenneth Lo, Carl Prothman, Simon Robinson, John Timney, Khin Walker, Warren Wiltsie, Adrian Young

Editorial Board: Steve Anglin, Dan Appleman, Gary Cornell, James Cox, Tony Davis, John Franklin, Chris Mills, Steven Rycroft, Dominic Shakeshaft, Julian Skinner, Martin Streicher, Jim Sumser, Karen Watterson, Gavin Wray, John Zukowski

Assistant Publisher: Grace Wong

Project Manager: Sofia Marchant

Copy Editor: Scott Carter

Production Manager: Kari Brooks

Production Editor: Kelly Winquist

Proofreader: Greg Teague

Compositor: Dina Quan

Cover Designer: Kurt Krames

Manufacturing Manager: Tom Debolski

Distributed to the book trade in the United States by Springer-Verlag New York, Inc., 175 Fifth Avenue, New York, NY, 10010 and outside the United States by Springer-Verlag GmbH & Co. KG, Tiergartenstr. 17, 69112 Heidelberg, Germany.

In the United States: phone 1-800-SPRINGER, email orders@springer-ny.com, or visit http://www.springer-ny.com. Outside the United States: fax +49 6221 345229, email orders@springer.de, or visit http://www.springer.de.

For information on translations, please contact Apress directly at 2560 Ninth Street, Suite 219, Berkeley, CA 94710. Phone 510-549-5930, fax 510-549-5939, email info@apress.com, or visit http://www.apress.com.

The source code for this book is available to readers at http://www.apress.com in the Downloads section. You will need to answer questions pertaining to this book in order to successfully download the code.

Contents

Contents

Contents

About the Author

Dave Sussman is a developer, trainer and author, living in a quiet country village in Oxfordshire, surrounded by nothing but fields and trees. One day soon he intends to stop working so hard and get some form of social life.

Introduction

This book provides a comprehensive guide to the ways in which ADO can be used in all kinds of applications. It demonstrates the use of ADO both in Web applications written using ASP, and in compiled applications written using Visual Basic and other languages. It also includes a reference section for fast access to detailed lists of the properties, methods, and events available in ADO.

What Is ADO?

If you are new to data-access programming with Microsoft technologies, you may not yet be aware of ADO, although it's hard not to have come across it if you've had anything at all to do with ASP programming. ADO stands for **ActiveX Data Objects** (although it's sometimes–mistakenly–called **Active Data Objects**).

ADO is a set of COM components that provides programmatic access to Microsoft's latest underlying data-access technologies. You can use ADO through almost any programming or scripting language, as long as it can instantiate and use COM components.

ADO is based on an underlying data access technology called **OLE DB** (Object Linking and Embedding Database). This is a defined set of COM interfaces that all data sources can implement through special drivers (or **providers**), thereby exposing their data content in a uniform way. OLE DB relies on a COM Interface (API), which is designed for use with languages like C++. ADO abstracts developers from the complex details of the OLE DB interfaces by providing a simplified set of COM-based components and interfaces that can be called from a far wider range of languages.

In other words, ADO gives us a standard way of managing data from all kinds of data stores, not just relational databases. In Chapter 1, I expand on these concepts to show you just how useful this whole approach is when building data-access applications.

The design of ADO has also been driven by the ever-increasing role and importance of the Internet in application development. ADO provides a range of techniques with which remote data access can be achieved over the Internet by using a Web browser or through custom applications written in a range of programming languages.

What Is This Book About?

This book covers the broad outlines and purpose of ADO as the Microsoft data access technology of the future. It also describes the new features included in ADO version 2.8 (which is only a security update, so it doesn't contain many new features).

It covers advanced ADO topics and acts as a vital reference on syntax and semantics for working with ADO. It describes the ADO Extensions for Data Definition Language and Security (ADOX), and the Jet Replication Objects for dealing with multiple copies of Access databases and replicating the data between them. It also introduces ADO for Multidimensional Data (ADO MD), which allows connection to Online Analytical Processing (OLAP) engines, such as Microsoft's Analysis Services, that ship with SQL Server.

In addition, this book explains how ADO fits into **Windows Distributed interNet Architecture** (DNA)–Microsoft's picture for distributed data-oriented applications–and describes the advantages of ADO over other existing Microsoft data-access technologies.

Finally, this book shows how ADO interfaces with the core OLE DB data-access driver model to provide connectivity with a wide range of data stores. This can include messaging systems, text files, and specific nonstandard data formats, as well as the more usual relational databases. In fact, anything can be considered a data store if an OLE DB Provider exists for it.

Who Is This Book For?

This book is a reference guide for the ADO programmer; it's primarily aimed at demonstrating and explaining the features of ADO and the ways that they can be used. As such, it isn't a beginner's guide–although if you have programmed any data-access applications in the past, you'll be able to use it to get up-to-speed with ADO.

In particular, the book is aimed at application developers who already use Microsoft's data-access methods in their applications, but want to take full advantage of ADO's features. It includes all the information required for reasonably experienced developers to start using ADO within their Web pages and distributed applications. Finally, it is ideal for existing ADO users who need to be quickly up-to-date with version 2.8.

What Does It Cover?

In this book, I've avoided discussion of ASP and data-handling programming in COM components (with the exception of the techniques directly connected with using ADO). As a result, the code examples are concise and are designed to demonstrate ADO techniques rather than to build entire applications. However, I do provide pointers to other information sources to indicate the kind of things that can be achieved.

The book offers users an easy-to-follow tutorial and reference to ADO by splitting the whole topic into neat and intuitive segments. This also makes it easier to find specific information later as you come to use ADO in real-world applications. To help out, a comprehensive quick-reference section is also included. It lists the properties, methods, and events of each object found in ADO, ADOX, RDS, JRO, and ADO MD, together with other useful information.

The segmentation of the book looks like this:

❏   Introduction to ADO and what's new in ADO 2.8

❏   Connecting to data stores with or without the `Connection` object (including a discussion of driver technologies)

❏   The `Command` object and techniques for executing queries against a data store

❏   Using the `Recordset` object to control recordsets and cursors, and how they are used to retrieve data from a data store

❏   A review of the `Record` and `Stream` objects

❏   Collections of objects, including the `Fields` and `Errors` collections

❏   Remote data access, showing how ADO can be used in Web-based and distributed applications

❏   Using ADOX for data definition and security

❏   Using ADOMD for multidimensional representation of data

❏   Using JRO for compaction, replication, and refreshing of data

❏   Data shaping, events, and offline usage

❏   Examination of ADO performance by comparing cursor and locking types

What Do I Need to Use This Book?

ADO has been available for some time, and it is installed with a whole range of other applications and development environments. The shipping of ADO has followed this path:

Version	Released With
1.5	Windows NT 4.0 Option Pack and IE 4.01
2.0	Visual Studio 6.0 Windows NT 4.0 Service Pack 4 (full install) Microsoft Data Access Components 2.0 (MDAC 2.0)
2.1	Office 2000 MDAC 2.1 SQL Server 7

Table continues on the following page

Version	Released With
2.5	Windows 2000 (all versions) MDAC 2.5
2.6	SQL Server 2000 MDAC 2.6
2.7	Windows XP SQL Server Service Pack 3a MSDE Service Pack 3a MDAC 2.7
2.8	Windows Server 2003 MDAC 2.8

In the meantime, if you don't have version 2.8 of ADO, you can download it from the Microsoft Data Access site at http://www.microsoft.com/data/. The Microsoft Data Access Components (MDAC) contains all of the components required for a particular version.

I provide the source code for the samples that you'll see in this book on our Web site, and you can even run some of them directly from there to save you the trouble of installing them on your own machine. You can get the code samples from the Support page of the Apress Web site, at http://support.apress.com/. This site also contains a range of other resources and reference material that you might find useful, including other books that demonstrate ADO applications.

To run the samples yourself and build applications that use ADO, you will require only your usual preferred development tools; check your development tool for its compatibility with ADO. To build Web-based or intranet-based applications that use ASP, this will be just a Web server that supports ASP 3.0, which means Windows 2000. For the remote data access examples in Chapter 9, the browser should be Internet Explorer 4.x or higher.

To build compiled applications that don't use the Internet or your own intranet, but rely on communication over a traditional LAN, you'll need just your own choice of programming language development tool. This will also be required if you want to build custom business components for Internet- or intranet-based applications.

Which Programming Language Do I Use?

Because ADO is COM-based, it is language-neutral; in other words, it can be used in any programming language that supports the instantiation of ActiveX/COM objects. This includes Visual Basic, C++, Delphi, Java, and scripting languages such as JavaScript, JScript, and VBScript—as used in client-side browser and server-side ASP programming.

I've provided some guidance about how to use various languages to access ADO objects in Chapter 1. I then use a Visual Basic–like syntax for each part of the ADO object model. I decided against including samples in each language, because this really breaks up the flow of text. However, I've put together a package of samples that demonstrate ADO usage in a number of languages: Visual Basic, ASP/VBScript, ASP/JScript, and Visual C++. You'll find these samples and supporting documentation on our Web site at http://support.apress.com/.

Conventions

We have used a number of different styles of text and layout in the book to help differentiate between the different kinds of information. Here are examples of the styles we use and an explanation of what they mean:

Bullets appear indented, with each new bullet marked as follows:

❑ **Important Words** are in a bold type font.

❑ Words that appear on the screen in menus like the File or Window menus are in a similar font to the one that you see on screen.

❑ Keys that you press on the keyboard, like *Ctrl* and *Enter*, are in italics.

Code has several fonts. If it's a word that we're talking about in the text, for example, when discussing the For...Next loop, it's in this font. If it's a block of code that you can type in as a program and run, then it's also in a gray box:

```
objRec.Open "authors", objConn, adOpenKeyset, _
        adLockOptimistic, (adCmdTable OR adAsyncFetch)
```

Sometimes you'll see code in a mixture of styles, like this:

```
<OBJECT CLASSID="clsid:BD96C556-65A3-11D0-983A-00C04FC29E33"
        ID="dsoBookList" HEIGHT=0 WIDTH=0>
    <PARAM NAME="Server" VALUE="http://www.yourserver.com">
    <PARAM NAME="Connect" VALUE="SERVER="http://dataserver.com;
        DRIVER={SQL Server};DATABASE=yourdb;UID=anon;PWD=">
    <PARAM NAME="SQL" VALUE="SELECT * FROM BookList">
</OBJECT>
```

The code with a white background is code we've already looked at and that we don't wish to examine further.

Advice, hints, and background information come in an italicized, indented font like this.

> **Important pieces of information come in boxes like this.**

I demonstrate the syntactical usage of methods, properties, and so on by using the following format:

```
Recordset.Find(Criteria, [SkipRecords], [SearchDirection], [Start])
```

Here, the square brackets indicate optional parameters.

Customer Support

I've tried to make this book as accurate and useful as possible, but what really matters is what the book actually does for you. Please let us know your views, either by returning the reply card at the back of the book, or by writing to us at support@apress.com.

The **source code** for this book—including ADO samples in C++, Visual Basic, and scripting languages—is available for download at http://support.apress.com/.

I've made every effort to ensure there are no errors in this book. However, to err is human, and we recognize the need to keep you informed of errors as they're spotted and corrected. **Errata sheets** for all our books are available at http://support.apress.com/. If you find an error that hasn't already been reported, please let us know by mailing support@apress.com and including the ISBN number, page number, and details of the error.

Our Web site acts as a focus for other information and support, including the code from all our books, sample chapters, and previews of forthcoming titles.

1

What Is ADO?

ActiveX Data Objects (ADO) and Object Linking and Embedding Database (OLE DB), its underlying technology, currently play a big part in data access. Microsoft has unequivocally committed its future to it, and rightly so. The paperless office has yet to appear, but the amount of data stored on computer systems increases every day. This is illustrated by the rate at which the Web is expanding—and that's just the public face of data. Much more data is hidden from general view in corporate applications or intranets.

This chapter describes the terms and technology behind ADO. If you need to start coding straight away, you could skip to the relevant chapters, but your understanding will be better if you have a good foundation.

So, to give you that good foundation, there are several important topics I will discuss in this chapter:

- ❑   What I mean by "data"
- ❑   What I mean by a "data store"
- ❑   How ADO fits with existing data access strategies
- ❑   Data access in the client/server world

ADO is central to Microsoft's data access strategy, so it's important to understand why it came about and what sort of a future it has. I'll be looking at these issues too.

What is Data?

If you've got a few spare minutes some time, open Windows Explorer and have a look around your hard drive. Make a mental note of how many separate pieces of information you've got: databases, documents, spreadsheets, e-mail messages, HTML and Active Server Pages (ASP) documents, etc.

Quite a lot, eh? They are all pockets of data, but are stored in different forms. This might seem obvious, but traditionally data has been thought of as being stored only in a database; if you built a business application, the data had to be in a database. Although a large proportion of existing data may be contained in databases, why should the remaining data be excluded from our grasp? In fact, as computers become more powerful, the term "data" is starting to include multimedia items such as music and video, as well as objects and the more typical document-based data.

So, by "data" I mean any piece of information whatever its contents. Whether it's your address book, your monthly expenses spreadsheet, or a pleading letter to the taxman, it's all data.

What Are Data Stores?

Now that I have established what I consider data to be, the definition of a data store might be fairly obvious—it's a place in which data is kept. However, there is much more to data stores than you might think. Instead of looking at your hard disk, let's look at mine to see what I've got installed:

❑ **Databases:** I consider these the traditional store of data—I've got both SQL Server and Access databases, which I use to store everything from accounts and invoicing to sample databases for books.

❑ **Spreadsheets:** Financial data with year-end figures for my tax returns and bills.

❑ **Mail and News:** I use Outlook and Outlook Express to handle my mail and Internet news.

❑ **Documents:** This is the largest portion of data on my machine, containing all my personal letters and documents, and chapters for books (including this one).

❑ **Graphics:** Screen captures and pictures for books.

❑ **Internet:** HTML and ASP pages containing samples and applications.

❑ **Reference Material:** Including MSDN and encyclopedias.

So that's the actual data, but how is it stored? Well, the databases are self-contained, so they are their own data store. The reference material is, by and large, stored in its own format, so that could also be considered a data store. The mail and news hold data on their own as well, so they are data stores. Everything else is stored as files; therefore, the file system itself becomes a data store (OK, the data it stores is in myriad formats, but it's all stored in the same way: folders and documents).

You could even include my CD-ROM drive and tape backup unit. The CD-ROM uses the standard documents and folders format, so this could be considered part of the file system data store, but the tape backup has its own format, so it could be considered a data store too.

Numerous other data stores exist, from mainframe file systems to databases and mail. As an enterprise becomes bigger it also must include user-account databases and other machines attached to the network, such as printers and scanners. Each of these things may not be data stores themselves, but as items of data, they'll be contained in a data store somewhere.

About Universal Data Access

Universal Data Access (UDA) is Microsoft's strategy for dealing with all this data. It's aimed at providing high-performance access to a variety of data stores. Cynics might suspect this to be an attempt to shoehorn another Microsoft technology into the scene, but let's consider the modern business.

To have a successful business, you must be flexible and adapt to change. How do you know when to change? There's no simple rule, but most companies make decisions by asking a few questions: How much can we sell? How much *are* we selling? How much are our competitors selling? What's the profit margin? What does research show about what customers want? Statistical analysis can answer questions like these, but what is the source of the statistics? That's right, data. But you've already seen that data is stored in many different ways, and there is no central way of accessing it all. UDA offers an easy-to-use methodology that allows access to multiple sources of data in a single way. Build in high performance and support for existing data access methods, and you're on your way to something that could make a real difference. It's important to remember that UDA is simply Microsoft's *strategy* for accessing data, not a technology. UDA is physically implemented as a collection of four technologies: ADO, OLE DB, Remote Data Services (RDS), and Open Database Connectivity (ODBC). Collectively, these four technologies are known as the Microsoft Data Access Components (MDAC). This means that you don't have to bundle all your data into a single data store. Here's how it can work.

When building an application, you can make sure it uses ADO for its data access, and ADO will talk to all the data sources required. This means that programming is easier, because you need learn only one programming syntax, as shown in the following illustration. Because ADO provides fast, transparent access to different types of data, there's no reason to use any other method.

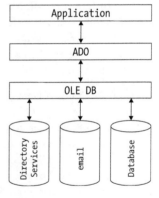

You can clearly see what Microsoft intends when you look at the three main design goals for the Data Access Components:

❑   Meeting the key customer requirements, such as performance, reliability, and broad industry support

❑   Giving access to the widest range of data sources through a common interface

❑   Providing an easy migration path for existing data access technologies

So far they seem to be meeting these objectives admirably.

This method contrasts with Oracle, which is pushing Universal Server, in which all data will be stored under one central (proprietary) data store. The ultimate aim is the same: broader access to data. The Oracle approach involves a bigger initial investment in data conversion and translation as the data is imported to the store. But once that investment has been made, the data will be easy to access. Of course, ADO can access Oracle databases.

In terms of superiority, it's difficult to choose between the two methods; the best method for you will depend upon your business needs and current computer systems. Bear in mind though, these points:

❑   With UDA you can write code today to access most major data stores and develop your own OLE DB Provider to access those data stores that don't already provide support for UDA technologies.

❑   Data conversion is very costly and error prone. Additionally, it rarely results in a fully integrated solution–something much needed for the businesses of today to become the e-businesses of tomorrow.

❑   New data types and data stores are emerging all the time. Instead of waiting on Oracle or other vendors to write data migration tools, you can write data access code to retrieve and manipulate the data in its native data store and in its native format.

Existing Technologies

Before I explain why ADO came about, I'll quickly describe some existing technologies and show you how they fit into the picture.

❑   **DB-Library (DBLib):** This is the underlying technology for connecting to SQL Server. It is primarily designed for C, but is often used in Visual Basic. Because it is specific to SQL Server, it is extremely fast and functional. For this very reason, however, it doesn't allow access to any other source of data. Other databases, such as Oracle and Sybase, have similar native communication libraries.

❑   **ODBC:** Open Database Connectivity (ODBC) was the first step on the road to a universal data access strategy. ODBC was designed (by Microsoft and other database management system [DBMS] vendors) as a cross-platform, database-independent method for accessing data in any relational database through the use of an Application Program Interface (API), known as the ODBC API. Although ODBC was designed for multidatabase use, it is often used only on single relational databases. From a programmer's point of view, ODBC, like DBLib, is also complex to use because it was a low-level library. ODBC is also restricted to data sources that support SQL, and is therefore not suitable for non-SQL based data stores, although ODBC Drivers exist that allow access to text files.

❑   **DAO:** The Data Access Objects (DAO), introduced with Microsoft Access, provided a strictly hierarchical set of objects for manipulating data in Jet and other Indexed Sequential Access Method (ISAM) and SQL databases. These objects were first available with Visual Basic 3.0 and quickly became the most commonly used data access method for early Visual Basic programs. DAO also had the advantage of being able to sit on top of ODBC, which allowed it to communicate with many different databases.

❑   **RDO:** Aimed as the successor to DAO for Visual Basic programmers, Remote Data Objects (RDO) is a thin layer that sits atop ODBC to allow better access to server databases, such as SQL Server. This brought the flexibility of ODBC with a much easier programming model than DBLib or the ODBC API, but like DAO it has a strictly hierarchical programming model.

RDO also brought the world of remote database servers to the world of many programmers. RDO and ODBC share the same relationship as ADO and OLE DB: a thin layer on top of an underlying data access mechanism.

❑ **ODBCDirect:** An extension to DAO, ODBCDirect combined portions of DAO and RDO. It allows programmers to use the DAO programming model and also allows access to ODBC data sources without having the Jet database engine loaded.

❑ **JDBC:** Java Database Connectivity (JDBC) was designed as another DBMS-neutral API especially for use in Java applications.

The problems with these technologies are very simple. DBLib and ODBC are low-level APIs and therefore, for many programmers, are complex to use. DAO and RDO offer the user another interface to ODBC, but this introduces another layer of code to go through, which can decrease performance. Moreover, all these technologies suffer from a very strict and hierarchical model, which adds extra overhead to programming and execution.

They are also more or less constrained to providing access to relational databases, although Microsoft Excel and simple text documents could also be used as data sources when using ODBC. ODBC drivers have also been produced for object-oriented and hierarchical databases to expose the data in a relational form with rows and columns.

What Is OLE DB?

OLE DB is designed to be the successor to ODBC. You might be asking, why do we need a successor? Well, there are three main trends at the moment. The first, fairly obviously, is the Internet. The second is the increasing amount of data being stored in a nonrelational form, such as Exchange Server and file systems. The third is Microsoft's desire for a world in which all object usage is handled through their Component Object Model (COM). In fact, OLE DB encourages the use of componentization, allowing database functionality and data handling to be encapsulated into components.

Because of its distributed nature, the Internet brings a different aspect to standard data access. Applications are now being written on a truly global scale, and you can no longer guarantee that the data you access is stored on your local network. This means that you need to consider carefully the *way* you access data and the *type* of data you access. The new business opportunity of e-commerce has meant that selling becomes a whole new ball game—you can now have an application that shows pictures of your products, plays music, and even videos, all running over the Web. The Web is also more distributed (and often less reliable) than conventional networks, so your data access method must take this into account. You can't, for example, assume that your client and server remain connected at all times during an application; in the stateless nature of the Web, this doesn't make sense.

OLE DB is a technology designed to solve some of these problems, and over time it will gradually replace ODBC as the central data access method. OLE DB is the guts of the new data access strategy, but because it allows access to existing ODBC Data Sources, OLE DB provides an easy migration path.

Why ADO?

OLE DB is a COM-based set of object-oriented interfaces, so it is too complex for a large portion of the programming community to use, or it is not suitable because they use programming languages that don't have access to custom COM interfaces. For example, accessing OLE DB directly requires C++ because of the OLE DB interface's complexity. ADO is the higher-level model that most people will use, because it allows access from dual-interface COM components that can be accessed from Visual Basic and scripting languages. It equates fairly well to the DAO level, where you create an object and call its methods and properties. As a COM component, it can be used from any language that supports COM, such as Visual Basic, VBA, scripting languages, and Visual C++.

So now my diagram looks even more enticing:

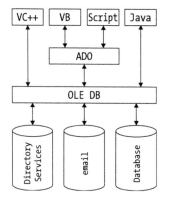

Various languages all have the ability to use a central data access strategy. Some languages (like Java and Visual C++) can talk directly to OLE DB in addition to talking to the easier ADO–although we'll be looking at only the ADO layer here.

ADO also improves speed and ease of development by providing an **object model** that allows data to be retrieved from a data source with as little as one line of code.

ADO addresses another pressing need that has been created by the increasing use of the Web as an application medium. Conventional applications are generally connected to their data store via a Local Area Network (LAN). They can open a connection to the data and keep that connection open throughout the life of the program. Consequently, the data store knows who is connecting. Many applications also process data on the client–perhaps a set of records that the user is browsing through or updating. Because the client is connected to the server–the data source–there's no trouble updating the data.

On the Web, however, the underlying HTTP protocol is stateless. No permanent connection between client and server exists If you think about the way the Web works, you'll realize why this is a problem:

1. You request a Web page in your browser.

2. The Web server receives the request, runs any server-side script, then sends the page back to you, and the connection is closed.

That's it. As soon as this is over, the Web server forgets about you. Admittedly, with ASP you can store some sort of session state, but it's not very sophisticated. How then, with this disconnected network, do you provide a system that allows data to be updated on the client and sent back to the server? This is where ADO comes in, with *disconnected recordsets*. This technology allows the recordset to be disassociated from the server and reassociated at a later date. Additionally, you can update, insert, and delete records on the disconnected recordsets locally, and update the central set of records (the server) at a later date. In fact, disconnected recordsets don't have to be associated with a database at all–they can be manually created and used as a data store in much the same way as collections are. Manually created recordsets, however, cannot be used to update data stores.

The use of client-side data manipulation also allows you to sort data, find records, and generally manage recordsets without resorting to additional trips to the server. Although this idea primarily fits with the nature of Web applications, it can work just as well for the standard type of applications running on a LAN, and can reduce network traffic.

ADO and ADO.NET

Because Microsoft is pushing its .NET technology very heavily, you might wonder what role ADO has to play in the future. The answer is: a big role. A huge amount has been invested in existing technologies (i.e., those that aren't .NET). This means that ADO is still important. So if you're developing applications that use ADO, don't worry that it will suddenly disappear; Microsoft is committed to supporting it for a very long time.

Data Providers and Data Consumers

OLE DB introduces two new terms that help to explain how OLE DB and ADO fit together:

❑ A **Data Consumer** is something that uses (or consumes) data. Strictly speaking, ADO is actually a consumer, because it uses data provided by OLE DB.

❑ A **Data Provider** is something that provides data. This isn't the physical source of the data, but the mechanism that connects you to the physical data store. The provider may get the data directly from the data store, or it may go through another layer (such as ODBC) to get to the data store.

The initial set of OLE DB providers supplied with MDAC 2.8 consists of:

❑ **Directory Services,** for stored resource data, such as Active Directory. With Windows 2000, the Directory Service allows access to user information and network devices.

❑ **Index Server,** for Microsoft Index Server. This will be particularly useful as Web sites grow, because indexed data will be available.

❑ **Site Server Search,** for Microsoft Site Server. Again for use with Web sites, especially large, complex sites, where Site Server is used to maintain them.

- ❑ **Oracle**, for Oracle databases. Connecting to Oracle has never been particularly easy with Microsoft products, but a native driver will simplify access to existing Oracle data stores.

- ❑ **SQL Server**, for Microsoft SQL Server, allows access to data stored in SQL Server.

- ❑ **Data Shape**, for hierarchical recordsets. This allows creation of master/detail type recordsets, which allow drilling down into detailed data.

- ❑ **Persisted Recordset**, for locally saved recordsets and recordset marshaling.

- ❑ **OLAP**, for accessing Online Analytical Processing data stores.

- ❑ **Internet Publishing**, for accessing Web resources that support Microsoft FrontPage Server Extensions or Distributed Authoring and Versioning (DAV).

- ❑ **Remoting Provider**, for connecting to data providers on remote machines.

This is just the standard providers supplied by Microsoft; other vendors have created their own. For example, a company called ISG provides an OLE DB provider that allows connections to multiple data stores at the same time. Oracle provides an OLE DB provider, which it claims is better than Microsoft's Oracle provider, and most other database suppliers have OLE DB providers for their databases.

OLE DB also provides a few other services, such as a query processor and a cursor engine, so these can be used at the client. There are two reasons for this. First, it frees the actual provider from providing the service, so the service can be smaller and faster. Second, it makes it available as a client service. This means that cursor handling can be provided locally, which is an important function of disconnected recordsets and Remote Data Services. Another advantage of the Cursor Service is that, as a client-based service, it can provide a more uniform set of features across all providers. Also, the persistence provider (MSPersist)–introduced in ADO 2.5–has the ability to persist a recordset to a stream.

> Note that Jet and ODBC desktop drivers are not included in ADO versions 2.6 and above. For more details on this, please visit http://support.microsoft.com/ and search for Knowledgebase article number 271908. For the ODBC examples in this book, you must install ADO 2.5 before installing a later version.

Providers and Drivers

It's important to understand how OLE DB Providers relate to ODBC Drivers, especially because an OLE DB Provider exists for ODBC, which seems somehow confusing. Take a look at this diagram, which shows the difference between providers and drivers:

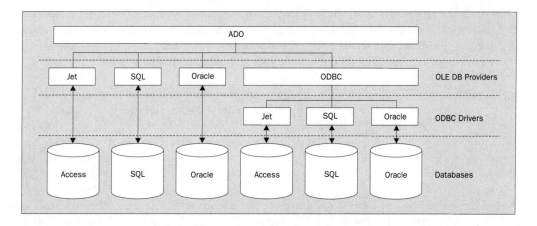

This distinctly shows the two layers. You can use OLE DB Providers to access data sources, including ODBC data sources. This allows OLE DB to access data for which there is an ODBC Driver, but no native OLE DB Provider (such as DAV or Directory Services). Note that the ODBC provider is deprecated, and although it will still work and is still supported, it may not be in the future. For example, no new changes will be made to the OLE DB Provider for ODBC, it is not supported from ADO.NET, and it will not be supported on 64-bit operating systems.

> The essential distinction is that Providers are for OLE DB and Drivers are for ODBC.

Windows Distributed interNet Application Architecture (Windows DNA)

DNA is the strategy that Microsoft is defining as the ideal way to write distributed, n-tier, client/server applications. One of the interesting things about this strategy is that it's really just a set of ideas and suggestions, rather than a complex, locked-in solution. It's not a new idea, but some really good tools now make creating this type of application relatively easy.

The basic premise is to partition your application into at least **three tiers, illustrated in this diagram**:

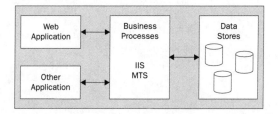

The first tier is the **user interface tier**–this is what the user sees, and could be a Web page or another type of application written in any language. The second tier is where the **business rules** or processes lie; these determine where the data comes from, what rules apply to the data, and how it should be returned to the user interface. The third tier is the **data layer**–the actual data source.

The great thing about DNA is that it aims to be language-independent; it all hinges around COM (COM+ in Windows 2000 and later). COM allows easy object creation and re-use. Any component that supports COM will fit into this picture, so you can write your application in ASP and JavaScript, Visual Basic, Visual C++, Delphi, or any language that supports COM. Likewise, your business components can be in any language, so you can program in your preferred environment; there's no need to learn a new language.

In the preceding diagram, you can see that Internet Information Server (IIS) and Microsoft Transaction Server (MTS) are mentioned in the Business Processes tier. IIS supplies the connection from Web applications to components, which could be MTS components or standalone components (that is, components not managed by MTS). The great advantage of MTS is that it makes your middle tier very easy to manage; you can just create a component and install it in MTS. Once you've done that, it becomes available to all applications that can call components. You can access the components on remote machines using DCOM, MTS, or HTTP (with RDS). You also get the added advantage of transaction processing and easy scalability without having to program it yourself. The user interface can then be built in any language that supports COM.

ADO Availability

The Microsoft Data Access Components (MDAC) are available as a separate download from the Microsoft Web site at http://www.microsoft.com/data. The file name is MDAC_TYPE.EXE.

If you're unsure what version of ADO, or any of its components, you've got installed, download the Component Checker from http://www.microsoft.com/data/download.htm. This utility will give you a complete list of ADO DLLs and their version numbers. You can also use the Version property of the Connection object (see Chapter 3).

New Features

ADO 2.5 and 2.6 have a host of new features that make programming easier and extend the goal of Universal Data Access. This section only summarizes them; I deal with them in more detail in later chapters.

ADO 2.5

The Record Object

The Record object is designed to deal with Document Source Providers, which are OLE DB Providers that don't access databases, but provide data from semistructured data stores. Two examples of this are Microsoft's Exchange Server 2000 and Internet Information Server 5.0; both are sources of large amounts of data, and the OLE DB Provider for Internet Publishing allows you to access the data storage structure and the stored objects themselves.

The primary purpose of the Record object is to map a node in a tree-like structure of a document source. It works in conjunction with the Recordset but is not directly applicable to relational data sources.

The Stream Object

The Stream object is a component that wraps the COM IStream interface, allowing easy access to streams of memory. This provides a way to transfer Recordsets directly to other components (such as the ASP 3.0 Request and Response objects) that support streams. The Stream is also used with Document Source Providers to allow access to file contents.

ADO 2.6

Command Streams

Command streams allow a Stream object to be used as the source of a command. A good example of this is a Stream containing an XML command to be executed against SQL Server 2000.

Results in Streams

Along with command streams, ADO 2.6 allows the results of a data query to be returned into a Stream object. This is particularly useful for obtaining XML data directly from SQL Server 2000.

Dialect Property

This identifies the syntax rules the provider uses when parsing strings or streams. Its main use is for XML-generated recordsets, where the dialect identifies what form of XML the recordset is stored in.

Single Row Resultsets

Because of the way ADO worked, singleton commands (commands that return only a single row) were always a performance hit, but ADO 2.6 has improved the performance of such commands.

Field Status Values

The Status property of the Field object is now filled with information to help with the dreaded "Errors Occurred" error.

SQL Variant Support for Cursor Service

Extended support for variant types has been added to the OLE DB Cursor Service.

ADOX Group and User Properties

The Properties collection has been added to the ActiveX Data Objects Extensions (ADOX) Group and User properties to allow access to provider-specific properties.

ADO MD UniqueName support

The UniqueName property can now be used to access ActiveX Data Objects Multidimensional ADO MD objects. This means that parent collections no longer need to be populated to retrieve schema objects.

ADO 2.7

ADO 2.7 didn't introduce any new features; it simply provided support for 64-bit operating systems.

ADO 2.8

ADO 2.8 is simply a security update done as part of the Microsoft Secure Computing initiative. In some cases this has meant a break in backward compatibility, but the benefits of the added security outweigh these breaking changes.

The first of these changes is that code able to access the disk (such as the Stream object or opening or saving a Recordset from a file) is limited to trusted sites. Additionally, the file source must be a physical file or URL (and not a printer or serial port, for example). This checking occurs only on Windows 2000, Windows Server 2003, and Windows XP.

The second change ensures that the ActiveCommand property of a Recordset cannot be read when running in Internet Explorer. This stops malicious script from hijacking the command.

The third main change affects the handling of integrated security. Depending upon settings, providers could reuse existing connections and credentials to access other servers. For sites not in the Trusted Sites zone, untrusted providers cause security dialogs to be shown to the user. If the user accepts that the data is coming from an untrusted source, or if the data is coming from a trusted source, connection is permitted depending upon certain conditions detailed in the following table:

IE Settings for authentication and login	Provider supports "Integrated Security"		Provider does not support "Integrated Security"
	UID & PWD are specified	SSPI	(JOLT, MSDASQL, MSPersist)
	(SQLOLEDB)	(no UID & PWD)	
Automatic login with current user name and password	Allow connection	Allow connection	Allow connection
Prompt for user name and password	Allow connection	Fail connection	Fail connection
Automatic logon only in Intranet zone	Allow connection	Prompt with security warning	Prompt with security warning
Anonymous logon	Allow connection	Fail connection	Fail connection

The final security feature covers session pooling, which now uses access tokens instead of just the Security Identifier (SID) to determine if the requested connection matches an existing pooled connection.

Deprecated Components

The following ADO components are deprecated in version 2.8, which means that they are still supported, but may be removed in the future.

❑ ODBC Provider (MSDASQL). You should use native OLE DB Providers instead of ODBC. Although deprecated, the OLE DB Provider for ODBC is still the default provider.

❑ Remote Data Services (RDS). You should replace RDS use with the Simple Object Access Protocol (SOAP) toolkit, which is an open, XML-based standard.

❑ Jet and Replication Objects (JRO). Because the Jet OLD DB Provider was removed from MDAC 2.6, no new releases are planned, and they will not be available in future MDAC releases.

❑ AppleTalk and Banyan Vines SQL Network Libraries. You should replace their use with TCP/IP.

❑ 16-bit ODBC support. You should migrate to 32-bit data sources.

Examples

Because this is primarily a reference book, I'll give you a few documented samples of code so that you can see what's possible and how some of the components fit together. You can use this as a sort of "table of contents" to the rest of the book, where the various aspects are covered in more detail. A later section of this chapter provide more detail about language specifics, so I use Visual Basic here because it's easy to read and understand.

Example 1

The following section of Visual Basic code creates a connection to SQL Server, opens a recordset, and then adds some details from the recordset to a listbox:

```
' Define two object variables
' The object model is discussed in Chapter 2
Dim objConn      As ADODB.Connection
Dim objRs        As ADODB.Recordset
Set objConn = New ADODB.Connection
Set objRs   As New ADODB.Recordset

' Open a connection to the pubs database using the
' SQL Server OLE DB Provider
' Connection strings are discussed in Chapter 2
' The Connection object is discussed in Chapter 3
objConn.Open "Provider=SQLOLE DB; Data Source=Tigger; " & _
             "Initial Catalog=pubs; User Id=sa; Password="

' Open a recordset on the 'authors' table
' The Recordset is discussed in Chapter 5
objRs.Open "authors", objConn, adOpenForwardOnly, _
           adLockReadOnly, adCmdTable

' Loop while we haven't reached the end of the recordset
' The EOF property is set to True when we reach the end
While Not objRs.EOF
    ' Add the names to the listbox, using the default Fields collection
    ' The Fields collection is discussed in Chapter 6
    List1.AddItem objRs.Fields("au_fname") & " " & _
                  objRs.Fields("au_lname")
    ' Move to the next record
    objRs.MoveNext
Wend

' Close the objects
objRs.Close
objConn.Close

' Release the memory associated with the objects
Set objRs = Nothing
Set objConn = Nothing
```

Example 2

This example runs a SQL statement and doesn't expect a set of records to be returned. It also uses an ODBC Data Source Name called pubs, which has been set up previously.

```
' Define the object variable
Dim objConn      As ADODB.Connection
Set objConn = New ADODB.Connection

' Open a connection to the pubs database using the
' OLE DB Provider for ODBC
objConn.Open "DSN=pubs; UID=sa; PWD="

' Run a SQL UPDATE statement to update book prices by 10%
objConn.Execute "UPDATE titles SET price = price * 1.10" _
           , , adExecuteNoRecords + adCmdText

' Close the connection
objConn.Close

' Release the memory associated with the objects
Set objConn = Nothing
```

Example 3

This example runs a stored query in Access, passing in some parameters:

```
' Declare the object variables
' The Command object is discussed in Chapter 4
' The Parameter object is discussed in Chapter 4
Dim objConn      As ADODB.Connection
Dim objCmd       As ADODB.Command
Dim objRs        As ADODB.Recordset
Dim objParam     As ADODB.Parameter
Set objConn = New ADODB.Connection
Set objCmd = New ADODB.Command

' Open a connection to an Access pubs database,
' using the Access OLE DB provider
objConn.Open "Provider=Microsoft.Jet.OLE DB.4.0; " & _
                        "Data Source=C:\temp\pubs.mdb"
' Create a new Parameter, called RequiredState
Set objParam = objCmd.CreateParameter("RequiredState", _
                          adChar, _
                          adParamInput, 2, "CA")

' Add the Parameter to the Parameters collection of the Command object
objCmd.Parameters.Append objParam

' Set the active connection of the command to the open Connection object
Set objCmd.ActiveConnection = objConn

' Set the name of the stored query that is to be run
objCmd.CommandText = "qryAuthorsBooksByState"

' Set the type of command
```

```
    objCmd.CommandType = adCmdStoredProc

    ' Run the stored query and set the recordset which it returns
    Set objRs = objCmd.Execute

    ' Loop through the recordset, adding the items to a listbox
    While Not objRs.EOF
        List1.AddItem objRs.Fields("au_fname") & " " & _
                      objRs.Fields("au_lname") & _
                      ": " & objRs.Fields("title")
        objRs.MoveNext
    Wend

    ' Close the recordset and connection
    objRs.Close
    objConn.Close

    ' Reclaim the memory from the objects
    Set objRs = Nothing
    Set objCmd = Nothing
    Set objParam = Nothing
    Set objConn = Nothing
```

Example 4

This example uses the `Fields` collection of the recordset to loop through all of the fields in a recordset, then prints the details in the debug window:

```
    ' Declare the object variables
    Dim objRs       As ADODB.Recordset
    Dim objFld      As ADODB.Field
    Set pbjRs = New ADODB.Recordset

    ' Open a recordset on the 'authors' table using the
    ' OLE DB Driver for ODBC
    ' without using a connection
    objRs.Open "authors", "DSN=pubs", _
               adOpenForwardOnly, adLockReadOnly, adCmdTable

    ' Loop through the Fields collection printing the
    ' name of each Field
    ' The Fields collection is discussed in Chapter 6
    For Each objFld In objRs.Fields
        Debug.Print objFld.Name; vbTab;
    Next
    Debug.Print

    ' Loop through the records in the recordset
    While Not objRs.EOF
        ' Loop through the fields, this time printing out
        ' the value of each field
        For Each objFld In objRs.Fields
            Debug.Print objFld.Value; vbTab;
        Next
        Debug.Print
        objRs.MoveNext
```

```
        Wend

        ' Close the recordset and release the memory
        objRs.Close
        Set objRs = Nothing
        Set objFld = Nothing
```

Example 5

This is an ADOX example; it uses a `Catalog` and its associated `Tables` collection to list the tables in a data store:

```
        ' Declare the object variables
        Dim objCat      As ADOX.Catalog
        Dim objTable    As ADOX.Table
        Dim strConn     As String
        Set objCat = New ADOX.Catalog

        ' set the connection string
        strConn="Provider=Microsoft.Jet.OLE DB.4.0; Data Source=C:\temp\pubs.mdb"

        ' point the catalog at a data store
        objCat.ActiveConnection = strConn

        ' loop through the tables collection
        For Each objTable In objCat.Tables
            Debug.Print objTable.Name
        Next

        ' clean up
        Set objTable = Nothing
        Set objCat = Nothing
```

Example 6

This example also shows ADOX, and uses a `Catalog`, its `Tables` collection, and the `Indexes` and `Columns` collections for a table to print a list of columns for the index:

```
        Dim objCat      As ADOX.Catalog
        Dim objTbl      As ADOX.Table
        Dim objIdx      As ADOX.Index
        Dim objCol      As ADOX.Column
        Dim strConn     As String
        Set objCat = New ADOX.Catalog

        ' set the connection string
        strConn="Provider=Microsoft.Jet.OLE DB.4.0; Data Source=C:\temp\pubs.mdb"

        ' point the catalog at a data store
        objCat.ActiveConnection = strConn

        ' loop through the tables
        For Each objTbl In objCat.Tables
            ' has the table got indexes
            If objTbl.Indexes.Count > 0 Then
                Debug.Print objTbl.Name
```

```
         ' loop through the indexes
         For Each objIdx In objTbl.Indexes
              Debug.Print vbTab; objIdx.Name; vbTab;
                              objIdx.PrimaryKey
              'loop through the columns in the index
              For Each objCol In objIdx.Columns
                   Debug.Print vbTab; vbTab; objCol.Name
              Next
         Next
    End If
Next

' clean up
Set objCol = Nothing
Set objTbl = Nothing
Set objIdx = Nothing
Set objCat = Nothing
```

Language Differences

I've tried to make this book relatively language-independent. Because ADO can be used by any programming language that supports COM, deciding which language to use for the samples in this book becomes sticky. To help the widest possible audience, I've stuck with a pseudo-code type style. For example, in the examples that show something being printed, I've just used Print. You can then substitute the command for your language of choice. The different methods for several common languages and environments are described here:

Language	Method	Notes
Visual Basic	`Debug.Print "message"`	Prints the text to the debug window
	`MsgBox "message"`	Pops up a window with the text
ASP & VBScript	`Response.Write "message"`	Returns the text to the browser
ASP & JavaScript	`Response.Write ("message");`	Returns the text to the browser
VBScript	`document.write "message"`	Inserts message into the HTML document
	`MsgBox "message"`	Pops up a window with the text
JavaScript	`document.write ("message");`	Inserts message into the HTML document
	`alert ("message");`	Pops up a window with the text

Although I've tried to make our samples as language-independent as possible, you'll notice that most of the samples in the book use a Visual Basic/VBScript style–because I see this as the greatest market for ADO usage. However, the samples should be easy to translate into your favorite language.

If you want to use ADO in a variety of languages, have a look at the document entitled *Implementing ADO with Various Development Languages* at http://msdn.microsoft.com/library/techart/msdn_adorosest.htm.

A set of samples in a variety of languages is also available from the support page on the Apress Web site at http://support.apress.com/.

Creating Objects

Creating the ADO objects is one area where pseudo-code doesn't really work too well. Significant differences exist, even between such apparently similar languages as Visual Basic and VBScript. Therefore, this section is devoted to the act of creating objects. I describe in some detail how it's done in each of the five languages where I think ADO will have most impact.

This isn't intended as a full explanation of all the objects and how they are used in each language; instead, it is a demonstration of the major differences between several of the most common languages.

Visual Basic

Before you can create an ADO object in Visual Basic, make sure you have a reference to the ActiveX Data Objects Database (ADODB) library set. From the Project menu, select References, and then choose Microsoft ActiveX Data Objects 2.8 Library. The ADO Extensions (ADOX) are in the library labeled Microsoft ADO Ext. 2.8 for DDL and Security. You can create objects three ways. The first is:

```
Dim objRs As New ADODB.Recordset
```

This creates the object reference immediately, but the object is not instantiated until the first property or method is called. This means that instead of being instantiated when declared, the object is instantiated later in the code–which can lead to debugging problems. A better solution is to use this method:

```
Dim objRs As ADODB.Recordset
Set objRs = New ADODB.Recordset
```

This creates a variable of the type Recordset, and then the Set line instantiates the object. The third method is the older style, using late binding, and is less used these days (and also doesn't require a reference to the ADODB library to be set):

```
Dim objRs As Object
Set objRs = CreateObject("ADODB.Recordset")
```

After an object has been created, invoking the methods and properties is extremely simple. For example:

```
objRs.Cursorlocation = adUseClient
objRs.Open "authors", objConn, adOpenStatic, _
                            adLockBatchOptimistic, adCmdTable
```

The ad constants are automatically available to you in Visual Basic once you have referenced the ADO library (as described previously).

Looping through a recordset is just a question of using the MoveNext method and checking the EOF property:

```
While Not objRs.EOF
  Debug.Print objRs("field_name")
  objRs.MoveNext
Wend
```

ASP/VBScript

Creating objects in VBScript is different from Visual Basic because VBScript doesn't have variable types (all variables are of Variant type) or support for adding references to type libraries (although it does use the Visual Basic syntax for assigning object variables using Set). Therefore, there's no need to define the variables, although it's better to define them for ease of code maintenance and reliability:

```
Dim objRs
Set objRs = Server.CreateObject("ADODB.Recordset")
```

This creates a Recordset object in ASP script code.

You can also use the <% Option Explicit %> command to ensure that variables are required to be defined.

Using the object follows the same procedure as for Visual Basic:

```
objRs.CursorLocation = adUseClient
objRs.Open "authors", objConn, adOpenStatus, _
                          adLockBatchOptimistic, adCmdTable
```

The only difference here is that the constants are not automatically available; this is because scripting languages do not have access to the type library and its constants. You have two options. The first is to use the integer values that these constants represent. The problem with this is that your code becomes sprinkled with various numbers whose meaning is not obvious to the reader. For example, without ADO's predefined constants, the previous statement would read:

```
objRs.CursorLocation = 3
objRs.Open "authors", objConn, 1, 3, 2
```

This makes your code harder to read, and therefore harder to maintain.

The second option is to include the constants in your ASP script; this means that you can use the constant names instead of their values. You can include the ADO constants with the following line:

```
<!- #INCLUDE FILE="adovbs.inc"->
```

The include file, adovbs.inc, is installed in the default directory of Program Files\Common Files\System\ADO. It can be moved to your local ASP directory or referenced from a central virtual directory.

A better way to use the constants is to create a direct reference to the type library, using some meta data:

```
<!- METADATA TYPE="typelib"
FILE="C:\Program Files\Common Files\System\ADO\msado15.dll" ->
```

The advantage of this method is that you use the values from the ADO library itself rather than those from the include file. This means that you don't have to worry that the location (or even the contents) of the include file might change. Note that the name of the DLL is always `msado15.dll` regardless of which ADO version you have.

Looping through recordsets in VBScript is exactly the same as in Visual Basic:

```
While Not objRs.EOF
    Response.Write objRs.Fields("field_name").Value
    objRs.MoveNext
Wend
```

JScript

JScript has a syntax different from VBScript's, although much of the object usage is similar. The major thing to watch for is that JScript is case-sensitive. For example, to create a recordset in Jscript, you would use:

```
var objRs = Server.CreateObject("ADODB.Recordset");
```

Use of the methods and properties is also very similar:

```
objRs.CursorLocation = adUseClient;
objRs.Open ("authors", objConn, adOpenStatic, adLockBatchOptimistic,
        adCmdTable);
```

To loop through a recordset in Jscript, you would use:

```
while (!objRs.EOF)
{
    Response.Write (objRs("field_name"));
    objRs.MoveNext();
}
```

Visual C++

To use ADO within C++, you must import the ADO library:

```
#import "c:\program files\common files\system\ado\msado15.dll" \
    no_namespace \
    rename( "EOF", "adoEOF" )
```

You must make sure the file path points to the location of your version of the ADO DLL. The no_namespace keyword is added so that you don't have to scope the ADO names. The EOF property must be renamed because of an unfortunate name collision with the EOF constant defined in the Standard C library.

Object creation follows this syntax:

```
_ConnectionPtr         pConnection;
pConnection.CreateInstance( __uuidof( Connection ) );
_RecordsetPtr          pRecordSet;
pRecordSet.CreateInstance( __uuidof( Recordset ) );
```

.NET

Although .NET comes with a new data access strategy (ADO.NET), You still can use ADO within .NET if required. For this you must create a .NET wrapper to use the ADO COM components. In Visual Studio .NET you can do this simply by creating a reference to the ADO component; otherwise, you can use the tlbimp.exe tool supplied with .NET to create the wrapper. See the .NET documentation for more details. Once the wrapper is created, ADO use is exactly the same as non-.NET languages.

Summary

So far you've explored the principles of data access and the range of problems created by the increasing variety and location of data and users. You've seen a bird's eye view of the significance of ADO and its advantages, and briefly looked at the other data access technologies it builds on, replaces, or complements. In particular, you've considered:

❑　Data and data stores

❑　The existing technologies for accessing data, and Microsoft's scheme to streamline data access, UDA

❑　What OLE DB and ADO are, and how they tie in with each other

❑　The distinction between data providers and data consumers, and Microsoft's Distributed interNet Application Architecture framework for client/server solutions

❑　The new features of ADO 2.5 and 2.6

❑　The security changes introduced in ADO 2.8

❑　How to use the basics of ADO in a variety of languages

The next chapter discusses the ADO and ADOX object models.

2

The ADO Object Model

Like all other data-access technologies from Microsoft, ADO has a distinct object model that defines the objects and interfaces, and how the objects relate to each other. If you've done any database programming before, you are probably familiar with the general layout of these objects, because they lean heavily on the lessons learned from DAO and RDO. ADO has a good object model, but it is not as strict as its ancestors, so it gives the programmer a great deal more flexibility, thereby reducing development time. For example, in ADO you can create a recordset of data by using just a single line of code.

This has been achieved by flattening the object model. It's still shown in the documentation as a hierarchy (with a single object at the top), but some of the lower objects can exist in your code in their own right, without the need to create higher-level objects explicitly. This means that a programmer can use the object most suitable for a particular task without having to create many other objects that aren't really required in the program. If ADO requires these objects, it creates them and uses them behind the scenes—and you need never know that they are there.

The ADO Object Model

Versions prior to 2.5 have three main objects: the **Connection**, the **Command**, and the **Recordset**. No hierarchy exists among the three main objects, and you can create them independently of each other. Versions 2.5 and higher make two new objects available: the **Record** and the **Stream**. This diagram shows the relationships among these objects in the ADO model:

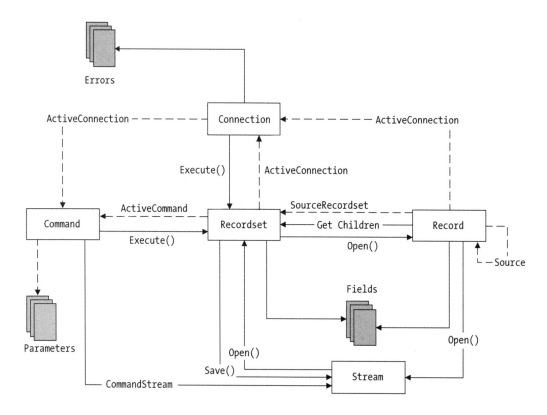

The objects shown as shaded are **collections**. Each collection can comprise zero or more instances of its associated object, as shown in the following table:

Collection	Associated Object
Errors	Error
Parameters	Parameter
Fields	Field
Properties	Property

Note that although the main five objects all can exist independently in our code, the collections must be derived from their parent objects. So (for example) a `Recordset` contains a `Fields` collection, which in turn contains zero-or-more `Field` objects.

Enumerating the objects in a collection is the same for all collections; you just have to use a loop variable of the appropriate type. For example, in Visual Basic the following construct will step through each and every object in the `Errors` collection:

```
Dim objErr As ADODB.Error
For Each objErr In objConn.Errors
    Debug.Print objErr.Description
Next
```

The same method can be used in VBScript, although you don't give the object variable a specific type, because VBScript variables are Variants. For example, in ASP you could use:

```
Dim objFld
For Each objFld In objRec.Fields
    Response.Write objFld.Name & "<BR>"
Next
```

In JScript you could use the Enumerator object. For example, in ASP you could use:

```
for(var objProp = new Enumerator(objConn.Properties);
        !objProp.atEnd(); objProp.moveNext() )
{
    Response.Write (objProp.item().Name + '<BR>');
}
```

The Main ADO Objects

The Connection Object

The Connection is actually the hub of ADO, because it provides the methods that allow us to connect to a data store. Note that when you create a Recordset or Command object, it is not necessary to create a connection first, because a Connection object is *automatically* created for you behind the scenes. What this means is that you can actually create a recordset or run a command with just a single line of code. For example:

```
rsAuthors.Open "authors", "DSN=pubs", adOpenStatic,
        adLockReadOnly, adCmdTable
```

This creates a recordset on the authors table from the pubs database, based on the ODBC Data Source Name (DSN) pubs. Although this example is using a Recordset object, it actually creates a connection underneath. In fact, you can create a separate and explicit Connection object from the one automatically created by ADO :

```
Set conPubs = objRec.ActiveConnection
```

This sort of mix-and-match approach to connection creation frees the programmer from a rigid structure and allows you to write the code in a way that is naturally easier.

Although this looks simple, you create a new connection every time you use a connection string to establish a connection to a data store (subject to connection pooling–see Chapter 3). If you will be running several commands or creating several recordsets, I recommend that you create a `Connection` object directly:

```
conPubs.Open "DSN=pubs; UID=sa; PWD="
```

or:

```
conPubs.Open "Provider=SQLOLEDB; Data Source=Piglet; " & _
             "Initial Catalog=pubs; User Id=sa; Password="
```

You can then use this `Connection` throughout your code without worrying about the number of connections you create. Not only is this more efficient, but it's faster too; once a connection to a data store is established, it can be reused.

One area where you shouldn't try to use a single connection is in the `Session` or `Application` scope in ASP pages. Creating an ADO object and storing it in a `Session` or `Application` variable has serious performance penalties if you want your ASP pages to scale. You can, however, store the connection string in `Session` or `Application` scope.

Once you have decided upon the provider, the properties of the `Connection` object allow you to see what kinds of facilities are available from the data provider. For example, picking the SQL Server provider allows you to see some of the properties for that provider, even before the connection is opened:

```
conPubs.Provider = "SQLOLEDB"
For Each objProp in conPubs.Properties
    Print objProp.Name
Next
```

Because ADO is designed to run against different data stores, it's often worth checking that a particular function is supported *before* you call it. You do this by examining the `Properties` collection of the `Connection` object. This is particularly useful when using ADO as part of a development or query tool that gives users the ability to connect to different data stores. You could also, for example, use some of the properties to define a schema if manually creating XML from the data.

The `Connection` object isn't just about connecting to, and holding information about, a data store. You can actually run commands and create recordsets with a `Connection` object too. For example:

```
conPubs.Execute "UPDATE titles SET price = price * 1.10", , _
                 adCmdText + adExecuteNoRecords
```

This would run a SQL UPDATE query. Alternatively, to run a command and return a read-only recordset:

```
Set rsAuthors = _
    objConn.Execute ("SELECT * FROM authors", , adCmdText)
```

So, not only can you use a `Recordset` object to connect to a data store, but you can also use a `Connection` object to create recordsets. It's all part of the "code as you want" strategy.

An ADO operation may generate more than one error, and these are stored in the `Connection` object's `Errors` collection, which is discussed in more detail in Chapter 8. Although you might think this breaks the flexibility of the object model, it gives a central place to find error information. Because the `Recordset` and `Command` objects have a connection underneath, it is extremely simple to access this error information without creating a `Connection` object.

The Command Object

The `Command` object is designed to run SQL statements (assuming the provider supports the `Command` object), especially those that require parameters. This is an important point, because the use of stored queries and procedures is a great way to improve speed and segment your application, and it fits naturally with Windows DNA.

Like the `Connection` object, the `Command` object can be used to run action queries that don't return a recordset, and for creating recordsets. Unlike the `Connection`, however, you'll need a couple more lines of code, because you cannot specify the command text in the same line as the line that specifies the command type:

```
objCmd.CommandText = "UPDATE titles SET price = price * 1.10"
objCmd.CommandType = adCmdText + adExecuteNoRecords
objCmd.Execute
```

To return a recordset, you use a similar style:

```
Set rsAuthors = objCmd.Execute
```

The greatest difference in command execution comes when using the `Parameters` collection, because this allows you to use stored procedures, queries, and template and parameterized queries saved in the data store. This removes the SQL code from your program, making it faster and easier to maintain. Using stored procedures, you can have SQL statements in a compiled form that perform a set of actions using the values you supply as parameters.

With a `Command`–if the data provider supports this facility–you can also save the command details for execution at a later date. This is known as a **prepared statement**, and it allows the precompiled command to be run many times within the same connection. Once you've finished with your connection, the saved commands are deleted automatically. You can also use a `Command` object more than once, and on different connections if you require (assuming that the command can be run on another connection). Just change the `ActiveConnection` property of the command to point to the new connection, then run the command again. If you wish to reuse the `Command` object, it's wise to close any active recordsets that were created as a result of the command's execution. This ensures that memory is deallocated correctly.

Another feature allows you to turn the command into a method of the `Connection` object, allowing you to build up a `Connection` object that contains many new methods. This is quite useful in client/server scenarios, because you could attach different commands to the connection depending upon user privilege. This is explained in more detail in Chapter 4.

> Unlike the `Connection` and `Recordset` objects, which must be supported by every OLE DB provider, a provider's decision to support the `Command` object is entirely optional. Consequently, not all OLE DB Providers support the `Command` object.

The Recordset Object

The `Recordset` object is probably the most frequently used object in ADO; consequently, it has more properties and methods than other objects. Like the `Command` object, a `Recordset` can exist on its own or be attached to a `Connection`:

```
rsAuthors.Open "authors", "DSN=pubs", adOpenStatic, _
        adLockReadOnly, adCmdTable
```

This opens a recordset using a new connection. To use an existing connection, simply substitute the connection string for the existing `Connection` object:

```
rsAuthors.Open "authors", conPubs, adOpenStatic, _
        adLockReadOnly, adCmdTable
```

This is the preferred method if you are creating several recordsets, because it means that the connection to the data store doesn't have to be established each time you create a recordset.

Another important point about the `Recordset` object is that it's the only way to specify the recordset's cursor type and lock type. If you use the `Execute` method of the `Connection` or `Command` object, it gives you the default cursor type, a read-only, forward-only cursor (often referred to as a firehose cursor, because the data is just "squirted" to the recordset). If you need to use a `Command` and require a different cursor type, then you can specify the `Command` object, instead of the table name or query text, as the source of the `Recordset`.

You use recordsets to examine and manipulate data from the data store. The `Recordset` object gives you facilities to move about through the records, find records, sort records in a particular order, and update records. You can perform updating in two modes: directly (changes are sent back to the data store as they are made) or in batches (changes are saved locally and then sent back to the data store all at once).

In client/server applications, you can also pass recordsets between the business-logic tier and the user-interface tier, where they can be manipulated locally. This saves database resources, which can be critical on large-scale applications, and it minimizes network traffic. These recordsets are called **disconnected recordsets**.

The Record Object

The `Record` object was introduced in version 2.5, and is used in conjunction with a new type of OLE DB Provider, called Document Source Providers. Document Source Providers are designed to enable access to data stores of semistructured data, such as file or mail systems. It was necessary to create a new object because of the way data is stored. In relational data stores, such as SQL Server or Access, we work using set-based data, where every row is in a rowset and has the same structure as the other rows. Semistructured data, on the other hand, doesn't follow this pattern, because each row might have a different structure. If you think about the structure of a Web site, then you'll start to understand how this works. A Web site generally consists of directories and files. If you look at the top-level directory for a site, you might see something like this:

File Name	Type
default.htm	File
Images	Directory
menu.xml	File

All three items here have some common properties, such as a name. However, they also have different properties; the directory doesn't have a size, but must indicate that it contains other files. These different properties are why we need a different object to cope with this sort of data. When dealing with semistructured data, the `Record` object maps onto individual files, and the `Recordset` object is mapped onto a collection of files.

To access a directory through a `Record` object, use the following syntax:

```
Dim recRoot      As New ADODB.Record
recRoot.Open "", "URL=http://localhost"
recRoot.Close
```

Specifying URL= tells ADO to use the Internet Publishing Provider.

The `Record` object not only allows access to files, but also gives management over them too. The `CopyRecord`, `MoveRecord`, and `DeleteRecord` methods give the ability to control files remotely.

The Stream Object

The `Stream` object is a wrapper around a memory manager (in fact it's based around the COM `IStream` interface) and gives control over the contents of the memory used to store an object. This might sound rather complex, but it has wide-ranging uses and is simple to use.

You can use a `Stream` in several ways. One way is in conjunction with a Document Source Provider (such as the OLE DB Provider for Internet Publishing) to provide access to file contents on a Web server. For example:

```
Dim stmFile      As New ADODB.Stream
Dim sContents    As String
stmFile.Open "URL=http://localhost/postinfo.html"
stmFile.Charset = "ascii"
sContents = stmFile.ReadText
stmFile.Close
```

This simply opens a file and reads the contents into a string. You also get the ability to write data out to the stream, where it is saved automatically to the file. This gives the ability to perform editing on remote files.

Stream objects have other roles. They can be used when saving and opening recordsets, and in conjunction with the Microsoft XML Parser.

The Other ADO Objects

The Field Object and the Fields Collection

A Field object contains details about a single field (or column) in a recordset. Such information includes the data type of the field, its width, and so on.

The Fields collection contains a reference to an ADO Field object for each field in a recordset, and there are two ways in which you can use this. The first is with existing recordsets, where you can examine each field, see its type, check its name, and so on. This is quite useful when you are unsure what exactly the recordset contains, and it can be useful in scripting when showing tables dynamically. Using the Fields collection allows you to find the name of each field. For example, in ASP script you could do this:

```
Response.Write "<TABLE>"
For Each objFld In objRec.Fields
   Response.Write "<TR><TD>" & objFld.Name & "</TD></TR>"
Next
Response.Write "</TABLE>"
```

This creates an HTML table showing which fields are in the recordset objRec. In fact, using a similar method, you could easily create a simple script routine that accepts any recordset and builds an HTML table from it. You could use the Fields collection to supply the table header, showing the column names, and the recordset to fill in table details.

Another use of the Fields collection is for creating programmatic, or fabricated, recordsets. In the past, arrays often were used when it was necessary to store several related items. The trouble with arrays is that you must manage the array manually; you can't add data to a new array element without first creating room in the array. Then came collections, to which you could add your own objects; but collections are also limited to objects and basic data types. So if you want to store some related items (records), but each item has different attributes (fields), you can use a fabricated recordset.

For example, imagine that you need to store details from a questionnaire. You could create a recordset like so:

```
rsNew.CursorLocation = adUseClient
rsNew.Fields.Append "Name", adVarChar, 50, adFldFixed
rsNew.Fields.Append "Age", adInteger, , adFldFixed
```

```
        rsNew.Fields.Append "Question1", adBoolean, , adFldFixed
        . . .
        rsNew.Fields.Append "Comments", adVarChar, 255, adFldFixed
```

The good thing about this method is that you can save the contents of this disconnected recordset to a file, and you can use it as a parameter for functions in business objects (just like recordsets obtained from OLE DB Providers).

The Error Object and the Errors Collection

An `Error` object contains details of a single error (or warning) returned from a data provider. Details include a description of the error, an error number, and the source object that raised the error. When a provider encounters an error or wishes to return information to the consumer, the details are placed in an `Error` object, and this is appended to the `Errors` collection.

The `Errors` collection holds all of the errors when a data provider generates an error or returns warnings in response to some failure. This is provided as a collection because a failure can generate more than one error. For example, the following statement generates two errors because X and Y are unknown columns:

```
        objConn.Open "DSN=pubs"
        Set objRec = objConn.Execute "SELECT X, Y FROM authors"
```

You could check the errors generated here by looping through the collection:

```
        For Each objErr In conPubs.Errors
           Print objErr.Description
        Next
```

If you don't have a predefined `Connection` object, you can use the `ActiveConnection` property of the `Command` or `Recordset`:

```
        rsAuthors.Open "SELECT X, Y FROM authors", "DSN=pubs", _
                    adOpenStatic, adLockReadOnly, adCmdTable
        For Each objErr In rsAuthors.ActiveConnection.Errors
           Print objErr.Description
        Next
```

As with the `Fields` collection, you could easily build a simple routine that centralizes error handling.

There is always an `Errors` collection, but it will be empty if no errors have occurred. `Error` objects remain in the collection until the next data access error occurs, when they are cleared and replaced by the new error details.

The Parameter Object and the Parameters Collection

A `Parameter` object contains details of a single parameter for a `Command` object. Some of these details include the name, data type, direction, and value of the parameter. A parameter can be one of the following types:

❑   An input parameter, which supplies values to the statement represented by the `Command` object

❑   An output parameter, which supplies values from the statement represented by the `Command` object

❑   An input and output parameter

❑   A return value, which supplies the return value from the statement represented by the `Command` object

The usage of the various parameter types is discussed in more detail in Chapter 4.

The `Parameters` collection is unique to the `Command` object and is one way of allowing you to pass parameters into and out of stored queries and procedures. When using parameters, you have two options. First, you can ask the data provider to fetch the parameters from the data source, and the `Parameters` collection will be filled in automatically for you:

```
objCmd.Parameters.Refresh
```

The downside of this is that it requires a trip to the server, which may cause your program to perform poorly, especially if you do this often. However, it's a great way of finding out what type and size the provider expects your parameters to be, and is very useful during development and debugging. You should note that not all OLE DB Providers (or ODBC Drivers) support the `Refresh` method.

The second option is to add the parameters to the collection manually, like so:

```
Set objParam = objCmd.CreateParameter ("ID", adInteger, _
                                adParamInput, 8, 147)
```

This creates an input parameter called `ID`, which is an integer (length 8 bytes) with a value of 147. Once created, the parameter can be appended to the `Parameters` collection:

```
objCmd.Parameters.Append objParam
```

Another good use of the `Refresh` method is, when first connecting to the data store, to cache the parameters details locally, perhaps in an array or in a user collection. This sort of approach allows you to write generic routines that process stored procedures.

The Property Object and the Properties Collection

A `Property` object contains provider-specific information about an object. We know that objects have a fixed set of properties, but one of the fundamentals of OLE DB and ADO is that it can talk to a variety of data providers, and these providers often have different ways of working, or they support different properties. If all providers had to support a fixed functionality, then OLE DB and ADO wouldn't really be very flexible; they would constitute the lowest common denominator of functionality. The solution is to provide a `Property` object for each provider-specific property, and a `Properties` collection to store all provider-specific properties.

For a `Connection`, the `Properties` collection contains a large amount of information about the facilities that the provider supports, such as the maximum number of columns in a `SELECT` statement, and what sort of outer join capabilities are supported. For a `Recordset`, there's just as much information, ranging from the current locking level to the asynchronous capabilities supported by the provider.

You can examine or set the value of an individual property by just using its name to index into the collection. For example:

```
Print conPubs.Properties("Max Columns in SELECT")
```

To examine all the properties, you can use a simple loop:

```
For Each objProp In conPubs.Properties
    Print objProp.Name
Next
```

You may well find that you never use this collection, unless you are writing an application that supports multiple data providers, in which case you may need to query the provider to examine what it supports.

The ADOX Object Model

The ADOX library contains extensions for Data Definition Language (DDL) and security, providing a way to access schema creation and modification and for accessing security credentials for the schema. Many data stores allow access to schema and security information, but they often differ in the command language used. ADOX abstracts these provider-specific details into a common set of objects, allowing a single code set to be used regardless of provider-specific syntax.

The ADOX (for DDL and Security) object model observes more hierarchy than does the ADO object model, but this is because of the nature of the objects it contains. This means there is a parent object and several child objects, as this diagram for the ADOX object model illustrates:

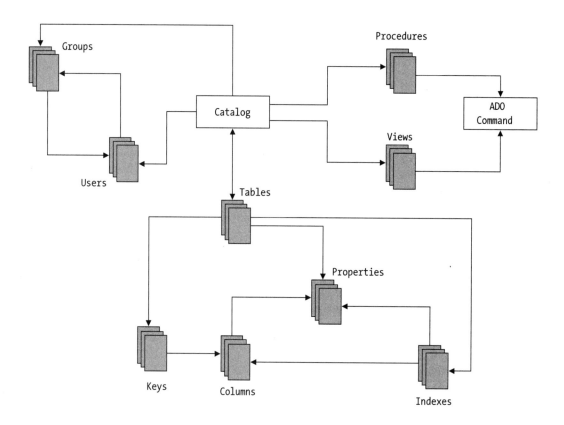

The Catalog Object

The Catalog object is a central repository, and is really just a container for all of the other objects. The Catalog object allows you to connect to a data store and examine the components comprising it. With the Catalog object, you can use the ActiveConnection property to specify the data store to which you want to connect, and then use the collections to obtain more detailed information. It's also possible to obtain and set the owner of various objects without using the collections.

To use a catalog, you just point to an existing Connection object or a Connection string. For example:

```
Dim objCatalog As New ADOX.Catalog
Set objCatalog.ActiveConnection = objConn
```

or:

```
objCatalog.ActiveConnection = "Provider=SQLOLEDB; . . ."
```

The Table Object and the Tables Collection

A `Table` object represents a single table, containing information such as the table name and the last change date, in a catalog. It is also a container for the `Indexes`, `Keys`, and `Columns` collections (described shortly).

The `Tables` collection contains `Table` objects—one for each table in the catalog. I provide an example of the `Tables` and `Columns` collections later in this section.

The Index Object and the Indexes Collection

An `Index` object contains the details for a single index on a table. It identifies attributes such as the index name, whether the index is unique, whether the index allows nulls, and so on. Using the `Index` object's `Columns` collection, you can see which columns comprise the index.

The `Indexes` collection contains all the `Index` objects for a particular `Table`. For example, the following code prints the indexes on a table and the columns that make up each index:

```
Dim objIndex  As ADOX.Index
Dim objColumn As ADOX.Column
For Each objIndex In objTbl.Indexes
   Print objIndex.Name
   For Each objColumn In objIndex.Columns
      Print objColumn.Name
   Next
Next
```

The Key Object and the Keys Collection

A `Key` object contains information regarding a table key. It identifies such items as its name, whether it is a primary or foreign key, the related table, and so on. Like the `Index` object, the `Key` object contains a collection of `Column` objects, identifying the columns that make up the key.

The `Keys` collection contains a list of keys for a table. For example, the following prints all the keys and columns for a table:

```
Dim objKey    As ADOX.Key
Dim objColumn As ADOX.Column
For Each objKey In objTabl.Indexes
   Print objKey.Name
   For Each objColumn In objKey.Columns
      Print objColumn.Name
   Next
Next
```

The Column Object and the Columns Collection

A `Column` object represents an individual column from a `Table`, `Index`, or `Key` object. In many respects it is similar to the ADO `Field` object, but rather than storing the details of a field, it holds the details of a stored column, such as its name, its data type, and so forth. For `Key` columns it contains details of the related columns, and for `Index` columns it contains details of the clustering and sorting. There is just one `Column` object, but what it contains depends upon its parent (`Table`, `Index`, or `Key`).

The `Columns` collection contains all the columns for a particular `Table`, `Key`, or `Index` object. For example, to see all the columns in a particular table, you would use this:

```
Dim objTbl As New ADOX.Table
Dim objCol As ADOX.Column
Set objTbl = objCatalog.Tables(0)
For Each objCol In objTbl.Columns
   Print objCol.Name
Next
```

The syntax is very similar when looping through all of the `Column` objects associated with an `Index` or a `Key` object.

The Group Object and the Groups Collection

A `Group` object identifies a security group. It contains a list of users in the catalog. Its main role is to allow the retrieval and setting of permission for a named group or for allowing access to the `Users` collection, which contains a list of all users belonging to this group.

The `Groups` collection contains a list of `Groups` that belong to a particular catalog, or a list of `Groups` that a particular user belongs to. For example, the following enumerates the `Groups` in a `Catalog`, and then the `Users` in a `Group`:

```
Dim objGroup As ADOX.Group
Dim objUser  As ADOX.User
For Each objGroup In objCatalog.Groups
   Print objGroup.Name
   For Each objUser In objGroup.Users
     Print objUser.Name
   Next
Next
```

Not all providers support the `Group` object and `Groups` collection. At the moment, the Jet provider gives the most comprehensive support.

The User Object and the Users Collection

A `User` object contains details of a single user of the data store and contains properties to retrieve or set the user name and the user's unique ID, and methods to read and write permissions. The `User` object also contains a `Groups` collection, which is a list of groups to which the user belongs. Be careful about writing recursive procedures that traverse the Users and Groups collections, because they point to each other.

The Users collection contains a list of all users in a catalog. For an example, refer to the preceding description of the Group object.

Not all providers support the User object and Users collection. At the moment, the Jet provider gives the most comprehensive support.

The Procedure Object and the Procedures Collection

A Procedure object identifies a stored procedure in a catalog. The Procedure object has very few properties, mainly because one of these properties represents an ADO Command object. The Procedure object identifies the details about the stored procedure (such as its name and when it was last modified), and the Command object identifies the internal details of the procedure (such as the SQL text).

The Procedures collection contains a Procedure object for each stored procedure in the Catalog. For example, to access a stored procedure and its SQL text, you could use the following code:

```
Dim objCmd As ADODB.Command
Set objCmd = objCat.Procedures("proc_name").Command
Print objCmd.CommandText
```

This uses the Command property of the Procedure object to reference a standard ADO Command object and print the text (command string) of the Command.

The View Object and the Views Collection

A View object identifies a single view in a Catalog, which is a set of records or a virtual table. Like the Procedure object, the View contains a Command object, allowing access to the view command.

The Views collection contains a list of View objects, one for each view in the catalog.

For example, to obtain all views in a catalog, you could do this:

```
Dim objView As ADOX.View
For Each objView In objCat.Views
    Print objView.Name
Next
```

Like the Procedure object, the View object also supports an ADO Command as a property. So, to access the details of the command, you could use similar code:

```
Dim objCmd As ADODB.Command
Set objCmd = objCat.Views("view_name").Command
Print objCmd.CommandText
```

This object and collection is also provider-dependent.

The Property Object and the Properties Collection

The `Property` object and `Properties` collection are identical to their ADODB equivalents.

ADOX Supported Features

ADOX is not supported by all providers, including those supplied by Microsoft. Currently, only the OLE DB Provider for Microsoft Jet fully supports ADOX. For the other Microsoft OLE DB providers, all features are supported *except* for those listed here:

Microsoft OLE DB Provider for SQL Server	
Object/Collection	**Feature Not Supported**
`Catalog` Object	`Create` method
`Tables` Collection	Properties for existing tables are read-only (properties for new tables can be read/write)
`Views` Collection	Not supported
`Procedures` Collection	`Append` method, `Delete` method, `Command` property
`Keys` Collection	`Append` method, `Delete` method
`Users` Collection	Not supported
`Groups` Collection	Not supported

Microsoft OLE DB Provider for ODBC	
Object/Collection	**Feature Not Supported**
`Catalog` Object	`Create` method
`Tables` Collection	`Append` method, `Delete` method; Properties for existing tables are read-only (properties for new tables can be read/write)
`Views` Collection	`Append` method, `Delete` method, `Command` property
`Procedures` Collection	`Append` method, `Delete` method, `Command` property
`Indexes` Collection	`Append` method, `Delete` method
`Keys` Collection	`Append` method, `Delete` method
`Users` Collection	Not supported
`Groups` Collection	Not supported

Microsoft OLE DB Provider for Oracle	
Object/Collection	**Feature Not Supported**
Catalog Object	Create method.
Tables Collection	Append method, Delete method; Properties for existing tables are read-only (properties for new tables can be read/write)
Views Collection	Append method, Delete method, Command property
Procedures Collection	Append method, Delete method, Command property
Indexes Collection	Append method, Delete method
Keys Collection	Append method, Delete method
Users Collection	Not supported
Groups Collection	Not supported

OLE DB Providers

I've already mentioned that ADO can connect to many different data providers, and this is because of OLE DB. Remember that ADO is just a layer sitting on top of OLE DB to hide the complexity. It seems sensible, though, to look at some of these OLE DB data providers in more detail. You need to see their differences, for although most of the ADO usage will be the same, OLE DB providers don't always support the same facilities. This is natural, because some of them are fundamentally very different. Most of the relational database providers, for example, will provide similar facilities, but other providers (such as for Internet Publishing) might not work the same way.

When you install MDAC, you are supplied with the following OLE DB providers:

Provider	Description
MSDASQL	Microsoft OLE DB Provider for ODBC: allows connection to existing ODBC data sources via either a System DSN or dynamically provided connection details. See Chapter 1 for how ODBC Drivers relate to OLE DB.
Microsoft.Jet.OLE DB.4.0	Microsoft OLE DB Provider for Jet: allows connections to be established directly to Microsoft Access databases, including Access 97 and Access 2000.
SQLOLEDB	Microsoft OLE DB Provider for SQL Server: allows connections to be established directly to Microsoft SQL Server databases.

Table continued on following page

Provider	Description
MSDAORA	Microsoft OLE DB Provider for Oracle: allows connections to be established to Oracle databases.
MSIDXS	Microsoft OLE DB Provider for Index Server: allows connections to be established to Microsoft Index Server.
ADSDSOObject	OLE DB Provider for Microsoft Directory Services: allows connections to be established to Directory Services such as the Windows 2000 Active Directory and the Windows NT 4 Directory Services.
MSDataShape	Microsoft OLE DB Data Shape Provider: provides the ability to create hierarchical recordsets.
MSPersist	Microsoft OLE DB Persistence Provider: allows recordsets to be saved or persisted and later reconstructed.
MSDAOSP	Microsoft OLE DB Simple Provider: allows connections to be established to custom OLE DB Providers that expose simple (relational) data.
MSDAIPP.DSO.1	Microsoft OLE DB Provider for Internet Publishing: allows connections to be established to DAV-compliant servers to aid publishing data on the Internet.

These are just the defaults supplied, some of which may not appear, depending upon your installation options. For example, Index Server does not act as a remote provider, and you can connect to only local Index Servers. Therefore, if you do not have Index Server on your machine, the MSIDXS may not be installed. Installation of versions later that 2.6 on top of an earlier version will not remove any deprecated providers, and these will not be installed on a clean MDAC 2.8 install.

You can find out which providers are available on your system by creating a new Data Link. This is similar to an ODBC DSN, but for OLE DB connections. By using Windows Explorer, you can create one in any directory simply by right-clicking (or selecting the File menu), picking New, and selecting Microsoft Data Link. This creates a file with a .udl extension, and you can then view its properties. If this option isn't available, you can create a text file and rename the extension to .udl. Open the UDL file by double-clicking it. From the Provider tab in the Data Link Properties window, you can see the available providers, as shown here:

In fact, using the Data Link is a good way to create connection strings if you are unfamiliar with them; you can even use them instead of a DSN within connection strings (see the next section). You can create a Data Link file, filling in the details onscreen, and then examine the resulting .udl file in Notepad.

Connection Strings

One of the major differences among the various OLE DB providers is found in the connection string: Different providers require different information to be able to make the connection to the data store.

ADO recognizes only four of the arguments in the connection string; the remaining arguments are passed on to the provider. The main argument you are interested in is `Provider`, which identifies the OLE DB provider to be used. The second argument is `File Name`, which can be used to point to an existing Data Link file. If you use a Data Link file, you can omit the `Provider` argument, because the Data Link file contains this information. The other two arguments (`Remote Provider` and `Remote Server`) relate to Remote Data Services; I describe them in detail in Chapter 9.

OLE DB Provider for the ODBC Drivers

The OLE DB Provider for ODBC is the default provider, so if you don't specify which one to use, this is what you'll get. If you *do* specify this provider explicitly in your connection string, you must give the rather obscure name `MSDASQL`. When using the OLE DB Provider for ODBC, you have three choices: use an existing ODBC System DSN, a DSN-less connection string, or an ODBC File DSN.

For a DSN-based connection, simply specify the data source name:

```
Provider=MSDASQL;DSN=data_source_name;
UID=user_id; PWD=user_password
```

For a DSN-less connection, the connection string varies with the database you are connecting to. It follows the same conventions as an ODBC connection string; in the **Control Panel**, you can see the parameters in the **ODBC** applet. One important option is the same for all ODBC connections, because it specifies the ODBC driver to use:

```
Provider=MSDASQL;Driver=
```

The name of the driver specified in the `Driver` attribute of the connection string will be one of those shown on the **Drivers** tab of the **ODBC Control Panel** applet. Your list of drivers may differ from those listed in this screen:

> *On Windows 2000 and Windows XP the ODBC Data Source Administrator, known as simply Data Sources (ODBC) on this platform, can be found under the Administrative Tools group. Regardless of platform, the list of ODBC Drivers installed on a given system can also be found in the system registry at* `HKEY_LOCAL_MACHINE\SOFTWARE\ODBC\ODBCINST.INI\ODBC Drivers`.

You should enclose the driver name in curly braces. Let's look at some examples.

Microsoft Access

To connect to Microsoft Access, your connection string would start like this:

```
Provider=MSDASQL;Driver={Microsoft Access Driver (*.mdb)}
```

You then must specify the full path and filename to the Access database by using the DBQ attribute:

```
Provider=MSDASQL;Driver={Microsoft Access Driver (*.mdb)};
DBQ=C:\mdb_name.mdb
```

Note: An interesting fact has recently come to light that causes the following error with the OLE DB Provider for ODBC:

Microsoft OLEDB Provider for ODBC Drivers error '80004005'

[Microsoft][ODBC Driver Manager] Data source name not found and no default driver specified

This seems to occur if you leave a space after the first semicolon in the connection string shown in the preceding code example, just before the Driver. So, this works:

```
Provider=MSDASQL;Driver={Microsoft Access Driver (*.mdb)};
DBQ=C:\mdb_name.mdb
```

But this doesn't:

```
Provider=MSDASQL; Driver={Microsoft Access Driver (*.mdb)};
DBQ=C:\mdb_name.mdb
```

Notice the space; it's hard to spot.

Of course, because this is the default OLE DB Provider, you can use the following string (without specifying the Provider) perfectly well:

```
Driver={Microsoft Access Driver (*.mdb)}; DBQ=C:\mdb_name.mdb
```

Microsoft SQL Server

To connect to SQL Server by using the OLE DB Provider for ODBC (MSDASQL), you must supply a little more information:

- ❏ Server is the name of the SQL Server

- ❏ Database is the database name

- ❏ UID is the SQL Server user ID

- ❏ PWD is the password for the SQL Server user ID

For example:

```
Provider=MSDASQL;Driver={SQL Server}; Server=Tigger;
Database=pubs; UID=sa; PWD=
```

Microsoft Excel

You can connect to a Microsoft Excel (any version) spreadsheet three ways. The first is by specifying the sheet name as the source of the `Recordset`:

```
objRs.Open "[Sheet1$]", objConn, adOpenDynamic, _
    adOpenStatic, adCmdTable
```

The second is by specifying the sheet name with a row and column area:

```
objRs.Open "Select * from `Sheet1$A2:C4`", oConn, _
    adOpenStatic, adLockBatchOptimistic, adCmdText
```

The third is by specifying a range name:

```
objRs.Open "Select * from myRange1", oConn, adOpenStatic, _
    adLockBatchOptimistic, adCmdText
```

To use the range method, you must first make sure that a range has been specified in the spreadsheet. This range should enclose all the data that you wish to select, and it equates to the recordset. You can have any number of ranges in a spreadsheet. To create a range, you select the cells in the spreadsheet and enter the name in the range box.

You then specify the range as the `Source` parameter of the `Recordset`'s `Open` method:

```
objRec.Open "Authors", objConn
```

In all three cases, the connection string must specify Microsoft Excel as the ODBC driver and the spreadsheet name as the data store name:

```
Provider=MSDASQL;Driver={Microsoft Excel Driver (*.xls)};
DBQ=C:\xls_name.xls
```

Text Files

Text files are slightly different from Excel files in the following respect: In the connection string, you specify the directory where the text file resides, rather than the text file itself:

```
Provider=MSDASQL;Driver={Microsoft Text Driver (*.txt; *.csv)};
DBQ=C:\directory_name
```

You then specify the text file as the name of the recordset to open:

```
objRec.Open "TextFile.txt", objConn
```

OLE DB Provider for Jet

When using the provider for Jet, you must specify only the database name in the Data Source attribute of the connection string:

```
Provider=Microsoft.Jet.OLEDB.4.0; Data Source=C:\mdb_name.mdb
```

If you have a system database, you can use the `Properties` collection to set this before opening the connection, but you must specify the provider first:

```
conDB.Provider = "Microsoft.Jet.OLEDB.4.0"
conDB.Properties("Jet OLEDB:System database") = _
                            "C:\system_db_name"
conDB.Open "Data Source=C:\pubs\pubs.mdb"
```

A database password is also set in this way:

```
objConn.Properties("Jet OLEDB:Database Password") = "LetMeIn"
```

OLE DB Provider for SQL Server

When establishing connections to SQL Server databases using the Microsoft OLE DB Provider for SQL Server (SQLOLEDB), the Data Source attribute is used to specify the name or address of the SQL Server. Consequently, an additional attribute named `Initial Catalog` is used to specify the name of the database for which the connection will be made:

```
Provider=SQLOLEDB; Data Source=server_name;
Initial Catalog=database_name; User Id=user_id; Password=user_password
```

For example:

```
Provider=SQLOLEDB; Data Source=Tigger; Initial Catalog=pubs;
User Id=sa; Password=
```

OLE DB Provider for Index Server

For Index Server you need to specify only the provider name, unless you have multiple catalogs in use under Index Server. In this case you use the `Data Source` to specify the required catalog:

```
Provider=MSIDXS; Data Source=catalog_name
```

OLE DB Provider for Internet Publishing

The Internet Publishing provider allows you to connect to servers that support either the Microsoft FrontPage Server Extensions or DAV (also known as WebDAV or HTTP-DAV) protocol. This allows you to use ADO to query the servers for directory contents, resources, and so on, as well as to update these resources. You use the `Data Source` attribute to specify the name of the Web server:

```
Provider=MSDAIPP.DSO.1; Data Source=http://web.server.name
```

Alternatively, you can add URL= to the front of the Data Source you are opening, which tells ADO that the Internet Publishing provider is being used. For example:

```
recRoot.Open "", "URL=http://web.server.name"
```

Data Link Files

A Data Link file can contain connection details for any OLE DB Provider. Data Link files have a .udl suffix and allow the connection details to be stored in a file rather than being embedded in an application. Data Link files can be created by using Windows Explorer. Under Windows 2000 and Windows XP, you should create a Text File, and then rename the suffix to .udl. Double-clicking this file opens the Data Link Properties dialog. Under previous versions of Windows (and ADO), you can select New Data Link File from the Explorer context menu.

To use a Data Link file as a connection string, simply set the File Name option to point to the .udl file:

```
objConn.Open "File Name=C:\temp\pubs.UDL"
```

Asynchronous Processing

Asynchronous processing was a new feature in ADO 2.0 and allows commands to be executed at the same time as other commands. This is particularly useful when creating very large recordsets or running a query that may take a long time, because you can continue with another task and allow ADO to tell you via an event when the command has finished. You can also cancel a long-running command if you wish. Events can also be used to perform preprocessing and postprocessing around certain ADO operations, such as opening a Recordset or establishing a Connection.

> Note that ASP scripting languages do not support events on the server. Client-side script does support events.

Events

For ADO, only the Recordset and Connection objects support events. There are generally two types of events:

❑ Will... events–those called before an operation starts

❑ ...Complete events–those called after it has completed

A few other events are called after an event has completed, but they are not part of the Will... and ...Complete event pairs.

A Will... event is called just before the action starts. It gives you the chance to examine the details of the action, and to cancel the action if you decide not to run it. The ...Complete event is called just after the action completes, even if the operation was cancelled. If it was cancelled, the Errors collection is filled with details of why it was cancelled.

The Will... events generally have an argument, adStatus, indicating the status of the event. You can set this argument to adStatusCancel before the method ends, to cancel the action that caused the event. For example, suppose a connection generated a WillConnect event; setting adStatus to adStatusCancel will cancel the connection. The ConnectComplete event will then be called, with a status indicating that the connection failed.

The nature of events means that there can be several Will... events that could result from a single action. Although all of these will be called, there is no guaranteed order in which this will happen.

Event Pairings

The way the Will... and ...Complete events are generated can often be confusing, especially in terms of what happens when you wish to cancel the operation that raised the event. The action triggers the Will... event, which has its own event procedure. This code runs, and then the action itself is run. After the action is finished, the ...Complete event is triggered, which runs its event procedure. Once that has completed, execution will continue at the line after the action. The following diagram shows this using Connection events when opening a connection:

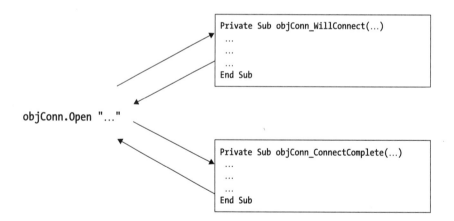

In the WillConnect event procedure, you can decide whether you want this action (that is, the objConn.Open) to occur or not. The event procedure has a parameter called adStatus, which you can use. If you set this to adStatusCancel before the event procedure finishes, the action is cancelled. The ConnectComplete event will still run, but its parameters will indicate that an error has occurred. For example, the following diagram shows how this can be trapped:

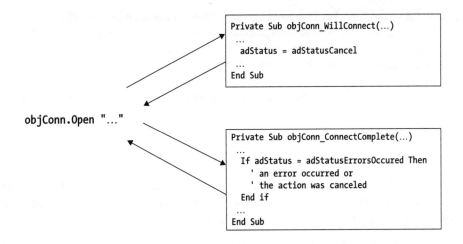

The important thing to note is that the ConnectComplete event is still generated, but the connection does not actually take place. Some actions may generate more than one event, so what happens then? Well, the Will... event is always generated before its associated ...Complete event, but when two Will... events exist, the order in which they are generated is not guaranteed. If you cancel the action from within an event procedure, and this happens to run as the first event procedure, then the second set of event procedures (both the Will... and the ...Complete) are never generated. For example, imagine a recordset where you have events to detect when fields and records change, as shown here:

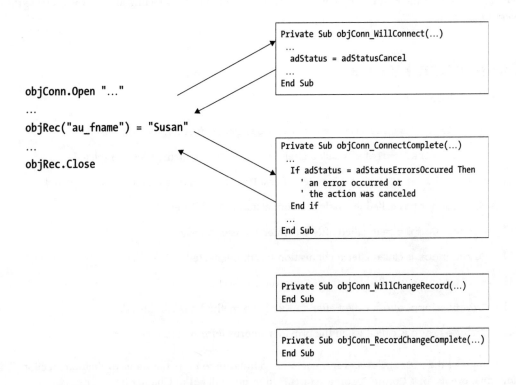

Here the action has been canceled in the WillChangeRecord event procedure. The RecordChangeComplete event procedure runs, but indicates that an error occurred, and the actual action, that of setting the field value is not executed. The WillChangeRecord and RecordChangeComplete event procedures are not run.

These diagrams use Visual Basic, but language choice is not crucial; it's the order of events that's important.

Events in Visual Basic

To use events within Visual Basic, you declare a variable by using the WithEvents keyword. This must be a module/form/class/control level or global variable, because WithEvents is invalid within procedures:

```
Private WithEvents m_rsAuthors As ADODB.Recordset
```

Note that the New keyword is omitted when using this syntax, because you can't instantiate objects at the same time as declaring the variable with events. You must do this separately:

```
Set m_rsAuthors = New ADODB.Recordset
```

Once you have declared the variable, the object will appear in the objects list in the code combo and in a list of events in the event drop-down list (for a selected object). Selecting an event will create the event procedure.

Connection Events

There are nine Connection events:

- ❑ BeginTransComplete is called after a BeginTrans method has completed.

- ❑ CommitTransComplete is called after a CommitTrans method has completed.

- ❑ RollbackTransComplete is called after a RollbackTrans method has completed.

- ❑ WillConnect is called just before a connection is established.

- ❑ ConnectComplete is called after a connection is established.

- ❑ Disconnect is called after a connection has disconnected.

- ❑ WillExecute is called before an Execute method is run.

- ❑ ExecuteComplete is called after an Execute method has completed.

- ❑ InfoMessage is called when the provider returns information messages.

An example of the ...Complete events could be to indicate to users the status of their connection. The individual events for a Connection are discussed in more detail in Chapter 3.

Recordset Events

The Recordset has more events than the Connection:

❑ FetchProgress is called periodically during an asynchronous recordset creation.

❑ FetchComplete is called when the recordset has been fully populated with its records.

❑ WillChangeField is called before an action causes a field to change.

❑ FieldChangeComplete is called after an action caused a field to change.

❑ WillMove is called before an action causes the current record to change.

❑ MoveComplete is called after an action caused the current record to change.

❑ EndOfRecordset is called when there is an attempt to move beyond the end of the recordset.

❑ WillChangeRecord is called before an action causes the data in the current record to change.

❑ RecordChangeComplete is called after an action caused the data in the current record to change.

❑ WillChangeRecordset is called before an action causes a change to an aspect of the record-set (such as a filter).

❑ RecordsetChangeComplete is called after an action caused the recordset to change.

The Will... events can be used to notify the user that an action may change data or may change the underlying records in the recordset.

A word of caution when using the new ADO Data Control in Visual Basic 6: This automatically updates records when using the video-style buttons to move around the records. This differs from the standard Data Control. If you change a field, then the WillChangeField event is called, and if the value is not correct, you can cancel the action. However, it is the Update that is cancelled, not the move. It's not a major problem, but something to bear in mind.

The individual events for a Recordset are discussed in more detail in Chapter 5.

Object Usage

Some people are confused about when to use which object. After all, the Connection, Command, and Recordset objects are all capable of returning a recordset of data. There are only a few hard-and-fast rules, but in general, here's what you should do:

❑ If you only ever need to run queries that don't return a recordset, and those queries are not parameterized statements (such as stored procedures) with output parameters, then use the Connection object and the Execute method.

❑ If you need to use stored procedures with output parameters, you must use the Command object.

❑ If you need to specify the cursor type or lock type, then you must use a Recordset object.

❑ If you are creating only one or two recordsets of data, then you can use the Recordset to implicitly establish a connection to a data store by passing in a connection string in the ActiveConnection parameter of a Recordset object's Open method.

❑ If you are creating two or more recordsets, then explicitly create a Connection object first, then reuse the Connection object when opening the Recordset objects. Remember that each time you connect to a data store with a connection string, a new connection is opened or retrieved from the connection pool.

Summary

This chapter has introduced the ADO object model, examined how you go about connecting to data stores, and looked at the connection strings for a variety of OLE DB providers. It has also briefly introduced asynchronous processing and the use of events, the details of which are covered in the Chapters 3 and 5, where the Connection and Recordset objects are discussed in more detail.

Most of the rest of the book is concerned with the properties, methods, and events of the various ADO objects and related libraries, such as ADOX, ADOMD, and Jet Replication Objects (JRO).

3

The Connection Object

The `Connection` object is what connects the consumer to the provider; it's the link between the program and the data. As you've already seen, the flat model of ADO means that `Connection` objects don't need to be created explicitly. Instead, you can pass a connection string directly to a `Command` or `Recordset` object, and ADO will create the `Connection` object for you. However, explicitly creating a `Connection` object is worthwhile if you are planning to retrieve data from the data source more than once, because you won't have to establish a fresh connection each time.

Connection Pooling

In the newsgroups during the early days of ADO, there was a lot of talk about connection pooling and whether the benefits really are worthwhile. One of the most time-consuming operations you can perform is the act of connecting to a data store, so anything that speeds this up is defined as "a good thing."

Connection pooling means that ADO will not actually destroy `Connection` objects unless it really needs to. The signal for destroying a `Connection` object is dictated by a timeout value; if the connection hasn't been reused within the allotted time, it is destroyed. Here's how it works. Suppose you open a connection, perform some data access, and close the connection. From your point of view, the connection is closed. But underneath, OLE DB keeps the connection in a pool, ready for it to be used again. If you decide that you need to open a connection to the same data store again, you will be given a `Connection` object from the pool of connections, and ADO *doesn't* have to perform all of the expensive data store stuff again. You may not necessarily get the exact same connection object back, but you'll get one that matches the same connection details that you previously used. In fact, existing objects will be given to anyone who requests them, so connection pooling is even more effective in a multi-user system.

One important point to note about connection pooling is that connections will be reused only if they match the exact connection details. So on multi-user systems, if you specify the same data store but use different user names and passwords, you will create a new connection rather than having one reused from the pool. This may seem like a disadvantage, but pooling must be done this way to avoid breaking security; it just wouldn't be right to reuse a connection based on different user details. You could, of course, create a generic user and perform all of your data access through this user, thus maximizing the use of pooling. Under version 2.8 an access token check is performed before the SID when creating pooled sessions. This ensures that delegated credentials are used correctly.

You should also realize that connection pooling is *not* the same as connection sharing. An individual connection is not shared among multiple connection requests. Pooling means that *closed* connections are reused; open connections are not.

You can test to see whether connection pooling really is working by using a tool to monitor the active connections to a data store. For example, with Microsoft SQL Server you can use SQL Trace. Executing the following code shows only one connection being opened:

```
For iLoop = 1 To 5
        objConn.Open strConn
        objConn.Close
    Next
```

However, if you turn off connection pooling, you'll find that the five connections are opened and then immediately closed, one after another.

Although you probably wouldn't want to, you can turn off connection pooling by adding the attribute OLE DB Services = -2 to the end of the connection string:

```
    strConn = " . . .; OLE DB Services = -2"
```

Alternatively, you can achieve the same result by setting the Connection object's Properties entry equal to -2 as in this example:

```
    objConn.Properties("OLE DB Services") = -2
```

This property takes values from the DBPROPVAL_OS constants (see Appendix B). If you've already flicked to the back of the book to find the constant with a value of -2, you'll notice there isn't one. There is, however, a constant to turn on connection pooling, so to turn it off you must use some binary arithmetic. Take the value for turning on connection pooling and perform a logical NOT operation on it.

DBPROPVAL_OS_RESOURCEPOOLING has a value of 1, so:

```
    DBPROPVAL_OS_RESOURCEPOOLING = 00000001
    NOT DBPROPVAL_OS_RESOURCEPOOLING = 11111110
```

and this equals -2.

If you're using an include file that contains these constants, you can use this format:

```
objConn.Properties("OLE DB Services") = DBPROPVAL_OS_ENABLEALL AND _
                                (NOT DBPROPVAL_OS_RESOURCEPOOLING)
```

This says we want all services enabled, apart from resource pooling.

> *The* `Properties` *collection is discussed in more detail in Chapter 8.*

For ODBC connections, the **ODBC Control Panel** applet controls connection pooling.

Connection State

One important point to note about connection pooling is that the connection state is reset when the connection is returned to the pool. This means that if you have set any properties for the connection, the values of these properties will return to their default values. So, even though pooling returns the same connection to you, you cannot rely upon the connection's previous state.

Methods of the Connection Object

Now let's take a look at how to work with the `Connection` object. The remainder of this chapter looks at the methods, properties, collections, and events that this object makes available to us. Let's begin with the methods.

The BeginTrans Method

The `BeginTrans` method begins a new transaction.

```
Level = Connection.BeginTrans()
```

A transaction provides atomicity to a series of data changes to a recordset (or recordsets) within a connection, allowing all of the changes to take place at once, or not at all. Once a transaction has been started, any changes to a recordset attached to the `Connection` are cached until the transaction is either completed or abandoned. At that stage, all of the changes will be either written to the underlying data store (if the transaction is committed) or discarded (if the transaction is aborted).

The return value indicates the level of nested transactions. This will be 1 for a top-level transaction and will be incremented by 1 for each subsequent contained transaction. You can ignore this value if you don't need to keep track of transaction levels.

Not all providers support transactions, and calling this method against a provider that does not support transactions will generate an error. To check that transactions are supported, you can check the `Transaction DDL` dynamic property of the connection's `Properties` collection. For example:

```
intSupported = objConn.Properties("Transaction DDL")
If intSupported = DBPROPVAL_TC_ALL Then
    ' transactions are fully supported
    objConn.BeginTrans
End If
```

`DBPROPVAL_TC_ALL` has a value of 8. The constants are explained in more detail in Appendix B, and the `Properties` collection in Appendix C.

For a good description of transactions, check out the MSDN article titled *Microsoft SQL Server: An Overview of Transaction Processing Concepts and the MS DTC*, available at http://msdn.microsoft.com/library/backgrnd/html/msdn_dtcwp.htm.

Nested Transactions

Nested transactions allow you to have transactions within transactions, and allow you to segment your work in a more controlled manner. For example, consider the situation shown in this diagram of nested transactions:

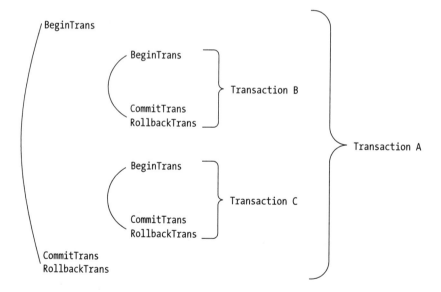

Transaction A starts; this is the first transaction, and no changes made within this transaction will be visible outside of the transaction (unless dirty reads are being used, which allow you to read values before a transaction is committed). Then Transaction B starts, and the nesting level is now 2. While B is running, the changes in B are not visible to Transaction A. When Transaction B finishes, it either commits or rolls back; at this stage, A can see the changes made in B, but processes outside of Transaction A cannot. The same happens with C; its changes will not be visible to A until C commits or rolls back. Once A commits, all the changes in A, B, and C are visible to other processes. Note that if A rolls back its changes, it rolls back transactions B and C, irrespective of whether they have committed or not.

It's possible to use connection attributes (set the `Attributes` property to include `adXactCommitRetaining`) to force transactions to start automatically on commit and rollback, and this can have serious consequences when nesting transactions. This is because every time you commit or rollback a transaction, a new one is automatically started. Imagine some code like this:

```
objConn.BeginTrans          ' start first transaction
    objConn.BeginTrans      ' start nested transaction
        ' do some processing
    objConn.CommitTrans     ' commit nested transaction
```

If auto-transaction mode is in place, then as soon as this nested transaction is committed, another nested transaction is started. You don't have a way to commit a transaction without it starting another, so you can never get back to the level 1 transaction.

You might never use nested transactions (or be able to for that matter—some providers, including the Provider for ODBC, don't support them), but it's good to be aware that this problem can arise.

> **The best way to build transactional systems is to utilize the facilities of MTS, where you don't need to write any code to start or end transactions. MTS also allows for distributed transactions, allowing applications to be distributed across machines.**

See also the `CommitTrans` method and the `RollbackTrans` method.

The Cancel Method

This method cancels the execution of a pending, asynchronous `Execute` or `Open` operation.

```
Connection.Cancel
```

This is particularly useful when writing applications that allow a user to specify connection details, or when users explicitly log on to a connection. If, after a certain delay, the connection has not been established, you can inform the user and offer the option of canceling the connection attempt. For example, in Visual Basic you could open the connection asynchronously and offer the user a Cancel button, which would call this method.

The Close Method

This method closes an open connection and any dependent objects.

```
Connection.Close
```

Closing a connection does not remove it from memory, and you can change its settings and reopen it. To free the object from memory (assuming no one else is using the object), you must set the object variable to `Nothing`. For example:

```
objConn.Close
Set objConn = Nothing
```

To avoid getting an error when trying to close a connection that is not open, you can check the `Connection` object's `State` property:

```
If objConn.State = adStateOpen Then
   objConn.Close
End If
Set objConn = Nothing
```

When the connection's `Close` method is called, associated recordsets and commands behave differently. Any `Recordset` objects associated with the connection are closed. Any `Command` objects associated with the connection will persist, but the `ActiveConnection` parameter will be cleared, thus disassociating the command from any connection.

When the `Close` method is called, any pending changes in `Recordset` objects associated with the connection will be cancelled. If you call the `Close` method while a transaction is in progress, an error will be generated. This is a run-time error, number 3246, saying that the `Connection` object cannot be explicitly closed while in a transaction. In comparison, if a `Connection` object falls out of scope, any incomplete transactions will be rolled back, and in this case *no* error is generated.

The CommitTrans Method

This method saves any pending changes and ends the current transaction.

```
Connection.CommitTrans
```

All changes made since the previous `BeginTrans` will be written to the data store. This only affects the most recently opened transaction, and you must resolve lower-level transactions before resolving higher-level ones. So, if you are nesting transactions, you cannot start two transactions and then `Commit` or `Abort` the outer transaction without first `Committing` or `Aborting` the inner transaction, because they refer to the same connection.

If the `Connection` object's `Attributes` property is set to `adXactCommitRetaining`, the provider automatically starts a new transaction after a `CommitTrans` call.

See also the `BeginTrans` method and the `RollbackTrans` method.

The Execute Method

This method executes the query, SQL statement, stored procedure, or provider-specific text.

```
Set Recordset = _
      Connection.Execute(CommandText, _
                          [RecordsAffected], [Options])
```

Parameter	Type	Description
CommandText	String	Contains the SQL statement, table name, stored procedure name, or provider-specific text to execute
RecordsAffected (Optional)	Long	For action commands, a variable into which the provider returns the number of records that the operation affected
Options (Optional)	Long	A value that indicates how the provider should interpret the CommandText argument (adCmdUnspecified default value)

`Options` can be one or more of the `CommandTypeEnum` constants:

❏ adCmdText, for a SQL string

❏ adCmdTable, for a table name, whose columns are returned via a SQL command

❏ adCmdTableDirect, for a table name, whose columns are all returned

❏ adCmdStoredProc, for a stored procedure name

❏ adCmdFile, for a saved recordset

❏ adCmdUnknown, for an unknown command type

❏ adCmdUnspecified, to indicate the command type is unspecified (ADO will work out the command type itself, but this will lead to poorer performance, so you should always explicitly set the command type.)

You can also add the following `ExecuteOptionEnum` modifiers to `Options`:

❏ adAsyncExecute, for asynchronous execution

❏ adAsyncFetch, for asynchronous fetching

❏ adAsyncFetchNonBlocking, for asynchronous fetching that does not block

❏ adExecuteNoRecords, for a non-row returning command

More details of these options appear under the CommandType property in Chapter 4.

The Execute method returns a new Recordset object, even if it is not used. If the command did not return any rows, the recordset will be empty. If you specify the adExecuteNoRecords option, a null recordset is returned. The Recordset object returned is always a forward-only, read-only cursor (often called a firehose cursor). However, you can specify different cursor types by using the Open method of the Recordset object instead of the Connection's Execute method.

You can use this method with or without some arguments, and with or without it returning a recordset. For example, to return a recordset, you could use this syntax:

```
strCommandText = "SELECT * FROM authors"
Set rsAuthors = objConn.Execute (strCommandText, , adCmdText)
```

If the statement specified in the strCommandText parameter does not return any rows, then you should include the adCmdExecuteNoRecords option; this can improve performance, because the null recordset is not automatically returned:

```
strCommandText = "UPDATE titles SET price = price * 1.10"
objConn.Execute strCommandText, , adCmdText + adExecuteNoRecords
```

To supply multiple values, you add them together.

If you want to find out how many records were affected by the command, you can use the RecordsAffected argument, passing in a variable. This is especially useful for action queries, where a recordset is not returned:

```
strCommandText = "UPDATE titles SET Price = Price * 1.10"
objConn.Execute strCommandText, lngRecsAffected, adCmdText
Print lngRecsAffected & " were updated."
```

If you are using RecordsAffected and you find that it always returns –1 when you expect a different value, check if data store options are stopping the return of this information. SQL Server, for example, has a SET NOCOUNT ON statement, which stops the number of rows affected by a command from being returned. Check that this option is not set anywhere in your command (you might not realize it's there if you are using a stored procedure), and check that it's not set as a global database variable.

To have the command executed asynchronously, you can also add one of the asynchronous flags to the Options argument. For example:

```
objConn.Execute strCommandText, lngRecsAffected, _
                             adCmdText + adAsyncExecute
```

An ExecuteComplete event will be raised when this operation finishes. This happens even if the command is executed synchronously, but is more useful when asynchronous operations are in use.

The Open Method

This method opens a connection to a data source so that commands can be executed against it.

```
Connection.Open([ConnectionString], [UserID], _
                [Password], [Options])
```

Parameter	Type	Description
Connection String (optional)	String	Connection information
UserID (optional)	String	User name to use when connecting
Password (optional)	String	User password to use when connecting
Options (optional)	Long	Extra connection options (adConnectUnspecified default value)

Options can be one of the ConnectOptionEnum constants. At the moment, the only constants supported are adAsyncConnect (which indicates the connection should be made asynchronously) and adConnectUnspecified (the default, which indicates a synchronous connection is to be made).

The ConnectionString property takes its value from the ConnectionString argument if used.

Values passed in the UserID and Password arguments override similar values passed in the ConnectionString argument—unless the Password you supply in the argument is blank, in which case the ConnectionString password still seems to take effect.

Under version 2.8, connecting to the data source depends upon the zone in which the data source originates and whether the provider supports Integrated Security (SQL, MSDataShape, Remote, and Directory Services). If the provider supports Integrated Security and the user credentials are supplied as part of the connection string, the connection is always allowed. If the provider supports Integrated Security and the credentials aren't supplied (i.e., the current user credentials are used), or the provider doesn't support Integrated Security, then the connection depends upon the IE settings for user authentication and logon, which can be:

❑ Automatic logon with current user name and password–the connection is allowed.

❑ Prompt for user name and password–the connection is not allowed.

❑ Automatic logon only in Intranet zone–the user is prompted with a security warning.

❑ Anonymous logon–the connection is not allowed.

Some typical connections strings are shown in the following examples. For the ODBC Provider connecting to an Access database, you would use:

```
Driver={Microsoft Access Driver (*.mdb)}; DBQ=database_file
```

The DBQ argument points to the physical path name of the Access database. To connect to SQL Server, again using ODBC, you would use:

```
Driver={SQL Server}; Server=server_name;
        Database=database_name;
        UID=user_name; PWD=user_password
```

Switching over to the native OLE DB drivers, connecting to Access would be like this:

```
Provider=Micrsoft.Jet.OLEDB.4.0; Data Source=database_file
```

For SQL Server, using the native driver, it would be:

```
Provider=SQLOLEDB; Data Source=server_name; Initial
        Catalog=database_name; User Id=user_name; Password=user_password
```

More details of the different connection strings you can use for the more common OLE DB Providers appear under the ConnectionString property and in Chapter 2.

The OpenSchema Method

This method obtains database schema information from the provider.

```
Set Recordset = Connection.OpenSchema(Schema, _
                                [Criteria], [SchemaID])
```

Parameter	Type	Description
Schema	SchemaEnum (Long)	The type of schema query to run
Criteria (Optional)	Variant	An array of query constraints for each Schema option (generally the column names and values to filter on)
SchemaID (Optional)	Variant	The GUID for a provider-specific schema query not defined by the OLE DB specification

Each value of SchemaEnum has a specific set of criteria values. This large list is included in Appendix B.

This method is most useful for obtaining table and procedure names from a data store. For example:

```
Set rsTables = objConn.OpenSchema(adSchemaTables)
While Not rsTables.EOF
  Debug.Print rsTables("TABLE_NAME")
  Debug.Print rsTables("TABLE_TYPE")
  rsTables.MoveNext
Wend
```

The various schemas are examined in detail in Appendix D.

For multidimensional (OLAP) providers using adSchemaMembers, the restrictions can be either the columns in the members schema or one of the MDTREEOP constants, as defined in Appendix L.

An alternative method of obtaining schema information is to use the ADOX library, as discussed in Chapter 10.

The RollbackTrans Method

This method cancels any changes made during the current transaction and ends the transaction.

```
Connection.RollbackTrans
```

All changes made since the previous BeginTrans will be cancelled. This affects only the most recently opened transaction, and like CommitTrans, you must resolve lower-level transactions before resolving higher-level ones.

Also, if the Connection object's Attributes property is set to adXactCommitAbort, the provider automatically starts a new transaction after a RollbackTrans call.

Also see the BeginTrans method and the CommitTrans method.

Properties of the Connection Object

The Attributes Property

This property indicates the transactional facilities of a Connection object.

```
Long = Connection.Attributes
Connection.Attributes = Long
```

Its value can be one or more of the adXactAttributeEnum constants:

❑   adXactCommitRetaining, to ensure that a new transaction is started automatically after a CommitTrans

❑   adXactAbortRetaining, to ensure that a new transaction is started automatically after a RollbackTrans

❑   A combination of both, to indicate that a new transaction is started automatically after an existing transaction is finished

Note that not all providers support this property.

In Visual Basic you can combine two or more values by ORing them together:

```
objConn.Attributes = adXactCommitRetaining OR adXactAbortRetaining
```

Beware of automatic transaction enlistment when using nested transactions, because this can lead to problems when committing the higher-level transactions. For more details on this see the *Nested Transactions* subsection of the discussion of the BeginTrans method, earlier in this chapter.

The CommandTimeout Property

This property indicates how long, in seconds, to wait while executing a command before terminating the command and generating an error. The default is 30.

```
Long = Connection.CommandTimeout
Connection.CommandTimeout = Long
```

If the timeout period is reached before the command completes execution, an error is generated and the command cancelled. Setting this property to zero will force the provider to wait indefinitely.

For example, the following code will ensure that an error is generated if the command doesn't complete within 10 seconds:

```
objConn.CommandTimeout = 10
```

Note that the Command object's CommandTimeout property does *not* inherit the value set here. So the CommandTimeout property of a Connection object applies only to statements executed through the use of the Execute method.

The ConnectionString Property

This property contains the details used to create a connection to a data source.

```
String = Connection.ConnectionString
Connection.ConnectionString = String
```

ADO supports only the following five arguments in the connection string (all other arguments are ignored by ADO and passed directly to the provider):

❑ Provider= identifies the name of the provider

❑ File Name= identifies the name of the provider-specific file containing connection information (for example, a UDL file)

❑ Remote Provider= is the name of a provider that should be used when opening a client-side connection (this applies only to RDS)

❑ Remote Server= is the path name of the server that should be used when opening a client-side connection (this applies only to RDS)

❑ URL= is the absolute URL identifying a resource, such as a file or directory

The provider can change the connection string while the connection is being established, because it fills in some of its own details.

You cannot pass both the Provider and File Name arguments. Specifying a File Name will cause ADO to load the specified Data Link (.udl) file, which contains all of the necessary connection information. For more information about Data Link files, see Chapter 2.

Under version 2.8, reading of the ConnectionString property has the following actions:

1. If the connection is open, the connection string is obtained from the underlying OLE DB provider.

2. The dynamic property "Persist Security Info" (OLE DB property DBPROP_AUTH_PERSIST_ SENSITIVE_AUTHINFO) is checked. If true, then the password information is returned along with the connection string; otherwise, the password information is omitted.

Some examples of various connection strings are shown here. For the ODBC provider connecting to Microsoft Access:

```
Driver={Microsoft Access Driver (*.mdb)}; DBQ= database_name
```

For the ODBC provider connecting to Microsoft SQL Server:

```
Driver={SQL Server}; Server=server_name; _
        Database=database_name;
        UID=user_name; PWD=password
```

You can also use an existing DSN. To use a DSN called pubs, you would specify this connection string:

```
DSN=pubs; UID=sa; PWD=
```

The pros and cons of using a DSN versus a full ODBC connect string are discussed in Chapter 14.

When using the OLE DB provider for ODBC, notice that you can omit the Provider option (because it is the default).

For the OLE DB provider connecting to Microsoft Access:

```
Provider=Microsoft.Jet.OLEDB.4.0; Data Source=database_name
```

For the OLE DB provider connecting to Microsoft SQL Server:

```
Provider=SQLOLEDB; Data Source=server_name;
         Initial Catalog=database_name; User Id=user_name;
         Password=user_password
```

For example, to connect to a SQL Server using the OLE DB Provider, you would do something like this:

```
objConn.ConnectionString = "Provider=SQLOLEDB; " & _
                           "Data Source=TIGGER;" & _
                           "Initial Catalog=pubs; " & _
                           "User Id=davids; Password=letmein"
objConn.Open
```

If, when you open a connection, you pass the connection details into the `ConnectionString` argument, then the `ConnectionString` property will be filled in with these details.

For more information on connection strings, refer to Chapter 2.

The ConnectionTimeout Property

This property indicates how long, in seconds, to wait while trying to establish a connection before aborting the attempt and generating an error. The default is 15 seconds.

```
Long = Connection.ConnectionTimeout
Connection.ConnectionTimeout = Long
```

If the timeout period expires before the connection opens, an error is generated and the connection cancelled. Setting this property to zero will force the provider to wait indefinitely.

You cannot set this property once the connection has been established.

The CursorLocation Property

This property sets or returns the location of the cursor engine.

```
CursorLocationEnum = Connection.CursorLocation
Connection.CursorLocation = CursorLocationEnum
```

You can set this property to one of the following `CursorLocationEnum` values:

❑   `adUseClient`, to use a client-side cursor

❑   `adUseClientBatch`, to use a client-side cursor

❑   `adUseServer`, to use a server-side cursor

❑   adUseNone, to indicate no cursor services are used (included for backward compatibility and should not be used)

A disconnected recordset can be achieved only by setting the `CursorLocation` property to `adUseClient`.

A `Recordset` created against the `Connection` object will inherit the value set here.

Changing the `CursorLocation` property has no effect on existing `Recordsets` associated with a `Connection`.

The performance issues surrounding various cursor types are discussed in Chapter 14.

The DefaultDatabase Property

This property indicates the default database for a `Connection` object.

```
String = Connection.DefaultDatabase
Connection.DefaultDatabase = String
```

You can access objects in other databases by fully qualifying the objects, if the data source or provider supports this.

For example, when using Microsoft SQL Server, you can create two recordsets on different databases:

```
objConn.DefaultDatabase="pubs"

rsOne.Open "authors", objConn, _
                 adOpenKeyset, adLockReadOnly, adCmdTable

rsTwo.Open "Sales.dbo.Orders", objConn, _
                 adOpenKeyset, adLockReadOnly, adCmdTable
```

The first uses the `authors` table from the default `pubs` database, and the second uses the `Orders` table in the `Sales` database. Note that this option is not available when using the RDS client-side `Connection` objects.

The IsolationLevel Property

This property indicates the level of transaction isolation for a `Connection` object.

```
IsolationLevelEnum = Connection.IsolationLevel
Connection.IsolationLevel = IsolationLevelEnum
```

The isolation level allows you to define how other transactions interact with yours, and whether they can see your changes and vice versa.

This value comes into effect only when you call the BeginTrans method. The provider may return the next greater level of isolation if the requested level is not available.

The value can be one of the IsolationLevelEnum constants:

❑ adXactUnspecified indicates that the provider is using a different isolation level to the one you specified, but it cannot determine which level.

❑ adXactChaos indicates that a higher-level transaction has control over the records. This means that you cannot overwrite any pending changes from another user.

❑ adXactBrowse or adXactReadUncommitted allows you to view uncommitted changes in another transaction. Be careful when using either of these values, because the changes in another transaction have not been committed; therefore, they could be rolled back, leaving you with invalid values.

❑ adXactCursorStability or adXactReadCommitted (the default) indicates that you can view changes in other transactions only after they have been committed. This guarantees the data's state. However, new records and deleted records will be reflected in your recordset.

❑ adXactRepeatableRead doesn't allow you to see changes made from other transactions unless you re-query the recordset. Once you have re-queried the recordset, you can see new records that might have been added by other users to the records that compose your recordset.

❑ adXactIsolated or adXactSerializable indicates that transactions are completely isolated from each other. This means that all concurrent transactions will produce the same effect as if each transaction were executed one after the other.

The Mode Property

This property indicates the available permissions for modifying data in a Connection.

```
ConnectModeEnum = Connection.Mode
Connection.Mode = ConnectModeEnum
```

The value can be one of the ConnectModeEnum constants:

❑ adModeUnknown (default) indicates that permissions cannot be determined, or haven't been set yet.

❑ adModeRead grants read-only permissions.

❑ adModeWrite grants write-only permissions.

❑ adModeReadWrite grants read/write permissions.

❑ adModeRecursive indicates that the adShare permissions should be applied recursively.

❑ adModeShareDenyRead prevents other users from opening a connection with read permissions.

- ❏ `adModeShareDenyWrite` prevents other users from opening a connection with write permissions.

- ❏ `adModeShareExclusive` prevents other users from opening a connection.

- ❏ `adModeShareDenyNone` allows users to open a connection with any permissions and ensures that neither read nor write permissions can be denied to other users.

You can use this property to set or return the provider access permission for the current connection.

You cannot set this property on open connections, and not all providers support all options.

The Provider Property

This property indicates the name of the provider for a `Connection` object.

```
String = Connection.Provider
Connection.Provider = String
```

It also can be set by the contents of the `ConnectionString` property.

Note that specifying the provider in more than one place can have unpredictable results. Microsoft doesn't actually specify what "unpredictable" means in this case, but it's probably best to set this in only one place. The `Provider` property must be set before trying to access any provider-specific dynamic properties; otherwise, the default OLE DB Provider for ODBC is assumed.

If no provider is specified, the default is MSDASQL, the Microsoft OLE DB Provider for ODBC. The providers supplied with MDAC 2.6 are:

- ❏ **MSDASQL** for ODBC
- ❏ **MSIDXS** for Index Server (if Index Server is installed)
- ❏ **ADSDSOObject** for Active Directory Services
- ❏ **Microsoft.Jet.OLEDB.4.0** for Microsoft Jet databases, both Access 2000 and earlier version
- ❏ **SQLOLEDB** for SQL Server
- ❏ **MSDAORA** for Oracle
- ❏ **MSDataShape** for the Microsoft Data Shape with hierarchical recordsets(discussed in more detail in Chapter 11)
- ❏ **MSDAIPP.DSO.1** for Internet Publishing
- ❏ **MSDAOSP** for developing simple OLE DB providers that expose data in simple tabular (row/column) format

❑   **MSPersist** for persisting or saving a `Recordset` to a file or object that supports the standard COM `IStream` interface (such as ASP's `Request` or `Response` objects or ADO's `Stream` object)

Remember that providers aren't deleted when a later version is installed, so upgrading to 2.8 will still show the providers from an earlier version.

The various `Provider` and `ConnectionString` options are discussed in more detail under the `ConnectionString` property, and in Chapter 2.

The State Property

This property describes whether the `Connection` object is open or closed. For asynchronous connections it also indicates whether the state is connecting, opening, or retrieving.

```
Long = Connection.State
```

This will be one of the following `ObjectStateEnum` constants:

❑   `adStateOpen` for an open connection

❑   `adStateClosed` for a closed connection

❑   `adStateConnecting` for an asynchronous connection still connecting to a provider

❑   `adStateExecuting` for an asynchronous connection executing a command

❑   `adStateFetching` for an asynchronous connection fetching data

You can use the `State` property to ensure that you don't generate errors when closing a connection. For example, to ensure that a transaction is committed:

```
If objConn.State = adStateOpen Then
    objConn.CommitTrans
    objConn.Close
End If
```

The Version Property

This property indicates the version number of the MDAC components.

```
String = Connection.Version
```

Note that the provider's version number can be obtained from the `Connection` object's `Properties` collection.

This property is read-only.

Events of the Connection Object

Connection events can be quickly summarized as follows:

- ❑ `BeginTransComplete` is raised after a transaction has begun.

- ❑ `CommitTransComplete` is raised after a transaction has been committed.

- ❑ `ConnectComplete` is raised after the connection has been established.

- ❑ `Disconnect` is raised after a connection has been closed.

- ❑ `ExecuteComplete` is raised after an `Execute` method call has completed.

- ❑ `InfoMessage` is raised when the provider returns extra information.

- ❑ `RollbackTransComplete` is raised after a transaction has been rolled back.

- ❑ `WillConnect` is raised just before the connection is established.

- ❑ `WillExecute` is raised just before a statement is executed.

These events work in both synchronous and asynchronous modes.

All events will have a bidirectional parameter, `adStatus`, to indicate the status of the event. This is of type `EventStatusEnum`, and on entry to the procedure can be one of the following constants:

- ❑ `adStatusOK` indicates that the action that caused the event was successful.

- ❑ `adStatusErrorsOccured` indicates that errors or warnings occurred, in which case the `Errors` collection should be checked.

- ❑ `adStatusCantDeny` indicates on a `Will...` event that you cannot cancel the action that generated the event, and on a `...Complete` event indicates that the action was cancelled.

- ❑ `adStatusUnwantedEvent` indicates that the action that generated the event should no longer generate events.

On a `Will...` event (and assuming `adStatusCantDeny` is not set), before the procedure exits you can set `adStatus` to `adStatusCancel` to cancel the action that caused this event. This also generates an error indicating the event has been cancelled. For example, assume that you have moved from one record to the next; this will raise a `WillMove` event on the recordset. If you decide not to move to another record, you can set `adStatus` to `adStatusCancel`, and the `Move` action will be cancelled. This allows you to cancel actions where the data is incorrect.

When using `Will...` events, one thing to watch for is implicit method calls. Taking the preceding `Move` as an example, if the current record has been edited, then ADO implicitly calls `Update`. In this case you might get more than one `Will...` event. I discuss this in more detail in Chapter 5.

If you no longer wish to receive events for a particular action, then before the procedure exits, you can set `adStatus` to `adStatusUnwantedEvent`, and they will no longer be generated.

The BeginTransComplete Event

This event fires after a `BeginTrans` method call finishes executing.

```
BeginTransComplete(TransactionLevel, pError, _
                   adStatus, pConnection)
```

Parameter	Type	Description
TransactionLevel	Long	Contains the new transaction level of the `BeginTrans` that caused the event
pError	Error	An `Error` object that describes the error that occurred if adStatus is `adStatusErrorsOccurred` (not set otherwise)
adStatus	EventStatus Enum (Long)	Identifies the status of the message
pConnection	Connection	The `Connection` object upon which the `BeginTrans` was executed

You can use this to trigger other operations dependent upon the transaction having been started. For example, you might like to build a transaction monitoring system, and you could log the start of the transaction in this event.

The CommitTransComplete Event

This event fires after a `CommitTrans` method call finishes executing.

```
CommitTransComplete(pError, adStatus, pConnection)
```

Parameter	Type	Description
pError	Error	An `Error` object that describes the error that occurred if adStatus is `adStatusErrorsOccurred` (not set otherwise)
adStatus	EventStatus Enum (Long)	Identifies the status of the message
pConnection	Connection	The `Connection` object upon which the `CommitTrans` was executed

You can use this to trigger other operations that are dependent upon the transaction having been completed successfully, such as updating log files or an audit trail.

The ConnectComplete Event

This event fires after a connection is established.

```
ConnectComplete(pError, adStatus, pConnection)
```

Parameter	Type	Description
pError	Error	An Error object that describes the error that occurred if adStatus is adStatusErrorsOccurred (not set otherwise)
adStatus	EventStatusEnum (Long)	Identifies the status of the event
pConnection	Connection	The Connection object for which this event applies

You can use the ConnectComplete event to examine the details of the connection and whether it completed successfully. For example, the following Visual Basic example shows how you could use the ConnectComplete event:

```
Private Sub objConn_ConnectComplete( _
             ByVal pError As ADODB.Error, _
             adStatus As ADODB.EventStatusEnum, _
             ByVal pConnection As ADODB.Connection)
   Select Case adStatus
   Case adStatusErrorsOccurred
      Print "Errors occurred whilst attempting to connect."
      Print "Connection String is: " & _
            pConnection.ConnectionString
      Print "Error description: " & pError.Description
   Case adStatusOK
      Print "Connection successful."
   End Select
End Sub
```

The nonhighlighted code is the definition of the event procedure and is automatically created by Visual Basic. (For more on using events with Visual Basic, see Chapter 2.)

The Disconnect Event

This event fires after a connection is closed.

```
Disconnect(adStatus, pConnection)
```

Parameter	Type	Description
adStatus	EventStatusEnum (Long)	Identifies the status of the event
pConnection	Connection	The Connection object for which this event applies You can use this to examine whether the disconnection was successful.

You can also use it to track users as they log on to and off from data sources. It can also be useful to alert users when a connection drops unexpectedly.

The ExecuteComplete Event

This event fires after a statement has finished executing.

```
ExecuteComplete(RecordsAffected, pError, _
                adStatus, pCommand, _
                pRecordset, pConnection)
```

Parameter	Type	Description
Records Affected	Long	A Long variable into which the provider returns the number of records that the operation affected
pError	Error	An Error object that describes the error that occurred if adStatus is adStatusErrorsOccurred (not set otherwise)
adStatus	EventStatus Enum (Long)	Identifies the status of the event
pCommand	Command	Command object for which this event applies (may not be set if a Command object was not used)
pRecordset	Recordset	Recordset object upon which the Execute was run (may be empty if a non-recordset-returning command was run, such as an action query)
pConnection	Connection	Connection object upon which the Execute method was called

This allows you to examine whether the command completed successfully and how many records it affected. You can use this instead of the Execute method's RecordsAffected argument. The following Visual Basic code shows the use of this event:

```
Private Sub objConn_ExecuteComplete( _
        ByVal RecordsAffected As_Long, _
        ByVal pError As ADODB.Error, _
```

```
            ByVal adStatus As ADODB.EventStatusEnum, _
            ByVal pCommand As ADODB.Command, ByVal pRecordset As _
            ADODB.Recordset, ByVal pConnection As ADODB.Connection)
        If adStatus = adStatusOK Then
            Print RecordsAffected & _
                    " records were affected by this command."
        End If

    End Sub
```

The nonhighlighted code is the Visual Basic generated event procedure.

The InfoMessage Event

This event fires whenever a connection event operation completes successfully and the provider returns additional information, such as a warning.

```
    InfoMessage(pError, adStatus, pConnection)
```

Parameter	Type	Description
pError	Error	An Error object that describes the error that occurred if adStatus is adStatusErrorsOccurred (not set otherwise)
adStatus	EventStatusEnum (Long)	Identifies the status of the event
pConnection	Connection	Connection object upon which the statement was executed

The parameters define what type of information message this is. This is particularly useful when dealing with ODBC data sources, especially to SQL Server, because it returns informational messages that could be logged in an audit trail.

For example, you could connect to the pubs database on SQL server with this connect string:

```
    Driver={SQL Server}; Server=Tigger; Database=pubs; UID=sa; PWD=
```

and then put this code into the InfoMessage event procedure:

```
    Private Sub oConn_InfoMessage(ByVal pError As ADODB.Error, _
            adStatus As ADODB.EventStatusEnum, _
            ByVal pConnection As ADODB.Connection)
        Dim objError As ADODB.Error

        Debug.Print pError.Description

        For Each objError In pConnection.Errors
            Debug.Print vbtab; objError.Description
```

```
        Next
    End Sub
```

On my server, the above code generates the following warnings when connecting to the pubs database in SQL Server using the OLE DB Provider for ODBC:

```
[Microsoft][ODBC SQL Server Driver]
   [SQL Server]Changed database context to 'master'.
[Microsoft][ODBC SQL Server Driver]
   [SQL Server]Changed database context to 'master'.
[Microsoft][ODBC SQL Server Driver]
   [SQL Server]Changed language setting to 'us_english'.
[Microsoft][ODBC SQL Server Driver]
   [SQL Server]Changed database context to 'pubs'.
```

In general, this event can be used to track connection messages or actions on the connection that return the ODBC SQL_SUCCESS_WITH_INFO result.

The RollbackTransComplete Event

This event fires after a RollbackTrans method call has finished executing.

```
RollbackTransComplete(pError, adStatus, pConnection)
```

Parameter	Type	Description
pError	Error	An Error object that describes the error that occurred if adStatus is adStatusErrorsOccurred (not set otherwise)
adStatus	EventStatusEnum (Long)	Identifies the status of the event
pConnection	Connection	The Connection object upon which the RollbackTrans method was called

You can use this event to trigger other operations that depend upon the transaction having failed, such as writing to log files. For example:

```
Private Sub objConn_RollbackTransComplete( _
                ByVal pError As ADODB.Error, _
                adStatus As ADODB.EventStatusEnum, _
                ByVal pConnection As ADODB.Connection)

    Print "Transaction was rolled back. " & _
        "Changes have not been saved."

End Sub
```

This could be extremely useful in nightly batch jobs.

The WillConnect Event

This event fires before a connection is opened, indicating that the connection is about to be established.

```
WillConnect(ConnectionString, UserID, Password, _
            Options, adStatus, pConnection)
```

Parameter	Type	Description
Connection String	String	Connection information
UserID	String	User name to use when connecting
Password	String	User password to use when connecting
Options	Long	Extra connection options, as passed into the Options parameter of the Connection object's Open method
adStatus	EventStatus Enum (Long)	Identifies the status of the event
pConnection	Connection	Connection object for which this event applies

The parameters supplied can be changed before the method returns–for instance if the user has specified certain connection attributes, but you wish to change them. As an example, imagine an application that allowed the user to specify connection details. You could prevent them from connecting as a certain user, but allow the connection to be established as another:

```
Private Sub objConn_WillConnect(ConnectionString As String, _
        UserID As String, Password As String, _
        Options As Long, _
        adStatus As ADODB.EventStatusEnum, _
        ByVal pConnection As ADODB.Connection)

    If adStatus = adStatusOK Then
        Select Case UserID
        Case "sa"
            Print "Connection as system " & _
                  "administrator not allowed."
            adStatus = adStatusCancel
        Case "Guest"
            UserID = "GuestUser"
            Password = "GuestPassword"
        End Select
    End If

End Sub
```

This stops the user trying to connect as sa and cancels the connection attempt. If a user tries to connect as Guest, then the user ID is changed to GuestUser and the connection proceeds. This allows you to have a set of real user details that are hidden, while exposing a viewable set of user details.

The WillExecute Event

This event fires before a pending command executes on the connection.

```
WillExecute(Source, CursorType, LockType, _
            Options, adStatus, pCommand, _
            pRecordset, pConnection)
```

Name	Type	Description
Source	String	The SQL command or stored procedure name
CursorType	CursorTypeEnum (Long)	Type of cursor for the recordset that will be opened (if adOpenUnspecified, cursor type cannot change)
LockType	LockTypeEnum (Long)	Lock type for the recordset that will be opened (if adLockUnspecified, lock type cannot be changed)
Options	Long	Options that can be used to execute the command or open the recordset, as passed into the Options argument
adStatus	EventStatusEnum (Long)	Identifies the status of the event
pCommand	Command	Command object for which this event applies (may be empty if a Command object was not being used)
pRecordset	Recordset	Recordset object for which this event applies (will be empty Recordset object if no recordset returned by Execute method)
pConnection	Connection	Connection object for which this event applies

The execution parameters can be modified in this procedure, because it is called before the command executes.

This is particularly useful when building user-query type applications where the user has the ability to set details of the connection, because it allows you to examine the parameters and modify them if necessary. For example:

```
Private Sub objConn_WillExecute(Source As String, _
        CursorType As ADODB.CursorTypeEnum, _
        LockType As ADODB.LockTypeEnum, _
            Options As Long, adStatus As ADODB.EventStatusEnum, _
            ByVal pCommand As ADODB.Command, _
            ByVal pRecordset As ADODB.Recordset, _
            ByVal pConnection As ADODB.Connection)

    If Source = "SalaryDetails" Then
        Print " Nice try, but you're not " & _
                "allowed to look at these"
        adStatus = adStatusCancel
    End If

End Sub
```

The preceding code cancels the event if someone tries to connect to the `SalaryDetails` table.

You can also use this technique to protect against *ad hoc* insertions and deletions, and it is an easy way to build business logic into the connection. A better way to protect against this sort of amendment to data or tables is to implement proper security and to use a three-tier business model, where data access is only possible through controlled operations.

Collections of the Connection Object

The collections are discussed in depth in Chapter 8.

The Errors Collection

This collection contains all `Error` objects created in response to a single failure involving the provider.

```
Connection.Errors
```

The `Errors` collection is only cleared by ADO when another ADO operation generates an error.

Note that along with errors, the `Errors` collection often contains warnings and other informational messages from the provider. For this reason, it's a good idea to use the `Errors` collection's `Clear` method before certain operations; this ensures that warnings are relevant to the most recent operation. In particular, you should use the technique on a `Recordset` object's `Resync`, `UpdateBatch`, and `CancelBatch` methods, or on its `Filter` property. On a `Connection` object, use this technique for the `Open` method. Explicitly clearing the errors allows you to use the `Count` property of the collection to quickly identify whether errors have occurred.

The Properties Collection

This collection contains all `Property` objects for a `Connection` object.

```
Properties = Connection.Properties
```

The `Properties` collection is discussed in more detail in Chapter 8, and a full list of the available properties is in Appendix C.

The Command Object

Although the `Connection` object allows the execution of commands (such as SQL statements or stored procedures) against a data store, the `Command` object has greater functionality and flexibility, especially when stored procedures are being used. It's not actually a requirement that data providers support the `Command` object, although all the major providers do.

You might be required to pass parameters into stored procedures or stored queries and, as you'll see in this chapter, there's more than one way to do this. One method involves the use of the `Parameters` collection, which allows complete control over the individual parameters passed to a procedure or query. It's for this reason that the `Parameters` collection is covered in this chapter (rather than with the other collections in Chapter 8).

> When using stored procedures that have output parameters, you must use a
> `Command` object. The `Command` object's `Parameters` collection allows the passing
> of parameters into and out of stored procedures, as well as allowing a recordset to
> be passed back to the application.

Methods of the Command Object

The Cancel Method

This method cancels execution of a pending asynchronous `Execute` method call.

```
Command.Cancel
```

The `Cancel` method is particularly useful when allowing users to submit their own asynchronous queries, because these can often have long execution times, and you may wish to provide them with a Cancel button on the screen.

The CreateParameter Method

This method creates and returns a reference to a new `Parameter` object.

```
Set Parameter = Command.CreateParameter([Name], [Type],
                                        [Direction],
                                        [Size], [Value])
```

The method's arguments are all optional:

Parameter	Type	Description
Name	String	Name of the parameter
Type	DataTypeEnum (Long)	Data type of the parameter (default value is adEmpty)
Direction	ParameterDirectionEnum (Long)	Direction of the parameter (default value is adParamInput)
Size	Long	Maximum length of the parameter value in characters or bytes
Value	Variant	Value for the parameter

The `ParameterDirectionEnum` constants list is as follows:

❑ `adParamUnknown` indicates that the direction of the parameter is unknown.

❑ `adParamInput` indicates that the parameter is an input parameter to the command.

❑ `adParamOutput` indicates that the parameter is an output parameter from the command.

❑ `adParamInputOutput` indicates that the parameter is both an input to and an output from the command.

❑ `adParamReturnValue` indicates that the parameter is a return value from the command.

The `DataTypeEnum` list is quite large, and is included in Appendix B.

Use `CreateParameter` to create the parameters that are to be passed to stored procedures and stored queries. You can use `CreateParameter` two ways: the first is with all of its arguments, and the second is without any arguments. For example, the following two sets of code are logically equivalent ways of assigning specific values to a `Parameter` object's properties:

```
Set objParam = objCmd.CreateParameter("ID", adInteger, _
                                      adParamInput, 8, _
                                      123 )
```

and:

```
Set objParam = objCmd.CreateParameter
objParam.Name = "ID"
objParam.Type = adInteger
objParam.Direction = adParamInput
objParam.Size = 8
objParam.Value = 123
```

Note that both code examples do not add the parameter to the `Parameters` collection of the `Command` object concerned. For this, you must call the `Append` method of the `Command` object, and pass a reference to the `Parameter` object that is to be added to the `Parameters` collection. For example:

```
objCmd.Parameters.Append objParam
```

Multiple parameter objects can be appended to the `Parameters` collection of a `Command` object. However, if you attempt to append a `Parameter` object that does not have a specific value assigned to at least one of its properties, an error will be generated. I'll discuss the `Parameter` object itself later in this chapter.

If the `NamedParameters` property is `True`, the names of the `Parameter` objects in the `Parameters` collection are used to match the parameters to the parameters in the underlying command. If the `NamedParameters` property is set to `False` (the default), then the parameters in the `Parameters` collection are matched to those in the stored procedure or query by the order in which they're listed. In particular, this means that the name you assign to a `Parameter` in the collection (via the `CreateParameter` method or the `Name` property) need not be the same as the corresponding parameter name within the procedure or query. It's the *order* of parameters that's important, not the names, although it's best to use similar (or the same) names both in the collection and in the procedure or query.

The Execute Method

This method executes the query, SQL statement, or stored procedure specified in the `CommandText` property, or the command specified in the `CommandStream` property.

```
[Set Recordset = ]Command.Execute([RecordsAffected],
                                  [Parameters],
                                  [Options])
```

Parameter	Type	Description
RecordsAffected	Long	A Long variable into which the provider returns the number of records that the operation affected
Parameters	Variant	An array of parameter values passed to the statement specified in the Command's CommandText property (Output parameters don't return correct values if passed here.)
Options	Long	A value that indicates how the provider should interpret the CommandText or CommandStream properties of the Command object (default value is -1)

You can use RecordsAffected to determine how many records were affected by the command executed. For example:

```
objCmd.CommandText = "UPDATE titles " & _
                     "SET royalty = royalty * 1.10"
objCmd.Execute lngRecs
Print "Number of records affected by command: "
Print lngRecs
```

Parameter values passed in the Parameters argument will override any values in a Command's Parameters collection. For example:

```
objCmd.Parameters.Refresh
objCmd.Parameters("@FirstParam") = "abc"
objCmd.Execute , Array("def")
```

This command will use def as the value for the @FirstParam parameter, instead of the value abc supplied in the Parameters collection.

Options can be one of the following CommandTypeEnum constants:

❑ adCmdText indicates that the command text is to be interpreted as a text command, such as a SQL statement.

❑ adCmdTable indicates that the command text is to be interpreted as the name of a table.

❑ adCmdTableDirect indicates that the command text is to be interpreted directly as a table name. This allows ADO to switch some internal options to provide more efficient processing. (See the section on the CommandType property.)

❑ adCmdStoredProc indicates that the command text should be interpreted as the name of a stored procedure or stored query.

❑ adCmdUnknown indicates that the nature of the command text is unknown.

Additionally, you can add one or more of the ExecuteOptionEnum constants:

❏   adAsyncExecute indicates that the command should be executed asynchronously.

❏   adAsyncFetch indicates that after the initial batch of rows is fetched, remaining rows are fetched asynchronously.

❏   adAsyncFetchNonBlocking indicates that asynchronous fetching is used. However, if the requested row has not yet been fetched, the last row fetched is supplied instead.

❏   adExecuteNoRecords indicates that the command does not return any records. Any returned rows are discarded.

❏   adExecuteRecord indicates that the result of the command is a single row and should be returned as a Record object.

❏   adExecuteStream indicates that the results of the command should be returned as a Stream object.

For asynchronous operations you can add adAsyncExecute to the Options argument to make the command execute asynchronously, and adAsyncFetch or adAsyncFetchNonBlocking to force the recordset to be returned asynchronously:

```
objCmd.Execute  , , adCmdTable OR adAsyncExecute _
                           OR adAsyncFetch
```

Using streams as command input and output was a new feature of ADO 2.6. The difference is that you use the CommandStream property to specify the stream containing the command to be executed. You can also use the dynamic property Output Stream to specify a stream into which the command's output should be placed. For example:

```
' construct the SQL query
sSQL = "<ROOT xmlns:sql=" & _
                    "'urn:schemas-microsoft.com:xml-sql'>" & _
          "<sql:query>SELECT * FROM authors FOR XML AUTO" & _
          "</sql:query>" & _
        "</ROOT>"

' place the query in the stream
stmQuery.WriteText sSQL, adWriteChar
stmQuery.Position = 0

objCmd.CommandStream = stmQuery
objCmd.Dialect = "{5D531CB2-E6Ed-11D2-B252-00C04F681B71}"
objCmd.Properties("Output Stream") = stmOutput
objCmd.Execute
```

At this stage the stream stmOutput contains the command's results. In ASP you could use the Response object here:

```
objCmd.Properties("Output Stream") = Response
```

This would stream the command output directly to the browser. If using the XPATH `Dialect`, you can also set the following dynamic properties:

Dynamic Property	Description
Mapping Schema	XML schema that maps XML elements and attributes to tables and columns
Base Path	Directory containing the mapping schema

Properties of the Command Object

The ActiveConnection Property

This property indicates the `Connection` object to which the `Command` object currently belongs.

```
Set Connection = Command.ActiveConnection
Set Command.ActiveConnection = Connection
Command.ActiveConnection = String
String = Command.ActiveConnection
```

This can be a valid `Connection` object or a connection string, and must be set before the `Execute` method is called; otherwise, an error will occur.

There is a subtle difference between using an existing `Connection` object and a connection string when setting the `ActiveConnection`. For example, consider the following code:

```
objConn.Open "Provider=Microsoft.Jet.OLEDB.4.0; " & _
                         "Data Source=C:\ADO\ADOTest.mdb"
Set objCmd.ActiveConnection = objConn

objCmd.ActiveConnection = "Provider=" & _
                                "Microsoft.Jet.OLEDB.4.0; " & _
                         "Data Source=C:\ADO\ADOTest.mdb"
```

These code fragments both appear to do the same thing; however, the first uses an existing `Connection` object, whereas the second will implicitly create a new connection. Connection pooling, however, may reuse an existing connection if it can speed up the connection in this second case.

In Visual Basic, if you set the value of `ActiveConnection` to `Nothing`, the `Command` object is disassociated from the connection but remains active. However, note what happens to the parameters. If the provider supplied the parameters (i.e., via the `Refresh` method of the `Parameters` collection), the `Parameters` collection will be cleared. On the other hand, if the parameters were created and appended manually, they are left intact. This could be useful if you have several commands with the same parameters.

The CommandStream Property

This property, new in ADO 2.6, identifies the `Stream` object containing the command details.

```
Variant = Command.CommandStream
Command.CommandStream = Variant
```

The `CommandStream` can be any valid `Stream` or an object that supports the `IStream` interface. For example, in an ASP page the input stream (`Request`) might contain the command details. Because the ASP `Request` object supports the standard COM `IStream` interface in ASP version 3.0, the following code allows us to assign the contents of the `Request` object to the `CommandStream` property:

```
<%
Set cmdC = Server.CreateObject("ADODB.Command")
Set objCmd.CommandStream = Request

objCmd.ActiveConnection = ". . ."
objCmd.Dialect = ". . ."
objCmd.Execute , , adExecuteStream
%>
```

The dynamic property `Output Stream` allows a command's output to be placed into a stream. For example, the preceding code could be modified to output the results of the command to the `Response` object:

```
<%
Set objCmd = Server.CreateObject("ADODB.Command")

Set objCmd.CommandStream = Request

objCmd.ActiveConnection = ". . ."
objCmd.Dialect = ". . ."
objCmd.Properties("Output Stream") = Response
objCmd.Execute , , adExecuteStream
%>
```

The `CommandStream` and `CommandText` properties are mutually exclusive; setting one clears the other.

The CommandText Property

This property contains the text of a command to be issued against a data provider.

```
String = Command.CommandText
Command.CommandText = String
```

This can be a SQL statement, a table name, a stored procedure name, or a provider-specific command, and the default is an empty string. For example, to set the command text to a SQL string, you can do the following:

```
objCmd.CommandText = "SELECT * FROM authors " & _
                     "WHERE state = 'CA'"
```

You can pass parameters into a stored procedure in SQL Server a number of ways. One way is to use the parameters contained in the `Parameters` collection. Another way is to pass the stored procedure and its arguments as a text command:

```
objCmd.CommandText = "usp_MyProcedure ('abc', 123)"
objCmd.CommandType = adCmdStoredProc
Set objRs = objCmd.Execute()
```

This method is sometimes quicker to code than using the `Parameters` collection, although you obviously have no way to use output parameters with this method. Alternatively, you could use the `Parameters` argument of the `Execute` method:

```
objCmd.CommandText = "usp_MyProcedure"
objCmd.CommandType = adCmdStoredProc
Set objRs = objCmd.Execute (, Array("abc", 123))
```

If you set the `Command` object's `Prepared` property to `True`, then the command will be compiled and stored by the provider (if it supports prepared statements) before executing. This prepared statement is retained by the provider for the duration of the connection. If you are using the SQL Server provider, this may create a temporary stored procedure for you (if you have the `Use Procedure for Prepare` dynamic property in the `Connection` object's `Properties` collection, as discussed in Appendix C). This is particularly useful when the same command must be executed several times but with different parameters.

The `Parameters` collection is explained in more detail later in this chapter.

The `CommandStream` and `CommandText` properties are mutually exclusive; setting one clears the other.

The CommandTimeout Property

This property indicates how long, in seconds, to wait while executing a command before terminating the command and generating an error. The default is 30 seconds.

```
Long = Command.CommandTimeout
Command.CommandTimeout = Long
```

An error will be generated if the timeout value is reached before the command completes execution, and the command will be cancelled. If you are using Visual Basic and ADO events, the `ExecuteComplete` event be fires when the error is generated, and you can check the `pError` argument to detect the error. You can also trap the error and examine the error details.

This property bears no relation to the `Connection` object's `CommandTimeout` property; it is not inherited from the connection.

The CommandType Property

This property indicates the type of the `Command` object.

```
CommandTypeEnum = Command.CommandType
Command.CommandType = CommandTypeEnum
```

The `CommandTypeEnum` constants are defined under the `Execute` method and in Appendix B.

You should use this property to optimize the processing of the command, because it informs the provider what sort of command you will execute before that command is actually performed. This allows the provider to decide what to do in advance; this often increases performance because ADO doesn't have to figure out the type of command.

The distinction between `adCmdTable` and `adCmdTableDirect` is quite subtle. Consider the following:

```
objCmd.CommandText = "authors"
objCmd.CommandType = adCmdTable
```

This actually sends `SELECT * FROM authors` to the provider. In contrast, consider this code:

```
objCmd.CommandText = "authors"
objCmd.CommandType = adCmdTableDirect
```

This only sends the statement `authors` to the provider. Some providers may not support direct table names and may require explicit SQL statements.

The performance implications of these options are discussed in more detail in Chapter 14.

The Dialect Property

This property identifies the dialect to be used for the `CommandStream` or `CommandText` properties.

```
String = Command.Dialect
Command.Dialect = String
```

The `Dialect` property is a Globally Unique Identifier (GUID) and is provider-dependent, allowing the provider to support multiple dialects. The default dialect is standard SQL, identified by the following GUID:

```
{C8B521FB-5CF3-11CE-ADE5-00AA0044773D}
```

For the SQL XML format supported by SQL Server 2000, you would use the following GUID:

```
{5D531CB2-E6Ed-11D2-B252-00C04F681B71}
```

For XPATH support, you should use:

```
{EC2A4293-E898-11D2-B1B7-00C04F680C56}
```

Consult your provider documentation to find out any provider-specific dialects.

More details about XML interaction can be found in the ADO help files.

The Name Property

This property indicates the name of the Command object.

```
String = Command.Name
Command.Name = String
```

In many cases you probably won't use this property, but it could be used to uniquely identify a Command object in a collection of commands. For example, imagine an application that allows users to build up a number of commands. You could store these in a collection and use the commands' Name property to identify them. Think about the query window in SQL Server; you could build quite a good emulation of this by using ADO to connect to multiple data sources and using a collection to store various command objects.

Commands as Connection Methods

There is a rarely noted feature that goes like this: if you name a Command object, then associate the command with a Connection object, the Connection object inherits a method corresponding to the name of the Command. This is a dynamic method, which doesn't show up as part of the object's methods or properties within code editors such as Visual Basic.

Let's consider an example. Suppose you have two types of user, a Clerk and a Manager, and both types need to look at employee details. Managers are allowed to see the salary details, but the humble clerks are not. You have decided to use stored procedures to encapsulate all your SQL logic, so you have two possibilities. The first is to build a single SQL statement to return the employee details, and have it check whether the user is a manager or a clerk. Your user then calls a business object that fetches the data, as shown in this diagram of three-tier architecture with the logic in the server:

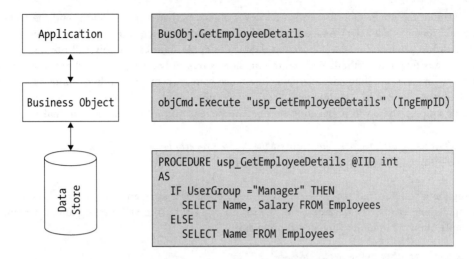

Note that you now have a business rule built into the SQL. In many cases this is not a problem (and indeed could be deemed good practice), but this doesn't always fit everyone's needs. You may find that you'd rather not put business rules into your SQL code. For instance, in this example, you also must work out details such as how to establish which group the user belongs to. That's not a particularly complex problem, but here's an alternative situation that keeps all the business logic in the same place–the business object–as this diagram shows:

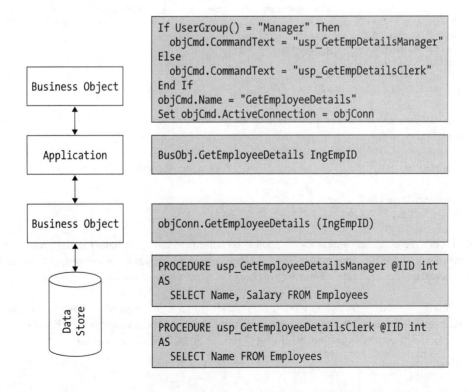

In this situation, the application first calls a business object, perhaps when it starts, and the business object establishes the role: clerk or manager. This sets the appropriate stored procedure and attaches the command as a method of the connection. Later, the application can simply call the business object that calls this new method. Because the method is one of two stored procedures, the correct stored procedure is run. Although this seems like more code, it actually simplifies some programming. It puts the business logic in a component where it is easily reused, and it also makes the stored procedures simpler; these will now run faster because there is no run-time decision to make.

> *When using this method, you must set the Name property before setting the* `ActiveConnection`*; otherwise, an error occurs.*

One thing that's not documented very clearly—or very often—is that when using this method, the newly named procedure accepts the parameters of the stored procedure, and an extra argument: a recordset. For example, imagine the following stored procedure:

```
CREATE PROCEDURE usp_TestProcOne
     @sAuLName varchar(40)
AS
     SELECT * FROM authors
     WHERE   au_lname = @sAuLName
```

You could call this using the following code:

```
strConn = "Provider=SQLOLEDB; Data Source=SQL7Server; " & _
          "Initial Catalog=TestData; User Id=sa; Password="
objConn.Open strConn
objCmd.CommandText = "usp_TestProcOne"
objCmd.CommandType = adCmdStoredProc
objCmd.Name = "TestProc"
Set objCmd.ActiveConnection = objConn
objConn.TestProc "Ringer", objRec
```

This passes `Ringer` into the stored procedure as the parameter, and the results are returned in the recordset `objRec`.

Another shortcut is simply to call the stored procedure name directly against the connection:

```
objConn.Open " . . ."
objConn.usp_TestProcOne "Ringer", objRec
```

If ADO doesn't recognize the command, it passes the command and parameters to the provider to see if it can handle it. If the provider recognizes the command, the command is executed; otherwise, an error is generated. Note that this, of course, will result in poorer performance.

One particularly interesting feature of named commands is that a variation of it allows you to retrieve output parameters of a stored procedure, even when the provider doesn't support it. This is covered in more detail in the "Retrieving Output Parameters" section at the end of the chapter.

The NamedParameters Property

This property indicates whether parameter names should be passed to the provider.

```
Boolean = Command.NamedParameters
Command.NamedParameters = Boolean
```

Setting this property to True means that ADO will pass the name of each parameter to the provider, where the name will be used to match up the parameters. If the value is False (the default), parameters are interpreted in the order created. It is more efficient to add parameters by position because, when adding by name, ADO has to match the parameters to their underlying counterparts.

The Prepared Property

This property indicates whether or not to save a compiled version of a command before execution.

```
Boolean = Command.Prepared
Command.Prepared = Boolean
```

The default value of the property is False. You should set it to True when the command is to be repeated several times. Although the compilation process will be slower during the first command execution, subsequent executions will be quicker because the command text does not have to be parsed and the execution plan can be reused.

If you're using the SQL Server provider, and you set the Use Procedure for Prepare dynamic property of the Connection object to True, a temporary stored procedure will be created for prepared commands. If you find that you need to prepare a lot of statements, consider moving the SQL into a stored procedure, because this will be more efficient than preparing statements.

> Use Procedure for Prepare *is one of the provider-specific dynamic properties of the* ADO Connection *object. For more on ADO's dynamic properties and how to use them, see Appendix C.*

If you are creating prepared commands against SQL Server and not disconnecting, you should ensure that the temporary database (tempdb) has enough space to accommodate the stored procedures.

The State Property

This property describes whether the Command object is open, closed, or currently processing a command.

```
Command.State = ObjectStateEnum
```

`State` can be one of the following `ObjectStateEnum` constants:

- ❏ `adStateClosed` indicates that the command is closed.
- ❏ `adStateOpen` indicates that the command is open.
- ❏ `adStateExecuting` indicates that the command is executing.
- ❏ `adStateFetching` indicates that the command is fetching records.
- ❏ `adStateConnecting` indicates that the command is connecting to the provider.

Using the `State` property allows you to detect the current state of the command. For example, to detect if the `Command` is still executing an asynchronous query, you could use this line:

```
If objCmd.State = adStateExecuting Then
    Print "Command is still executing"
End If
```

Collections of the Command Object

The Parameters Collection

This collection contains all the `Parameter` objects for a `Command` object.

```
Parameters = Command.Parameters
```

The `Parameters` collection is most often used when passing arguments to stored procedures or queries. `Parameter` objects are appended to this collection by use of the `Append` method:

```
Set objParam = objCmd.CreateParameter("ID", adInteger, _
                                        adParamInput, 8, 123)
objCmd.Append objParam
```

You can iterate through the objects in this collection in Visual Basic or VBScript by using the `For Each...Next` command. For example:

```
For Each objParam In objCmd.Parameters
    Print objParam.Name
Next
```

If your provider is capable of describing the parameters of a stored procedure or query, then you can use the `Refresh` method to have the provider fill in the `Parameters` collection for you:

```
objCmd.Parameters.Refresh
```

The `Parameters` collection is discussed more fully in "The Parameters Collection" section later in this chapter.

Other collections, and their methods and properties, are covered in more detail in Chapter 8.

The Properties Collection

This collection contains all of the provider-specific, dynamic `Property` objects for a `Command` object:

```
Properties = Command.Properties
```

The Parameter Object

The `Parameter` object comprises all of the information for a single parameter to be used in a stored procedure or query, and is really used only in conjunction with the `Command` object and its associated `Parameters` collection.

Methods of the Parameter Object

This section details the methods of the Parameter object.

The AppendChunk Method

This method appends data to a large or binary `Parameter` object.

```
Parameter.AppendChunk Data
```

Parameter	Type	Description
Data	Variant	Data to be appended to the parameter

The first `AppendChunk` call after editing the parameter details writes data to the parameter, overwriting any existing data. Subsequent calls add to existing data. Although the documentation states that a parameter must support long data for this method to work, this doesn't appear to be compulsory for SQL Server. You can check the `Attributes` property (see the following section) to see if it contains `adParamLong`, which will indicate if it supports long data.

This method is most often used when storing images in tables. A full discussion of using images with `AppendChunk` appears at the end of Chapter 8.

The `Parameter` object's `AppendChunk` method is functionally equivalent to the `AppendChunk` method of the `Field` object, and it works the same way. The only difference is that you are dealing with a different base object.

Properties of the Parameter Object

This section details the properties of the Parameter object.

The Attributes Property

This property indicates one or more characteristics of a `Parameter` object.

```
ParameterAttributesEnum = Parameter.Attributes
Parameter.Attributes = ParameterAttributesEnum
```

This can be one or more of these `ParameterAttributesEnum` values:

❑   `adParamSigned` indicates that the parameter will accept signed values. This is the default.

❑   `adParamNullable` indicates that the parameter will accept null values.

❑   `adParamLong` indicates that the parameter accepts long data, such as binary data.

You can combine these values by using a logical `OR` statement:

```
objParam.Attributes = adParamNullable OR adParamLong
```

Setting `adParamLong` doesn't appear to be compulsory for binary data. A SQL Server stored procedure with a parameter of type `image` will accept long data without this set.

The Direction Property

This property indicates whether the `Parameter` object represents an input parameter, an output parameter, or an input/output parameter, or if the parameter is a return value from a stored procedure.

```
ParameterDirectionEnum = Parameter.Direction
Parameter.Direction = ParameterDirectionEnum
```

`ParameterDirectionEnum` can be one of the following values:

❑   `adParamUnknown` indicates that the direction of the parameter is not known.

❑   `adParamInput` indicates that the parameter is to pass information to the stored procedure or query.

❑   `adParamOutput` indicates that the parameter is to receive information from the stored procedure or query.

❑   `adParamInputOutput` indicates that the parameter can be used to pass information to, and return information from, a stored procedure or query.

❑   `adParamReturnValue` indicates that the parameter will contain the return value of the stored procedure or query.

In a SQL Server stored procedure, you would declare an output parameter by appending OUTPUT to the parameter declaration. For example, the following SQL code creates a stored procedure with input and output parameters and return values:

```
CREATE PROCEDURE usp_GetValues
       @PubID char(4),          -- indicates an input parameter
       @Value integer OUTPUT    -- indicates an output parameter
   AS
   BEGIN
       . . . .
   RETURN 123                   -- indicates the return value
```

The return value is always the first parameter (index position zero) in the Parameters collection and is named RETURN_VALUE. If you're creating parameters, you must create the return value first:

```
objCmd.CreateParameter   "RETURN_VALUE", adVarInteger, _
                         adParamReturnValue, 8, lngRetVal
```

The return value should be declared as a long integer. If you use Refresh, then a return value parameter is always created, irrespective of whether the stored procedure returns a value with the RETURN statement.

You can also set this property by using the Direction argument of the Command object's CreateParameter method.

Microsoft Access does not support output parameters or return values.

The Name Property

This property indicates the Parameter object's name.

```
String = Parameter.Name
Parameter.Name = String
```

This just identifies the parameter name within the Parameters collection, and doesn't have to be the same as the parameter's name as defined in the stored procedure or query–but it makes sense to keep these the same. This makes the code more readable and easier to maintain.

You can also set this property by using the Name argument of the Command object's CreateParameter method.

Once the Parameter object has been appended to the Parameters collection, this property becomes read-only, because its name becomes its key in the Parameters collection.

The NumericScale Property

This property indicates the scale of numeric values for the `Parameter` object.

```
Byte = Parameter.NumericScale
Parameter.NumericScale = Byte
```

The numeric scale indicates how many digits are to the right of the decimal point.

Both the `NumericScale` and `Precision` properties are required to process SQL data of numeric type correctly. Both Oracle and SQL Server 7.0 support numeric types, using both native OLE DB Providers and the OLE DB Provider for ODBC.

Furthermore, note that the `NumericScale` and `Precision` properties cannot be set via the `Command` object's `CreateParameter` method. If you need to set these properties (for example, in the scenario described in the previous paragraph), you must create an explicit `Parameter` object and set its properties before appending it to the `Parameters` collection.

The Precision Property

This property indicates the degree of precision for numeric values in the `Parameter` object.

```
Byte = Parameter.Precision
Parameter.Precision = Byte
```

The precision indicates the maximum number of digits used to represent a numeric value.

The `Precision` property, like the `NumericScale` property, is required for the correct processing of SQL data of numeric type—as supported by both Oracle and SQL Server 7.0, using both native OLE DB Providers and the OLE DB Provider for ODBC. There's more about this in the previous section on the `NumericScale` property.

The Size Property

This property indicates the maximum size, in bytes or characters, of a `Parameter` object.

```
Long = Parameter.Size
Parameter.Size = Long
```

Watch out for a few things when using the `Size` property:

❑ For variable-length parameters (such as character strings or binary data), you must always set the `Size` so that the provider knows how much space to allocate for the parameter. If you don't specify the size, an error is generated.

❑ If you use the `Parameters` collection's `Refresh` method to force the provider to fill in the parameter details, the `Size` for variable-length parameters may be at their maximum potential size, and memory may be allocated for these parameters accordingly.

❑ For binary data you have to be quite specific about the size of the parameter. For example, if a SQL Server stored procedure has a parameter of type image, and you Refresh the parameters, the size of this parameter is returned as 2147483647. If you create the parameters yourself and use this size, and then use AppendChunk to add the data to the parameter, there are no problems, but creating the parameter with the actual size of the binary data doesn't work. That's because Size is the *maximum* size of the parameter, not its actual size.

The Type Property

This property indicates the data type of the Parameter object.

```
DataTypeEnum = Parameter.Type
Parameter.Type = DataTypeEnum
```

A full list of the DataTypeEnum values is shown in Appendix B, but the following table lists the data types used by the SQL Server and Jet providers and shows how the underlying data store's data types map to those of ADO. The empty table cells indicate that there is no direct mapping between the two database types.

SQL Server 6.5	SQL Server 7.0	SQL Server 2000	Access 97	Access 2000	Enum Value
binary	binary	binary	Binary		adBinary
varbinary	varbinary	varbinary			adVarBinary
char			Text		adVarChar
	char	char			adChar
varchar	varchar	varchar			adVarChar
datetime	datetime	datetime			adDBTimeStamp
smalldatetime	smalldatetime	smalldatetime			adDBTimeStamp
float			Single	Single	adSingle
real	real	real			adSingle
int	int	int	Long Integer	Long Integer	adInteger
smallint	smallint	smallint	Integer	Integer	adSmallInt
tinyint	tinyint	tinyint	Byte	Byte	adUnsignedTinyInt
money	money	money	Currency	Currency	adCurrency
smallmoney	smallmoney	smallmoney	Currency	Currency	adCurrencys
bit	bit	bit	Yes/No	Yes/No	adBoolean
timestamp					adVarBinary

Table continues on the following page

SQL Server 6.5	SQL Server 7.0	SQL Server 2000	Access 97	Access 2000	Enum Value
text			Memo		adVarChar
image			OLE Object		adVarBinary
	float	float	Double	Double	adDouble
			Date/ Time	Date/ Time	adDate
	unique identifier	unique identifier	Replication ID	Replication ID	adGUID
			Value		adEmpty
	nvarchar	nvarchar		Text	adVarWChar
				Memo	adLongVar WChar
	ntext	ntext		Hyper link	adLongVar WChar
	decimal	decimal		Decimal	adNumeric
	numeric	numeric			adNumericge
	image	image		OLE Object	adLongVar Binary
	nchar	nchar			adWChar
	text	text			adLongVar Char
	timestamp	timestamp			adBinary
		bigint			adBigInt
		sql_ variant			adVariant

There are a few interesting (and often confusing) things to note. For example, date parameters in SQL Server don't map to the obvious adDate data type, but rather to the adDBTimeStamp data type. Also, the timestamp maps to adVarBinary for SQL Server 6.5 and adBinary for SQL Server 7.0. You should also note that adInteger maps to Visual Basic's Long data type; it doesn't fit VB's Integer type. If the parameters are of the wrong type, they can cause your commands to fail.

If you wish to create your parameters by using the CreateParameter method, but you're having trouble matching data types or sizes, then the simplest fix is to temporarily call the Refresh method and examine the Parameters collection. You can do this in VBScript by looping through the collection or by using the Locals window in Visual Basic. You can then copy the values that ADO has used and amend your code accordingly. Don't forget to remove the Refresh once you've sorted out your parameters, because leaving it in will cause a performance penalty.

You can find more on data types in Appendix E.

The Value Property

This property indicates the value assigned to the `Parameter` object.

```
Variant = Parameter.Value
Parameter.Value = Variant
```

This is the default property and can be omitted if desired.

The value of a parameter can be read only once, and the recordset should be closed before you read the value (depending upon the `Output Parameter Availability` dynamic property of the `Connection`). Reading a value more than once returns an empty value. For more details on this, see the "Retrieving Output Parameters" section on parameter values at the end of this chapter.

For a parameter holding binary data, you can use the `Value` property to set its value instead of using the `AppendChunk` method. For example:

```
objRec.Parameters("@Logo").Value = varChunk
```

A full description of using binary data appears at the end of Chapter 8.

The Parameters Collection

When dealing with stored procedures or queries that accept arguments, you have three options:

❑   Use the `Command` object's `Execute` method, passing in the parameters as an array of values into the second argument of this method. Not all providers support this.

❑   Use the `Command` object's `Execute` method, passing the parameters in the `Command`'s `Parameters` collection.

Use the `Command` object's `Execute` method, passing the parameter values as part of the command text. In many cases the first is acceptable (and is in fact easier to code), but the one restriction of this is that you can't return any values from your stored procedure. For example, suppose you have a stored procedure like this:

```
CREATE PROCEDURE usp_AuthorsByState
    @RequiredState    char(2),
    @ID               integer    OUTPUT
AS
BEGIN
    SELECT *
    FROM    authors
    WHERE   state = @RequiredState

    SELECT @ID=123

    RETURN 456
END
```

This procedure does three things:

1. It returns a recordset using one of the parameters to restrict the rows that are returned.

2. It sets the output parameter to an arbitrary value (123 in this case).

3. It returns another arbitrary value (456 in this case).

Although the output value and return value are falsely constructed, it illustrates two common techniques for returning information from a stored procedure.

If you wished to call this stored procedure *without* using the Parameters collection, you could do so using code like this:

```
objCmd.CommandText = "usp_AuthorsByState"
objCmd.CommandType = adCmdStoredProc
Set objRec = objCmd.Execute (, Array("CA", lngID))
```

This simply calls the procedure, passing in two arguments: CA to filter the recordset and lngID (a long integer) to be used as the output parameter. This works fine, because ADO builds a Parameters collection from the values you supply. However, note that the output parameter (lngID) is never populated with the output value, and there's also no way to access the return value. So although this method is extremely easy to use, it doesn't give you the functionality that the Parameters collection does.

There's a caveat to this approach: If you reference the Parameters collection before calling the Execute method, the Parameters collection is then Refreshed automatically for you. For example:

```
objCmd.CommandText = "usp_AuthorsByState"
objCmd.CommandType = adCmdStoredProc
Print "Parameter Count = " & objCmd.Parameters.Count
```

During the Print statement, ADO automatically calls a Refresh and populates the Parameters collection. The key point is that there are *three* parameters, not two: the return value, the input parameter (the required state), and the output parameter (the ID value). This means that the next line might fail, because it doesn't use enough parameters:

```
Set objRec = objCmd.Execute (, Array("CA", lngID))
```

However, this line works:

```
Set objRec = objCmd.Execute (, Array(lngRV, "CA", lngID))
```

This shows that if you manually populate the Parameters collection or use the Array method, you don't need to worry about the return parameter. However, if you Refresh the Parameters collection (or if it is refreshed implicitly for you), you'll find that the return value becomes the first parameter in the collection.

Note that not all providers or versions of SQL Server may support this automatic refresh (or indeed the `Refresh` method itself). If using SQL Server 6.5, ensure that you have installed the latest Catalog Procedures. See the SQL Books online for more details on this.

Differences from ADO 2.0

The automatic refreshing of parameters in ADO 2.1 onward is different from what occurred in ADO 2.0. Using an explicit `Refresh` works for both the OLE DB Provider for ODBC and the OLE DB Provider for SQL in both versions of ADO. However, using the implicit refresh gives different results.

I've used the following code to test the automatic refresh facility in ADO 2.0 and ADO 2.1 onward:

```
objCmd.CommandText = "usp_AuthorsByState"
objCmd.CommandType = adCmdStoredProc
Print "Parameter Count = " & objCmd.Parameters.Count
```

If you are using SQL Server 6.5 (and you haven't updated your Catalogs), only the OLE DB Provider for ODBC will return the correct parameter information to the `Parameters` collection. If you *have* updated your catalogs, or if you're using SQL Server 7, then there are differences between the ways that the two versions of ADO handle the parameters. The following list shows which combinations of ADO, providers, and data stores support automatic refreshing of parameters:

ADO Version	Provider	SQL Server	Supported
2.0	OLE DB for ODBC	6.5	Yes
		7.0	Yes
	OLE DB for SQL	6.5	Yes
		7.0	No
2.1 onward	OLE DB for ODBC	6.5	Yes
		7.0	No
		2000	No
	OLE DB for SQL	6.5	No
		7.0	No
		2000	No

Don't think that this removal of functionality is a detrimental step. In this case it is a deliberate (and documented) move to improve performance and reduce network traffic.

Parameter Types in ASP

When using the array method in ASP scripting languages, you must make sure that any variables used for output parameters have the correct data type. When you declare variables in scripting languages, they are **variants**, and this may not match the correct parameter type. The output parameter must have the correct type, even though you can't actually use it. For example, in VBScript:

```
Dim lngID
Set objRec = objCmd.Execute (, Array(lngRV, "CA", lngID))
```

This produces an error, which indicates that a parameter object has not been supplied. That's because lngID is a variant and doesn't have a default type or value. However, this section of code works:

```
Dim lngID
lngID = 1
Set objRec = objCmd.Execute (, Array(lngRV, "CA", lngID))
```

This forces the variant to hold the correct data type; it gives lngID a sub-type of Integer, which is compatible with the integer type declared in the stored procedure (SQL Server integers map to Longs in Visual Basic and in scripting languages).

The Parameters collection contains a Parameter object for each parameter in a stored procedure, including the return value if the procedure has one. It has only two properties and three methods.

Methods of the Parameters Collection

The Append Method

This method appends a Parameter object to the Parameters collection.

```
Parameters.Append(Object)
```

Parameter	Type	Description
Object	Parameter	Parameter object to be appended to the collection

Parameters are created by using the CreateParameter method, and you must set the Type property before calling this method. For example:

```
Set objParam = objCmd.CreateParameter
objParam.Name = "Name"
objParam.Type = adVarChar
objParam.Direction = adParamInput
objParam.Size = 25
objParam.Value = "Janine"
objCmd.Parameters.Append objParam
```

Although more cumbersome to use than the `Refresh` method to build a parameter list, this method is much more efficient, because it minimizes the total number of calls made to the provider.

You can create a parameter with just one line by using the following:

```
Set objParam = objCmd.CreateParameter("State",adChar,adParamInput,2,"CA")
```

You can combine the `Append` and `CreateParameter` methods into a single statement:

```
objCmd.Parameters.Append _
        objCmd.CreateParameter("State",adChar,adParamInput,2,"CA")
```

The Delete Method

This method deletes a `Parameter` object from the `Parameters` collection.

```
Parameters.Delete(Index)
```

Parameter	Type	Description
Index	Variant	Number or name of the `Parameter` object to be removed from the collection

You must use the `Parameter` object's index or its `Name` when deleting a parameter. You cannot use an object variable. For example, we can delete the parameter called `ID` by using this line:

```
objCmd.Parameters.Delete ("ID")
```

Here's another example. This line deletes the first parameter in the collection:

```
objCmd.Parameters.Delete (0)
```

The Refresh Method

This method updates the `Parameter` objects in the `Parameters` collection.

```
Parameters.Refresh
```

This has the impact of querying the data provider for details of the parameters, such as the name, size, direction, and so on. You can then access the parameters by name or ordinal number by indexing into the collection. For example:

```
objCmd.Parameters.Refresh
objCmd.Parameters(0).Value = 1
objCmd.Parameters("@FirstName") = "Janine"
```

You should use this method only when willing to accept the performance hit of the provider re-querying the data source for the parameter details. This is especially important if the same set of parameters is used frequently.

You can use this method quite effectively by querying the provider for the parameters once—for example, at the start of the program. You could then copy the parameter details into a global variable (perhaps an array or a collection, or even a local, fabricated recordset), where it can be used many times during the program. The advantage with this method is that you don't have to keep repeating `CreateParameter` calls, and you can create a generic piece of code to run a command. In addition, you can change the stored procedure without having to change the code that runs the command. The disadvantage is, of course, the delay as the program starts while the parameters are read in. However, you may consider this delay worthwhile, because it gives you a good chance to display that fancy splash screen you've always wanted!

If you access the `Parameters` collection (for example, setting the value of a parameter) without having created your own `Parameters` for a command, ADO will call `Refresh` automatically to fill the collection. Not all providers support the `Refresh` method.

The performance issues regarding `Refresh` are discussed in Chapter 14.

Properties of the Parameters Collection

The Count Property

This property indicates the number of `Parameter` objects in the `Parameters` collection.

```
Long = Parameters.Count
```

You can use the Visual Basic or VBScript `For Each...Next` command to iterate through the parameters collection without using the `Count` property. For languages that do not support enumeration of collections, you can use this property in a loop.

The Item Property

This property allows indexing into the `Parameters` collection to reference a specific `Parameter` object.

```
Parameter = Parameters.Item(Index)
```

Name	Type	Description
Index	Variant	Number or name of the parameter within the collection

This is the default property and can be omitted. For example, the following lines are identical:

```
objCmd.Parameters.Item(1)
```

```
objCmd.Parameters(1)
```

```
objCmd.Parameters("@FirstName")
```

Retrieving Output Parameters

The ability to return information from stored procedures in parameters is extremely useful, but you should be aware of some points. The first is whether output parameters are supported at all by the provider–Access doesn't support them. The second is at what stage the output parameters are available, and for this there are two choices:

1. The parameter is available as soon as the command has been executed.

2. The parameter is available only after the recordset has been closed.

This latter option is the one you must watch for, because in that case, ADO will read the parameter values from the provider only once. This means that if you read the parameter before closing the recordset, then close it, and then try to read the parameter value again, the value may not be available.

You can check to see which of the modes your provider supports by examining the Output Parameter Availability dynamic property for the connection. This will return one of the three DBPROPVAL_OA constant values:

❑ DBPROPVAL_OA_ATEXECUTE indicates that the parameters are available after the command has been executed. This has a value of 2.

❑ DBPROPVAL_OA_ATROWRELEASE indicates that the parameters are available after the recordset has been closed. This has a value of 4, and is the option supported by SQL Server.

❑ DBPROPVAL_OA_NOTSUPPORTED indicates that output parameters are not supported. This has a value of 1.

You could check these values with code like this:

```
Set objCmd.ActiveConnection = objConn

objCmd.CommandText = "usp_ProcedureWithOutputParam"
objCmd.CommandType = adCmdStoredProc
objCmd.Parameters.Append objCmd.CreateParameter("RETURN_VALUE", _
                                adInteger, adParamReturnValue)
Set objRec = objCmd.Execute

intParamAvail = objConn.Properties("Output Parameter Availability")
If intParamAvail = DBPROPVAL_OA_ATROWRELEASE Then
     ' parameter not available until recordset is closed
```

```
        objRec.Close
   End If
   intRV = objCmd.Parameters("ReturnValue")
```

This isn't a problem with commands that do not return recordsets, because there is no recordset to close.

Output Parameters Without Closing Recordsets

There are two solutions to the problem of parameters not being available until the recordset is closed. The first is simply a matter of using client-side cursors, which allows the parameters to be immediately available.

The second method involves the naming of stored procedures by using the Command object's Name property. You've already seen that code similar to this is allowed:

```
strConn = "Provider=SQLOLEDB; Data Source=SQL7Server; " & _
          "Initial Catalog=TestData; User Id=sa; Password="
objConn.Open strConn

objCmd.CommandText = "usp_AStoredProcedure"
objCmd.CommandType = adCmdStoredProc
Set objParam = objCmd.CreateParameter("ID", adInteger, _
                                    adParamInput, 8, 123)
objCmd.Parameters.Append objParam
Set objParam = _
      objCmd.CreateParameter("Name", adVarChar, _
                                adParamInput, 25, "Janine")
objCmd.Parameters.Append objParam
objCmd.Name = "StoredProcedureName"
Set objCmd.ActiveConnection = objConn

objConn.StoredProcedureName
```

This was never well documented, but what's even less well documented is that you can pass the arguments to the stored procedure and a recordset object like so:

```
objConn.StoredProcedureName Argument1, Argument2, objRec
```

The arguments are accepted by the stored procedure in the normal way, and the recordset object is filled accordingly. As soon as this command is executed, you can access the return and output parameters even though the recordset is still open.

As a word of warning, you shouldn't really rely on this procedure; because it's not documented, there's no way of telling whether this will continue to work in future versions of ADO.

5

The Recordset Object

The recordset is really all about data, so it's at the very heart of ADO. A recordset contains all the columns and rows returned from a specific action.

Methods of the Recordset Object

The AddNew Method

This method creates a new row for an updateable `Recordset` object.

```
Recordset.AddNew([FieldList], [Values])
```

Parameter	Type	Description
FieldList	Variant	A single name or an array of names or ordinal positions of the fields in the new row
Values	Variant	A single value or an array of values for the fields in the new row (if `FieldList` is an array, must also be an array with same number of elements)

You can use `AddNew` only when the recordset supports addition of new rows. You can check this by examining the `Supports` method:

```
If objRs.Supports(adAddNew) Then
    ' recordset supports additions
End If
```

You can use AddNew in two ways. The first is without any arguments, which places the current row pointer on the new row. You can then set values to the fields for the new row and save the changes with Update if using immediate update mode, or with UpdateBatch if using batch update mode (LockType = adLockBatchOptimistic). When you are adding a new row and have set the various fields for the row, you can also save the changes by moving off the row. Calling MoveFirst or MoveLast will move to the beginning or end of the recordset, respectively. Calling MoveNext will place you at EOF, and calling MovePrevious will move you to the row before the new row.

The second method uses the arguments, allowing you to pass in an array of fields and values. For example, the following line adds a new row filling in one field:

```
objRs.AddNew "author", "Jan Lloyd"
```

The following line adds one row, but fills in two fields:

```
objRs.AddNew Array("author", "year born"), _
             Array("Jan Lloyd", 1969)
```

If you are using arguments to supply both the field names and values, and batch update mode is not being used, then the changes are effective immediately–that is, there is no need to perform the Update method. ADO will automatically call the Update method if you use AddNew while editing the current row or adding a new row. You can check the EditMode property for the value of adEditAdd to determine if this is so.

However, if you are using batch update mode, you must still call the UpdateBatch method to update the data source.

If you're using the array method to add rows (as shown in the preceding example), you must ensure that both arrays contain the same number of arguments, and that the details of the arrays are in the correct order. The array method is also particularly good when creating (fabricating) your own recordsets.

AutoNumber and Identity Fields

The following question is probably one of the most frequently asked questions about ADO, and it's of particular interest to people converting from DAO:

When using AutoNumber *and* Identity *fields, how do you add a new row and then get the key value for the newly added row?*

Unfortunately, there's not always a simple answer; it depends on the provider you are using and details like the cursor location, cursor type, locking method, and indexes on the table.

ADO states that after adding a new row, when you then Update that row, the cursor is placed on the newly added row. This is exactly what you need, but the Identity or AutoNumber value may not be available. For example, code such as this may not produce the desired result:

```
objRs.AddNew
objRs("field_name") = "field_value"
objRs.Update

Print objRs("ID")
```

This assumes that ID is an automatically incrementing field.

The table below indicates which combinations of providers and target databases support retrieval of auto-incrementing fields:

Provider	Target	Indexed	Cursor Location	Cursor Type	Lock Type
ODBC	Access (all versions)	Yes	Server	Keyset	Pessimistic Optimistic
		No	Server	Keyset	Pessimistic Optimistic
		Yes & No	Client	All	Optimistic BatchOptimistic
	SQL Server 6.5	Yes	Server	Keyset	Pessimistic Optimistic
	SQL Server 7.0	Yes	Server	Keyset	Pessimistic Optimistic
		Yes	Client	All	Pessimistic Optimistic
		No	Client	All	Pessimistic Optimistic
	SQL Server 2000	Yes	Server	Keyset	Pessimistic Optimistic
			Client	ForwardOnly	Pessimistic

Table continues on the following page

Provider	Target	Indexed	Cursor Location	Cursor Type	Lock Type
Jet 4.0	Access 97	Yes	Server	All	All
		No	Server	All	All
	Access 2000 (and higher)	Yes	Server	All	All
		Yes	Client	All	Pessimistic Optimistic
		No	Server	All	All
		No	Client	All	Pessimistic Optimistic
SQL OLEDB	SQL Server 6.5	Yes	Server	Keyset	Pessimistic Optimistic
	SQL Server 7.0	Yes	Client	All	Pessimistic Optimistic
	SQL Server 2000	No	Client	All	Pessimistic Optimistic

Any combination not shown in the list does not support the availability of the auto-number field.

Obtaining the identity value directly works only when adding rows directly using AddNew; it will not work if you use commands and SQL INSERT statements.

Using @@IDENTITY

If using SQL Server and you need to use a combination that does not support the auto-number field, then you can use the global value that represents the latest IDENTITY value added. Using this, you can obtain the value you need. For example, in a stored procedure you could do this:

```
CREATE PROCEDURE usp_AddAuthor
    @sAuLName    varchar(25),
    @sAuFName    varchar(25)
AS
BEGIN
    INSERT INTO authors (au_lname, au_fname)
    VALUES (@sAuLName, @sAUFName)

    RETURN @@IDENTITY
END
```

This adds a new row and then returns the IDENTITY field just used. You can then run this stored procedure by using a Command object and access the return value through the first member (index 0) in the `Parameters` collection. Alternatively, you can return the identity value as an output parameter. You can also use this technique when running straight SQL queries.

One thing to watch when using this technique: `@@IDENTITY` is a global variable and represents the last `IDENTITY` value updated, irrespective of the table. So if you have an `INSERT` trigger on a table, and the table that the trigger inserts into has an identity field, then `@@IDENTITY` will reflect this value rather than the one you intended. To get around this it's best to use the `SCOPE_IDENTITY()` function, which returns the identity value for the scope of the current insert.

Because the server handles this facility, you can use this with any type of cursor and location.

The Cancel Method

This method cancels execution of a pending asynchronous `Open` operation.

```
Recordset.Cancel
```

This is particularly useful when allowing users to submit queries, because you can use it to give them an opportunity to cancel the query if they feel it is taking too long.

If you call the `Cancel` method on a recordset that was not opened asynchronously, an error will be generated.

The CancelBatch Method

This method cancels a pending batch update when in batch update mode.

```
Recordset.CancelBatch([AffectRecords])
```

Name	Type	Description
AffectRecords	AffectEnum	Determines which rows will be affected by the batch cancel (default is adAffectAll)

The `AffectEnum` value can be one of the following constants:

❑   `adAffectCurrent` cancels updates for the current row.

❑   `adAffectGroup` cancels updates for rows that match the current `Filter`, which must be set before using this option.

❑   `adAffectAll` cancels all pending updates, even those not shown because of a `Filter`.

❑   `adAffectAllChapters` cancels all pending updates in child (chapter) recordsets when using shaped data.

Be careful when using adAffectGroup. With this setting, rows that do not match the current filter are *not* cancelled; if your Filter is not set as you intend, it's possible you'll fail to cancel all of the pending changes you wanted to.

Always check the Errors collection after performing this method. It's a good way to catch underlying conflicts, such as a row being deleted. Conflict resolution is discussed in more detail later in this chapter in the "Conflict Resolution" section under the Save method.

It's always sensible to set the current row position to a known row after this call, because the current row can be left in an unknown position after a CancelBatch method call.

The CancelUpdate Method

This method cancels any changes made to the current row or to a new row prior to calling the Update method.

```
Recordset.CancelUpdate
```

This is used when in normal update mode, and it cancels changes to the current row only.

You can use this to cancel the addition of a new row, in which case the current row becomes the row you were on before adding the new row.

The Clone Method

This method creates a duplicate Recordset object from an existing Recordset object.

```
Set Recordset_Clone = Recordset.Clone([LockType])
```

Name	Type	Description
LockType	LockTypeEnum	Lock type to apply to the new recordset (default value is adLockUnspecified)

In this case LockTypeEnum is a subset of the full list of constants and should have one of these two values:

❑ adLockUnspecified indicates that the cloned recordset should have the same lock type as the original recordset.

❑ adLockReadOnly indicates that the cloned recordset should be read-only.

It's important to note that this doesn't create two independent recordsets. Rather, it creates two pointers (which are Recordset objects) that both point to the same recordset. This lets you have two separate cursors open on the same set of rows, allowing you to move the row pointers independently. There is only one data set, so changes made through either the original recordset pointer or through the clone pointer appear in the other. The important thing to remember is that a `Recordset` object is just a pointer to a data set. Therefore, a `Clone` is just another pointer to the same data set.

Cloning recordsets is often more efficient than creating a new recordset with the same request criteria, because it avoids a trip to the server.

Cloning is allowed only on bookmarkable recordsets (for more on bookmarkable recordsets, see section on the `Bookmark` property later in this chapter). Bookmarks are valid in all clones. You can use the `Supports` method to determine if bookmarks are supported in the recordset:

```
If objRs.Supports(adBookmark) Then
    Set objRsClone = objRs.Clone
End If
```

If you make any changes to a recordset, those changes will be visible in all clones until the time you `Requery` the original recordset. At that stage the cloned recordset will no longer be synchronized with the original recordset (you effectively have two recordsets) and will contain the set of rows before the `Requery` took place.

The Close Method

This method closes the `Recordset` object and any dependent objects.

```
Recordset.Close
```

Beware of closing the recordset when changes are in place, because the following will occur:

❑   When in batch update mode, changes will be lost.

❑   When in immediate update mode, an error will be generated.

Closing a recordset does not free all of its resources from memory, and you should set its object variable to `Nothing` in VB (or to `null` in JScript) to achieve this:

```
Set objRs = Nothing
```

> The best method of using recordsets is to open the recordset as late as possible and close it (and free any associated resources) as early as possible, thus minimizing the amount of time the recordset is open. This can help conserve database resources.

To be absolutely sure that you protect against errors, you can also check to see whether the recordset is open before closing it:

```
If objRs.State = adStateOpen Then
    objRs.Close
End If
Set objRs = Nothing
```

The CompareBookmarks Method

This method compares two bookmarks and returns an indication of the relative values.

```
CompareEnum = Recordset.CompareBookmarks(Bookmark1, Bookmark2)
```

Parameter	Type	Description
Bookmark1	Variant	Bookmark of the first row to be compared
Bookmark2	Variant	Bookmark of the second row to be compared

CompareEnum will be one of the following constants:

❑ adCompareLessThan indicates that the first bookmark is before the second.

❑ adCompareEqual indicates that the bookmarks are equal.

❑ adCompareGreaterThan indicates that the first bookmark is after the second.

❑ adCompareNotEqual indicates that the bookmarks are not equal and not ordered.

❑ adCompareNotComparable indicates that it is not possible to compare the two bookmarks.

For more on setting bookmarks, see the section on the Bookmark property later in this chapter. The CompareBookmarks method is applicable only for comparing bookmarks from the same recordset or its clones. Even if two recordsets were created in exactly the same way, their bookmarks are not guaranteed to be the same.

Bookmarks are comparable across Sort and Filter method calls, because these do not change the rowset.

Note that this compares the actual bookmarks, not the values in the rows that the bookmarks point to.

The Delete Method

This method deletes the current row or group of rows.

```
Recordset.Delete([AffectRecords])
```

Parameter	Type	Description
AffectRecords	AffectEnum	Value that determines how many rows this method will affect (default value is adAffectCurrent)

The AffectEnum type can be one of the following constants:

❑   adAffectAllChapters deletes all chapters (child recordsets) associated with the row or group of rows. For more details on chapters, see Chapter 13.

❑   adAffectCurrent deletes only the current row.

❑   adAffectGroup deletes only rows that match the current Filter.

❑   adAffectAll deletes all rows.

Remember that when in batch update mode, the rows are only *marked* for deletion; they are not removed from the data store itself until UpdateBatch is called.

Once a row has been deleted, the current deleted row remains active until you move away from it. Attempting to access values from a deleted row will result in an error.

If the Recordset contains multiple tables, and the Unique Table dynamic property is set, then only rows from this unique table are deleted.

An error will be generated if the recordset does not support deletions. You can use the Supports method to determine if the recordset support deletions:

```
If objRs.Supports(adDelete) Then
    objRs.Delete
End If
```

You should also check the Errors collection, because the provider may return errors because of conflicts with the underlying data.

The Find Method

Searches the `Recordset` for a row that matches the specified criteria.

```
Recordset.Find(Criteria, [SkipRecords], _
               [SearchDirection], [Start])
```

Parameter	Type	Description
Criteria	String	Statement that specifies the column name, comparison operator, and value to use for the search (Only one criterion is supported, and multiple values by use of OR or AND will generate an error.)
SkipRecords	Long	The offset (from the current row, or from the bookmark specified by the Start parameter) from which point the search should begin (default value is 0)
Search Direction	SearchDirectionEnum	Indicates the direction of the search (default value is adSearchForward)
Start	Variant	Bookmark for the row from which the operation should begin.

`SearchDirection` can be one of the following `SearchDirectionEnum` constants:

❑ `adSearchForward` searches forward in the recordset.

❑ `adSearchBackward` searches backward in the recordset.

`Start` can be a valid bookmark, or you can use one of the `BookmarkEnum` constants:

❑ `adBookmarkCurrent` starts the search on the current row.

❑ `adBookmarkFirst` starts the search from the first row.

❑ `adBookmarkLast` starts the search from the last row.

`Criteria` follows the basic form of a SQL WHERE clause. For example:

```
state = 'CA'
```

```
age = 13
```

```
au_lname LIKE 'S*'
```

*Both * and % are acceptable as wildcard characters, although they can be used only at the end of the search string.*

If `Criteria` is met, the current row is positioned on the found row. If `Criteria` is not met, then:

❑   If you're searching forward, the current row is set to be the end of the recordset (and `EOF` is set).

❑   If you're searching backward, the current row is set to be the beginning of the recordset (and `BOF` is set).

For example:

```
objRs.Find "au_lname = 'Lloyd'"
If objRs.EOF Then
    Print "Record was not found"
End If
```

You can use `Criteria` to search for values that are less than, equal to, greater than, or like a particular value. For example:

```
objRs.Find "Price < 14.99"
objRs.Find "Price > 14.99"
objRs.Find "au_lname LIKE 'L*'"
```

The latter will find all values of au_lname that start with L.

Only single search values are allowed with `Find`. Using multiple search values with `AND` or `OR` generates an error. For example:

```
objRs.Find "au_lname = 'Lloyd' AND au_fname = 'Janine'"
```

This is invalid and will generate an error. This is one area where the direct migration from DAO to ADO will cause problems.

If you do need to use multiple criteria values, then your only choice is to create a new recordset or use a `Filter`, which does accept multiple values.

Not all providers support the `Find` method, so you can use the `Supports` method to identify whether this is supported by the recordset:

```
If objRs.Supports(adFind) Then
    objRs.Find "au_lname = 'Lloyd'"
End If
```

The GetRows Method

This method retrieves multiple rows of a `Recordset` object into a multidimensional array.

```
Variant = Recordset.GetRows([Rows], [Start], [Fields])
```

Parameter	Type	Description
Rows	Long	Indicates how many rows to retrieve. The default is adGetRowsRest, which indicates that all remaining rows in the recordset should be fetched.
Start	Variant	The bookmark for the row from which the operation should begin. The default is the current row.
Fields	Variant	A single field name, an ordinal position, an array of field names, or an array of ordinal values representing the fields that should be fetched. The default is to fetch all fields.

Start can be a valid bookmark, or one of the BookmarkEnum constants:

❑ adBookmarkCurrent starts the search on the current row.

❑ adBookmarkFirst starts the search from the first row.

❑ adBookmarkLast starts the search from the last row.

The array returned by the GetRows call is automatically sized to fit the requested columns and rows. The columns are placed into the first dimension of the array, and the rows placed into the second. For example:

```
varRec = objRs.GetRows
intCols = UBound(varRec, 1)
intRows = UBound(varRec, 2)

For intRow = 0 To intRows
    For intCol = 0 To intCols
        Print varRec(intCol, intRow)
    Next
Next
```

Although this is not the obvious way around, this column/row order has been used to allow backward compatibility with DAO and RDO. In fact, the main reason for this is that it's easy to modify the second dimension of an array to add more data, but it's much harder to modify the first dimension once data is in the array. Any values that do not make sense to store in an array, such as chapters or images, are given empty values.

For Fields, you can specify either a single field name or an array of fields to be returned. Here are a couple of examples:

```
varRec = objRs.GetRows (, , "au_lname")

varRec = objRs.GetRows (, , Array("au_lname", "au_fname"))
```

If using the latter method, the order in which the columns are placed in the array dictates the order in which they are returned.

After you call `GetRows`, the next unread row becomes the current row. If there are no more rows, `EOF` is set.

When dealing with a large recordset, you may find that calling `GetRows` several times with a smaller number of rows is more efficient than calling it once to retrieve all rows. For example, if calling `GetRows` on a table with 1,000 rows, it might be quicker to call it 10 times using 100 as the number of rows to retrieve (depending upon the cursor type and location) rather than retrieving all rows at once. This is examined in more detail in Chapter 14.

The GetString Method

This method returns a `Recordset` as a string.

```
String = Recordset.GetString([StringFormat], [NumRows], _
                             [ColumnDelimiter], _
                             [RowDelimiter],
                             [NullExpr])
```

Parameter	Type	Description
StringFormat	StringFormat Enum	The format in which the recordset should be returned (default is adClipString)
NumRows	Long	The number of rows to be returned from the recordset (If this is not specified, or if it is greater than the number of rows in the recordset, all rows will be returned.)
Column Delimiter	String	The delimiter to use between columns (default is the TAB character)
RowDelimiter	String	The delimiter to use between rows (default is the CARRIAGE RETURN character)
NullExpr	String	Expression to use in place of NULL value (default is an empty string)

The only valid value for `StringFormatEnum` is `adClipString`. You can use this method quite effectively to populate text boxes in Visual Basic or to quickly create HTML tables in ASP. For example, the following code shows how to fill a text box (named `Text1`, with its `MultiLine` property set to `True`):

```
Dim objConn As New ADODB.Connection
Dim objRs  As New ADODB.Recordset

objConn.Open "Provider=SQLOLEDB; Data Source=Tigger; " & _
            "Initial Catalog=pubs; User ID=sa; Password="

objRs.Open "select au_lname from authors", objConn, _
```

```
                    adOpenForwardOnly, adLockReadOnly, adCmdText

    Text1.Text = objRs.GetString (,,,vbCrLf)

    objRs.Close
    objConn.Close
    Set objRs = Nothing
    Set objConn = Nothing
```

The next example shows how to quickly create an HTML table:

```
    NBSPACE = chr(160)
    Set objConn = Server.CreateObject("ADODB.Connection")
    Set objRs = Server.CreateObject("ADODB.Recordset")

    objConn.Open "Provider=SQLOLEDB; Data Source=Tigger; " & _
                 "Initial Catalog=pubs; User ID=sa; Password="

    objRs.Open "authors", objConn, _
                 adOpenForwardOnly, adLockReadOnly, adCmdTable

    Response.Write "<TABLE BORDER=1><TR><TD>"
    Response.Write objRs.GetString (adClipString, -1, _
                                "</TD><TD>", _
                                "</TD></TR><TR><TD>", _
                                NBSPACE)
    Response.Write "</TD></TR></TABLE>"

    objRs.Close
    objConn.Close
    Set objRs = Nothing
    Set objConn = Nothing
```

This saves having to loop through the Fields collection to manually build the table.

Only row data is saved to the string, not schema data. You cannot, therefore, reopen a recordset from this string.

The Move Method

Moves the position of the current row pointer in a Recordset.

```
    Recordset.Move(NumRecords, [Start])
```

Parameter	Type	Description
NumRecords	Long	The number of rows the current row position moves
Start	Variant	The bookmark for the row from which the operation should begin (default value is adBookmarkCurrent)

`Start` can be a valid bookmark, or one of the `BookmarkEnum` constants:

❑   `adBookmarkCurrent`, to start the search on the current row

❑   `adBookmarkFirst`, to start the search from the first row

❑   `adBookmarkLast`, to start the search from the last row

You can supply a negative number for `NumRecords` to move backwards in the recordset. For example, to move backwards three rows you could do this:

```
objRs.Move -3
```

You should be aware that forward-only recordsets will not allow moving backwards, and may not allow moving forwards by any number other than 1. You can use the `Supports` method to check for this:

```
If objRs.Supports(adMovePrevious) Then
    objRs.Move -3
End If
```

If your recordset has a `CacheSize` other than 1, you are allowed to move within the rows in the cache but not to rows outside the cache.

If you move past the beginning or end of the recordset, then you will be positioned on `BOF` or `EOF`, and the properties set accordingly. A subsequent call to `Move` beyond the start or end of the recordset will generate an error, as will trying to `Move` in an empty recordset.

If the current row has been changed, and `Update` not called, then a move will implicitly call `Update`. You should call `CancelUpdate` before calling `Move` if you do not wish to keep the changes.

The MoveFirst Method

This method moves the current row pointer to the first row in the `Recordset`.

```
Recordset.MoveFirst
```

This moves to the first nondeleted row in the recordset and sets `BOF` if all rows are deleted or if there are no rows in the recordset.

Before issuing a `MoveFirst`, you should check to see whether the recordset supports moving to the first row. For example:

```
If objRs.Supports(adMoveFirst) Then
    objRs.MoveFirst
End If
```

> **Be aware that some providers (for example, SQL Server 6.5 and 7.0) implement the** `MoveFirst` **by resubmitting the query to the database server; this has the effect of reopening the recordset, thus placing you back on the first row. This happens only with server-side cursors. This could cause serious performance degradation if the command you are running takes a long time. SQL Server 2000 has a smarter cursor engine and does not resubmit the query.**

If the current row has been changed, but you haven't yet called `Update`, then a `MoveFirst` will implicitly call `Update`. If you do not wish to keep such changes, call `CancelUpdate` before calling `MoveFirst`.

The MoveLast Method

This method moves the current row to the last row in the `Recordset`.

```
Recordset.MoveLast
```

This moves to the last nondeleted row in the recordset and sets `EOF` if all rows are deleted or if the recordset is empty.

Before issuing a `MoveLast`, check to see whether the recordset supports moving to the last row. For example:

```
If objRs.Supports(adMoveLast) Then
    objRs.MoveLast
End If
```

You may encounter one odd problem when using server-based cursors for read-only, forward-only recordsets. Your provider may say that `MoveLast` is supported, but moving to the last row generates the following message:

The rowset does not support fetching backwards.

This seems a misleading error, and may result from the way `MoveLast` is implemented—by using a built-in bookmark on the last row. So this error could result from the fact that forward-only, read-only cursors don't support bookmarks, even though the error message doesn't imply this. I've no confirmation of this, but it seems a sensible reason.

If the current row has been changed, and `Update` not called, a `MoveLast` will implicitly call `Update`. Call `CancelUpdate` before calling `MoveLast` if you do not wish to keep the changes.

The MoveNext Method

This method moves the current row to the next row in the `Recordset`.

```
Recordset.MoveNext
```

If you try to move past the last row in a recordset, the `EOF` property is set. Subsequent calls to `MoveNext` will generate an error.

If the current row has been changed, and `Update` not called, then a `MoveNext` will implicitly call `Update`. Call `CancelUpdate` before calling `MoveNext` if you do not wish to keep the changes.

The MovePrevious Method

This method moves the current row to the previous row in the `Recordset`.

```
Recordset.MovePrevious
```

If you try to move past the first row in a recordset, the `BOF` property is set. Subsequent calls to `MovePrevious` will generate an error.

You can use the `Supports` method to check whether `MovePrevious` can be used on the recordset:

```
If objRs.Supports(adMovePrevious) Then
    objRs.MovePrevious
End If
```

If the current row has been changed, and `Update` not called, then a `MovePrevious` will implicitly call `Update`. Call `CancelUpdate` before calling `MovePrevious` if you do not wish to keep the changes.

The NextRecordset Method

This method clears the current `Recordset` object and returns the next `Recordset` by advancing through a series of commands specified as the source of the recordset.

```
Set Recordset = Recordset.NextRecordset([RecordsAffected])
```

Parameter	Type	Description
Records Affected	Long	A variable into which the provider returns the number of rows affected by the operation

`RecordsAffected` is meaningful only for a recordset that does not return any rows.

This can be useful if you wish to build up a set of SQL statements and send them all to the provider in one go. However, not all of the data may be returned to the client in a single batch, and this may require a trip to the server for each recordset. Each SQL command will be executed when the `NextRecordset` command is issued. Issuing a `Close` on the recordset will close the recordset without executing any outstanding commands.

You could use this for returning separate lists to be used in combo boxes. For example, imagine the following code that creates a stored procedure:

```
CREATE PROCEDURE usp_ListBoxes
AS
BEGIN
     SELECT * FROM authors
     SELECT * FROM titles
END
```

Opening a recordset on this stored procedure would return the first command in the series. Once you've finished with the data from that recordset, you could issue a `NextRecordset` command to execute the next command. For example:

```
objRs.Open "usp_ListBoxes", objConn, adOpenForwardOnly, _
                         , adLockReadOnly, adCmdStoredProc

Set objRsTitles = objRs.NextRecordset
```

Notice that the preceding example returns the next recordset into a new recordset variable. You can also use the same variable:

```
Set objRs = objRs.NextRecordset
```

The next recordset can be returned in several states:

❑ As a closed recordset, but with rows (You can open the recordset and proceed as normal.)

❑ As a closed recordset (with no rows), for a recordset that does not return rows

❑ As an empty recordset (with no rows), where both BOF and EOF will be set

You should therefore check the `State` property and the `BOF` and `EOF` properties to determine the recordset's status. When there are no more recordsets, the recordset object will be set to `Nothing`.

There is one problem with this in Visual Basic, though, if you declare your variables in a particular format. For many years I have used the following format:

```
Dim objRs As New ADODB.Recordset
```

This causes the variable to be created if it is set to `Nothing`, which means that testing the recordset object variable for `Nothing` doesn't work. For example:

```
objConn.Open "Provider=SQLOLEDB; Data Source=Tigger;" & _
              " Initial Catalog=pubs; User Id=sa; Password="
objRs.Open "usp_ListBoxes", objConn, adOpenStatic, _
                              adLockOptimistic, adCmdStoredProc

Do
    ' do something with recordset
    Set objRs = objRs.NextRecordset
Loop While Not (objRs Is Nothing)
```

If you step through this routine in Visual Basic and look at the **Locals Window** when there are no more recordsets, you'll see that `objRs` is indeed `Nothing`. However, the test fails and sets the `objRs` from `Nothing` back to a variable with a value. The way around this is to check for the `ActiveCommand` property of the `Recordset`. So, change the end of the loop to:

```
Loop While Not (objRs.ActiveCommand Is Nothing)
```

This just seems to be a Visual Basic quirk, and a downloadable samples sample shows this in action.

Alternatively, if you code according to the currently recommended style, you'll avoid this problem. Declare and set your variables in two stages:

```
Dim objRs As ADODB.Recordset
Set objRs = New ADODB.Recordset
```

When using immediate update mode, a call to `NextRecordset` will generate an error if editing is in progress, so make sure that you have updated or cancelled the changes.

Closing the recordset will terminate any further pending commands.

Not all providers support multiple recordsets, so consult your provider documentation. Additionally, note that they are not applicable to client-side cursors.

The Open Method

This method opens a recordset.

```
Recordset.Open([Source], [ActiveConnection], [CursorType], _
              [LockType], [Options])
```

Parameter	Type	Description
Source	Variant	A valid Command object, a SQL statement, a table name, a stored procedure, a URL, a Stream object, or the file name of a persisted recordset

Table continues on the following page

Parameter	Type	Description
Active Connection	Variant	A valid `Connection` object or a connection string that identifies the connection to be used
CursorType	CursorType Enum	The cursor type that the provider should use when opening the recordset (If the provider doesn't support the requested cursor type, it may use a different type. The default value is `adOpenForwardOnly`.)
LockType	LockType Enum	The locking type (concurrency) that the provider should use when opening the recordset (default value is `adLockReadOnly`)
Options	Long	Indicates how the provider should interpret the `Source` argument if the `Source` argument represents something other than a `Command` object or a persisted Recordset (default value `adCmdText`)

`CursorTypeEnum` can be one of the following constants (these are covered in more detail under the `CursorType` property section later in this chapter):

❑ `adOpenForwardOnly` for a recordset that allows forward movement only

❑ `adOpenKeyset` for a keyset-type cursor

❑ `adOpenDynamic` for a dynamic-type cursor

❑ `adOpenStatic` for a static-type cursor

`LockTypeEnum` can be one of the following constants (these are covered in more detail under the `LockType` property section later in this chapter):

❑ `adLockReadOnly` for a read-only recordset

❑ `adLockPessimistic` for pessimistic locking

❑ `adLockOptimistic` for optimistic locking

❑ `adLockBatchOptimistic` for batch optimistic locking

`Options` can be one or more of the following `CommandTypeEnum` or `ExecuteOptionEnum` constants:

❑ `adCmdText` indicates that the command is a textual command.

❑ `adCmdTable` indicates that the command is a table name.

❑ `adCmdStoredProc` indicates that the command is a stored procedure.

- ❑ adCmdUnknown indicates that the command type is unknown.

- ❑ adCmdTableDirect indicates that the command is a table.

- ❑ adCmdFile indicates that the command is a saved recordset.

- ❑ adAsyncFetch fetches the records asynchronously.

- ❑ adAsyncFetchNonBlocking fetches the rows asynchronously, but without blocking the return.

- ❑ adAsyncExecute executes the command asynchronously.

The first five of these are discussed in more detail in Chapter 4, under the CommandType property. The constant adAsyncFetchNonBlocking is ignored if the recordset is opening a persisted recordset from a stream.

You can deal with persisted files in two ways. This first is by setting the Provider to MSPersist:

```
objRs.Open "c:\temp\authors.xml", "Provider=MSPersist"
```

The second is to use the adCmdFile argument:

```
objRs.Open "c:\temp\authors.xml", , , , adCmdFile
```

For ADO 2.8, additional security measures have been introduced into opening recordsets from files when ADO code is used within Internet Explorer. If the site is not part of a Trusted Zone, the code is blocked and access to local files is denied. Note that no warning dialogs are given, so you must ensure that sites requiring access are Trusted.

For URL usages, specify the absolute URL (or scope) as the Source:

```
objRs.Open "http://localhost/testsite"
```

For Stream usage, you can just specify the stream name:

```
objRs.Open stmData
```

In ASP pages you can use this to open recordsets persisted into the Request object from the browser:

```
objRs.Open Request, , , , adCmdFile
```

For asynchronous usage, you use a logical OR to add the asynchronous option. For example:

```
objRs.Open "authors", objConn,_
           adOpenKeyset, adLockOptimistic, _
           (adCmdTable OR adAsyncFetch)
```

You can then use the State property or the FetchComplete event to determine when the recordset has been fully populated.

The difference between adAsyncFetch and adAsyncFetchNonBlocking is what happens when you request a row that has not yet been fetched. If the recordset has been opened using adAsyncFetch and you request a row that hasn't been fetched yet, then the operation will wait until the requested row is available. If the recordset has been opened using adAsyncFetchNonBlocking and you request a row that hasn't been fetched yet, you are placed at the end of the recordset.

Note that this is the end of the recordset as it currently exists; because the recordset is being populated asynchronously, more rows may still need to be fetched. So in this mode, EOF is the last row that has been fetched, not the physical end of the set of rows.

Opening a recordset does not guarantee that there are any rows available. If you open a recordset with rows, you are automatically placed on the first row. If the recordset doesn't contain any rows, BOF and EOF will be True. Ideally, you should check for this before accessing the rows:

```
objRs.Open "select * from some_table", objConn
If Not objRs.EOF Then
    ' it is safe to access rows
End If
```

The Requery Method

This method updates the data in a Recordset object by reexecuting the query on which the object is based.

```
Recordset.Requery([Options])
```

Name	Type	Description
Options	Long	Indicates the options to use when re-querying the recordset (default value is adOptionUnsepecified)

This is equivalent to issuing a Close and Open. Because you cannot change the settings of the recordset, setting Options is merely an optimization issue to help ADO. The exception to this is if you add either of the asynchronous flags, adAsyncFetch or adAsyncFetchNonBlocking, which cause the Requery to be executed asynchronously.

If you Requery a recordset while editing an existing row or adding a new one, you will generate an error.

When using client-side cursors, you can only issue Resync (and not a Requery) against a non-read-only recordset.

The Resync Method

This method refreshes the data in the current `Recordset` object from the underlying database.

```
Recordset.Resync([AffectRecords], [ResyncValues])
```

Name	Type	Description
AffectRecords	AffectEnum	Determines how many rows will be affected (default value is adAffectAll)
ResyncValues	ResyncEnum	Specifies whether underlying values are overwritten (default value is adResyncAll)

`AffectRecords` can be one of the following `AffectEnum` constants:

❑ `adAffectCurrent` refreshes just the current row.

❑ `adAffectGroup` refreshes all rows in the current `Filter`.

❑ `adAffectAll` refreshes all rows in the recordset.

`ResyncValues` can be one of the following `ResyncEnum` constants:

❑ `adResyncAllValues` refreshes all of the value properties, effectively overwriting any pending updates.

❑ `adResyncUnderlyingValues` refreshes only the `UnderlyingValue` property.

Using `adResyncUnderlyingValues` allows you to repopulate the `UnderlyingValue` property without discarding any changes or the `OriginalValue` property. This is particularly useful for investigating optimistic update conflicts and is discussed in more detail later in this chapter, in the "Conflict Resolution" section for the Save method.

If the recordset contains multiple tables, and the `Unique Table` and `Resync Command` dynamic properties are set, then only rows from this unique table are resynchronized, using the command specified.

Not all providers support resynchronization, so use the `Supports` method before issuing a `Resync`:

```
If objRs.Supports(adResync) Then
    objRs.Resync
End If
```

Unlike the `Requery` method, the `Resync` method does not reexecute the underlying command.

The Save Method

This method saves the Recordset to a file.

```
Recordset.Save([Destination], [PersistFormat])
```

Name	Type	Description
Destination	Variant	Complete path name of the file where the recordset should be saved, or a Stream object
PersistFormat	PersistFormat Enum	The format in which the recordset should be saved (default value is adPersistADTG)

PersistFormat can be one of these:

❑ adPersistADTG saves the recordset in a proprietary binary format.

❑ adPersistXML saves the recordset as an XML file.

Using Save means the following actions will apply:

❑ Only rows in the current Filter are saved.

❑ If the recordset is being fetched asynchronously, the Save will be blocked until all rows are fetched.

❑ The first row becomes the current row once the save is complete.

Destination should be used for only the initial save. Subsequent saves on the same recordset will automatically save to the same file unless another filename is specified. Attempting to save over an existing file will generate an error. If Destination is omitted, the Source property will be used as the name of the file.

For streams, the Destination should be a valid Stream object or an object that supports the IStream interface. For example:

```
Dim stmData As New Stream
objRs.Save stmData, adPersistXML
```

or:

```
Dim domXML As New MSXML.Document
objRs.Save domXML, adPersistXML
```

In ASP this can be the Response object:

```
objRs.Save Response, adPersistXML
```

You cannot save in XML format from hierarchical recordsets based on parameterized queries (for example, a stored procedure with parameters), because the child recordsets are fetched only upon each row access of the parent. Pending updates in a hierarchical recordset also mean that you cannot save to XML.

You can use the Save method from a script executed by Microsoft Internet Explorer only when the Internet Explorer security settings are low or custom. For more details on this, see the article entitled *ADO and RDS Security Issues in Microsoft Internet Explorer*, available at MSDN Online (http://msdn.microsoft.com/)

For ADO 2.8 additional security measures have been introduced into saving recordsets from files when ADO code is used within Internet Explorer. If the site is not part of a Trusted Zone, the code is blocked and access to local files is denied. Note that no warning dialogs are given, so you must ensure that sites requiring access are Trusted. Additionally the source–whether a file name or a URL–must point to an actual file. Under earlier versions the source could be a non-disk-based file, such as a printer or serial port.

Recordset Persistence

The Save method of recordsets allows data to be saved to a local file and then reopened with the Open method. The great point about this is that it suddenly opens up the world of roving users. You now have the opportunity to provide the same application to both connected and disconnected users, and an easy way for them to switch states.

Imagine a sales situation where salespeople occasionally take their laptops on the road. You could provide a Work Offline option that saves their data locally. On the road, the application can open these persisted recordsets and work on them as normal. When the user connects back online, the master copy of the data can be updated with the offline data.

Here's some Visual Basic code that can do this:

```
objRs.CursorLocation = adUseClient
objRs.Save "c:\temp\OfflineData.dat"

' disconnect from connection and close connection
Set objRs.ActiveConnection = Nothing
objRs.Close
objConn.Close

' now re open in offline mode
objRs.Open "c:\temp\OfflineData.dat"
```

This could be executed when the user wishes to work offline. The recordset is saved locally, the connection and recordset closed, and then the local recordset opened. The user would be disconnected from the server and could continue as normal, although only the saved data would be available. Any new information, or information not saved, would become available only once the connection to the server was reestablished.

To get back online, you would do this:

```
' reconnect to the data source
strConn = "Provider=SQLOLEDB; Data Source=Tigger; " & _
          " Initial Catalog=pubs; User Id=sa; Password="
objRs.ActiveConnection = strConn

' update the master table with the offline changes
objRs.UpdateBatch
```

This connects the recordset to a connection and then uses `UpdateBatch` to update the master copy of the rows with the local copy. See the section on Conflict Resolution further on for more details on this.

You can see that this makes writing offline applications no different from writing an online application. You could have a simple flag that is set when the application is offline to indicate that the saved copies of the recordset are opened when the application starts.

This method also works in browser situations, because you can use the XMLHTTP object in IE to persist RDS client recordsets from the browser back to ASP pages. The web site has a sample that shows how this is done.

Conflict Resolution

Using client-side cursors and disconnected recordsets is great, especially because you have the ability to amend rows and send them back to the server to update the database master copy. One thing you must consider, however, is how to resolve conflicts between changes you've made to the data and any changes that other users might have caused.

If you think back to the offline code, we used `UpdateBatch` to update the master rows, and this will generate errors if any of the rows conflicted with underlying recordset changes. There are two ways to investigate this problem:

1. Have error trapping in the routine that calls `UpdateBatch`. You can then filter the recordset by using `adFilterConflictingRecords` to see which rows caused the problem.

2. Use the recordset events, and place some code in the `RecordChangeComplete` event. If errors are generated by conflicts, the recordset already will be filtered for you in the `RecordChangeComplete` event procedure.

If you choose the latter approach, your code could look like this:

```
Private Sub objRs_RecordChangeComplete( _
        ByVal adReason As ADODB.EventReasonEnum, _
        ByVal cRecords As Long, _
        ByVal pError As ADODB.Error, _
        adStatus As ADODB.EventStatusEnum, _
        ByVal pRecordset As ADODB.Recordset)
    Dim objFld      As ADODB.Field
```

```
            If adStatus = adStatusErrorsOccurred Then
                Print cRecords & " caused errors.:"
                For Each objFld In pRecordset.Fields
                    Debug.Print "Name"; vbTab; objFld.Name
                    Debug.Print "Value"; vbTab; objFld.Value
                    Debug.Print "UV"; vbTab; objFld.UnderlyingValue
                    Debug.Print "OV"; vbTab; objFld.OriginalValue
                Next
            End If

    End Sub
```

Of the event procedure arguments, `adStatus` indicates that an error occurred, and `cRecords` identifies the number of rows that failed. `pRecordset` is the recordset filtered to show only those conflicting rows.

You can also use the `Status` property of the `Field` object to determine the reason why a particular field caused the conflict. This is covered in more detail in Chapter 8.

For more details on the arguments for this event, see the `RecordChangeComplete` event procedure later in this chapter.

A small sample application showing these techniques is available as part of the downloadable samples.

The Seek Method

This method uses an `Index` to perform searches to locate specific rows.

```
    Recordset.Seek KeyValues, SeekOption
```

Parameter	Type	Description
KeyValues	Variant Array	Column values to search for
SeekOption	SeekEnum	Type of comparison to be made (default value is adSeekFirstEQ)

`SeekOption` takes its value from one of the following `SeekEnum` constants:

❑   `adSeekAfter` find the key just after the match.

❑   `adSeekAfterEQ` find the key equal to or just after the match.

❑   `adSeekBefore` find the key just before the match.

❑   `adSeekBeforeEQ` find the key equal to or just before the match.

- ❑ adSeekFirstEQ find the first key equal to the match.
- ❑ adSeekLastEQ find the last key equal to the match.

KeyValues is a variant array to allow for indexes that contain multiple columns.

If the row being sought is not found, no error is returned, and the current row is placed at EOF.

You use the Seek method in conjunction with the Index property. For example:

```
objRs.Index = "FullName"
objRs.Seek Array("Janine", "Lloyd"), adSeekFirstEQ
If objRs.EOF Then
    Print "Row not found"
End If
```

Not all providers support the Seek operation. To check this, use adSeek with the Supports method.

The Seek operation is supported only by server-based cursors (CursorLocation = adUseServer). This is because it uses the cursor service and indexes on the provider, rather than facilities of ADO.

The Supports Method

This method determines whether a specified Recordset object supports a particular functionality.

```
Boolean = Recordset.Supports(CursorOptions)
```

Parameter	Type	Description
CursorOptions	CursorOption Enum	One or more values to identify what functionality is supported

CursorOptions can take one or more of the following CursorOptionEnum constants:

- ❑ adAddNew indicates that the recordset supports addition of new rows via the AddNew method.
- ❑ adApproxPosition indicates that the recordset supports absolute position via the AbsolutePosition and AbsolutePage properties.
- ❑ adBookmark indicates that the recordset supports bookmarks via the Bookmark properties.
- ❑ adDelete indicates that the recordset supports row deletion via the Delete method.
- ❑ adFind indicates that the recordset supports the finding of rows via the Find method.
- ❑ adHoldRecords indicates that changes to the recordset will remain if you fetch more rows.
- ❑ adIndex indicates that you can use the Index property to set the current Index.

❑ adMovePrevious indicates that the recordset supports movement backward via the MoveFirst, MovePrevious, Move, or GetRows methods.

❑ adNotify indicates that the recordset supports notifications, and will return events.

❑ adResync indicates that the recordset allows the underlying data to be refreshed with the Resync method.

❑ adSeek indicates that you can use the Seek method to find rows by an Index.

❑ adUpdate indicates that the recordset allows records to be updated with the Update method.

❑ adUpdateBatch indicates that the recordset allows rows to be updated with the UpdateBatch method.

You can use the Supports method to find out which features a recordset makes available. For example, the following lines establish whether the recordset is updateable:

```
If objRs.Supports(adUpdate) Then
    ' recordset supports updates
End If
```

You can use Boolean logic to check for multiple values:

```
If objRs.Supports(adDelete Or adAddNew) Then
    ' recordset supports both Delete and AddNew
End If
```

Note that even if the recordset supports a particular feature, the underlying data may make the feature unavailable—and this may result in errors from the provider. For example, you may have a recordset based on a view where only certain columns are updateable; the recordset will support adUpdate, but certain columns may not allow updating. This means that you should really check the Errors collection after each operation.

The Update Method

This method saves any changes made to the current Recordset object.

```
Recordset.Update([Fields], [Values])
```

Parameter	Type	Description
Fields	Variant	A single name or Variant array representing the names or ordinal positions of the fields to be modified
Values	Variant	A single name or Variant array representing the values for the fields in the new or updated row

You can update fields in three ways. First, by assigning values to fields and then calling the `Update` method:

```
objRs("au_lname").Value = "Lloyd"
objRs("au_fname").Value = "Janine"
objRs.Update
```

Second, you can pass a single field name with a single value:

```
objRs.Update "au_lname", "Lloyd"
```

Third, you can pass multiple field names and multiple values:

```
objRs.Update Array("au_lname", "au_fname"),
             Array("Lloyd", "Janine")
```

The three methods are interchangeable. There's little difference between the methods unless updating multiple fields, in which case you should use the first or third methods. Each `Update` issues a command to the server, so you can make your code more efficient by issuing fewer updates.

Using any of the `Move` methods when editing a row will implicitly call `Update`.

If the recordset contains multiple tables, and the `Unique Table` dynamic property is set, then only rows from this unique table can be updated. This is discussed in more detail in the Dynamic Properties section at the end of the chapter.

The UpdateBatch Method

This method writes all pending batch updates to disk.

```
Recordset.UpdateBatch([AffectRecords])
```

Name	Type	Description
AffectRecords	AffectEnum	Determines how many rows will be affected (default value is adAffectAll)

`AffectRecords` can take any of the following `AffectEnum` constants:

❑   `adAffectCurrent` refreshes just the current row.

❑   `adAffectGroup` refreshes all rows in the current `Filter`.

❑   `adAffectAll` refreshes all rows in the recordset.

Using UpdateBatch allows changes to be cached until whenever you request the underlying data store to be updated. Caching starts when opening a recordset with adLockBatchOptimistic.

A failure to update will cause the Errors collection to be populated, and you can use the Filter property to see which rows failed. The failure could be caused by a conflict between a change made by you or a change made by another user. There's more on conflicts earlier in this chapter.

If the recordset contains multiple tables, the Unique Table dynamic property is set, and the Update Resync dynamic property is set to True, then a Resync is performed directly after the update.

The order in which updates occur on the provider is not guaranteed to be the same as the order in which they were performed on the client.

Properties of the Recordset Object

The AbsolutePage Property

This property specifies in which page the current row resides.

```
PositionEnum = Recordset.AbsolutePage
Long = Recordset.AbsolutePage
Recordset.AbsolutePage = PositionEnum
Recordset.AbsolutePage = Long
```

PositionEnum can be a valid page number or one of the following constants:

❑   adPosBOF indicates or positions the current row pointer at the beginning of the recordset.

❑   adPosEOF indicates or positions the current row pointer at the end of the recordset.

❑   adPosUnknown indicates that the current page is unknown. This could be because the record-set is empty, the provider does not support this property, or the provider cannot identify the current page.

When you set the value of the AbsolutePage property, the row pointer is set to the first row in the specified page. If you set the AbsolutePage property to 1, this moves to the first page of the recordset, and thus sets the row pointer to the first row in the recordset. This is used in conjunction with the PageSize property.

The AbsolutePosition Property

This property specifies the ordinal position of a Recordset object's current cursor position.

```
PositionEnum = Recordset.AbsolutePosition
Recordset.AbsolutePosition = PositionEnum
```

PositionEnum can be a valid row number or one of the following constants:

❑   adPosBOF indicates or positions the current row pointer at the beginning of the recordset.

❑   adPosEOF indicates or positions the current row pointer at the end of the recordset.

❑   adPosUnknown indicates that the current position is unknown. This could be because the recordset is empty, the provider does not support this property, or it cannot identify the current position.

You cannot use the absolute position to identify a row uniquely, because this value changes as rows are added and deleted. Of course, you could use AbsolutePosition to point to a row through the life of the recordset if your recordset does not allow additions or deletions. However, the AbsolutePosition is affected by the use of Sort and Index, because it points to a row at a particular position in the recordset and not to an individual row, irrespective of its position. If you need to identify a row throughout sorts and filters, use a bookmark.

The ActiveCommand Property

This property indicates the Command object that created the associated Recordset object.

```
Set Command = Recordset.ActiveCommand
```

When the recordset has been created from a command, you can use this property to access the Command object's properties and parameters. For example:

```
objCmd.CommandText = "usp_foo"

Print objRs.ActiveCommand.CommandText
```

This is particularly useful when you have been supplied with only the recordset, such as in the Visual Basic 6 Data Environment, which provides details of commands used to create recordsets. Because you can create these at design time, this property allows you to extract the details at run time.

If the recordset was not created from a command, then this property will be Null.

For ADO 2.8, access to the ActiveCommand property is blocked when running in Internet Explorer. This is irrespective of whether the site is from a Trusted Zone.

The ActiveConnection Property

This property indicates to which Connection object the specified Recordset object currently belongs.

```
Set Variant = Recordset.ActiveConnection
Set Recordset.ActiveConnection = Variant
```

```
Recordset.ActiveConnection = String
String = Recordset.ActiveConnection
```

The `ActiveConnection` can be set to a preexisting `Connection` object, in which case you use the `Set` form:

```
Set objRs.ActiveConnection = objConn
```

Alternatively, you can set the `ActiveConnection` by using a connection string, in which case an implicit `Connection` object is created for you:

```
objRs.ActiveConnection = "DSN=pubs"
```

This property will inherit the value from the `ActiveConnection` argument of an `Open` command, or from the `Source` property of a `Command`. The `ActiveConnection` property may also be modified by the provider to allow access to provider-specific connection information.

You can disassociate a client-side recordset from a connection by setting this property to `Nothing`. The recordset remains valid and can be reconnected to any `Connection` object at a later date.

The BOF Property

This property indicates whether the current row pointer is before the first row in a `Recordset` object.

```
Boolean = Recordset.BOF
```

If your recordset is empty, then the `BOF` and `EOF` properties will both be `True`.

The Bookmark Property

This property can be used to return a bookmark that uniquely identifies the current row in a `Recordset` object, or to set the current row pointer to the row identified by a valid bookmark.

```
Variant = Recordset.Bookmark
Recordset.Bookmark = Variant
```

Using the `Clone` method on a recordset gives two recordsets with interchangeable bookmarks. This means that bookmarks between cloned recordsets are identical. However, bookmarks from different recordsets (that is, noncloned, or cloned after the `Requery` method has been called) are not interchangeable, even if the recordsets were created from the same source or command.

You can use this property to store the position in the recordset temporarily, allowing you to return to that position later. For example:

```
varBkmk = objRs.Bookmark
' ... some processing that changes the current row ...
objRs.Bookmark = varBkmk
```

For example, this is quite useful when using the `Find` method (which positions you at EOF if the row you are searching for is not found):

```
varBkmk = objRs.Bookmark

objRs.Find "au_lname = 'Lloyd'"
If objRs.EOF Then
   Print "Row not found - now moving cursor " & _
         "from EOF to bookmarked
          row"
   objRs.Bookmark = varBkmk
End If
```

Bookmarks are generally supported only on keyset and static cursors and client-side cursors. Server-based dynamic cursors do not support bookmarks, because their membership is not fixed. Check the `adBookmark` value (using the recordset's `Supports` method) to verify this.

The CacheSize Property

This property indicates the number of rows from a `Recordset` object cached locally in memory. This defaults to 1.

```
Long = Recordset.CacheSize
Recordset.CacheSize = Long
```

The cache size affects how many rows from the recordset are fetched from the server in one go and held locally; this can affect performance and memory usage. When a recordset is first opened, only a certain number of rows (the number stored in `CacheSize`) are fetched locally, and the remaining rows are not fetched until required. If you move to a row that's not in the current cache, the provider will fetch another cache of rows. So, a cache larger than 1 is generally more efficient. Chapter 14 shows the speed difference between a cache of 1 and a larger value. Changing the size of the cache can have an effect on both client- and server-based cursors.

An important point to note is that rows in the cache do not reflect underlying changes made by other users until `Resync` is issued or until recordset navigation options cause those rows to be reread.

You can change the cache size during the life of a recordset, but the new size becomes effective only when the next cache of data is retrieved. A cache size of zero is not allowed and generates an error.

An undocumented feature, which is not officially supported, is that a negative cache size causes rows to be fetched backward from the current row, rather than forward.

The CursorLocation Property

This property sets or returns the location of the cursor engine.

```
CursorLocationEnum = Recordset.CursorLocation
Recordset.CursorLocation = CursorLocationEnum
```

`CursorLocationEnum` can be one of the following constants:

❑ `adUseClient` specifies the Microsoft Client cursor.

❑ `adUseServer` specifies the cursor support supplied by the data provider, assuming it supports server-based cursors.

Server-side cursors often support better concurrency than client-side cursors, because the actual provider handles concurrency control.

Client-side cursors must be used when creating disconnected recordsets.

The CursorType Property

This property indicates the type of cursor used in a `Recordset` object.

```
CursorTypeEnum = Recordset.CursorType
Recordset.CursorType = CursorTypeEnum
```

`CursorTypeEnum` can be one of the following constants:

❑ `adOpenForwardOnly` for a recordset that only allows forward movement one row at a time. It is therefore not possible to use anything other than `MoveNext` or `Move` with a value of 1 unless the `CacheSize` is greater than 1. Bookmarks are not supported on this cursor type, because absolute position is not a requirement.

❑ `adOpenKeyset` for a keyset-type cursor. This gives you a set of rows for which the data is up to date with the underlying data, but the number of rows may not be because additions and deletions may not be visible to the cursor. Keyset cursors work by storing the keys to the row of data, then fetching the data only when it is required. Therefore, the set of rows is fixed, but the data is not fixed. Deleted rows remain in the recordset, but are empty. Other users' insertions are not visible (because they weren't part of the original set of keys), but your insertions may be visible (if they match the rowset criteria). Movement is supported forward and backward.

❑ `adOpenDynamic` for a dynamic type cursor. The membership of rows in the recordset is not fixed. New rows added by any user will be visible, deleted rows will not be visible, and any data changes will be visible. Movement is supported forward and backward.

❑ `adOpenStatic` for a static type cursor, where the data is fixed at the time the cursor is created. Movement is supported forward and backward.

For keyset cursors, you can control the visibility of inserted and deleted rows by use of the following dynamic properties:

- ❑ `Remove Deleted Records` removes deleted rows from the keyset.

- ❑ `Own Inserts Visible` ensures that your inserts into the keyset are visible.

- ❑ `Other Inserts Visible` ensures that inserts by others are visible in the keyset.

Not all providers support all cursor types, and the actual cursor type used may depend on the cursor location. You should query the `CursorType` property after the recordset has been opened, to see what type the provider has used. The cursor types requested and supported by the main providers are included in Chapter 14.

The DataMember Property

This property specifies the name of the data member to be retrieved from the object referenced by the `DataSource` property.

```
String = Recordset.DataMember
Recordset.DataMember = String
```

Visual Basic's Data Environment uses this property to create data-bound controls. The `DataMember` identifies the object in the `DataSource` that will supply the recordset.

The DataSource Property

This property specifies an object containing data to be represented as a `Recordset` object.

```
Set Object = Recordset.DataSource
Set Recordset.DataSource = Object
```

Visual Basic's Data Environment uses this property to create data-bound controls. The `DataSource` identifies the object in the Data Environment to which the `DataMember` belongs.

The EditMode Property

This property indicates the editing status of the current row.

```
EditModeEnum = Recordset.EditMode
```

`EditModeEnum` will be one of the following constants:

- ❑ `adEditNone` indicates that the current row has no edits in progress.

- ❑ `adEditInProgress` indicates that the current row is being edited.

❑ adEditAdd indicates that the current row is being added (it's a new row).

❑ adEditDelete indicates the current row has been deleted.

You could use this in an interactive application that allows users to edit and move around rows. Because moving around rows intrinsically calls Update, you may want to offer the user the option of canceling or saving changes before moving to another row. For example, imagine a section of Visual Basic code that runs when a **Next Row** button is pressed:

```
If objRs.EditMode = adEditInProgress Then
    strMsg = "The current row has changed. " & _
             "Would you like to save the changes?"
    If MsgBox (strMsg, vbYesNo) = vbNo Then
        objRs.CancelUpdate
    End If
End If
objRs.MoveNext
```

This simply checks the edit mode before moving to another row.

The EOF Property

This property indicates whether the current row pointer is after the last row in a Recordset object.

```
Boolean = Recordset.EOF
```

The Filter Property

This property indicates a filter for data in the Recordset.

```
Variant = Recordset.Filter
Recordset.Filter = Variant
```

You can set the Filter property to a valid filter string, an array of bookmarks, or one of the following FilterGroupEnum constants:

❑ adFilterNone removes any current filter and shows all rows.

❑ adFilterPendingRecords (for batch update mode) shows only rows that have been changed but not yet sent to the server.

❑ adFilterAffectedRecords shows only rows affected by the last Delete, Resync, UpdateBatch, or CancelBatch.

❑ adFilterFetchedRecords shows rows in the current cache.

❑ adFilterPredicate shows deleted rows.

❑ adFilterConflictingRecords shows rows that caused a conflict during the last batch update attempt.

You can filter with an array of `Bookmarks`. This small section of Visual Basic code shows an example of this:

```
Dim avarBkmk(5)
avarBkmk(0) = objRs.Bookmark
' ...some more processing...
avarBkmk(1) = objRs.Bookmark
objRs.Filter = Array(avarBkmk(0), avarBkmk(1))
```

This can be quite useful when allowing users to select multiple rows from a list.

Using a normal string as a filter follows much the same syntax as a SQL WHERE clause, as the following examples show:

```
objRs.Filter = "au_lname = 'Lloyd'"
objRs.Filter = "au_lname LIKE 'L*'"
objRs.Filter = "Price > 10.99 AND Price < 15.99"
objRs.Filter = "InvoiceDate > #04/04/98#"
```

You'll notice that multiple conditions are allowed here, unlike the `Find` command. When using date fields, you must use the VBA syntax, surrounding the date with # symbols.

Once the `Filter` has been set, the cursor is placed on the first row in the newly filtered recordset.

To cancel a filter, call the `Filter` method again. This time, either use `adFilterNone` or specify an empty string (`""`):

```
objRs.Filter ""
```

The Index Property

This property indicates the name of the index currently in effect.

```
String = Recordset.Index
Recordset.Index = String
```

The `Index` property refers to a previously defined table index. This can be either an index that was created on the base table, or an ADOX `Index` object.

Changing an `Index` may change the current row position, which may therefore update the current row.

You cannot set the `Index` if a `Filter` has been set on the recordset, if the recordset is still processing an asynchronous operation, or from within a `WillChangeRecordset` or `RecordsetChangeComplete` event handler.

The `Index` property is not related to the indexing used by the dynamic `Optimize` property.

Not all providers support the `Index` property. To check this, you should use `adIndex` with the `Supports` method.

The LockType Property

This property indicates the type of locks placed on rows during editing.

```
LockTypeEnum = Recordset.LockType
Recordset.LockType = LockTypeEnum
```

`LockTypeEnum` can be one of the following constants:

❏ `adLockReadOnly` for a read-only recordset, where the provider does no locking and the data cannot be changed

❏ `adLockPessimistic` for pessimistic locking, where the provider attempts to lock edited rows at the data source

❏ `adLockOptimistic` for optimistic locking, where the provider locks rows on a row-by-row or page-by-page basis, when `Update` is called

❏ `adLockBatchOptimistic` for batch update mode, where locking occurs when `UpdateBatch` is called

Only `adLockBatchOptimistic` or `adLockReadOnly` are supported by client-side cursors. If you attempt to use any other lock type, you'll get `adLockBatchOptimistic`.

The locking method you choose is really going to depend upon the application. Because pessimistic locking locks the row at the data source as you start editing, you don't have to worry about a conflict with another user's changes unless the row is already locked when you try to lock it. However, this implies a permanent connection to the data store, which may be either impractical or impossible.

Optimistic locking gives you better resource management, but you then must cater for conflicts, because the lock doesn't actually occur until you try to `Update` the row. This means that someone else might have changed the row between the time that you started editing it and the time that you went to `Update` it. Because ADO doesn't know which copy is correct, it deals with this by generating an error, which can be trapped. This error number is -2147217885, but not all providers report error information correctly. To get the best error information, use the OLE DB Provider for ODBC.

Although batch locking can be used with server-based cursors, it's more useful with client cursors. This allows changes to multiple rows before committing them to the data store in a single batch.

The MarshalOptions Property

This property indicates which rows are to be marshaled back to the server.

```
MarshalOptionsEnum = Recordset.MarshalOptions
Recordset.MarshalOptions = MarshalOptionsEnum
```

`MarshalOptionsEnum` can be one of the following constants:

❑ `adMarshalAll` sends back to the server all rows (default).

❑ `adMarshalModifiedOnly` sends back to the server only those rows that have changed.

Marshaling is the term given to transferring a recordset between two processes. This could be between the client and the server in a two-tier system, or between the client and a middle-tier in an n-tier system.

This property is applicable only when using disconnected, client-side recordsets. By marshaling only the changed rows (as opposed to all rows), you can greatly improve performance. If only a few rows are modified locally, less data must be sent back to the server process.

You can use this quite effectively when using n-tier client-server architecture that uses a business object on the server to supply recordsets. These can be modified locally, and only the changed rows are sent back to the business processes for updating.

The MaxRecords Property

This property indicates the maximum number of rows that may be returned to a `Recordset` object as the result of a query.

```
Long = Recordset.MaxRecords
Recordset.MaxRecords = Long
```

You can set this property only while the recordset is closed. The `MaxRecords` property defaults to zero, which indicates that all rows should be returned.

This is quite useful for applications that allow users to submit queries, because you can limit the set of rows if it is too big.

Although this property is supported, not all providers may implement it.

The PageCount Property

This property indicates how many pages of data the `Recordset` object contains.

```
Long = Recordset.PageCount
```

The recordset will consist of a number of pages; each page contains a number of rows equal to `PageSize`, except for the last page, which may contain fewer rows. If the `PageSize` is not set, `PageCount` will be -1.

The `PageCount` property allows you to move quickly to the last page in a recordset:

```
objRs.AbsolutePage = objRs.RecordCount/objRs.PageCount
```

This positions your row pointer on the first row of the last page. Note that not all providers support the `PageCount` property.

The PageSize Property

Indicates how many rows constitute one page in the `Recordset`.

```
Long = Recordset.PageSize
Recordset.PageSize = Long
```

You can use this to change the number of rows in a page. For example, imagine a Web application that shows search results from Microsoft Index Server. You could allow the user to page through these rows and to specify how many rows should be seen in each page.

The page size doesn't correspond to the cache size. The cache is a way of managing the transfer of a number of rows from the server to the client. In comparison, the page size is merely a logical structure that can be used for display purposes. The page size allows you an easy way to access a group of rows next to each other in the recordset.

Not all providers support `PageSize`.

The RecordCount Property

This property indicates the current number of rows in the `Recordset` object.

```
Long = Recordset.RecordCount
```

The `RecordCount` will be accurate only for recordsets that support approximate positioning or bookmarks. In practice this is generally all cursor types except server-side, forward-only cursors, and server-side, dynamic cursors. If the row count cannot be accurately determined, it is set to −1. You can test to see if the recordset supports approximate positioning or bookmarks by using the `Supports` method:

```
If objRs.Supports(adBookmark Or adApproxPosition) Then
    ' RecordCount will be accurate
End If
```

If the `Recordset` does not support approximate positioning or bookmarks, it must be fully populated before an accurate `RecordCount` value can be returned. One way to achieve this is by using `MoveLast` to move to the last row in the recordset, assuming the recordset supports `MoveLast`. If `MoveLast` is not supported, then all rows must be read before an accurate count can be determined. In general, static and keyset cursors return the correct count, as do dynamic cursors under certain providers, but forward-only cursors return –1.

If the recordset is being fetched asynchronously, the same rules apply. The `RecordCount` will be accurate if approximate position or bookmarks are supported, even if the asynchronous command is still running and the recordset has not been fully populated with rows. In this case the number of rows is the number returned so far.

The Sort Property

This property specifies one or more field names on which to sort the `Recordset`, and it specifies the direction of the sort.

```
String = Recordset.Sort
Recordset.Sort = String
```

The sort string should be a comma-separated list of columns to dictate the hierarchy of the sort order, each optionally followed by the sort direction. The default sort direction is `ASC`. For example:

```
objRs.Sort = "au_lname ASC, au_fname DESC"
```

You must use a client-side cursor (`CursorLocation = adUseClient`). Once the sort is set, a temporary index will be created for each field in the `Sort`. You can also force the creation of local indexes by setting the `Optimize` property (of the `Field` object's `Properties` collection) to be `True`. For example:

```
objRs("au_lname").Properties("Optimize") = True
```

This will create a local index, which will speed up sorting and searching.

The Source Property

This property indicates the command or SQL command for the data in a `Recordset` object.

```
String = Recordset.Source
Recordset.Source = String
Set Recordset.Source = Variant
```

This is useful for identifying the actual command text used to create the recordset, especially if it was created from a `Command` object.

The State Property

This property gives the state of the recordset in both synchronous and asynchronous mode. It indicates whether the recordset is open, closed, or whether it is executing an asynchronous operation.

```
ObjectStateEnum = Recordset.State
```

ObjectStateEnum can be one or more of the following constants:

- ❑ adStateClosed indicates that the recordset is closed.
- ❑ adStateOpen indicates that the recordset is open.
- ❑ adStateConnecting indicates that the recordset is connecting to the data store
- ❑ adStateExecuting indicates that the recordset is executing a command
- ❑ adStateFetching indicates that the recordset is fetching rows.

When the recordset is opened asynchronously, you should use logical operations to test these values. For example:

```
If (objRs.State And adStateFetching) = adStateFetching Then
   Print "Recordset is still fetching rows"
End If
```

A positive test for adStateExecuting or adStateFetching implies adStateOpen, but you cannot test for this alone.

The Status Property

This property indicates the current row's status with respect to batch updates or other bulk operations.

```
RecordStatusEnum = Recordset.Status
```

RecordStatusEnum can be one or more of the RecordStatusEnum constants shown in Appendix B.

The StayInSync Property

This property indicates, in a hierarchical Recordset object, whether a reference to the child row should change when the parent row changes.

```
Boolean = Recordset.StayInSync
Recordset.StayInSync = Boolean
```

The default for this is True; if set to False, a reference to a child recordset will remain pointing to the old recordset, even though the parent row may have changed.

Hierarchical recordsets are covered in more detail in Chapter 13, in the discussion on Data Shaping.

Events of the Recordset Object

ADO 2.6 and later supports notifications, which allow providers to notify the application when certain events occur. Event ordering is covered in Chapter 2, and examples of event usage are available on the supporting Web site.

Event Status

All events will have a bidirectional parameter, adStatus, to indicate the status of the event. This is of type EventStatusEnum, and can be one of the following constants:

- ❑ adStatusOK indicates that the action that caused the event was successful.

- ❑ adStatusErrorsOccured indicates that errors or warnings occurred, in which case the Errors collection should be checked.

- ❑ adStatusCantDeny indicates that you cannot cancel the action that generated the event on a Will... event, or indicates that the action was cancelled on a ...Complete event.

- ❑ adStatusUnwantedEvent indicates that the action that generated the event should no longer generate events.

On a Will... event (and assuming adStatusCantDeny is not set), before the procedure exits, you can set adStatus to adStatusCancel to cancel the action that caused this event. This also generates an error indicating that the event has been cancelled. For example, assume that you have moved from one row to the next; this will raise a WillMove event on the recordset. If you decide not to move to another row, you can set adStatus to adStatusCancel, and the Move action will be cancelled. This allows you to perhaps cancel actions where the data is incorrect.

When using Will... events, watch for implicit method calls. Take the preceding Move as an example: If the current row has been edited, then ADO implicitly calls Update. In this case you might get more than one Will... event.

If you no longer wish to receive events for a particular action, then before the procedure exits, you can set adStatus to adStatusUnwantedEvent, and they will no longer be generated for the current object instance.

The EndOfRecordset Event

This event fires when there is an attempt to move to a row past the end of the `Recordset`.

```
EndOfRecordset(fMoreData, adStatus, pRecordset)
```

Parameter	Type	Description
fMoreData	Boolean	Set to `True` if it is possible to append more data to `pRecordset` while processing this event
adStatus	EventStatusEnum	Identifies the message's status
pRecordset	Recordset	A reference to the `Recordset` object for which this event applies

While in this event procedure, more rows can be retrieved from the data store and appended to the end of the recordset. If you wish to do this, you should set the parameter `fMoreData` to `True`. After returning from this procedure, a subsequent `MoveNext` will allow access to the newly added rows. This can be useful if you wish to provide your own paging scheme, because you can read in the next batch of rows when the user attempts to move past the end of the current page of rows.

The FetchComplete Event

This event fires after all the rows in an asynchronous operation have been retrieved into the `Recordset`.

```
FetchComplete(pError, adStatus, pRecordset)
```

Parameter	Type	Description
pError	Error	An `Error` object describing the error that occurred if adStatus is adStatusErrorsOccurred (not set otherwise)
adStatus	EventStatusEnum	Identifies the message's status
pRecordset	Recordset	A reference to the `Recordset` object for which the rows were retrieved

This is most useful when the recordset is being fetched asynchronously, because it avoids the need to check the recordset's state periodically.

The FetchProgress Event

The provider periodically fires this event during an asynchronous operation to report how many rows have been retrieved so far.

```
FetchProgress(Progress, MaxProgress, adStatus, pRecordset)
```

Parameter	Type	Description
Progress	Long	The number of rows retrieved so far
MaxProgress	Long	The maximum number of rows expected to be retrieved
adStatus	EventStatusEnum	Identifies the message's status
pRecordset	Recordset	A reference to the Recordset object for which the rows are being retrieved

MaxProgess may not contain the total number of rows to be fetched if the recordset type does not support this.

This would be used for updating status indicators on user screens.

The provider determines when and why this event is raised.

The FieldChangeComplete Event

This event fires after the values of one or more Field objects have been changed.

```
FieldChangeComplete(cFields, Fields, pError, adStatus, pRecordset)
```

Parameter	Type	Description
cFields	Long	The number of Field objects within Fields
Fields	Variant	An array of Field objects with completed changes
pError	Error	Describes the error that occurred if adStatus is adStatusErrorsOccurred (not set otherwise)
adStatus	EventStatusEnum	Identifies the message's status.
pRecordset	Recordset	A reference to the Recordset object for which this event applies

You can use this to update status indicators or to trigger other actions that are dependent upon some fields being changed.

The MoveComplete Event

This event fires after the current position in the `Recordset` changes.

```
MoveComplete(adReason, pError, adStatus, pRecordset)
```

Parameter	Type	Description
adReason	EventReasonEnum	The reason for the event
pError	Error	An `Error` object describing the error that occurred if adStatus is adStatusErrorsOccurred (not set otherwise)
adStatus	EventStatusEnum	Identifies the message's status
pRecordset	Recordset	The `Recordset` object for which this event applies

adReason will be one of a subset of the `EventReasonEnum` constants:

❑   adRsnMoveFirst when a `MoveFirst` is issued

❑   adRsnMoveLast when a `MoveLast` is issued

❑   adRsnMoveNext when a `MoveNext` is issued

❑   adRsnMovePrevious when a `MovePrevious` is issued

❑   adRsnMove when a `Move` is issued

❑   adRsnRequery when a `Requery` is issued or a `Filter` is set

adReason might also assume the value of adRsnMove when the `AbsolutePage` or `AbsolutePosition` property is set, or a `Bookmark` is set, or a new row is added with `AddNew`. In addition, this value is generated when the recordset is opened.

These could also be generated when a child recordset has events and the parent recordset moves.

The RecordChangeComplete Event

This event fires after one or more rows change in the local recordset.

```
RecordChangeComplete(adReason, cRecords, pError, adStatus,
                     pRecordset)
```

Parameter	Type	Description
adReason	EventReasonEnum	Specifies the reason for the event
cRecords	Long	The number of rows changing
pError	Error	An Error object describing the error that occurred if adStatus is adStatusErrorsOccurred (not set otherwise)
adStatus	EventStatusEnum	Identifies the message's status
pRecordset	Recordset	The Recordset object for which this event applies, containing only the changed rows

adReason will be one of a subset of the EventReasonEnum constants:

- ❑ adRsnAddNew when an AddNew is issued
- ❑ adRsnDelete when a Delete is issued
- ❑ adRsnUpdate when an Update is issued
- ❑ adRsnUndoUpdate when an Update is cancelled with CancelUpdate or CancelBatch
- ❑ adRsnUndoAddNew when an AddNew is cancelled with CancelUpdate or CancelBatch
- ❑ dRsnUndoDelete when a Delete is cancelled with CancelUpdate or CancelBatch
- ❑ adRsnFirstChange when the row is changed for the first time

You could use this event for creation of an audit trail or for triggering other actions dependent upon the data having changed.

The RecordsetChangeComplete Event

This event fires after the Recordset has changed.

```
RecordsetChangeComplete(adReason, pError, adStatus, pRecordset)
```

Parameter	Type	Description
adReason	EventReasonEnum	Specifies the reason for the event
pError	Error	An Error object describing the error that occurred if adStatus is adStatusErrorsOccurred (not set otherwise)

Parameter	Type	Description
adStatus	EventStatusEnum	Identifies the message's status
pRecordset	Recordset	The Recordset object for which this event applies

adReason will be one of a subset of the EventReasonEnum constants:

- ❏ adRsnRequery when a Requery is issued
- ❏ adRsnReSynch when a Resync is issued
- ❏ adRsnClose when a Close is issued

The WillChangeField Event

This event fires before a pending operation changes the value of one or more Field objects.

```
WillChangeField(cFields, Fields, adStatus, pRecordset)
```

Parameter	Type	Description
cFields	Long	The number of Field objects within Fields
Fields	Variant	An array of Field objects with pending changes
adStatus	EventStatusEnum	Identifies the message's status
pRecordset	Recordset	The Recordset object for which this event applies

This can be useful for validating user input.

This event can fire as a result of these Recordset operations: setting the Value property, and calling the Update method with field and value array parameters.

The WillChangeRecord Event

This event fires before one or more rows in the Recordset change.

```
WillChangeRecord(adReason, cRecords, adStatus, pRecordset)
```

Parameter	Type	Description
adReason	EventReasonEnum	Specifies the reason for the event
cRecords	Long	The number of rows changing
adStatus	EventStatusEnum	Identifies the message's status
pRecordset	Recordset	The Recordset object for which this event applies

adReason will be one of a subset of the EventReasonEnum constants:

❑ adRsnAddNew when an AddNew is issued

❑ adRsnDelete when a Delete is issued

❑ adRsnUpdate when an Update is issued

❑ adRsnUndoUpdate when an Update is cancelled with CancelUpdate or CancelBatch

❑ adRsnUndoAddNew when an AddNew is cancelled with CancelUpdate or CancelBatch

❑ dRsnUndoDelete when a Delete is cancelled with CancelUpdate or CancelBatch

❑ adRsnFirstChange when the row is changed for the first time

You could use this when actions might change the record, and it can be used in parallel with WillChangeField.

The WillChangeRecordset Event

This event fires before a pending operation changes the Recordset.

```
WillChangeRecordset(adReason, adStatus, pRecordset)
```

Parameter	Type	Description
adReason	EventReasonEnum	Specifies the reason for the event
adStatus	EventStatusEnum	Identifies the message's status
pRecordset	Recordset	The Recordset object for which this event applies

adReason will be one of a subset of the EventReasonEnum constants:

- ❏ adRsnRequery when a Requery is issued

- ❏ adRsnReSynch when a Resync is issued

- ❏ adRsnClose when a Close is issued

You can use this to identify when an action would cause the underlying set of rows to change.

The WillMove Event

This event fires before a pending operation changes the current position in the Recordset.

```
WillMove(adReason, adStatus, pRecordset)
```

Parameter	Type	Description
adReason	EventReasonEnum	The reason for the event
adStatus	EventStatusEnum	Identifies the message's status
pRecordset	Recordset	The Recordset object for which this event applies

adReason will be one of a subset of the EventReasonEnum constants:

- ❏ adRsnMoveFirst when a MoveFirst is issued

- ❏ adRsnMoveLast when a MoveLast is issued

- ❏ adRsnMoveNext when a MoveNext is issued

- ❏ adRsnMovePrevious when a MovePrevious is issued

- ❏ adRsnMove when a Move or AddNew is issued, or AbsolutePage or AbsolutePosition is set, or the current row is moved by setting the Bookmark, or the recordset is opened

- ❏ adRsnRequery when a Requery is issued or a Filter is set

This allows you to identify when an action will cause the current row to change.

Collections of the Recordset Object

The Fields Collection

The `Fields` collection contains zero or more `Field` objects, each representing a field in the recordset, and is the default collection for a `Recordset`.

```
Recordset.Fields
```

You can iterate though the `Fields` collection to access each `Field` object individually:

```
For Each objField in objRs.Fields
    Print "Field name is " & objField.Name
Next
```

The `Fields` collection and `Field` object are discussed in more detail in Chapter 8.

The Properties Collection

The `Properties` collection contains `Property` objects, each representing an extended property supplied by the provider for the recordset.

```
Recordset.Properties
```

You can iterate through the `Properties` collection to access each `Property` object individually:

```
For Each objProp in objRs.Properties
    Print "property name is " & objProp.Name
Next
```

The `Properties` collection is discussed in more detail in Chapter 8 and Appendix C.

Dynamic Properties

A few dynamic properties are worth covering in a little detail here rather than in Appendix C, where you might miss them.

The Resync Command Property

The `Resync Command` property specifies a command string that the recordset's `Resync` method will use to refresh data in the `Unique Table`. This allows you to customize what happens when data in the `Unique Table` is resynchronized. For example, imagine that a recordset is created by the following query:

```
SELECT  *
FROM    publishers JOIN titles
ON      publishers.pub_id = titles.pub_id
```

Here, the Unique Table property should be set to titles, and its primary key, title_id, is the key that uniquely identifies rows in this recordset. You can specify that only rows from the Unique Table that match the non-unique table are resynchronized. This allows you to resynchronize the data for just the Unique Table, rather than data for the whole query.

The Resync Command would therefore be:

```
SELECT  *
FROM    publishers JOIN titles
ON      publishers.pub_id = titles.pub_id
WHERE   titles.title_id = ?
```

The Resync Command should be generally the same as the recordset definition, but with the addition of a WHERE clause parameterizing the primary key of the Unique Table. You add a question mark as the parameter, and ADO handles the matching of this to the non-unique table. In the preceding example, the result is that only the rows matching the original query are returned.

The rows affected by the Resync are dependent upon the Update Resync property, described shortly.

The Unique Catalog Property

The Unique Catalog property specifies the catalog (or database name, depending upon your database server terminology) containing the table named in the Unique Table property.

The Unique Schema Property

The Unique Schema property specifies the schema (or owner, depending upon your database server terminology) of the table named in the Unique Table property.

The Unique Table Property

The Unique Table property specifies the name of the base table upon which edits are allowed. This is required when recordsets are created from JOIN statements. For example, consider the following SQL statement:

```
SELECT  *
FROM    publishers JOIN titles
ON      publishers.pub_id = titles.pub_id
```

In this example you could set `Unique Table` to `titles` to indicate that `titles` is the table containing the unique information. For many-to-one queries, you generally set `Unique Table` to point to the many table, because this is the table that will contain unique keys for the recordset.

When `Unique Table` is set, the recordset's `AddNew`, `Delete`, `Resync`, `Update`, and `UpdateBatch` methods affect only the table named in this property.

Generally, you should set the `Unique Schema` or `Unique Catalog` properties before setting the `Unique Table` property, because the table, schema, and catalog names uniquely identify the base table.

The `Unique Table` is directly related to the `Resync Command` property.

The Update Resync Property

The `Update Resync` property specifies whether an implicit `Resync` method is called directly after an `UpdateBatch` method. This lets you choose which rows (if any) are resynchronized. One of the main reasons for the inclusion of these `Resync` properties is the need for client-cursor-based applications to have a better way of handling data changes, especially the insertion of new rows.

This property's values can be one or more of the `CEResyncEnum` constants:

❑ `adResyncNone` indicates that no `Resync` is performed.

❑ `adResyncAutoIncrement` indicates that a `Resync` is performed for all successfully inserted rows, including values of any auto-incrementing columns. This is the default.

❑ `adResyncConflicts` indicates that a `Resync` is performed for updated or deleted rows that failed because of concurrency conflicts.

❑ `adResyncUpdates` indicates that a `Resync` is performed for all rows that were updated successfully.

❑ `adResyncInserts` indicates that a `Resync` is performed for all rows that were successfully inserted, including values of any auto-incrementing columns.

❑ `adResyncAll` indicates that a `Resync` is performed for all rows with pending changes.

These constants are part of the standard ADO type library.

To set more than one value, you should join them together:

```
objRs.Properties("Update Resync") = adResyncUpdates OR adResyncInserts
```

6

The Record Object

The `Record` object is designed for use with Document Source Providers; the OLE DB Provider for Internet Publishing is the first to enable its use. Although this provider shipped with ADO 2.1, its functionality was severely limited, and it was only with the release of ADO 2.5 that all of its features were made available. The only change with version 2.6 was that the `Command` object can now return results into a `Record`.

> *The OLE DB Provider for Internet Publishing is a Web Distributed Authoring and Versioning (WebDAV) client, and will work against any WebDAV-enabled Web server. WebDAV is a W3C standard for document authoring over the Web. For more information on WebDAV, see* www.webdav.org.

Document Source Providers are those providers that allow access to document-based data stores (such as file systems), rather than relational data stores (such as databases). With relational data stores, it is easy to map between a set of data (such as a table or the results of a SQL statement) and a `Recordset` object. With document providers, however, this mapping becomes more difficult, because not every document contains the same properties. For example, in relational data, each row has the same structure as the previous row. There is the same number of columns, and each of the columns is the same. Nonrelational data doesn't follow this pattern, so it wouldn't be easy to try to use a `Recordset`. The general term for this type of data is semistructured data.

This is best explained by looking at the Internet Publishing Provider and using it to connect to a Web server (in this case Microsoft Internet Information Server 5.0). For example, consider the Web site structure shown in this diagram:

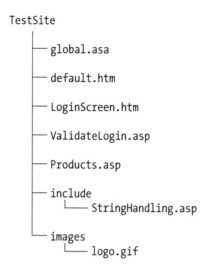

```
TestSite
    ├── global.asa
    ├── default.htm
    ├── LoginScreen.htm
    ├── ValidateLogin.asp
    ├── Products.asp
    ├── include
    │       └── StringHandling.asp
    └── images
            └── logo.gif
```

The structure comprises three directories and a number of different file types. Although these files have some common properties (such as a name), some properties are applicable only to certain types. For example, documents have a size, whereas a directory doesn't. Note that to obtain this sort of information from an IIS 5.0 Web site, directory browsing must be enabled.

In ADO terms, you would use both the Record and the Recordset objects; the Record object would map onto individual items, and the Recordset would contain collections of items. So a Record would hold the top-level directory, TestSite, and a Recordset would hold the files contained within that directory, including subdirectories. The Recordset contains information about only the common properties, such as name, last access time, and so on. Because these are common across all files (whether documents or directories), each row in the Recordset will have the same structure as the previous. However, each item (each row in the recordset) individually may have extra properties, and to access these you use a Record object, using the source of the Record as the current row in the Recordset.

The following pseudo-code should make this clearer:

```
Open directory as a Record.
Extract Recordset of children
Loop through rows in Recordset
    If the row points to a directory
        Open the sub-directory as a new Record
        Extract Recordset of children
        Loop . . .
    Else
        Print out details of file from Recordset
    End If
End Loop
```

A full set of samples on the supporting Web site (http://support.apress.com/) *shows how this works in more detail.*

Methods of the Record Object

The Cancel Method

This method cancels the execution of an asynchronous method call.

```
Record.Cancel
```

This method will cancel an Open, CopyRecord, DeleteRecord, or MoveRecord method call.

The Close Method

This method closes an open Record object.

```
Record.Close
```

The CopyRecord Method

This method copies a file or directory from one location to another.

```
String = Record.CopyRecord([Source], [Destination], [UserName],
                           [Password], [Options], [Async])
```

Name	Type	Description
Source	String	URL of the file or directory to be copied
Destination	String	URL of the location where the Source is to be copied
UserName	String	The user ID, if required, to authorize access to the Destination
Password	String	The user password, if required, to authorize access to the Destination
Options	CopyRecord OptionsEnum	Options to specify the behavior of the copy (default value is adCopyUnspecified)
Async	Boolean	Indicates whether or not the copy should be performed asynchronously (default value is False)

The Options can be one of the following:

- ❑ adCopyAllowEmulation uses a download/upload method if the copy fails.

- ❑ adCopyNonRecursive copies only the current directory, but no children.

❑   adCopyOverWrite overwrites an existing file or directory. If Destination is a directory, all children of that directory will be lost.

❑   adCopyUnspecified indicates that the default copy operation is performed.

By default, the copy operation is recursive, so if Source indicates a directory, all files and directories under Source will be copied. For example:

```
recRoot.CopyRecord "http://localhost/TestSite/", _
                 "http://localhost/LiveSite", _
                 "davids", "SneakYpAssword"
```

However, to copy only the files under the top-level directory, you would do this:

```
recRoot.CopyRecord "http://localhost/TestSite/", _
                 "http://localhost/LiveSite", _
                 "davids", "SneakYpAssword", _
                 adCopyNonRecursive
```

The values of Source and Destination must be different; otherwise, an error is generated. If no Source is provided, then the current Record object is taken as the source.

The return value is provider-dependent, but typically is the value of the Destination.

The DeleteRecord Method

This method deletes a file or directory and subdirectories.

```
Record.DeleteRecord([Source], [Async])
```

Name	Type	Description
Source	String	The URL of the file or directory to be deleted
Async	Boolean	Indicates whether the delete should be performed asynchronously (default value is False)

If Source is empty, the file or directory specified by the Record object is deleted; in this case, you should close the Record object after performing the delete, because subsequent behavior of the object is provider-dependent.

If a Recordset was used as a source for the Record, then the Recordset must be refreshed to reflect the deleted record. For example:

```
' open the root directory
recRoot.Open "http://localhost/TestSite"

' get a recordset of the files in that directory
```

```
      rsChildren = recRoot.GetChildren

    ' open a new Record, using the current row as the source.
    ' this gives us a Record pointing directly at the file
    recFile.Open rsChildren

    ' delete the file
    recFile.DeleteRecord
```

At this stage the file has been deleted, but it still exists as a row in the `Recordset`. To correct this you should do the following:

```
      rsChildren.Requery
```

The `Recordset` now accurately reflects the files in the directory.

The GetChildren Method

This method returns a `Recordset` containing the current `Record`'s files and directories.

```
    Set Recordset = Record.GetChildren
```

The provider determines the fields that make up the `Recordset`, for example:

```
    recRoot.Open "", "URL=http://localhost/TestSite"

    Set rsChildren = recRoot.GetChildren

    While Not rsChildren.EOF
       . . .
    Wend
```

The properties of files are available through the `Recordset`'s `Fields` collection. For example:

```
    Debug.Print rsChildren.Fields("RESOURCE_ABSOLUTEPARSENAME")
```

The `Fields` accessible through the OLE DB Provider for Internet Publishing are discussed at the end of this chapter. How to navigate down through a directory tree is also covered there.

The MoveRecord Method

This method moves a file or directory from one location to another.

```
    String = Record.MoveRecord([Source], [Destination], [UserName],
                          [Password], [Options], [Async])
```

Name	Type	Description
Source	String	The URL of the file or directory to be moved
Destination	String	The URL of the location where the Source is to be moved to
UserName	String	The user ID, if required, to authorize access to the Destination
Password	String	The user password, if required, to authorize access to the Destination
Options	MoveRecord OptionsEnum	Options to specify the behavior of the move (default value is adMoveUnspecified)
Async	Boolean	Indicates whether the move should be performed asynchronously (default value is False)

Options can be one of the following:

❑ adMoveAllowEmulation allows download, upload, and delete operations to simulate the move operation.

❑ adMoveDontUpdateLinks ensures that hypertext links of the source Record are not updated. Link updating is provider-specific.

❑ adMoveOverWrite overwrites the destination file or directory, if it exists.

❑ adMoveUnspecified performs the default move operation.

If Destination already exists, an error will be generated unless adMoveOverWrite is specified. For example:

```
recRoot.MoveRecord "http://localhost/TestSite/", _
                   "http://localhost/LiveSite", _
                   "davids", "SneakYpAssword", adMoveOverWrite
```

The values of Source and Destination must be different; otherwise, an error is generated.

Some changes to the current Record (or Recordset if that's where the Record originated—see the Open method for more details) will not be updated immediately. The ParentURL property is one example, and the Record must be closed (or re-queried) for this to reflect its new value, similar to the code shown for the DeleteRecord method.

The return value is provider-dependent, but typically is the value of the Destination.

The Open Method

This method opens a file or directory, or creates a new file or directory.

```
Record.Open([Source], [ActiveConnection], [Mode], [CreateOptions],
            [Options], [UserName], [Password])
```

Name	Type	Description
Source	Variant	The URL of the file or directory, a Command object, an Open Recordset object, or a string containing a table name or SQL statement
Active Connection	Variant	A connection string or open Connection object
Mode	ConnectMode Enum	The access mode for the Record (default value is adMoveUnknown)
CreateOptions	RecordCreate OptionsEnum	Indicates whether a file should be opened or created–ignored when Source is not a URL (default value is adFailIfNotExists)
Options	RecordOpen OptionsEnum	Specific options for the open command (default value is adOpenRecordUnspecified)
UserName	String	The user ID, if required, to authorize access to the Source
Password	String	The user password, if required, to authorize access to the Source

The ConnectModeEnum constants are discussed under the Mode property, and they specify what permissions are to be applied to the resource being opened.

CreateOptions can be one of the following RecordCreateOptionsEnum constants:

- ❏ adCreateCollection creates a new collection resource (for example, a directory).
- ❏ adCreateNonCollection creates a new simple resource (for example, a file).
- ❏ adCreateOverwrite forces an existing file or directory to be overwritten.
- ❏ adCreateStructDoc creates a new structured document.
- ❏ adFailIfNotExists, ensures that an error is generated if the Source does not exist.
- ❏ adOpenIfExists forces any existing file or directory to be opened (when added to the other adCreate options, apart from adCreateOverwrite).

Options can be one of the following RecordOpenOptionsEnum constants:

- ❑ adDelayFetchFields ensures that fields are not fetched until their first access.
- ❑ adDelayFetchStream ensures that the default stream is not fetched until requested.
- ❑ adOpenAsync opens the Record asynchronously.
- ❑ adOpenRecordUnspecified indicates that no specific open options are specified.
- ❑ adOpenSource opens the source of the resource, rather than its processed output (for example, an ASP file).

The Source argument can be one of the following:

- ❑ A URL pointing to the file or directory to be opened (This can be an absolute or relative URL. If a relative URL is used, then ActiveConnection defines the scope (root) of the relative URL.)
- ❑ An open Recordset object, whose current row identifies the URL to open
- ❑ A Command object that will return a single row (If more than one row is returned, the first row is used as the Source, and the Errors collection will have a warning added to it.)
- ❑ A SQL SELECT statement that returns a single row. (If more than one row is returned, the first row is used as the Source, and the Errors collection will have a warning added to it.)
- ❑ The name of a table

For example, the following all use URLs to open the Record:

```
rec.Open "http://localhost/testsite"
rec.Open "images", "URL=http://localhost/testsite"
rec.Open "default.htm", "URL=http://localhost/testsite"
```

The following uses an open Connection object:

```
conSite.Open "URL=http://localhost/testsite"
rec.Open "default.htm", conSite
```

The following opens a recordset, containing files in the images folder, and then opens a record using the recordset as the source. Because the recordset contains more than one row, the first row in the recordset (the first file in the images directory) is the file the Record opens:

```
rs.Open "images", "URL=http://localhost/testsite", _
                  , , adCmdTableDirect
rec.Open rs
```

This technique is also useful when traversing through directory structures, because the `GetChildren` method of the `Record` returns a `Recordset` of the child files:

```
recParent.Open "http://localhost/testsite"
Set rsChildren = rec.GetChildren
recChild.Open rsChilren
```

The following uses a SQL statement, where only a single row (in this case the first row) is returned into the `Record`:

```
strCon = "Provider=SQLOLEDB; Data Source=Eeyore; " & _
            "Initial Catalog=pubs; User ID=sa; Password="
rec.Open "SELECT * FROM authors", strCon, , , adOpenExecuteCommand
```

The following uses a `Command` object as the source:

```
strCon = "Provider=SQLOLEDB; Data Source=Eeyore; " & _
            "Initial Catalog=pubs; User ID=sa; Password="
cmd.CommandText = "usp_AuthorByID"
cmd.CommandType= adCmdStoredProc
cmd.Parameters.Append _
    cmd.CreateParameter("@au_id", adVarChar, _
                        adParamInput, 22, "172-32-1176")

rec.Open cmd, strCon, , , adOpenExecuteCommand
```

Or, if the `Command` already has the connection defined:

```
rec.Open cmd, , , , adOpenExecuteCommand
```

Properties of the Record Object

The ActiveConnection Property

This property identifies the connection string or `Connection` object to which the `Record` belongs.

```
String = Record.ActiveConnection
Record.ActiveConnection = String
Set Variant = Record.ActiveConnection
Set Record.ActiveConnection = Variant
```

Once the `Record` is open, this property is read-only.

The Mode Property

This property indicates the permissions used when opening the resource.

```
Record.Mode = ConnectModeEnum
ConnectModeEnum = Record.Mode
```

`ConnectModeEnum` can be one or more of the following constants:

- ❑ `adModeRead` indicates read-only permissions. This is the default value.

- ❑ `adModeReadWrite` indicates read and write permissions.

- ❑ `adModeRecursive` indicates that permission should be applied recursively.

- ❑ `adModeShareDenyNone` allows other users to open this resource with any permissions.

- ❑ `adModeShareDenyRead` prevents other users from opening the resource with read permissions.

- ❑ `adModeShareDenyWrite` prevents other users from opening the resource with write permissions.

- ❑ `adModeShareExclusive` prevents other users from opening the resource.

- ❑ `adModeUnknown` indicates that either the permissions have yet to be set, or that they cannot be identified.

- ❑ `adModeWrite` indicates write permissions.

When using the `adModeShare...` constants, you can add `adModeRecursive` to indicate that permissions should be applied recursively. This would apply the permissions to all children and subchildren of the resource when the record is opened.

For example, to apply read and write permissions recursively to a directory and its children:

```
recWeb.Mode = adModeReadWrite + adModeRecursive
recWeb.Open "URL=http://localhost/testsite"
```

This property cannot be changed once the `Record` is open.

When using a client-side (RDS) Connection, the `Mode` property can be set to only `adModeUnknown`.

The ParentURL Property

This property indicates the absolute URL of this `Record`'s parent.

```
String = Record.ParentURL
```

If the Record is the root URL of a Web site, this property will have a null value. If a SQL statement is used as the source of the Record, a run-time error will be generated when accessing this property.

This property is read-only.

The RecordType Property

This property identifies the type of the Record.

```
RecordTypeEnum = Record.RecordType
```

RecordTypeEnum can be one of the following constants:

❑   adSimpleRecord indicates a simple resource that does not contain children (a file).

❑   adCollectionRecord indicates a resource that contains children (a folder).

❑   adStructDoc indicates a COM-structured document.

This property is read-only.

The Source Property

This property indicates the item represented by the Record.

```
Set Variant = Record.Source
Set Record.Source = Variant
```

This property returns the value of the Source argument of the Open method, and therefore contains one of the following:

❑   An absolute or relative URL

❑   A reference to a Recordset object

❑   A reference to a Connection object

The State Property

This property indicates whether the Record is open or closed:

```
ObjectStateEnum = Record.State
```

`ObjectStateEnum` will be one or more of these constants:

❑ `adStateClosed` indicates that the `Record` is closed.

❑ `adStateOpen` indicates that the `Record` is open.

❑ `adStateConnecting` indicates that the `Record` is connecting.

❑ `adStateExecuting` indicates that the `Record` is executing a command.

❑ `adStateFetching` indicates that the `Record` is fetching rows of data.

A combination of values is possible if asynchronous operations are being used. For example, if an asynchronous command is executing, both `adStateOpen` and `adStateExecuting` would be set. This could be tested by:

```
If (rec.State And adStateOpen) = adStateOpen Then
    ' The record is open
    If (rec.State And adStateExecuting) = adStateExecuting Then
        ' . . . but it's still executing a command
```

This property is read-only.

Collections of the Record Object

The Fields Collection

This collection contains a `Field` object for each field in the record.

```
Fields = Record.Fields
```

For URL-based `Records`, the `Field` objects are mapped from file properties and URL directories, such as the MIME type, the URL, and so on (the full list is shown a little later). For non–URL-based `Records`, the `Field` objects are mapped from the underlying provider. For example, a `Record` opened from a SQL query would have the `Fields` mapped from the database columns returned in the query.

When indexing into the `Fields` collection, you can use a field number, a field name, or, for the `Record` object, one of the `FieldEnum` constants:

❑ `adDefaultStream` returns the default stream of the Record.

❑ `adRecordURL` returns the absolute URL of the Record.

The `Field` object is discussed in more detail in Chapter 8.

The Properties Collection

This collection contains a `Property` object for each provider specific property.

```
Properties = Record.Properties
```

This is discussed in more detail in Chapter 8.

Fields of a Record

This section details the fields supplied by the OLE DB Provider for Internet Publishing when `Record` objects are opened from URLs.

Field	Type	Description
CHAPTERED_CHILDREN	adVarWChar	Indicates the rowset chapter containing the children of the resource (not used by the OLE DB Provider for Internet Publishing)
DEFAULT_DOCUMENT	adVarWChar	URL of the default document for a folder
RESOURCE_ABSOLUTEPARSENAME	adVarWChar	The absolute URL, including path
RESOURCE_CONTENTCLASS	adVarWChar	The likely use of the resource
RESOURCE_CONTENTLANGUAGE	adVarWChar	The resource language
RESOURCE_CONTENTTYPE	adVarWChar	MIME type of the resource
RESOURCE_CREATIONTIME	adFileTime	The time the resource was created
RESOURCE_DISPLAYNAME	adVarWChar	Display name of the resource
RESOURCE_ISCOLLECTION	adBoolean	Indicates whether the resource is a collection (has children)
RESOURCE_ISHIDDEN	adBoolean	Indicates whether the resource is hidden
RESOURCE_ISMARKEDFOROFFLINE	adBoolean	Indicates whether the resource is marked for offline usage
RESOURCE_ISREADONLY	adBoolean	Indicates whether the resource is read-only
RESOURCE_ISROOT	adBoolean	Indicates whether the resource is the root of a collection

Table continues on the following page

Field	Type	Description
RESOURCE_ISSTRUCTURED DOCUMENT	adBoolean	Indicates whether the resource is a structured document, such as a Word document
RESOURCE_LASTACCESSTIME	adFileTime	The time the resource was last accessed
RESOURCE_LASTWRITETIME	adFileTime	The time the resource was updated
RESOURCE_PARENTNAME	adVarWChar	URL of the parent resource
RESOURCE_PARSENAME	adVarWChar	URL of the resource
RESOURCE_STREAMSIZE	adUnsigned BigInt	Size of the default stream

DAV Fields

Some Fields begin with DAV. These are for Distributed Authoring and Versioning, and they map onto the existing Fields in the following way:

Field	DAV Field
RESOURCE_PARSENAME	DAV:lastpathsegment
RESOURCE_PARENTNAME	DAV:parentname
RESOURCE_ABSOLUTEPARSENAME	DAV:href
RESOURCE_ISHIDDEN	DAV:ishidden
RESOURCE_ISREADONLY	DAV:isreadonly
RESOURCE_CONTENTTYPE	DAV:getcontenttype
RESOURCE_CONTENTCLASS	DAV:getcontentclass
RESOURCE_CONTENTLANGUAGE	DAV:getcontentlanguage
RESOURCE_CREATIONTIME	DAV:creationtime
RESOURCE_LASTACCESSTIME	DAV:lastaccessed
RESOURCE_LASTWRITETIME	DAV:getlastmodified
RESOURCE_STREAMSIZE	DAV:getcontentlength
RESOURCE_ISCOLLECTION	DAV:iscollection
RESOURCE_ISSTRUCTUREDDOCUMENT	DAV:isstructureddocument

Field	DAV Field
DEFAULT_DOCUMENT	DAV:defaultdocument
RESOURCE_DISPLAYNAME	DAV:displayname
RESOURCE_ISROOT	DAV:isroot

The reason for two sets of properties is that Internet Publishing is built on top of a protocol called WebDAV, and IIS 5.0 is a WebDAV server. It's therefore possible to use any WebDAV client to access IIS 5.0, so it must support the official set of DAV properties.

7

The Stream Object

The Stream object is designed for much the same purpose as the COM IStream interface, and it provides a way to read and write file contents or data streams of. Support for streams is not only available in this separate object, but also has been built into the Command and Recordset objects, allowing greater flexibility when using ADO with other technologies, such as XML and ASP.

Stream objects can be used for several purposes:

❑   To store data internally within applications. Because the Stream is a simple memory manager, you can create Stream objects to store arbitrary amounts of data, such as XML, text, and so on.

❑   In conjunction with the OLE DB Provider for Internet Publishing (discussed in more detail in the previous chapter) and the Record object. Because the Record object allows access to and manipulation of remote files, the Stream adds the ability to access the contents of these files. Together, the two give full support for remote file editing over HTTP.

❑   As a way of transferring data to other applications that support Streams, such as ASP 3.0, where the Request and Response objects both have stream support.

There's nothing to stop you from also using streams in your own applications to provide other applications or developers easy data access. The supporting Web site (http://support.apress.com) has an application that uses the Stream objects.

> **Streams do not perform caching of data, and are intrinsically linked to their underlying objects. This means that it's not necessary to flush the contents either periodically or before closing a stream. Data written to a stream is automatically flushed to the underlying object.**

Methods of the Stream Object

The Cancel Method

This method cancels the execution of an asynchronous `Open` method call.

```
Stream.Cancel
```

If the `adOpenStreamAsync` flag was specified on the `Open` method call, `Cancel` allows the open to be aborted before it has completed.

The Close Method

This method closes an open `Stream` object.

```
Stream.Close
```

You can use the `State` property to determine if the stream is open before attempting to close it.

```
If stmData.State = adStateOpen Then
    stmData.Close
End If
```

It's not necessary to flush the stream before closing, because the close automatically performs a `Flush`.

The CopyTo Method

This method copies a specified number of characters or bytes from one stream to another.

```
Stream.CopyTo(DestStream, [CharNumber])
```

Name	Type	Description
DestStream	Stream	The destination `Stream` object into which characters are to be copied
CharNumber	Long	The number of bytes or characters to copy (The default is −1, which indicates that all characters or bytes from the current stream position to the end of the stream should be copied.)

The start position of the copy for both the source and destination streams is determined by the current position in the stream as specified in the `Position` property. After the copy, the `Position` is immediately after the last byte copied. Data in the destination stream is overwritten.

For the destination stream, one of two things happens to the end of the stream:

❑ It is left where it is if the number of bytes copied is less than were remaining. That is, copying does not truncate the destination stream; to do this, you would use the SetEOS method.

❑ It is extended if the number of bytes copied is greater than were remaining. That is, the destination stream increases in size, then ends immediately after the copied data.

For example:

```
Dim stmSource    As New ADODB.Stream
Dim stmTarget    As New ADODB.Stream

stmTarget.Open

stmSource.Open "URL=http://localhost/testsite/default.htm"

stmSource.CopyTo stmTarget
```

You cannot copy from a binary stream to a text stream, although you can copy from a text stream to a binary stream.

The Flush Method

This method forces the stream's contents into its underlying object.

```
Stream.Flush
```

The buffer is flushed continuously by ADO, so it's only necessary to use this method call when you want to force the changes to be written to the underlying object. For example, use this method if you change the contents of a stream opened from a file, and you want those changes to be immediately available.

The LoadFromFile Method

This method loads the contents of a file into the stream.

```
Stream.LoadFromFile(FileName)
```

Name	Type	Description
FileName	String	A UNC format string containing the file to be loaded

You must open the Stream before loading contents into it, at which time the current contents are overwritten, and the end of the stream (EOS) is set to the end of the loaded contents. The beginning of the stream becomes the current position. For example:

```
stmSource.Open "URL=http://localhost/testsite/default.htm"
stmSource.LoadFromFile "D:\temp\NewDefault.htm"
```

If the Stream object is associated with a URL, this association still exists. Only the contents of the stream change. In the preceding example the stream is still attached to the default.htm file, but now the contents of that file are the contents that were originally in NewDefault.htm.

With ADO 2.8, additional security measures have been introduced into loading a stream from a file when ADO code is used within Internet Explorer. If the site is not part of a Trusted Zone, the code is blocked and access to local files is denied. Note that no warning dialogs are given, so you must ensure that sites requiring access are Trusted.

The Open Method

This method opens a Stream object.

```
Stream.Open([Source], [Mode], [Options], _
            [UserName], [Password])
```

Name	Type	Description
Source	Variant	Either the URL of the resource to be opened, or a Record object whose default stream is used as the source
Mode	ConnectModeEnum	The access mode used when opening the stream. (default value is adModeUnknown)
Options	StreamOpenOptionsEnum	Additional options identifying how the stream should be opened
UserName	String	The user ID if security credentials are required to access to the resource
Password	String	Password for the user ID

The Mode argument can be one of the ConnectModeEnum constants, as detailed under the Mode property.

The Options argument can be one or more of the StreamOpenOptionsEnum constants:

❑ adOpenStreamAsync opens the stream asynchronously.

❑ adOpenStreamFromRecord indicates that the Source argument specifies a Record object, whose default stream should be used.

❑   adOpenStreamUnspecified indicates that the default options should be used. This is the default value and means that synchronous operation is performed, with the source being supplied by a URL.

If a Record object is used as the source, then the security credentials (UserName and Password properties) and the Mode property are ignored. Instead, these properties are taken from the underlying Record object.

For example, to open a stream from a URL:

```
Dim stmSource     As New ADODB.Stream

stmSource.Open "URL=http://localhost/testsite/default.htm"
```

To use a Record as the source (which is why the source is a Variant):

```
Dim stmSource     As New ADODB.Stream
Dim recRoot       As New ADODB.Record

recRoot.Open "default.htm", "URL=http://localhost/testsite"

stmSource.Open recRoot
```

The Read Method

This method reads a number of bytes from a binary stream.

```
Variant = Stream.Read([NumBytes])
```

Name	Type	Description
NumBytes	Long	The number of bytes to read from the stream (default value is −1)

The NumBytes argument can be the actual number of bytes or one of the StreamReadEnum constants:

❑   adReadAll reads all characters from the current position to the end of the stream. This is the default value, and is the same as omitting this argument.

❑   adReadLine reads only the next line. The LineSeparator identifies the character that separates lines.

Only the remaining bytes are read from the stream if the number requested is larger than the number remaining. A Null value is returned if no more bytes remain.

If the number of bytes is not specified, then all remaining bytes are returned.

After reading, the current position in the stream is the byte after the last one read, or the end of the stream if all bytes are read (in which case the EOS property is set to True).

The ReadText Method

This method reads a number of characters from a text stream.

```
String = Stream.ReadText(NumChars)
```

Name	Type	Description
NumChars	Long	The number of characters to read from the Stream (default value is -1)

The NumChars argument can be the actual number of characters or one of the StreamReadEnum constants:

❑   adReadAll reads all characters from the current position to the end of the stream. This is the default value, and is the same as omitting this argument.

❑   adReadLine reads only the next line. The LineSeparator identifies the character that separates lines.

Only the remaining characters are read from the stream if the number requested is larger than the number remaining. A Null value is returned if no more characters remain.

For example:

```
strContents = stmData.ReadText
```

You may have to set the Charset property of the stream before reading data from it, because the default character set is Unicode.

If the number of characters is not specified, then all remaining characters are returned.

The SaveToFile Method

This method saves the contents of a binary stream to a file.

```
Stream.SaveToFile(FileName, Options)
```

Name	Type	Description
FileName	String	The fully qualified name of the file in UNC format
Options	SaveOptionsEnum	Indicates whether a new file should be created or existing files overwritten

The `Options` argument can be one of the `SaveOptionsEnum` constants:

- ❏ `adSaveCreateNotExist` creates a new file only if the file doesn't already exist. This is the default value.

- ❏ `adSaveCreateOverWrite` overwrites an existing file.

After saving, the stream's position is placed at the beginning.

If the `Stream` object is associated with a URL, this association still exists. For example:

```
stmSource.Open "URL=http://localhost/testsite/default.htm"
stmSource.SaveToFile "D:\temp\OldDefault.htm"
```

Here `stmSource` is still associated with the `default.htm` file. The `SaveToFile` method simply copies the contents of a stream to a local file, and doesn't reassociate the stream with that new file.

With ADO 2.8, additional security measures have been introduced into saving a stream to a file when ADO code is used within Internet Explorer. If the site is not part of a Trusted Zone, the code is blocked and access to local files is denied. No warning dialogs are given, so you must ensure that sites requiring access are Trusted.

The SetEOS Method

This method sets the current position to be the end of the stream.

```
Stream.SetEOS
```

Any bytes or characters after the current position are truncated.

This is useful when used after `Write`, `WriteText`, or `CopyTo` method calls, which do not set the end of the stream. For example:

```
stmData.WriteText "Some new text"
stmData.SetEOS
```

The SkipLine Method

When reading text streams, this method skips a line, including the line separator character.

```
Stream.SkipLine
```

The `LineSeparator` property is used to identify the character that separates lines.

For example, imagine processing a text configuration file where, if the first character is #, the line is a comment and should be skipped:

```
Dim stmFile As ADODB.Stream
Dim sChar   As String

Set stmFile = New ADOD.Stream

stmFile.Type = adTypeTxt
stmFile.Charset = "ascii"
stmFile.LineSeparator = adCRLF
stmFile.ReadFromFile "c:\temp\config.txt"

While Not stmFile.EOS
    ' read the first character to check for the comment
    sChar = stmFile.ReadText(1)
    If sChar = "#" Then
        stmFile.SkipLine
    Else
        Debug.Print sChar & stmFile.ReadText(adReadLine)
    End If
Wend
stmFile.Close
```

You cannot skip beyond the end of a stream; you will just remain at EOS if you attempt this, and no error will be generated.

The Write Method

This method writes data to a binary stream.

```
Stream.Write(Buffer)
```

Name	Type	Description
Buffer	Variant	The array of bytes to be written to the stream

After the write, the current stream position is the byte after the last one just written. The end of the stream is not set when you use this method unless you write beyond the end of the existing contents.

The WriteText Method

This method writes characters to a text stream.

```
Stream.WriteText(Data, [Options])
```

Name	Type	Description
Data	String	The string containing the characters to be written to the stream
Options	StreamWriteEnum	Identifies whether line separators are written after the specified string

`Options` can be one of the `StreamWriteEnum` constants:

- ❏ `adWriteChar` just writes the supplied string characters.

- ❏ `adWriteLine` writes the supplied string characters and then the `LineSeparator` character.

For example:

```
stmData.WriteText "This is the new stream contents."
```

After the write, the current stream position is the character after the last one just written. The end of the stream is not set when you use this method unless you write beyond the end of the existing contents.

Properties of the Stream Object

The Charset Property

This property identifies the character set into which the text stream contents should be translated.

```
Stream.Charset = String
String = Stream.Charset
```

The default value is `Unicode`, but other values can include `ascii`, `windows-1252`, and so on. The full range of supported character sets is held under the following registry key:

```
HKEY_CLASSES_ROOT\MIME\Database\Charset
```

If the stream is open, then you must be at the start of the stream before setting this property. It is ignored for binary streams, because these are handled by way of bytes rather than characters.

The EOS Property

This property indicates whether the current position is at the end of the stream.

```
Boolean = Stream.EOS
```

Similar in use to the EOF property of Recordsets, this can be used to identify when the end of the stream has been reached:

```
While Not stmData.EOS
    Debug.Print stmData.ReadText(adReadLine)
Wend
```

The LineSeparator Property

This property identifies the character used to separate lines in the stream:

```
Stream.LineSeparator = LineSeparatorEnum
LineSeparatorEnum = Stream.LineSeparator
```

This value is used when specifying adReadLine in the Read or ReadText methods, and is also used by the SkipLine method.

The default value is adCRLF. Other values are adCR and adLF.

The Mode Property

This property identifies the mode used to open the stream.

```
Stream.Mode = ConnectModeEnum
ConnectModeEnum = Stream.Mode
```

ConnectModeEnum can be one or more of the following constants:

❑   adModeRead indicates read-only permissions. This is the default value.

❑   adModeReadWrite indicates both read and write permissions.

❑   adModeShareDenyNone allows other users with any permissions to open this resource.

❑   adModeShareDenyRead prevents other users with read permissions from opening the resource.

❑   adModeShareDenyWrite prevents other users with write permissions from opening the resource.

❑   adModeShareExclusive prevents other users from opening the resource.

- ❑ adModeUnknown indicates that either the permissions have yet to be set or that they cannot be identified.

- ❑ adModeWrite indicates write permissions.

When using the adModeShare options, you can also specify adModeRecursive to make the permissions be set recursively.

The Position Property

This property identifies the current position within the stream.

```
Stream.Position = Long
Long = Stream.Position
```

The position of the first byte or character in the stream is zero, and all other positions are an offset from this. You cannot use a negative value to move backward through the stream; to do this, you can specify the current position and subtract the number of bytes you wish to move backward.

Specifying a Position beyond the end of the stream will increase the stream's size, and any new bytes will be null unless the stream is read-only; in this case, Position is set to the supplied (but meaningless) number, and no error is generated.

Position is always the number of bytes, so for multibyte character sets, you may have to divide the position by the number of bytes in each character to get the actual character number.

The Size Property

This property identifies the size, in bytes, of the stream.

```
Long = Stream.Size
```

If the size of the stream is unknown, -1 is returned.

The stream's size is limited only by system resources, although the value returned by the Size property will never exceed the value of a Long.

The State Property

This property indicates whether the stream is open or closed.

```
ObjectStateEnum = Stream.State
```

This can be one of the `ObjectStateEnum` constants:

- ❏ `adStateClose` indicates that the stream is closed.

- ❏ `adStateOpen` indicates that the stream is open.

The Type Property

This property identifies the stream's type.

```
Stream.Type = StreamTypeEnum
StreamTypeEnum = Stream.Type
```

`StreamTypeEnum` can be one of two constants:

- ❏ `adTypeBinary` indicates a binary stream.

- ❏ `adTypeText` indicates a text stream. This is the default value.

If you set an empty stream's type to be text and then write binary data to it, the type is changed to binary. Writing text to a binary stream does not change the type, because the text data is just accepted as a string of bytes. You can set the type only when at the beginning of the stream.

Collections of the Stream Object

The `Stream` object has no collections.

8

Collections

Nearly everything you do in ADO uses a collection of some sort. Even the simple task of opening a `Recordset` gives you a collection of fields. When looking at collections, you must look at two things:

❑   The collection itself

❑   The objects in the collection

You'll find that the ADO collections and objects are named sensibly, where the collection is the plural and the object the singular:

Object	Collection
Error	Errors
Field	Fields
Parameter	Parameters
Property	Properties

This chapter is divided into three main sections covering the `Error` object and the `Errors` collection, the `Field` object and the `Fields` collection, and the `Property` object and the `Properties` collection. The `Parameter` object and `Parameters` collection were discussed in Chapter 4. At the end of this chapter, you can find shorter sections covering indexing and the retrieval and storage of images.

The Error Object

An `Error` object is used to hold all the details pertaining to a single error, warning, or informational message from an OLE DB provider, and therefore contains only data access errors. For example, consider the following two sections of code:

```
strConn = "Provider=SQLOLEDB; Data Source=(local); " & _
          "Initial Catalog=pubs; User ID=sa"
objRs.Open "select foo from authors", strConn

strConn = "Provider=SQLSERVER; Data Source=(local); " & _
          "Initial Catalog=pubs; User ID=sa"
objRs.Open "select * from authors", strConn
```

The first example generates errors from the provider (`foo` is a not a valid column in the authors table), and the second example generates an exception (the `Provider` attribute in the connection string is incorrect).

`Error` objects are stored together in the `Errors` collection, which in turn belongs to the `Connection` object. This means that if you want to access the errors, you must refer to the `Errors` collection of the connection on which they were generated. For example, if you have an explicit connection object called `objConn`, you can access the first error in the collection as follows:

```
objConn.Errors(0).Description
```

Here's another example. If you had a `Recordset` object without an explicit connection, you can use the recordset's `ActiveConnection` property to get access to the errors:

```
objRec.ActiveConnection.Errors(0).Description
```

Because each `Error` object contains a single error, and the provider can return multiple errors, you should really iterate through the entire `Errors` collection to see all of the possible errors. In Visual Basic, for example, you would do this:

```
Dim objErr As ADODB.Error

For Each objErr in objConn.Errors
    Print "Error: " & objErr.Description
Next
```

Methods of the Error Object

The `Error` object has no methods.

Properties of the Error Object

The Description Property

This property is a description string associated with the error.

```
String = Error.Description
```

This is the default property of the `Error` object, so it can be omitted if required. The following two lines of code, for example, are equivalent in action (although not readability):

```
Print objConn.Errors(0).Description
```

```
Print objConn.Errors(0)
```

The HelpContext Property

This property indicates the `ContextID` in the help file for the associated error, if one exists.

```
Long = Error.HelpContext
```

You can use this property if you wish to integrate your application with the standard Windows help system. You can do this by calling the Windows help functions, then using the `HelpContext` to identify the ID number of the help description.

If no further help is available, this property will have the value `0`.

The HelpFile Property

This property indicates the name of the help file, if one exists.

```
String = Error.HelpFile
```

Use this in conjunction with the `HelpContext` property when interacting with the Windows help system. If no help file exists, this will be an empty string.

The NativeError Property

This property indicates provider-specific error code for the associated error.

```
Long = Error.NativeError
```

This is useful for identifying errors produced, say, in stored procedures. The native error will be the *underlying* error code. So, if an error is generated in the data store, it's this error that is returned via the `NativeError` property. This is useful for tracking down the error in the provider documentation, because the `NativeError` is the error code returned by the data provider.

The Number Property

This property indicates the number that uniquely identifies an `Error` object.

```
Long = Error.Number
```

This is a unique ADO number (equivalent to the Windows API `HRESULT`) that corresponds to the error condition. For example, many database-related errors will generate their own error number, which is stored in the `NativeError` property, and the ADO `Number` property probably will be set to one of the following nonspecific errors:

❑ `-2147217900` (hex 80040E14): "The command contained one or more errors"

❑ `-2147467259` (hex 80004005): "Unspecified error"

In either case, you can deduce that an underlying object caused the error.

If an `Error` object represents a warning (rather than an error), its `Number` property will be 0. A full list of the error numbers is included in Appendix P.

The Source Property

This property indicates the name of the object or application that originally generated the error.

```
String = Error.Source
```

This could come from the class name of an object, the provider, or ADO. For example, ADO errors will be in this form:

```
ADODB.ObjectName
```

where `ObjectName` is the ADO object that generated the error. You'll notice that, in the errors shown in the section on Error Examples later in this chapter, the `Source` doesn't follow this form; this is because those errors were generated by the provider.

The SQLState Property

This property indicates the SQL state for a given `Error` object.

```
String = Error.SQLState
```

This will contain the five-character SQL error code if the error occurred during a SQL command. If the error doesn't have a specific SQL error code, this may be blank. Consult your provider's SQL documentation for a list of these error codes.

The SQL state error codes are defined by the SQL Access Group and the X/Open Group, and are a standard for SQL error messages. Most database documentation will contain a list of SQL error messages.

The Errors Collection

The Errors collection contains zero or more Error objects, each representing a single error from the provider. Certain error events may produce more than one error event, so each is placed in its own error object, but the collection of errors relates to a single provider error.

Methods of the Errors Collection

The Clear Method

This method removes all Error objects from the Errors collection.

```
Errors.Clear
```

This is called automatically when an error occurs, so the new error information can be entered. It is ADO (rather than the provider) that performs this clearing; this enables the provider to supply multiple error details in response to a single error condition. There's no way to stop this happening; if you need to keep error information, you can store it in a custom data store, such as a collection or recordset.

You might think that this method is a bit superfluous if the Errors collection is cleared automatically, but some actions cause the Errors collection to be filled with warning information. This specifically affects the recordset's Resync, UpdateBatch, and CancelBatch methods, where records may have been deleted at the source while you were editing them.

Another case of this is miscellaneous warnings from the provider. For example, look at the following lines of Visual Basic code:

```
Dim objRs As New ADODB.Recordset
objRs.Open "authors", "DSN=pubs", _
           adOpenDynamic, adLockOptimistic, adCmdTable
```

This may appear fairly innocuous, but running this may fill in an Error in the Errors collection of the recordset's ActiveConnection property. For SQL Server, you get the following:

```
Description:   [Microsoft][ODBC SQL Server Driver]
               Cursor concurrency changed
HelpContext:   0
HelpFile:
NativeError:   0
Number:   0
Source:   Microsoft OLE DB Provider for ODBC Drivers
SQLState:   01S02
```

There's nothing wrong here; it's just that when you create a `Recordset` object, the cursor type is initially `adForwardOnly`. But here a different type is requested, so the provider kindly tells you that it has changed the cursor type. These warnings are dependent upon the provider and data store. You can differentiate between errors and warnings in your `Errors` collection by checking for an error number of zero (signifying a warning) in your error routines.

Clearing the `Errors` collection before an operation allows you to see easily if that operation generated errors (or warnings), because you can easily check the `Count` property after the operation.

The Refresh Method

This method updates the `Error` objects with information from the provider.

```
Errors.Refresh
```

You can use this to ensure that the `Errors` collection contains the latest set of error information from the provider. Having said that, I've yet to come across a situation where the collection isn't populated and needs refreshing.

Properties of the Errors Collection

The Count Property

This property indicates the number of `Error` objects in the `Errors` collection.

```
Long = Errors.Count
```

You should use the Visual Basic or VBScript `For Each...Next` command to iterate through the `Errors` collection without using the `Count` property. For example:

```
If Errors.Count > 0 Then
    For Each objErr In objConn.Errors
        Print objErr.Number & " " & objErr.Description
    Next
End If
```

The Item Property

This property allows indexing into the `Errors` collection to reference a specific `Error` object.

```
Error = Errors.Item(Index)
```

Name	Type	Description
Index	Variant	The number of the error in the collection (zero based)

This is the default property of the `Errors` collection and can be omitted. For example, both of the following lines are logically identical:

```
objConn.Errors.Item(0)
```

```
objConn.Errors(0)
```

If you're coding in a scripting language, you should specify the `Item` property; omitting `Item` causes a small performance penalty, because an extra internal call to `IDispatch` is required to query the interface. In fact, using the `Item` property in every language increases readability.

Error Examples

The following piece of Visual Basic code shows a good way to list all of the errors in the `Errors` collection:

```
Public Sub ErrorTest()
   ' set the error handling on
   On Error GoTo ShowErrors

   Dim objConn    As ADODB.Connection
   Dim strConn    As String
   Set objConn = New ADODB.Connection

   ' set the connection string
   strConn = "put your connection string here"

   objConn.Open strConn
   objConn.Execute "UPDATE pub_info SET pub_id='1111' " & _
                   "WHERE pub_id='9999'"

   objConn.Close
   Set objConn = Nothing

   Exit Sub

ShowErrors:

   ' check for the connection failing
   If objConn.State = adStateClosed Then
     Debug.Print "Connection could not be opened: " & _
                       Err.Description
     Set objConn = Nothing
     Exit Sub
   End If

   ' is it really an ado error?
   If objConn.Errors.Count = 0 Then
     Debug.Print "Error: " & Err.Description
   Else
     Dim objErr As ADODB.Error
     For Each objErr In objConn.Errors
```

```
            Debug.Print "Description:"; vbTab; objErr.Description
            Debug.Print "HelpContext:"; vbTab; objErr.HelpContext
            Debug.Print "HelpFile:"; vbTab; objErr.HelpFile
            Debug.Print "NativeError:"; vbTab; objErr.NativeError
            Debug.Print "Number:"; vbTab; objErr.Number
            Debug.Print "Source:"; vbTab; objErr.Source
            Debug.Print "SQLState:"; vbTab; objErr.SQLState
        Next
    End If

    objConn.Close
    Set objConn = Nothing
End Sub
```

This uses the pubs database and tries to run a SQL statement that violates referential integrity.

If you run this command using different OLE DB providers and data stores, you'll get similar (but not quite the same) results, as the following subsections show. The descriptions have been wrapped to make it easier to read; normally, its one long string.

OLE DB Provider for ODBC to SQL Server

When using the OLE DB provider for ODBC connected to SQL Server, you will notice that two errors are generated. The first is an error indicating the exact nature of the error, and the second indicates that the command has been aborted. You can clearly see the SQL Server error numbers and descriptions:

```
Description: [Microsoft][ODBC SQL Server Driver]
             [SQL Server]UPDATE statement conflicted
             with COLUMN FOREIGN KEY constraint
             'FK_pub_info_pub_id_2AEA69DC'. The conflict
             occurred in database 'pubs',
             table 'publishers', column 'pub_id'
HelpContext:    0
HelpFile:
NativeError:    547
Number:    -2147217900
Source:    Microsoft OLE DB Provider for ODBC Drivers
SQLState:    23000

Description: [Microsoft][ODBC SQL Server Driver]
             [SQL Server]Command has been terminated.
HelpContext:    0
HelpFile:
NativeError:    3621
Number:    -2147217900
Source:    Microsoft OLE DB Provider for ODBC Drivers
SQLState:    01000
```

You can also see that the ADO error number is the same; this corresponds to "The command contained one or more errors," so it's important that you use the `NativeError` property to identify the exact problem.

A full list of ADO error numbers and descriptions is included in Appendix P.

OLE DB Provider for ODBC to Access

When using the OLE DB provider for ODBC to connect to an Access database with the same structure, you get only one error–the actual error that occurred. The Access ODBC driver doesn't send back an extra error.

```
Description:    [Microsoft][ODBC Microsoft Access Driver]
                    You can't add or change a record because a
                related record is required in table
                'publishers'.
HelpContext:    0
HelpFile:
NativeError:    -1613
Number:     -2147217900
Source:     Microsoft OLE DB Provider for ODBC Drivers
SQLState:    23000
```

SQL Server Provider

When using the native OLE DB provider for SQL Server, you get two errors–almost identical to the ODBC details:

```
Description:    UPDATE statement conflicted with
                COLUMN FOREIGN KEY constraint
                'FK_pub_info_publishers'. The conflict occurred
                in database 'pubs', table 'publishers',
                column 'pub_id'.
HelpContext:    0
HepFile:
NativeError:    547
Number:     -2147217900
Source:     Microsoft OLE DB Provider for SQL Server
SQLState:    23000

Description:    The statement has been aborted.
HelpContext:    0
HepFile:
NativeError:    3621
Number:     -2147217900
Source:     Microsoft OLE DB Provider for SQL Server
SQLState:    01000
```

Jet Provider

For the OLE DB provider for Jet, you get only one error, but you get a full description of it:

```
Description:  You can't add or change a record because a related
              record is required in table 'publishers'.
HelpContext:    5003000
HelpFile:
NativeError:    -535037517
Number:    -2147467259
Source:    Microsoft JET Database Engine
SQLState:    3201
```

Notice that the ADO error number is slightly different; this corresponds to "Unspecified error." Also notice that the NativeError property returns a different error number than for the ODBC case, although both these error numbers correspond to "Application-defined or object-defined error."

The Field Object

A Field object represents a single field (or column) in a Recordset object or Record object. When you open a recordset, you'll find a Fields collection that contains zero or more Field objects. This Fields collection will contain a Field object for each column in the recordset and, as you move through the rows, the Fields collection changes its contents to represent the fields of the chosen record.

Although Field objects can exist on their own, they are really only useful when used in conjunction with a Recordset object. Unless creating your own recordsets (with the Recordset object's Append method) where you create fields, you'll generally be dealing with existing Field objects. You can reference these in several ways. The first is by accessing the Field directly through the Fields collection, as shown in the following examples, where the data types of some Field objects are printed:

```
Print objRs.Fields(0).Type
```

```
Print objRs.Fields("FirstName").Type
```

The Fields collection is the default collection of a recordset and can therefore be omitted, if desired:

```
Print objRs("FirstName").Type
```

Second, you can use a Field object explicitly in your code:

```
Dim objFld As ADODB.Field

Set objFld = objRs.Fields("FirstName")
Print objFld.Type
```

The advantage of doing this is realized in situations where you are referencing the field several times. Using a reference to a `Field` object in a separate variable, as opposed to referencing the field in the collection, is more efficient.

Third, you can use the `Item` property of the `Fields` collection:

```
Print objRs.Fields.Item("FirstName")
```

All of these methods are functionally equivalent, although there may be performance differences. Using the `Item` property is faster in scripting languages, and using a `Field` object will be faster if you plan to reference several properties or methods of a single field.

Methods of the Field Object

The AppendChunk Method

This method appends data to a large or binary `Field` object.

```
Field.AppendChunk(Data)
```

Name	Type	Description
Data	Variant	The data to be appended to the object

The first call to `AppendChunk` (after you start editing a field) writes data to the field, overwriting any existing data in the buffer. Subsequent calls add to existing data.

You can use `AppendChunk` only if the `Attributes` property includes `adFldLong`.

This is most often used when dealing with images, large text fields, or binary large objects (BLOBs) stored in databases. A full discussion of this appears at the end of this chapter.

The GetChunk Method

This method returns all or a portion of the contents of a large or binary `Field` object.

```
Variant = Field.GetChunk(Length)
```

Name	Type	Description
Length	Long	The number of bytes or characters to be retrieved

The first call returns data beginning at the start of the field. Subsequent calls start where the last call left off, unless you read the value of another field, in which case a call to GetChunk for the current field starts at the beginning of the field again.

You can use GetChunk only if the Attributes property includes adFldLong.

Like AppendChunk, this is most often used with images, and a full discussion appears at the end of the chapter.

Properties of the Field Object

The ActualSize Property

This property indicates the actual length, in bytes, of a field's value.

```
Long = Field.ActualSize
Field.ActualSize = Long
```

Use this property when you need to set or find out how long a field actually is (rather than how long it *can* be—for that, use the DefinedSize property). For fixed length data types, these two properties will be the same, but they may be different for variable-length data.

The Attributes Property

This property indicates characteristics of a Field object.

```
Long = Field.Attributes
```

This will be one or more of the following FieldAttributeEnum values:

- ❑ adFldMayDefer indicates that the field's contents are not retrieved from the provider along with the rest of the data, but are only retrieved when referenced. This is particularly useful for recordsets containing large BLOBs, where the BLOB may not be referenced.

- ❑ adFldUpdatable indicates that the field can be updated.

- ❑ adFldUnknownUpdatable indicates that the provider doesn't know whether the field can be updated.

- ❑ adFldFixed indicates that the field contains fixed-length data.

- ❑ adFldIsNullable indicates that Null values can be used when writing to the field.

- ❑ adFldMayBeNull indicates that the field may contain a Null value when you read from the field.

❑ adFldLong indicates that AppendChunk and GetChunk can be used on the field, because it contains long binary data.

❑ adFldRowID indicates that the field contains a row ID that cannot be updated. This doesn't indicate the Access AutoNumber or SQL Server IDENTITY fields, but rather an internal row number field, which is unique across the database. Oracle has these natively, but many other data stores don't.

❑ adFldRowVersion indicates a field that uniquely identifies the version of the row, such as a SQL Timestamp field.

❑ adFldCacheDeferred indicates that the values for this field will be cached once it has been read for the first time, and reading the value again will read from the cache.

❑ adNegativeScale indicates that the values for this field have a negative scale.

❑ adKeyColumn indicates that this field is part of a key.

❑ adFldIsChapter indicates that this field is a chaptered recordset.

❑ adFldIsCollection indicates that this field is a collection object (when used with the Internet Publishing Provider).

❑ adFldIsDefaultStream indicates that this field points to the default stream for the object.

❑ adFldIsRowURL indicates that the field contains the URL of the underlying resource (when used with the Internet Publishing Provider).

❑ adFldUnspecified indicates that the provider cannot specify the attributes.

Because this property can be a combination of values, it may not directly match one of the above constants. To check that a value is set, use a procedure like this:

```
If (Field.Attributes AND ad_constant) = ad_constant Then
    Print "field supports that attribute"
End If
```

For example, to check to see if a field might contain Null values:

```
Set objField = objRs.Fields("field_that_might_be_null")
If (objField.Attributes And adFldMayBeNull) = _
                                    adFldMayBeNull Then
    Print "Field may contain a null"
End If
```

Note that this property is read/write when fabricating your own recordsets, and becomes read-only once this fabricated recordset is opened. For new Field objects added to a Record object, you can set the Attributes only once the Value has been set and the Fields collection's Update method has been called to force the provider to append the field.

The DataFormat Property

This property identifies the format in which the data should be displayed.

```
Set DataFormatObject = Field.DataFormat
Set Field.DataFormat = DataFormatObject
```

This is useful only when used in conjunction with Visual Basic 6 or Visual J++ 6, which include the `DataFormat` object. This object contains several properties to identify the type of data the object holds and the way in which it should be displayed. For example, in Visual Basic 6 you could do this:

```
Set txtDate.DataFormat = objRs.Fields("InvoiceDate").DataFormat
```

For more information on this, consult the Visual Basic 6 or Visual J++ 6 documentation.

The DefinedSize Property

This property indicates the defined size (in bytes) of the `Field` object.

```
Long = Field.DefinedSize
```

For variable-width fields this indicates the maximum width of the field, as opposed to the `ActualSize` property that identifies the actual size. For example, a SQL Server column declared as `varchar(20)` would have a `DefinedSize` of 20, irrespective of the actual size of the text it contains.

Note that this field is read/write when creating your own recordsets and becomes read-only once the fabricated recordset is opened.

The Name Property

This property indicates the name of the `Field` object.

```
String = Field.Name
```

This is a necessary field when creating your own `Field` objects to add to the existing `Fields` collection, or when creating a new recordset.

It is also useful when dynamically creating tables in ASP Script code or filling grids manually in Visual Basic. For example, in ASP you could create a table header using the `Name` property:

```
Response.Write "<TABLE><THEAD><TR>"
For Each objField In objRs.Fields
    Response.Write "<TH>" & objField.Name & "</TH>"
Next
Response.Write "</TR></THEAD>"
```

You could then go on to create the rest of the table by using the values from the recordset.

Note that this field is read/write when creating your own recordsets and becomes read-only once the fabricated recordset is opened. For new `Field` objects added to a `Record` object, you can set the `Name` only once the `Value` has been set and the `Fields` collection's `Update` method has been called to force the provider to append the field.

The NumericScale Property

This property indicates the scale of numeric values for the `Field` object.

```
Byte = Field.NumericScale
```

For numeric data, this identifies how many digits are stored to the right of the decimal place. For nonnumeric data, this will be 0 or 255, depending upon the provider and field type.

Note that this field is read/write when creating your own recordsets and becomes read-only once the fabricated recordset is opened.

The OriginalValue Property

This property indicates the value of a `Field` object that existed in the record before any changes were made.

```
Variant = Field.OriginalValue
```

The original value is the value stored in the field before any changes were saved to the provider. This allows the provider simply to return to the original value when you do a `CancelBatch` or `CancelUpdate` method call. For example:

```
' Assume when read that the field contains a value of 10.99
Set objField = objRs.Fields("Price")
objField.Value = 15.99
Print objField.OriginalValue        ' Prints 10.99
Print objField.Value                ' Prints 15.99
objRs.CancelUpdate
Print objField.Value                ' Prints 10.99
```

For related information, see the `UnderlyingValue` and `Value` properties.

This property is read-only.

The Precision Property

This property indicates the degree of precision for numeric values in the `Field` object.

```
Byte = Field.Precision
```

The precision is the maximum number of digits that will be used. For nonnumeric fields, this is 255.

Note that this field is read/write when creating your own recordsets and becomes read-only once the fabricated recordset is opened.

The Status Property

This property indicates the status of the `Field` after it has been appended to the `Fields` collection.

```
FieldStatusEnum = Field.Status
```

The set of constants in `FieldStatusEnum` is quite large, and is included in Appendix B.

You can use this value to determine whether `Field` objects have been successfully appended to the `Fields` collection of a `Record` object. Changes to the collection are cached until the `Update` is called, at which point the `Status` is set to one or more of the `FieldStatusEnum` values. For example, if you don't have permission to insert or delete fields, you can check the `Status` in the following way:

```
If (fld.Status And adFieldPermissionDenied) = _
                            adFieldPermissionDenied Then
    Debug.Print "Permission denied while ";

    If (fld.Status And adFieldPendingInsert) = _
                            adFieldPendingInsert Then
        Debug.Print "adding a field"
    End If

    If (fld.Status And adFieldPendingDelete) = _
                            adFieldPendingDelete Then
        Debug.Print "deleting a field"
    End If
End If
```

For `Field` objects belonging to a `Recordset`, this always returns `adFieldOK`.

The Type Property

This property indicates the data type of the `Field` object.

```
DataTypeEnum = Field.Type
```

The data type will be one of the `DataTypeEnum` values, such as `adInteger` or `adVarChar`. Because this list is quite long, we've included it in Appendix B. Not all providers support all data types, but when creating recordsets, you should be able to use all types, and the provider will compensate for any types it doesn't support by converting them into an equivalent supported type. When creating your own recordsets, use the data type most appropriate to the type of data you wish to store.

Note that this field is read/write when creating your own recordsets and becomes read-only once the fabricated recordset is opened.

The UnderlyingValue Property

This property indicates a `Field` object's current value in the database.

```
Variant = Field.UnderlyingValue
```

The underlying value differs from the original value, because this property holds the current value of the field as stored in the cursor. This would, for example, hold the value if another user changed a field's value. So if you call the `Resync` method, your fields will get repopulated with values from the `UnderlyingValue` property.

The `UnderlyingValue` is really only useful for those situations where your cursor will not see data changes made by other users, such as in batch operations. In particular this will be:

❑   All client-side updateable cursors

❑   Server-based keyset cursors, except for the OLE DB Provider for Jet

> *Interestingly, there is a difference between server-side keysets and static cursors for the OLE DB Provider for SQL Server—despite the fact they both actually use keyset cursors. When requesting a keyset cursor, you get a keyset cursor, and it supports* `UnderlyingValue`. *However, when requesting a static cursor, you are returned a keyset cursor, but it doesn't support* `UnderlyingValue`. *If you examine the dynamic properties of the recordset under these two conditions, you'll see that the properties are not the same, which seems to indicate that the properties are not updated when the server changes the cursor type.*

This property is particularly useful when dealing with conflicts between values that you have changed and values that other users have changed. I examine conflict resolution in more detail in Chapter 5.

For related information, see the `OriginalValue` and `Value` properties.

The Value Property

This property indicates the value assigned to the `Field` object.

```
Variant = Field.Value
Field.Value = Variant
```

This indicates the current value of the field and may not reflect the value stored in the database. This is noticeable in situations where client-cursors or server-based static cursors are used, where the data you have in your recordset doesn't reflect the current state of records in the database (that is to say, another user might have changed the values). The difference between the three value fields is quite simple:

❑   `Value` contains the current value of the field in your current recordset. So if you've made any changes to the field, they will be reflected in the `Value`.

❑ `OriginalValue` contains the value of the field as it was before you made any changes.

❑ `UnderlyingValue` contains the value of the field, as stored in the database, which might include changes made by other users.

This is the default property of a field and can be omitted if required. For example, the following lines of code are functionally equivalent:

```
Print objRs("FirstName").Value
```

```
Print objRs("FirstName")
```

```
Print objRs.Fields("FirstName")
```

If you are appending fields to the `Fields` collection of a `Record`, then the `Value` property must be set and the `Update` method called before any other properties of the `Field`.

You might need to specify the `Value` property when using collections. For example, consider the following Visual Basic code:

```
Dim colNames As New Collection

colNames.Add objRs.("FirstName"), "Name1"
Debug.Print colNames("Name1")
objRs.MoveNext
Debug.Print colNames("Name1")
```

You might expect the same name to be printed twice, because you probably assume that the name was the only thing to be stored in the collection. However, it's actually the `Field` object that is stored in the collection, and the `Field` object just points to a particular field in the recordset. So, when you move to the next row, the `Field` reflects those changes. If you want to store the actual field contents in the collection, you must do this:

```
Dim colNames As New Collection

colNames.Add objRs.("FirstName").Value, "Name1"
```

For related information, see the `UnderlyingValue` and `OriginalValue` properties.

Collections of the Field Object

The Properties Collection

This collection contains all the `Property` objects for a `Field` object.

```
Field.Properties
```

The `Properties` collection contains all of the properties associated with a particular field. This is discussed in more detail in Appendix C.

The Fields Collection

This collection contains zero or more `Field` objects. In existing recordsets there will be one `Field` object for each column in the recordset. When creating new recordsets, you append `Field` objects to the `Fields` collection.

The `Fields` collection is the default collection of the `Recordset` object, which means that you don't need to specify its name. For example, the following two lines are functionally equivalent:

```
objRs.Fields("FirstName")
```

```
objRs("FirstName")
```

For `Fields` of the `Record` object, you can also use the `FieldEnum` constants to index into the collection:

```
objRs.Fields(adDefaultStream)
```

```
objRs.Fields(adRecordURL)
```

These constants return the default stream and the URL of the underlying object.

Scripting languages will suffer a slight performance penalty when omitting the default collection name.

Methods of the Fields Collection

The Append Method

This method appends a `Field` object to the `Fields` collection.

```
Fields.Append(Name, Type, [DefinedSize], [Attrib])
```

Name	Type	Description
Name	String	The name of a new field object
Type	DataTypeEnum	The data type of the new field (default value is adEmpty)
Defined Size	Long	The defined size in characters or bytes of the new field (For fixed-length data types, the default value for the defined size is derived from Type; otherwise, it is 0.)
Attrib	FieldAttributeEnum	The attributes for the new field (default value is adFldUnspecified)

You should set the `CursorLocation` property to `adUseClient` before calling this method, because you cannot append fields to an existing recordset created from a data store.

You cannot append fields of the following types: `adArray`, `adChapter`, `adEmpty`, `adPropVariant`, and `adUserDefined`. Also, although `adIDispatch`, `adIUnknown`, and `adIVariant` can be appended, the results could be unpredictable. These data types will have no use for the majority of ADO programmers, but have been included for completeness.

If you are appending fields to the `Fields` collection of a `Record`, remember that the `Value` property must be set and the `Update` method called before any other properties of the `Field`.

This is quite useful for those situations where you would like some data to be processed as a recordset, but it is not so useful in a data store, and there is no provider for accessing it. You could create a recordset and append your own fields to it. For example:

```
Dim objRs    As New ADODB.Recordset

objRs.CursorLocation = adUseClient
objRs.Fields.Append "Name", adVarChar, 25, adFldMayBeNull
objRs.Fields.Append "Age", adInteger, 8, adFldFixed
```

Calling this method for an open recordset, or a recordset in which the `ActiveConnection` property has been set, will generate a run-time error. This applies even if the recordset has been disconnected from a data store.

Creating Recordsets

Creating recordsets actually has some very interesting uses, some of which have nothing to do with databases or large stores of data. Consider the following:

❑   You have a source of data for which there is no OLE DB provider, but you want to provide a consistent access to this data for your programmers. You could create a component that reads this data in, then creates a recordset that is exposed to the caller of the component.

❑   You are creating a multitier client/server application that needs to pass data around from tier to tier, but you don't want it to be bound up creating arrays and odd structures. You could create a recordset that contains the data and have the recordset passed around. This does, however, rely on having ADO installed on the client.

❑   You are using Microsoft Message Queue Server (MSMQ) and need to pass data in the messages. The body of an MSMQ message must be a string of data or an object that can persist its data, and ADO 2.6 and later can do this. It's not actually the object itself that is passed, but its data and state. Suppose you have a group of traveling sales staff who regularly need to send sales reports back to base. Instead of having to connect back to the server to update the data, they could pass their data back and forth as a message, which means that the data is available to be processed whenever the server is free.

Creating a recordset is simply a matter of appending fields to an empty recordset not connected to a data source. For example, in Visual Basic this could be done with the following code:

```
Dim objRs        As New ADODB.Recordset

objRs.Fields.Append "OrderNumber", adVarChar, 10
objRs.Fields.Append "OrderDate", adVarChar, 20
```

This just creates a recordset with two fields, both holding text data, which can be Null. At this stage you have a closed recordset, so you can open it and add data as though it were a recordset created from a data source. For example:

```
objRs.Open
objRs.AddNew
objRs.Fields("OrderNumber").Value = 1
objRs.Fields("OrderDate") = Now()
objRs.Update
```

The CancelUpdate Method

This method cancels pending changes made to the Fields collection when adding fields to a Record object.

```
Fields.CancelUpdate
```

Any pending field inserts, deletions, or changes are cancelled, and the fields are returned to their previous values. The Status property is set to adFieldOK after this method call.

The Delete Method

This method deletes a Field object from the Fields collection.

```
Fields.Delete(Index)
```

Name	Type	Description
Index	Variant	The name or index number of the Field object to delete

You can use this to delete fields that you have added to your own recordset. For example:

```
objRs.Fields.Delete("Age")
```

Note that there is no way to check if a field exists in the collection without referring to the field. In that case, a run-time error will be generated (error 3265), which you must trap.

You cannot use this method on an open recordset.

The Refresh Method

This method updates the `Field` objects in the `Fields` collection.

```
Fields.Refresh
```

Using this method has no visible effect. You should use the `Recordset` object's `Requery` method to retrieve changes.

The Resync Method

This method refreshes the data in the `Fields` collection of a `Record` object.

```
Fields.Resync ResyncValues
```

`ResyncValues` can be one of the `ResyncEnum` constants:

❑   `adResyncAllValues` resynchronizes all values

❑   `adResyncUnderlyingValues` resynchronizes only the `UnderlyingValue` property

If the `Status` of a `Field` is `adFieldPendingUnknown` or `adFieldPendingInsert`, then `Resync` has no effect.

The `Status` value of a `Field` is only modified if an error occurs during synchronization.

The Update Method

This method saves (to the underlying data store) any pending changes made to the `Fields` collection of a `Record` object.

```
Fields.Update
```

Changes made to the `Fields` collection of a `Record` object are not made permanent until this method is called.

Properties of the Fields Collection

The Count Property

This property indicates the number of `Field` objects in the `Fields` collection.

```
Long = Fields.Count
```

In Visual Basic or VBScript you can use the `For Each...Next` command to iterate through the `Fields` collection without referring to the `Count` property.

This property is read-only.

The Item Property

This property allows indexing into the `Fields` collection to reference a specific `Field` object.

```
Field = Fields.Item(Index)
```

Name	Type	Description
Index	Variant	The name or index number of the item in the collection

This is the default property of the `Fields` collection and can be omitted. For example, the following lines are equivalent:

```
objRs.Fields.Item(1)
```

```
objRs.Fields(1)
```

```
objRs.Fields("FirstName")
```

```
objRs.Fields.Item("FirstName")
```

Because `Fields` is the default collection, you don't need to specify it in your code:

```
objRs("FirstName")
```

The Property Object

A `Property` object contains the attributes of a single property, for any of the following objects:

- ❑ Connection
- ❑ Command
- ❑ Record
- ❑ Recordset
- ❑ Field

Each of these objects contains a `Properties` collection, which, in turn, contains zero or more `Property` objects. It's important to realize that these do not contain the standard properties for an object, but rather the extended, or provider-specific, properties. In use, this generally means provider-specific characteristics, such as Jet-specific features for the Access provider. The documentation for the Provider should detail these properties.

A detailed list of properties is included in Appendix C.

Methods of the Property Object

The `Property` object has no methods.

Properties of the Property Object

The Attributes Property

This property indicates characteristics of a `Property` object.

```
Long = Property.Attributes
```

The `Attributes` can be one or more of the `PropertyAttributesEnum` values:

❑   `adPropNotSupported` indicates that the provider does not support the property.

❑   `adPropRequired` indicates that this property must be specified before the data source is initialized.

❑   `adPropOptional` indicates that this property does not have to be specified before the data source is initialized.

❑   `adPropRead` indicates that the property can be read by the user.

❑   `adPropWrite` indicates that the property can be set by the user.

For example, before you connect to SQL Server you can examine the `Attributes` of the `User ID` property in the `Properties` collection:

```
Print objConn.Properties("User ID").Attributes
```

This gives a value of 1537, which is a combination of some of the constants listed previously:

Attribute	Binary Value	Decimal Value
adPropRequired	00000000001	1
adPropRead	01000000000	512
adPropWrite	10000000000	1024
Total:	11000000001	1537

You don't have to worry about the numbers, because you can test the attributes by using the constants:

```
intAttr = objConn.Properties("User ID").Attributes
If (intAttr AND adPropRequired) = adPropRequired Then
    ' Property is required
End If
```

The Name Property

This property indicates the name of the Property object.

```
String = Property.Name
```

This is the name by which the provider knows the property.

The Type Property

This property indicates the data type of the Property object.

```
DataTypeEnum = Property.Type
```

For example, the User ID property of a connection has a value of adBStr, which indicates a string.

The list of constants for DataTypeEnum is quite large, so it is provided in Appendix B.

The Value Property

This property indicates the value assigned to the Property object.

```
Variant = Property.Value
Property.Value = Variant
```

Some properties may be read-only and do not allow you to set the `Value`, so you should check the `Attributes` beforehand:

```
intAttr = objConn.Properties("property_name").Attributes
If (intAttr AND adPropWrite) = adPropWrite Then
   objConn.Properties("property_name").Value = some_value
End If
```

This is the default property of the `Property` object and can be omitted if desired.

The Properties Collection

The `Properties` collection contains zero or more `Property` objects to indicate the extended properties of the applicable object. You can examine all of the properties by enumerating through the collection. For example:

```
For Each objProp In objConn.Properties
      Print objProp.Name
Next
```

This is a particularly good way to find out which extended properties are supported by a provider.

Methods of the Properties Collection

The Refresh Method

This method updates the `Property` objects in the `Properties` collection with the details from the provider.

```
Properties.Refresh
```

The `Refresh` method is useful for the `Properties` collection because the default provider is the OLE DB Provider for ODBC: If you have set the `Provider` property to point to a different provider, you must `Refresh` the properties to ensure that they are applicable to the changed provider.

Properties of the Properties Collection

The Count Property

This property indicates the number of `Property` objects in the `Properties` collection.

```
Long = Properties.Count
```

You can use the Visual Basic or VBScript For Each...Next command to iterate through the properties collection without using the Count property. For languages that do not support enumeration of collections, you can use this property in a loop.

The Item Property

This property allows indexing into the Properties collection to reference a specific Property object.

```
Property = Properties.Item(Index)
```

Name	Type	Description
Index	Variant	The number or name of the property in the collection (zero-based)

This is the default property of the Properties collection and can be omitted. For example, the following lines are equivalent:

```
object.Properties.Item(1)
```

```
object.Properties(1)
```

```
object.Properties("property_name")
```

Indexing

ADO 2.0 introduced the concept of **local indexing** for client cursors. This is achieved by using one of the Field object's dynamic properties, called Optimize. The way it works is that you decide which field you want to index, then set the Optimize property to True. For example:

```
Set objField = objRs("au_lname")
objField.Properties("Optimize") = True
```

You don't have to use a Field object, because you can just access the properties directly from the recordset's field:

```
objRs("au_lname").Properties("Optimize") = True
```

This creates a local index, which will improve sorting and finding records. Setting the property to False will delete the index.

Future versions of ADO were expected to provide an Indexes collection and Index objects, which would help you manage local indexes and give you greater control over them. With the release of .NET and ADO.NET it seems unlikely this will now be introduced.

Using Images with ADO

This can be one of the most confusing aspects of using databases, because it never seems to be quite as intuitive as it should be. Many people say that storing images in databases isn't the most efficient use of the database, and that it can be slow. However, there are times when you need to do this, such as when you have legacy data or if a third party supplies your data to you.

I think a preferable solution is to store the images on disc as files, and just store the file name in the database. Here are the reasons why:

1. As a rule, databases aren't designed to store large binary data, and therefore the storage and handling of them can be slower than it is for other fields.

2. Keeping images separate allows them to be updated more easily. For example, when you have different people designing your images, it's easier to just have the designers save the files to a directory, rather than having them access the database (to which they would need permissions).

3. There's currently no easy way to stream images directly from a database into another location in an application. For example, in HTML an image must come from an HTTP address, and in Visual Basic applications, images or icons can be loaded only from files or resource files.

These are just my opinions, and shouldn't deter you from storing images in a database if you want to.

Images and Parameters

Here are a few simple rules to follow when using images with parameters:

❑ If reading and writing images from disc, then you should read into, and write from, a `Byte` array.

❑ The ADO `Parameter` object's `Type` should be `adVarBinary`.

❑ The ADO `Parameter` object's `Length` should be the maximum size of the binary data. For a SQL Server `image` or an Access OLE Object parameter, this is 2,147,483,647.

❑ Either set the `Value` property directly or use `GetChunk` and `AppendChunk` to get the image data into your ADO `Parameter`.

One thing to watch out for when dealing with images using stored procedures in SQL Server is that your procedure cache might not be big enough to allow the use of large images. In this case you'll get error 701, and you should consult the SQL Server documentation for details of how to increase this cache.

Following are a few examples to show how this works.

Using Parameters to Store Images

The following shows how you could read an image from a file and store it in a SQL Server database. I use Visual Basic to grab the image file and a stored procedure to place it in the database. Here's the stored procedure:

```
CREATE PROCEDURE usp_UpdateLogo
     @PubID    char(4),
     @Logo     image
AS
     UPDATE    pub_info
     SET       logo = @Logo
     WHERE     pub_id = @PubID
```

This simply updates the logo field for the publisher ID supplied.

The code to call this procedure from Visual Basic could look like this:

```
Dim objConn      As New ADODB.Connection
Dim objCmd       As New ADODB.Command
Dim bytChunk()   As Byte
Dim varChunk     As Variant

' open bitmap file
Open "c:\temp\wrox.bmp" For Binary As #1

' resize the byte array, read in the data space, and close it.
ReDim bytChunk(LOF(1))
Get #1, , bytChunk()
varChunk = StrConv(bytChunk, vbUnicode)
Erase bytChunk
Close #1

' connect to data store
objConn.Open "Provider=SQLOLEDB; Data Source=Tigger; " & _
             "Initial Catalog=pubs; User ID=sa; Password="

' set up command
With objCmd
    Set .ActiveConnection = objConn
    .CommandText = "usp_UpdateLogo"
    .CommandType = adCmdStoredProc

    ' create the parameters
    .Parameters.Append .CreateParameter("@PubID", adVarChar, _
                            adParamInput, 4, "0736")
    .Parameters.Append .CreateParameter("@Logo", adVarBinary, _
                            adParamInput, 2147483647)

    ' set the parameter value
    ' use either this command, which is commented out
    ' .Parameters("@Logo").Value = varChunk


    ' or this one
```

```
        .Parameters("@Logo").AppendChunk varChunk

      ' now run the command
      .Execute
End With

objConn.Close

Set objCmd = Nothing
Set objConn = Nothing
```

Passing the Image in Smaller Chunks

You may find that reading the whole image file into memory at once wastes resources, especially considering how large images can be. You can break this down into smaller chunks and use AppendChunk to append chunks of the image into the parameter. The Visual Basic code from the previous example would be modified like this:

```
Dim objConn           As New ADODB.Connection
Dim objCmd            As New ADODB.Command
Dim bytChunk(512)     As Byte                    ' Note the size
Dim varChunk          As Variant

' open bitmap file
Open "c:\temp\wrox.bmp" For Binary As #1

' don't read the image file yet

' connect to data store
objConn.Open "Provider=SQLOLEDB; Data Source=Tigger; " & _
             "Initial Catalog=pubs; User ID=sa; Password="

' set up command
With objCmd
    .ActiveConnection = objConn
    .CommandText = "usp_UpdateLogo"
    .CommandType = adCmdStoredProc

    ' create the parameters
    .Parameters.Append .CreateParameter("@PubID", adVarChar, _
                                adParamInput, 4, "0736")
    .Parameters.Append .CreateParameter("@Logo", adVarBinary, _
                                adParamInput, 2147483647)

    ' continue reading from file whilst we haven't hit EOF
    While Not EOF(1)
        ' Read in a small chunk. The amount read is determined
        ' by the size of the byte array we are reading into
        Get #1, , bytChunk()

        ' Append the smaller array to the parameter
        .Parameters("@Logo").AppendChunk bytChunk()
    Wend
```

```
        ' run the command
        .Execute
    End With

    objConn.Close
    Close #1

    Set objCmd = Nothing
    Set objConn = Nothing
```

This performs exactly the same action, only using a small chunk of memory to repeatedly read in from the image file. You may find this marginally slower, but it uses memory and network resources more efficiently.

Using Parameters to Retrieve Images

If you want to retrieve images from a database via a stored procedure, the first thing to note is that it's *not* possible to assign an image to a variable (at least, not with SQL Server). This means that you cannot have a stored procedure like this:

```
    CREATE PROCEDURE usp_FetchLogo
        @PubID    char(4),
        @Logo     image OUTPUT
    AS
        SELECT    @Logo = logo
        FROM      pub_info
        WHERE     pub_id = @PubID
```

Instead, if you need to extract images using a stored procedure, you must return a recordset, even if that recordset contains only one row and one field.

Images and Fields

Using images with `Recordset` fields is very similar to using `Parameters`.

Storing Images in Fields

To store images directly into fields simply requires a call to the `AppendChunk` method. The following Visual Basic code shows this:

```
    Dim objConn     As New ADODB.Connection
    Dim objCmd      As New ADODB.Command
    Dim objRs       As ADODB.Recordset
    Dim bytChunk()  As Byte

    ' open bitmap file
    Open "c:\temp\single.bmp" For Binary As #1

    ' resize the byte array, read in the data, and close it.
```

```
ReDim bytChunk(LOF(1))
Get #1, , bytChunk()
Close #1


' open the connection
objConn.Open "Provider=SQLOLEDB; Data Source=Tigger; " & _
             "Initial Catalog=pubs; User ID=sa; Password="

With objCmd
    ' set the commmand properties
    .ActiveConnection = objConn
    .CommandText = "usp_FetchLogo"
    .CommandType = adCmdStoredProc
    ' create the parameters
    .Parameters.Append .CreateParameter("@PubID", adVarChar, _
                              adParamInput, 4, "0736")

    ' create and open a new recordset
    Set objRs = New ADODB.Recordset
    objRs.Open objCmd, , adOpenDynamic, adLockOptimistic, _
                              adCmdStoredProc
End With

' update the logo field, passing in the image
objRs("logo").AppendChunk (bytChunk)
objRs.Update

objRs.Close
objConn.Close

Set objRs = Nothing
set objCmd = Nothing
Set objConn = Nothing
```

In this case, I've used a stored procedure called usp_FetchLogo to fetch the image from the database. The SQL code for usp_FetchLogo is shown later in this chapter.

Smaller Chunks

Using a smaller chunk size to conserve the memory resources on the client is quite simple too.

```
Dim objConn         As New ADODB.Connection
Dim objCmd          As New ADODB.Command
Dim objRs           As ADODB.Recordset
Dim bytChunk(512)   As Byte                    ' note the size

' don't read the bitmap file yet

' open the connection
objConn.Open "Provider=SQLOLEDB; Data Source=Tigger; " & _
             "Initial Catalog=pubs; User ID=sa; Password="

With objCmd
    ' set the command properties
    .ActiveConnection = objConn
```

```
            .CommandText = "usp_FetchLogo"
            .CommandType = adCmdStoredProc

            ' create the parameters
            .Parameters.Append .CreateParameter("@PubID", adVarChar, _
                                       adParamInput, 4, "0736")

            ' create and open the recordset
            Set objRs = New ADODB.Recordset
            objRs.Open objCmd, , adOpenDynamic, adLockOptimistic, _
                                       adCmdStoredProc
        End With
```

```
        ' open bitmap file
        Open "c:\temp\chunks.bmp" For Binary As #1

        ' whilst we haven't reached the end of the image file
        While Not EOF(1)
            ' Read in a small chunk. The amount read is determined
            ' by the size of the byte array we are reading into
            Get #1, , bytChunk()

            ' append this small array to the field
            objRs("logo").AppendChunk (bytChunk)
        Wend
        Close #1
```

```
        ' update the field
        objRs.Update

        objRs.Close
        objConn.Close

        Set objRs = Nothing
        Set objCmd = Nothing
        Set objConn = Nothing
```

Retrieving Images from Fields

This task is extremely simple when using the Value of the field or the GetChunk method. This Visual Basic code shows how it can be done:

```
        Dim objConn     As New ADODB.Connection
        Dim objCmd      As New ADODB.Command
        Dim objRs       As ADODB.Recordset
        Dim bytChunk()  As Byte

        ' open the connection
        objConn.Open "Provider=SQLOLEDB; Data Source=Tigger; " & _
                     "Initial Catalog=pubs; User ID=sa; Password="

        With objCmd
            ' set up the command
            .ActiveConnection = objConn
```

```
            .CommandText = "usp_FetchLogo"
            .CommandType = adCmdStoredProc


        ' create the parameters
        .Parameters.Append .CreateParameter("@PubID", adVarChar, _
                                    adParamInput, 4, "0736")

        ' now run the command
        Set objRs = objCmd.Execute
    End With


    ' extract the logo into a variable
    bytChunk = objRs("logo")


    ' store the image to a file and load it into a picture box
    ' Note: Visual Basic has no method to accept the image
    '        directly from the variable so you have to save
    '        it to disk first
    Open "c:\temp\image.bmp" For Binary As #1
    Put #1, , bytChunk()
    Close #1
    Picture1.Picture = LoadPicture("c:\temp\image.bmp")

    objRs.Close
    objConn.Close

    Set objRs = Nothing
    Set objCmd = Nothing
    Set objConn = Nothing
```

This example used a Command object and parameters, but you could equally use just a recordset and return a whole set of records with images.

Smaller Chunks

One of the disadvantages of using the preceding method is that, for a large image (such as a 24-bit full-color picture), it requires a large amount of memory on the client and is not particularly efficient. If you think about how large images can be, there seems little point in clogging up the user machine with a large amount of dynamic storage.

To alleviate this problem, you can use GetChunks and limit the amount it reads. For example, the above Visual Basic code could be rewritten like this:

```
Dim objConn     As New ADODB.Connection
Dim objCmd      As New ADODB.Command
Dim objRs       As ADODB.Recordset
Dim bytChunk()  As Byte
Dim varChunk    As Variant

' open the connection
objConn.Open "Provider=SQLOLEDB; Data Source=Tigger; " & _
             "Initial Catalog=pubs; User ID=sa; Password="
```

```
With objCmd
    ' set up the command
    .ActiveConnection = objConn
    .CommandText = "usp_FetchLogo"
    .CommandType = adCmdStoredProc

    ' create the parameters
    .Parameters.Append .CreateParameter("@PubID", adVarChar, _
                                adParamInput, 4, "0736")

    ' now run the command
    Set objRs = objCmd.Execute
End With
```

```
' open the output file
Open "c:\temp\barf.bmp" For Binary As #1

' read in the first chunk
varChunk = objRs("logo").GetChunk(512)

' GetChunk returns Null if there is no more data
While Not IsNull(varChunk)
    ' convert the data to a byte array and write
    ' it to the file
    bytChunk = varChunk
    Put #1, , bytChunk()

    ' read in the next chunk
    varChunk = objRs("logo").GetChunk(512)
Wend
```

```
' close the file and load the picture
Close #1
Picture1.Picture = LoadPicture("c:\temp\barf.bmp")

objRs.Close
objConn.Close

Set objRs = Nothing
Set objCmd = Nothing
Set objConn = Nothing
```

You might think that this is much slower, but the delay is hardly noticeable.

Retrieving Images into a Stream

The new feature of allowing the results of a Command to be stored in a Stream is particularly suited to images, because it avoids the need to have code to handle the file. For example, the following code creates and opens a new Stream object, into which the results of the usp_FetchLogo stored procedure are stored. The contents of the Stream are then written directly to a file:

```
Dim objConn     As New ADODB.Connection
Dim objCmd      As New ADODB.Command
Dim objStm      As New Stream
```

```
' open the connection
objConn.Open "Provider=SQLOLEDB; Data Source=Tigger; " & _
             "Initial Catalog=pubs; User ID=sa; Password="


' open the stream
objStm.Open

With objCmd
    ' set up the command
    .ActiveConnection = objConn
    .CommandText = "usp_FetchLogo"
    .CommandType = adCmdStoredProc

    ' create the parameters
    .Parameters.Append .CreateParameter("@PubID", adVarChar, _
                                   adParamInput, 4, "0736")

    ' set the output stream
    .Properties("Output Stream") = objStm

    ' now run the command
    objCmd.Execute , , adExecuteStream
End With

' save the file
objStm.SaveToFile "c:\temp\image.bmp"

objConn.Close

Set objCmd = Nothing
Set objConn = Nothing
```

Images Using ASP

The same sort of procedure to push an image to the browser is just as simple in ASP. I'll start with a stored procedure to fetch the image:

```
CREATE PROCEDURE usp_FetchLogo
    @lPubID   int
AS
    SELECT    logo
    FROM      pub_info
    WHERE     pub_id = @lPubId
```

Now imagine an ASP page called GetLogo.asp:

```
<!--METADATA TYPE="TypeLib" FILE="C:\Program Files\Common
➥Files\SYSTEM\ADO\MSADO15.DLL"-->
<%
    ' turn on buffering and set the mime type
    Response.Buffer = True
    Response.ContentType = "image/bmp"
```

```
        Dim objConn
        Dim objCmd
        Dim objRs
        Dim bytChunk
        Dim sID
```

```
        ' get the required id
        sID = Request.QueryString("pub_id")

        Set objConn = Server.CreateObject("ADODB.Connection")
        Set objCmd = Server.CreateObject("ADODB.Command")
        Set objRs = Server.CreateObject("ADODB.Recordset")

        ' open the connection
        objConn.Open "Provider=SQLOLEDB; Data Source=Tigger; " & _
                     "Initial Catalog=pubs; User ID=sa; Password="

        ' set the command details
        objCmd.ActiveConnection = objConn
        objCmd.CommandText = "usp_FetchLogo"
        objCmd.CommandType = adCmdStoredProc

        objCmd.Parameters.Append objCmd.CreateParameter("@PubID", _
                                 adVarChar, adParamInput, 4, sID)

        ' run the command and extract the logo
        Set objRs = objCmd.Execute
        bytChunk = objRs("logo")

        ' write image to the browser
        Response.BinaryWrite bytChunk
        Response.End
    %>
```

You could use this from another ASP page as the source of the image tag. For example:

```
    <IMG SRC="GetLogo.asp?pub_id=0736">
```

When the page is loaded, the GetLogo.asp page is called to fetch the image from the database.

9

Remote Data Services

Remote Data Services (RDS) differs from ADO in that RDS is a set of objects designed to work in the browser and provide client-side data facilities. It sits on top of ADO and works in Internet Explorer, providing a way to handle data within DHTML and to easily allow data to be displayed in HTML elements. RDS not only allows data to be displayed, but also allows data updates and provides methods for updating the original data store. In effect, RDS provides an offline copy of the data.

This chapter covers the RDS objects, such as the Data Space Objects, Data Source Objects, and so on, but doesn't give an exhaustive tutorial of their workings.

Note that from ADO 2.8 onward, RDS is deprecated, although it will continue to be supported. Microsoft advises using the SOAP toolkit instead. ADO 2.8 does not ship with the `handunsf.reg` file, which when run allowed the server to run in unsafe mode. For more details, see the Knowledge Base article number 818490.

RDS Support

The use of RDS is browser-dependent, and only the Microsoft Internet Explorer browser (version 4 onward) fully supports RDS. If you'd like to use RDS but need to support other browsers, the MSDN site has a good article describing this at http://msdn.microsoft.com/workshop/dbdwnlvl.asp.

You should also be aware that applications using RDS might have to contend with different versions of RDS on the client. Internet Explorer 4 shipped with RDS 1.5, and Internet Explorer 5, Office 2000, and Visual Studio 6 shipped with RDS 2.0. RDS 2.5 shipped with Windows 2000, and was also available as a download.

For information on general compatibility issues, you should read the following knowledge-base articles, available from http://support.microsoft.com:

❑   Q216389–Maintaining Binary Compatibility in Components with ADOR

❑   Q195049–Maintain Binary Compatibility in Components Exposing ADO

❑   Q201580–ADO 2.0 and ADO 2.1 Binary Compatibility

At the time of writing, there were no other issues concerning compatibility.

You can obtain the latest versions of ADO and RDS at http://www.microsoft.com/data.

RDS Objects

Because RDS uses both client- and server-side components, they are best described in conjunction with a diagram of the RDS component relationship:

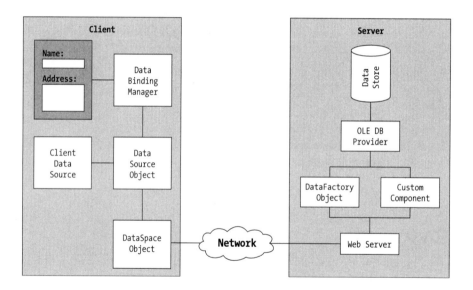

At the server we have the following:

❑   **Data Store,** which is the source of the data

❑   **Data Factory Object** or **Custom Component,** which supply only the requested data (The custom component can be any COM-compliant component.)

❑   **Web Server,** which provides the interface from the server to the client

This means that you must have certain facilities installed on your Web server. The NT 4.0 Option Pack supplies RDS 1.5, and versions 2.0 and 2.1 are available for download. Windows 2000 comes with

ADO 2.5, and versions 2.5, 2.6, 2.7, and 2.8 are available for download at
http://www.microsoft.com/data. See the section entitled "RDS Support" later in this chapter for more
details.

On the client side we have the following:

❑   **Data Space Object**, which takes the data from the Web server and makes it available to a Data
    Source object

❑   **Data Source Object**, which along with the **client data cache** holds the data on the client

❑   **Data Binding Manager**, which connects the Data Source Object to HTML Tags (See the Data
    Binding section later in the chapter for more details)

❑   **Client HTML tags**, which display the data

In the preceding diagram, the use of Client and Server is a *logical* separation, and does not have to
represent a physical separation of the two items. The Web server, for example, can exist on the same
machine as the client, which means that RDS-based applications can be created and tested on a single
machine. Also, certain Data Source Objects (such as the Tabular Data Control [TDC] and the XML
Data Control) can work with local data files and do not always require a server to supply the data.

In essence, RDS is just a way of handling data remotely. It provides a way for HTML pages to access
data from a remote data source, thereby allowing data changes and providing a way for data to be sent
back to the original data store. Its use is simplified by the fact that underneath each Data Source Object
is a standard ADO recordset. Because it is a disconnected recordset (that is, not permanently
connected to the data store) it uses the client cursor engine.

Data Source Objects

The simplest way to use RDS is through the use of a Data Source Object (DSO). A DSO provides the
data to the client interface, allowing it to be bound to HTML elements and manipulated directly by
way of an ADO `Recordset`.

Several Data Source Objects are available as part of the standard IE 4, 5, or 6 installation, or as a
separate download. They are generally created by use of the HTML `OBJECT` tag, for which an ActiveX
control has the general form:

```
<OBJECT CLASSID="clsid:class id of object"
        ID="id of HTML tag" HEIGHT="0" WIDTH="0">
    <PARAM NAME="parameter name" VALUE="parameter value">
    <PARAM NAME="parameter name" VALUE="parameter value">
</OBJECT>
```

Setting a unique `ID` allows data binding to take place, and using a `Height` and `Width` of zero ensures
that the control doesn't take up any space on the page. You can give a height and width, but because
the control doesn't have a visible interface, there's not much to see.

The parameter names correspond to the properties of the object, and are listed below with each object. For example:

```
<OBJECT CLASSID="clsid:BD96C556-65A3-11D0-983A-00C04FC29E33"
        ID="dsoAuthors" HEIGHT="0" WIDTH="0">
    <PARAM NAME="Server" VALUE="http://www.yourserver.com">
    <PARAM NAME="Connect" VALUE="DSN=pubs">
    <PARAM NAME="SQL" VALUE="SELECT * FROM authors">
</OBJECT>
```

You can also set the parameters (and call methods) from within script by referencing the properties:

```
<SCRIPT Language="JScript">
    dsoAuthors.Server = "http://www.yourserver.com";
    dsoAuthors.Connect = "DSN=pubs";

    dsoAuthors.SQL = "SELECT * FROM authors"
    dsoAuthors.Refresh;
</SCRIPT>
```

There are various security implications when using RDS. See the Security Issues section at the end of this chapter for more details.

I cover the following Data Source Objects:

❑   RDS Control, which is designed to handle data from SQL databases

❑   The Tabular Data Control (TDC), which is designed for data stored in text files

❑   Java Database Connectivity Control (JDBC), which is a DSO written in Java, and therefore available for use in other browsers

❑   Microsoft HTML Control, which is designed for data formatted in HTML

❑   XML Java Applet, which is another Java written applet, this time for XML data (It only provides read-only access to the data.)

❑   The XML Control, which is designed for data in XML form (The XML DSO is more commonly known as an XML Data Island.)

Remote Data Service Data Control

In older versions of RDS, the RDS Data Control was known as the Advanced Data Control (ADC). It is automatically installed with IE 4 or higher.

Class ID	BD96C556-65A3-11D0-983A-00C04FC29E33
Source	C:\Program Files\Common Files\System\MSADC\msadco.dll
Prog ID	RDS.DataControl

Instantiating the RDS Data Control

You instantiate the RDS Data Control with the use of an OBJECT tag, taking the following form:

```
<OBJECT CLASSID="clsid:BD96C556-65A3-11D0-983A-00C04FC29E33"
        ID="DataControl" WIDTH="0" HEIGHT="0">
  <PARAM NAME="Connect" VALUE="ConnectString">
  <PARAM NAME="Server" VALUE="ServerURL">
  <PARAM NAME="SQL" VALUE="SQLQueryString">
  <PARAM NAME="URL" VALUE="URLpath">
</OBJECT>
```

Methods of the RDS Data Control

The Cancel Method

This method cancels an asynchronous action.

```
datacontrol.Cancel
```

If data is being fetched asynchronously, for example when the FetchOptions property is set to adcFetchAsync or adcFetchBackground, then calling the Cancel method will cancel the fetching operation.

After this call, the ReadyState property is set to adcReadyStateLoaded and the Recordset will be empty.

The CancelUpdate Method

This method cancels changes made to the source recordset.

```
datacontrol.CancelUpdate
```

Because an RDS recordset is disconnected from the original data store, CancelUpdate ensures that any changes made to the recordset since the last Refresh or SubmitChanges method call will be discarded. The cache of changes is reset to empty, and any bound controls are refreshed with the original data.

The CreateRecordSet Method

This method creates an empty, disconnected recordset on the client.

```
Object = datacontrol.CreateRecordSet(varColumnInfos)
```

Parameter	Type	Description
varColumnInfos	Variant	An array of arrays defining the columns for the recordset

varColumnInfos should be a variant array, with each column of the inner array being defined by one of the following four elements:

- ❑   Name, for the name of the column

- ❑   Type, for the data type of the column

- ❑   Size, for the size of the column (for fixed-length types this must be -1)

- ❑   Nullability, to indicate if the column can contain a null value

For the data type, you should use one of the ADO DataTypeEnum values (except for adChapter, adDBFileTime, adEmpty, adFileTime, adIDispatch, adIUnknown, adLongVarChar, adPropVariant, adUserDefined, adVariant, and adVarNumeric, which are not supported). For a full list of these data types and their associated values, consult Appendix B.

The data type may be converted into an equivalent type, but you won't see this until the recordset is populated. The possible substitutions are:

Original Type	Substituted Type
adDBTimeStamp	adDate
adBSTR, adVarWChar, adLongVarWChar	adWChar
adChar, adVarChar	adLongVarChar
adLongVarBinary	adVarBinary

The column arrays should be appended to another array, which becomes the method argument. For example:

```
<SCRIPT LANGUAGE=" JScript">

function cmdCreateNew.onclick()
{
    var aField1 = Array(4);
    var aField2 = Array(4);
    var aField3 = Array(4);
    var aField4 = Array(4);
    var aCols = Array(4);

    // create the individual columns
    aField1[0] = "ID";           // name
    aField1[1] = 3;              // type - adInteger
    aField1[2] = -1;             // size
    aField1[3] = false;          // nullability
```

```
            aField2[0] = "FirstName";      // name
            aField2[1] = 202;              // type - adVarWChar
            aField2[2] = -1;               // size
            aField2[3] = false;            // nullability

            aField3[0] = "LastName";       // name
            aField3[1] = 202;              // type - adVarWChar
            aField3[2] = -1;               // size
            aField3[3] = false;            // nullability

            aField4[0] = "DateOfBirth";    // name
            aField4[1] = 7;                // type - adDate
            aField4[2] = -1;               // size
            aField4[3] = false;            // nullability

            // add the columns to an array
            aCols[0] = aField1;
            aCols[1] = aField2;
            aCols[2] = aField3;
            aCols[3] = aField4;


            // create a new recordset
            // dsoNew and dsoTest are data controls on the
            // page as OBJECT tags or created in code
            dsoNew.SourceRecordset = dsoTest.CreateRecordset (aCols);

            // add some data
            dsoNew.AddNew;
            dsoNew.Fields(0) = 1;
            dsoNew.Fields(1) = "Rob";
            dsoNew.Fields(2) = "Smith";
            dsoNew.Fields(3) = 68/03/05;
            dsoNew.Update;
    }
    </SCRIPT>
```

The recordset created is a standard ADO disconnected recordset.

The Move... Methods

These method move to the appropriate row in the recordset.

```
datacontrol.MoveFirst
datacontrol.MoveNext
datacontrol.MovePrevious
datacontrol.MoveLast
```

These methods are the same as the Recordset methods of the same name; they move to the first, next, previous, and last row in a recordset.

The Refresh Method

This method refreshes the data from the data source.

```
datacontrol.Refresh
```

Because RDS works in a disconnected environment, it's possible for the data it's using to become out of sync with the data in the original data source. Calling `Refresh` will update the current data.

The `Refresh` method will discard any unsaved changes and will position the recordset at the first record. Bound HTML elements will reflect the new data.

The Reset Method

This method resets the client-side recordset based on filter and sort criteria.

```
datacontrol.Reset(fRefilter)
```

Parameter	Type	Description
fRefilter	Boolean	Setting this to `True` applies the reset to any records already filtered, and setting this to `False` applies the `Filter` to the original set of data (default is `True`)

Use this method after setting the `FilterColumn`, `FilterCriterion`, `FilterValue`, `SortColumn`, or `SortDirection` properties to ensure that the filter is applied. For example:

```
datacontrol.FilterColumn = "au_fname"
datacontrol.FilterCriterion = "="
datacontrol.FilterValue = "Alex"
datacontrol.Reset(false)
```

This method will fail if there are unsaved changes in the data.

The SubmitChanges Method

This method sends pending changes to the data source.

```
datacontrol.SubmitChanges
```

When sending changes back to the data source, only the changes are sent, and one of two actions can occur. Either the changes will *all* succeed, or *all* will fail; it is not possible for some changes to succeed while others fail. For more information on failed changes, see the Conflict Resolution section in Chapter 5.

Properties of the RDS Data Control

The Connect Property

This property indicates an ADO connection string to connect to the data source.

```
datacontrol.Connect = String
String = datacontrol.Connect
```

For locally persisted files, the connection string can simply be:

```
Provider=MSPersist
```

The ExecuteOptions Property

This property indicates whether or not to use asynchronous execution.

```
datacontrol.ExecuteOptions = adcExecuteOptionEnum
adcExecuteOptionEnum = datacontrol.ExecuteOptions
```

The value can be one of the `adcExecuteOptionEnum` constants:

Constant	Value	Description
adcExecSync	1	Indicates that the command should be executed synchronously (default)
adcExecAsync	2	Indicates that the command should be executed asynchronously

Synchronous operations mean that control is not returned to the calling program until the data-fetching action has been completed. This means that when a data control on a page is running a command to fetch data from a data source, the data control waits until the command has been processed before continuing. Asynchronous operations return control as soon as the command has been sent to the data server.

The FetchOptions Property

This property indicates the type of fetching being used.

```
datacontrol.FetchOptions = adcFetchOptionEnum
adcFetchOptionEnum = datacontrol.FetchOptions
```

The value can be one of the following `adcFetchOptionEnum` constants:

Constant	Value	Description
adcFetchUpFront	1	Indicates that all records are fetched before control is given back to the application (default)
adcFetchBackground	2	Indicates that control is given back to the application as soon as the first batch of records has been fetched
adcFetchAsync	3	Indicates that control is given back to the application immediately, and that fetching of records continues in the background

If you are using `adcFetchBackground` and you try to access a record that has not yet been retrieved, the application will not regain control until the record has been fetched. So, your application blocks until the required record is available.

If you are using `adcFetchAsync` and try to access a record that has already been fetched, you will be placed on that record. If the record has not yet been fetched, control is given back to the application immediately; you will be placed on the closest record, and `EOF` will be set for the recordset. This means that when using `adcFetchAsync`, you should really check the `ReadyState` property before attempting to move to the end of the recordset; otherwise, you will just be moved to the last fetched record while other records are still being fetched.

The FilterColumn Property

This property indicates the column upon which filtering should take place.

```
datacontrol.FilterColumn = String
String = datacontrol.FilterColumn
```

Setting the `FilterColumn` property does not activate the filter. For this you need to use the `Reset` method, which applies the filter and changes the recordset to contain only the directed rows. The full recordset is maintained by RDS.

The FilterCriterion Property

This property indicates the criteria to be used for filtering.

```
datacontrol.FilterCriterion = String
String = datacontrol.FilterCriterion
```

The value for `FilterCriterion` can be one of the following:

❑ < for less than

❑ <= for less than or equal to

❑ = for equal to

- ❑ >= for greater than or equal to

- ❑ > for greater than

- ❑ <> for not equal to

Setting the `FilterCriterion` property does not activate the filter. For this you must use the `Reset` method.

The FilterValue Property

This property indicates the value to filter for.

```
datacontrol.FilterValue = String
String = datacontrol.FilterValue
```

Setting the `FilterValue` property alone does not activate the filter. To activate the filter, use the `Reset` method.

The Handler Property

This property indicates what handler to use.

```
datacontrol.Handler = String
String = datacontrol.Handler
```

The `Handler` enables custom logic to be executed on the server when RDS is used to work directly with remote OLE DB providers. This allows you to build your own custom server-side data handlers instead of using the default. One reason for doing this is to provide more control over requests and access rights.

The handler is a COM object that implements the `IDataFactoryHandler` interface, and it has only two methods: `GetRecordset` and `Reconnect`.

A detailed explanation of this feature appears in the MSDN Online article entitled *Using the Customization Handler Feature in RDS 2.0.*

The InternetTimeout Property

This property indicates the time in milliseconds to wait for HTTP requests.

```
datacontrol.InternetTimeout = Long
Long = datacontrol.InternetTimeout
```

It allows you to customize how long to wait before an error is generated. The default value is 300000, which is 5 minutes.

This doesn't override the server timeout facility. Whichever timeout is reached first is used.

The ReadyState Property

This property indicates the state of the control.

```
adcReadStateEnum = datacontrol.ReadyState
```

It can be one of the `adcReadStateEnum` values:

Constant	Value	Description
adcReadyStateLoaded	2	To indicate that the recordset is open, but no data has been received from the source
adcReadyStateInteractive	3	To indicate that the recordset is receiving data from the source
adcReadyStateComplete	4	To indicate that the recordset is fully populated and has received all of its data from the source

The Recordset Property

This property returns the ADO `Recordset` object underlying this data control.

```
Recordset = datacontrol.Recordset
```

The underlying recordset is a standard ADO `Recordset` object, so you can use the recordset methods to manipulate the records in the data control. For example, if using single table binding, you could have several buttons to perform the navigation:

```
<INPUT ID="cmdFirst" TYPE="BUTTON" VALUE="<<"
    onclick="dsoAuthors.Recordset.MoveFirst();">

<INPUT ID="cmdPrevious" TYPE="BUTTON" VALUE="<"
    onclick="dsoAuthors.Recordset.MovePrevious();">

<INPUT ID="cmdNext" TYPE="BUTTON" VALUE=">"
    onclick="dsoAuthors.Recordset.MoveNext();">

<INPUT ID="cmdLast" TYPE="BUTTON" VALUE=">>"
    onclick="dsoAuthors.Recordset.MoveLast();">
```

The Server Property

This property indicates the Web server URL.

```
datacontrol.Server = String
String = datacontrol.Server
```

The `Server` property can be a standard HTTP or HTTPS URL, the name of a machine (without the leading //) for DCOM use, or empty for local in-process use. For example:

```
datacontrol.Server = "http://www.apress.com"
```

If using HTTP, the name of the server must be the same as the name of the machine that the HTML or ASP has been downloaded from. This is a deliberate security restriction to ensure that only data from data stores on the same server are allowed.

The SortColumn Property

This property indicates the column upon which to perform sorting.

```
datacontrol.SortColumn = String
String = datacontrol.SortColumn
```

Once the `SortColumn` is set, the `SortDirection` should be set, and the `Reset` method called.

The SortDirection Property

This property indicates the direction in which to sort.

```
datacontrol.SortDirection = Boolean
Boolean = datacontrol.SortDirection
```

This value is `True` for ascending sorts and `False` for descending sorts. The `Reset` method applies the sort.

The SourceRecordset Property

This property sets the ADO `Recordset` to be used for the data control.

```
Set Recordset = datacontrol.SourceRecordset
Set datacontrol.SourceRecordset = Recordset
```

It allows you to set the source data of a data control to an existing ADO `Recordset`.

The SQL Property

This property indicates the SQL query string used to generate the data.

```
datacontrol.SQL = String
String = datacontrol.SQL
```

The SQL string uses the SQL dialect of the server.

Events of the RDS Data Control

The onerror Event

Raised if an event is generated whenever an error occurs during a data operation.

```
onerror(SCode, Description, Source, CancelDisplay)
```

Parameter	Type	Description
SCode	Integer	The status code of the error
Description	String	The error description
Source	String	The query or command that caused the error
CancelDisplay	Boolean	Allows you to prevent an error dialog being shown

If you set the CancelDisplay parameter to True in the onerror event procedure, no error dialog box is displayed. For example:

```
<SCRIPT LANGUAGE="JScript" FOR="dsoAuthors"
                         EVENT="onerror">
    // code to handle the error
    CancelDisplay = true;
</SCRIPT>
```

The onreadystatechange Event

Raised when the state of the Data Source Object changes, such as when a new set of data is loaded.

```
onreadystatechange
```

The event has no parameters with which to identify the state, but the this object refers to the active object. You can then examine the readyState property to see what the state is. For example, in JScript:

```
<SCRIPT LANGUAGE="JScript" FOR="dsoAuthors"
                         EVENT="onreadystatechange">

    if (this.readyState == 'complete')
        // data has been completely read in
</SCRIPT>
```

In VBScript you use the Me object (which is equivalent to the this object in JScript and refers to the active object):

```
<SCRIPT LANGUAGE="VBScript" FOR="dsoAuthors"
                         EVENT="onreadystatechange">
```

```
        If Me.readyState = 'complete' Then
            ' data has been completely read in
        End If
    </SCRIPT>
```

These are the `readyState` values:

❑   `uninitialized` indicates that the object is not initialized with data.

❑   `loading` indicates the that object is currently loading data.

❑   `interactive` indicates that the object has not fully loaded its data, although it can be interacted with.

❑   `complete` indicates that the control is completely loaded.

The Tabular Data Control

The Tabular Data Control (TDC) is automatically installed with Internet Explorer 4.0 or later, and is designed to handle data from text files.

Class ID	`333C7BC4-460F-11D0-BC04-0080C7055A83`
Source	`C:\WINNT\System32\tdc.ocx`
Prog ID	`TDCCtl.TDCCtl`

By default, the TDC will allow data to be loaded from only the same domain as the Web page, and any other domain will silently fail. This is a deliberate security restriction to protect against unauthorized access to private data. If you need to allow access to data files on other domains, you can add the following domain details to the beginning of the data file.

```
        domain_string: header_string "=" domain_list
        header_string: "@!allow_domains"
        domain_list: domain_spec [; domain_list ]
        domain_spec: *  |  [*.] domain | ipaddr
```

Wildcards are in domain names (*.apress.com), but they are not supported in IP addresses. For example, if Apress wanted to expose a text file, but only allow access from the `tigger` server on `ipona.co.uk` and all servers on `stonebroom.co.uk`, the domain details would be:

```
        @!allow_domains=tigger.ipona.co.uk;*.stonebroom.co.uk
```

These servers are not part of the Apress domain, but it's the data that controls where it can be seen.

Instantiating the TDC

To create an instance of the TDC within a Web page, you use the standard <OBJECT> tag using the CLASSID of the TDC, as shown here:

```
<OBJECT CLASSID="clsid:333C7BC4-460F-11D0-BC04-0080C7055A83"
                  ID="DataControl" WIDTH="0" HEIGHT="0">
    <PARAM NAME="DataURL" VALUE="composer.csv">
</OBJECT>
```

The parameter DataURL simply indicates the data source.

Methods of the Tabular Data Control

The Reset Method

This method updates the local recordset to reflect current filter and sort criteria.

```
datacontrol.Reset
```

Properties of the Tabular Data Control

The AppendData Property

This property identifies whether the new data replaces the existing recordset or is appended to the existing recordset.

```
datacontrol.AppendData = Boolean
Boolean = datacontrol.AppendData
```

If this is set to True, the new data is appended to the end of the existing recordset when the Reset method is called.

The default value is False.

The CaseSensitive Property

This property indicates whether string comparisons will be case sensitive.

```
datacontrol.CaseSensitive = Boolean
Boolean = datacontrol.CaseSensitive
```

The default value is True.

The CharSet Property

This property identifies the data's character set.

```
datacontrol.CharSet = String
String = datacontrol.CharSet
```

The default value is `windows-1252`. For more information on the available character sets, search on http://msdn.microsoft.com.

Character sets are particularly important when dealing with data containing non-English characters, such as umlauts, cedillas, and so forth. Correctly identifying the data's character set ensures that you won't receive errors when the data control tries to load the data. This is particularly important with XML data, because you may receive XML parsing errors if your data contains characters not included in your character set.

The DataURL Property

This property indicates the data file's URL.

```
datacontrol.DataURL = String
String = datacontrol.DataURL
```

The EscapeChar Property

This property indicates the escape character used in the source data file.

```
datacontrol.EscapeChar = String
String = datacontrol.EscapeChar
```

The Tabular Data Control is designed to take textual data in a tabular form, with columns and rows being separated by special characters, and a special character to distinguish text data. These characters are defined by the `FieldDelim`, `RowDelim`, and `TextQualifier` properties. If your data must contain one of these characters, then the character should be escaped, which is accomplished by placing the `EscapeChar` in front of it. For example, suppose you have some data in the following form:

```
ID,FirstName,LastName,Address
1,Jan,Lloyd,14 Coniston Close, Borden, Hants
2,Nigel,Futter,23a Lemington Road, Risely, Beds
```

There are four columns separated by commas, but the fourth column has commas in it. Because the comma is the column delimiter, any commas within columns must be escaped, like so:

```
ID,FirstName,LastName,Address
1,Jan,Lloyd,14 Coniston Close\, Borden\, Hants
2,Nigel,Futter,23a Lemington Road\, Risely\, Beds
```

In this instance, you could set the properties of the TDC as follows:

```
dataControl.FieldDelim = ","
dataControl.EscapeChar = "\"
```

The FieldDelim Property

This property identifies the character that delimits columns in the data file.

```
datacontrol.FieldDelim = String
String = datacontrol.FieldDelim
```

Only a single character can be used, and it defaults to a comma. For example, to change this to a colon:

```
datacontrol.FieldDelim = ":"
```

The Filter Property

This property indicates the filter that will be applied to data.

```
datacontrol.Filter = String
String = datacontrol.Filter
```

The `Filter` property is similar to a SQL WHERE clause without the WHERE. For example:

```
dataControl.Filter = "LastName=Lloyd"
```

To filter on wildcards, you can use the asterisk:

```
dataControl.Filter = "LastName=L*"
```

The Language Property

This property specifies the data file's language.

```
datacontrol.Language = String
String = datacontrol.Language
```

The default language is eng-us.

The ReadyState Property

This property indicates the control state as data is received.

```
datacontrol.ReadyState = Long
Long = datacontrol.ReadyState
```

ReadyState can be one of the following ADCReadyStateEnum constants:

Constant	Value	Description
adcReadyStateComplete	4	All the available rows have arrived, or an error prevented (more) data from arriving.
adcReadyStateInteractive	3	Rows are still arriving from the server.
adcReadyStateLoaded	2	The control is loaded and waiting to fetch rows from the server.

The RowDelim Property

This property specifies the character that delimits each row in the data file.

```
datacontrol.RowDelim = String
String = datacontrol.RowDelim
```

Only a single character can be used, and it defaults to carriage return. For example, to use the ~ character as a row delimiter:

```
dataControl.RowDelim = "~"
```

The Sort Property

This property specifies the data file's sort order.

```
datacontrol.Sort = String
String = datacontrol.Sort
```

For the sort order, you specify the column names as a comma-delimited list. The default order is ascending, but you can insert a minus sign (–) before each column to sort in a descending order. For example:

```
dataControl.Sort = "LastName,FirstName,-Age"
```

The TextQualifier Property

This property indicates the character that is used to enclose text fields.

```
datacontrol.TextQualifier = String
String = datacontrol.TextQualifier
```

If some of your columns contain characters that might be column delimiters, you can either escape the delimiters (see discussion of the EscapeChar property, earlier in this chapter) or use a text qualifier around the column. For example:

```
ID,FirstName,LastName,Address
1,Jan,Lloyd,14 Coniston Close, Borden, Hants
2,Nigel,Futter,23a Lemington Road, Risely, Beds
```

There are only four columns, separated by commas, but the fourth column has commas in it. Using a text qualifier ensures that the commas are not seen as column delimiters:

```
ID,FirstName,LastName,Address
1,Jan,Lloyd,"14 Coniston Close, Borden, Hants"
2,Nigel,Futter,"23a Lemington Road, Risely, Beds"
```

The default is the double quote mark ("). Naturally, your fields cannot include characters the same as the qualifier; otherwise, the end of the text field is assumed, and any additional data is taken as part of the next field.

245

The UseHeader Property

This property indicates whether the data file's first row contains heading information, such as column names and data types.

```
datacontrol.UseHeader = Boolean
Boolean = datacontrol.UseHeader
```

The simplest form just shows column names:

```
ID,FirstName,LastName,Address
1,Jan,Lloyd,"14 Coniston Close, Borden, Hants"
2,Nigel,Futter,"23a Lemington Road, Risely, Beds"
```

The heading row can optionally contain data types for the columns. For example:

```
ID:Int,FirstName:String,LastName:String,Address:String
1,Jan,Lloyd,"14 Coniston Close, Borden, Hants"
2,Nigel,Futter,"23a Lemington Road, Risely, Beds"
```

The data type can be one of the following:

❑   String for textual data (default)

❑   Date for dates

❑   Boolean for Yes/No or True/False

❑   Int for whole numbers

❑   Float for floating point numbers

For Date fields, you can add a space and then D, M, or Y to indicate the date style. The TDC assumes that dates are numbers separated by characters, so any character date separator will work. For example:

```
Name:String, DateOfBirth:Date YMD
Dave,66/06/11
Rob,68.03.05
```

For Boolean values, the following applies:

❑   A value of Yes, True, 1, -1, or any *non-zero number* is interpreted as True. This is case insensitive.

❑   A value of No, False, or 0 is interpreted as False.

Events of the Tabular Data Control

The onreadystatechange Event

This event is triggered when the `ReadyState` property changes. You can use this to detect when the TDC has fully loaded the data into the Data Source Object.

The event has no parameters with which to identify the state, but the `this` object refers to the active object (that is, the data control). For example:

```
<SCRIPT LANGUAGE="JScript" FOR="dsoAuthors"
                        EVENT="onreadystatechange">
    if (this.readyState == 'complete')
        // data has been completely read in
</SCRIPT>
```

The Java Data Base Connectivity Control (JDBC)

The Java Data Base Connectivity Control (also known as the Java Data Base Control or the Java DSO) is a Data Source Object written entirely in Java, and is therefore available for browsers other than Microsoft Internet Explorer, such as Netscape Navigator or Opera. All other DSOs use the HTML `OBJECT` tag, but the Java DSO is created with an `APPLET` tag.

The Java DSO is available as either compiled class files or as source, so you can extend it if required. Downloads for the Java DSO seem to have disappeared from Microsoft and MSDN, so you may have to hunt around for this control.

If you want to learn more about JDBC, consult a specialist book.

Instantiating the JDBC Object

```
<APPLET CODE="JDC.class" ID="dsoAuthors" WIDTH=0 HEIGHT=0>
  <PARAM NAME=cabbase VALUE= "jdc.cab">
  <PARAM NAME="dbURL" VALUE="jdbc:odbc:pubs">
  <PARAM NAME="showUI" VALUE="false">
  <PARAM NAME="sqlStatement" VALUE="select * from authors">
  <PARAM NAME="allowInsert" VALUE="true">
  <PARAM NAME="allowDelete" VALUE="true">
  <PARAM NAME="allowUpdate" VALUE="false">
  <PARAM NAME="user" VALUE="">
  <PARAM NAME="password" VALUE="">
  <PARAM NAME="filterColumn" VALUE="">
  <PARAM NAME="filterCriterion " VALUE="">
  <PARAM NAME="filterValue " VALUE="">
  <PARAM NAME="driver" VALUE="">
</APPLET>
```

You can obtain the JDC CAB file from MSDN at http://msdn.microsoft.com/downloads/
c-frame.htm?928521190764#/downloads/samples/internet/default.asp.

Methods of the Java DSO

The apply Method

This method applies a sort or a filter to the DSO's recordset.

```
datacontrol.apply()
```

For example:

```
dataControl.filterColumn = "au_lname";
dataControl.filterCriterion = "=";
dataControl.filterValue = "Homer";
dataControl.apply();
```

The commitChanges Method

The `commitChanges` method is implemented as a stub and will raise an error if called. Because this method cannot be implemented in a generic way, Microsoft has left this to be implemented by the user if required. In other words, it exists but doesn't work.

Properties of the Java DSO

The allowInsert Property

This property indicates whether or not inserts (that is, new rows) are allowed against the DSO.

```
datacontrol.allowInsert = Boolean
Boolean= datacontrol.allowInsert
```

Inserts affect only the local data and are not sent to the server. The current Java DSO doesn't allow updates to the data source. See the `CommitChanges` method just described for more details.

The allowDelete Property

This property indicates whether or not deletes are allowed against the DSO.

```
datacontrol.allowDelete = Boolean
Boolean= datacontrol.allowDelete
```

Deletes affect only the local data and are not sent to the server.

The allowUpdate Property

This property indicates whether or not updates are allowed against the DSO.

```
datacontrol.allowUpdate = Boolean
Boolean = datacontrol.allowUpdate
```

Updates affect only the local data and are not sent to the server.

The cabbase Property

This property specifies the data control's code location

```
datacontrol.cabbase = String
String = datacontrol.cabbase
```

This is a general APPLET property that identifies the location of the applet code. The applet will be downloaded if it is not already installed on the client. For example:

dataControl.cabbase = "http:/www.apress.com/cabs/jdso.cab"

The dbURL Property

This property identifies the ODBC DSN that supplies the data.

```
datacontrol.dbURL = String
String = datacontrol.dbURL
```

The connect string takes the following form:

jdbc: *subprotocol*: *subname*

The driver Property

This property indicates which JDBC Bridge driver to use.

```
datacontrol.driver = String
String = datacontrol.driver
```

The JDBC Bridge is what interfaces the JDBC calls to a data source. The Java Software Developers Kit (SDK) ships with an ODBC bridge, allowing you to use JDBC to access ODBC data sources.

The filterColumn Property

This property indicates the column index or name to filter on.

```
datacontrol.filterColumn = String
String = datacontrol.filterColumn
```

The filterCriterion Property

This property indicates the filter criteria.

```
datacontrol.filterCriterion = String
String = datacontrol.filterCriterion
```

The value for FilterCriterion can be one of these:

❑   < for less than

❑   <= for less than or equal to

❑   = for equal to

❑   >= for greater than or equal to

❑   > for greater than

❑   <> for not equal to

The filterValue Property

This property indicates the value to filter on.

```
datacontrol.filterValue = String
String = datacontrol.filterValue
```

The password Property

This property indicates the user password needed to connect to the data store.

```
datacontrol.password = String
String= datacontrol.password
```

The preloadRows Property

This property indicates the number of rows to preload before loading asynchronously.

```
datacontrol.preloadRows = Long
Long = datacontrol.preloadRows
```

When loading data synchronously, this property indicates the number of rows initially loaded before the rest of the rows are loaded asynchronously.

The showUI Property

This property indicates whether a user interface for the applet should be displayed.

```
datacontrol.showUI = Boolean
Boolean = datacontrol.showUI
```

The Java DSO does not have a user interface.

The sortColumn Property

This property indicates the column number or name upon which to sort.

```
datacontrol.sortColumn = String
String = datacontrol.sortColumn
```

The sortDirection Property

This property indicates the direction in which to sort.

```
datacontrol.sortDirection = String
String = datacontrol.sortDirection
```

The sqlStatement Property

This property indicates the SQL statement used to return the data.

```
datacontrol.sqlStatement = String
String = datacontrol.sqlStatement
```

The user Property

This property indicates the user name needed to connect to the data source.

```
datacontrol.user = String
String = datacontrol.user
```

Events of the Java DSO

The Java DSO does not implement any events directly, although some DSO events are available through the APPLET. See the section on DHTML Events later in this chapter for more details.

The MSHTML DSO

The MSHTML DSO is part of Internet Explorer and allows a DSO to be created based upon HTML tags. To be included in the data, the HTML tags must include an ID attribute. When parsing an HTML page, unique ID attributes become the columns, and the values within the tags become the column values. Separate rows are created by having tags with the same ID attribute. The parser ignores the actual HTML tag type; only the ID and the data are important.

Here is an example of an HTML data file:

```
<DIV ID="PersonID">101</DIV>
<SPAN ID="FirstName">Jan</SPAN>
<H1 ID="LastName">Lloyd</H1>
<PRE ID="PersonID">104</PRE>
<SPAN ID="FirstName">Rob</SPAN>
<H2 ID="LastName">Smith</H2>
```

Each unique ID field would translate to a column, resulting in three columns: PersonID, FirstName, and LastName. The data set would have two rows because there are two sets of tags with the same ID fields. The actual HTML tag is ignored, as are HTML tags without an ID attribute.

The data is taken sequentially from the top down.

Class ID	25336921-03F9-11CF-8FD0-00AA00686F13
DLL	%SystemRoot%\System32\mshtml.dll
Prog ID	htmlfile_FullWindowEmbed

Instantiating the MSHTML DSO

```
<OBJECT ID="dsoAuthors" DATA="HTMLFile.html" HEIGHT="0" WIDTH="0">
</OBJECT>
```

The DATA attribute points to the HTML file containing the data.

Methods of the MSHTML DSO

The MSHTML DSO does not have any methods.

Properties of the MSHTML DSO

The Recordset Property

This property returns the ADO Recordset object underlying this data control.

```
Recordset = datacontrol.Recordset
```

The underlying recordset is a standard ADO Recordset object, so you can use the Recordset methods to manipulate the records in the data control. For example, if using single table binding, you could have several buttons to perform the navigation:

```
<INPUT ID="cmdFirst" TYPE="BUTTON" VALUE="<<"
    onclick="dsoAuthors.Recordset.MoveFirst();">

<INPUT ID="cmdPrevious" TYPE="BUTTON" VALUE="<"
    onclick="dsoAuthors.Recordset.MovePrevious();">

<INPUT ID="cmdNext" TYPE="BUTTON" VALUE=">"
    onclick="dsoAuthors.Recordset.MoveNext();">

<INPUT ID="cmdLast" TYPE="BUTTON" VALUE=">>"
    onclick="dsoAuthors.Recordset.MoveLast();">
```

Events of the MSHTML DSO

The MSHTML DSO does not have any distinct events, although it responds to the standard data binding events discussed in the Events section of this chapter.

The XML Java Applet in IE 4

The XML DSO Java Applet ships with IE 4 and provides read-only access to XML data. It's particularly useful for hierarchical data.

A known problem with the XML DSO is that, when binding hierarchical data to HTML tables in a situation where you have a parent record with different child records, the second child record is not bound correctly. A way around this is to use the C++ XML DSO, which can be instantiated either in an `OBJECT` tag or from within code. The C++ XML DSO is covered under the IE 5 section.

Instantiating the Java Applet

```
<APPLET CODE="com.ms.xml.dso.XMLDSO.class" ID="dsoAuthors"
                         HEIGHT="0" WIDTH="0" MAYSCRIPT="True">
   <PARAM NAME="URL" VALUE="XMLDataFile.xml">
   <PARAM NAME="SCHEMA" VALUE="SchemaFile.xml">
</APPLET>
```

The Java Applet has a visible interface, so you can give it a height and width (60 and 400 perhaps). The interface shows trace messages showing successful loading of the XML data or error messages. Rather conveniently, the interface is green when successful and red for errors.

You can also directly embed XML between the `APPLET` tags:

```
<APPLET CODE="com.ms.xml.dso.XMLDSO.class" ID="dsoAuthors"
         HEIGHT="0" WIDTH="0" MAYSCRIPT="True">
<?xml version="1.0"?>
<AUTHORS>
  <AUTHOR>
    <au_id>101</au_id>
    <au_fname>Jan</au_fname>
    <au_lname>Lloyd</au_lname>
  </AUTHOR>
  <AUTHOR>
    <au_id>104</au_id>
    <au_fname>Rob</au_fname>
    <au_lname>Smith</au_lname>
  </AUTHOR>
</AUTHORS>
</APPLET>
```

Essentially, the Java DSO is a forerunner of the XML Data Island in IE 5.

Methods of the IE 4 XML DSO

The clear Method

This method clears the data from the DSO.

```
datacontrol.clear
```

After this control, the data control is empty.

The getDocument Method

This method returns the loaded document.

```
datacontrol.getDocument
```

This is synonymous with the Document property.

The getError Method

This method returns the most recent error encountered by the DSO.

```
datacontrol.getError
```

This is synonymous with the Error property.

The getSchema Method

This method returns the XML schema of the DSO.

```
datacontrol.getSchema (Format)
```

Parameter	Type	Description
Format	Boolean	True to format the schema, False to return the schema without formatting

Formatting the schema simply adds white space to make it more readable.

The getXML Method

This method returns the XML data.

```
datacontrol.getXML (Format)
```

Parameter	Type	Description
Format	Boolean	True to format the XML data, False to return the XML data without formatting

Formatted data appears neatly embedded (just like IE 5 does when you view an XML file), whereas unformatted means that the XML is just returned as is, with no formatting.

The init Method

This method reloads the XML Data.

```
datacontrol.init
```

If the URL PARAM exists, then the VALUE is used to reload the XML data. If no URL PARAM exists, the XML data is taken to be inline, between the APPLET tags. If no XML exists, no action is taken.

The load Method

This method loads the XML specified in the supplied file.

```
datacontrol.load (File)
```

Parameter	Type	Description
File	String	The URL of the XML Data document

For local URLs, the `load` method is dependent upon your browser's security settings, which may not allow access to the local drives.

This differs from the `init` method because you can specify the XML data's source, whereas the `init` method only reloads existing data.

The save Method

This method saves the XML to a file.

```
datacontrol.save (File)
```

Parameter	Type	Description
File	String	The file name to save the XML into.

For local URLs, the `save` method is dependent upon your browser's security settings, which may not allow access to the local drives.

The setRoot Method

This method sets the root of the document for the DSO.

```
datacontrol.setRoot (elem)
```

Parameter	Type	Description
elem	Element	The element to set as the root node of the DSO

The updateSchema Method

This method updates the SCHEMA whenever the document is changed.

```
datacontrol.updateSchema
```

This method is automatically called by the `clear`, `load`, and `setRoot` methods.

Properties of the IE 4 XML DSO

The Document Property

This method returns a DOM `document` object containing the DSO document.

```
Object = datacontrol.Document
```

This is synonymous with the `getDocument` method.

The Error Property

This method returns the most recent error description encountered by the DSO.

```
String = datacontrol.Error
```

This is synonymous with the `getError` method.

The URL Property

This method identifies the URL of the data's source.

```
datacontrol.URL = String
String = datacontrol.URL
```

Events of the XML DSO

The Java XML DSO does not implement any events directly, although DSO events are available through the `APPLET`. See the section on Events later in this chapter for more details.

The XML Tag in IE 5

Internet Explorer 5 natively supports XML by way of an `XML` tag. The technique of embedding XML Data into HTML is called using XML Data Islands, and there are two ways to specify the data. The first is to use the `SRC` attribute to specify `XML` data file's name:

```
<XML ID="dsoAuthors" SRC="authors.xml"></XML>
```

Alternatively, you can embed the XML data between the `XML` tags:

```
<XML ID="dsoAuthors"
<?xml version="1.0"?>
<AUTHORS>
  <AUTHOR>
    <au_id>101</au_id>
    <au_fname>Jan</au_fname>
    <au_lname>Lloyd</au_lname>
  </AUTHOR>
  <AUTHOR>
    <au_id>104</au_id>
    <au_fname>Rob</au_fname>
```

```
        <au_lname>Smith</au_lname>
    </AUTHOR>
</AUTHORS>
</XML>
```

Class ID 5	50dda30-0541-11d2-9ca9-0060b0ec3d39
DLL	%SystemRoot%\System32\msxml.dll
Prog ID	Microsoft.XMLDSO

Instantiating the XML DSO as an Object

Because XML is handled by MSXML, which is a COM object, it can also be created by using an HTML OBJECT tag.

```
<OBJECT CLASSID="clsid:550dda30-0541-11d2-9ca9-0060b0ec3d39"
        ID="dsoAuthors" HEIGHT="0" WIDTH="0">
</OBJECT>
```

This method also works for the XML DSO in IE 4.

Code

You can also create and load the XML DSO from code:

```
<SCRIPT LANGUAGE="JavaScript">
function window.onload()
{
  var docAuthors = XMLDSO.XMLDocument;
  docAuthors.loadXML("authors.xml")
}
</SCRIPT>
```

or:

```
<SCRIPT LANGUAGE="JavaScript">
function window.onload()
{
  var docAuthors = new ActiveXDocument("Microsoft.xmldom");
  docAuthors.loadXML("authors.xml")
}
</SCRIPT>
```

Methods of the IE 5 XML DSO

The XML DSO does not implement any methods directly, although the DSO does expose the XML Document object, which allows loading and parsing of XML.

257

> For more details on this, consult an XML DOM reference book, such as Wrox's
> *XML IE 5 Programmer's Reference* (**ISBN 1861001576**) or Apress's *XML Programming
> using the Microsoft XML Parser* (**ISBN 1893115429**).

Properties of the IE 5 XML DSO

The JavaDSOCompatible Property

This property indicates whether the DSO behaves in a way that is compatible with the Java XML
DSO supplied with IE 4.

```
datacontrol.JavaDSOCompatible = Boolean
Boolean = datacontrol.JavaDSOCompatible
```

A value of `True` indicates that the same behavior as the IE 4 Java DSO is applied when parsing XML.
The default value is `False`, which uses the new parsing mode. See the "Parsing Rules" section for
more details on how the XML is parsed into rows and columns.

The readyState Property

This property indicates the state of the DSO with regard to its data.

```
String = datacontrol.readyState
```

Values for the `readyState` are:

- ❑ `uninitialized` indicates that the object is not initialized with data.

- ❑ `loading` indicates that the object is loading data.

- ❑ `interactive` indicates that the object has not fully loaded its data, although it can be
  interacted with.

- ❑ `complete` indicates that the data is completely loaded.

The XMLDocument Property

This property returns or sets the XML DOM `Document` for the data control.

```
datacontrol.XMLDocument = XMLDOMDocument
XMLDOMDocument = datacontrol.XMLDocument
```

This allows you access to the `DOMDocument` object, allowing manipulation of the XML through the
DOM. For example:

```
var doc = dsoXMLBooklist.XMLDocument;
var el = doc.getElementsByTagName("CATEGORY").item(0);
alert(el.xml);
```

This searches for XML tags by name and retrieves the first tag that matches.

258

Events of the XML DSO

The XML DSO does not implement any events directly, although DSO events are available through the OBJECT. See the section on DHTML Events later in this chapter for more details.

Parsing Rules

There are set rules for how the XML data is parsed into rows and columns:

❑ Each sub-element and attribute becomes a column in the same row.

❑ The column name is the sub-element or attribute name, unless the parent element has an attribute and sub-element of the same name. In this case, an exclamation mark (!) is added to the beginning of the column name.

❑ A column based on an attribute is always a simple column, that is, one containing normal string or number data.

❑ If an element has sub-elements or attributes, the column becomes a row column. This corresponds to a chapter column in a hierarchical recordset.

❑ Multiple instances of sub-elements under different parents use different rules. If any instance implies a row, then all instances become rows. If all instances imply a column, then the element becomes a column.

❑ Each row has an extra column called $Text. This contains the sub-elements of the row concatenated together. This is particularly useful when your XML elements have attributes and you wish to bind data to HTML elements. This is explained in more detail further on in the "Data Binding" section.

When in Java Compatibility mode, the rules are simpler:

❑ Any element that contains another element is a row.

❑ Text-only elements are columns.

❑ Attributes are ignored.

If you want to define your own rules as to how the XML elements are converted into rows or columns, you need to add a Document Type Definition (DTD) to the XML data:

```
<XML ID="dsoAuthors"
<?xml version="1.0" ?>
<!DOCTYPE AUTHORS [
    <!ELEMENT AUTHORS (AUTHOR+)>
    <!ELEMENT AUTHOR (au_id, au_fname, au_lname)>
    <!ELEMENT au_id (#PCDATA)>
    <!ELEMENT au_fname (#PCDATA)>
    <!ELEMENT au_lname (#PCDATA)>
]>

<AUTHORS>
```

```
<AUTHOR>
  <au_id>101</au_id>
  <au_fname>Jan</au_fname>
  <au_lname>Lloyd</au_lname>
</AUTHOR>
<AUTHOR>
  . . .
</AUTHORS>
```

RDS DataSpace

The DataSpace object is responsible for creating a client-side proxy to communicate with the server, and often goes hand-in-hand with the DataFactory object. When you use a DSO, a DataSpace object is created behind the scenes on the client, connecting to the Web server automatically (a bit like a proxy/stub). The DataSpace performs the marshaling and facilitates the packaging, unpackaging, and transport of the data from the client to the server, and vice-versa.

Class ID	BD96C556-65A3-11D0-983A-00C04FC29E36
Source	C:\Program Files\Common Files\System\MSADC\msadco.dll
Prog ID	RDS.DataSpace

Instantiating the RDS DataSpace Object

```
<OBJECT CLASSID="clsid:BD96C556-65A3-11D0-983A-00C04FC29E36"
        ID="dspDataSpace" HEIGHT="0" WIDTH="0">
</OBJECT>
```

Methods of the DataSpace Object

The CreateObject Method

This method creates a server-side object.

```
variant = dataspace.CreateObject (ProgID, Connection)
```

Name	Type	Description
ProgID	String	The Program ID (ProgID or class string) of the object to create
Connection	String	Connection details of the Web server or machine name

The connection details can be a URL for a Web server, a UNC name for a machine, or an empty string for a local, in-process business object. For example:

```
dfFactory = dspSpace.CreateObject ("RDSServer.DataFactory",
                                   "http://servername.com");
```

This creates an instance of the `DataFactory` component (explained shortly) on the Web server servername.com. If you use an ASP file instead of an HTML file, you can use the `ServerVariables` method of the `Request` object to extract the name of the Web server:

```
dfFactory = dspSpace.CreateObject ("RDSServer.DataFactory",
            http://<%=Request.ServerVariables("SERVER_NAME")%>");
```

You are not limited to creating the `DataFactory` with this method; you can create any COM object. This is discussed in more detail in the "DataSpace and DataFactory Usage" section later in this chapter.

Properties of the DataSpace Object

The InternetTimeout Property

This property indicates the HTTP timeout in milliseconds.

```
dataspace.InternetTimeout = Long
Long = dataspace.InternetTimeout
```

When creating proxy objects, the `DataSpace` will wait for the amount of time specified in this property. If no response is received from the server, an error is generated. The default value is 300000 (5 minutes).

Events of the DataSpace Object

The `DataSpace` object has no events.

RDS DataFactory

The `DataFactory` is the server-side part of the proxy process being used to marshal data from the server to the client. You can use the `DataFactory` to execute SQL queries on the server and return the data to the client.

Although the `DataFactory` is a server-side object, you can instantiate it with a command in the HTML in the client page:

```
dfFactory = dspSpace.CreateObject ("RDSServer.DataFactory",
                                   "http://servername.com");
```

Class ID	9381D8F5-0288-11d0-9501-00AA00B911A5
Source	C:\Program Files\Common Files\System\MSADC\msadcf.dll
Prog ID	RDSServer.DataFactory

Methods of the DataFactory Object

The ConvertToString Method

This method converts a recordset into a MIME64 string that represents the recordset data.

```
String = DataFactory.ConvertToString(Recordset)
```

Parameter	Type	Description
Recordset	Recordset	An ADO Recordset to convert to a string

This method was useful in early versions of ADO (pre 2.0) when you needed to transfer a recordset between server and client. Recordsets from ADO 2.0 onwards can now marshal themselves across HTTP, so this method is less used.

The CreateRecordSet Method

This method creates and returns an empty disconnected recordset.

```
Object = DataFactory.CreateRecordSet(ColumnInfos)
```

Parameter	Type	Description
ColumnInfos	Variant	An array of arrays containing the column details

ColumnInfos should be a variant array, with each column being defined by four array elements:

❑ Name is the name of the column.

❑ Type is the data type of the column.

❑ Size is the size of the column (fixed-length types must be -1)

❑ Nullability indicates if the column can contain a null value.

For the data type, you should use one of the ADO DataTypeEnum values (except for adChapter, adDBFileTime, adEmpty, adFileTime, adIDispatch, adIUnknown, adLongVarChar, adPropVariant, adUserDefined, adVariant, and adVarNumeric, which are not supported). For a full list of these data types and their associated values, see Appendix B.

The column arrays should be appended to another array, which becomes the method argument. For example:

```
<SCRIPT LANGUAGE="JavaScript">

function cmdCreateNew.onclick()
{
    var aField1 = Array(4);
    var aField2 = Array(4);
    var aField3 = Array(4);
    var aField4 = Array(4);
    var aCols = Array(4);

    // create the individual columns
    aField1[0] = "ID";            // name
    aField1[1] = 3;               // type - adInteger
    aField1[2] = -1;              // size
    aField1[3] = false;           // nullability

    aField2[0] = "FirstName";     // name
    aField2[1] = 202;             // type - adVarWChar
    aField2[2] = -1;              // size
    aField2[3] = false;           // nullability

    aField3[0] = "LastName";      // name
    aField3[1] = 202;             // type - adVarWChar
    aField3[2] = -1;              // size
    aField3[3] = false;           // nullability

    aField4[0] = "DateOfBirth";   // name
    aField4[1] = 7;               // type - adDate
    aField4[2] = -1;              // size
    aField4[3] = false;           // nullability

    // add the columns to an array
    aCols[0] = aField1;
    aCols[1] = aField2;
    aCols[2] = aField3;
    aCols[3] = aField4;

    // create a new recordset
    recNew = dataFactory.CreateRecordset (aCols);
}
</SCRIPT>
```

The Query Method

This method executes a SQL query and creates a `Recordset`.

```
Recordset = DataFactory.Query(Connection, Query)
```

Parameter	Type	Description
Connection	String	The data store's connection details
Query	String	The SQL query to run

The `Query` string should be in the native database format. For example:

```
dfFactory = dspSpace.CreateObject ("RDSServer.DataFactory",
                                    "http://servername.com");
recAuthors = dfDataFactory.Query ("DSN=pubs",
                                    "SELECT * FROM authors");
```

The SubmitChanges Method

Given a recordset with pending changes, this method submits them to the database identified in the connection string.

```
DataFactory.SubmitChanges(Connection, Recordset)
```

Parameter	Type	Description
Connection	String	The data store's connection details
Recordset	Recordset	The Recordset containing the changes

When sending changes back to the data source, only the changes are sent, and one of two actions can occur: All of the changes succeed, or all of them fail. It is not possible for some changes to succeed and others fail. Handling of errors is covered in Chapter 5, in the discussion on Conflict Resolution.

Properties of the DataFactory Object

The `DataFactory` has no properties.

Events of the DataFactory Object

The `DataFactory` has no events.

DataSpace and DataFactory Usage

The `DataSpace` and `DataFactory` perform the client and server ends of the data marshaling. Using the two together with a data control, it's easy to get data from a server, allow the user to modify it, and then send those changes back to the server. All this can be performed over HTTP, and therefore allows the creation of genuine Web applications.

In its simplest form you can use the `DataFactory` on the server to perform your data access:

```
<!-- normal RDS DataControl object, no parameters set -->
<OBJECT ID="dsoDataControl"
        CLASSID="clsid:BD96C556-65A3-11D0-983A-00C04FC29E33">
</OBJECT>

<!-- client-side RDS DataSpace object -->
<OBJECT ID="dspSpace"
        CLASSID="CLSID:BD96C556-65A3-11D0-983A-00C04FC29E36">
</OBJECT>

<SCRIPT LANGUAGE="JavaScript">

  // create a DataFactory object
  dfFactory = dspSpace.CreateObject("RDSServer.DataFactory",
                                          "http://servername.com");

  // create a recordset using the DataFactory
  recAuthors = dfFactory.Query("DSN=pubs",
                                    "SELECT * FROM authors");

  // assign the recordset to the DataControl
  dsoDataControl.SourceRecordset = recAuthors;

</SCRIPT>
```

This does expose one flaw: The connection details are visible at the client. A way around this is to use a custom business component. This will be a COM-compliant object (and therefore only available in IE), or perhaps an ActiveX DLL written in Visual Basic and hosted on the server.

```
<!-- normal RDS DataControl object, no parameters set -->
<OBJECT ID="dsoDataControl"
        CLASSID="clsid:BD96C556-65A3-11D0-983A-00C04FC29E33">
</OBJECT>

<!-- client-side RDS DataSpace object -->
<OBJECT ID="dspSpace"
        CLASSID="CLSID:BD96C556-65A3-11D0-983A-00C04FC29E36">
</OBJECT>

<SCRIPT LANGUAGE="JavaScript">

  // create a custom business object
  objWroxBooks = dspSpace.CreateObject("Apress.Books",
                                    "http://servername.com");

  // create a recordset using the business object
  recAuthors = objWroxBooks.GetAuthors();

  // assign the recordset to the DataControl
  dsoDataControl.SourceRecordset = recAuthors;

</SCRIPT>
```

The business object should return a disconnected, client-side recordset.

DHTML Events

When using Data Source Objects in HTML pages, the DSO extends the DHTML event model with events of its own. Although these appear as part of the DSO, they are in fact implemented by DHTML, and therefore appear on all HTML elements that can be sources of data.

The following table lists the events that are generated by the DSO:

Event	Cancelable	Applies To
onbeforeupdate	True	bound elements
onafterupdate	False	bound elements
onrowenter	False	DSO
onrowexit	True	DSO
onbeforeunload	False	window
ondataavailable	False	DSO
ondatasetcomplete	False	DSO
ondatasetchanged	False	DSO
onerrorupdate	True	bound elements
onreadystatechange	False	DSO
oncellchange	False	DSO
onrowsinserted	False	DSO
onrowsdelete	False	DSO

All events are raised (that is, bubble) to parent objects, apart from onbeforeunload, which applies to the window object and therefore has no parent.

The oncellchange, onrowsinserted, onrowsdelete events were new for IE 5.

Events marked as cancelable allow cancellation of the event, and thus can be used to prevent certain actions taking place. For example, canceling the onbeforeupdate event can prevent data changes taking place.

The onbeforeupdate Event

This event is fired when an element is about to lose focus and the data in that element has been changed.

It is not fired if the data is changed from within scripting code.

Returning `False` from the event procedure will cancel the event, and stop the user leaving a data-bound field. For example:

```
<SCRIPT FOR=txtDateOfBirth EVENT=onbeforeupdate>

    if ( some test on the date here)
        bRV = false;
    else
        bRV = true;

    event.cancelBubble = true;

    return bRV;

</SCRIPT>
```

In this example, the `onbeforeupdate` of the `txtDateOfBirth` field is used, which performs some validation upon the entered date before the update takes place. The validation sets a variable to be `true` if the date is valid or `false` if invalid. This value is used as the return value for the procedure, which prevents the update from taking place and prevents the user from leaving the field. The `cancelBubble` method is set to `true` to prevent this event from being raised to parent objects.

The onafterupdate Event

This event fires after the data has been transferred to the data provider. If the `onbeforeupdate` event is canceled, this event does not fire.

The onrowenter Event

This event fires when a new row of data becomes the current row. You can use this to process the data before it is shown (perhaps to format it) or to update other elements on the page.

The onrowexit Event

This event fires before the current record pointer moves to a new row. This could happen if you use recordset navigation, if you delete the current record, or if you leave the page.

You can use this event to perform validation at the record level. In a similar way to the example in the `onbeforeupdate` event, you could perform validation for the fields in an entire row, rather than validating each field.

The onbeforeunload Event

This event fires before the current page becomes unloaded. This could be caused by navigating to another page, using the browser's Back or Forward buttons, Refreshing the page, submitting a request from a FORM element, or selecting from the Favorites folder.

This event cannot be cancelled.

The ondataavailable Event

This event is fired by the DSO when records are available for use. This does not guarantee that all the records are available (in asynchronous operations); it indicates only that some are available.

The event may fire several times or may not fire at all. This depends upon the DSO.

The ondatasetcomplete Event

This event fires when all the data is loaded into the DSO.

This event object has a property, reason, which identifies the download state. These are the values:

❑   0 indicates a successful data download.

❑   1 indicates an aborted data download.

❑   2 indicates a failed data download.

For example:

```
function dsoAuthors.ondatasetcomplete()
{
  if (event.reason == 2)
    alert ("Failed to load data");
}
```

The ondatasetchanged Event

This event is fired after a new data set is requested or when the current data set of is filtered or sorted.

The data might not be available when this event fires, but the meta data (fields, data types, etc.) will be available.

You could use this event to dynamically populate other controls.

The onerrorupdate Event

This event fires when an error occurs while transferring data from the server to the client.

If this event is cancelled, system dialog boxes describing the error are not shown.

The onreadystatechange Event

This event fires when the state of the DSO changes. You can examine the readyState property of the this object (or the Me object in VBScript) to identify the state, which will be one the following:

❑   uninitialized indicates that the object is not initialized with data.

❑   loading indicates that the object is loading its data.

❑ `interactive` indicates that the object can be interacted with even though it is not fully loaded.

❑ `complete` indicates that the data is completely loaded.

The oncellchange Event

This event is fired when data changes in any element. You can use the `dataFld` property to indicate which field changed.

The onrowsdelete Event

This event is fired before rows are deleted. Although the event is not cancelable, you can use the `bookmarks` collection to examine the deleted records.

The onrowsinserted Event

This event is fired after rows are added. Although the event is not cancelable, you can use the `bookmarks` collection to examine the new records.

Data Binding

There are many HTML fields that can be bound to DSOs. Four attributes affect data binding:

❑ `DATASRC` indicates the DSO supplying the data. You should use the `ID` of the DSO, with a hash (#) symbol in front of the `ID` value.

❑ `DATAFLD` indicates the field in the DSO to bind to.

❑ `DATAFORMATAS` indicates how the bound data is to be formatted.

❑ `DATAPAGESIZE` indicates the number of rows to show when using tabular data binding.

This table shows which elements support data binding:

HTML Element	Bound Property	Update Data?	Tabular Binding?	Display as HTML?
A	href	No	No	No
APPLET	PARAM	Yes	No	No
BUTTON	innerText and innerHTML	No	No	Yes
DIV	innerText and innerHTML	No	No	Yes
FRAME	src	No	No	No
IFRAME	src	No	No	No

Table continues on the following page

HTML Element	Bound Property	Update Data?	Tabular Binding?	Display as HTML?
IMG	src	No	No	No
INPUT TYPE=CHECKBOX	checked	Yes	No	No
INPUT TYPE=HIDDEN	value	Yes	No	No
INPUT TYPE=LABEL	value	Yes	No	No
INPUT TYPE=PASSWORD	value	Yes	No	No
INPUT TYPE=RADIO	checked	Yes	No	No
INPUT TYPE=TEXT	value	Yes	No	No
LABEL	innerText and innerHTML	No	No	Yes
LEGEND	innerText and innerHTML	No	No	No
MARQUEE	innerText and innerHTML	No	No	Yes
OBJECT	param	Yes	No	No
SELECT	text of selected option	Yes	No	No
SPAN	innerText and innerHTML	No	No	Yes
TABLE	none	No	Yes	No
TEXTAREA	value	Yes	No	No

Tabular Binding

Tabular data binding involves the use of TABLE elements. The table is bound to a DSO, and the table cells are bound to individual columns. For example:

```
<TABLE DATASRC="#dsoAuthors">
  <THEAD>
   <TR>
      <TH>ID</TH>
      <TH>First Name</TH>
      <TH>Last Name</TH>
   </TR>
  </THEAD>
  <TBODY>
   <TR>
      <TD><SPAN DATAFLD="au_id"></SPAN></TD>
      <TD><SPAN DATAFLD="au_fname"></SPAN></TD>
      <TD><SPAN DATAFLD="au_lname"></SPAN></TD>
   </TR>
  </TBODY>
</TABLE>
```

The table is automatically created, with the number of rows being determined by the number of rows in the recordset. To limit the number of rows, you can use the DATAPAGESIZE attribute:

```
<TABLE ID="tblAuthors" DATASRC="#dsoAuthors" DATAPAGESIZE="10">
<THEAD>
  <TR>
    <TH>ID</TH>
    <TH>First Name</TH>
    <TH>Last Name</TH>
  </TR>
</THEAD>
<TBODY>   <TR>
    <TD><SPAN DATAFLD="au_id"></SPAN></TD>
    <TD><SPAN DATAFLD="au_fname"></SPAN></TD>
    <TD><SPAN DATAFLD="au_lname"></SPAN></TD>
  </TR>
</TBODY>
</TABLE>
```

You can then add buttons to move through the pages:

```
<INPUT TYPE="BUTTON" ID="cmdNextPage" VALUE=">P"
                          onclick="tblAuthors.nextPage();">
<INPUT TYPE="BUTTON" ID="cmdPreviousPage" VALUE="<P"
                          onclick="tblAuthors.previousPage();">
```

Single Record Binding

Single record binding involves displaying a single record at a time. Each HTML element that is to bind to data specifies both the DATASRC and the DATAFLD attributes. For example:

```
ID: <INPUT TYPE="TEXT" DATASRC="#dsoAuthors"
                      DATAFLD="au_id" SIZE="6"><P>
First Name: <INPUT TYPE="TEXT" DATASRC="#dsoAuthors"
                                DATAFLD="au_fname" SIZE="20"><P>
Last Name: <INPUT TYPE="TEXT" DATASRC="#dsoAuthors"
                              DATAFLD="au_lname" SIZE="20"><P>
Title: <SELECT DATASRC="#dsoAuthors"
              DATAFLD="au_title" SIZE="4">
          <OPTION>Mr
          <OPTION>Mrs
          <OPTION>Miss
      </SELECT><P>
```

To navigate through the recordset, you can add a series of buttons:

```
<INPUT TYPE="BUTTON" ID="cmdFirst" VALUE="<<"
                      onclick="dsoAuthors.recordset.MoveFirst();">
<INPUT TYPE="BUTTON" ID="cmdPrevious" VALUE="<"
                      onclick="dsoAuthors.recordset.MovePrevious();">
<INPUT TYPE="BUTTON" ID="cmdNext" VALUE=">"
                      onclick="dsoAuthors.recordset.MoveNext();">
<INPUT TYPE="BUTTON" ID="cmdLast" VALUE=">>"
                      onclick="dsoAuthors.recordset.MoveLast();">
```

Because the HTML elements are bound to the data source, moving through the data source refreshes the UI.

Formatting Data

You can use the DATAFORMATAS property to specify how the data from the DSO is to be formatted. A value of HTML means that any HTML elements in the data are applied, and a value of TEXT means that any HTML elements are shown as plain text.

For example:

```
<TABLE DATASRC="#dsoAuthors" DATAPAGESIZE="10">
  <TR>
    <TD><SPAN DATAFLD="au_id"></SPAN></TD>
    <TD><SPAN DATAFLD="au_fname" DATAFORMATAS="HTML"></SPAN></TD>
    <TD><SPAN DATAFLD="au_lname"></SPAN></TD>
  </TR>
</TABLE>
```

This allows formatting, such as <B> or <I> tags to emphasize or italicize text, to be embedded within the data.

Updating Data

Many DSOs can update the server with any changes made to the data. This is simply a matter of calling the submitChanges method of the DSO. For example:

```
<INPUT TYPE="BUTTON" ID="cmdSubmit" VALUE="Submit"
                     onclick="dsoAuthors.submitChanges();">
```

When using the DataFactory directly, you also use the submitChanges method, but you must also specify the connection information and the recordset as arguments:

```
<SCRIPT LANGAUGE="JavaScript">
function cmdSubmit.onclick()
{
  dfFactory.SubmitChanges("DSN=pubs", dsoAuthors.recordset);
}
</SCRIPT>
```

If you are using a custom business object, then you must provide a custom method to accept the changed recordset. For example, a Visual Basic component could implement a method like this:

```
Public Sub UpdateRecords (oRec As ADODB.Recordset)
    ' set the connection to the data store
    ' assumes g_sConnect is a global string previously set
    oRec.ActiveConnection = m_sConnect
```

```
        ' now update the source data
        oRec.UpdateBatch
    End Sub
```

This could be called from the same page that created the custom object:

```
<SCRIPT LANGUAGE="JavaScript">
function cmdUpdate.onclick()
{
   ' get the recordset
   oRec = dsoAuthors.Recordset

   ' marshal only changed records
   oRec.MarshalOptions = 1;    ' adMarshalModifiedOnly

   ' call custom component method
   objWroxBooks.UpdateRecords (oRec)
}
</SCRIPT>
```

Security Issues

If using MTS as part of your data application, you need to read the article *FIX: MTS Impersonation Returns Incorrect Caller When Using RDS* at http://support.microsoft.com/default.aspx?scid=kb;en-us;184702. This details a large security hole in RDS. Upgrading to at least MDAC 2.1 Service Pack 2 will cure the problem.

Beginning with RDS version 2.0, a new set of security features based around a configuration file was added. When RDS is installed, an INI file called msdfmap.ini is placed in your Windows (or WINNT) folder. This file allows you to completely customize the settings for the DataFactory when it is instantiated by a client. Consult the RDS documentation for full details of this, and this series of MSDN articles:

❑ *Using the Customization Handler Feature in RDS 2.0*

❑ *Remote Data Service in MDAC 2.0*

❑ *Security and Your Web Server*

❑ *ADO and RDS Security Issues in Microsoft Internet Explorer*

With IE 6 Service Pack 1b, the behavior of ActiveX controls has been changed. By default, ActiveX controls will be loaded only if they do not contain any parameters, or if they do contain parameters, but those parameters do not reference data external to the page. For more details on this, see the MSDN article titled *Changes to the Default Handling of ActiveX Controls by Internet Explorer*.

Custom Business Objects

Microsoft's IIS has security settings that restrict which objects can be instantiated by the `DataSpace` object's `CreateObject` method. If using custom business objects, you must add the details of these objects to the registry.

> **Remember to back up the Registry before making any changes to it.**

This is the simplest way is to create a `.reg` file:

```
REGEDIT4
[HKEY_CLASSES_ROOT\CLSID\{your_component_guid}\Implemented
Categories\{7DD95801-9882-11CF-9FA9-00AA006C42C4}]
[HKEY_CLASSES_ROOT\CLSID\{your_component_guid}\Implemented
Categories\{7DD95802-9882-11CF-9FA9-00AA006C42C4}]
[HKEY_LOCAL_MACHINE\System\CurrentControlSet\Services\W3SVC\
Parameters\ADCLaunch\your_component_class_string]
```

The first line tells `regedit` that this is a valid `.reg` file. The next two entries enable the **Safe for Scripting** setting, and the third allows IIS to instantiate the component on the server. Note that each entry should be on one line, not wrapped like the code shown here. Place the file on the server machine, then double-click it to merge the values into the registry.

10

ADOX Objects and Collections

This chapter deals with the ADO Extensions for Data Definition and Security (ADOX). This was the big new feature of ADO 2.1, and allows the manipulation of the data store's metadata through ADO objects and methods, thereby removing the necessity to learn the explicit syntax of the data provider.

This is made possible because the ADOX objects abstract the data store's objects into an easily workable form. For example, most databases have users and groups to deal with security issues; to allow these to be easily accessed by developers, ADOX has `User` and `Group` objects.

Here's a look at the object model again:

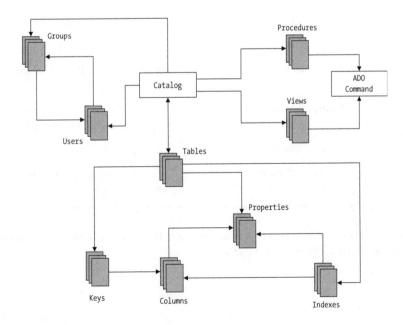

The ADOX objects are described individually. Because the handling of collections is the same for each collection, they have been included as a single section at the end of the chapter.

> **For ADOX 2.6, the only new feature was the addition of a Properties collection to the User and Group objects.**

Of the OLE DB providers currently available, the Jet provider has the fullest support for ADOX. Other providers may not support all properties and methods. The following table shows which features are *not* supported for the SQL Server and Oracle providers:

Provider	Object/Collection	Feature *Not* Supported
SQL Server	Catalog Object	Create method.
	Groups Collection	Not supported
	Procedures Collection	Append method, Delete method, Command property
	Tables Collection	Properties are read only for existing tables
	Users Collection	Not supported
	Views Collection	Not supported
Oracle	Catalog Object	Create method
	Groups Collection	Not supported
	Indexes Collection	Append method, Delete method
	Keys Collection	Append method, Delete method
	Procedures Collection	Append method, Delete method, Command property
	Tables Collection	Append method, Delete method. (Properties are read only for existing tables.)
	Users Collection	Not supported
	Views Collection	Append method, Delete method, Command property

If you wish to use ADOX against a different provider, consult the provider-specific documentation for more details on supported properties for ADOX.

The Catalog Object

The `Catalog` object is the parent for all objects because it deals with catalog or data store information. The `Catalog` can be equated to a single connection to a data store, and the objects underneath the `Catalog` are the objects (metadata) within that data store.

Methods of the Catalog Object

The Create Method

This method creates a new catalog. In most cases this means the creation of a new database.

```
String = Catalog.Create(ConnectString)
Set Connection = Catalog.Create(ConnectString)
```

Name	Type	Description
ConnectString	String	The connection string for the catalog to be created

The return value is either a connection string or an ADO `Connection` object, depending upon how you call the method. For example, the following line of code sets `strConn` to the connection string of the new database:

```
Dim objCat     As New ADOX.Catalog
Dim strConn    As String

strConn = objCat.Create("Provider=Microsoft.Jet.OLEDB.4.0;" & _
                        "Data Source=C:\temp\newdb.mdb")
```

The following code, however, sets `objConn` to a `Connection` object:

```
Dim objCat     As New ADOX.Catalog
Dim objConn    As ADODB.Connection

Set objConn = objCat.Create("Provider=Microsoft.Jet.OLEDB.4.0; " & _
                        "Data Source=C:\temp\newdb.mdb")
```

If you use a scripting language (such as VBScript), where variables are all `Variants`, then the `Set` keyword determines what type of variable you receive from the `Create` method. Without using `Set`, you get a string (the connection string), and with `Set`, you get a pointer to a `Connection` object.

The GetObjectOwner Method

This method retrieves the user or group name of the owner of the specified object.

```
String = Catalog.GetObjectOwner(ObjectName, ObjectType, [ObjectTypeId])
```

Name	Type	Description
ObjectName	String	The name of the object
ObjectType	ObjectTypeEnum	The type of the object
ObjectTypeId	Variant	A GUID (If the object type is provider-specific and not a standard OLE DB object type, ObjectType must be set to adPermObjProviderSpecific.)

ObjectType can be one of the following constants :

❑ adPermObjColumn specifies the object as a column.

❑ adPermObjDatabase specifies the object as a database.

❑ adPermObjProcedure specifies the object as a procedure.

❑ adPermObjProviderSpecific specifies the object as a provider-specific type.

❑ adPermObjTable specifies the object as a table.

❑ adPermObjView specifies the object as a view.

> For scripting languages, these constants are not in the include files supplied with ADO. They are available in Appendix I, as well as an include file from the supporting Web site.

Note that to use this method with the Jet provider, you must explicitly set a security database. For example:

```
strConn = "Provider=Microsoft.Jet.OLEDB.4.0; " & _
          "Data Source=C:\temp\pubs.mdb; " & _
          "Jet.OLEDB:System Database=" & _
          "c:\Program Files\Microsoft Office\Office\System.mdw"

objCat.ActiveConnection = strConn
Print objCat.GetObjectOwner ("authors", adPermObjTable)
```

The SQL Server provider does not support this method.

The SetObjectOwner Method

This method sets the user or group as the owner of the specified object.

```
Catalog.SetObjectOwner(ObjectName, ObjectType, UserName, [ObjectTypeId])
```

Name	Type	Description
ObjectName	String	The name of the object
ObjectType	ObjectTypeEnum	The type of the object
OwnerName	String	The name of the User or Group who will be the new owner of the object
ObjectTypeId	Variant	A GUID (If the object type is provider-specific and not a standard OLE DB object type, ObjectType must be set to adPermObjProviderSpecific.)

ObjectType can be one of the following constants:

❑   adPermObjColumn specifies the object as a column.

❑   adPermObjDatabase specifies the object as a database.

❑   adPermObjProcedure specifies the object as a procedure.

❑   adPermObjProviderSpecific specifies the object as a provider-specific type.

❑   adPermObjTable specifies the object as a table.

❑   adPermObjView specifies the object as a view.

To set the new owner of a table, you would use this method like this:

```
objCat.SetObjectOwner "authors", adPermObjTable, "Jan"
```

Note that to use this method with the Jet Provider, you must explicitly set a security database.

Properties of the Catalog Object

The ActiveConnection Property

This property sets or retrieves the information detailing the connection to the data store.

```
String = Catalog.ActiveConnection
Catalog.ActiveConnection = String
Set Connection = Catalog.ActiveConnection
Set Catalog.ActiveConnection = Connection
```

The connection details can either be a valid ADO connection string or an ADO Connection object. For example, either of the two following constructs is valid:

```
strConn = "Provider=Microsoft.Jet.OLEDB.4.0; " & _
          "Data Source=c:\temp\pubs.mdb"
objConn.Open strConn
Set objCat.ActiveConnection = objConn
```

```
strConn = "Provider=Microsoft.Jet.OLEDB.4.0; " & _
          "Data Source=c:\temp\pubs.mdb"
objCat.ActiveConnection strConn
```

Setting the ActiveConnection property to Nothing will close the catalog.

Collections of the Catalog Object

The objects that make up the Collections are briefly mentioned here, but are covered in more detail under each object heading.

The Tables Collection

This collection returns a collection of the tables contained in this catalog.

```
Set Tables = Catalog.Tables
```

This is the default collection.

The Groups Collection

This collection returns a collection of the user group accounts contained in this catalog.

```
Set Groups = Catalog.Groups
```

The Users Collection

This collection returns a collection of the user accounts contained in this catalog.

```
Set Users = Catalog.Users
```

The Procedures Collection

This collection returns a collection of the stored procedures contained in this catalog.

```
Set Procedures = Catalog.Procedures
```

The Views Collection

This collection returns a collection of the views contained in this catalog.

```
Set Views = Catalog.Views
```

The Table Object

The `Table` object contains all the details (such as columns, keys, and so on) for a single table. It's equivalent to looking at the table in design view in the database and seeing the properties.

Methods of the Table Object

The `Table` object has no methods.

Properties of the Table Object

The DateCreated Property

This property identifies the date the table was created.

```
Variant = Table.DateCreated
```

The DateModified Property

This property identifies the date the table was last modified.

```
Variant = Table.DateModified
```

The Name Property

This property is the name of the table.

```
Table.Name = String
String = Table.Name
```

The ParentCatalog Property

This property identifies the parent catalog for the table.

```
Set Catalog = Table.ParentCatalog
Set Table.ParentCatalog = Catalog
```

You can use the `ParentCatalog` property to set provider-specific properties before the table is added to the catalog. For example:

```
Dim objCat As New ADOX.Catalog
Dim objTbl As New ADOX.Table

objCat.ActiveConnection = _
        "Provider=Microsoft.Jet.OLEDB.4.0; " & _
        "Data Source=c:\temp\pubs.mdb"

objTbl.Name = "tblNewTable"
objTbl.Columns.Append "FirstName", adVarWChar, 25
objTbl.Columns.Append "LastName", adVarWChar, 25
objTbl.Columns.Append "Age", adInteger

Set objTbl.ParentCatalog = objCat
objTbl.Properties("Jet.OLEDB:Table Validation Rule") = _
            "[Age]>18"
objTbl.Properties("Jet.OLEDB:Table Validation Text") = _
            "Age must be over 18"

objCat.Tables.Append objTbl

Set objTbl = Nothing
Set objCat = Nothing
```

The Type Property

This property identifies the type of table.

```
String = Table.Type
```

This can be one of the following strings:

❑ TABLE for a normal table

❑ SYSTEM TABLE for a provider system table

❑ GLOBAL TEMPORARY for a temporary table

Collections of the Table Object

The Columns Collection

This collection contains a `Column` object for each column in the table.

```
Set Columns = Table.Columns
```

You can use the `Columns` collection to find the details for each `Column`.

This is the default collection.

The Indexes Collection

This collection contains an `Index` object for each index associated with the table.

```
Set Indexes = Table.Indexes
```

The Keys Collection

This collection contains a `Key` object for each key associated with the table.

```
Set Keys = Table.Keys
```

The Properties Collection

This collection contains a `Property` object for each provider-specific property of the table.

```
Set Properties = Table.Properties
```

The `Properties` collection is covered in more detail in Chapter 8, and a full list of ADOX properties appears in Appendix J.

The Index Object

The `Index` object contains all of the details for a single index on a table.

Methods of the Index Object

The `Index` object has no methods.

Properties of the Index Object

The Clustered Property

This property indicates whether the `Index` is clustered.

```
Index.Clustered = Boolean
Boolean = Index.Clustered
```

By default, indexes are not clustered.

You can set this property only before appending an `Index` to the `Indexes` collection.

Clustered indexes mean that the data is stored in the same physical order as the index, which speeds up access to the data. Not all databases support clustered indexes. For more information on this, consult the Microsoft Press book *Inside SQL Server 2000* (ISBN 0735609985).

The IndexNulls Property

This property indicates what happens to index entries containing Null values.

```
Index.IndexNulls = AllowNullsEnum
AllowNullsEnum = Index.IndexNulls
```

AllowNullsEnum can be one of the following constants:

❑   adIndexNullsAllow ensures that key columns with Null values have index values. The index entry will itself be Null.

❑   adIndexNullsDisallow ensures that if the key columns are Null, index entries are not allowed. Attempting to insert a record with Null values in a key column will generate an error. This is the default value.

❑   adIndexNullsIgnore allows Null values in key columns, but they are ignored, and an index entry is not created.

❑   adIndexNullsIgnoreAny allows Null values in any part of the key (for multiple columns), but they are ignored, and an index entry is not created.

You cannot change this property on Index objects that already exist in the Indexes collection.

The Name Property

This property sets or retrieves the name of the Index.

```
Index.Name = String
String = Index.Name
```

This is the default property.

The PrimaryKey Property

This property indicates whether or not the Index is the table's primary key.

```
Index.PrimaryKey = Boolean
Boolean = Index.PrimaryKey
```

The default value is False, and you can set this value only for Index objects that have not yet been added to the Indexes collection.

The Unique Property

This property indicates whether the keys in the Index must be unique.

```
Index.Unique = Boolean
Boolean = Index.Unique
```

The default value is False, and you can set this value only for Index objects that have not yet been added to the Indexes collection.

Collections of the Index Object

The Columns Collection

This collection contains a Column object for each column that exists in the Index.

```
Set Columns = Index.Columns
```

Although a single column comprises many indexes, it's important to remember that multiple columns are supported by (probably) all databases.

The Properties Collection

This collection contains a Property object for each provider-specific property that exists in the index.

```
Set Properties = Index.Properties
```

The Key Object

The Key object represents a table key, which may be primary, foreign, or unique.

Methods of the Key Object

The Key object has no methods.

Properties of the Key Object

The DeleteRule Property

This property indicates what happens when a primary key is deleted.

```
Key.DeleteRule = RuleEnum
RuleEnum = Key.DeleteRule
```

`RuleEnum` can be one of the following constants:

- ❏ `adRICascade` indicates that deletes are cascaded, meaning that subtables (that is the "many" table in a "one-to-many" join) are also deleted. This avoids the problem of orphaned records.

- ❏ `adRINone` indicates that deletes are not cascaded. This is the default value and will result in orphaned records.

- ❏ `adRISetDefault` indicates that the foreign key should be set to its default value for deletes, and will result in orphaned records.

- ❏ `adRISetNull` indicates that the foreign key should be set to null for deletes, and will result in orphaned records.

You can set this value on keys only before you add them to the `Keys` collection.

The Name Property

This property indicates the `Key`'s name.

```
Key.Name = String
String = Key.Name
```

The RelatedTable Property

If the key is foreign, this property represents the foreign table's name.

```
Key.RelatedTable = String
String = Key.RelatedTable
```

To identify the column in the related table, you use the `RelatedColumn` property of the `Column` object. For example:

```
objKey.RelatedTable = "sales"
objKey.Columns("store_id").RelatedColumn = "store_id"
```

The Type Property

This property indicates the `Key`'s type.

```
Key.Type = KeyTypeEnum
KeyTypeEnum = Key.Type
```

`KeyTypeEnum` can be one of the following constants:

- ❏ `adKeyForeign` indicates that the key is foreign.

- ❏ `adKeyPrimary` indicates that the key is primary.

- ❏ `adKeyUnique` indicates that the key is unique.

The UpdateRule Property

This property indicates what should happen when primary keys are updated.

```
Key.UpdateRule = RuleEnum
RuleEnum = Key.UpdateRule
```

`RuleEnum` can be one of the following constants:

❑ `adRICascade` indicates that updates are cascaded.

❑ `adRINone` indicates that updates are not cascaded. This is the default value.

❑ `adRISetDefault` indicates that the foreign key should be set to its default value for updates.

❑ `adRISetNull` indicates that the foreign key should be set to null for updates.

You can set this value on keys only before you add them to the `Keys` collection.

Collections of the Key Object

The Columns Collection

This collection contains a `Column` object for each column in the key.

```
Columns = Key.Columns
```

The Column Object

The `Column` object relates to an individual column, or field, in a `Key`, `Table`, or `Index`.

Methods of the Column Object

The `Column` object has no methods.

Properties of the Column Object

The Attributes Property

This property retrieves or sets a `Column`'s individual characteristics.

```
Column.Attributes = ColumnAttributesEnum
ColumnAttributesEnum = Column.Attributes
```

`ColumnAttributesEnum` can be one or both of the following values:

- ❑ `adColFixed` indicates that the column is of a fixed length.

- ❑ `adColNullable` indicates that the column may contain `Null` values.

The default value of `ColumnAttributesEnum` has neither of these attributes set. You should use bitwise operations to set multiple values or to retrieve individual attributes. For example, to set both attributes:

```
Set objCol = objTable.Columns("state")
objCol.Attributes = adColFixed Or adColNullable
```

And to check for a single attribute:

```
If (objCol.Attributes And adColFixed) = adColFixed Then
    Print "The column is of a fixed width"
End If
```

The DefinedSize Property

This property sets or retrieves the maximum size (in characters) of a column.

```
Column.DefinedSize = Long
Long = Column.DefinedSize
```

For variable-length columns, this indicates the maximum amount of data that the column may contain. It defaults to zero, and a value is not explicitly required for fixed length data types. For example:

```
objCol.Type = adInteger

objCol.Type = adVarChar
objCol.DefinedSize = 10
```

In the latter case, the `DefinedSize` must be set, because a variable character type must have a specified length.

You can set this value on `Column` objects only before they are appended to the `Columns` collection.

The Name Property

This property sets or retrieves the name of a column.

```
Column.Name = String
String = Column.Name
```

For example:

```
objCol.Name = "Age"
objCol.Type = adInteger
```

This is the default property.

The NumericScale Property

This property sets or retrieves the scale for a numeric column.

```
Column.NumericScale = Byte
Byte = Column.NumericScale
```

This is applicable to columns only of type adNumeric or adDecimal, and any value in this property will be ignored for all other column types.

The NumericScale defines how many digits are stored to the right of the decimal place, and is used in conjunction with the Precision property.

The default value is 0.

The ParentCatalog Property

This property sets or retrieves the Catalog to which this column belongs.

```
Set Catalog = Column.ParentCatalog
Set Column.ParentCatalog = Catalog
```

The ParentCatalog property allows you to set provider-specific properties before the column is appended to the Columns collection. For example:

```
strConn = "Provider= Microsoft.Jet.OLEDB.4.0; " & _
          "Data Source=c:\temp\pubs.mdb"
objCat.ActiveConnection = strConn

objTbl.Columns.Append "Name", adVarWChar
objCol.Name = "Age"
objCol.Type = adInteger

Set objCol.ParentCatalog = objCat
objCol.Properties("Jet.OLEDB:Column Validation Rule") = _
                                    ">18"
objCol.Properties("Jet.OLEDB:Column Validation Text") = _
                                "Age must be over 18"
objTbl.Columns.Append objCol

objCat.Tables.Append objTbl
```

You can set this value on Column objects only before they are appended to the Columns collection.

The Precision Property

This property sets or retrieves the maximum precision of data in the column.

```
Column.Precision = Long
Long = Column.Precision
```

This is applicable only to columns that are numeric and is ignored for other column types.

The default value is 0.

The RelatedColumn Property

For foreign key columns, this property sets or retrieves the name of the column in the related table.

```
Column.RelatedColumn = String
String = Column.RelatedColumn
```

You can set this value on Column objects only before they are appended to the Columns collection.

An error will be generated if you try to read this value for columns that are not part of keys. The only way to tell if a Column is part of a key is to check the Columns collection for a Key.

The SortOrder Property

For a Column in an Index, this property indicates the order in which the Column is sorted.

```
Column.SortOrder = SortOrderEnum
SortOrderEnum = Column.SortOrder
```

SortOrderEnum can be one of the following:

❑   adSortAscending sorts in ascending order.

❑   adSortDescending sorts in descending order.

The default sort order is ascending.

Accessing this property on a column that is not part of an index will generate an error.

The Type Property

This property sets or retrieves the data type for the values that will be held in the column.

```
Column.Type = DataTypeEnum
DataTypeEnum = Column.Type
```

Because of its size, the listing for DataTypeEnum is not shown here; it is provided in Appendix B.

The default value is adVarWChar. Not all providers support all data types, and you should use Appendix E as a guide for picking the correct type for your provider.

You can set this value on Column objects only before they are appended to the Columns collection.

> *The difference between* adVarChar *and* adVarWChar *(and, indeed, other types containing a W) is that the W types support Unicode, allowing for extended character sets. Jet 4 fully supports Unicode, so these W types are now the default over their non-Unicode equivalents.*

Collections of the Column Object

The Properties Collection

This collection contains all the Property objects for the Column.

```
Set Properties = Column.Properties
```

The Properties collection contains provider-specific properties and behaves exactly the same as the Properties collection of ADO discussed in Chapter 8. A full list of ADOX properties is available in Appendix J.

The Group Object

The group object identifies a security group account. As a general rule, most databases support the symmetrical nature of groups and users, where a Group can contain many users, and each User can belong to many groups. This allows you to set permission for a group as a whole rather than for individual users.

Methods of the Group Object

The GetPermissions Method

This method retrieves the group permissions for an object or for a class of object.

```
RightsEnum = Group.GetPermissions(Name, ObjectType, [ObjectTypeId])
```

Name	Type	Description
Name	Variant	The object name for which the permissions are to be retrieved
ObjectType	ObjectTypeEnum	The type of object
ObjectTypeId	Variant	A GUID (If the object type is provider-specific and not a standard OLE DB object type, ObjectType must be set to adPermObjProviderSpecific.)

ObjectType can be one of the following ObjectTypeEnum constants:

❑ adPermObjColumn specifies the object as a column.

❑ adPermObjDatabase specifies the object as a database.

❑ adPermObjProcedure specifies the object as a procedure.

❑ adPermObjProviderSpecific specifies the object as a provider-specific type.

❑ adPermObjTable specifies the object as a table.

❑ adPermObjView specifies the object as a view.

The return value is a combination of one or more RightsEnum constants, a list of which appears in Appendix I. You can test for individual permissions by using bitwise operations:

```
lngPerms = objGroup.GetPermissions ("authors", adPermObjTable)
If (lngPerms And adRightReadDesign) = adRightReadDesign Then
    Print "You have permissions to read the table design"
End If
```

You can also test for multiple permissions:

```
lngPerms = objGroup.GetPermissions ("authors", adPermObjTable)
If (lngPerms And adRightReadDescign = adRightReadDesign) Or
   (lngPerms And adRightWriteDesign = adRightWriteDesign) Then
    Print "You can read from and write to the table design"
End If
```

Substituting Null for the Name parameter allows you to examine the permissions on the container. For example, the following shows the permissions on the Tables container, identifying what permissions the group has for new tables:

```
lngPerms = objGroup.GetPermissions (Null, adPermObjTable)
```

The SetPermissions Method

This method sets the group permissions for an object, or for a class of object.

```
Group.SetPermissions(Name, ObjectType, Action, Rights,
                     [Inherit], [ObjectTypeId])
```

Name	Type	Description
Name	Variant	The name of the object for which to set permissions
ObjectType	ObjectTypeEnum	The object type
Action	ActionEnum	The type of permission action to set
Rights	RightsEnum	The individual permissions to set
Inherit	InheritTypeEnum	Indicates the type of permissions inheritance for containers and objects (default is adInheritNone)
ObjectTypeId	Variant	A GUID (If the object type is provider-specific and not a standard OLE DB object type, ObjectType must be set to adPermObjProviderSpecific.)

ObjectType can be one of the following ObjectTypeEnum constants:

❑ adPermObjColumn specifies the object as a column.

❑ adPermObjDatabase specifies the object as a database.

❑ adPermObjProcedure specifies the object as a procedure.

❑ adPermObjProviderSpecific specifies the object as a provider-specific type.

❑ adPermObjTable specifies the object as a table.

❑ adPermObjView specifies the object as a view.

Action can be one of the following ActionEnum constants:

❑ adAccessDeny denies the specific permissions to the Group or User.

❑ adAccessGrant grants the specific permissions to the Group or User. This grants an individual permission and will leave other permissions in effect.

❑ adAccessRevoke revokes any specific access rights to the Group or User.

❑ adAccessSet sets the exact permissions for the Group or User. Any existing permissions will be replaced by the new set of permissions.

`Rights` can be one or more of the `RightsEnum` constants (see list in Appendix I) and indicates the permissions to be set on the object for the group.

`Inherit` allows you to specify whether containers inherit permissions from the contained object; it can be one of the `InheritTypeEnum` constants:

❑ `adInheritBoth` indicates that objects and other containers inherit permissions for the object.

❑ `adInheritContainers` indicates that other containers inherit permissions for the object.

❑ `adInheritNone` indicates that no permissions are inherited.

❑ `adInheritNoPropogate` indicates that the `adInheritObjects` and `adInheritContainers` permissions are not propagated to child objects.

❑ `adInheritObjects` indicates that permissions are inherited only by objects that are not containers.

To set more than one right, combine them:

```
lngRights = adRightInsert Or adRightUpdate
objGroup.SetPermissions "authors", adPermObjTable, adAccessGrant, lngRights
```

If you wish to set the permissions for the container, you can supply `Null` for the name:

```
lngRights = adRightInsert Or adRightUpdate
objGroup.SetPermissions Null, adPermObjTable, adAccessGrant, lngRights
```

This sets the rights on the `Tables` container to allow inserts and updates.

Properties of the Group Object

The Name Property

This property sets or retrieves the name of the group account.

```
Group.Name = String
String = Group.Name
```

This is the default property.

The ParentCatalog Property

This property identifies the parent catalog to which this group belongs.

```
Set Catalog = Group.Name
```

Collections of the Group Object

The Users Collection

This collection contains all the user accounts that belong to this group.

```
Set Users = Group.Users
```

To list all the users in a particular group, you can use the `For...Each` construct.

The Properties Collection

This collection contains a `Property` object for each provider-specific property of the group.

```
Set Properties = Group.Properties
```

The `Properties` collection is covered in more detail in Chapter 8, and a full list of ADOX properties appears in Appendix J.

The User Object

The `User` object contains the details of a single user account.

Methods of the User Object

The ChangePassword Method

This method allows the user password to be changed.

```
User.ChangePassword(OldPassword, NewPassword)
```

Name	Type	Description
OldPassword	String	The existing user password
NewPassword	String	The new user password

To clear a password or to represent a blank password, use an empty string. For example, to clear the password for a user:

```
objUser.ChangePassword "abc123", ""
```

The GetPermissions Method

This method retrieves the user permissions on an object.

```
RightsEnum = User.GetPermissions(Name, ObjectType, [ObjectTypeId])
```

Usage of the GetPermission method for a User object is exactly the same as the GetPermissions method for the Group object.

The SetPermissions Method

This method sets the user permissions for an object or for a class of object.

```
User.SetPermissions(Name, ObjectType, Action, Rights, [Inherit],
[ObjectTypeId])
```

Usage of the SetPermissions method for a User object is exactly the same as the SetPermissions method for the Group object.

Properties of the User Object

The Name Property

This property identifies the name of the user.

```
User.Name = String
String = User.Name
```

This is the default property.

The ParentCatalog Property

This property identifies the parent catalog to which this user belongs.

```
Set Catalog = User.Name
```

Collections of the User Object

The Groups Collection

This collection contains a Group object for each group to which the user belongs.

```
Set Groups = User.Groups
```

The Properties Collection

This collection contains a `Property` object for each provider-specific property of the user.

```
Set Properties = User.Properties
```

The `Properties` collection is covered in more detail in Chapter 8, and a full list of ADOX properties appears in Appendix J.

The Procedure Object

The `Procedure` object contains the details of a stored procedure. It does not directly contain the SQL text associated with the stored procedure, but just identifies the procedure in the catalog—that is, the meta data. To access the SQL that makes up the procedure, use the `Command` property of the `Procedure` object.

Methods of the Procedure Object

The `Procedure` object has no methods.

Properties of the Procedure Object

The Command Property

This property indicates an ADO `Command` object that contains the procedure details.

```
Set Command = Procedure.Command
Set Procedure.Command = Command
```

The following providers do *not* support the `Command` property and will return an error if you try to reference it:

❑ OLE DB Provider for SQL Server

❑ OLE DB Provider for ODBC

❑ OLE DB Provider for Oracle

For providers that support the `Command` interface, you can set and retrieve the command details by using the ADO `Command` properties:

```
Set objCmd = objCat.Procedures("qryPriceDetails")
Print objCmd.CommandText
```

Or you can update the procedure:

```
objCmd.CommandText = "UPDATE Products SET Price = Price * 1.05"
Set objCat.Procedures("qryUpdatePrices") = objCmd
```

This is the default property.

The DateCreated Property

This property indicates the date the procedure was created.

```
Variant = Procedure.DateCreated
```

You must Refresh the collection to see this value for newly appended procedures.

The DateModified Property

This property indicates the date the procedure was last modified.

```
Variant = Procedure.DateModified
```

You must Refresh the collection to see this value for newly appended procedures.

The Name Property

This property indicates the name of the procedure.

```
String = Procedure.Name
```

The View Object

The View object contains details of views in the catalog. For Microsoft Access, this includes standard select queries.

Methods of the View Object

The View object has no methods.

Properties of the View Object

The Command Property

This property indicates an ADO Command object that contains the view details.

```
Set Command = View.Command
Set View.Command = Command
```

.

The following providers do *not* support the Command property and will return an error if you try to reference it:

❑   OLE DB Provider for SQL Server

❑   OLE DB Provider for ODBC

❑   OLE DB Provider for Oracle

For providers that support the Command interface, you can set and retrieve the command details by using the ADO Command properties:

```
Set objCmd = objCat.Views("vwTradePriceList")
Print objCmd.CommandText
```

Or you can set the command text:

```
objCmd.CommandText = "SELECT Product, TradePrice " & _
                     "FROM Products"
Set objCat.Views("vwTradePriceList").Command = objCmd
```

This is the default property.

The DateCreated Property

This property identifies the date the view was created.

```
Variant = View.DateCreated
```

The DateModified Property

This property identifies the date the view was last modified.

```
Variant = View.DateModified
```

The Name Property

This property identifies the name of the view.

```
String = View.Name
```

Collections

The handling of ADOX collections is similar to that of ADOX objects, so they have been included here as a single section.

This following table details the objects and their collections.

ADOX Object	Collections
Catalog	Tables, Groups, Users, Procedures, Views
Table	Columns, Indexes, Keys, Properties
Index	Columns, Properties
Key	Columns
Column	Properties
Group	Users, Properties
User	Groups, Properties
Procedure	
View	

The differences between the collections are:

❑ The `Properties` collection is a read-only collection, and therefore does not have an `Append` or `Delete` method. The `Properties` collection is the same as the ADO `Properties` collection and is detailed in Chapter 8.

❑ The remaining collections have different `Append` methods, which are detailed in the following sections.

Enumerating collections can be achieved with the `For...Each` statement in Visual Basic or VBScript, or the `Enumerator` object in JScript. C++ users should use standard enumerators to access each element in the collection.

Methods of a Collection

The Append Method

The Append method appends an object to the collection.

The Columns Collection

The Append method of the Columns collection adds a new Column to the collection.

```
Columns.Append(Item, [Type], [DefinedSize])
```

Name	Type	Description
Item	Variant	A Column object to append, or the name of the new column to append
Type	DataTypeEnum	The data type of the column (default is adVarWChar)
DefinedSize	Long	The maximum column size (default is 0)

Because of its size, the listing for DataTypeEnum is not shown here; it appears in Appendix B.

The Append method can take one of two forms. The first is to append an existing Column object to the collection:

```
objColumn.Name = "FirstName"
objColumn.Type = adVarWChar
objColumn.DefinedSize = 25
objTable.Columns.Append objColumn
```

The second method is to define the column name:

```
objTable.Columns.Append "FirstName", adVarWChar, 25
```

The Groups Collection

The Append method of the Groups collection adds a new Group to the collection.

```
Groups.Append(Item)
```

Name	Type	Description
Item	Variant	A Group object, or the name of the group to be added

You can specify either a valid Group object or just the name of a group in this method. For example, the following are equivalent:

```
objGroup.Name = "Finance"
objCat.Groups.Append objGroup
```

```
objCat.Groups.Append "Finance"
```

The Indexes Collection

The Append method of the Indexes collection adds a new Index to the collection.

```
Indexes.Append(Item, [Columns])
```

Name	Type	Description
Item	Variant	An Index object, or the name of the index to append
Columns	Variant	A variant array listing the column names contained in the Index

You can specify either an existing Index object or the name that the new index is to have:

```
objIndex.Name = "NameIndex"
objIndex.Columns.Append "FirstName", adVarWChar, 10
objIndex.Columns.Append "LastName", adVarWChar, 10
objTable.Indexes.Append objIndex
```

```
objTable.Indexes.Append "NameIndex", Array("FirstName", "LastName")
```

If your index consists of only a single column, then you can omit the Array usage:

```
objTable.Indexes.Append "FirstNameIndex", "FirstName"
```

The Keys Collection

The Append method of the Keys collection adds a new key to the collection.

```
Keys.Append(Item, [Type], [Column], [RelatedTable], [RelatedColumn])
```

Name	Type	Description
Item	Variant	A Key object, or the name of the key to append
Type	KeyTypeEnum	The type of the key (default is adKeyPrimary)
Column	Variant	The column to which the key applies
RelatedTable	String	For a foreign key, the Table to which the key points
RelatedColumn	String	For a foreign key, the Column in the RelatedTable to which the key points

The key `Type` can be one of the `KeyTypeEnum` constants:

- ❑ `adKeyForeign` indicates that the key is foreign.

- ❑ `adKeyPrimary` indicates that the key is primary.

- ❑ `adKeyUnique` indicates that the key is unique.

The item being appended can either be a valid `Key` object or the name of the key:

```
objKey.Name = "PKau_id"
objKey.Columns.Append "au_id", adKeyPrimary
objTable("authors").Keys.Append objKey
```

```
objTable("authors").Keys.Append "PKau_id", adKeyPrimary, "au_id"
```

When dealing with foreign keys, you should set the `RelatedTable` and `RelatedColumn` arguments accordingly to point to the primary key:

```
objTable("authors").Keys.Append "FKpub_id", adKeyForeign, _
                    "pub_id", "publishers", "pub_id"
```

The Procedures Collection

The `Append` method of the `Procedures` collection adds a new procedure to the collection.

```
Procedures.Append(Name, Command)
```

Name	Type	Description
Name	String	The name of the new procedure
Command	Object	An ADO `Command` object containing the procedure details

As with the `Command` property, this method is not supported by all providers. In such cases, you can easily create new stored procedures:

```
objCmd.Name.CommandText = "UPDATE . . ."
objCat.Procedures.Append "UpdateValues", objCmd
```

The Tables Collection

The `Append` method of the `Tables` collection adds a new `Table` to the collection.

```
Tables.Append(Item)
```

Name	Type	Description
Item	Variant	A `Table` object, or the name of the table to add

The `Item` can be either a valid `Table` object or the name of the table to be added:

```
objTable.Name = "Contacts"
objCat.Tables.Append objTable
```

```
objCat.Tables.Append "Contacts"
```

The Users Collection

The `Append` method of the `Users` collection adds a new user to a group or to a catalog.

```
Users.Append(Item, [Password])
```

Name	Type	Description
Item	Variant	A user object, or the name of the user to add
Password	String	The user password

The `Item` can be either a valid `User` object or the name of a user:

```
objUser.Name = "Jan"
objCat.Users.Append objUser
```

```
objCat.Users.Append "Jan", "Vouvray"
```

You must ensure that a `User` is added to the `Catalog` before adding the `User` to a `Group`. This is because the `User` must have a valid user account before it can be added to a `Group`.

The Views Collection

The `Append` method of the `Views` collection adds a new view to the catalog.

```
Views.Append(Name, Command)
```

Name	Type	Description
Name	String	The name of the new procedure
Command	Object	An ADO Command object containing the procedure details

As with the `Command` property, this method is not supported by all providers. In these cases, you can easily create new views:

```
objCmd.Name.CommandText = "SELECT . . ."
objCat.Views.Append "GetValues", objCmd
```

The Delete Method

This method deletes an object from the collection. The syntax is the same for all collections.

```
Collection.Delete(Item)
```

Name	Type	Description
Item	Variant	The number or name of the object to be deleted

Item can either be the number (that is, its position in the collection) or the name of the object to delete. For example, to delete a View from the Views collection, you could use either of these lines:

```
objCat.Views.Delete(0)
```

```
objCat.Views.Delete("qrySalesByQuarter")
```

The Refresh Method

This method refreshes the collection from the provider, ensuring that any deleted objects are no longer shown and that new objects are available. The syntax is the same for all collections.

```
Collection.Refresh
```

Using Refresh ensures that any changes being made by other users of the Catalog are reflected in your collection objects.

Properties of a Collection

The Count Property

This property identifies the number of objects within the collection.

```
Long = Collection.Count
```

For example, to determine the number of tables within a Catalog, you could use this code:

```
Print objCatalog.Tables.Count
```

The Item Property

This property allows indexing by either name or number into the collection.

```
Set Object = Collection.Item(Item)
```

Name	Type	Description
Item	Variant	The name of the object, or its number

This is the default method and can be omitted. For example, in indexing into the `Columns` collection, both of the following are equivalent:

```
Set objColumn = objTable.Columns ("Name")
```

```
Set objColumn = objTable.Columns.Item("Name")
```

11

ADO Multidimensional

The ADO MD library is a companion to the standard ADO library, and is specially developed to integrate with On Line Analytical Processing (OLAP) servers. The best way to think about OLAP is to think of spreadsheets. You could compare a normal spreadsheet to a standard database table; you have rows and columns in both. OLAP data also has rows and columns, but is more like the Pivot Table in Microsoft Excel. OLAP is designed for performing complex analysis, such as calculations, summaries, etc. more easily than can be done with SQL. Some of the analysis you can perform with OLAP is perfectly easy with a spreadsheet (in fact the Pivot Table in Excel is very similar to OLAP analysis), but when the data starts becoming large, the handling of the spreadsheet becomes more complex.

To understand OLAP, you really need an example, so let's take one of the SQL Server default databases: pubs. Suppose you want to see the book sales for each Publisher, grouped by State and City, and sub-grouped by the period of sale (Year, Quarter, Month, Day). What you are aiming for is something like this—multidimensional data bound to a hierarchical grid:

+ State	- Year	- Quarter	+ Month	All Publishers	Algodata Infosystems	Binnet & Hardley
All Geography	- 1994	- Quarter 3	Quarter 3 Total	163	15	40
			+ September	163	15	40
	All Dates	All Dates Total		275	65	90
	- 1992		1992 Total	80		80
		- Quarter 2	Quarter 2 Total	80		80
+ CA			+ June	80		80
	+ 1993	1993 Total		110	65	10
	- 1994		1994 Total	85		
		- Quarter 3	Quarter 3 Total	85		
			+ September	85		
	All Dates	All Dates Total		80	65	15
	- 1992		1992 Total			
		- Quarter 2	Quarter 2 Total			
+ OR			+ June			
	+ 1993	1993 Total		55	55	
	- 1994		1994 Total	25	10	15
		- Quarter 3	Quarter 3 Total	25	10	15
			+ September	25	10	15

This sort of data analysis is possible with standard SQL queries, or even by using the Pivot Table in Excel, but there's a better way: Use an OLAP server that can take raw data (from any data source) and transform it into easily accessible structures. That transformation is one of the key points of OLAP. It makes producing this type of analysis very easy and efficient by providing a language similar to SQL that is more powerful for this kind of procedure, and by internally storing selected data in different structures that make such analyses more efficient to perform.

These OLAP structures come in two sets and map onto the ADO MD objects. The first set represents how the OLAP server stores the data, and it consists of the following objects:

❑ Catalog, which is the container for all OLAP objects. This identifies the OLAP server and the actual data server that supplies the original data. Although this chapter uses Microsoft SQL Server and Microsoft's OLAP Server, there is no reason for them to be from the same supplier; the ADO MD objects don't require a specific OLAP server.

❑ CubeDef, which is a container for a set of data. The CubeDef used in producing the previous screenshot is called AllSales and contains the structures that identify the States, Dates (Years, Quarters, and Months), and Publishers. A CubeDef doesn't represent how the data is shown; it just represents what the structures are and what they contain. The name CubeDef suggests only three axes of data, but that's not the case; more than three are allowed.

❑ Dimension, which is a distinct set of items giving you a way to break down data. The preceding screen shows several distinct Dimension objects: Geography (to identify the States and Cities), Dates (to identify the date of the book sales), and Publishers (to identify the book publishers). The Dimensions give us the headings on both axes of the diagram. Moreover, as you can see, Dimensions can be nested, which gives a hierarchy.

❑ Hierarchy, which identifies the relationship of the items within a Dimension. So, for the Dates dimension we have three Hierarchy objects: Year, Quarter, and Month. The hierarchies give us subheadings.

❑ Level, which identifies the elements in an individual Hierarchy. For the Dates dimension we have a Hierarchy called Year; each year in the Dimension is a Level. Likewise, there is a Level for each Publisher.

❑ Member, which represents a unique item in a Level. This is equivalent to the cells in the diagram. A Member is unique in an OLAP structure because it represents the intersection of the Levels.

The second set of OLAP structures represent the data as it is actually being displayed. So if you run a query against an OLAP server, you get a set of data comprising:

❑ CellSet, which represents the whole set of data. This would be equivalent to the entire preceding diagram.

❑ Axis, which represents one of the physical axes of the CellSet. For example, the preceding diagram would require an Axis for the rows (the y-axis) and another Axis for the columns (the x-axis).

❏   Cell, which is a single cell. In the preceding diagram, a Cell would represent the quantity sold.

❏   Position, which is an individual row or column.

❏   Measure, which is a quantitative, numerical column, and is usually the name of the item shown in each cell. It's the *actual data to be shown*. In the preceding diagram, the Measure is the quantity of books sold.

Many (although not all) of the objects I've listed here are contained within collections. The ADO MD object model illustrates how these objects relate to each other in this diagram:

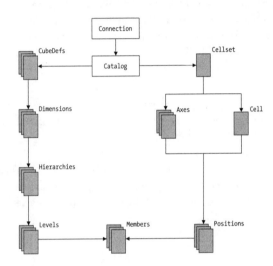

This might all seem to be just another confusing way to represent data. However, OLAP servers give you the ability to manipulate data much more easily than most relational databases. Abstracting the data into known terms (Geography, Sales, Publishers) makes the data more accessible for users because they are less reliant upon knowing the physical structure of the data in the database.

Multi-Dimension Extensions

SQL Server 7.0 and newer versions implement Multi-Dimension Extensions (MDX), which is a set of SQL extensions that allow processing of OLAP queries. For example, the set of data I showed at the beginning of this chapter could be generated with the following:

```
SELECT    Publishers.Members ON COLUMNS,
CROSSJOIN (Geography.Members, Dates.Members) ON ROWS
FROM      AllSales
```

Although different from standard SQL, it's not hard to understand. The first line indicates that the Publishers are to be shown on the columns (that's the x-axis). The second line indicates that it is a cross-join, so for each Publisher, you want to show something on the rows (the y-axis). In this case, you want to see the Geography (States) and the Dates (Years and Quarters). This is what makes OLAP so powerful, as it's easy to say "for each one of these, show me this and that." It allows you to join related sets of data in an easily viewed form. The third line just identifies where the data comes from.

The MDX extensions allow the use of OLAP names (Members, Levels, and so on) in SQL queries. For more information on MDX, consults the SQL Server documentation.

OLAP Servers

To use ADO MD, you need access to an OLAP server. Several OLAP servers available, but Microsoft SQL Server comes with an OLAP server as standard, so check out the documentation. The OLAP server for SQL Server is extremely easy to set up and use, and you can obtain it (along with SQL Server itself) as a time-limited evaluation. The limit is 120 days, which should give you plenty of time to get to know it.

> **For SQL Server 2000, the OLAP Services are called Analysis Services.**

To use ADO with OLAP, install the Client components (which include the PivotTable Service) when you install the OLAP Services. The PivotTable Service is the service that provides the interface from ADO into the OLAP Service. The SQL Server installation CD contains a set of ADO MD examples in a variety of languages.

The Catalog Object

A Catalog object contains the CubeDefs that make up a multidimensional query. The Catalog identifies the OLAP server that contains the structures to be used for OLAP queries.

Methods of the Catalog Object

The Catalog object has no methods

Properties of the Catalog Object

The ActiveConnection Property

This property identifies the ADO Connection to the OLAP data provider.

```
Set Connection = Catalog.ActiveConnection
Set Catalog.ActiveConnection = Connection
```

```
String = Catalog.ActiveConnection
Catalog.ActiveConnection = String
```

This can be an existing ADO `Connection` object or an ADO connection string. For example:

```
Provider=MSOlap; Data Source=Eeyore; Initial Catalog=Pubs; User ID=sa;
➥Password=
```

The Name Property

This property identifies the name of the catalog.

```
String = Catalog.Name
```

This property is defined by the OLAP server; you cannot change it.

Collections of the Catalog Object

The CubeDefs Collection

This collection contains a `CubeDef` for each multidimensional query in the catalog.

```
CubeDefs = Catalog.CubeDefs
```

You can use the `CubeDefs` collection to access individual `CubeDef` objects:

```
Set objCubeDef = objCatalog.CubeDefs("AllSales")
```

The Microsoft OLAP Server/Analysis Services installs the FoodMart sample, which has six CubeDefs.

The CubeDef Object

A `CubeDef` object contains the related dimensions from a cube of multidimensional data.

Methods of the CubeDef Object

The GetSchemaObject Method

This method returns the schema object from the CubeDef.

```
Object = CubeDef.GetSchemaObject(eObjType, bsUniqueName)
```

Name	Type	Description
eObjType	adObjectTypeEnum	The type of object to retrieve
bsUniqueName	String	The UniqueName of the object to retrieve

eObjType can be one of the adObjectTypeEnum constants:

❑ adObjectTypeDimension retrieves a Dimension object.

❑ adObjectTypeHierarchy retrieves a Hierarchy object.

❑ adObjectTypeLevel retrieves a Level object.

❑ adObjectTypeMember retrieves a Member object.

The Schema object will be a Dimension, Hierarchy, Level, or Member object. The GetSchemaObject method allows you to retrieve it directly without knowing where it is in the hierarchy of objects.

This method was new to ADO 2.6 and allows direct access to the object by way of its unique name.

Properties of the CubeDef Object

The Description Property

This property contains descriptive text for the CubeDef.

```
String = CubeDef.Description
```

The Name Property

This property identifies the name of the CubeDef.

```
String = CubeDef.Name
```

You can use the Name property to index into the Catalog object's CubeDefs collection:

```
Set objCubeDef = objCatalog.objCubeDefs("AllSales")
```

Collections of the CubeDef Object

The Dimensions Collection

This collection contains a Dimension object for each dimension in the CubeDef.

```
Dimensions = CubeDef.Dimensions
```

For example, the `AllSales` `CubeDef` in the example diagram has three dimensions: `Geography`, `Publishers`, and `Dates`.

The Properties Collection

This collection contains a `Property` object for each provider-specific property.

```
Properties = CubeDef.Properties
```

This works in the same way as the `Properties` collection for the ADO objects, where the provider implements specific functionality that cannot be covered by the ADO MD objects.

The Dimension Object

A `Dimension` object represents a single dimension from a cube in a multidimensional query.

Methods of the Dimension Object

The `Dimension` object has no methods.

Properties of the Dimension Object

The Description Property

This property contains descriptive text for the `Dimension`.

```
String = Dimension.Description
```

The Name Property

This property identifies the name of the `Dimension`.

```
String = Dimension.Name
```

You can use the `Name` property to index into the `Dimensions` collection of the `CubeDef` object:

```
Set objDimension = objCubeDef.Dimensions("Geography")
```

The UniqueName Property

This property indicates the unique name for the Dimension.

```
String = Dimension.UniqueName
```

Because of the complexity of dimensions, it's possible that you may find yourself using two (or more) Dimension objects with the same Name property. In such cases, you can use UniqueName to provide an unambiguous name for each Dimension object.

The need for a UniqueName is unlikely to arise with dimensions, because they are the highest objects in the hierarchy, but it may be necessary in other circumstances. You'll get a better understanding of this by looking up the UniqueName property of the Level object described later on.

Collections of the Dimension Object

The Hierarchies Collection

This collection contains a Hierarchy object for each hierarchy in the dimension.

```
Hierarchies = Dimension.Hierarchies
```

For instance, in the pubs database example, the Dates dimension has a Dates hierarchy.

The Properties Collection

This collection contains a Property object for each provider-specific property.

```
Properties = Dimension.Properties
```

This works in the same way as the Properties collection for the ADO objects, where the provider implements specific functionality that cannot be covered by the ADO MD objects.

The Hierarchy Object

A Hierarchy object identifies a single way in which data from a Dimension can be represented. This is often called an aggregation or a roll-up.

Methods of the Hierarchy Object

The Hierarchy object has no methods.

Properties of the Hierarchy Object

The Description Property

This property provides descriptive text for the Hierarchy.

```
String = Hierarchy.Description
```

The Name Property

This property identifies the Hierarchy object within the Hierarchies collection of a Dimension.

```
String = Hierarchy.Name
```

The UniqueName Property

This property provides a unique name with which to identify the Hierarchy in the collection.

```
String = Hierarchy.UniqueName
```

The UniqueName property allows you to identify a Hierarchy object by assigning a unique name to it, which is particularly useful when you have multiple Hierarchy objects possessing the same Name. It allows you to have multiple Hierarchy objects with the same name if the situation demands. Look up the UniqueName property of the Level object.

Collections of the Hierarchy Object

The Levels Collection

This collection contains a Level object for each level in the hierarchy.

```
Levels = Hierarchy.Levels
```

For example, the Dates hierarchy has the following Levels: All, Year, Quarter, Month, and Day. When this hierarchy was created (using the wizard in the Analysis Services Manager), it was identified as a time dimension using the order date (ord_date) as the date field. The wizard knows this is a date and automatically creates the necessary levels that belong to a date. This allows analysis on any part of the date.

The Properties Collection

This collection contains a Property object for each provider-specific property.

```
Properties = Hierarchy.Properties
```

This works in the same way as the `Properties` collection for the ADO objects, where the provider implements specific functionality that cannot be covered by the ADO MD objects.

The Level Object

A `Level` object identifies a single step (or layer of aggregation) in a `Hierarchy`.

Methods of the Level Object

The `Level` object has no methods.

Properties of the Level Object

The Caption Property

This property identifies the text that is written on the screen when the `Level` is displayed.

```
String = Level.Caption
```

The Depth Property

This property identifies how deep in the hierarchy this `Level` is.

```
Integer = Level.Depth
```

The `Level` object's `Depth` property is the number of levels between the hierarchy's root of the hierarchy and the `Level` object. For example, in the diagram at the beginning of this chapter, we have is a `Hierarchy` object called `Dates`. The levels of this hierarchy (and their depths) are as follows:

Level Name	Depth
(All)	0
Year	1
Quarter	2
Month	3
Day	4

The Description Property

This property provides a textual description of the Level.

```
String = Level.Description
```

The Name Property

This property identifies the name of the Level.

```
String = Level.Name
```

The UniqueName Property

This property provides a unique name for the Level.

```
String = Level.UniqueName
```

The UniqueName allows for multiple Level objects that have the same Name.

For example, assume you have two Levels that are date-based—perhaps order date and restocking date. Each Level has a hierarchy of date information like so:

OrderDate	RestockDate
All	All
Year	Year
Quarter	Quarter
Month	Month
Day	Day

If you have just the hierarchy name (the Name property), you won't know which Level it belongs to. The UniqueName property combines the name of the current object with the names of all parent objects. So, if you show the table again, this time with the UniqueName, you will get this:

OrderDate	RestockDate
[OrderDate].[All]	[RestockDate].[All]
[OrderDate].[Year]	[RestockDate].[Year]
[OrderDate].[Quarter]	[RestockDate].[Quarter]
[OrderDate].[Month]	[RestockDate].[Month]
[OrderDate].[Day]	[RestockDate].[Day]

Square brackets surround each part of the hierarchy, and periods separate them from other parts of the hierarchy. It is this naming convention that allows each object to be uniquely named.

Collections of the Level Object

The Members Collection

This collection contains a `Member` object for each unique row or column in the `Level` object.

```
Members = Level.Members
```

For example, consider the Month `Level`. The initial thought is that this should contain 12 Members, one for each month, but that's not the case. In fact, it contains a month only if there is data for that month. So, what you get is this:

- ❑   June, from 1992
- ❑   February, from 1993
- ❑   March, from 1993
- ❑   May, from 1993
- ❑   October, from 1993
- ❑   December, from 1993
- ❑   September, from 1994

This illustrates that you cannot make assumptions about what levels will be available just from the object name. It's the data that defines what's available.

The Properties Collection

This collection contains a `Property` object for each provider-specific property.

```
Properties = Level.Properties
```

This works in the same way as the `Properties` collection for the ADO objects, where the provider implements specific functionality that cannot be covered by the ADO MD objects.

The Member Object

A `Member` object represents the data in a `Dimension`.

Methods of the Member Object

The Member object has no methods.

Properties of the Member Object

The Caption Property

This property identifies the text that is written to the screen when the Member is used in a hierarchical query.

```
String = Member.Caption
```

The ChildCount Property

This property identifies how many child members the Member object contains.

```
Long = Member.ChildCount
```

You can reach the child members via the Children property.

The Children Property

This property identifies the child members of which this Member is the parent.

```
Members = Member.Children
```

To make this clearer, look again at the diagram at the beginning of this chapter and consider the Dates hierarchy. This has levels for the different types of date measurement (all dates, years, quarters, months, and days). OLAP allows you to look at data in a variety of different ways because each Member (in the Members collection of each Level) has a collection of sub-Member objects, which are the children of the current Member. You can see this more clearly in this table:

Level Name	Member	Child Member
(All)	All Dates	1992
		1993
		1994

Table continues on the following page

Level Name	Member	Child Member
Year	1992	Quarter 2
	1993	Quarter 1
		Quarter 2
		Quarter 4
	1994	Quarter 3
Quarter	Quarter 2	June
	Quarter 1	February
		March
	Quarter 2	May
Month	June	15
	May	22
		24

The Description Property

This property provides descriptive text for the member.

```
String = Member.Description
```

The DrilledDown Property

This property indicates whether the Level has been drilled down.

```
Boolean = Member.DrilledDown
```

This property shows whether the Member is contained in the deepest level of the hierarchy, that is, whether you have *drilled down* as far as possible. If so, this property returns True. Otherwise, the Member possesses child members, and this property returns False.

The LevelDepth Property

This property identifies how deep this Member is within the Level's hierarchy.

```
Long = Member.LevelDepth
```

The `LevelDepth` property is the same as the `Depth` property for the `Level`, and it is included for a `Member` because you can access `Member` objects from their positions in a `CellSet`, and not just from the `Levels` collection.

The LevelName Property

This property indicates the name of the `Level` to which the `Member` belongs.

```
String = Member.LevelName
```

The Name Property

This property indicates the name of the `Member`.

```
String = Member.Name
```

The Parent Property

This property indicates the parent object of this `Member`.

```
Member = Member.Parent
```

In the preceding discussion of the `Children` property, the table illustrates the concept of the parent-child relationship among `Member` objects.

The ParentSameAsPrev Property

This property identifies whether the parent of this member is the same as the parent of the preceding `Member` in the `Members` collection.

```
Boolean = Member.ParentSameAsPrev
```

You can use this property to identify siblings, or `Member` objects that are on the same level.

The Type Property

This property identifies the type of the `Member`.

```
MemberTypeEnum = Member.Type
```

`MemberTypeEnum` can be one of the following constants:

- ❑ `adMemberRegular` indicates that the member is data that has come directly from the data source.

- ❏ adMemberMeasure indicates that the member is a Measure, and represents a quantitative attribute.

- ❏ adMemberFormula indicates the member is calculated from a formula.

- ❏ adMemberAll indicates that the member represents all members for a given level.

- ❏ adMemberUnknown indicates that the type is unknown.

The default is adMemberRegular.

The UniqueName Property

This property indicates the unique name for the Member.

```
String = Member.UniqueName
```

Following on from the list of Levels shown in the Levels collection, you can see how the list of unique names shows the complete hierarchy of objects and ensures that no duplicate names ever exist:

```
[Dates].[All Dates].[1992].[Quarter 2].[June]
[Dates].[All Dates].[1993].[Quarter 1].[February]
[Dates].[All Dates].[1993].[Quarter 1].[March]
[Dates].[All Dates].[1993].[Quarter 2].[May]
[Dates].[All Dates].[1993].[Quarter 4].[October]
[Dates].[All Dates].[1993].[Quarter 4].[December]
[Dates].[All Dates].[1994].[Quarter 3].[September]
```

Collections of the Member Object

The Properties Collection

Contains a Property object for each provider-specific property.

```
Properties = Member.Properties
```

This works in the same way as the Properties collection for the ADO objects, where the provider implements specific functionality that cannot be covered by the ADO MD objects.

The Cell Object

A cell represents a single item of data at the intersection of a number of Axes in a CellSet. This is much like a cell in a spreadsheet, and is uniquely identified by the Positions along the Axes.

Methods of the Cell Object

The Cell object has no methods.

Properties of the Cell Object

The FormattedValue Property

This property indicates the formatted value of the cell.

```
Cell.FormattedValue = String
String = Cell.FormattedValue
```

The value from this property is the Value property formatted according to its type.

The Ordinal Property

The Ordinal property uniquely identifies a cell within a CellSet.

```
Long = Cell.Ordinal
```

The CellSet notionally identifies each cell as though the CellSet is a multidimensional array, and each array element has a unique number. Cells are numbered starting from zero, and the Ordinal can be used in the Item property of the CellSet to quickly locate a cell.

For the exact formula used to calculate the cell Ordinal, consult the ADO MD documentation.

The Value Property

This property indicates the value contained within the cell.

```
Cell.Value = Variant
Variant = Cell.Value
```

Collections of the Cell Object

The Positions Collection

This collection contains a collection of Position objects.

```
Positions = Cell.Positions
```

Each Cell comprises a number of Axes, and each Axis contains a number of Position objects. Each Position object uniquely identifies a row or column in the Axis.

You can use the `Positions` collection to iterate through each `Position`:

```
For Each objPos In objCell.Positions
    Print objPos.Name
Next
```

The Properties Collection

This collection contains an ADO `Property` object for each provider-specific property.

```
Properties = Cell.Properties
```

This works in the same way as the `Properties` collection for the ADO objects, where the provider implements specific functionality that cannot be covered by the ADO MD objects.

The CellSet Object

A `CellSet` object contains the results of a multidimensional query against an OLAP server. It contains collections of `Cell` objects, a collection of `Axis` objects, and details of the connection and query.

Methods of the CellSet Object

The Close Method

This method closes an open `CellSet`.

```
CellSet.Close
```

Closing a `CellSet` will release any child collections associated with the `CellSet`.

The Open Method

This method opens a new `CellSet` based upon a multidimensional query.

```
CellSet.Open([DataSource], [ActiveConnection])
```

Parameter	Type	Description
DataSource	Variant	The multidimensional query that will retrieve the data
ActiveConnection	Variant	Either an ADO `Connection` object or an ADO connection string

The `DataSource` argument corresponds to the `Source` property of the `CellSet`. Multidimensional queries use their own variant of the SQL language (which is a standard). For example:

```
strQuery = "SELECT [Books].MEMBERS ON ROWS," & _
                " [Stores].MEMBERS ON COLUMNS" & _
            " FROM [PubsOLAP]"

objCellSet.Open strQuery, objConn
```

For more information on multidimensional queries, consult the appropriate documentation, such as the SQL Server OLAP documentation, the MDX documentation in the Data Access SDK, or the MDAC Web site, at http://www.microsoft.com/data.

The `ActiveConnection` argument corresponds to the `ActiveConnection` property.

Properties of the CellSet Object

The ActiveConnection Property

This property identifies the connection to which the `CellSet` or `Catalog` belongs.

```
Set Connection = CellSet.ActiveConnection
Set CellSet.ActiveConnection = Connection
String = CellSet.ActiveConnection
CellSet.ActiveConnection = String
```

This can be a valid ADO `Connection` object or an ADO connection string. As with ADO, if the string method is used, a new connection is made.

If the `ActiveConnection` argument of the `Open` method was used to specifythe connection, then the `ActiveConnection` property inherits the value from the argument.

The FilterAxis Property

This property indicates the filtering information for the `CellSet`.

```
Axis = CellSet.FilterAxis
```

If filtering has been used to restrict the data returned during the query, the `FilterAxis` property will return an `Axis` object, usually containing one row, with the filter information.

The Item Property

This property allows indexing into the `CellSet` to reference a specific `Cell` object.

```
Set Cell = CellSet.Item(Index)
```

Parameter	Type	Description	Default
Index	Variant	The number of the Cell in the collection (zero-based)	

This is the default property, which means that its name can be omitted when called. For example, the following lines are equivalent:

```
Set objCell = objCellSet.Item(1)
```

```
Set objCell = objCellSet(1)
```

The Source Property

This property identifies the multidimensional query used to return the data.

```
Variant = CellSet.Source
CellSet.Source = Variant
```

If the DataSource argument of the Open method was used to specify the query, the Source property inherits its value from the argument.

The State Property

Identifies the current state of the CellSet.

```
Long = CellSet.State
```

The State can be one of the following ADO ObjectStateEnum constants:

❑   adStateOpen indicates that the CellSet is open.

❑   adStateClosed indicates that the CellSet is closed.

Collections of the CellSet Object

The Axes Collection

This collection contains an Axis object for each axis in the CellSet.

```
Axes = CellSet.Axes
```

This collection will always contain at least one Axis object. You can iterate through the Axes collection to examine the data in the CellSet. For example, consider the following OLAP query:

```
SELECT Publishers.Members ON COLUMNS,
       Geography.Members  ON ROWS,
       Dates.Members      ON PAGES
FROM   AllSales
```

This creates three `Axis` objects in the collection: `Publishers`, `Geography`, and `Dates`.

The Properties Collection

This collection contains an ADO `Property` object for each provider-specific property.

```
Properties = CellSet.Properties
```

This works in the same way as the `Properties` collection for the ADO objects, where the provider implements specific functionality that cannot be covered by the ADO MD objects.

The Axis Object

An `Axis` object is an axis from the `Axes` collection of a `CellSet`. It represents the rows and columns of data in a query.

Methods of the Axis Object

The `Axis` object has no methods.

Properties of the Axis Object

The DimensionCount Property

This property returns the number of `Dimensions` on this `Axis`.

```
Long = Axis.DimensionCount
```

The Name Property

This property returns the name of the `Axis`.

```
String = Axis.Name
```

Collections of the Axis Object

The Positions Collection

This collection contains `Position` objects.

```
Positions = Axis.Positions
```

Using the `Positions` collection allows you to iterate through the unique rows and columns in a query.

The Properties Collection

This collection contains an ADO `Property` object for each provider-specific property.

```
Properties = Axis.Properties
```

This works in the same way as the `Properties` collection for the ADO objects, where the provider implements specific functionality that cannot be covered by the ADO MD objects.

The Position Object

A `Position` object contains the members of those dimensions that identify a point along a specific axis. For example, consider the following OLAP query:

```
SELECT  Publishers.Members ON COLUMNS,
        Geography.Members   ON ROWS,
        Dates.Members       ON PAGES
  FROM  AllSales
```

Suppose you examine just one set of members—Geography, for example. In this case, the `Positions` collection will contain an entry for each unique column:

```
[Geography].[All Geography]
[Geography].[All Geography].[CA]
[Geography].[All Geography].[CA].[Fremont]
[Geography].[All Geography].[CA].[Los Gatos]
[Geography].[All Geography].[CA].[Tustin]
[Geography].[All Geography].[OR]
[Geography].[All Geography].[OR].[Portland]
[Geography].[All Geography].[WA]
[Geography].[All Geography].[WA].[Remulade]
[Geography].[All Geography].[WA].[Seattle]
```

A `Position` contains the members and levels that allow a row or column to be uniquely identified.

Methods of the Position Object

The `Position` object has no methods.

Properties of the Position Object

The Ordinal Property

This property identifies a position along an axis.

```
Long = Position.Ordinal
```

The `Ordinal` is a unique identifier for a position and corresponds to the `Index` of the position in the `Positions` collection.

Collections of the Position Object

The Members Collection

This collection contains a `Member` object for each member in the `Position` object.

```
Members = Position.Members
```

The ADO MD Collections

All collections in ADO MD have the same properties and work in the same way. The objects and their collections are listed here:

Object	Contains Collections
Catalog	CubeDefs
CubeDef	Dimensions, Properties
Dimension	Hierarchies, Properties
Hierarchy	Levels, Properties
Level	Members, Properties
Member	Children, Properties
CellSet	Axes, Properties

Table continues on the following page

Object	Contains Collections
Axis	Positions, Properties
Cell	Positions, Properties
Position	Members

Note that these collections do not offer any events or collections of their own.

Collection Methods

The Refresh Method

This method updates the collection from the provider to ensure that it contains the latest objects.

```
Collection.Refresh
```

Collection Properties

The Count Property

This property indicates the number of objects in the collection.

```
Long = Collection.Count
```

The Item Property

This property allows indexing into the collection to reference a specific object.

```
Set Object = Collection.Item(Index)
```

Parameter	Type	Description
Index	Variant	The number or name of the object in the collection (zero-based)

This is the default property, which means that its name may be omitted when called. For example, the following lines (which use the Positions collection) are equivalent:

```
Set objPosition = objPositions.Item(1)
```

```
Set objPosition = objPositions(1)
```

12

Jet Replication Objects

The Jet Replication Objects (JRO, in `msjro.dll`) allow you to manipulate the replication features of a database through a simple set of objects. Although JRO is part of ADO, it applies only when replicating Access databases (to and from other Access databases, as well as to and from SQL Server). Replication allows you to have a number of copies of the same database and the ability to synchronize changes between them. This is particularly useful in situations where the database user might be absent from the office but still requires database access. Users leaving the office can take a copy with them on a laptop computer, then synchronize changes when they return. Replication doesn't take place in real time, but must be initiated by the user, so there is no performance hit.

JRO lets you:

- ❏ Compact databases
- ❏ Set passwords and encryption on databases
- ❏ Create replica databases
- ❏ Synchronize replica sets
- ❏ Control the memory cache

Replication allows you to create any number of copies of a database in which changes may be shared and synchronized between the copies. These copies are called the **replica set**, and you can replicate between any members in a replica set.

One of the replicated databases in a replica set database is designated the **design master**. Changes to objects (tables, queries, and so on) can be made only in the design master. Any replica in the replica set can be the design master (by default it's the first replica created), but you can have only one design master at any time.

A database may be defined as replicable, but not actually be replicated. This just means that the database *can* be replicated if desired, but it isn't at the moment.

If replication is used with Access 2000 and SQL Server 7.0 onward, then you can get full, bidirectional data replication between the Access and SQL Server databases. For more details on this, and other areas of replication, consult the documentation of Microsoft Office, Microsoft SQL Server, and Microsoft Office Developer Edition. The JRO object model looks like this:

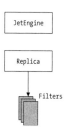

> *If you'd like to learn more about Access replication, Microsoft Press devotes a chapter to it in* Microsoft Jet Database Engine Programmer's Guide (Second Edition). *It doesn't discuss JRO at all, but covers what happens to Access databases during the replication process, and how you can best use replication. In fact, if you're an Access programmer, it's worth getting the book anyway; it contains lots of useful information.*

Creating Replica Databases

Creating a replica database is extremely simple and only involves selecting the Create Replica... option from the Tools menu, as shown here:

Creating a replica can be done only on a closed database, so Access will ask you if it's OK to do this. You are then asked if you'd like a backup copy of the database made. It's always wise to say "yes" to this question, because creating the replica results in changes to the database, and you cannot change a replicated database back into a nonreplicated database.

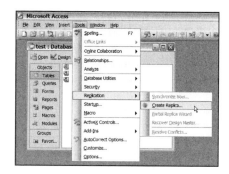

You are then asked for the name and location of the replica database, and Access goes ahead and creates it. The current copy then becomes the design master.

The Replica Object

The `Replica` object represents a copy of a replicated database. Using a replica database is simply a matter of instantiating the `Replica` object:

```
Dim objRep As JRO.Replica
Set objRep = New JRO.Replica
```

Once the object is created, you can the set the `ActiveConnection` property and call the methods.

Methods of the Replica Object

The CreateReplica Method

This method creates a replica of any database that is replicable (that allows itself to be replicated).

```
Replica.CreateReplica(ReplicaName, Description,
                      [ReplicaType], [Visibility],
                      [Priority], [Updatability])
```

Parameter	Type	Description
ReplicaName	String	The name and path of the replica to be created
Description	String	A description of the newly replicated database
ReplicaType	ReplicaTypeEnum	Indicates the type of the replica database to create (default is jrRepTypeFull)
Visibility	VisibilityEnum	Indicates the visibility of the new replica database (For more details, see the Visibility property. Default is jrRepVisibilityGlobal.)
Priority	Long	The priority of the database for use in conflict resolution (For more details, see the Priority property. Default is –1.)
Updatability	UpdatabilityEnum	Indicates the type of updates allowed in the new replica database (default is jrRepUpdFull)

ReplicaType can be one of the following ReplicaTypeEnum constants:

❑ jrRepTypeFull indicates a full replica; this is the default.

❑ jrRepTypePartial indicates a partial replica.

Visibility can be one of the following VisibilityEnum constants:

❑ jrRepVisibilityGlobal indicates a global replica.

❑ jrRepVisibilityLocal indicates a local replica.

❑ jrRepVisibilityAnon indicates an anonymous replica.

For more information on these options, refer to section on the Visibility property.

`Updatability` can be one of the following `UpdatabilityEnum` constants:

❑ `jrRepUpdFull` indicates that the new replica allows changes to the schema and records.

❑ `jrRepUpdReadOnly` indicates that the new replica does not allow changes to the schema and records.

For example:

```
Dim objDB As JRO.Replica
Set objDB = New JRO.Replica

objDB.ActiveConnection = _
        "Provider=Microsoft.Jet.OLEDB.4.0; Data Source=C:\Temp\pubs.mdb"
objDB.CreateReplica _
        "C:\Temp\NewReplica.mdb", "A new replica", jrRepTypePartial
```

You can only create a replica of the source database if the source database is replicable—that is, its `ReplicaType` property must not be `jrRepTypeNotReplicable`.

The GetObjectReplicability Method

This method identifies whether the object is replicated, or if it has been marked so as to be replicated the next time synchronization between replicas takes place.

```
Boolean = Replica.GetObjectReplicability(objectName, objectType)
```

Parameter	Type	Description
objectName	String	The name of the object
objectType	String	The type of the object

`objectName` identifies the object that is to be tested for replicability. The `objectType` is the container name in Access, so this will be `Tables`, `Queries`, `Forms`, `Reports`, `Macros`, or `Modules`.

If `objectName` is contained in a nonreplicable database, the `GetObjectReplicability` method will return `True`, because the object will be replicable if the database is made replicable. This method doesn't actually take account of the replicability of the database itself—just the requested object.

A value of `False` indicates that the database is replicable, but that the object itself is not replicable.

For example:

```
If objDB.GetObjectReplicability("authors", "tables") = True Then
    Print "The authors table may be replicated in the future"
End If
```

The MakeReplicable Method

This method adjusts the properties of the database to allow it to be replicated.

```
Replica.MakeReplicable([connectionString], [columnTracking])
```

Parameter	Type	Description
connectionString	String	The full path of the database that is to be made replicable
columnTracking	Boolean	Indicates whether changes are tracked by row or column (default is True, indicating column tracking)

The source database must be opened exclusively before it can be made replicable.

The PopulatePartial Method

This method populates a partial replica.

```
Replica.PopulatePartial(FullReplica)
```

Parameter	Type	Description
FullReplica	String	The full path of the replica database to be populated with data

You can only replicate a database if it is replicable–that is, its ReplicaType property must not be jrRepTypeNotReplicable.

For full details on the implications of replication, including conflict resolution and orphaned records, you should consult the Jet documentation.

The SetObjectReplicability Method

This method sets whether an object will be replicated (in the event of a call to the CreateReplica method).

```
Replica.SetObjectReplicability(objectName, objectType, _
                         replicability)
```

Parameter	Type	Description
objectName	String	The name of the object to replicate
objectType	String	The type of the object
replicability	Boolean	Set to True to make this a replicable object or False to keep the object local

Note that if the database has not been marked for replication, all of its objects are replicable by default unless SetObjectReplicability is used to mark them otherwise. This is to allow all objects to be automatically replicated once the database is made replicable.

For example:

```
objDB.SetObjectReplicability "authors", "tables", False
```

The object type is the container name in Access, so this will be Tables, Queries, Forms, Reports, Macros, or Modules.

The Synchronize Method

This method synchronizes two replica databases from the same replica set.

```
Replica.Synchronize(target, [syncType], [syncMode])
```

Parameter	Type	Description
target	String	The full path of the target replica database with which the current database will synchronize, or the name of a Synchronizer to manage the target replica database, or the Internet server on which the target replica is located
syncType	SyncTypeEnum	The type of synchronization to be performed (default is jrSyncTypeImpExp)
syncMode	SyncModeEnum	The synchronization method to be used (default is jrSyncModeIndirect)

syncType can be one of the following SyncTypeEnum constants:

❑   jrSyncTypeExport exports changes from the current database to the target database.

❑   jrSyncTypeImport imports changes from the target database into the current database.

❑   jrSyncTypeImpExp exchanges changes between the current database and the target database.

syncMode can be one of the following SyncModeEnum constants:

❑ jrSyncModeIndirect indicates that indirect synchronization is to take place. This is where the target parameter contains the name of the synchronizer that will perform the remote synchronization, and is best used over poor or inconsistent lines, such as WANs or modem lines.

❑ jrSyncModeDirect indicates that direct synchronization is to take place. Here, both databases are opened together and the appropriate changes made.

❑ jrSyncModeInternet indicates that synchronization will take place over the Internet. Here, the target parameter will contain the URL of the Internet server on which the target database is located.

Synchronization is simply a matter of exchanging records that have changed between databases. Direct is the most common method, where you have the two Access replicas available on the local network. In this case, Access checks each replicable object to see whether it needs to be copied to the other database. The Internet mode performs a similar operation, but allows the target database to be located on an Internet server. The Indirect mode allows synchronization to take place even when the target database is unavailable, perhaps through a known poor connection, such as a slow WAN link or modem. In this case, the changes aren't directly made to the target database, but are instead placed in a "drop-box" (such as a shared folder), where they can be picked up at a later date by the target database.

If the synchronization process detects conflicts, it will create a table containing the conflicting records. This will be the same name of the original table, but with _Conflict added. See the ConflictTables property for more information.

Properties of the Replica Object

The ActiveConnection Property

This property indicates the ADO Connection string or object.

```
Set Object = Replica.ActiveConnection
Set Replica.ActiveConnection = Object
String = Replica.ActiveConnection
Replica.ActiveConnection = String
```

You can use the standard ADO formats for this. Here are a couple of examples:

```
objDB.ActiveConnection = _
    "Provider=Microsoft.Jet.OLEDB.4.0; " & _
    "Data Source=C:\temp\pubs.mdb"
```

```
Set objDB.ActiveConnection = objConn
```

The ConflictFunction Property

This property points to the name of a function that will be used to perform conflict resolution.

```
Replica.ConflictFunction = String
String = Replica.ConflictFunction
```

This function allows you to specify your own method for resolving conflicts. The default action is for Access to call its built-in conflict resolver. This is a fairly simple routine and is based on the version number of the record (stored in a field added to the table when the replica is created). Every time a change is made to a record, this field is incremented, and Access uses the difference in version numbers to determine which record contains the data that wins the update. The assumption used is that the record whose version number has changed the most is the correct record. If both records contain the same version number, then the `ReplicaID` property of the replica set is used, and the lowest one wins.

If you wish to use your own conflict resolution function, use something like:

```
objDB.ConflictFunction = "MyConflictResolver()"
```

Your function should be a public function (not a sub) in the database, and its job is to look through the replica tables and work out which record is the correct one. If you intend to do this, you must think very carefully about what determines the correct record. The Access method is simplistic but logical. You can't rely on things such as the date the record was changed, because dates on different machines might be different (especially if they are in different time zones).

The function you build will have to open both tables and check each field in each record to see whether any changes have been made. If so, then you'll need some form of business logic to pick the correct record, or you will need to provide a user interface that displays both records and lets the user decide which is correct.

The ConflictTables Property

This property identifies the list of tables that contain conflict information.

```
Recordset = Replica.ConflictTables
```

If conflict errors are generated during synchronization, a table containing the conflicting rows is created, and the `ConflictTables` property will contain a recordset comprising two columns. The first column, TABLE_NAME, indicates the first table, which contains the original data; the second column, CONFLICT_TABLE_NAME, indicates the table containing the conflicting rows. You can then open the conflicting table, fetch a conflicting row of data, and compare it with the original row from the original table.

For example, imagine synchronizing a database with a table called `authors`. If there were any conflicts, a table containing the conflicting rows, called `authors_Conflict`, would be created. In this case, the `ConflictTables` would contain:

TABLE_NAME	CONFLICT_TABLE_NAME
authors	authors_Conflict

The DesignMasterId Property

This property is the unique ID of the design master database.

```
Replica.DesignMasterId = Variant
Variant = Replica.DesignMasterId
```

This property is created automatically at the time a database is set to be the design master. The DesignMasterId is a GUID value.

Each replica in a replica set has a GUID, which is used to uniquely identify it. The only values for DesignMasterId are GUIDs from other replicas in the replica set.

The Priority Property

This property identifies the relative priority of a replica during conflict resolution.

```
Long = Replica.Priority
```

During conflict resolution, the following applies:

- ❑ The replica with the highest Priority value wins. Priorities range from 0 to 100.

- ❑ If the Priority values are equal, the replica with the highest ReplicaID wins.

The default priority for global replicas is 90 percent of the priority of the parent replica. The value for local and anonymous replicas is zero.

The ReplicaId Property

This property is a unique identifier for a replica database.

```
Variant = Replica.ReplicaId
```

This value is a GUID, which is automatically generated at the time the replica is created.

The ReplicaType Property

This property identifies the type of the replica database.

```
ReplicaTypeEnum = Replica.ReplicaType
```

`ReplicaTypeEnum` can be one of the following constants:

☐ `jrRepTypeNotReplicable` identifies that the database is not replicable. This is the default.

☐ `jrRepTypeDesignMaster` indicates that the database is the design master.

☐ `jrRepTypeFull` indicates that the database is a full replica.

☐ `jrRepTypePartial` indicates that the database is a partial replica.

A value of `jrRepTypeNotReplicable` does not mean that the database can never be replicated, but that it has not yet been made replicable. You can use the `MakeReplicable` method to make the database replicable at run-time.

The RetentionPeriod Property

This property identifies the number of days for which replica histories should be kept.

```
Replica.RetentionPeriod = Long
Long = Replica.RetentionPeriod
```

A replica set retains details of changes for the number of days (from 5 to 32,000) specified in this property.

The default value is dependent on how the database was made replicable. If the database was made replicable with the Replication Manager, RDO, or ADO, the `RetentionPeriod` value defaults to 60. If the database was made replicable with Access, the `RetentionPeriod` value defaults to 1,000.

You can set this property at any time, but only on a design master database.

The Visibility Property

This property indicates the visibility of the database.

```
VisibilityEnum = Replica.Visibility
```

`VisibilityEnum` can be one of the following constants:

☐ `jrRepVisibilityGlobal` indicates a global replica.

☐ `jrRepVisibilityLocal` indicates a local replica.

☐ `jrRepVisibilityAnon` indicates an anonymous replica.

A global replica is typically the design master, and is allowed to synchronize with any replicas in the replica set. A local or anonymous replica can synchronize only with a global replica, and not other replicas in the set. The difference between a local and an anonymous replica is that the global replica can see local replicas, but not anonymous ones. This is useful in situations where you have a central hub that is the global replica, which, perhaps automatically, performs the replication process with other replicas in the set, but not with anonymous ones, because it cannot see them. The user of the anonymous replica can then synchronize at will. This allows databases to be part of a replica set but not take part in the standard synchronization process, thereby allowing them to be synchronized when required.

For more information on replica schemes, consult the Access documentation.

Collections of the Replica Object

The Filters Collection

This collection contains a `Filter` object for each filter specifying replication information.

```
Set Filters = Replica.Filters
```

There's more on the `Filters` collection later in this chapter, but first I'll look at what an individual `Filter` object can do.

The Filter Object

A `Filter` object specifies the details of a filter that limits the records transferred during replication. This allows you to create partial replicas containing a subset of the main database. A partial replica is still bidirectional, but with less data.

Don't confuse the `Filter` object with the `Filter` method of the ADO `Recordset` object; the two are not related. `Filter` objects are created by adding them to the `Filters` collection of the `Replica` object.

Methods of the Filter Object

There are no methods for the `Filter` object.

Properties of the Filter Object

The FilterCriteria Property

This property sets or returns the string that controls the filter.

```
String = Filter.FilterCriteria
```

The filter string is a standard SQL WHERE clause without the WHERE keyword. The filter determines only which records in a table are replicated, but not which tables. For this, you must set the table so that it isn't replicable.

The filter criteria are set in the Append method of the Filters collection.

The FilterType Property

This property indicates the type of the filter.

```
FilterTypeEnum = Filter.FilterType
```

FilterTypeEnum can be one of the following constants:

- ❑   jrFilterTypeRelationship indicates that the filter is based on a relationship.

- ❑   jrFilterTypeTable indicates that the filter is based on a table.

The filter type is set in the Append method of the Filters collection.

The TableName Property

This property identifies the table to which the Filter applies.

```
String = Filter.TableName
```

When the filter is based on a one-to-many relationship, the table name is the table on the many side of a join.

The filter table name is set in the Append method of the Filters collection.

The Filters Collection

The Filters collection contains a Filter object for each filter applicable to the replication process. You cannot create more than one filter of the same type on a table.

Methods of the Filters Collection

The Append Method

This method adds a new filter to the collection.

```
Filters.Append(TableName, FilterType, FilterCriteria)
```

Parameter	Type	Description
TableName	String	The name of the table to which the filter applies, or (if the filter is based on a relationship) the name of the table on the many side of a join
FilterType	FilterTypeEnum	The type of filter
FilterCriteria	String	The SQL clause that makes up the filter

The `FilterType` can be one of the following constants:

❑ `jrFilterTypeRelationship` indicates that the filter is based on a relationship.

❑ `jrFilterTypeTable` indicates that the filter is based on a table.

Using the filter types specified here, you can create filters that apply either to tables or to relationships. For example, the following creates a filter based upon a table:

```
objDB.Filters.Append "authors", _
        jrFilterTypeTable, "state='CA'"
```

The second example creates a filter based upon a join:

```
objDB.Filters.Append "authors", _
        jrFilterTypeRelationship, "qryPublishersAuthors"
```

For the `FilterCriteria`, you specify the query that makes up the relationship, and for the `TableName`, you specify the table that is on the many side of the relationship.

The Delete Method

This method deletes a `Filter` object from the collection.

```
Filters.Delete(Item)
```

Parameter	Type	Description
Item	Variant	The index number or table name of the `Filter` object to be deleted

The Refresh Method

This method refreshes the collection so that changes are visible.

```
Filters.Refresh
```

Properties of the Filters Collection

The Count Property

This property returns the number of `Filter` objects in the collection.

```
Long = Filters.Count
```

The Item Property

This property allows indexing into the collection by either name or number.

```
Filter = Filters.Item(Item)
```

Parameter	Type	Description
Item	Variant	The name of the `Filter` or its index number

This is the default method, which means that the method name can be omitted when the method is called. For example, the following expressions are equivalent:

```
objReplica.Filters("Name")
```

```
objReplica.Filters.Item("Name")
```

The JetEngine Object

The `JetEngine` object gives you control of the Jet database engine.

Methods of the JetEngine Object

The CompactDatabase Method

This method copies and compacts a database into a new database.

```
JetEngine.CompactDatabase(SourceConnection, DestConnection)
```

Parameter	Type	Description
SourceConnection	String	An ADO Connection string identifying the database that is to be compacted
DestConnection	String	An ADO Connection string identifying the new database that is to be created from the compaction

Using this method, you cannot compact in-place—that is, you cannot compact a database into itself. You must specify the database name and location of the new database to be created, or an error will be generated. For example:

```
objJE.CompactDatabase "Provider=Microsoft.Jet.OLEDB.4.0; " & _
                      "Data Source=C:\temp\pubs.mdb", _
                      "Provider=Microsoft.Jet.OLEDB.4.0; " & _
                      "Data Source=C:\temp\newpubs.mdb"
```

The connection string only allows a limited set of provider-specific properties; all other properties are ignored. The allowed properties are:

Property	Source	Destination
Provider	✔	✔
Data Source	✔	✔
User Id	✔	
Password	✔	
Locale Identifier		✔
Jet OLEDB:Database Password	✔	✔
Jet OLEDB:Engine Type	✔	✔
Jet OLEDB:Registry Path	✔	
Jet OLEDB:System Database	✔	
Jet OLEDB:Encrypt Database		✔
Jet OLEDB:Don't Copy Locale on Compact		✔
Jet OLEDB:Compact Without Relationships		✔
Jet OLEDB:Compact Without Replica Repair		✔

These properties are added to the connection string in the usual way. For example:

```
objJE.CompactDatabase "Provider=Microsoft.Jet.OLEDB.4.0; " & _
                      "Data Source=C:\temp\pubs.mdb; " & _
                      "User Id=davids; Password=abc123", _
                      "Provider=Microsoft.Jet.OLEDB.4.0; " & _
                      "Data Source=C:\temp\newpubs.mdb;" & _
                      "Jet OLEDB:Encrypt Database=True"
```

For more details on these properties, consult the ADO Properties collection in Appendix C.

The RefreshCache Method

RefreshCache allows you to force any pending writes to the database and refresh the memory with the latest data from the database.

```
JetEngine.RefreshCache(Connection)
```

Parameter	Type	Description
Connection	Connection	An open ADO Connection object for which the cache should be refreshed

In high multi-user applications, you can use this method to free memory locks.

13

Data Shaping

This chapter gives you a comprehensive look at Data Shaping. The Data Shape Provider originally shipped with ADO 2.0. It provides a way to arrange sets of related data hierarchically, and it provides an efficient way to transfer related sets of data from the server to a client. ADO 2.1 added some new features to the Data Shape Provider:

❑   **Hierarchy Reshaping** allows the creation of new hierarchies based upon existing data.

❑   **Grandchild Aggregates and Grouping** allows aggregation of the values of specific grandchildren in a hierarchy into a higher aggregation level.

❑   **Parameterized Computed Children** allows an aggregate level to be inserted between a parent and parameterized child.

Examples of these are shown later in the chapter.

The easiest way to understand data shaping is to use another term often employed: **hierarchical recordsets**. Think about all of those times that you've had master and detail recordsets; publishers and books are a good example. The easiest way to imagine this is to think of the Windows file system, where you have folders and subfolders. In data shaping terms, you have recordsets and subrecordsets.

Take a look at this diagram, which shows a shape I want to achieve (not its actual structure) involving publishers, titles, and sales from the SQL Server default pubs database:

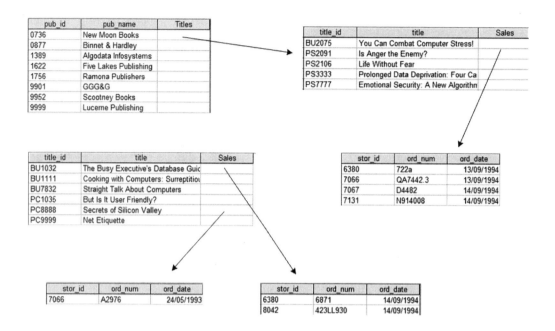

This could be created with the following SHAPE command:

```
SHAPE {SELECT * FROM publishers}
APPEND ((SHAPE {SELECT * FROM titles}
    APPEND ({SELECT * FROM sales}
    RELATE title_id TO title_id))
RELATE pub_id TO pub_id)
```

What this produces is a recordset for the publishers, with an extra column containing another recordset for titles. The Titles recordset also has an extra column for the Sales recordset. These child recordsets are often called **chapters**, and the data type of the column would be adChapter. In this example only three recordsets are created—one each for Sales, Titles, and Publishers. What the shaping service does is provide a way to map the relational structure of primary and foreign keys in a table with a parent-child relationship.

The child column actually contains the details that relate the parent to the child, and when you access the child column, the child recordset is filtered so only the correct rows are shown. So, creating the this sample hierarchy against SQL Server, you can see (using SQL Trace in SQL 6.5 or in SQL 7) three statements sent to the server:

```
select * from publishers
select * from titles
select * from sales
```

All these are sent in one command and returned as multiple recordsets. All of the data is sent back at once. The client has only three recordsets, so resource usage is kept to a minimum, although the amount of data could still be substantial.

The Data Shape Provider performs no optimization on the SQL statements sent to the server. For example, consider the following SHAPE command:

```
SHAPE {select * from publishers where state = 'ca'}
APPEND ({select * from titles}
RELATE pub_id TO pub_id)
```

This returns two recordsets, the first containing details of all publishers where the state is ca, and the second containing all titles. This isn't a joined query, so the titles query returns all titles, not just those for publishers in ca. The data shaping actually takes place on the client, and the actual Data Provider is just the supplier of data.

Child Data Caching

You can force the Data Shape Provider to query the data source for the child data each time a parent row is accessed. To do this, set the Cache Child Rows dynamic property to False:

```
objRs.Properties("Cache Child Rows") = False
```

Normally, this property is True, which tells the local cursor service to cache the child data. By setting it to False, you ensure that the cursor service re-queries the data provider for new information each time a parent row is accessed. This ensures that the data for the child is up-to-date, but it does impose a performance penalty, although the initial load might be quicker.

Child Recordsets

When you access a row in the parent recordset, the child recordset automatically reflects the values related to the parent. In fact, the child recordset is closed and reopened with the new values.

You can change this behavior so that when you move to a new record, the child recordset does not change. This behavior is controlled by the StayInSync property of the Recordset. Setting this to True (the default) keeps the child recordset synchronized with its parent. Setting it to False ensures that no synchronization takes place. For example:

```
objRs.StayInSync = False
```

One use of this is if you want to move around the parent recordset without the overhead of the child recordset being available.

Using Data Shaping

You must remember two important things if you want to use data shaping:

❑   You must use the MSDataShape provider. Your provider that supplies the data becomes the Data Provider.

❑   You must use a special Data Shape language, which is a superset of SQL.

If you've got Visual Basic 6, there's a really quick way to produce your shape commands by using the Data Environment Designer (select the **Project** menu and **Add Data Environment**). The Data Environment Designer can write your SHAPE commands for you, saving you from having to worry about the syntax, but it's worthwhile learning it anyway, especially if you are working in ASP and may not have Visual Basic installed. You'll see examples of the designer later in the chapter.

The Shape Language

The SHAPE command has its own formal grammar, which we won't list here (it's included in the ADO documentation that is installed when you install the Microsoft Data Access Components), but I'll go through the way you use this command. Your shape command will generally look something like this:

```
SHAPE {parent_command} [[AS] table_alias]
APPEND ({child_command} [[AS] child_table_alias]
        RELATE parent_column TO child_column) [[AS] column_name]
```

This defines the parent and the child, and how they relate. The parent_command and child_command are the statements that define the parent and child recordsets. In most cases these will be SQL statements, but they can be any command appropriate to the OLE DB Provider in use. You can happily omit the table_alias, but the column_name is extremely useful because it defines the name of the column containing the child recordset. Take the pubs database and show an example using publishers and titles:

```
SHAPE {SELECT * FROM publishers}
APPEND ({SELECT * FROM titles}
        RELATE pub_id TO pub_id) AS recTitles
```

So, the first line is the parent; this will be a list of publishers:

```
SHAPE {SELECT * FROM publishers}
```

For each publisher, you want a list of titles, so you APPEND a query that lists the titles:

```
APPEND ({SELECT * FROM titles}
```

Now you identify how the two commands are linked. This is the primary key in the parent table and the foreign key in the child table:

```
RELATE pub_id TO pub_id) AS recTitles
```

The alias used here is what the new column will be called. The Data Shape Provider creates this new column on the parent, and for each entry, this column contains a recordset of its own.

Here's a simple piece of VB code that creates a shape and navigates through the records in both the parent and the child (you'll need to change the connect string to point to your server for this):

```
Dim objConn      As ADODB.Connection
Dim objRs        As ADODB.Recordset
Dim objRsTitle   As ADODB.Recordset
Dim strShape     As String

Set objConn = New ADODB.Connection
Set objRs = New ADODB.Recordset

' use the data shape provider,
' with SQL Server as the source of the data
objConn.Provider = "MSDataShape"
objConn.Open "Data Provider=SQLOLEDB; Data Source=Tigger; " & _
             "Initial Catalog=pubs; User Id=sa; Password="

' define our shape string and open the recordset
strShape = "SHAPE {SELECT * FROM publishers}" & _
           " APPEND ({SELECT * FROM titles}" & _
           " RELATE pub_id TO pub_id) AS recTitles"
objRs.Open strShape, objConn

' loop through the parent records
While Not objRs.EOF
    Debug.Print objRs("pub_name")

    ' set the recordset for the child
    ' records and loop through them
    Set objRsTitle = objRs("recTitles").Value
    While Not objRsTitle.EOF
        Debug.Print vbTab; objRsTitle("title")
        objRsTitle.MoveNext
    Wend
    objRs.MoveNext
Wend

objRs.Close
objConn.Close
Set objRs = Nothing
Set objConn = Nothing
Set objRsTitle = Nothing
```

The first thing to notice is that the `Data Provider` is set to the name of the OLE DB Provider that actually supplies the data, and we set the `Provider` property to `MSDataShape`. So the actual OLE DB Provider is `MSDataShape`; its job is to get the data from somewhere else and shape it. This means we have to tell the Data Shape Provider where we want the actual data to come from; here this is accomplished through the `Data Provider` part of the connection string. This means that the Data Shape Provider can take data from any OLE DB provider.

The `SHAPE` command becomes the source of our recordset, and you can loop through this as normal. Notice that I use a second recordset to point to the child recordset, which is stored as a column in the first recordset. The `Value` of this column is the child recordset. This produces the following output:

New Moon Books
   You Can Combat Computer Stress!
   Is Anger the Enemy?
   Life Without Fear
   Prolonged Data Deprivation: Four Case Studies
   Emotional Security: A New Algorithm
Binnet & Hardley
   Silicon Valley Gastronomic Treats
   The Gourmet Microwave
   The Psychology of Computer Cooking
   Computer Phobic AND Non-Phobic Individuals: Behavior Variations
   Onions, Leeks, and Garlic: Cooking Secrets of the Mediterranean
   Fifty Years in Buckingham Palace Kitchens
   Sushi, Anyone?
Algodata Infosystems
   The Busy Executive's Database Guide
   Cooking with Computers: Surreptitious Balance Sheets
   Straight Talk About Computers
   But Is It User Friendly?
   Secrets of Silicon Valley
   Net Etiquette
Five Lakes Publishing
Ramona Publishers
GGG&G
Scootney Books
Lucerne Publishing

Notice that some records don't have child records. In such cases, an empty recordset is created.

You don't have to assign a different variable to hold the child recordset to a `Recordset` object if you don't want to. Instead, you can access the child recordset directly:

```
objRs("recTitles").Value.Fields("title")
```

Multiple Children

The preceding example uses publishers and titles, but a parent recordset is not restricted to only one child recordset. For example, the publishers also have employees, and you may wish to include this information in the data schema:

```
SHAPE {SELECT * FROM publishers}
APPEND ({SELECT * FROM titles}
        RELATE pub_id TO pub_id) AS rsTitles,
       ({SELECT * FROM employee}
        RELATE pub_id TO pub_id) AS rsEmployees
```

This follows the same rules as the preceding example, but I am appending two commands. The parent is publishers, to which you can APPEND two select queries (separated by a comma), giving them the names rsTitles and rsEmployees. The syntax for these is the same, indicating the relationship of the parent to the child:

```
SHAPE {parent_command} [[AS] table_alias]
APPEND ({child_command_1} [[AS] child_table_1_alias]
   RELATE parent_column TO child_column_1) [[AS] column_name_1],
        {child_command_2} [[AS] child_table_2_alias]
   RELATE parent_column TO child_column_2) [[AS] column_name_2]
```

The recordset would now have two extra columns representing child recordsets, which you could use in the same way as in the previous Visual Basic example where I looped through the records. Access to the child recordsets would be as follows:

```
Set objRsTitles = objRs("rsTitles").Value
Set objRsEmps = objRs("rsEmployees").Value
```

Grandchildren

Data shaping doesn't have to be limited to sets of data one level deep. Each child record can have its own children, thus allowing you to nest to arbitrary depths. For example, suppose you wanted to add the sales for each title, showing the date purchased and the number sold. The SHAPE command now becomes:

```
SHAPE {SELECT * FROM publishers}
APPEND (( SHAPE {SELECT * FROM titles}
    APPEND ({SELECT * FROM sales}
    RELATE title_id TO title_id) AS rsSales)
RELATE pub_id TO pub_id) AS rsTitles
```

This just adds another APPEND and RELATE command to relate the new child table to its parent. So now you could change your code accordingly. Add a new variable declaration:

```
Dim objRsSales As ADODB.Recordset
```

And then add the loop to print the sales:

```
Set objRsTitle = objRs("rsTitles").Value
While Not objRsTitle.EOF
    Debug.Print vbTab; objRsTitle("title")
    Set objRsSales = objRsTitle("rsSales").Value
    While Not objRsSales.EOF
        Debug.Print vbTab; vbTab; objRsSales("ord_date");
                            vbTab; objRsSales("qty")
        objRsSales.MoveNext
    Wend
    objRsTitle.MoveNext
Wend
```

What you now see is this:

Binnet & Hardley
   Silicon Valley Gastronomic Treats
      12/12/93   10
   The Gourmet Microwave
        14/09/94   25
      14/09/94   15
   The Psychology of Computer Cooking
   Computer Phobic AND Non-Phobic Individuals: Behavior Variations
      29/05/93   20
   Onions, Leeks, and Garlic: Cooking Secrets of the Mediterranean
      15/06/92   40

The SQL statement is not limited to just SELECT *, and you can use almost any SQL statement you like. The only restriction is that you must have matching columns in the parent and child SELECTs, but this is not different from a normal SQL join or subquery.

Summarizing with Shapes

The Data Shape language also has a way to produce summary information, allowing your parent to hold summary details, and the children hold the individual details. This is really useful for those drill-down situations in management information systems where you show a total, and then can drill down into the details. For example, imagine that you wanted to find out the total sales of each book subject area, and be able to see the sales for individual titles.

For this type of Data Shape, you must use a different form of the shaping language:

```
SHAPE {child_command} [[AS] table_alias]
COMPUTE aggregate_field_list
BY group_field_list
```

For example, you could construct a shape command like this:

```
SHAPE {SELECT * FROM titles}  AS rsTitlesSales
COMPUTE TitlesSales, SUM(TitlesSales.ytd_sales) AS NumberSold
BY type
```

The first line is familiar; you are creating a shape, and it is to be called `rsTitlesSales`. You want to sum the `ytd_sales` column of this shape, grouping on the `type` column. Your parent recordset will contain three columns:

- ❏ `type`, the column we grouped on

- ❏ `NumberSold`, the column we summed

- ❏ `rsTitlesSales`, the child recordset

The child recordset contains the SQL statement from the first line and, as a result of this, everything in the `titles` table.

You could access the result with code like this:

```
While Not objRs.EOF
    Debug.Print objRs("type"); vbTab; objRs("NumberSold")

    Set objRsSales = objRs("rsTitlesSales").Value
    While Not objRsSales.EOF
        Debug.Print vbTab; objRsSales("title"); _
                    vbTab; objRsSales("ytd_sales")
        objRsSales.MoveNext
    Wend
    objRs.MoveNext
Wend
```

And the results it produces would be like this:

```
business    30788
   The Busy Executive's Database Guide   4095
   Cooking with Computers: Surreptitious Balance Sheets   3876
   You Can Combat Computer Stress!   18722
   Straight Talk About Computers   4095
mod_cook    24278
   Silicon Valley Gastronomic Treats   2032
   The Gourmet Microwave   22246
```

Stored Procedures

In addition to using SELECT queries in your shape commands, you can also use stored procedures. For example, imagine two stored procedures:

```
CREATE PROCEDURE usp_AllPublishers
AS
    SELECT *
    FROM    publishers
```

and:

```
CREATE PROCEDURE usp_TitlesByPubID
    @PubID char(4)
AS
    SELECT *
    FROM    titles
    WHERE   pub_id = @PubID
```

The first just returns all publishers, and the second returns all titles for a given publisher. You could create a shape command to use these two as follows:

```
SHAPE {{CALL dbo.usp_AllPublishers }}
APPEND ({{CALL dbo.usp_TitlesByPubID( ?) }}
RELATE pub_id TO  PARAMETER 0) AS rsTitlesByPubID
```

Notice that instead of the SELECT commands used in previous examples, there is now a call to the stored procedures; the statement is passed directly through to the OLE DB Provider (SQL Server in this case), and therefore uses the appropriate provider syntax. The stored procedure for the child takes a parameter. Because the parameter is to be filled in by the parent, we RELATE the pub_id field to the parameter–the foreign key of the child. The shape command processor automatically takes care of filling in this parameter for each child recordset. Although this might look good, be aware that this can have a detrimental effect on performance, because the child stored procedure is executed each time it is referenced. If you have stored procedures that are children, all parameters must participate in the relationship.

If you wanted the parent stored procedure to accept an argument, such as the country, then it could be written like this:

```
CREATE PROCEDURE usp_PublishersByCountry
    @Country varchar(30)
AS
    SELECT *
    FROM    publishers
    WHERE   country = @Country
```

The shape command would now become:

```
SHAPE {{CALL dbo.usp_PublishersByCountry( ?) }}
APPEND ({{CALL dbo.usp_TitlesByPubID( ?) }}
RELATE pub_id TO  PARAMETER 0) AS rsTitlesByPubID
```

You can pass a parameter into this command in three ways. The first is to add it in manually:

```
SHAPE {{CALL dbo.usp_PublishersByCountry('USA') }}
APPEND ({{CALL dbo.usp_TitlesByPubID( ?) }}
RELATE pub_id TO  PARAMETER 0) AS rsTitlesByPubID
```

The second is to create a `Command` object and use the `Parameters` collection:

```
strShape = "SHAPE {{CALL dbo.usp_PublishersByCountry(?) }}" & _
           "APPEND ({{CALL dbo.usp_TitlesByPubID(?) }}" & _
           "RELATE pub_id TO PARAMETER 0) AS rsTitlesByPubID "

objCmd.CommandText = strShape
objCmd.Parameters.Append objCmd.CreateParameter("@Country", _
                            adVarChar, adParamInput, 30, "USA")
Set objCmd.ActiveConnection = objConn
Set objRs = objCmd.Execute
```

The third is again to use a `Command` object, but this time pass the parameter into the `Execute` method:

```
objCmd.CommandText = strShape
Set objRs = objCmd.Execute  (, Array("USA"))
```

You can pass in multiple parameters by using any of these methods.

Parameter-Based Shapes

When using a parameter-based hierarchy, the data is not fetched all at once when the command is executed. When the parent row is accessed, the parameter query is executed with the parameter details from the parent. This data is then cached locally. This means that there will be a trip back to the server to fetch data the first time a new row is accessed. However, this approach can be much more efficient if the user is interested in only a subset of parent rows, because only the required child rows will be fetched. This contrasts with a nonparameter-based shape where all of the child rows are fetched.

You can change this behavior by setting the `Cache Child Rows` dynamic property, as discussed earlier.

Updating Shaped Recordsets

Using data shaping doesn't mean that your recordsets behave any differently from normal recordsets. Assuming that your recordset allows updating, then you can treat shaped recordsets as you would normally: adding, updating, and deleting records. For example:

```
Set objRsTitles = objRs("titles").Value
objRsTitles("qty") = objRsTitles("qty") + 1
objRsTitles.Update
```

This sets a variable, objRsTitles, to point to the child recordset, then updates a value. Changing the relating field in the parent recordset means that the child recordset will become orphaned. Likewise, changing the relating field in the child recordset will stop it being related to its previous parent, and it may end up being related to a different parent.

Data Shaping in Visual Basic 6

Now that you've seen the hard way to create shape commands, you won't be surprised to find that Visual Basic 6 has a quick way to do this through its Data Environment Designer. To create a Data Shape command, you first add a command to the Data Environment. I created a connection to the pubs database, then added a command pointing to the publishers table. You can do this by selecting the connection, right-clicking the mouse, selecting **Add Command**, and adding the command details. You'll have to enter SQL query details via the **General** tab of the **Properties...** of the command. The following diagram shows the Data Environment Designer once a command (called publishers) has been added:

Then you add a child command (right-click on the existing publishers command). In this case we'll write a command to query the titles table. With child commands, you must specify the relationship (after adding the SQL query details into the **General** tab's **SQL Statement** box), as shown here:

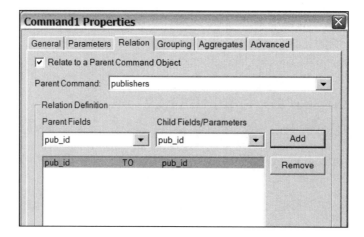

Once the child command has been added, you'll see it appear under its parent, as shown here:

If you then right-click on the parent, you can pick Hierarchy Info... from the menu to see the SHAPE command, as shown here:

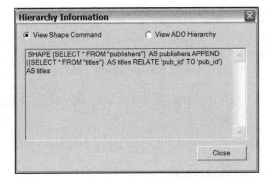

Another great thing about Visual Basic 6 is that it has a grid, the Hierarchical FlexGrid, which binds directly to hierarchical recordsets, allowing you to drill down to the child data, as shown here:

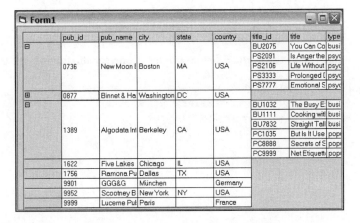

Why Data Shaping?

All of this might seem very smart, but what's the real use, especially when you can achieve the same result by joining the tables? Well, imagine a parent recordset that has 100 rows and 10 columns. It has a child recordset containing 10 rows per parent row. Now look at a normal SQL join:

```
SELECT * FROM parent INNER JOIN child
ON parent.id = child.id
```

For each row on the *many* side, there will also be a row containing 10 columns from the *one* side. Those 10 columns from the *one* side will be the same for each of the 10 rows on the *many* side. That's an awful lot of wasted network traffic and data handling.

If you use data shaping, then the parent row is included only once, so instead of 1,000 rows containing the parent data, you have only 100. You still have 1,000 rows of child data, but the parent data is not repeated. Overall, it's smaller, easier to manage, and produces less network traffic when marshaled as a disconnected recordset. However, you should be aware of the way that data shaping actually works.

When you create a simple relation (for example, the relation between `publishers` and `titles`), both tables will be fetched before the hierarchy is created. A new field (a pointer to the child recordset) is added to the parent recordset, and when the child is referenced, a filter is applied to the child recordset. This means that all child recordsets are fetched in advance; so, if the child recordsets are large, you might find that this is slower than a normally joined recordset, and may lead to more network congestion. The only way around this is to use a parameterized child recordset, where the child rows are fetched only when accessed.

Reshaping Hierarchies

Reshaping allows you to reuse existing recordsets held by the shape provider, allowing them to become children of new `SHAPE` commands. If the new `SHAPE` command doesn't require new data from the original data provider, the shaping is performed entirely within the shape provider on the client; otherwise, the data is fetched from the provider. This reshaping allows you write applications that allow users to manipulate data without the necessity of fetching it again.

The easiest way to understand this is via a few examples. Consider the following `SHAPE` command:

```
SHAPE {SELECT * FROM titles} AS rsTitles
      APPEND ({SELECT * FROM sales} AS rsSales
            RELATE title_id TO title_id)
```

This will give the standard shape structure shown here:

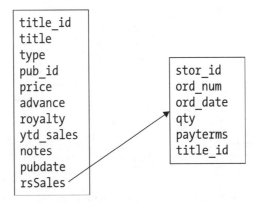

Here I have a recordset containing the details from the `titles` table. The last column, `rsSales`, is a chapter column containing the recordset of the `sales` table.

A new recordset can be created by using a new `SHAPE` command:

```
SHAPE rsSales
        COMPUTE rsSales, SUM(rsSales.qty) AS Sum_qty1 BY stor_id
```

This creates a reshaped structure with a summary in the parent, as shown here:

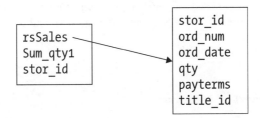

The existing `rsSales` recordset is reshaped, with a new parent being added, which contains summary details of the sales quantity. The original recordset is unchanged by this new shape.

Another parent addition could be:

```
SHAPE {SELECT * FROM publishers}
        APPEND (rsTitles RELATE pub_id TO pub_id)
```

This creates a new shape using the publishers as the top level and appending the already existing shape `rsTitles` to it:

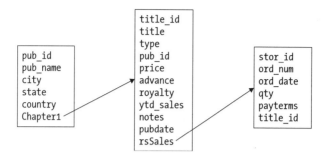

Notice that the APPENDed chapter has been given the default name of `Chapter1`. This is because in the preceding code fragment, I didn't use the AS clause to assign a specific name to `rsTitles`.

You can also use reshaping to gain access to all the records in a child recordset. For example, consider this shape command:

```
SHAPE {SELECT * FROM titles} as rsTitles
       APPEND (({SELECT * FROM sales} AS rsSales
              RELATE title_id TO title_id)
```

When you access the child recordset, you only ever see the records related to the parent. However, you know that two recordsets exist—one for the parent and one for the child—and that it's just filtering that takes place to show the correct records. Because reshaping allows access to recordsets without requerying the data provider, you can use the following SHAPE command to access the complete set of records for the child:

```
SHAPE rsSales
```

This would give you a recordset of all sales items.

Limitations

Reshaping allows quite a lot of flexibility, but it has some limitations:

❑   You cannot APPEND new columns to an existing shaped recordset.

❑   You cannot reshape parameterized recordsets.

Usage

The actual commands to reshape are no different from those used to create an initial shape. For example, consider the following Visual Basic code:

```
        objConn.Open strConn

        strShape = "SHAPE {SELECT * FROM titles} as rsTitles" & _
                   "APPEND ({SELECT * FROM sales} AS rsSales" & _
                   "RELATE title_id TO title_id)"

        objRs.Open strShape, objConn

        objRs1.Open "SHAPE rsSales " & _
                    "COMPUTE rsSales, SUM(rsSales.qty) BY stor_id", objConn

        objRs2.Open "SHAPE {select * from publishers} " & _
                    "APPEND (rsTitles RELATE pub_id TO pub_id)", objConn
```

Once the original recordset has been opened, the Data Shape Provider caches the shape details, and they then become available for use in reshaping, unless the recordset is closed.

Grandchild Aggregates

When using aggregation to produce summary values, you are not limited to just one level, and you can aggregate multiple levels down by including the full object hierarchy. For example, imagine you wanted to list the quantity of books sold, broken down by publisher, store, and book. Something like this:

New Moon Books	208
You Can Combat Computer Stress!	35
Fricative Bookshop	35
Is Anger the Enemy?	108
Eric the Read Books	3
Barnum's	75
News & Brews	10
Doc-U-Mat: Quality Laundry and Books	20
Life Without Fear	25
Doc-U-Mat: Quality Laundry and Books	25
Prolonged Data Deprivation: Four Case Studies	15
Doc-U-Mat: Quality Laundry and Books	15
Emotional Security: A New Algorithm	25
Doc-U-Mat: Quality Laundry and Books	25
Binnet & Hardley	150
Silicon Valley Gastronomic Treats	10
Fricative Bookshop	10
The Gourmet Microwave	40
Doc-U-Mat: Quality Laundry and Books	25

So, what you need is a structure like the one in this diagram:

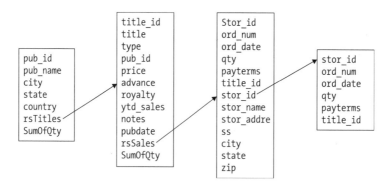

If the quantity sold is only held at the bottom level, then you need to be able to sum this value from the parent and the grandparent. Here's the SHAPE command:

```
SHAPE {SELECT * FROM publishers}
    APPEND ((SHAPE {SELECT * FROM titles}
        APPEND ({SELECT * FROM sales INNER JOIN
                    stores on sales.stor_id = stores.stor_id}
        RELATE title_id TO title_id) AS rsSales, SUM(rsSales.qty)
                AS SumOfQty)
        RELATE pub_id TO pub_id) AS rsTitles, SUM(rsTitles.rsSales.qty)
                As SumOfQty
```

The SUM statement at the bottom applies to the parent, so it includes the names for both the child and the grandchild. You can produce the table of data with the following Visual Basic code:

```
objRsPubs.Open strShape, objConn

While Not objRsPubs.EOF
    Debug.Print objRsPubs("pub_name")& "~~~" & objRsPubs("SumOfQty")
    Set objRsTitles = objRsPubs("rsTitles").Value
    While Not objRsTitles.EOF
        Debug.Print "~" & objRsTitles("title") & _
                    "~~" & objRsTitles("SumOfQty")
        Set objRsStoreSales = objRsTitles("rsSales").Value
        While Not objRsStoreSales.EOF
            Debug.Print "~~" & objRsStoreSales("stor_name") & _
                        "~" & objRsStoreSales("qty")
            objRsStoreSales.MoveNext
        Wend
        objRsTitles.MoveNext
    Wend
    objRsPubs.MoveNext
Wend
```

I've used the tilde symbol (~) to separate the columns being produced; this makes it easy to convert into a Word table.

Parameterized Computed Children

If a SHAPE command has a child based on a parameterized stored procedure, there's no reason why you can't have an intermediate table to perform grouping on certain values in the procedure. For example, imagine you want to show the book titles grouped by book type and by publisher. Something like this:

```
New Moon Books
        business
                You Can Combat Computer Stress!
        psychology
                Is Anger the Enemy?
                Life Without Fear
                Prolonged Data Deprivation: Four Case Studies
                Emotional Security: A New Algorithm
Binnet & Hardley
        mod_cook
                Silicon Valley Gastronomic Treats
                The Gourmet Microwave
        psychology
                Computer Phobic AND Non-Phobic Individuals: Behavior Variations
        trad_cook
                Onions, Leeks, and Garlic: Cooking Secrets of the Mediterranean
                Fifty Years in Buckingham Palace Kitchens
                Sushi, Anyone?
```

The code used to produce this is similar to the parent/child/grandchild example shown earlier.

This diagram shows the structure that will give this analysis:

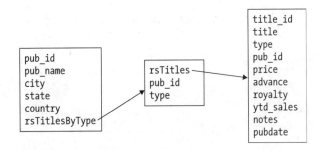

This is easy to do with three SQL commands, but suppose you want to use a parameterized query for the book titles so that you always see the latest data? Here's the SHAPE command:

```
SHAPE {{CALL usp_PublishersByCountry(?)}}
    APPEND ((SHAPE {{CALL usp_TitlesByPubID(?)}} AS rsTitles
        COMPUTE rsTitles By pub_id, type)
        RELATE pub_id TO PARAMETER 0) AS rsTitlesByType
```

The advantage of using a COMPUTE statement for the book types is that the COMPUTE is based upon the child. Because the child is a parameterized query, it always shows the latest data–therefore, so does the COMPUTE. If a new book is added with a new book type, this is automatically reflected by the COMPUTE.

Creating New Shapes

The shape language allows you to create shaped recordsets that are not bound to a data provider. This is useful if you want to create a local store of complex, structured data, perhaps to replace collections.

To create a new shape, you must set the Data Provider option in the connection string to none:

```
Provider=MSDataShape; Data Provider=none
```

You can then construct your recordset in the SHAPE command:

```
SHAPE APPEND
    NEW adChar(4) AS pub_id,
    NEW adVarChar(40) AS pub_name,
    NEW adVarChar(20) AS city,
    NEW adChar(2)      AS state,
    NEW adVarChar(30) AS country,
    ((SHAPE APPEND
        NEW adVarChar(6)  AS title_id,
        NEW adVarChar(80) AS title,
        NEW adCurrency    AS price,
        NEW adChar(4)     AS pub_id)
    RELATE pub_id TO pub_id) AS rsTitles
```

You can then open the recordset and add records. Here's an example in Visual Basic:

```
' open the new shape
objRs.Open strShape, "Provider=MSDataShape; Data Provider=none", _
                adOpenStatic, adLockOptimistic

' add some records
With objRs
    .AddNew
    .Fields("pub_id") = "1234"
    .Fields("pub_name") = "APress"
    .Fields("city") = "Berkeley"
    .Fields("state") = "CA"
    .Fields("country") = "USA"
    .Update
End With

' now some children
Set objRsT = objRs("rsTitles").Value
With objRsT
    .AddNew
    .Fields("title_id") = "0288"
```

```
        .Fields("title") = "ADO Prog Ref"
        .Fields("price") = 29.99
        .Update
        .AddNew
        .Fields("title_id") = "2182"
        .Fields("title") = "A Programmer's Guide To SQL"
        .Fields("price") = 49.99
        .Update
    End With
```

Once created, the shaped recordset behaves exactly like a shaped recordset created from a data provider.

Dynamic Properties

The shape provider now has some new dynamic properties to help with the shape service. These apply to the `Recordset` and are set by using the dynamic `Properties` collection:

```
    objRs.Properties("property_name") = value
```

The Name Property

The `Name` property is a read-only property that identifies the name of the `Recordset` in a shape. The recordset name is generally defined by the `AS` keyword in the shape language; if this is omitted, the shape provider will generate a name for you. For example, the following code fragment has a parent recordset named `rsTitles` and a child recordset named `rsSales`:

```
    SHAPE {SELECT * FROM titles} AS rsTitles
        APPEND ({SELECT * FROM sales} AS rsSales
                RELATE title_id TO title_id)
```

The Unique Reshape Names Property

The `Unique Reshape Names` property specifies whether unique values for the name are generated. For example, a `SHAPE` command that assigned the same name (using the `AS` keyword) to two different recordsets can be forced to be unique by setting this property to `True`.

14

Performance

This chapter looks at one of the most critical issues for all data store programmers: **performance**. Microsoft has stated that one of its goals for ADO was to achieve the best performance possible. However, during testing and through its various versions, the newsgroups have contained several messages regarding poor performance. What I plan to do here is show you whether those criticisms were justified.

Most of the performance statistics were generated using a Test Tool built especially for this purpose in Visual Basic 6. The source code for this tool is available from the Apress Web site (http://support.apress.com), along with a test Access database, some SQL Scripts for creating the test database in SQL Server, and an Access database for logging the results.

This tool is provided as-is, with no warranty of its fitness for purpose. You can use it as you find it, or extend it in your own environment. For obvious reasons, I can't guarantee the same results on your systems. At the end of this chapter you'll see how this tool works, but we won't cover it in depth. Its sole purpose is to run various queries under different conditions, and to time them. Not all tests were carried out using this tool, and I created several tools just for testing purposes; some of these are also available on the Web site.

The tests were primarily run on a Dell Dimension 8100, Pentium 4 1.8MHz, with 512MB memory and 2 IDE disks in RAID 1 format, running Windows XP Professional. I tested Access 2000 and SQL Server 2000 database, both of which were on the same machine.

All tests were run on this single machine, so those involving client cursors don't have the added network lag to contend with. Although this is less realistic, it ensures that only the difference between cursor types (and not the network) is tested. This is important because network traffic can vary widely from situation to situation, and it's unlikely that my machines–6 of them–would ever give any kind of useful indication. It would therefore be wrong for me to say "these timings take into account network usage" when this is quite clearly not the case. So, when running the tests yourself, make sure you allow for this.

One further thing to note is that ADO and the data stores were not under any stress here. The tests were performed in a single-user environment, and you may experience different results if your server and data store are being used heavily. The tests were run 10 times and the results averaged to take account of cached data. The standard deviations were generally very small.

For the majority of tests, the following table was used:

Column	Type	Length
KeyCol	int (IDENTITY)	
Description	varchar	(50)
ForeignKey	int	
TextField	varchar	(10)
CurrencyField	money	
BitField	bit	

There were several copies of this table, all with varying amounts of dummy data. When testing ADO, you should use your own tables and data to get a more accurate picture.

I've tried to explain why some of the tests give the results that they do—although in some cases this is not possible simply because I don't know what OLE DB and the providers are actually doing underneath. It would be nice to have these details explained, but as ADO programmers, it's not really necessary. As long as we know which mechanisms to use to give us best performance, and we have a way of testing that, we should be relatively happy.

Cursor Type, Location, and Locking

Here are three questions often asked by beginners and experienced users alike:

❑ What's the best cursor type to use?

❑ Should I use server-side or client-side cursors?

❑ What locking scheme should I use?

Like many design questions, the answer is always the same: it depends. The cursor type and location that you choose will affect not only performance, but also the functionality. So, although in some cases it's easy to establish a particular cursor type as the fastest, it may not be the type that best suits your particular business needs.

The OLE DB Provider for Jet

The following charts show the results from opening and closing a table by using the OLE DB Provider for Access. The code used for this test is simple:

```
objRs.Open "table_name", objConn
objRs.Close
```

We timed only this fragment of the code, adding the various locking modes and cursor types to the `Open` command. This was run 10 times (that is, I performed the `Open`/`Close` combination 10 times), and I averaged the times. I took an average in this way in all of the tests performed to ensure that the first run didn't distort the results because of data not being cached. However, bear in mind that many applications perform a single table access and may not "hit" that table again. This is another reason why you need to perform testing in your own application situations.

Times are given in milliseconds.

Server-Side Cursors

This graph was produced by using server-side cursors, with a table holding 100 rows.

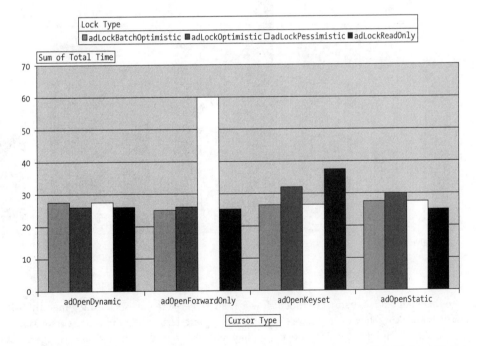

You might wonder why there is so little difference between the cursor types. Recall that when you use server-side cursors, Access supports only keyset cursors (unless you specify a read-only recordset). So if you are locking your recordset, Access will always return a keyset cursor—no matter what cursor type you request. Oddly, a forward-only Recordset with pessimistic locking is twice as slow as other lock types; I can only assume that it's something to do with the pessimistic locking mechanism that's unique to forward movement.

You might also expect that larger tables would have an impact, but the times are almost exactly the same, even for a table of the same type with 100,000 records! The lack of difference in speed when using larger tables is because, if you are using server-side cursors, only the first batch of data is read into the recordset. Consequently, it doesn't matter how many records there are when you open the table. And that's an important point. This test is essentially just opening and closing the table without reading any data in.

Client-Side Cursors

The following graph shows the speed using client-side cursors, with the test table holding 100 rows.

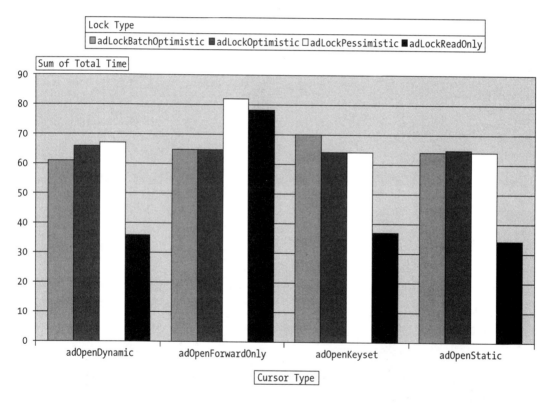

You can see that client-side cursors are much slower than server-side cursors, being generally twice as slow. Relatively speaking, however, cursors with no locking are faster than the other cursor types. Client-side cursors are inherently slower because they actually copy the entire data set (regardless of its size) into a cache on the local machine, using the memory and disk space if necessary. This is why they are named client-side cursors; the cursor facility is located in the central OLE DB handler rather than being provided by the data store.

Comparing locking cursors, you can see that the read-only cursor is faster than the other two locking types (optimistic and pessimistic), and between the latter two, there is very little difference. The graphs also suggest that there's little difference between the cursor types. You might wonder at this, but note that when locking is required, the OLE DB Provider for Jet supports only static cursors. Therefore, whatever cursor type you request, you'll always get a static cursor back. In fact, a static cursor is the only cursor type that really makes sense when dealing with client-side cursors. The `Errors` collection of the `Connection` object may well have a warning indicating that the cursor type is different from that requested, although this will depend upon the provider.

The reasons for the time differences between read-only and updateable locking should be fairly clear. With read-only cursors, Jet can stream out the data without having to keep track of the records, because it knows that no changes will ever take place. Obviously, this is going to be faster than trying to keep track of the changes. For updateable cursors, the cursor type must be changed–but this fact can be ignored, because you can see that for a static cursor, the timings are approximately the same.

Have a look at the same test over a table with 1,000 rows:

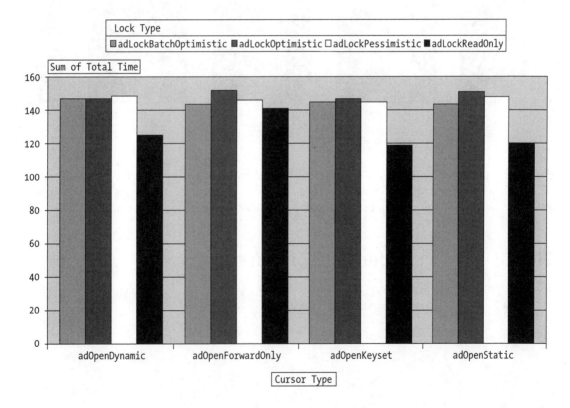

Again, not much difference between the locking types, but the difference in speed between read-only access and read/write access is not as marked as before. The overall times have increased, reflecting that much more data is being pushed to the client, as compared to the server-side cursors, where there was little difference.

With 50,000 records, the result looks like this:

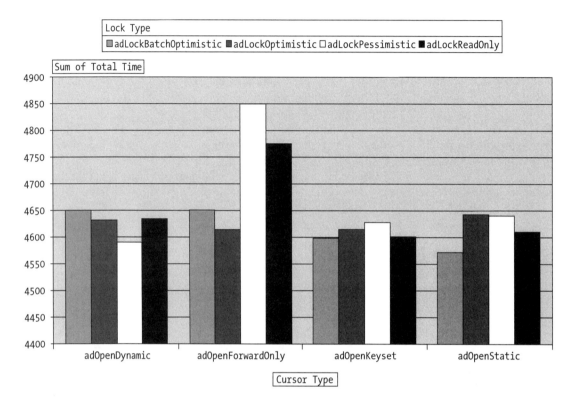

Now we see some more interesting results, with a much greater variation between the various cursor types and locking mechanisms. I've no explanation for this difference, especially because Jet really is using only one cursor type. Again, the average times have increased to reflect the amount of data.

The OLE DB Provider for SQL Server

The same tests for SQL Server show remarkably different results. Again, these are comprised of opening and closing a recordset 10 times, then taking the average figure.

Server-Side Cursors

SQL Server provides full support for server-side cursors.

The following graph shows the results for a table of 100 rows on SQL 2000.

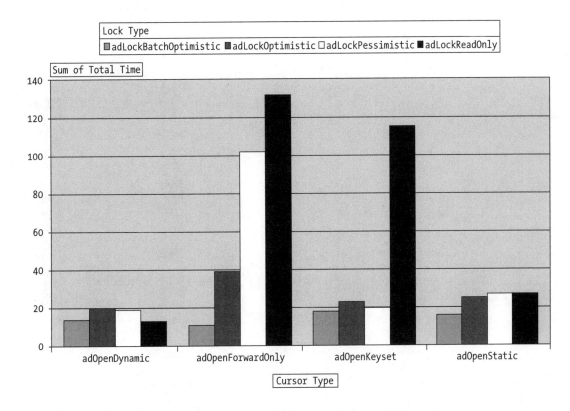

An issue with SQL Server 6.5 (not shown in the graph) is that there was a dramatic improvement in performance when using dynamic and forward-only cursors rather than keyset and static cursors. The reason for this is simple: In SQL Server 6.5, both keyset and static cursors require a copy of the data to be put into SQL Server's temporary database (tempdb) before the cursor is created. In fact, a keyset cursor puts only the keys and the first buffer full of data into temporary storage. SQL Server 7.0 and SQL Server 2000 don't appear to suffer from this problem, except with read-only cursors. However, any relative difference between cursor types on the same version indicates a difference in how the cursor type is handled.

You can see how this has a marked effect as the number of rows increases. For a table with 1,000 rows, the change is significant:

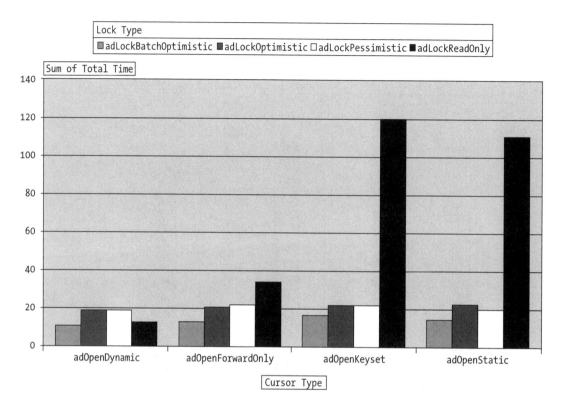

The difference between keyset and static forward-only cursors, and other cursor combinations is now obvious.

Client-Side Cursors

So how does this compare with client-side cursors, given that all the client-side cursor types were slower in Jet? For the initial test of 100 rows, I got the results shown here:

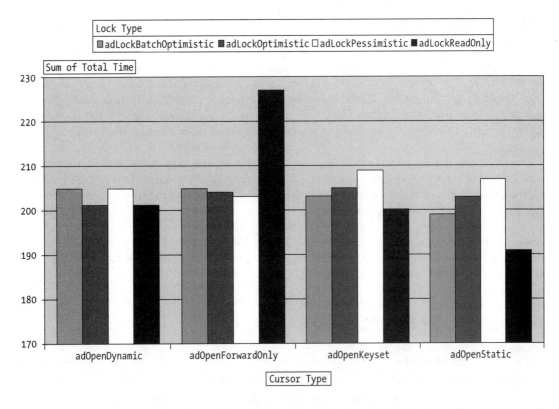

These seem to bear out what we know about client cursors; they are slower because all the data is read into the client. Overall, the performance is close for all cursor types and lock types, and this remains true as I scaled the table up to 50,000 rows. On the other hand, the overall speed is slower than server-based dynamic and forward-only cursors (as expected), because all the data is returned to the client.

> *If you want to learn more about SQL Server cursor types and how they are used, the best description by far appears in Microsoft Press's Inside Microsoft SQL Server 2000 (ISBN 0735609985). In fact, this book is full of extremely useful information for the SQL Server developer.*

The OLE DB Provider for ODBC

For ODBC, the tests show similar results for the cursor types, locations, and locking mechanisms. I'll be contrasting the OLE DB Provider for ODBC against the native driver later in this chapter.

Cursor Summary

Despite the figures you've seen so far, it's not always possible to use the faster method, because it may not meet your needs. For example, although server-side cursors are quicker to open, they don't always provide the same functionality that client-side cursors do, and cannot be used if you need to disconnect your recordsets. In the n-tier world of client-server development, you may well be using disconnected recordsets to pass data between the various tiers in your application, so you'll have to use client cursors. If this is the case, then you want to minimize the amount of data being passed around.

With locking, you can see that in most cases read-only mode is faster, as you would expect. Use this to your advantage if you are just providing data-browsing capabilities. If you need both browsing and editing in your application, it's worth considering using read-only cursors for browsing, then opening another recordset with a writable cursor for editing.

You've seen that in some cases the cursor type you get is not necessarily the one you requested; this depends upon the provider, the cursor location, and the locking mechanism used. The following tables describe the cursor type that you receive according to these conditions.

OLE DB Provider for SQL Server

adUseServer (Indexed Table)

Lock Type	Cursor Type Requested			
	Forward-Only	Keyset	Dynamic	Static
Read-Only	Forward-Only	Keyset	Dynamic	Static
Pessimistic	Forward-Only	Keyset	Dynamic	Keyset
Optimistic	Forward-Only	Keyset	Dynamic	Keyset
Batch Optimistic	Forward-Only	Keyset	Dynamic	Keyset

adUseServer (Non-Indexed Table)

Lock Type	Cursor Type Requested			
	Forward-Only	Keyset	Dynamic	Static
Read-Only	Forward-Only	Static	Dynamic	Static
Pessimistic	Forward-Only	Dynamic	Dynamic	Keyset
Optimistic	Forward-Only	Dynamic	Dynamic	Keyset
Batch Optimistic	Forward-Only	Dynamic	Dynamic	Keyset

adUseClient

Lock	Type Cursor Type Requested			
	Forward-Only	**Keyset**	**Dynamic**	**Static**
Read-Only	Static	Static	Static	Static
Pessimistic	Static	Static	Static	Static
Optimistic	Static	Static	Static	Static
Batch Optimistic	Static	Static	Static	Static

OLE DB Provider for Jet

adUseServer

Lock Type	Cursor Type Requested			
	Forward-Only	**Keyset**	**Dynamic**	**Static**
Read-Only	Forward-Only	Keyset	Static	Static
Pessimistic	Keyset	Keyset	Keyset	Keyset
Optimistic	Keyset	Keyset	Keyset	Keyset
Batch Optimistic	Keyset	Keyset	Keyset	Keyset

adUseClient

Lock Type	Cursor Type Requested			
	Forward-Only	**Keyset**	**Dynamic**	**Static**
Read-Only	Static	Static	Static	Static
Pessimistic	Static	Static	Static	Static
Optimistic	Static	Static	Static	Static
Batch Optimistic	Static	Static	Static	Static

OLE DB Provider for ODBC with SQL Server

adUseServer (Indexed Table)

Lock Type	Cursor Type Requested			
	Forward-Only	**Keyset**	**Dynamic**	**Static**
Read-Only	Forward-Only	Keyset	Dynamic	Static
Pessimistic	Forward-Only	Keyset	Dynamic	Keyset
Optimistic	Forward-Only	Keyset	Dynamic	Keyset
Batch Optimistic	Forward-Only	Keyset	Dynamic	Keyset

adUseServer (Non-Indexed Table)

Lock Type	Cursor Type Requested			
	Forward-Only	**Keyset**	**Dynamic**	**Static**
Read-Only	Forward-Only	Static	Dynamic	Static
Pessimistic	Forward-Only	Static	Dynamic	Static
Optimistic	Forward-Only	Static	Dynamic	Static
Batch Optimistic	Forward-Only	Static	Dynamic	Static

adUseClient

Lock Type	Cursor Type Requested			
	Forward-Only	**Keyset**	**Dynamic**	**Static**
Read-Only	Static	Static	Static	Static
Pessimistic	Static	Static	Static	Static
Optimistic	Static	Static	Static	Static
Batch Optimistic	Static	Static	Static	Static

OLE DB Provider for ODBC with Access

adUseServer

Lock Type	Cursor Type Requested			
	Forward-Only	**Keyset**	**Dynamic**	**Static**
Read-Only	Forward-Only	Keyset	Keyset	Static
Pessimistic	Forward-Only	Keyset	Keyset	Keyset
Optimistic	Forward-Only	Keyset	Keyset	Keyset
Batch Optimistic	Forward-Only	Keyset	Keyset	Keyset

adUseClient

Lock Type	Cursor Type Requested			
	Forward-Only	**Keyset**	**Dynamic**	**Static**
Read-Only	Static	Static	Static	Static
Pessimistic	Static	Static	Static	Static
Optimistic	Static	Static	Static	Static
Batch Optimistic	Static	Static	Static	Static

Moving Through Records

Because you very rarely just open and close a recordset, you need to look at moving through records, where the cursor type and mode can also have an effect on performance. The time taken to open and close the recordset were not included as part of the timing – only movement through the recordset was included.

You can get at the data in a recordset two main ways. The first is to use MoveNext to move from one end of the recordset to the other, and the second is to use GetRows to read the data into an array. For client-based cursors (of any type and locking mode) the figures were extremely close between using MoveNext and GetRows. This is because the data is already on the client, and in both cases, the client cursor service is fetching the data from its local cache. For server-based cursors, however, there are differences.

GetRows can also be used to fetch a smaller number of rows, and this operation is repeated until the whole recordset is read. However, the method I've used here, called GetRows(chunked), is less common; it involves fetching data in batches. Consider a table of 1,000 rows, on SQL Server 2000 (the figures were very similar for optimistic, batch optimistic and pessimistic locking modes), as shown in this graph:

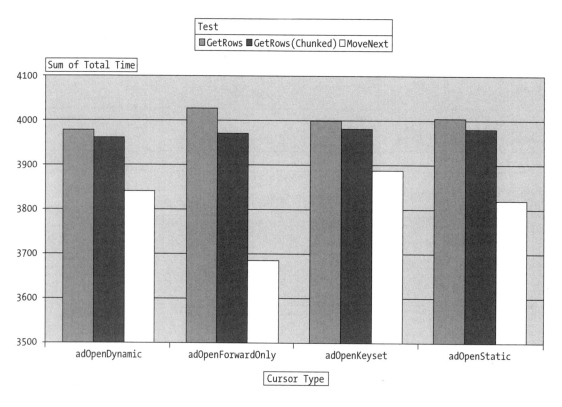

Here you can see that MoveNext is clearly the fastest method, but that using GetRows with small chunks is faster than trying to retrieve all the records into an array at once. However, the difference is minor, so you may not consider the extra effort involved worthwhile. The interesting figures come when you use a read-only cursor, as shown in the next graph. This is the same 1,000 rows using SQL Server 2000:

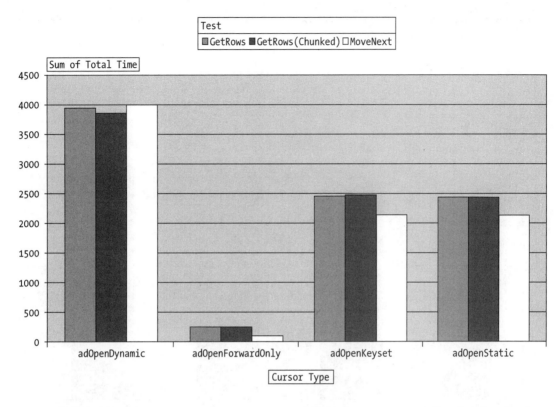

A forward-only cursor brings a vast improvement in speed, because using server-based, forward-only cursors makes use of the SQL Server native cursor (firehose), which is much faster than other cursor types. With other providers, you're unlikely to see this difference.

Cache Size

The Recordset object's CacheSize property identifies how many records are fetched at once and stored in a local cache on the client. The default value for this property is 1, so with a large table you are able to fetch each record individually (if you desire). This could be quite time consuming if moving through the records. For example, imagine a table with 1,000 rows. If the CacheSize property is equal to 1, then it would require 1,000 fetches to create a recordset on this table and move through all 1,000 rows. If the CacheSize property were equal to 100, the same task would take only 10 fetches (each visit fetching 100 records).

The following graph shows the results of changing the cache size for a client-side read-only cursor on a table of 1,000 rows in SQL 2000.

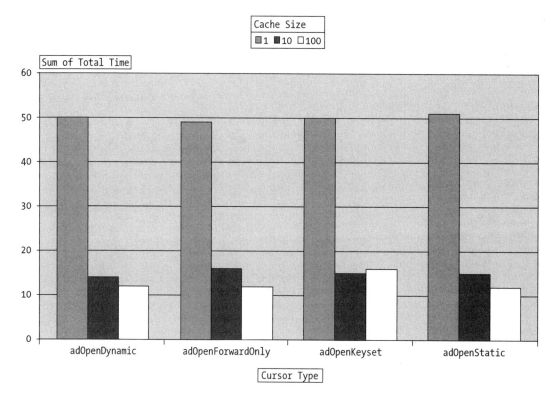

Notice that using a larger cache size is much faster. In some cases there's very little difference between a cache size of 10 and 100, so you'll need to experiment. For server-side cursors the results are even more significant:

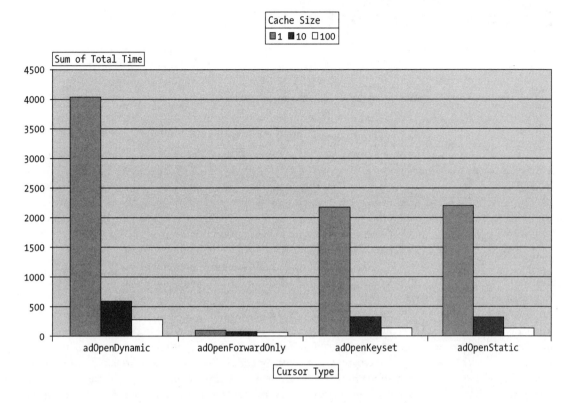

Here you can see that moving from a cache size of 1 to 10 has a dramatic effect, and for some cursor types this can be improved even more by increasing the cache size to 100.

Although you might never fetch 1,000 rows directly for processing, the cache size can have a big impact even on small tables. For processing large tables, you are nearly always better off building SQL statements and executing them on the server. Also, the cache size can be affected by the amount of data in the row being fetched. A larger row will result in more data being fetched into the cache, thus using more resources.

Stored Procedure or Direct SQL?

Many people often put SQL statements directly into their programs, and there are a couple of reasons why:

❏ They feel it keeps together everything required to run the program.

❏ They are unsure about stored procedures and the benefits they can bring.

Using stored procedures not only allows you to alter them without affecting your program, but also brings the performance advantage of compiled SQL. When you run SQL statements, they are parsed by SQL Server and then executed. The SQL engine must carry this out every time the statement is used, unless it's been prepared. When you create a stored procedure, the SQL is converted into a compiled form, thus eliminating this step when the procedure is run. In addition, stored procedures are placed into a procedure cache, which is an in-memory store of the compiled SQL; this improves performance even more. Of course, if your table statistics change frequently, then the stored execution plan for stored procedures could become out-of-date. This is another reason why good test data is so important; compiling stored procedures against nonrealistic (or empty) data can result in a suboptimal execution plan being generated.

You can bring the stored procedure benefit to straight SQL text strings by setting the `Prepared` property of the `Command` object before execution, but this is useful only if you intend to run the command several times on the same connection. With `Prepared` set to `True`, a prepared statement is created the first time the command is run, and subsequent runs of the command on the same connection will use the prepared statement. So the first run will be slower, but subsequent runs will be quicker. In ASP, you will not notice any benefit in using prepared statements, because you should always work in a disconnected mode—creating database connections as you require them, which means subsequent runs of the SQL will use a new connection, and will therefore prepare a new statement.

On SQL Server 6.5, prepared statements are compiled into temporary stored procedures. On SQL Server 7.0 and later, prepared statements are fully supported.

Consider the following SQL statement, using the `pubs` database, to analyze sales by publisher, state, and author:

```
SELECT publishers.pub_name, publishers.state,
       (au_lname + ', ' + au_fname) AS author,
       Sum(sales.qty) AS SumOfqty
FROM (publishers INNER JOIN titles
                    ON publishers.pub_id = titles.pub_id)
    INNER JOIN (authors INNER JOIN titleauthor
                    ON authors.au_id = titleauthor.au_id)
    ON titles.title_id = titleauthor.title_id
INNER JOIN sales ON titles.title_id = sales.title_id
GROUP BY publishers.pub_name, publishers.state,
       (au_lname + ', ' + au_fname)
```

Executing this statement 10 times on the same connection gave the results shown in this graph:

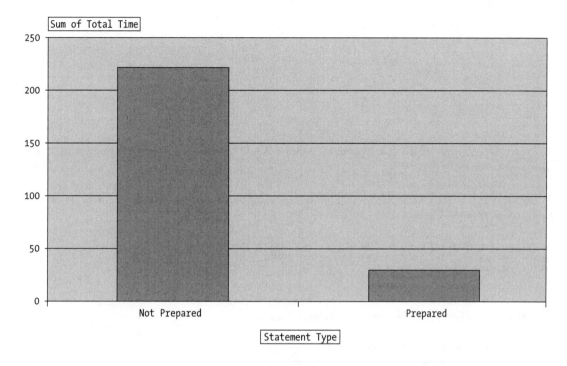

You can clearly see that prepared statements are faster for concurrent executions. Simple SQL statements may yield less impressive performance improvements because the SQL optimizer will have less to do.

Parameters

When I started using ADO, I had a lot of trouble using parameters, partly because of the data types. I then discovered the Refresh method, and I started to use this during development to print out details of what the parameters should be. If you use SQL Trace when connecting to SQL Server, you can clearly see that using Refresh can have a big overhead as it makes a trip back to the server to get the parameters. However, I did wonder what the speed difference was between the following three methods:

❑   Using direct SQL

❑   Using the Parameters argument of the Command's Execute method

❑   Using the Parameters collection

For example, consider the pubs database supplied with SQL Server. A stored procedure could contain the following commands:

```
CREATE PROCEDURE usp_SalesTest
      @iQty           int,
      @sPayTerms      varchar(12)
AS
      SELECT    *
      FROM      sales
      WHERE     qty = @iQty
      OR        payterms = @sPayTerms
```

There are several ways to call this, assuming you wish to search for 20 for the quantity and Net 60 for the payment terms.

A Command object was created for each of the three tests, giving three sections of code. For the direct SQL statement, I used:

```
objCmd.CommandText = "SELECT * FROM sales WHERE qty=20 OR" & _
                         "payterms='Net 60'"
objCmd.CommandType = adCmdText
Set objRs = objCmd.Execute
```

Passing the parameters into the Execute method, I used:

```
objCmd.CommandText = "usp_SalesTest"
objCmd.CommandType = adCmdStoredProc
Set objRs = objCmd.Execute(, Array(20, "Net 60"))
```

To create a Parameters collection, I used:

```
objCmd.CommandText = "usp_SalesTest"
objCmd.CommandType = adCmdStoredProc
objCmd.Parameters.Append objCmd.CreateParameter("@iQty", _
                         adInteger, adParamInput, 8, 20)
objCmd.Parameters.Append objCmd.CreateParameter("@sPayTerms", _
                         adVarChar, adParamInput, 12, "Net 60")
Set objRs = objCmd.Execute
```

Again, these were run 10 times and the average taken, and each set of runs executed three times, closing the connection between runs. This test proved inconclusive, with only negligible differences between the three methods. The Parameter method has the advantage of making the parameters explicit, and of course you have to use this method if you require output parameters. Many databases don't support the extraction of parameters, so you might have to use explicit parameters–that is, create them explicitly with CreateParameter.

Connection Pooling

There's nothing to say here about the use of connection pooling except that it works. Don't turn it off unless you have explicit reasons to do so. For applications that reuse connections, such as ASP, connection pooling can be a big benefit because you are generally connecting to the database as the same user, and therefore pooled connections are regularly reused.

Performance Summary

The first thing to remember is that these figures only show certain traits under certain circumstances, so don't rely on them. Perform your own analysis using your own data and see what results you achieve. Also make sure that you test your application under circumstances similar to those in which it will run–that is, on a well-used network, on a server that is heavily used, on a database with multiple users, and so on. You can use this chapter as a guideline for some of the criteria to test.

Having said that, there are some key points that I've established from these tests:

❑   When opening recordsets, server-side cursors are generally quicker than client-side cursors because less data is initially being transferred. However, the fetching of data is then slower, because the data is retrieved from the server rather than from the local cache.

❑   If you need to use disconnected recordsets, then you'll have to use client-side cursors. In this case, try and keep the amount of data transferred to a minimum. For example, don't do "select *" when you need only a couple of columns.

❑   If using SQL Server 6.5 and server-side cursors, using dynamic or forward-only cursors is more efficient when selecting data. This is because the data is not initially copied into tempdb. For SQL Server 7.0 and 2000, this effect is greatly reduced.

❑   Use the native OLE DB providers; they are quicker and offer more functionality than the ODBC ones. However, if using Oracle you may want to use the OLE DB Provider for ODBC, because it has greater functionality than the OLE DB Provider for Oracle.

❑   Use the correct cursor types. If you're not going to change any data, use read-only cursors. Don't waste the resources of the data store.

There is also the performance aspect of performing large batch jobs on the server and transferring data to the client only when required. These are general ways to improve application performance; use them in conjunction with any ADO performance enhancements.

The Performance Test Tool

As mentioned at the beginning of this chapter, this tool is intended to help you do your own performance tests. It began its life in the form of a few small routines used to help decide a few issues, and it has grown into the program now available from http://support.apress.com. I considered expanding this into a large test suite, and supplying it as a fully finished program, but then decided that–as a programmer–this is probably not what you really want. Therefore, I've decided to give it away as it stands. Bear in mind that it's a far-from-complete product, has little or no error handling, and has some options that won't work under all conditions. Having said that, it does perform basic tests fairly well.

The opening screen allows you to connect to a data store:

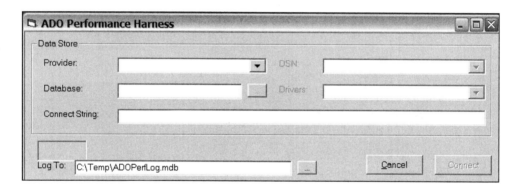

Here you can pick a provider (and, if using ODBC, pick a DSN or a driver). The Connect String box will supply some default values, and you should overwrite these with your specific values before connecting. The Log To box allows you to pick the database to log timings to. Currently, this is an Access database, but there's no reason why you couldn't convert the code to use another database.

Once you've connected, you get to the main timing screen:

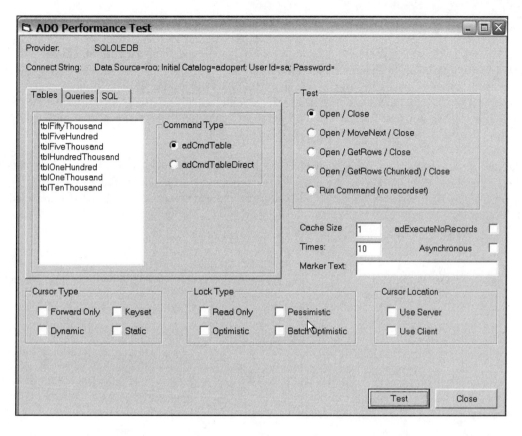

The tab control allows you to select from tables, queries, or your own SQL text. To the right, you pick which test you want to run, but remember that some may not be suitable for SQL queries that don't return recordsets. Below this, you can select whether records are to be returned. The asynchronous option isn't implemented, and was added to give you the opportunity to supply this. You can specify the number of times that the test is run, and add some marker text (to be written to the logging database) so that you can identify individual tests. At the bottom of the screen, you can pick the cursor type, lock type, and cursor location. To run a test, you must select at least one of each, and you can pick more options to allow several tests to be compared.

The logging database just consists of one simple table into which the results are written. The graphs in this chapter were produced by pulling the figures from this table into Excel; it's often easier to appreciate the performance differences in visual form, so you may wish to consider doing the same.

Summary

In this chapter, I've shown you the results of my experimentation with the various options available in ADO. In particular, you've seen the performance implications of using different data providers and the often significant differences given by the various cursor types and locking options. To finish, I discussed the VB tool used to run the tests, and encouraged you to download and use it, or customize it for your own purposes. You can download it from our Web site: you'll find the samples page that supports this book at http://support.apress.com.

With this consideration of the performance implications of ADO, our discussion of ADO is complete. The appendices that follow this chapter are intended to provide a reference for using ADO. The documentation Microsoft supplies is not quite complete, and wherever possible I have tried to include undocumented features.

ADO Object Summary

Microsoft ActiveX Data Objects Library Reference

Properties and methods new to version 2.6 are shown in **bold** in the first column.

> **All properties are read/write unless otherwise stated.**

The Objects

The Main Objects	Description
Command	A Command object is a definition of a specific command that you intend to execute against a data source.
Connection	A Connection object represents an open connection to a data store.
Recordset	A Recordset object represents the entire set of records from a base table, the results of an executed command, or a fabricated recordset. At any given time, the "current record" of a Recordset object refers to a single record within the recordset.
Record	A Record object represents a single resource (file or directory) made available from a Document Source Provider, or a single row from a singleton query.

Table continues on the following page

The Main Objects	Description
Stream	A Stream object is an implementation of the IStream COM interface to allow reading and writing to blocks of memory. In conjunction with the OLE DB Provider for Internet Publishing, it allows access to the contents of resources (files) made available from a Document Source Provider. It can also be used to accept the output from executed Commands.

The Other Objects	Description
Error	An Error object contains the details of a data access error pertaining to a single operation involving the provider.
Field	A Field object represents a single column of data within a common data type (Recordset or Record).
Parameter	A Parameter object represents a single parameter or argument associated with a Command object based on a parameterized query or stored procedure.
Property	A Property object represents a single dynamic characteristic of an ADO object that is defined by the provider.

The Collections	Description
Errors	The Errors collection contains all of the Error objects created in response to a single failure involving the provider.
Fields	A Fields collection contains all of the Field objects for a Recordset or Record object.
Parameters	A Parameters collection contains all the Parameter objects for a Command object.
Properties	A Properties collection contains all the Property objects for a specific instance of an ADO object.

The Command Object

Methods of the Command Object	Return Type	Description
Cancel		Cancels execution of a pending `Execute` or `Open` call
CreateParameter	Parameter	Creates a new `Parameter` object
Execute	Recordset	Executes the query, SQL statement, or stored procedure specified in the `CommandText` property

> **Note that the `CommandStream` and `NamedParameters` properties were new to ADO 2.6.**

Properties of the Command Object	Return Type	Description
ActiveConnection	Variant	Indicates to which `Connection` object the command currently belongs
CommandStream	Variant	Identifies the `Stream` object that contains the commands to be issued against a data provider
CommandText	String	Contains the text of a command to be issued against a data provider
CommandTimeout	Long	Indicates how long to wait, in seconds, while executing a command before terminating the command and generating an error (default is 30)
CommandType	CommandTypeEnum	Indicates the type of command specified by the `Command` object
Dialect	String	A Globally Unique Identifier (GUID) that identifies the command dialect to be used by a particular command
Name	String	Indicates the name of the `Command` object
NamedParameters	Boolean	Indicates whether the Parameter names are sent to the provider or whether Parameters are identified by their position in the collection
Prepared	Boolean	Indicates whether to save a compiled version of a command before execution
State	Long	Describes whether the `Command` object is open or closed (read-only)

Collections of the Command Object	Return Type	Description
Parameters	Parameters	Contains all of the Parameter objects for a Command object
Properties	Properties	Contains all of the Property objects for a Command object

The Connection Object

Methods of the Connection Object	Return Type	Description
BeginTrans	Integer	Begins a new transaction
Cancel		Cancels the execution of a pending asynchronous Execute or Open operation
Close		Closes an open connection and any dependent objects
CommitTrans		Saves any changes and ends the current transaction
Execute	Recordset	Executes the query, SQL statement, stored procedure, or provider-specific text
Open		Opens a connection to a data store so that provider-specific statements (such as SQL statements) can be executed against it
OpenSchema	Recordset	Obtains database schema information from the provider
RollbackTrans		Cancels any changes made during the current transaction and ends the transaction

Properties of the Connection Object	Return Type	Description
Attributes	Long	Indicates one or more characteristics of a Connection object (default is 0)
CommandTimeout	Long	Indicates how long, in seconds, to wait while executing a command before terminating the command and generating an error (default is 30)
ConnectionString	String	Contains the information used to establish a connection to a data source
ConnectionTimeout	Long	Indicates how long, in seconds, to wait while establishing a connection before terminating the attempt and generating an error (default is 15)
CursorLocation	CursorLocationEnum	Sets or returns the location of the cursor engine
DefaultDatabase	String	Indicates the default database for a Connection object.
IsolationLevel	IsolationLevelEnum	Indicates the level of transaction isolation for a Connection object
Mode	ConnectModeEnum	Indicates the available permissions for modifying data in a Connection
Provider	String	Indicates the name of the provider for a Connection object
State	ObjectStateEnum	Describes whether the Connection object is open, closed, or currently executing a statement (read-only)
Version	String	Indicates the ADO version number (read-only)

Collections of the Connection Object	Return Type	Description
Errors	Errors	Contains all Error objects created in response to a single failure involving the provider
Properties	Properties	Contains all of the Property objects for a Connection object

Events of the Connection Object	Description
BeginTransComplete	Fired after a BeginTrans operation finishes executing
CommitTransComplete	Fired after a CommitTrans operation finishes executing
ConnectComplete	Fired after a connection opens
Disconnect	Fired after a connection closes
ExecuteComplete	Fired after a command has finished executing
InfoMessage	Fired whenever a ConnectionEvent operation completes successfully and additional information is returned by the provider
RollbackTransComplete	Fired after a RollbackTrans operation has finished executing
WillConnect	Fired before a connection starts
WillExecute	Fired before a pending command executes on the connection

The Error Object

Properties of the Error Object	Return Type	Description
Description	String	A description string associated with the error (read-only)
HelpContext	Integer	Indicates the ContextID in the help file for the associated error (read-only)
HelpFile	String	Indicates the name of the help file (read-only)
NativeError	Long	Indicates the provider–specific error code for the associated error (read-only)

Table continues on the following page

Properties of the Error Object	Return Type	Description
Number	Long	Indicates the number that uniquely identifies an Error object (read-only)
Source	String	Indicates the name of the object or application that originally generated the error (read-only)
SQLState	String	Indicates the SQL state for a given Error object by using a five character string that follows the ANSI SQL standard (read-only)

The Errors Collection

Methods of the Errors Collection	Return Type	Description
Clear		Removes all of the Error objects from the Errors collection
Refresh		Updates the Error objects with information from the provider

Properties of the Errors Collection	Return Type	Description
Count	Long	Indicates the number of Error objects in the Errors collection (read-only)
Item	Error	Allows indexing into the Errors collection to reference a specific Error object (read-only)

The Field Object

Methods of the Field Object	Return Type	Description
AppendChunk		Appends data to a large or binary Field object (such as an image or text field in SQL Server)
GetChunk	Variant	Returns all or a portion of the contents of a large or binary Field object (such as an image or text field in SQL Server)

Properties of the Field Object	Return Type	Description
ActualSize	Long	Indicates the actual length of a field's value (read-only)
Attributes	Long	Indicates one or more characteristics of a Field object
DataFormat	Variant	Identifies the format in which data should be displayed
DefinedSize	Long	Indicates the defined size of the Field object
Name	String	Indicates the name of the Field object
NumericScale	Byte	Indicates the scale of numeric values for the Field object
OriginalValue	Variant	Indicates the value of a Field object that existed in the record before any changes were made (read-only)
Precision	Byte	Indicates the degree of precision for numeric values in the Field object (read-only)
Status	FieldStatusEnum	Identifies the current state of the Field object (read-only)
Type	DataTypeEnum	Indicates the data type of the Field object
UnderlyingValue	Variant	Indicates a Field object's current value in the database (read-only)
Value	Variant	Indicates the value assigned to the Field object

Collections of the Field Object	Return Type	Description
Properties	Properties	Contains all of the Property objects for a Field object

The Fields Collection

Methods of the Fields Collection	Return Type	Description
Append		Appends a Field object to the Fields collection
CancelUpdate		Cancels any changes made to the Fields collection of a Record object
Delete		Deletes a Field object from the Fields collection
Refresh		Updates the Field objects in the Fields collection
Resync		Resynchronizes the values of the Fields collection of a Record object with values from the data provider
Update		Confirms any changes made to Field objects in the Fields collection of a Record object

Properties of the Fields Collection	Return Type	Description
Count	Long	Indicates the number of Field objects in the Fields collection (read-only)
Item	Field	Allows indexing into the Fields collection to reference a specific Field object (read-only)

The Parameter Object

Methods of the Parameter Object	Return Type	Description
AppendChunk		Appends data to a large or binary Parameter object (such as an image or text field in SQL Server)

Properties of the Parameter Object	Return Type	Description
Attributes	Long	Indicates one or more characteristics of a Parameter object
Direction	ParameterDirection Enum	Indicates whether the Parameter object represents an input parameter, an output parameter, or an input/output parameter, or if the parameter is a return value from a statement
Name	String	Indicates the name of the Parameter object
NumericScale	Byte	Indicates the scale of numeric values for the Parameter object
Precision	Byte	Indicates the degree of precision for numeric values in the Parameter object
Size	Long	Indicates the maximum size (in bytes or characters) of a Parameter object
Type	DataTypeEnum	Indicates the data type of the Parameter object
Value	Variant	Indicates the value assigned to the Parameter object

Collections of the Parameter Object	Return Type	Description
Properties	Properties	Contains all of the Property objects for a Parameter object

The Parameters Collection

Methods of the Parameters Collection	Return Type	Description
`Append`		Appends a `Parameter` object to the `Parameters` collection
`Delete`		Deletes a `Parameter` object from the `Parameters` collection
`Refresh`		Updates the `Parameter` objects in the `Parameters` collection

Properties of the Parameters Collection	Return Type	Description
`Count`	`Long`	Indicates the number of `Parameter` objects in the `Parameters` collection (read-only)
`Item`	`Parameter`	Allows indexing into the `Parameters` collection to reference a specific `Parameter` object (read-only)

The Properties Collection

Methods of the Properties Collection	Return Type	Description
`Refresh`		Updates the `Property` objects in the `Properties` collection with the details from the provider

Properties of the Properties Collection	Return Type	Description
`Count`	`Long`	Indicates the number of `Property` objects in the `Properties` collection (read-only)
`Item`	`Property`	Allows indexing into the `Properties` collection to reference a specific `Property` object (read-only)

The Property Object

Properties of the Property Object	Return Type	Description
Attributes	Long	Indicates one or more characteristics of a Property object
Name	String	Indicates the name of the Property object (read-only)
Type	DataTypeEnum	Indicates the data type of the Property object
Value	Variant	Indicates the value assigned to the Property object

The Record Object

Methods of the Record Object	Return Type	Description
Cancel		Cancels any pending asynchronous method call
Close		Closes the currently open Record
CopyRecord	String	Copies a file, or a directory and its contents, to a new location
DeleteRecord		Deletes a file, or a directory and its contents
GetChildren	Recordset	Returns a Recordset containing the child resources of the Record's underlying resource
MoveRecord	String	Moves a resource and its contents to a new location
Open		Opens an existing resource, or creates a new resource

Properties of the Record Object	Return Type	Description
ActiveConnection	Variant	Identifies the connection details for the resource (can be a connection string or a Connection object)
Mode	ConnectModeEnum	Indicates the permissions used when opening a Record

Table continues on the following page

Properties of the Record Object	Return Type	Description
ParentURL	String	Identifies the absolute URL of the parent of the current Record
RecordType	RecordTypeEnum	Indicates whether the record type is a directory, a simple file, or a complex file
Source	Variant	Identifies the Record source (either a URL or a reference to a Recordset object)
State	ObjectStateEnum	Indicates whether the Record is open, closed, or a statement is currently executing

Collections of the Record Object	Return Type	Description
Fields	Fields	Contains a Field object for each property of the resource
Properties		Contains all of the Property objects for the current Record object

The Recordset Object

Methods of the Recordset Object	Return Type	Description
AddNew		Creates a new record for an updateable Recordset object
Cancel		Cancels execution of a pending asynchronous Open operation
CancelBatch		Cancels a pending batch update
CancelUpdate		Cancels any changes made to the current record, or to a new record, prior to calling the Update method

Table continues on the following page

Methods of the Recordset Object	Return Type	Description
Clone	Recordset	Creates a duplicate Recordset object from an existing Recordset object
Close		Closes the Recordset object and any dependent objects, including clones
CompareBookmarks	CompareEnum	Compares two bookmarks and returns an indication of the relative values
Delete		Deletes the current record or group of records
Find		Searches the Recordset for a record that matches the specified criteria
GetRows	Variant	Retrieves multiple records of a Recordset object into an array
GetString	String	Returns a Recordset as a string
Move		Moves the position of the current record in a Recordset
MoveFirst		Moves the position of the current record to the first record in the Recordset
MoveLast		Moves the position of the current record to the last record in the Recordset
MoveNext		Moves the position of the current record to the next record in the Recordset
MovePrevious		Moves the position of the current record to the previous record in the Recordset
NextRecordset	Recordset	Clears the current Recordset object and returns the next Recordset by advancing to the next in a series of commands
Open		Opens a Recordset
Requery		Updates the data in a Recordset object by reexecuting the query on which the object is based
Resync		Refreshes the data in the Recordset object with the current data from the underlying data store

Table continues on the following page

Methods of the Recordset Object	Return Type	Description
Save		Saves the Recordset to a file, a Stream, or any object that supports the standard COM IStream interface (such as the ASP Response object)
Seek		Searches the recordset index to locate a value
Supports	Boolean	Determines whether a specified Recordset object supports particular functionality
Update		Saves any changes made to the current Recordset object.
UpdateBatch		Writes all pending batch modifications (updates, inserts, and deletes) to the underlying data store

Properties of the Recordset Object	Return Type	Description
AbsolutePage	PositionEnum	Specifies the page in which the current record resides
AbsolutePosition	PositionEnum	Specifies the ordinal position of the Recordset object's current record
ActiveCommand	Object	Indicates the Command object that created the associated Recordset object (read-only)
ActiveConnection	Variant	Indicates the Connection object to which the Recordset object currently belongs
BOF	Boolean	Indicates whether the record pointer is pointing before the first record in the Recordset object (read-only)
Bookmark	Variant	Returns a bookmark that uniquely identifies the current record in the Recordset object, or sets the record pointer to point to the record identified by a valid bookmark

Table continues on the following page

Properties of the Recordset Object	Return Type	Description
CacheSize	Long	Indicates the number of records from the Recordset object that are cached locally in memory
CursorLocation	CursorLocationEnum	Sets or returns the location of the cursor engine
CursorType	CursorTypeEnum	Indicates the type of cursor used in the Recordset object.
DataMember	String	Specifies the name of the data member to be retrieved from the object referenced by the DataSource property
DataSource	Object	Specifies an object containing data to be represented by the Recordset object
EditMode	EditModeEnum	Indicates the editing status of the current record (read-only)
EOF	Boolean	Indicates whether the record pointer is pointing beyond the last record in the Recordset object (read-only)
Filter	Variant	Indicates a filter for data in the Recordset
Index	String	Identifies the name of the index currently being used
LockType	LockTypeEnum	Indicates the type of locks placed on records during editing
MarshalOptions	MarshalOptionsEnum	Indicates which records are to be marshaled back to the server, or across thread or process boundaries
MaxRecords	Long	Indicates the maximum number of records that can be returned to the Recordset object from a query—default is zero (no limit)

Table continues on the following page

Properties of the Recordset Object	Return Type	Description
PageCount	Long	Indicates how many pages of data are contained in the Recordset object (and is thus dependent on the values of PageSize and RecordCount) (read-only)
PageSize	Long	Indicates how many records constitute one page in the Recordset
RecordCount	Long	Indicates the current number of records in the Recordset object (read-only)
Sort	String	Specifies one or more field names the Recordset is sorted on, and the direction of the sort
Source	String	Indicates the statement used to populate the data in the Recordset object
State	Long	Indicates whether the recordset is open, closed, or whether it is executing an asynchronous operation (read-only)
Status	Integer	Indicates the status of the current record with respect to batch updates or other bulk operations (read-only)
StayInSync	Boolean	Indicates, in a hierarchical Recordset object, whether the parent row should change when the set of underlying child records changes (read-only)

Collections of the Recordset Object	Return Type	Description
Fields	Fields	Contains all of the Field objects for the Recordset object
Properties	Properties	Contains all of the Property objects for the current Recordset object

Events of the Recordset Object	Description
EndOfRecordset	Fired when there is an attempt to move to a row past the end of the Recordset
FetchComplete	Fired after a Recordset has been populated with all the rows from an asynchronous operation
FetchProgress	Fired periodically during a lengthy asynchronous operation to report how many rows have been retrieved.
FieldChangeComplete	Fired after the value of one or more Field objects has been changed
MoveComplete	Fired after the position in the Recordset changes.
RecordChangeComplete	Fired after one or more records change
RecordsetChangeComplete	Fired after the Recordset has changed
WillChangeField	Fired before a pending operation changes the value of one or more Field objects
WillChangeRecord	Fired before one or more rows in the Recordset change
WillChangeRecordset	Fired before a pending operation changes the Recordset
WillMove	Fired before a pending operation changes the current position in the Recordset

The Stream Object

Methods of the Stream Object	Return Type	Description
Cancel		Cancels any pending asynchronous commands
Close		Closes the current Stream
CopyTo		Copies a number of characters or bytes into another Stream object
Flush		Forces the contents of the buffer into the underlying object
LoadFromFile		Loads the contents of a file into the Stream object

Table continues on the following page

Methods of the Stream Object	Return Type	Description
Open		Opens a `Stream` object from a URL or a `Record` object
Read	Variant	Reads a number of bytes from the `Stream`
ReadText	String	Reads a number of characters from the `Stream`
SaveToFile		Saves the contents of a `Stream` to a file
SetEOS		Sets the position that identifies the end of the stream
SkipLine		Skips a line when reading in a text stream. Uses the `LineSeparator` property to identify the end of line character
Write		Writes binary data to the stream
WriteText		Writes text data to the stream

Properties of the Stream Object	Return Type	Description
Charset	String	Indicates the character set to translate the `Stream` contents into
EOS	Boolean	Indicates whether the end of the `Stream` has been reached
LineSeparator	LineSeparatorEnum	Identifies the binary character that separates lines
Mode	ConnectModeEnum	Identifies the permissions used when opening the `Stream`
Position	Long	Identifies the current position with the `Stream`
Size Stream	Long	Indicates, in bytes, the size of the
State	ObjectStateEnum	Indicates whether the `Stream` is open or closed
Type	StreamTypeEnum	Indicates whether the `Stream` contains binary or text data

ADO Method Calls—Quick Reference

Command Object Methods

```
Command.Cancel
Parameter = Command.CreateParameter([Name As String], _
               [Type As DataTypeEnum], _
               [Direction As ParameterDirectionEnum], _
               [Size As Integer], _
               [Value As Variant])
Recordset = Command.Execute([RecordsAffected As Variant], _
               [Parameters As Variant], [Options As Long])
```

Connection Object Methods

```
Long = Connection.BeginTrans
Connection.Cancel
Connection.Close
Connection.CommitTrans
Recordset = Connection.Execute(CommandText As String, _
               [RecordsAffected As Variant], [Options As Long])
Connection.Open([ConnectionString As String], [UserID As String], _
               [Password As String], [Options As Long])
Recordset = Connection.OpenSchema(Schema As SchemaEnum, _
               [Restrictions As Variant], [SchemaID As Variant])
Connection.RollbackTrans
```

Errors Collection Methods

```
Errors.Clear
Errors.Refresh
```

Field Object Methods

```
Field.AppendChunk(Data As Variant)
Variant = Field.GetChunk(Length As Long)
```

Fields Collection Methods

```
Fields.Append(Name As String, Type As DataTypeEnum, _
               [DefinedSize As Long], _
               [Attrib As FieldAttributeEnum], _
               [FieldValue As Variant])
Fields.CancelUpdate
Fields.Delete(Index As Variant)
Fields.Refresh
Fields.Resync([ResyncValues As ResyncEnum])
Fields.Update
```

Parameter Object Methods

```
Parameter.AppendChunk(Val As Variant)
```

Parameters Collection Methods

```
Parameters.Append(Object As Object)
Parameters.Delete(Index As Variant)
Parameters.Refresh
```

Properties Collection Methods

```
Properties.Refresh
```

Record Object Methods

```
Record.Cancel
Record.Close
String = Record.CopyRecord([Source As String], _
            [Destination As String], _
            [UserName As String], [Password As String], _
            [Options As CopyRecordOptionsEnum], [Async As Boolean])
Record.DeleteRecord([Source As String], [Async As Boolean])
Recordset = Record.GetChildren
String = Record.MoveRecord([Source As String], _
            [Destination As String], _
            [UserName As String], [Password As String], _
            [Options As MoveRecordOptionsEnum], [Async As Boolean])
Record.Open([Source As Variant], [ActiveConnection As Variant], _
            [Mode As ConnectModeEnum], _
            [CreateOptions As RecordCreateOptionsEnum], _
            [Options as RecordOpenOptionsEnum], _
            [UserName As String], _
            [Password As String])
```

Recordset Object Methods

```
Recordset.AddNew([FieldList As Variant], [Values As Variant])
Recordset.Cancel
Recordset.CancelBatch([AffectRecords As AffectEnum])
Recordset.CancelUpdate
Recordset = Recordset.Clone([LockType As LockTypeEnum])
Recordset.Close
CompareEnum = Recordset.CompareBookmarks(Bookmark1 As Variant, _
            Bookmark2 As Variant)
Recordset.Delete([AffectRecords As AffectEnum])
Recordset.Find(Criteria As String, [SkipRecords As Long], _
            [SearchDirection As SearchDirectionEnum], _
            [Start As Variant])
Variant = Recordset.GetRows([Rows As Long], [Start As Variant], _
            [Fields As Variant])
String = Recordset.GetString(StringFormat As StringFormatEnum, _
            [NumRows As Long], [ColumnDelimeter As String], _
            [RowDelimeter As String], [NullExpr As String])
Recordset.Move(NumRecords As Long, [Start As Variant])
Recordset.MoveFirst
Recordset.MoveLast
```

```
Recordset.MoveNext
Recordset.MovePrevious
Recordset = Recordset.NextRecordset([RecordsAffected As Variant])
Recordset.Open([Source As Variant], _
               [ActiveConnection As Variant], _
               [CursorType As CursorTypeEnum], _
               [LockType As LockTypeEnum], _
               [Options As Long])
Recordset.Requery([Options As Long])
Recordset.Resync([AffectRecords As AffectEnum], _
                  [ResyncValues As ResyncEnum])
Recordset.Save([FileName As String], _
                [PersistFormat As PersistFormatEnum])
Recordset.Seek(KeyValues As Variant, SeekOption As SeekEnum)
Boolean = Recordset.Supports(CursorOptions As CursorOptionEnum)
Recordset.Update([Fields As Variant], [Values As Variant])
Recordset.UpdateBatch([AffectRecords As AffectEnum])
```

Stream Object Methods

```
Stream.Cancel
Stream.Close
Stream.CopyTo(DestStream As Stream, [CharNumber As Long])
Stream.Flush
Stream.LoadFromFile(FileName As String)
Stream.Open([Source As Variant], [Mode As ConnectModeEnum], _
             [Options As StreamOpenOptionsEnum], _
             [UserName As String], _
             [Password As String])
Variant = Stream.Read([NumBytes As Long])
String = Stream.ReadText([NumChars As Long])
Stream.SaveToFile(FileName As String, [Options As SaveOptionsEnum])
Stream.SetEOS
Stream.SkipLine
Stream.Write(Buffer As Variant)
Stream.WriteText(Data As String, [Options As StreamWriteEnum])
```

B

ADO Constants

Standard Constants

The following constants are predefined by ADO. For scripting languages these are included in adovbs.inc or adojava.inc, which you can find in the Program Files\Common Files\System\ado directory. In ASP you can either include these files or use the METADATA tag:

```
<!- METADATA TYPE="typelib" FILE="C:\Program Files\Common Files\
System\ado\msado15.dll" ->
```

This should appear on a single line, and you'll have to put the correct path in. Don't worry about the name of the DLL; it's the current version, whatever its name.

In Visual Basic, these constants are included automatically when you reference the ADO library.

AffectEnum

Name	Value	Description
adAffectAll	3	Operation affects all records in the recordset
adAffectAllChapters	4	Operation affects all child (chapter) records
adAffectCurrent	1	Operation affects only the current record
adAffectGroup	2	Operation affects records that satisfy the current Filter property

BookmarkEnum

Name	Value	Description
adBookmarkCurrent	0	Starts at the current record (default)
adBookmarkFirst	1	Starts at the first record
adBookmarkLast	2	Starts at the last record

CEResyncEnum

Name	Value	Description
adResyncAll	15	Resynchronizes the data for each pending row
adResyncAutoIncrement	1	Resynchronizes the auto-increment values for all successfully inserted rows (default)
adResyncConflicts	2	Resynchronizes all rows for which an update or delete operation failed because of concurrency conflicts
adResyncInserts	8	Resynchronizes all successfully inserted rows, including the values of their identity columns
adResyncNone	0	No resynchronization performed
adResyncUpdates	4	Resynchronizes all successfully updated rows

CommandTypeEnum

Name	Value	Description
adCmdFile	256	Indicates that the provider should evaluate CommandText as a previously persisted file
adCmdStoredProc	4	Indicates that the provider should evaluate CommandText as a stored procedure
adCmdTable	2	Indicates that the provider should generate a SQL query to return all rows from the table named in CommandText
adCmdTableDirect	512	Indicates that the provider should return all rows from the table named in CommandText

Table continues on the following page

Name	Value	Description
adCmdText	1	Indicates that the provider should evaluate CommandText as textual definition of a command, such as a SQL statement
adCmdUnknown	8	Indicates that the type of command in CommandText unknown
adCmdUnspecified	-1	The command type is unspecified

CompareEnum

Name	Value	Description
adCompareEqual	1	The bookmarks are equal.
adCompareGreaterThan	2	The first bookmark is after the second.
adCompareLessThan	0	The first bookmark is before the second.
adCompareNotComparable	4	The bookmarks cannot be compared.
adCompareNotEqual	3	The bookmarks are not equal and not ordered.

ConnectModeEnum

Name	Value	Description
adModeRead	1	Indicates read-only permissions
adModeReadWrite	3	Indicates read/write permissions
adModeRecursive	4194304	Applies permissions recursively
adModeShareDenyNone	16	Prevents others from opening connection with any permissions
adModeShareDenyRead	4	Prevents others from opening connection with read permissions
adModeShareDenyWrite	8	Prevents others from opening connection with write permissions
adModeShareExclusive	12	Prevents others from opening connection
adModeUnknown	0	Indicates that the permissions have not yet been set or cannot be determined (default)
adModeWrite	2	Indicates write-only permissions

ConnectOptionEnum

Name	Value	Description
adAsyncConnect	16	Opens the connection asynchronously
adConnectUnspecified	-1	Connection mode unspecified

ConnectPromptEnum

Name	Value	Description
adPromptAlways	1	Always prompt for connection information.
adPromptComplete	2	Only prompt if not enough information was supplied.
adPromptCompleteRequired	3	Only prompt if not enough information was supplied, but disable any options not directly applicable to the connection.
adPromptNever	4	Never prompt for connection information (default).

CopyRecordOptionsEnum

Name	Value	Description
adCopyAllowEmulation	4	Use a download/upload if the copy fails.
adCopyNonRecursive	2	Copy only the current directory, but no children.
adCopyOverWrite	1	Overwrite an existing file or directory.
adCopyUnspecified	-1	The default copy operation is performed (default).

CursorLocationEnum

Name	Value	Description
adUseClient	3	Uses client-side cursors supplied by the local cursor library
adUseNone	1	Uses no cursor services
adUseServer	2	Uses data provider driver supplied cursors (default)

CursorOptionEnum

Name	Value	Description
adAddNew	16778240	The AddNew method is supported for the addition of new records.
adApproxPosition	16384	Support for the AbsolutePosition and AbsolutePage properties is available to allow cursor positioning.
adBookmark	8192	Support for the Bookmark property is available to access specific records.
adDelete	16779264	The Delete method is supported for the deletion of records.
adFind	524288	The Find method is supported to find records.
adHoldRecords	256	More records can be retrieved or the next retrieve position can be changed, without committing all pending changes.
adIndex	8388608	The Index property is supported to set the current index.
adMovePrevious	512	The MoveFirst, MovePrevious, Move, and GetRows methods are supported.
adNotify	262144	The recordset supports Notifications.
adResync	131072	The cursor can be updated with the data visible in the underlying database with the Resync method.
adSeek	4194304	The Seek method is supported to find records by an index.
adUpdate	16809984	The Update method is supported to modify existing records.
adUpdateBatch	65536	The UpdateBatch or CancelBatch methods are supported to transfer changes to the provider in groups.

CursorTypeEnum

Name	Value	Description
adOpenDynamic	2	Opens a dynamic type cursor
adOpenForwardOnly	0	Opens a forward-only type cursor (default)
adOpenKeyset	1	Opens a keyset type cursor
adOpenStatic	3	Opens a static type cursor
adOpenUnspecified	-1	Indicates an unspecified value for cursor type

DataTypeEnum

Name	Value	Description
adArray	8192	Array of data types
adBigInt	20	8-byte signed integer
adBinary	128	Binary value
adBoolean	11	Boolean value
adBSTR	8	Null-terminated character string
adChapter	136	Chapter type indicating a child recordset
adChar	129	String value
adCurrency	6	Currency value (an 8-byte signed integer scaled by 10,000, with four digits to the right of the decimal point)
adDate	7	Date value (Double precision floating point value where the whole part is the number of days since December 30 1899, and the fractional part is the fraction of the day)
adDBDate	133	Date value (yyyymmdd)
adDBTime	134	Time value (hhmmss)
adDBTimeStamp	135	Date-time stamp (yyyymmddhhmmss plus a fraction in nanoseconds)
adDecimal	14	Exact numeric value with fixed precision and scale
adDouble	5	Double-precision floating point value

Table continues on the following page

Name	Value	Description
adEmpty	0	No value specified
adError	10	32-bit error code
adFileTime	64	DOS/Win32 file time (the number of 100-nanosecond intervals since Jan 1, 1601)
adGUID	72	Globally unique identifier
adIDispatch	9	Pointer to an IDispatch interface on an OLE object
adInteger	3	4-byte signed integer
adIUnknown	13	Pointer to an IUnknown interface on an OLE object
adLongVarBinary	205	Long binary value
adLongVarChar	201	Long String value
adLongVarWChar	203	Long Null-terminated string value
adNumeric	131	Exact numeric value with a fixed precision and scale
adPropVariant	138	Variant not equivalent to an Automation variant
adSingle	4	Single-precision floating point value
adSmallInt	2	2-byte signed integer
adTinyInt	16	1-byte signed integer
adUnsignedBigInt	21	8-byte unsigned integer
adUnsignedInt	19	4-byte unsigned integer
adUnsignedSmallInt	18	2-byte unsigned integer
adUnsignedTinyInt	17	1-byte unsigned integer
adUserDefined	132	User-defined variable
adVarBinary	204	Binary value
adVarChar	200	String value
adVariant	12	Automation Variant
adVarNumeric	139	Variable-width exact numeric with a signed scale value
adVarWChar	202	Null-terminated Unicode character string
adWChar	130	Null-terminated Unicode character string

EditModeEnum

Name	Value	Description
adEditAdd	2	Indicates that the AddNew method has been invoked and the current record in the buffer is a new record that hasn't been saved to the database
adEditDelete	4	Indicates that the Delete method has been invoked
adEditInProgress	1	Indicates that data in the current record has been modified but not saved
adEditNone	0	Indicates that no editing is in progress

ErrorValueEnum

Name	Value	Description
adErrBoundToCommand	3707	The application cannot change the ActiveConnection property of a Recordset object with a Command object as its source.
adErrCannotComplete	3732	The server cannot complete the operation.
adErrCantChangeConnection	3748	Connection denied, as the characteristics differ from the connection in use.
adErrCantChangeProvider	3220	The requested provider is different from the one in use.
adErrCantConvertvalue	3724	The data value cannot be converted. The reason is something other than an overflow or sign mismatch.
adErrCantCreate	3725	Value cannot be set or retrieved. The reason is an unknown data type or insufficient resources.
adErrCatalogNotSet	3747	A valid ParentCatalog is required.
adErrColumnNotOnThisRow	3726	The record does not contain this field.
adErrDataConversion	3421	The application is using a value of the wrong type for the current application.

Table continues on the following page

Name	Value	Description
adErrDataOverflow	3721	The value is too large for the field.
adErrDelResOutOfScope	3738	Deleting the requested URL is not allowed as it is outside of the record scope.
adErrDenyNotSupported	3750	Sharing restrictions are not supported by the provider.
adErrDenyTypeNotSupported	3751	The requested sharing restriction is not supported by the provider.
adErrFeatureNotAvailable	3251	The operation requested by the application is not supported by the provider.
adFieldsUpdateFailed	3749	An update to the Fields collection failed. The Status property of the Field objects will contain more information.
adErrIllegalOperation	3219	The operation requested by the application is not allowed in this context.
adErrIntegrityViolation	3719	Changing the value conflicts with the integrity constraints of the field.
adErrInTransaction	3246	The application cannot explicitly close a Connection object while in the middle of a transaction.
adErrInvalidArgument	3001	The application is using arguments that are the wrong type, are out of the acceptable range, or are in conflict with one another.
adErrInvalidConnection	3709	The application requested an operation on an object with a reference to a closed or invalid Connection object.
adErrInvalidParamInfo	3708	The application has improperly defined a Parameter object.
adErrInvalidTransaction	3714	The coordinating transaction has not started or is invalid.
adErrInvalidURL	3729	The supplied URL is invalid.
adErrItemNotFound	3265	ADO could not find the object in the collection.

Table continues on the following page

423

Name	Value	Description
adErrNoCurrentRecord	3021	Either BOF or EOF is True, or the current record has been deleted. The operation requested by the application requires a current record.
adErrNotExecuting	3715	The operation is not executing.
adErrNotReentrant	3710	The operation is not reentrant.
adErrObjectClosed	3704	The operation requested by the application is not allowed if the object is closed.
adErrObjectInCollection	3367	Can't append. Object already in collection.
adErrObjectNotSet	3420	The object referenced by the application no longer points to a valid object.
adErrObjectOpen	3705	The operation requested by the application is not allowed if the object is open.
adErrOpeningFile	3002	The requested file could not be opened.
adErrOperationCancelled	3712	The operation was cancelled.
adErrOutOfSpace	3734	The provider cannot obtain enough space to complete the operation.
adErrPermissionDenied	3720	Insufficient permissions to complete the operation.
adErrPropConflicting	3742	The property value conflicts with the related property.
adErrPropInvalidColumn	3739	This field cannot have the property applied to it.
adErrPropInvalidOption	3740	The property attribute is invalid.
adErrPropInvalidValue	3741	The property value is invalid.
adErrPropNotAllSettable	3743	The property cannot be set, perhaps because it is read-only.
adErrPropNotSet	3744	An optional property value was not set.
adErrPropNotSettable	3745	A read-only property was not set.
adErrPropNotSupported	3746	The property is not supported by the provider.

Table continues on the following page

Name	Value	Description
adErrProviderFailed	3000	The requested operation failed to be performed by the provider.
adErrProviderNotFound	3706	ADO could not find the specified provider.
adErrReadFile	3003	The file could not be read.
adErrResourceExists	3731	The destination URL already exists.
adErrResourceLocked	3730	The resource specified by the URL is locked by another process.
adErrResourceOutOfScope	3735	The supplied URL is outside the scope of the current record.
adErrSchemaViolation	3722	The value conflicts with the constraints or data type of the field.
adErrSignMismatch	3723	The value is signed and the data type is unsigned.
adErrStillConnecting	3713	The operation is still connecting.
adErrStillExecuting	3711	The operation is still executing.
adTreePermissionDenied	3728	Current permissions are not sufficient to access the tree or sub-tree.
adErrUnavailable	3736	The operation failed and the status is unavailable.
adErrUnsafeOperation	3716	The operation is unsafe under these circumstances.
adErrURLDoesNotExist	3727	The URL, or the parent of the destination URL, does not exist.
adErrURLNamedRowDoesNotExist	3737	The record named by this URL does not exist.
adErrVolumeNotFound	3733	The device indicated by the URL cannot be found.
adErrWriteFile	3004	Failed to write to the file.
adWrnSecurityDialog	3717	This is for internal use only and should not be used. It's included for completeness.
adWrnSecurityDialogHeader	3718	This is for internal use only and should not be used. It's included for completeness.

EventReasonEnum

Name	Value	Description
adRsnAddNew	1	A new record is to be added.
adRsnClose	9	The object is being closed.
adRsnDelete	2	The record is being deleted.
adRsnFirstChange	11	The record has been changed for the first time.
adRsnMove	10	A Move has been invoked and the current record pointer is being moved.
adRsnMoveFirst	12	A MoveFirst has been invoked and the current record pointer is being moved
adRsnMoveLast	15	A MoveLast has been invoked and the current record pointer is being moved.
adRsnMoveNext	13	A MoveNext has been invoked and the current record pointer is being moved.
adRsnMovePrevious	14	A MovePrevious has been invoked and the current record pointer is being moved.
adRsnRequery	7	The recordset was re-queried.
adRsnResynch	8	The recordset was resynchronized.
adRsnUndoAddNew	5	The addition of a new record has been cancelled.
adRsnUndoDelete	6	The deletion of a record has been cancelled.
adRsnUndoUpdate	4	The update of a record has been cancelled.
adRsnUpdate	3	The record is being updated.

EventStatusEnum

Name	Value	Description
adStatusCancel	4	Request cancellation of the operation that is about to occur.
adStatusCantDeny	3	A Will event cannot request cancellation of the operation about to occur.
adStatusErrorsOccurred	2	The operation completed unsuccessfully, or a Will... event cancelled the operation.
adStatusOK	1	The operation completed successfully.
adStatusUnwantedEvent	5	Events for this operation are no longer required.

ExecuteOptionEnum

Name	Value	Description
adAsyncExecute	16	The operation is executed asynchronously.
adAsyncFetch	32	The records are fetched asynchronously.
adAsyncFetchNonBlocking	64	The records are fetched asynchronously without blocking subsequent operations.
adExecuteNoRecords	128	CommandText is a command or stored procedure that does not return rows (always combined with adCmdText or adCmdStoreProc).
adExecuteRecord	2048	The CommandText property of the command returns a single row and should be returned as a Record object.
adExecuteStream	1024	Results of the command should be returned as a Stream object. The output stream is defined by the Output Stream dynamic property.
adOptionUnspecified	-1	The command is unspecified.

FieldAttributeEnum

Name	Value	Description
adFldCacheDeferred	4096	Indicates that the provider caches field values and that subsequent reads are done from the cache
adFldFixed	16	Indicates that the field contains fixed-length data
adFldIsChapter	8192	Indicates that the field contains a chaptered value (a recordset)
adFldIsCollection	262144	Indicates that the field represents a resource made up of other resources, such as a directory
adFldIsDefaultStream	131072	Indicates that the field contains the default stream for the resource
adFldIsNullable	32	Indicates that the field accepts Null values
adFldIsRowURL	65536	Indicates that the field is a URL representing a resource
adFldKeyColumn	32768	Indicates that the field is part of a key column
adFldLong	128	Indicates that the field is a long binary field, and that the AppendChunk and GetChunk methods can be used
adFldMayBeNull	64	Indicates that you can read Null values from the field
adFldMayDefer	2	Indicates that the field is deferred (that is, the field values are not retrieved from the data source with the whole record, but only when you access them)
adFldNegativeScale	16384	Indicates that the field has a negative scale
adFldRowID	256	Indicates that the field is some kind of record ID
adFldRowVersion	512	Indicates that the field is a time or date stamp used to track updates
adFldUnknownUpdatable	8	Indicates that the provider cannot determine if you can write to the field
adFldUnspecified	-1	Indicates that attributes of the field are unspecified
adFldUpdatable	4	Indicates that you can write to the field

FieldEnum

Name	Value	Description
adDefaultStream	-1	When used to index into the `Fields` collection, returns the default `Stream` object associated with the `Record`
adRecordURL	-2	When used to index into the `Fields` collection, returns the absolute URL for the current `Record`

FieldStatusEnum

Name	Value	Description
adFieldAlreadyExists	26	The field already exists.
adFieldBadStatus	12	An incorrect status value was received by OLE DB from ADO.
adFieldCannotComplete	20	The server of the source URL could not complete the operation.
adFieldCannotDeleteSource	23	The source could not be deleted after a move operation.
adFieldCantConvertValue	2	The field cannot be set or retrieved without data loss.
adFieldCantCreate	7	The field could not be created because of a provider limitation (for example, on the number of fields).
adFieldDataOverflow	6	The provider returned data that overflowed the field data type.
adFieldDefault	13	The default value for the field has been used to set the value.
adFieldDoesNotExist	16	The requested field does not exist.
adFieldIgnore	15	This field was skipped when setting values.
adFieldIntegrityViolation	10	The field is calculated or derived, and the value cannot be set.

Table continues on the following page

Name	Value	Description
adFieldInvalidURL	17	The URL is invalid.
adFieldIsNull	3	The provider returned a Null value.
adFieldOK	0	The field was successfully added or deleted.
adFieldOutOfSpace	22	The provider was unable to allocate enough space to complete the operation.
adFieldPendingChange	262144	The value of the field has changed, or the field has been removed and added with another data type. Calling Update will confirm the change.
adFieldPendingDelete	131072	The field has been marked for deletion, but will not be deleted until Update is called.
adFieldPendingInsert	65536	The field is a new field, but will not be added until Update is called.
adFieldPendingUnknown	524288	The field status has been set, but the provider cannot determine why.
adFieldPendingUnknownDelete	1048576	The field status has been set to delete the field, but the provider cannot determine why. The field will be deleted after an Update.
adFieldPermissionDenied	9	The field cannot be modified, because it is read-only.
adFieldReadOnly	24	The field in the data store is read-only.
adFieldResourceExists	19	A resource at the specified URL already exists.
adFieldResourceLocked	18	The specified resource is locked by another process.
adFieldResourceOutOfScope	25	The source or destination URL is outside the scope of the record.
adFieldSchemaViolation	11	The value conflicts with the schema constraint.

Table continues on the following page

Name	Value	Description
adFieldSignMismatch	5	The provider returned a signed value, but the ADO field type is unsigned.
adFieldTruncated	4	The data was truncated when retrieved from the data store.
adFieldUnavailable	8	The provider could not determine the value from the data source (for example, a new record).
adFieldVolumeNotFound	21	The volume of the URL was not found.

FilterGroupEnum

Name	Value	Description
adFilterAffectedRecords	2	Allows you to view only records affected by the last Delete, Resync, UpdateBatch, or CancelBatch method
adFilterConflictingRecords	5	Allows you to view the records that failed the last batch update attempt
adFilterFetchedRecords	3	Allows you to view records in the current cache
adFilterNone	0	Removes the current filter and restores all records to view
adFilterPendingRecords	1	Allows you to view only the records that have changed but have not been sent to the server (applicable only for batch update mode)
adFilterPredicate	4	Allows you to view records that failed the last batch update attempt

GetRowsOptionEnum

Name	Value	Description
adGetRowsRest	-1	Retrieves the remainder of the rows in the recordset

IsolationLevelEnum

Name	Value	Description
adXactBrowse	256	Indicates that from one transaction you can view uncommitted changes in other transactions
adXactChaos	16	Indicates that you cannot overwrite pending changes from more highly isolated transactions
adXactCursorStability	4096	Indicates that from one transaction you can view changes in other transactions only after they have been committed (default)
adXactIsolated	1048576	Indicates that transactions are conducted in isolation from other transactions
adXactReadCommitted	4096	Same as adXactCursorStability
adXactReadUncommitted	256	Same as adXactBrowse
adXactRepeatableRead	65536	Indicates that from one transaction you cannot see changes made in other transactions, but that re-querying can bring new recordsets
adXactSerializable	1048576	Same as adXactIsolated
adXactUnspecified	-1	Indicates that the provider is using a different IsolationLevel than specified, but that the level cannot be identified

LineSeparatorEnum

Name	Value	Description
adCR	13	The carriage return character
adCRLF	-1	The carriage return and line feed characters
adLF	10	The line feed character

LockTypeEnum

Name	Value	Description
adLockBatchOptimistic	4	Optimistic batch updates
adLockOptimistic	3	Optimistic locking, record by record (The provider locks records when Update is called.)
adLockPessimistic	2	Pessimistic locking, record by record (The provider locks the record immediately upon editing.)
adLockReadOnly	1	Read-only, data cannot be modified (default)
adLockUnspecified	-1	Clone created with same lock type as original

MarshalOptionsEnum

Name	Value	Description
adMarshalAll	0	Indicates that all rows are returned to the server (default)
adMarshalModifiedOnly	1	Indicates that only modified rows are returned to the server

MoveRecordOptionsEnum

Name	Value	Description
adMoveAllowEmulation	4	Use download, upload, delete operations to simulate the move operation.
adMoveDontUpdateLinks	2	Do not update hypertext links of the source record. Updating of links is provider-specific.
adMoveOverWrite	1	Overwrite the destination file or directory, even if it exists.
adMoveUnspecified	-1	Perform the default move operation (default).

ObjectStateEnum

Name	Value	Description
adStateClosed	0	Indicates that the object is closed (default)
adStateConnecting	2	Indicates that the object is connecting
adStateExecuting	4	Indicates that the object is executing a command
adStateFetching	8	Indicates that the recordset rows are being fetched
adStateOpen	1	Indicates that the object is open

ParameterAttributesEnum

Name	Value	Description
adParamLong	128	Indicates that the parameter accepts long binary data
adParamNullable	64	Indicates that the parameter accepts Null values
adParamSigned	16	Indicates that the parameter accepts signed values (default)

ParameterDirectionEnum

Name	Value	Description
adParamInput	1	Indicates an input parameter (default)
adParamInputOutput	3	Indicates both an input and an output parameter
adParamOutput	2	Indicates an output parameter
adParamReturnValue	4	Indicates a return value
adParamUnknown	0	Indicates parameter direction is unknown

PersistFormatEnum

Name	Value	Description
adPersistADTG	0	Persists data in Advanced Data TableGram format (default)
adPersistXML	1	Persists data in XML format

PositionEnum

Name	Value	Description
adPosBOF	-2	The current record pointer is at BOF.
adPosEOF	-3	The current record pointer is at EOF.
adPosUnknown	-1	The Recordset is empty, or the current position is unknown, or the provider does not support the AbsolutePage property.

PropertyAttributesEnum

Name	Value	Description
adPropNotSupported	0	Indicates that the property is not supported by the provider
adPropOptional	2	Indicates that the user does not need to specify a value for this property before the data source is initialized
adPropRead	512	Indicates that the user can read the property
adPropRequired	1	Indicates that the user must specify a value for this property before the data source is initialized
adPropWrite	1024	Indicates that the user can set the property

RecordCreateOptionsEnum

Name	Value	Description
adCreateCollection	8192	Creates a new collection resource (for example, a directory)
adCreateNonCollection	0	Creates a new simple resource (for example, a file)
adCreateOverwrite	67108864	When added to the other adCreate options, forces any existing file or directory to be overwritten
adCreateStructDoc	-2147483648	Creates a new structured document
adFailIfNotExists	-1	Generates an error if the source does not exist
adOpenIfExists	335544322	When added to the other adCreate options (except adCreateOverwrite), forces any existing file or directory to be opened

RecordOpenOptionsEnum

Name	Value	Description
adDelayFetchFields	32768	Do not fetch fields until their first access.
adDelayFetchStream	16384	Do not fetch the default stream until requested.
adOpenAsync	4096	Open the record asynchronously.
adOpenExecuteCommand	65536	The source of the record is a Command object.
adOpenRecordUnspecified	-1	No specific open options are specified.
adOpenSource	8388608	Open the source of the resource rather than its processed output (for example, an ASP file).

RecordStatusEnum

Name	Value	Description
adRecCanceled	256	The record was not saved, because the operation was cancelled.
adRecCantRelease	1024	The new record was not saved, because of existing record locks.
adRecConcurrencyViolation	2048	The record was not saved, because optimistic concurrency was in use.
adRecDBDeleted	262144	The record has already been deleted from the data source.
adRecDeleted	4	The record was deleted.
adRecIntegrityViolation	4096	The record was not saved, because the user violated integrity constraints.
adRecInvalid	16	The record was not saved, because its bookmark is invalid.
adRecMaxChangesExceeded	8192	The record was not saved, because there were too many pending changes.
adRecModified	2	The record was modified.
adRecMultipleChanges	64	The record was not saved, because it would have affected multiple records.

Table continues on the following page

Name	Value	Description
adRecNew	1	The record is new
adRecObjectOpen	16384	The record was not saved, because of a conflict with an open storage object.
adRecOK	0	The record was successfully updated.
adRecOutOfMemory	32768	The record was not saved, because the computer has run out of memory.
adRecPendingChanges	128	The record was not saved, because it refers to a pending insert.
adRecPermissionDenied	65536	The record was not saved, because the user has insufficient permissions.
adRecSchemaViolation	131072	The record was not saved, because it violates the structure of the underlying database.
adRecUnmodified	8	The record was not modified.

RecordTypeEnum

Name	Value	Description
adCollectionRecord	1	The record represents a collection resource, such as a directory.
adSimpleRecord	0	The record represents a simple resource, such as a text or HTML file.
adStructDoc	2	The record represents a structured document.

ResyncEnum

Name	Value	Description
adResyncAllValues	2	Data is overwritten, and pending updates are cancelled (default).
adResyncUnderlyingValues	1	Data is not overwritten, and pending updates are not cancelled.

SaveOptionsEnum

Name	Value	Description
adSaveCreateNotExist	1	Create a new file if one doesn't already exist (default).
adSaveCreateOverWrite	2	Overwrite the file if it already exists.

SchemaEnum

Because of a misspelling in the type library, adSchemaReferentialConstraints *is included twice—once for the original spelling and once for the corrected spelling*

Name	Value	Description
adSchemaActions	41	Request action information.
adSchemaAsserts	0	Request assert information.
adSchemaCatalogs	1	Request catalog information.
adSchemaCharacterSets	2	Request character set information.
adSchemaCheckConstraints	5	Request check constraint information.
adSchemaCollations	3	Request collation information.
adSchemaColumnPrivileges	13	Request column privilege information.
adSchemaColumns	4	Request column information.
adSchemaColumnsDomainUsage	11	Request column domain usage information.
adSchemaCommands	42	Request command information.
adSchemaConstraintColumnUsage	6	Request column constraint usage information.
adSchemaConstraintTableUsage	7	Request table constraint usage information.

Table continues on the following page

Name	Value	Description
adSchemaCubes	32	For multidimensional data, view the Cubes schema.
adSchemaDBInfoKeywords	30	Request the keywords from the provider.
adSchemaDBInfoLiterals	31	Request the literals from the provider.
adSchemaDimensions	33	For multidimensional data, view the Dimensions schema.
adSchemaForeignKeys	27	Request foreign key information.
adSchemaFunctions	40	Request function information.
adSchemaHierarchies	34	For multidimensional data, view the Hierarchies schema.
adSchemaIndexes	12	Request index information.
adSchemaKeyColumnUsage	8	Request key column usage information.
adSchemaLevels	35	For multidimensional data, view the Levels schema.
adSchemaMeasures	36	For multidimensional data, view the Measures schema.
adSchemaMembers	38	For multidimensional data, view the Members schema.
adSchemaPrimaryKeys	28	Request primary key information.
adSchemaProcedureColumns	29	Request stored procedure column information.
adSchemaProcedureParameters	26	Request stored procedure parameter information.
adSchemaProcedures	16	Request stored procedure information.
adSchemaProperties	37	For multidimensional data, view the Properties schema.
adSchemaProviderSpecific	-1	Request provider-specific information.
adSchemaProviderTypes	22	Request provider type information.

Table continues on the following page

Name	Value	Description
adSchemaReferentialContraints	9	Request referential constraint information.
adSchemaReferentialConstraints	9	Request referential constraint information.
adSchemaSchemata	17	Request schema information.
adSchemaSets	43	Request set information.
adSchemaSQLLanguages	18	Request SQL language support information.
adSchemaStatistics	19	Request statistics information.
adSchemaTableConstraints	10	Request table constraint information.
adSchemaTablePrivileges	14	Request table privilege information.
adSchemaTables	20	Request information about the tables.
adSchemaTranslations	21	Request character set translation information.
adSchemaTrustees	39	Request trustee information.
adSchemaUsagePrivileges	15	Request user privilege information.
adSchemaViewColumnUsage	24	Request column usage in views information.
adSchemaViews	23	Request view information.
adSchemaViewTableUsage	25	Request table usage in views information.

SearchDirectionEnum

Name	Value	Description
adSearchBackward	-1	Search backward from the current record.
adSearchForward	1	Search forward from the current record.

SeekEnum

Name	Value	Description
adSeekAfter	8	Seek the key just after the match.
adSeekAfterEQ	4	Seek the key equal to or just after the match.
adSeekBefore	32	See the key just before the match.
adSeekBeforeEQ	16	Seek the key equal to or just before the match.
adSeekFirstEQ	1	Seek the first key equal to the match.
adSeekLastEQ	2	Seek the last key equal to the match.

StreamOpenOptionsEnum

Name	Value	Description
adOpenStreamAsync	1	Open the stream asynchronously.
adOpenStreamFromRecord	4	Use the contents of an already open Record object as the resource to open.
adOpenStreamUnspecified	-1	Open the stream with default options (default).

StreamReadEnum

Name	Value	Description
adReadAll	-1	Read the entire contents of the stream, starting at the current position and ending at the end of the stream (default).
adReadLine	-2	Read the next line from the stream (uses the LineSeparator property to determine the end of the line).

StreamTypeEnum

Name	Value	Description
adTypeBinary	1	The stream contains binary data.
adTypeText	2	The stream contains text data (default).

StreamWriteEnum

Name	Value	Description
adWriteChar	0	Write the text string to the stream.
adWriteLine	1	Write the text string and a line separator (as defined by the LineSeparator property) to the stream.

StringFormatEnum

Name	Value	Description
adClipString	2	Rows are delimited by user-defined values.

XactAttributeEnum

Name	Value	Description
adXactAbortRetaining	262144	The provider will automatically start a new transaction after a RollbackTrans method call.
adXactAsyncPhaseOne	524288	Perform an asynchronous commit.
adXactCommitRetaining	131072	The provider will automatically start a new transaction after a CommitTrans method call.
adXactSyncPhaseOne	1048576	Perform a synchronous commit.

Miscellaneous Constants

These values are not included in the standard adovbs.inc include file (and are not automatically supplied when using Visual Basic), but can be found in adocon.inc (for ASP) and adocon.bas (for Visual Basic) from the supporting Web site.

Many of these may not be necessary for you as an ADO programmer, but they are included here for completeness. They are only really useful as bitmask values for entries in the Properties collection.

DB_COLLATION

Name	Value	Description
DB_COLLATION_ASC	1	The sort sequence for the column is ascending.
DB_COLLATION_DESC	2	The sort sequence for the column is descending.

DB_IMP_LEVEL

Name	Value	Description
DB_IMP_LEVEL_ANONYMOUS	0	The client is anonymous to the server, and the server process cannot obtain identification information about the client and cannot impersonate the client.
DB_IMP_LEVEL_DELEGATE	3	The process can impersonate the client's security context while acting on behalf of the client. The server process can also make outgoing calls to other servers while acting on behalf of the client.
DB_IMP_LEVEL_IDENTIFY	1	The server can obtain the client's identity, and can impersonate the client for ACL checking, but cannot access system objects as the client.
DB_IMP_LEVEL_IMPERSONATE	2	The server process can impersonate the client's security context while acting on behalf of the client. This information is obtained upon connection and not on every call.

DB_MODE

Name	Value	Description
DB_MODE_READ	1	Read-only
DB_MODE_READWRITE	3	Read/write (equal to DB_MODE_READ + DB_MODE_WRITE)
DB_MODE_SHARE_DENY_NONE	16	Prevents read and write access from being denied to others
DB_MODE_SHARE_DENY_READ	4	Prevents others from opening in read mode
DB_MODE_SHARE_DENY_WRITE	8	Prevents others from opening in write mode
DB_MODE_SHARE_EXCLUSIVE	12	Prevents others from opening in read/write mode (equal to DB_MODE_SHARE_DENY_WRITE + DB_MODE_SHARE_DENY_WRITE)
DB_MODE_WRITE	2	Write-only

DB_PROT_LEVEL

Name	Value	Description
DB_PROT_LEVEL_CALL	2	Authenticates the source of the data at the beginning of each request from the client to the server
DB_PROT_LEVEL_CONNECT	1	Authenticates only when the client establishes the connection with the server
DB_PROT_LEVEL_NONE	0	Performs no authentication of data sent to the server
DB_PROT_LEVEL_PKT	3	Authenticates that all data received is from the client
DB_PROT_LEVEL_PKT_INTEGRITY	4	Authenticates that all data received is from the client and has not been changed in transit
DB_PROT_LEVEL_PKT_PRIVACY	5	Authenticates that all data received is from the client, that it has not been changed in transit, and protects the privacy of the data by encrypting it

DB_PT

Name	Value	Description
DB_PT_FUNCTION	3	Function–there is a returned value.
DB_PT_PROCEDURE	2	Procedure–there is no returned value.
DB_PT_UNKNOWN	1	It is not known whether there is a returned value.

DB_SEARCHABLE

Name	Value	Description
DB_ALL_EXCEPT_LIKE	3	The data type can be used in a WHERE clause with all comparison operators except LIKE.
DB_LIKE_ONLY	2	The data type can be used in a WHERE clause only with the LIKE predicate.
DB_SEARCHABLE	4	The data type can be used in a WHERE clause with any comparison operator.
DB_UNSEARCHABLE	1	The data type cannot be used in a WHERE clause.

DBCOLUMNDESCFLAG

Name	Value	Description
DBCOLUMNDESCFLAG_CLSID	8	The CLSID portion of the column description can be changed when altering the column.
DBCOLUMNDESCFLAG_COLSIZE	16	The column size portion of the column description can be changed when altering the column.
DBCOLUMNDESCFLAG_DBCID	32	The DBCID portion of the column description can be changed when altering the column.
DBCOLUMNDESCFLAG_ITYPEINFO	2	The type information portion of the column description can be changed when altering the column.

Table continues on the following page

Name	Value	Description
DBCOLUMNDESCFLAG_PRECISION	128	The precision portion of the column description can be changed when altering the column.
DBCOLUMNDESCFLAG_PROPERTIES	4	The property sets portion of the column description can be changed when altering the column.
DBCOLUMNDESCFLAG_SCALE	256	The numeric scale portion of the column description can be changed when altering the column.
DBCOLUMNDESCFLAG_TYPENAME	1	The type name portion of the column description can be changed when altering the column.
DBCOLUMNDESCFLAG_WTYPE	64	The data type portion of the column description can be changed when altering the column.

DBCOLUMNFLAGS

Name	Value	Description
DBCOLUMNFLAGS_CACHEDEFERRED	4096	The value of a deferred column is cached when it is first read.
DBCOLUMNFLAGS_ISCHAPTER	8192	The column contains a Chapter value.
DBCOLUMNFLAGS_ISFIXEDLENGTH	16	All data in the column is of a fixed length.
DBCOLUMNFLAGS_ISLONG	128	The column contains a BLOB value that contains long data.
DBCOLUMNFLAGS_ISNULLABLE	32	The column can be set to Null, or the provider cannot determine whether the column can be set to Null.
DBCOLUMNFLAGS_ISROWID	256	The column contains a persistent row identifier.
DBCOLUMNFLAGS_ISROWVER	512	The column contains a timestamp or other row versioning data type.

Table continues on the following page

Name	Value	Description
DBCOLUMNFLAGS_MAYBENULL	64	Nulls can be got from the column.
DBCOLUMNFLAGS_MAYDEFER	2	The column is deferred.
DBCOLUMNFLAGS_WRITE	4	The column may be updated.
DBCOLUMNFLAGS_WRITEUNKNOWN	8	It is not known if the column can be updated.

DBLITERAL

Name	Value	Description
DBLITERAL_INVALID	0	An invalid value
DBLITERAL_BINARY_LITERAL	1	A binary literal in a text command
DBLITERAL_CATALOG_NAME	2	A catalog name in a text command
DBLITERAL_CATALOG_SEPARATOR	3	The character that separates the catalog name from the rest of the identifier in a text command
DBLITERAL_CHAR_LITERAL	4	A character literal in a text command
DBLITERAL_COLUMN_ALIAS	5	A column alias in a text command
DBLITERAL_COLUMN_NAME	6	A column name used in a text command or in a data-definition interface
DBLITERAL_CORRELATION_NAME	7	A correlation name (table alias) in a text command
DBLITERAL_CURSOR_NAME	8	A cursor name in a text command
DBLITERAL_ESCAPE_PERCENT_PREFIX	9	The character used in a LIKE clause to escape the character returned for the DBLITERAL_LIKE_PERCENT literal
DBLITERAL_ESCAPE_PERCENT_SUFFIX	29	The escape character, if any, used to suffix the character returned for the DBLITERAL_LIKE_PERCENT literal

Table continues on the following page

Name	Value	Description
DBLITERAL_ESCAPE_UNDERSCORE_PREFIX	10	The character used in a LIKE clause to escape the character returned for the DBLITERAL_LIKE_UNDERSCORE literal
DBLITERAL_ESCAPE_UNDERSCORE_SUFFIX	30	The escape character, if any, used to suffix the character returned for the DBLITERAL_LIKE_UNDERSCORE literal
DBLITERAL_INDEX_NAME	11	An index name used in a text command or in a data-definition interface
DBLITERAL_LIKE_PERCENT	12	The character used in a LIKE clause to match zero or more characters
DBLITERAL_LIKE_UNDERSCORE	13	The character used in a LIKE clause to match exactly one character
DBLITERAL_PROCEDURE_NAME	14	A procedure name in a text command
DBLITERAL_SCHEMA_NAME	16	A schema name in a text command
DBLITERAL_SCHEMA_SEPARATOR	27	The character that separates the schema name from the rest of the identifier in a text command
DBLITERAL_TABLE_NAME	17	A table name used in a text command or in a data-definition interface
DBLITERAL_TEXT_COMMAND	18	A text command, such as a SQL statement
DBLITERAL_USER_NAME	19	A user name in a text command
DBLITERAL_VIEW_NAME	20	A view name in a text command
DBLITERAL_QUOTE_PREFIX	15	The character used in a text command as the opening quote for quoting identifiers that contain special characters
DBLITERAL_QUOTE_SUFFIX	28	The character used in a text command as the closing quote for quoting identifiers that contain special characters

DBPARAMTYPE

Name	Value	Description
DBPARAMTYPE_INPUT	1	The parameter is an input parameter.
DBPARAMTYPE_INPUTOUTPUT	2	The parameter is both an input and an output parameter.
DBPARAMTYPE_OUTPUT	3	The parameter is an output parameter.
DBPARAMTYPE_RETURNVALUE	4	The parameter is a return value.

DBPROMPT

Name	Value	Description
DBPROMPT_COMPLETE	2	Prompt the user only if more information is needed.
DBPROMPT_COMPLETEREQUIRED	3	Prompt the user only if more information is required. Do not allow the user to enter optional information.
DBPROMPT_NOPROMPT	4	Do not prompt the user.
DBPROMPT_PROMPT	1	Always prompt the user for initialization information.

DBPROPVAL_AO

Name	Value	Description
DBPROPVAL_AO_RANDOM	2	Columns can be accessed in any order.
DBPROPVAL_AO_SEQUENTIAL	0	All columns must be accessed in sequential order determined by the column ordinal.
DBPROPVAL_AO_SEQUENTIALSTORAGEOBJECTS	1	Columns bound as storage objects can be accessed only in sequential order as determined by the column ordinal.

DBPROPVAL_ASYNCH

Name	Value	Description
DBPROPVAL_ASYNCH_ BACKGROUNDPOPULATION	8	The rowset is populated asynchronously in the background.
DBPROPVAL_ASYNCH_INITIALIZE	1	Initialization is performed asynchronously.
DBPROPVAL_ASYNCH_ POPULATEONDEMAND	32	The consumer prefers to optimize for getting each individual request for data returned as quickly as possible.
DBPROPVAL_ASYNCH_PREPOPULATE	16	The consumer prefers to optimize for retrieving all data when the row set is materialized.
DBPROPVAL_ASYNCH_ RANDOMPOPULATION	4	Rowset population is performed asynchronously in a random manner.
DBPROPVAL_ASYNCH_ SEQUENTIALPOPULATION	2	Rowset population is performed asynchronously in a sequential manner.

DBPROPVAL_BG

Name	Value	Description
DBPROPVAL_GB_COLLATE	16	A COLLATE clause can be specified at the end of each grouping column.
DBPROPVAL_GB_CONTAINS_SELECT	4	The GROUP BY clause must contain all non-aggregated columns in the select list. It can contain columns that are not in the select list.
DBPROPVAL_GB_EQUALS_SELECT	2	The GROUP BY clause must contain all nonaggregated columns in the select list. It cannot contain any other columns.
DBPROPVAL_GB_NO_RELATION	8	The columns in the GROUP BY clause and the select list are not related. The meaning on nongrouped, nonaggregated columns in the select list is data source dependent.
DBPROPVAL_GB_NOT_SUPPORTED	1	GROUP BY clauses are not supported.

DBPROPVAL_BI

Name	Value	Description
DBPROPVAL_BI_CROSSROWSET	1	Bookmark values are valid across all rowsets generated on this table.

DBPROPVAL_BMK

Name	Value	Description
DBPROPVAL_BMK_KEY	2	The bookmark type is key.
DBPROPVAL_BMK_NUMERIC	1	The bookmark type is numeric.

DBPROPVAL_BO

Name	Value	Description
DBPROPVAL_BO_NOINDEXUPDATE	1	The provider is not required to update indexes based on inserts or changes to the rowset. Any indexes need to be re-created following changes made through the rowset.
DBPROPVAL_BO_NOLOG	0	The provider is not required to log inserts or changes to the rowset.
DBPROPVAL_BO_REFINTEGRITY	2	Referential integrity constraints do not need to be checked or enforced for changes made through the rowset.

DBPROPVAL_BP

Name	Value	Description
DBPROPVAL_BP_NOPARTIAL	2	Fail the bulk operation if there is a single error.
DBPROPVAL_BP_PARTIAL	1	Allow the bulk operation to partially complete, possibly resulting in inconsistent data.

DBPROPVAL_BT

Name	Value	Description
DBPROPVAL_BT_ DEFAULT	0	Use the value defined in the dynamic property Jet OLEDB:Global Bulk Transactions.
DBPROPVAL_BT_NOBULKTRANSACTIONS	1	Bulk operations are not transacted.
DBPROPVAL_BT_BULKTRANSACTION	2	Bulk operations are transacted.

DBPROPVAL_CB

DBPROPSET_DATASOURCEINFO has two instances of DBPROPVAL_CB. The values in the following table are for DBPROP_CONCATNULLBEHAVIOR.

Name	Value	Description
DBPROPVAL_CB_NON_NULL	2	The result is the concatenation of the non-Null valued column or columns.
DBPROPVAL_CB_NULL	1	The result is Null valued.

DBPROPVAL_CB

DBPROPSET_DATASOURCEINFO has two instances of DBPROPVAL_CB. The values in the following table are for DBPROP_PREPAREABORTBEHAVIOR.

Name	Value	Description
DBPROPVAL_CB_DELETE	1	Aborting a transaction deletes prepared commands.
DBPROPVAL_CB_PRESERVE	2	Aborting a transaction preserves prepared commands.

DBPROPVAL_CD

Name	Value	Description
DBPROPVAL_CD_NOTNULL	1	Columns can be created non-nullable.

DBPROPVAL_CL

Name	Value	Description
DBPROPVAL_CL_END	2	The catalog name appears at the end of the fully qualified name.
DBPROPVAL_CL_START	1	The catalog name appears at the start of the fully qualified name.

DBPROPVAL_CO

Name	Value	Description
DBPROPVAL_CO_BEGINSWITH	32	Provider supports the BEGINSWITH and NOTBEGINSWITH operators.
DBPROPVAL_CO_CASEINSENSITIVE	8	Provider supports the CASEINSENSITIVE operator.
DBPROPVAL_CO_CASESENSITIVE	4	Provider supports the CASESENSITIVE operator.
DBPROPVAL_CO_CONTAINS	16	Provider supports the CONTAINS and NOTCONTAINS operators.
DBPROPVAL_CO_EQUALITY	1	Provider supports the following operators: LT, LE, EQ, GE, GT, NE.
DBPROPVAL_CO_STRING	2	Provider supports the BEGINSWITH operator.

DBPROPVAL_CS

Name	Value	Description
DBPROPVAL_CS_COMMUNICATIONFAILURE	2	The DSO is unable to communicate with the data store.
DBPROPVAL_CS_INITIALIZED	1	The DSO is in an initialized state and able to communicate with the data store.
DBPROPVAL_CS_UNINITIALIZED	0	The DSO is in an uninitialized state.

DBPROPVAL_CU

Name	Value	Description
DBPROPVAL_CU_DML_STATEMENTS	1	Catalog names are supported in all Data Manipulation Language statements.
DBPROPVAL_CU_INDEX_DEFINITION	4	Catalog names are supported in all index definition statements.
DBPROPVAL_CU_PRIVILEGE_ DEFINITION	8	Catalog names are supported in all privilege definition statements.
DBPROPVAL_CU_TABLE_DEFINITION	2	Catalog names are supported in all table definition statements.

DBPROPVAL_DF

Name	Value	Description
DBPROPVAL_DF_INITIALLY_DEFERRED	1	The foreign key is initially deferred.
DBPROPVAL_DF_INITIALLY_IMMEDIATE	2	The foreign key is initially immediate.
DBPROPVAL_DF_NOT_DEFERRABLE	3	The foreign key is not deferrable.

DBPROPVAL_DL

Name	Value	Description
DBPROPVAL_DL_OLDMODE	0	Mode used in previous versions of the Jet database
DBPROPVAL_DL_ALCATRAZ	1	Mode used in Jet 4 and later, allowing row level locking

DBPROPVAL_DST

Name	Value	Description
DBPROPVAL_DST_MDP	2	The provider is a multidimensional provider (MD).
DBPROPVAL_DST_TDP	1	The provider is a tabular data provider (TDP).
DBPROPVAL_DST_TDPANDMDP	3	The provider is both a TDP and a MD provider.
DBPROPVAL_DST_DOCSOURCE	4	The provider is a document source (Internet Publishing Provider).

DBPROPVAL_GU

Name	Value	Description
DBPROPVAL_GU_NOTSUPPORTED	1	URL suffixes are not supported. This is the only option supported by the Internet Publishing Provider in this version of ADO.
DBPROPVAL_GU_SUFFIX	2	URL suffixes are generated by the Internet Publishing Provider.

DBPROPVAL_HT

Name	Value	Description
DBPROPVAL_HT_DIFFERENT_ ATALOGS	1	The provider supports heterogeneous joins between catalogs.
DBPROPVAL_HT_DIFFERENT_ ROVIDERS	2	The provider supports heterogeneous joins between providers.

DBPROPVAL_IC

Name	Value	Description
DBPROPVAL_IC_LOWER	2	Identifiers in SQL are case insensitive and are stored in lowercase in system catalog.
DBPROPVAL_IC_MIXED	8	Identifiers in SQL are case insensitive and are stored in mixed case in system catalog.
DBPROPVAL_IC_SENSITIVE	4	Identifiers in SQL are case sensitive and are stored in mixed case in system catalog.
DBPROPVAL_IC_UPPER	1	Identifiers in SQL are case insensitive and are stored in uppercase in system catalog.

DBPROPVAL_IN

Name	Value	Description
DBPROPVAL_IN_ALLOWNULL	0	The index allows Null values to be inserted.
DBPROPVAL_IN_DISALLOW NULL	1	The index does not allow entries where the key columns are Null. An error will be generated if the consumer attempts to insert a Null value into a key column.
DBPROPVAL_IN_IGNOREANY NULL	4	The index does not insert entries containing Null keys.
DBPROPVAL_IN_IGNORENULL	2	The index does not insert entries where some column key has a Null value.

DBPROPVAL_IT

Name	Value	Description
DBPROPVAL_IT_BTREE	1	The index is a B+ tree.
DBPROPVAL_IT_CONTENT	3	The index is a content index.
DBPROPVAL_IT_HASH	2	The index is a hash file using linear or extensible hashing.
DBPROPVAL_IT_OTHER	4	The index is some other type of index.

DBPROPVAL_JCC

Name	Value	Description
DBPROPVAL_JCC_PASSIVESHUTDOWN	1	New connections to the database are disallowed.
DBPROPVAL_JCC_NORMAL	2	Users are allowed to connect to the database.

DBPROPVAL_LG

Name	Value	Description
DBPROPVAL_LG_PAGE	1	Use page locking.
DBPROPVAL_LG_ALCATRAZ	2	Use row-level locking.

DBPROPVAL_MR

Name	Value	Description
DBPROPVAL_MR_CONCURRENT	2	More than one rowset created by the same multiple results object can exist concurrently.
DBPROPVAL_MR_NOTSUPPORTED	0	Multiple results objects are not supported.
DBPROPVAL_MR_SUPPORTED	1	The provider supports multiple results objects.

DBPROPVAL_NC

Name	Value	Description
DBPROPVAL_NC_END	1	Nulls are sorted at the end of the list, regardless of the sort order.
DBPROPVAL_NC_HIGH	2	Nulls are sorted at the high end of the list.
DBPROPVAL_NC_LOW	4	Nulls are sorted at the low end of the list.
DBPROPVAL_NC_START	8	Nulls are sorted at the start of the list, regardless of the sort order.

DBPROPVAL_NP

Name	Value	Description
DBPROPVAL_NP_ABOUTTODO	2	The consumer will be notified before an action (the Will event).
DBPROPVAL_NP_DIDEVENT	16	The consumer will be notified after an action (the Complete event).
DBPROPVAL_NP_FAILEDTODO	8	The consumer will be notified if an action failed (a Will or Complete event).
DBPROPVAL_NP_OKTODO	1	The consumer will be notified of events.
DBPROPVAL_NP_SYNCHAFTER	4	The consumer will be notified when the rowset is resynchronized.

DBPROPVAL_NT

Name	Value	Description
DBPROPVAL_NT_MULTIPLEROWS	2	For methods that operate on multiple rows, and generate multiphased notifications (events), the provider calls OnRowChange once for all rows that succeed and once for all rows that fail.
DBPROPVAL_NT_SINGLEROW	1	For methods that operate on multiple rows, and generate multiphased notifications (events), the provider calls OnRowChange separately for each phase for each row.

DBPROPVAL_OA

Name	Value	Description
DBPROPVAL_OA_ATEXECUTE	2	Output parameter data is available immediately after the Command.Execute returns.
DBPROPVAL_OA_ATROWRELEASE	4	Output parameter data is available when the rowset is released. For a single rowset operation, this is when the rowset is completely released (closed). For a multiple rowset operation, this is when the next rowset if fetched. The consumer's bound memory is in an indeterminate state before the parameter data becomes available.
DBPROPVAL_OA_NOTSUPPORTED	1	Output parameters are not supported.

DBPROPVAL_OO

Name	Value	Description
DBPROPVAL_OO_BLOB	1	The provider supports access to BLOBs as structured storage objects.
DBPROPVAL_OO_DIRECTBIND	16	The provider supports direct binding to BLOBs.
DBPROPVAL_OO_IPERSIST	2	The provider supports access to OLE objects through OLE.
DBPROPVAL_OO_SCOPED	8	Row objects implement scoped operations.
DBPROPVAL_OO_SINGLETON	32	The provider supports singleton selects.

DBPROPVAL_ORS

Name	Value	Description
DBPROPVAL_ORS_TABLE	0	The provider supports opening tables.
DBPROPVAL_ORS_INDEX	1	The provider supports opening indexes.
DBPROPVAL_ORS_INTEGRATEDINDEX	2	The provider supports both the table and index in the same open method.
DBPROPVAL_ORS_STOREDPROC	4	The provider supports opening rowsets over stored procedures.
DBPROPVAL_ORS_HISTOGRAM	8	The provider supports opening rowsets over histograms.

DBPROPVAL_OS

Name	Value	Description
DBPROPVAL_OS_ENABLEALL	-1	All services should be invoked (default).
DBPROPVAL_OS_RESOURCEPOOLING	1	Resources should be pooled.
DBPROPVAL_OS_TXNENLISTMENT	2	Sessions in an MTS environment should be enlisted automatically in a global transaction where required
DBPROPVAL_OS_CLIENT_CURSOR	4	Disable client cursor.
DBPROPVAL_OS_DISABLEALL	0	All services should be disabled.
DBPROPCAL_OS_AGR_AFTERSESSION	8	Only session level aggregation of resources should be invoked.

DBPROPVAL_PT

Name	Value	Description
DBPROPVAL_PT_GUID	8	The GUID is used as the persistent ID type.
DBPROPVAL_PT_GUID_NAME	1	The GUID Name is used as the persistent ID type.
DBPROPVAL_PT_GUID_PROPID	2	The GUID Property ID is used as the persistent ID type.
DBPROPVAL_PT_NAME	4	The Name is used as the persistent ID type.
DBPROPVAL_PT_PGUID_NAME	32	The Property GUID name is used as the persistent ID type.
DBPROPVAL_PT_PGUID_PROPID	64	The Property GUID Property ID is used as the persistent ID type.
DBPROPVAL_PT_PROPID	16	The Property ID is used as the persistent ID type.

DBPROPVAL_RD

Name	Value	Description
DBPROPVAL_RD_RESETALL	-1	The provider should reset all states associated with the data source, with the exception that any open object is not released.

DBPROPVAL_RT

Name	Value	Description
DBPROPVAL_RT_APTMTTHREAD	2	The DSO is apartment threaded.
DBPROPVAL_RT_FREETHREAD	1	The DSO is free threaded.
DBPROPVAL_RT_SINGLETHREAD	4	The DSO is single threaded.

DBPROPVAL_SQ

Name	Value	Description
DBPROPVAL_SQ_COMPARISON	2	All predicates that support subqueries support comparison subqueries.
DBPROPVAL_SQ_CORRELATEDSUBQUERIES	1	All predicates that support subqueries support correlated subqueries.
DBPROPVAL_SQ_EXISTS	4	All predicates that support subqueries support EXISTS subqueries.
DBPROPVAL_SQ_IN	8	All predicates that support subqueries support IN subqueries.
DBPROPVAL_SQ_QUANTIFIED	16	All predicates that support subqueries support quantified subqueries.

DBPROPVAL_SQL

Name	Value	Description
DBPROPVAL_SQL_ANDI89_IEF	8	The provider supports the ANSI SQL89 IEF level.
DBPROPVAL_SQL_ANSI92_ENTRY	16	The provider supports the ANSI SQL92 Entry level.
DBPROPVAL_SQL_ANSI92_FULL	128	The provider supports the ANSI SQL92 Full level.
DBPROPVAL_SQL_ANSI92_INTERMEDIATE	64	The provider supports the ANSI SQL92 Intermediate level.
DBPROPVAL_SQL_CORE	2	The provider supports the ODBC 2.5 Core SQL level.
DBPROPVAL_SQL_ESCAPECLAUSES	256	The provider supports the ODBC escape clauses syntax.
DBPROPVAL_SQL_EXTENDED	4	The provider supports the ODBC 2.5 EXTENDED SQL level.
DBPROPVAL_SQL_FIPS_TRANSITIONAL	32	The provider supports the ANSI SQL92 Transitional level.
DBPROPVAL_SQL_MINIMUM	1	The provider supports the ODBC 2.5 EXTENDED SQL level.
DBPROPVAL_SQL_NONE	0	SQL is not supported.
DBPROPVAL_SQL_ODBC_CORE	2	The provider supports the ODBC 2.5 Core SQL level.
DBPROPVAL_SQL_ODBC_EXTENDED	4	The provider supports the ODBC 2.5 EXTENDED SQL level.
DBPROPVAL_SQL_ODBC_MINIMUM	1	The provider supports the ODBC 2.5 EXTENDED SQL level.
DBPROPVAL_SQL_SUBMINIMUM	512	The provider supports the DBGUID_SQL dialect and parses the command text according to SQL rules, but does not support either the minimum ODBC level or the ANSI SQL92 Entry level.

DBPROPVAL_SS

Name	Value	Description
DBPROPVAL_SS_ILOCKBYTES	8	The provider supports IlockBytes.
DBPROPVAL_SS_ISEQUENTIALSTREAM	1	The provider supports IsequentialStream.
DBPROPVAL_SS_ISTORAGE	4	The provider supports Istorage.
DBPROPVAL_SS_ISTREAM	2	The provider supports IStream.

DBPROPVAL_SU

Name	Value	Description
DBPROPVAL_SU_DML_STATEMENTS	1	Schema names are supported in all Data Manipulation Language statements.
DBPROPVAL_SU_INDEX_DEFINITION	4	Schema names are supported in all index definition statements.
DBPROPVAL_SU_PRIIVILEGE_ DEFINITION	8	Schema names are supported in all privilege definition statements.
DBPROPVAL_SU_TABLE_DEFINITION	2	Schema names are supported in all table definition statements.

DBPROPVAL_TC

Name	Value	Description
DBPROPVAL_TC_ALL	8	Transactions can contain DDL and Data Manipulation Language statements in any order.
DBPROPVAL_TC_DDL_COMMIT	2	Transactions can contain only Data Manipulation Language statements. The transaction will be committed if a table or index is modified within a transaction.
DBPROPVAL_TC_DDL_IGNORE	4	Transactions can contain only Data Manipulation Language statements. Any attempt to modify a table or index within a transaction is ignored.

Table continues on the following page

Name	Value	Description
DBPROPVAL_TC_DDL_LOCK	16	Transactions can contain both Data Manipulation Language and table or index modifications. The table or index will be locked until the transaction completes.
DBPROPVAL_TC_DML	1	Transactions can only contain Data Manipulation Language statements. DDL statements within a transaction cause an error.
DBPROPVAL_TC_NONE	0	Transactions are not supported.

DBPROPVAL_TI

Name	Value	Description
DBPROPVAL_TI_BROWSE	256	Changes made by other transactions are visible before they are committed.
DBPROPVAL_TI_CHAOS	16	Transactions cannot overwrite pending changes from more highly isolated transactions (default).
DBPROPVAL_TI_CURSORSTABILITY	4096	Changes made by other transactions are not visible until those transactions are committed
DBPROPVAL_TI_ISOLATED	1048576	All concurrent transactions will interact only in ways that produce the same effect as if each transaction were entirely executed one after the other.
DBPROPVAL_TI_READCOMMITTED	4096	Changes made by other transactions are not visible until those transactions are committed.
DBPROPVAL_TI_READUNCOMMITTED	256	Changes made by other transactions are visible before they are committed.
DBPROPVAL_TI_REPEATABLEREAD	65536	Changes made by other transactions are not visible.
DBPROPVAL_TI_SERIALIZABLE	1048576	All concurrent transactions will interact only in ways that produce the same effect as if all transactions were entirely executed sequentially.

DBPROPVAL_TR

Name	Value	Description
DBPROPVAL_TR_ABORT	16	The transaction preserves its isolation context (it preserves its locks if that is how isolation is implemented) across the retaining abort.
DBPROPVAL_TR_ABORT_DC	8	The transaction may either preserve or dispose of isolation context across a retaining abort.
DBPROPVAL_TR_ABORT_NO	32	The transaction is explicitly not to preserve its isolation across a retaining abort.
DBPROPVAL_TR_BOTH	128	Isolation is preserved across both a retaining commit and a retaining abort.
DBPROPVAL_TR_COMMIT	2	The transaction preserves its isolation context (it preserves its locks if that is how isolation is implemented) across the retaining commit.
DBPROPVAL_TR_COMMIT_DC	1	The transaction may either preserve or dispose of isolation context across a retaining commit.
DBPROPVAL_TR_COMMIT_NO	4	The transaction is explicitly not to preserve its isolation across a retaining commit.
DBPROPVAL_TR_DONTCARE	64	The transaction may either preserve or dispose of isolation context across a retaining commit or abort (default).
DBPROPVAL_TR_NONE	256	Isolation is explicitly not to be retained across either a retaining commit or abort.
DBPROPVAL_TR_OPTIMISTIC	512	Optimistic concurrency control is to be used.

DBPROPVAL_TS

Name	Value	Description
DBPROPVAL_TS_CARDINALITY	1	Column and tuple cardinality information on columns in a statistic are supported.
DBPROPVAL_TS_HISTOGRAM	2	Histogram information on the first column of a statistic is supported.

DBPROPVAL_UP

Name	Value	Description
DBPROPVAL_UP_CHANGE	1	Indicates that SetData is supported
DBPROPVAL_UP_DELETE	2	Indicates that DeleteRows is supported
DBPROPVAL_UP_INSERT	4	Indicates that InsertRow is supported

JET_ENGINETYPE

Name	Value	Description
JET_ENGINETYPE_UNKNOWN	0	Database type unknown
JET_ENGINETYPE_JET10	1	Jet 10
JET_ENGINETYPE_JET11	2	Jet 11
JET_ENGINETYPE_JET2X	3	Jet 2x
JET_ENGINETYPE_JET3X	4	Jet 3x
JET_ENGINETYPE_JET4X	5	Jet 4x
JET_ENGINETYPE_DBASE3	10	DBase III
JET_ENGINETYPE_DBASE4	11	DBase IV
JET_ENGINETYPE_DBASE5	12	DBase V
JET_ENGINETYPE_EXCEL30	20	Excel 3
JET_ENGINETYPE_EXCEL40	21	Excel 4
JET_ENGINETYPE_EXCEL50	22	Excel 5 (Excel 95)
JET_ENGINETYPE_EXCEL80	23	Excel 8 (Excel 97)
JET_ENGINETYPE_EXCEL90	24	Excel 9 (Excel 2000)
JET_ENGINETYPE_EXCHANGE4	30	Exchange Server
JET_ENGINETYPE_LOTUSWK1	40	Lotus 1
JET_ENGINETYPE_LOTUSWK3	41	Lotus 3
JET_ENGINETYPE_LOTUSWK4	42	Lotus 4

Table continues on the following page

Name	Value	Description
JET_ENGINETYPE_PARADOX3X	50	Paradox 3.x
JET_ENGINETYPE_PARADOX4X	51	Paradox 4.5
JET_ENGINETYPE_PARADOX5X	52	Paradox 5.x
JET_ENGINETYPE_PARADOX7X	53	Paradox 7.x
JET_ENGINETYPE_TEXT1X	60	Text
JET_ENGINETYPE_HTML1X	70	HTML

MD_DIMTYPE

Name	Value	Description
MD_DIMTYPE_MEASURE	2	A measure dimension
MD_DIMTYPE_OTHER	3	Neither a time nor a measure dimension
MD_DIMTYPE_TIME	1	A time dimension
MD_DIMTYPE_UNKNOWN	0	Unclassifiable dimension

SQL_FN_NUM

Name	Value	Description
SQL_FN_NUM_ABS	1	The ABS function is supported by the data source.
SQL_FN_NUM_ACOS	2	The ACOS function is supported by the data source.
SQL_FN_NUM_ASIN	4	The ASIN function is supported by the data source.
SQL_FN_NUM_ATAN	8	The ATAN function is supported by the data source.
SQL_FN_NUM_ATAN2	16	The ATAN2 function is supported by the data source.

Table continues on the following page

Name	Value	Description
SQL_FN_NUM_CEILING	32	The CEILING function is supported by the data source.
SQL_FN_NUM_COS	64	The COS function is supported by the data source.
SQL_FN_NUM_COT	128	The COT function is supported by the data source.
SQL_FN_NUM_DEGREES	262144	The DEGREES function is supported by the data source.
SQL_FN_NUM_EXP	256	The EXP function is supported by the data source.
SQL_FN_NUM_FLOOR	512	The FLOOR function is supported by the data source.
SQL_FN_NUM_LOG	1024	The LOG function is supported by the data source.
SQL_FN_NUM_LOG10	524288	The LOG10 function is supported by the data source.
SQL_FN_NUM_MOD	2048	The MOD function is supported by the data source.
SQL_FN_NUM_PI	65536	The PI function is supported by the data source.
SQL_FN_NUM_POWER	1048576	The POWER function is supported by the data source.
SQL_FN_NUM_RADIANS	2097152	The RADIANS function is supported by the data source.
SQL_FN_NUM_RAND	131072	The RAND function is supported by the data source.
SQL_FN_NUM_ROUND	4194304	The ROUND function is supported by the data source.
SQL_FN_NUM_SIGN	4096	The SIGN function is supported by the data source.
SQL_FN_NUM_SIN	8192	The SIN function is supported by the data source.
SQL_FN_NUM_SQRT	10384	The SQRT function is supported by the data source.
SQL_FN_NUM_TAN	32768	The TAN function is supported by the data source.
SQL_FN_NUM_TRUNCATE	8388608	The TRUNCATE function is supported by the data source.

SQL_FN_STR

Name	Value	Description
SQL_FN_STR_ASCII	8192	The ASCII function is supported by the data source.
SQL_FN_STR_BIT_LENGTH	524288	The BIT_LENGTH function is supported by the data source.
SQL_FN_STR_CHAR	16384	The CHAR function is supported by the data source.
SQL_FN_STR_CHAR_LENGTH	1048576	The CHAR_LENGTH function is supported by the data source.
SQL_FN_STR_CHARACTER_LENGTH	2097152	The CHARACTER_LENGTH function is supported by the data source.
SQL_FN_STR_CONCAT	1	The CONCAT function is supported by the data source.
SQL_FN_STR_DIFFERENCE	32768	The DIFFERENCE function is supported by the data source.
SQL_FN_STR_INSERT	2	The INSERT function is supported by the data source.
SQL_FN_STR_LCASE	64	The LCASE function is supported by the data source.
SQL_FN_STR_LEFT	4	The LEFT function is supported by the data source.
SQL_FN_STR_LENGTH	16	The LENGTH function is supported by the data source.
SQL_FN_STR_LOCATE	32	The LOCATE function is supported by the data source.
SQL_FN_STR_LOCATE_2	65536	The LOCATE_2 function is supported by the data source.
SQL_FN_STR_LTRIM	8	The LTRIM function is supported by the data source.

Table continues on the following page

470

Name	Value	Description
SQL_FN_STR_OCTET_LENGTH	4194304	The OCTET_LENGTH function is supported by the data source.
SQL_FN_STR_POSITION	8388608	The POSITION function is supported by the data source.
SQL_FN_STR_REPEAT	128	The REPEAT function is supported by the data source.
SQL_FN_STR_REPLACE	256	The REPLACE function is supported by the data source.
SQL_FN_STR_RIGHT	512	The RIGHT function is supported by the data source.
SQL_FN_STR_RTRIM	1024	The RTRIM function is supported by the data source.
SQL_FN_STR_SOUNDEX	131072	The SOUNDEX function is supported by the data source.
SQL_FN_STR_SPACE	262144	The SPACE function is supported by the data source.
SQL_FN_STR_SUBSTRING	2048	The SUBSTRING function is supported by the data source.
SQL_FN_STR_UCASE	4096	The UCASE function is supported by the data source.

SQL_FN_SYS

Name	Value	Description
SQL_FN_SYS_DBNAME	2	The DBNAME system function is supported.
SQL_FN_SYS_IFNULL	4	The IFNULL system function is supported.
SQL_FN_SYS_USERNAME	1	The USERNAME system function is supported.

SQL_OJ

Name	Value	Description
SQL_OJ_ALL_COMPARISON_OPS	64	The comparison operator in the ON clause can be any of the ODBC comparison operators. If this is not set, only the equals (=) comparison operator can be used in an outer join.
SQL_OJ_FULL	4	Full outer joins are supported.
SQL_OJ_INNER	32	The inner table (the right table in a left outer join or the left table in a right outer join) can also be used in an inner join. This does not apply to full out joins, which do not have an inner table.
SQL_OJ_LEFT	1	Left outer joins are supported.
SQL_OJ_NESTED	8	Nested outer joins are supported.
SQL_OJ_NOT_ORDERED	16	The column names in the ON clause of the outer join do not have to be in the same order as their respective table names in the OUTER JOIN clause.
SQL_OJ_RIGHT	2	Right outer joins are supported.

SQL_SDF_CURRENT

Name	Value	Description
SQL_SDF_CURRENT_DATE	1	The CURRENT_DATE system function is supported.
SQL_SDF_CURRENT_TIME	2	The CURRENT_TIME system function is supported.
SQL_SDF_CURRENT_TIMESTAMP	4	The CURRENT_TIMESTAMP system function is supported.

SSPROP_CONCUR

Name	Value	Description
SSPROP_CONCUR_LOCK	4	Use row locking to prevent concurrent access.
SSPROP_CONCUR_READ_ONLY	8	The rowset is read-only. Full concurrency is supported.
SSPROP_CONCUR_ROWVER	1	Use row versioning to determining concurrent access violations. The SQL table or tables must contain a timestamp column.
SSPROP_CONCUR_VALUES	2	Use the values of columns in the rowset.

SSPROPVAL_USEPROCFORPREP

Name	Value	Description
SSPROPVAL_USEPROCFORPRE_OFF	0	A temporary stored procedure is not created when a command is prepared.
SSPROPVAL_USEPROCFORPRE_ON	1	A temporary stored procedure is created when a command is prepared. Temporary stored procedures are dropped when the session is released.
SSPROPVAL_USEPROCFORPREP_ON_DROP	2	A temporary stored procedure is created when a command is prepared. The procedure is dropped when the command is unprepared, or a new command text is set, or when all application references to the command are released.

ADO Properties Collection

The Properties collection deals with dynamic properties specific to the provider. All ADO objects have a fixed set of properties (such as Name), but because ADO is designed for use with different providers, a way was needed to allow providers to specify their own properties. The Properties collection contains these properties, and this appendix deals with which properties are supported by which providers, and what these properties actually do.

Some of the properties refer to rowsets. This is just the OLE DB term for Recordsets.

Property Usage

As you can see from the tables in this appendix, there are very many properties. However, using them is actually quite simple. You simply index into the Properties collection by using the property name itself. For example, to find out the name the provider gives to procedures, you could do this:

```
Print objConn.Properties("Procedure Term")
```

For SQL Server, this returns stored procedure, and for Access this returns STORED QUERY.

You can iterate through the entire set of properties very simply:

```
For Each objProp In objConn.Properties
    Print objProp.Name
    Print objProp.Value
Next
```

This will print out the property names and values.

For those properties that return custom types, you must identify whether these return a bitmask or a simple value; the property description identifies this, because it says "one of" or "one or more of." In the first case, the property will just return a single value. For example, to find out whether your provider supports output parameters on stored procedures, you can query the Output Parameter Availability property. This is defined as returning values of type DBPROPVAL_OA, which are as follows:

Constant	Value
DBPROPVAL_OA_ATEXECUTE	2
DBPROPVAL_OA_ATROWRELEASE	4
DBPROPVAL_OA_NOTSUPPORTED	1

Examining this property when connected to SQL Server gives you a value of 4, indicating that output parameters are available when the recordset is closed. Access, on the other hand, returns a value of 1, indicating that output parameters are not supported.

For those properties that return bitmask, you'll need to use Boolean logic to identify which values are set. For example, to query the provider and examine what features of SQL are supported, you can use the SQL Support property. For Access this returns 512, which corresponds to DBPROPVAL_SQL_SUBMINIMUM, indicating that not even the ANSI SQL92 Entry level SQL facilities are provided. On the other hand, SQL Server returns 283, but there isn't a single value for this, so it must be a combination of values. In fact, it corresponds to the sum of the following:

Constant	Value
DBPROPVAL_SQL_ESCAPECLAUSES	256
DBPROPVAL_SQL_ANSI92_ENTRY	16
DBPROPVAL_SQL_ANDI89_IEF	8
DBPROPVAL_SQL_CORE	2
DBPROPVAL_SQL_MINIMUM	1

To see whether a specific value is set, use the Boolean AND operator. For example:

```
lngSQLSupport = oConn.Properties("SQL Support")
If (lngSQLSupport AND DBPROPVAL_SQL_CORE) = DBPROPVAL_SQL_CORE Then
    'core facilities are supported
End If
```

A full description of the constants appears in Appendix B.

Property Support

The following table shows a list of all OLE DB properties and indicates which are supported by three widely used drivers: the Microsoft OLE DB driver for Jet, the Microsoft OLE DB driver for ODBC, and the Microsoft OLE DB driver for SQL Server. Because this list contains dynamic properties, not every property may show up under all circumstances. Other providers may also implement properties not listed in this table.

A tick (✓) indicates that the property is supported, and a blank space indicates it is not supported. Note that support for recordset properties may depend upon the locking type, cursor type, and cursor location.

> *Note: This list doesn't include the* Iproperty *(such as* IRowset, *etc.) properties. Although these are part of the collection, they are not particularly useful for the ADO programmer.*

For the *Object Type* column, the following applies:

❑   RS = Recordset

❑   R = Record

❑   C = Connection

❑   CM = Command

❑   F = Field

Property Name	Object Type	ODBC	Jet	SQL	Internet Publishing (IIS5)	MSDataShape	Persist	Remote	Indexing Service	Directory Services	Exchange	Oracle
Access Order	RS/CM	✓	✓	✓		✓	✓	✓	✓	✓		✓
Accessible Procedures	C	✓										
Accessible Tables	C	✓										
Active Sessions	C	✓	✓	✓	✓				✓	✓	✓	✓
Active Statements	C	✓										
ADSI Flag	C									✓		
Allow Native Variant	C			✓								
Alter Column Support	C		✓	✓								
Always use content index	RS								✓			
Append-Only Rowset	RS	✓	✓	✓		✓	✓	✓	✓	✓		
Application Name	C			✓								
Asynchable Abort	C	✓	✓	✓							✓	✓
Asynchable Commit	C	✓	✓	✓							✓	✓
Asynchronous Processing	C					✓						
Asynchronous Rowset Processing	RS	✓	✓	✓		✓	✓	✓	✓	✓	✓	
Auto Recalc	RS	✓	✓	✓		✓	✓	✓	✓	✓		
Auto Translate	C			✓								
Autocommit Isolation Levels	C	✓	✓	✓		✓	✓	✓	✓	✓	✓	✓
Background Fetch Size	RS	✓	✓	✓	✓	✓	✓	✓	✓	✓		
Background Thread Priority	RS	✓	✓	✓	✓	✓	✓	✓	✓	✓		
Base Path	CM			✓								
BASECATALOGNAME	F	✓	✓	✓	✓	✓	✓	✓	✓	✓		✓

Table continues on the following page

Property Name	Object Type	ODBC	Jet	SQL	Internet Publishing (IIS5)	MSDataShape	Persist	Remote	Indexing Service	Directory Services	Exchange	Oracle
BASECOLUMNNAME	F	✓	✓	✓	✓	✓	✓	✓	✓	✓		✓
BASESCHEMANAME	F	✓	✓	✓	✓	✓	✓	✓	✓	✓		✓
BASETABLEINSTANCE	F			✓								
BASETABLENAME	F	✓	✓	✓	✓	✓	✓	✓	✓	✓		✓
Batch Size	RS	✓	✓	✓	✓	✓	✓	✓	✓	✓		
Bind Flags	C				✓	✓						
BLOB accessibility on Forward-Only cursor	RS	✓										
Blocking Storage Objects	RS/CM	✓	✓	✓		✓	✓	✓	✓	✓		✓
Bookmark Information	RS/CM	✓		✓								
Bookmark Type	RS/CM	✓	✓	✓		✓	✓	✓	✓	✓	✓	
Bookmarkable	RS/CM	✓	✓	✓	✓	✓	✓	✓	✓	✓	✓	
Bookmarks Ordered	RS	✓	✓	✓		✓	✓	✓	✓	✓	✓	
Cache Aggressively	C				✓							
Cache Authentication	C		✓			✓		✓				
Cache Child Rows	RS	✓	✓	✓		✓	✓	✓	✓	✓		
Cache Deferred Columns	RS	✓	✓	✓		✓	✓	✓	✓	✓	✓	✓
CALCULATIONINFO	F	✓	✓	✓		✓	✓	✓	✓	✓		
Catalog Location	C	✓	✓	✓					✓	✓		✓
Catalog Term	C	✓	✓	✓					✓	✓		✓
Catalog Usage	C	✓		✓					✓	✓		✓

Table continues on the following page

Property Name	Object Type	ODBC	Jet	SQL	Internet Publishing (IIS5)	MSDataShape	Persist	Remote	Indexing Service	Directory Services	Exchange	Oracle
Change Inserted Rows	RS/CM	✓	✓	✓		✓	✓	✓			✓	
Chapter	C						✓					
CLSID	F	✓										
COLLATINGSEQUENCE	F	✓	✓									
Column Definition	C	✓	✓	✓					✓			✓
Column Privileges	RS/CM	✓	✓	✓		✓	✓	✓	✓	✓	✓	
Column Set Notification	RS/CM	✓	✓	✓		✓	✓	✓	✓	✓		
Column Writable	RS	✓	✓	✓		✓	✓	✓	✓	✓		
Command Properties	C						✓					
Command Time Out	RS/CM		✓	✓	✓	✓	✓	✓	✓	✓	✓	
Command Type	CM			✓								
COMPFLAGS	F			✓								
COMPUTEMODE	F	✓		✓								
Connect Timeout	C	✓		✓	✓	✓	✓	✓		✓		
Connection Status	C	✓		✓								✓
Content Type	CM			✓								
Current Catalog	C	✓	✓	✓						✓		✓
Current DFMode	C							✓				
Current Language	C			✓								
Cursor Auto Fetch	RS/CM			✓								

Table continues on the following page

Property Name	Object Type	ODBC	Jet	SQL	Internet Publishing (IIS5)	MSDataShape	Persist	Remote	Indexing Service	Directory Services	Exchange	Oracle
Cursor Engine Version	RS	✓	✓	✓		✓	✓	✓	✓	✓		
Data Provider	C					✓						
Data Source	C	✓	✓	✓	✓	✓		✓	✓	✓	✓	✓
Data Source Name	C	✓	✓	✓						✓	✓	✓
Data Source Object Threading Model	C	✓	✓	✓		✓		✓	✓	✓	✓	✓
Datasource Type	C				✓						✓	
DATETIMEPRECISION	F	✓		✓								
DBMS Name	C	✓	✓	✓					✓		✓	✓
DBMS Version	C	✓	✓	✓	✓	✓	✓					
DEFAULTVALUE	F	✓										
Defer Column	RS/CM	✓	✓	✓		✓	✓	✓	✓	✓	✓	✓
Defer Prepare	CM			✓								
Defer scope and security testing	RS								✓			
Delay Storage Object Updates	RS/CM	✓	✓	✓		✓	✓	✓	✓	✓		
Determine Key Columns For Rowset	RS/CM											✓
DFMode	C							✓				
DOMAINCATALOG	F	✓										
DOMAINNAME	F	✓										
DOMAINSCHEMA	F	✓										
Driver Name	C	✓										

Table continues on the following page

Property Name	Object Type	ODBC	Jet	SQL	Internet Publishing (IIS5)	MSDataShape	Persist	Remote	Indexing Service	Directory Services	Exchange	Oracle
Driver ODBC Version	C	✓										
Driver Version	C	✓										
Enable Fastload	C		✓									
Encrypt Password	C		✓			✓		✓		✓		
Extended Properties	C	✓	✓	✓		✓		✓		✓		✓
Fastload Options	RS/CM			✓								
Fetch Backwards	RS/CM	✓	✓	✓	✓	✓	✓	✓	✓	✓	✓	✓
File Usage	C	✓										
Filter Operations	RS	✓	✓	✓		✓	✓	✓	✓	✓		
Find Operations	RS	✓	✓	✓		✓	✓	✓	✓	✓		
Force no command preparation when executing a parameterized command	RS	✓										
Force no command reexecution when failure to satisfy all required properties	RS	✓										
Force no parameter rebinding when executing a command	RS	✓										
Force SQL Server Firehose Mode cursor	RS	✓										
Generate a Rowset that can be marshaled	RS	✓										
General Timeout	C	✓		✓								

Table continues on the following page

Property Name	Object Type	ODBC	Jet	SQL	Internet Publishing (IIS5)	MSDataShape	Persist	Remote	Indexing Service	Directory Services	Exchange	Oracle
Generate URL	C				✓							
GROUP BY Support	C	✓	✓	✓					✓			✓
Handler	C							✓				
HASDEFAULT	F	✓										
Heterogeneous Table Support	C	✓	✓	✓					✓			✓
Hidden Columns	RS/CM	✓	✓	✓		✓	✓	✓	✓	✓		✓
Hold Rows	RS/CM	✓	✓	✓	✓	✓	✓	✓	✓	✓	✓	✓
Identifier Case Sensitivity	C	✓	✓	✓								✓
Ignore Cached Data	C				✓							
Immobile Rows	RS/CM	✓	✓	✓		✓	✓	✓	✓	✓	✓	
Impersonation Level	C					✓		✓				
Include SQL_FLOAT, SQL_DOUBLE, and SQL_REAL in QBU WHERE clauses	RS	✓										
Initial Catalog	C	✓		✓		✓		✓				
Initial Fetch Size	RS	✓	✓	✓		✓	✓	✓	✓	✓		
Initial File Name	C			✓								
Integrated Security	C			✓		✓		✓		✓		
Integrity Enhancement Facility	C	✓										
Internet Timeout	C							✓				
ISAUTOINCREMENT	F	✓	✓	✓		✓	✓	✓	✓			✓

Table continues on the following page

Property Name	Object Type	ODBC	Jet	SQL	Internet Publishing (IIS5)	MSDataShape	Persist	Remote	Indexing Service	Directory Services	Exchange	Oracle
ISCASESENSITIVE	F	✓	✓	✓								
Isolation Levels	C	✓	✓	✓					✓		✓	✓
Isolation Retention	C	✓	✓	✓					✓		✓	✓
ISSEARCHABLE	F	✓		✓								
ISUNIQUE	F	✓										
Jet OLEDB:Bulk Transactions	RS		✓									
Jet OLEDB:Compact Reclaimed Space Amount	C		✓									
Jet OLEDB:Compact Without Replica Repair	C		✓									
Jet OLEDB:Connection Control	C		✓									
Jet OLEDB:Create System Database	C		✓									
Jet OLEDB:Database Locking Mode	C		✓									
Jet OLEDB:Database Password	C		✓									
Jet OLEDB:Don't Copy Locale on Compact	C		✓									
Jet OLEDB:Enable Fat Cursors	RS		✓									
Jet OLEDB:Encrypt Database	C		✓									
Jet OLEDB:Engine Type	C		✓									
Jet OLEDB:Exclusive Async Delay	C		✓									
Jet OLEDB:Fat Cursor Cache Size	RS		✓									

Table continues on the following page

Property Name	Object Type	ODBC	Jet	SQL	Internet Publishing (IIS5)	MSDataShape	Persist	Remote	Indexing Service	Directory Services	Exchange	Oracle
Jet OLEDB:Flush Transaction Timeout	C		✓									
Jet OLEDB:Global Bulk Transactions	C		✓									
Jet OLEDB:Global Partial Bulk Ops	C		✓									
Jet OLEDB:Grbit Value	RS		✓									
Jet OLEDB:Implicit Commit Sync	C		✓									
Jet OLEDB:Inconsistent	RS		✓									
Jet OLEDB:Lock Delay	C		✓									
Jet OLEDB:Lock Retry	C		✓									
Jet OLEDB:Locking Granularity	RS		✓									
Jet OLEDB:Max Buffer Size	C		✓									
Jet OLEDB:Max Locks Per File	C		✓									
Jet OLEDB:New Database Password	C		✓									
Jet OLEDB:ODBC Command Time Out	C		✓									
Jet OLEDB:ODBC Parsing	C		✓									
Jet OLEDB:ODBC Pass-Through Statement	RS		✓									
Jet OLEDB:Page Locks to Table Lock	C		✓									
Jet OLEDB:Page Timeout	C		✓									

Table continues on the following page

Property Name	Object Type	ODBC	Jet	SQL	Internet Publishing (IIS5)	MSDataShape	Persist	Remote	Indexing Service	Directory Services	Exchange	Oracle
Jet OLEDB:Partial Bulk Ops	RS		✓									
Jet OLEDB:Pass Through Query Bulk-Op	RS		✓									
Jet OLEDB:Pass Through Query Connect String	RS		✓									
Jet OLEDB:Recycle Long-Valued Pages	C		✓									
Jet OLEDB:Registry Path	C		✓									
Jet OLEDB:Reset ISAM Stats	C		✓									
Jet OLEDB:Sandbox Mode	C		✓									
Jet OLEDB:SFP	C		✓									
Jet OLEDB:Shared Async Delay	C		✓									
Jet OLEDB:Stored Query	RS		✓									
Jet OLEDB:System database	C		✓									
Jet OLEDB:Transaction Commit Mode	C		✓									
Jet OLEDB:Use Grbit	RS		✓									
Jet OLEDB:User Commit Sync	C		✓									
Jet OLEDB:Validate Rules On Set	RS		✓									
Keep Identity	RS/CM			✓								
Keep Nulls	RS/CM			✓								
KEYCOLUMN	F	✓	✓	✓		✓	✓	✓	✓	✓		✓
Like Escape Clause	C	✓										

Table continues on the following page

Property Name	Object Type	ODBC	Jet	SQL	Internet Publishing (IIS5)	MSDataShape	Persist	Remote	Indexing Service	Directory Services	Exchange	Oracle
Literal Bookmarks	RS/CM	✓	✓	✓		✓	✓	✓	✓	✓	✓	
Literal Row Identity	RS/CM	✓	✓	✓		✓	✓	✓	✓	✓	✓	✓
Locale Identifier	C	✓	✓	✓	✓	✓		✓	✓	✓	✓	✓
Location	C	✓				✓		✓	✓	✓		
Lock Mode	RS/CM		✓	✓								
Lock Owner	C				✓							
Maintain Change Status	RS	✓	✓	✓	✓	✓	✓	✓	✓	✓		
Maintain Property Values	C						✓					
Mapping schema	CM			✓								
Mark For Offline	C				✓							
Mask Password	C		✓		✓		✓					
Max Columns in Group By	C	✓										
Max Columns in Index	C	✓										
Max Columns in Order By	C	✓										
Max Columns in Select	C	✓										
Max Columns in Table	C	✓										
Maximum BLOB Length	RS/CM			✓								
Maximum Index Size	C	✓	✓	✓								✓
Maximum Open Chapters	C			✓					✓			✓
Maximum Open Rows	RS/CM	✓	✓	✓		✓	✓	✓	✓	✓	✓	✓

Table continues on the following page

Property Name	Object Type	ODBC	Jet	SQL	Internet Publishing (IIS5)	MSDataShape	Persist	Remote	Indexing Service	Directory Services	Exchange	Oracle
Maximum Pending Rows	RS/CM	✓	✓	✓		✓	✓	✓	✓	✓		
Maximum Row Size	C	✓	✓	✓					✓	✓	✓	✓
Maximum Row Size Includes BLOB	C	✓	✓	✓								✓
Maximum Rows	RS/CM	✓	✓	✓		✓	✓	✓	✓	✓	✓	✓
Maximum Tables in SELECT	C	✓	✓	✓					✓			✓
Memory Usage	RS	✓	✓	✓		✓	✓	✓	✓	✓		
Mode	C	✓	✓		✓	✓		✓		✓	✓	
Multi-Table Update	C	✓	✓	✓								✓
Multiple Connections	C			✓								
Multiple Parameter Sets	C	✓	✓	✓			✓	✓				✓
Multiple Results	C	✓	✓	✓		✓		✓	✓		✓	✓
Multiple Storage Objects	C	✓	✓	✓					✓		✓	✓
Network Address	C			✓								
Network Library	C			✓								
Notification Granularity	RS/CM	✓	✓	✓		✓	✓	✓	✓	✓		✓
Notification Phases	RS/CM	✓	✓	✓		✓	✓	✓	✓	✓		✓
Null Collation Order	C	✓	✓	✓					✓			✓
Null Concatenation Behavior	C	✓	✓	✓								✓
Numeric Functions	C	✓										

Table continues on the following page

Property Name	Object Type	ODBC	Jet	SQL	Internet Publishing (IIS5)	MSDataShape	Persist	Remote	Indexing Service	Directory Services	Exchange	Oracle
Objects Transacted	RS/CM	✓	✓	✓		✓	✓	✓	✓	✓		✓
OCTETLENGTH	F	✓		✓								
ODBC Concurrency Type	RS	✓										
ODBC Cursor Type	RS	✓										
OLE DB Services	C	✓							✓			✓
OLE DB Version	C	✓	✓	✓	✓			✓	✓	✓	✓	✓
OLE Object Support	C	✓	✓	✓					✓	✓	✓	✓
OLE Objects	C				✓							
Open Rowset Support	C	✓	✓	✓								
OPTIMIZE	F	✓	✓	✓		✓	✓	✓	✓	✓		
ORDER BY Columns in Select List	C	✓	✓	✓					✓			✓
Others' Changes Visible	RS/CM	✓	✓	✓		✓	✓	✓	✓	✓	✓	✓
Others' Inserts Visible	RS/CM	✓	✓	✓		✓	✓	✓	✓	✓	✓	✓
Outer Join Capabilities	C	✓										
Outer Joins	C	✓										
Output encoding	CM			✓								
Output Parameter Availability	C	✓	✓	✓				✓	✓			✓
Output stream	CM			✓								
Own Changes Visible	RS/CM	✓	✓	✓		✓	✓	✓	✓	✓	✓	✓

Table continues on the following page

Property Name	Object Type	ODBC	Jet	SQL	Internet Publishing (IIS5)	MSDataShape	Persist	Remote	Indexing Service	Directory Services	Exchange	Oracle
Own Inserts Visible	RS/CM	✓	✓	✓		✓	✓	✓	✓	✓	✓	✓
Packet Size	C			✓								
Pass By Ref Accessors	C	✓	✓	✓					✓	✓	✓	✓
Password	C	✓	✓	✓	✓	✓		✓		✓	✓	✓
Persist Encrypted	C					✓						
Persist Format	C						✓					
Persist Schema	C						✓					
Persist Security Info	C	✓		✓		✓		✓				
Persistent ID Type	C	✓	✓	✓					✓	✓	✓	✓
Position on the last row after insert	RS	✓										
Prepare Abort Behavior	C	✓	✓	✓							✓	✓
Prepare Commit Behavior	C	✓	✓	✓							✓	✓
Preserve on Abort	RS/CM	✓	✓	✓		✓	✓	✓	✓	✓	✓	✓
Preserve on Commit	RS/CM	✓	✓	✓		✓	✓	✓	✓	✓	✓	✓
Procedure Term	C	✓	✓	✓								✓
Prompt	C	✓	✓	✓	✓	✓		✓	✓	✓		✓
Protection Level	C					✓		✓				
Protocol Provider	C				✓							
Provider Friendly Name	C	✓	✓	✓				✓	✓	✓		✓
Provider Name	C	✓	✓	✓	✓			✓	✓	✓	✓	✓

Table continues on the following page

Property Name	Object Type	ODBC	Jet	SQL	Internet Publishing (IIS5)	MSDataShape	Persist	Remote	Indexing Service	Directory Services	Exchange	Oracle
Provider Version	C	✓	✓	✓	✓			✓	✓	✓	✓	✓
Query Based Updates/Deletes/Inserts	RS	✓										
Query Restriction	RS								✓			
Quick Restart	RS/CM	✓	✓	✓		✓	✓	✓	✓	✓	✓	✓
Quoted Catalog Names	C			✓								
Quoted Identifier Sensitivity	C	✓		✓								✓
Read-Only Data Source	C	✓	✓	✓					✓	✓	✓	
Reentrant Events	RS/CM	✓	✓	✓		✓	✓	✓	✓	✓	✓	
RELATIONCONDITIONS	F	✓	✓	✓		✓	✓	✓	✓	✓		
Remote Provider	C							✓				
Remote Server	C							✓				
Remove Deleted Rows	RS/CM	✓	✓	✓		✓	✓	✓	✓	✓	✓	✓
Report Multiple Changes	RS/CM	✓	✓	✓		✓	✓	✓	✓	✓	✓	
Reshape Name	RS	✓	✓	✓	✓	✓	✓	✓				
Reset Connection	C			✓								
Reset Datasource	C	✓		✓					✓			
Resync Command	RS	✓	✓	✓		✓	✓	✓	✓	✓		
Return Pending Inserts	RS/CM	✓	✓	✓		✓	✓	✓	✓	✓		

Table continues on the following page

Property Name	Object Type	ODBC	Jet	SQL	Internet Publishing (IIS5)	MSDataShape	Persist	Remote	Indexing Service	Directory Services	Exchange	Oracle
Return PROPVARIANTs in variant binding	RS								✓			
Row Delete Notification	RS/CM	✓	✓	✓		✓	✓	✓	✓	✓		
Row First Change Notification	RS/CM	✓	✓	✓		✓	✓	✓	✓	✓		
Row Insert Notification	RS/CM	✓	✓	✓		✓	✓	✓	✓	✓		
Row Privileges	RS/CM	✓	✓	✓		✓	✓	✓	✓	✓	✓	
Row Resynchronization Notification	RS/CM	✓	✓	✓		✓	✓	✓	✓	✓		
Row Threading Model	RS/CM	✓	✓	✓		✓	✓	✓	✓	✓	✓	✓
Row Undo Change Notification	RS/CM	✓	✓	✓		✓	✓	✓	✓	✓		
Row Undo Delete Notification	RS/CM	✓	✓	✓		✓	✓	✓	✓	✓		
Row Undo Insert Notification	RS/CM	✓	✓	✓		✓	✓	✓	✓	✓		
Row Update Notification	RS/CM	✓	✓	✓		✓	✓	✓	✓	✓		
Rowset Conversions on Command	C	✓	✓	✓					✓	✓		✓
Rowset Fetch Position Change Notification	RS/CM	✓	✓	✓		✓	✓	✓	✓	✓		✓
Rowset Query Status	RS								✓			

Table continues on the following page

Property Name	Object Type	ODBC	Jet	SQL	Internet Publishing (IIS5)	MSDataShape	Persist	Remote	Indexing Service	Directory Services	Exchange	Oracle
Rowset Release Notification	RS/CM	✔	✔	✔		✔	✔	✔	✔	✔		✔
Schema Term	C	✔	✔	✔								✔
Schema Usage	C	✔	✔	✔								✔
Scroll Backwards	RS/CM	✔	✔	✔		✔	✔	✔	✔	✔	✔	✔
Server Cursor	RS/CM	✔	✔	✔		✔	✔	✔	✔	✔	✔	✔
Server Data on Insert	RS/CM		✔	✔								
Server Name	C	✔		✔								
Skip Deleted Bookmarks	RS/CM	✔	✔	✔		✔	✔	✔	✔	✔	✔	
Sort Order Name	C			✔								
SORTID	F			✔								
Special Characters	C	✔										
SQL Content Query Locale String	RS								✔			
SQL Grammar Support	C	✔										
SQL Support	C	✔	✔	✔					✔	✔	✔	✔
Qsqlxmlx.dll Progid	C			✔								
SS Stream Flags	CM			✔								
Stored Procedures	C	✔										
String Functions	C	✔										

Table continues on the following page

Property Name	Object Type	ODBC	Jet	SQL	Internet Publishing (IIS5)	MSDataShape	Persist	Remote	Indexing Service	Directory Services	Exchange	Oracle
Strong Row Identity	RS/CM	✓	✓	✓		✓	✓	✓	✓	✓	✓	✓
Structured Storage	C	✓	✓	✓					✓		✓	✓
Subquery Support	C	✓	✓	✓					✓			✓
System Functions	C	✓										
Table Statistics Support												
Table Term	C	✓	✓	✓							✓	✓
Tag with column collation when possible	C											
TDSCOLLATION	F			✓								
Time/Date Functions	C	✓										
Transact Updates	C						✓					
Transaction DDL	C	✓	✓	✓					✓		✓	✓
Treat As Offline	C				✓							
Unicode Comparison Style	C			✓								
Unicode Locale ID	C			✓								
Unique Catalog	RS	✓	✓	✓		✓	✓	✓	✓	✓		
Unique Reshape Names	C					✓						
Unique Rows	RS/CM	✓	✓	✓		✓	✓	✓	✓	✓		✓
Unique Schema	RS	✓	✓	✓		✓	✓	✓	✓	✓		
Unique Table	RS	✓	✓	✓		✓	✓	✓	✓	✓		
Updatability	RS/CM	✓	✓	✓	✓	✓	✓	✓	✓	✓	✓	

Table continues on the following page

Property Name	Object Type	ODBC	Jet	SQL	Internet Publishing (IIS5)	MSDataShape	Persist	Remote	Indexing Service	Directory Services	Exchange	Oracle
Update Criteria	RS	✓	✓	✓		✓	✓	✓	✓	✓		
Update Resync	RS	✓	✓	✓		✓	✓	✓	✓	✓		
URL Generation	C										✓	
Use Bookmarks	RS/CM	✓	✓	✓	✓	✓	✓	✓	✓	✓	✓	✓
Use Encryption for Data	C			✓								
Use Procedure for Prepare	C			✓								
User ID	C	✓	✓	✓	✓	✓		✓		✓	✓	✓
User Name	C	✓	✓	✓						✓		✓
Window Handle	C	✓	✓	✓	✓	✓		✓	✓	✓		✓
Workstation ID	C			✓								
XML root	CM			✓								
XSL	CM			✓								

Object Properties

This section details the properties by object type, including the enumerated values that they support. These values are not included in the standard adovbs.inc include file (and are not automatically supplied when using Visual Basic), but can be found in adoconvb.inc and adoconjs.inc (for ASP, in VBScript and JScript format) and adocon.bas (for Visual Basic) from the supporting Web site.

Some properties in this list are undocumented, and I've had to make an educated guess as to their purpose. I've marked these properties with a hash (#) in their description field.

The Connection Object's Properties

Property Name	Description	Data Type
Access Permissions	Identifies the permissions used to access the data source. Read/write.	`ConnectMode Enum`
Accessible Procedures	Identifies accessible procedures. Read-only.	`Boolean`
Accessible Tables	Identifies accessible tables. Read-only.	`Boolean`
Active Sessions	The maximum number of sessions that can exist at the same time. A value of 0 indicates no limit. Read-only.	`Long`
Active Statements	The maximum number of statements that can exist at the same time. Read-only.	`Long`
Allow Native Variant	For SQL Variant columns, identifies whether the data is returned as a SQL Variant or an OLE DB Variant. Default value is `False`.	`Boolean`
Alter Column Support	Identifies which portions of the column can be altered.	`DBCOLUMNDES CFLAG`
Application Name	Identifies the client application name. Read/write.	`String`
Asynchable Abort	Whether transactions can be aborted asynchronously. Read-only.	`Boolean`
Asynchable Commit	Whether transactions can be committed asynchronously. Read-only.	`Boolean`
Asynchronous Processing	Specifies the asynchronous processing performed on the rowset. Read/write.	`DBPROPVAL_ ASYNCH`
Auto Translate	Indicates whether OEM/ANSI character conversion is used. Read/write.	`Boolean`
Autocommit Isolation Level	Identifies the transaction isolation level while in auto-commit mode. Read/write.	`DBPROPVAL_OS`
Bind Flags	Identifies the binding behavior for resources. Allows binding to the results of a resource rather than the resource itself.	`DBBINDUR LFLAG`
Cache Aggressively	Identifies whether the provider will download and cache all properties of the resource and its stream.	`Boolean`

Table continues on the following page

Property Name	Description	Data Type
Cache Authentication	Whether the data source object can cache sensitive authentication information, such as passwords, in an internal cache. Read/write.	Boolean
Catalog Location	The position of the catalog name in a table name in a text command. Returns 1 (DBPROPVAL_CL_START) if the catalog is at the start of the name (such as Access with \Temp\Database.mdb), and 2 (DBPROPVAL_CL_END) if the catalog is at the end of name (such as Oracle with ADMIN.EMP@EMPDATA). Read/write.	DBPROPVAL_CL
Catalog Term	The name the data source uses for a catalog, such as "catalog" or "database." Read/write.	String
Catalog Usage	Specifies how catalog names can be used in text commands. A combination of zero or more of the DBPROPVAL_CU constants. Read/write.	DBPROPVAL_CU
Column Definition	Defines the valid clauses for the definition of a column. Read/write.	DBPROPVAL_CD
Command Properties	Indicates the values that will be added to the string of properties by the MSRemote provider.	String
Connect Timeout	The amount of time, in seconds, to wait for the initialization to complete. Read/write.	Long
Connection Status	The status of the current connection. Read-only.	DBPROPVAL_CS
Current Catalog	The name of the current catalog. Read/write.	String
Current DFMode	Identifies the actual version of the Data Factory on the server. Can be: "21" (the default) for version 2.1 "20" for version 2.0 "15" for version 1.5	String
Current Language	Identifies the language used for system messages selection and formatting. The language must be installed on the SQL Server or initialization of the data source fails. Read/write.	String
Data Provider	For a shaped (hierarchical) recordset, this identifies the provider that supplies the data.	String
Data Source	The name of the data source to connect to. Read/write.	String

Table continues on the following page

Property Name	Description	Data Type
Data Source Name	The name of the data source. Read-only.	String
Data Source Object	Threading Model Specifies the threading models supported by the data source object. Read-only.	DBPROPVAL_RT
Datasource Type	The type of data source.	DBPROPVAL_DST
DBMS Name	The name of the product accessed by the provider. Read-only.	String
DBMS Version	The version of the product accessed by the provider. Read-only.	String
DFMode	Identifies the Data Factory mode. Can be: "21" (the default) for version 2.1 "20" for version 2.0 "15" for version 1.5	String
Driver Name	Identifies the ODBC driver name. Read-only.	String
Driver ODBC	Version Identifies the ODBC driver version. Read-only.	String
Driver Version	Identifies the Driver ODBC version. Read-only.	String
Enable Fastload	Indicates whether bulk-copy operations can be used between the SQL Server and the consumer.	Boolean
Encrypt Password	Whether the consumer required that the password be sent to the data source in an encrypted form. Read/write.	Boolean
Extended Properties	Contains provider-specific, extended connection information. Read/write.	String
File Usage	Identifies the usage count of the ODBC driver. Read-only.	Long
Generate URL	Identifies the level of support of the Internet Server for generating URL suffixes.	DBPROPVAL_GU
General Timeout	The number of seconds before a request times out. This applies to requests other than the connection opening or a command execution.	Long
GROUP BY Support	The relationship between the columns in a GROUP BY clause and the non-aggregated columns in the select list. Read-only.	DBPROPVAL_BG
Handler	The name of the server-side customization program, and any parameters the program uses.	String

Table continues on the following page

Property Name	Description	Data Type
Heterogeneous Table Support	Specifies whether the provider can join tables from different catalogs or providers. Read-only.	DBPROPVAL_HT
Identifier Case Sensitivity	How identifiers treat case. Read-only.	DBPROPVAL_IC
Ignore Cached Data	Identifies whether the provider should ignore any cached data for this resource.	Boolean
Impersonation Level	Identifies the level of client impersonation the server can take while performing actions on behalf of the client.	DB_IMP_LEVEL
Initial Catalog	The name of the initial, or default, catalog to use when connecting to the data source. If the provider supports changing the catalog for an initialized data source, a different catalog name can be specified in the Current Catalog property. Read/write.	String
Initial File Name	The primary file name of an attachable database. #	String
Integrated Security	Contains the name of the authentication service used by the server to identify the user. Read/write.	String
Integrity Enhancement Facility	Indicates whether the data source supports the optional Integrity Enhancement Facility. Read-only.	Boolean
Internet Timeout	The maximum number of milliseconds to wait before generating an error.	Long
Isolation Levels	Identifies the supported transaction isolation levels. Read-only.	DBPROPVAL_TI
Isolation Retention	Identifies the supported transaction isolation retention levels. Read-only.	DBPROPVAL_TR
Jet OLEDB:Compact Reclaimed Space Amount	The approximate amount of space that would be reclaimed by a compaction. This is not guaranteed to be exact.	Long
Jet OLEDB:Compact Without Replica Repair	Indicates whether or not to find and repair damaged replicas.	Boolean
Jet OLEDB:Compact Without Relationships	Indicates whether to copy relationships to the new database.	Boolean

Table continues on the following page

Property Name	Description	Data Type
Jet OLEDB:Connection Control	Identifies the state of the connection, indicating whether other users are allowed to connect to the database.	DBPROPVAL_JCC
Jet OLEDB:Create System Database	Indicates whether a system database is generated when creating a new data source.	Boolean
Jet OLEDB:Database Locking Mode	Identifies the mode to use when locking the database. The first person to open a database identifies the mode.	DBPROPVAL_DL
Jet OLEDB:Database Password	The database password. Read/write.	String
Jet OLEDB:Don't Copy Locale on Compact	Indicates that the database sort order should be used when compacting, rather than the locale.	Boolean
Jet OLEDB:Encrypt Database	Indicates whether or not to encrypt the new database.	Boolean
Jet OLEDB:Engine Type	Identifies the version of the database to open, or the version of the database to create.	JET_ENGINETYPE
Jet OLEDB:Exclusive Async Delay	The maximum time (in milliseconds) that Jet will delay asynchronous writes to disk when the database is open in exclusive mode.	Long
Jet OLEDB:Flush Transaction Timeout	Amount of time of inactivity before the asynchronous write cache is written to the disk.	Long
Jet OLEDB:Global Bulk Transactions	Identifies whether bulk operations are transacted.	DBPROPVAL_BT
Jet OLEDB:Global Partial Bulk Ops	Identifies whether Bulk operations are allowed with partial values. Read/write.	DBPROPVAL_BP
Jet OLEDB:Implicit Commit Sync	Indicates whether or not implicit transactions are written synchronously.	Boolean
Jet OLEDB:Lock Delay	The time to wait between lock attempts, in milliseconds.	Long
Jet OLEDB:Lock Retry	The number of attempts made to access a locked page.	Long
Jet OLEDB:Max Buffer Size	The largest amount of memory (in kilobytes) that can be used before it starts flushing changes to disk.	Long

Table continues on the following page

Property Name	Description	Data Type
Jet OLEDB:Max Locks Per File	The maximum number of locks that can be placed on a database. This defaults to 9500.	Long
Jet OLEDB:New Database Password	Sets the database password.	String
Jet OLEDB:ODBC Command Time Out	The number of seconds before remote ODBC queries timeout.	Long
Jet OLEDB:ODBC Parsing	Indicates whether or not Jet should attempt parsing of ODBC SQL syntax or only use native Jet syntax.	Boolean
Jet OLEDB:Page Locks to Table Lock	The number of page locks to apply to a table before escalating the lock to a table lock. A value of 0 means the lock will never be promoted.	Long
Jet OLEDB:Page Timeout	The amount of time (in milliseconds) that is waited before Jet checks to see if the cache is out of date with the database.	Long
Jet OLEDB:Recycle Long-Valued Pages	Indicates whether or not Jet aggressively tries to reclaim BLOB pages when they are freed.	Boolean
Jet OLEDB:Registry Path	The registry key that contains values for the Jet database engine. Read/write.	String
Jet OLEDB:Reset ISAM Stats	Determines whether or not the ISAM statistics should be reset after the information has been returned.	Boolean
Jet OLEDB:Sandbox Mode	Indicates whether the database is in Sandbox mode. #	Boolean
Jet OLEDB:Shared Async Delay	The maximum time (in milliseconds) to delay asynchronous writes when in multi-user mode.	Long
Jet OLEDB:System database	The path and file name for the workgroup file. Read/write.	String
Jet OLEDB:Transaction Commit Mode	A value of 1 indicates that the database commits updates immediately rather than caching them.	Long
Jet OLEDB:User Commit Sync	Indicates whether or not explicit user transactions are written synchronously.	Boolean
Like Escape Clause	Identifies the LIKE escape clause. Read-only.	String
Locale Identifier	The locale ID of preference for the consumer. Read/write.	Long

Table continues on the following page

Property Name	Description	Data Type
Location	The location of the data source to connect to. Typically, this will be the server name. Read/write.	String
Lock Owner	The string to show when you lock a resource and other users attempt to access that resource. Ignored for the WEC protocol, used with FrontPage Server Extensions. Read/write.	String
Log text and image writes	Identifies whether writes to text and image fields are logged in the transaction log. Read/write.	Boolean
Maintain Property Values	Indicates whether the property values are persisted along with the data when saving a recordset. Default is True. #	Boolean
Mark For Offline	Indicates that the URL can be marked for offline use. #	Integer
Mask Password	The consumer requires that the password be sent to the data source in masked form. Read/write.	Boolean
Max Columns in Group By	Identifies the maximum number of columns in a GROUP BY clause. Read-only.	Long
Max Columns in Index	Identifies the maximum number of columns in an index. Read-only.	Long
Max Columns in Order By	Identifies the maximum number of columns in an ORDER BY clause. Read-only.	Long
Max Columns in Select	Identifies the maximum number of columns in a SELECT statement. Read-only.	Long
Max Columns in Table	Identifies the maximum number of columns in a table. Read-only.	Long
Maximum Index Size	The maximum number of bytes allowed in the combined columns of an index. This is 0 if there is no specified limit or the limit is unknown. Read-only.	Long
Maximum Open Chapters	The maximum number of chapters that can be open at any one time. If a chapter must be released before a new chapter can be opened, the value is 1. If the provider does not support chapters, the value is 0. Read-only.	Long

Table continues on the following page

Property Name	Description	Data Type
Maximum OR Conditions	The maximum number of disjunct conditions that can be supported in a view filter. Multiple conditions of a view filter are joined in a logical OR. Providers that do not support joining multiple conditions return a value of 1, and providers that do not support view filters return a value of 0. Read-only.	Long
Maximum Row Size	The maximum length of a single row in a table. This is 0 if there is no specified limit or the limit is unknown. Read-only.	Long
Maximum Row Size	Includes BLOB Identifies whether Maximum Row Size includes the length for BLOB data. Read-only.	Boolean
Maximum Sort Columns	The maximum number of columns that can be supported in a View Sort. This is 0 if there is no specified limit or the limit is unknown. Read-only.	Long
Maximum Tables in SELECT	The maximum number of tables allowed in the FROM clause of a SELECT statement. This is 0 if there is no specified limit or the limit is unknown. Read-only.	Long
Mode	Specifies the access permissions. Read/write.	DB_MODE
Multi-Table Update	Identifies whether the provider can update rowsets derived from multiple tables. Read-only.	Boolean
Multiple Connections	Identifies whether the provider silently creates additional connections to support concurrent Command, Connection, or Recordset objects. This applies only to providers that must spawn multiple connections, and not to providers that support multiple connections natively. Read/write.	Boolean
Multiple Parameter Sets	Identifies whether the provider supports multiple parameter sets. Read-only.	Boolean
Multiple Results	Identifies whether the provider supports multiple results objects and what restrictions it places on those objects. Read-only.	DBPROPVAL_MR
Multiple Storage Objects	Identifies whether the provider supports multiple open-storage objects simultaneously. Read-only.	Boolean

Table continues on the following page

Property Name	Description	Data Type
Network Address	Identifies the network address of the SQL Server. Read/write.	String
Network Library	Identifies the name of the Net-Library (DLL) used to communicate with SQL Server. Read/write.	String
Null Collation Order	Identifies where nulls are sorted in a list. Read-only.	DBPROPVAL_NC
Null Concatenation Behavior	How the data source handles concatenation of Null-valued character data type columns with non-Null valued character data type columns. Read-only.	DBPROPVAL_CB
Numeric Functions	Identifies the numeric functions supported by the ODBC driver and data source. Read-only.	SQL_FN_NUM
OLE DB Services	Specifies the OLE DB services to enable. Read/write.	DBPROPVAL_OS
OLE DB Version	Specifies the version of OLE DB supported by the provider. Read-only.	String
OLE Object Support	Specifies the way in which the provider supports access to BLOBs and OLE objects stored in columns. Read-only.	DBPROPVAL_OO
OLE Objects	Indicates the level of binding support for OLE objects.	DBPROPVAL_OO
Open Rowset Support	Indicates the level of support for opening rowsets.	DBPROPVAL_ORS
ORDER BY Columns in Select List	Identifies whether columns in an ORDER BY clause must be in the SELECT list. Read-only.	Boolean
Outer Join Capabilities	Identifies the outer join capabilities of the ODBC data source. Read-only.	SQL_OJ
Outer Joins	Identifies whether outer joins are supported. Read-only.	Boolean
Outer Join Capabilities	Identifies the outer join capabilities of the ODBC data source. Read-only.	SQL_OJ
Output Parameter Availability	Identifies the time at which output parameter values become available. Read-only.	DBPROPVAL_OA
Packet Size	Specifies the network packet size in bytes. It must be between 512 and 32767. The default is 4096. Read/write.	Long

Table continues on the following page

Property Name	Description	Data Type
Pass By Ref Accessors	Whether the provider supports the DBACCESSOR_PASSBYREF flag. Read-only.	Boolean
Password	The password to be used to connect to the data source. Read/write.	String
Persist Encrypted	Whether or not the consumer requires that the data source object persist sensitive authentication information, such as a password, in encrypted form. Read/write.	Boolean
Persist Format	Indicates the format for persisting data.	PersistFormat Enum
Persist Schema	Indicates whether the schema is persisted along with the data.	Boolean
Persist Security Info	Indicates whether the data source object is allowed to persist sensitive authentication information, such as a password, along with other authentication information. Read/write.	Boolean
Persistent ID Type	Specifies the type of DBID that the provider uses when persisting DBIDs for tables, indexes, and columns. Read-only.	DBPROPVAL_PT
Prepare Abort Behavior	Identifies how aborting a transaction affects prepared commands. Read-only.	DBPROPVAL_CB
Prepare Commit Behavior	Identifies how committing a transaction affects prepared commands. Read-only.	DBPROPVAL_CB
Procedure Term	Specifies the data source providers name for a procedure, such as "database procedure" or "stored procedure." Read-only.	String
Prompt	Specifies whether to prompt the user during initialization. Read/write.	DBPROMPT
Protection Level	The protection level of data sent between client and server. This property applies only to network connections other than RPC. Read/write.	DB_PROT_LEVEL
Protocol Provider	The protocol to use when using the IPP to connect to a resource. This should be WEC to use the FrontPage Web Extender Client protocol, and DAV to use the WebDAV protocol.	String

Table continues on the following page

Property Name	Description	Data Type
Provider Friendly Name	The friendly name of the provider. Read-only.	String
Provider Name	The file name of the provider. Read-only.	String
Provider Version	The version of the provider. Read-only.	String
Quoted Catalog Names	Indicates whether quoted identifiers are allowed for catalog names.	Boolean
Quoted Identifier Sensitivity	Identifies how quoted identifiers treat case. Read-only.	DBPROPVAL_IC
Read-Only Data Source	Indicates whether the data source is read-only. Read-only.	Boolean
Remote Provider	The data provider used to supply the data from a remote connection.	String
Remote Server	The name of the server supplying data from a remote connection.	String
Reset Datasource	Specifies the data source state to reset. Write only.	DBPROPVAL_RD
Rowset Conversions on Command	Identifies whether callers can inquire on a command, and about conversions supported by the command. Read-only.	Boolean
Schema Term	The name the data source uses for a schema, such as "schema" or "owner." Read-only.	String
Schema Usage	Identifies how schema names can be used in commands. Read-only.	DBPROPVAL_SU
Server Name	The name of the server. Read-only.	String
Sort on Index	Specifies whether the provider supports setting a sort order only for columns contained in an index. Read-only.	Boolean
Sort Order Name	Indicates the sort order to use for data types.	String
Special Characters	Identifies the data store's special characters. Read-only.	String
SQL Grammar Support	Identifies the SQL grammar level supported by the ODBC driver. No conformance is represented by 0, Level 1 conformance is indicated by 1, and Level 2 conformance is represented by 2. Read-only.	Long

Table continues on the following page

Property Name	Description	Data Type
SQL Support	Identifies the level of support for SQL. Read-only.	DBPROPVAL_SQL
SQLOLE execute a SET TEXTLENGTH	Identifies whether SQLOLE executes a SET TEXTLENGTH before accessing BLOB fields. Read-only. #	Boolean
Stored Procedures	Indicates whether stored procedures are available. Read-only.	Boolean
String Functions	Identifies the string functions supported by the ODBC driver and data source. Read-only.	SQL_FN_STR
Structured Storage	Identifies what interfaces the rowset supports on storage objects. Read-only.	DBPROPVAL_SS
Subquery Support	Identifies the predicates in text commands that support sub-queries. Read-only.	DBPROPVAL_SQ
System Functions	Identifies the system functions supported by the ODBC driver and data source. Read-only.	SQL_FN_SYS
Table Term	The name the data source uses for a table, such as "table" or "file." Read-only.	String
Time/Date Functions	Identifies the time/date functions supported by the ODBC driver and data source. Read-only.	SQL_SDF_ CURRENT
Table Statistics	Support Lists the table statistics that are available for a given table.	DBPROPVAL_TS
Tag with column collations when possible	If possible, use collation details specified on the columns.	Boolean
Transact Updates	Indicates whether an UpdateBatch method call is performed within a transaction. The default value is False.	Boolean
Transaction DDL	Indicates whether DDL statements are supported in transactions. Read-only.	DBPROPVAL_TC
Treat As Offline	Indicates whether the resource should be treated as an offline resource.	Boolean
Unicode Comparison Style	Determines the sorting options used for Unicode data.	Long
Unicode Locale ID	The locale ID to use for Unicode sorting.	Long

Table continues on the following page

Property Name	Description	Data Type
Unique Reshape Names	Indicates whether the value of a recordset's Name property would conflict with an existing name, resulting in a unique name being generated.	Boolean
URL Generation	Indicates whether the provider requires data store generated URLs.	DBPROPVAL_GU
Use Encryption for Data	Indicates whether the data is encrypted.	Boolean
Use Procedure for Prepare	Indicates whether SQL Server is to use temporary stored procedures for prepared statements. Read/write.	SSPROPVAL_ USEPROCFOR PREP
User Authentication mode	Indicates whether Windows NT Authentication is used to access SQL Server. Read/write.	Boolean
User ID	The User ID to be used when connecting to the data source. Read/write.	String
User Name	The User Name used in a particular database. Read-only.	String
Window Handle	The window handle to be used if the data source object needs to prompt for additional information. Read/write.	Long
Workstation ID	Identifies the workstation. Read/write.	String

The Recordset Object's Properties

Property Name	Description	Data Type
Access Order	Indicates the order in which columns must be accessed on the rowset. Read/write.	DBPROPVAL_AO
Always use content index	Indicates whether to use the content index to resolve queries, even if the index is out of date.	Boolean
Append-Only Rowset	A rowset opened with this property will initially contain no rows. Read/write.	Boolean
Asynchronous Rowset Processing	Identifies the asynchronous processing performed on the rowset. Read/write.	DBPROPVAL_ ASYNCH

Table continues on the following page

Property Name	Description	Data Type
Auto Recalc	Specifies when the MSDataShape provider updates aggregated and calculated columns. Read/write.	`ADCPROP_ AUTORECALC_ ENUM`
Background Fetch Size	The number of rows to fetch in each batch during asynchronous reads.	`Long`
Background thread Priority	The priority of the background thread for asynchronous actions. Read/write.	`ADCPROP_ ASYCTHREAD PRIORITY_ENUM`
Batch Size	The number of rows in a batch. Read/write.	`Integer`
BLOB accessibility on Forward-Only cursor	Indicates whether BLOB columns can be accessed irrespective of their position in the column list. If True, then the BLOB column can be accessed even if it is not the last column. If False, then the BLOB column can be accessed only if it the last BLOB column, and any non-BLOB columns after this column will not be accessible. Read/write.	`Boolean`
Blocking Storage Objects	Indicates whether storage objects might prevent use of other methods on the rowset. Read/write.	`Boolean`
Bookmark Information	Identifies additional information about bookmarks over the rowset. Read-only.	`DBPROPVAL_BI`
Bookmark Type	Identifies the bookmark type supported by the rowset. Read/write.	`DBPROPVAL_BMK`
Bookmarkable	Indicates whether bookmarks are supported. Read-only.	`Boolean`
Bookmarks Ordered	Indicates whether bookmarks can be compared to determine the relative position of their rows in the rowset. Read/write.	`Boolean`
Bulk Operations	Identifies optimizations that a provider may take for updates to the rowset. Read-only.	`DBPROPVAL_BO`
Cache Child Rows	Indicates whether child rows in a chaptered recordset are cached, or whether they are re-fetched when the rows are accessed. Read/write.	`Boolean`
Cache Deferred Columns	Indicates whether the provider caches the value of a deferred column when the consumer first gets a value from that column. Read/write.	`Boolean`

Table continues on the following page

Property Name	Description	Data Type
Change Inserted Rows	Indicates whether the consumer can delete or update newly inserted rows. An inserted row is assumed to be one that has been transmitted to the data source, as opposed to a pending insert row. Read/write.	Boolean
Column Privileges	Indicates whether access rights are restricted on a column-by-column basis. Read-only.	Boolean
Column Set Notification	Indicates whether changing a column set is cancelable. Read-only.	DBPROPVAL_NP
Column Writable	Indicates whether a particular column is writable. Read/write.	Boolean
Command Time Out	The number of seconds to wait before a command times out. A value of 0 indicates an infinite timeout. Read/write.	Long
Concurrency Control Method	Identifies the method used for concurrency control when using server-based cursors. Read/write.	SSPROPVAL_ CONCUR
Cursor Engine Version	Identifies the version of the cursor engine. Read-only.	String
Defer Column	Indicates whether the data in a column is not fetched until specifically requested. Read/write.	Boolean
Defer scope and security testing	Indicates whether or not the search will defer scope and security testing.	Boolean
Delay Storage Object Updates	When in delayed update mode, indicates if storage objects are also used in delayed update mode (i.e., whether they are updated immediately or whether updates are delayed). Read/write.	Boolean
Determine Key Columns For Rowset	Indicates whether or not key column is automatically identified, thus avoiding update errors due to changed values (see MSKB 270636)	Boolean
Fastload Options	Indicates the options to use when in Fastload mode.	String
Fetch Backward	Indicates whether a rowset can fetch backward. Read/write.	Boolean
Filter Operations	Identifies which comparison operations are supported when using Filter on a particular column. Read-only.	DBPROPVAL_CO

Table continues on the following page

Property Name	Description	Data Type
Find Operations	Identifies which comparison operations are supported when using Find on a particular column. Read-only.	DBPROPVAL_CO
FOR BROWSE versioning columns	Indicates that the rowset contains the primary key or a timestamp column. Only applicable with rowsets created with the SQL FOR BROWSE statement. Read/write.	Boolean
Force no command preparation when executing a parameterized command	Identifies whether or not a temporary statement is created for parameterized commands. Read/write. #	Boolean
Force no command reexecution when failure to satisfy all required properties	Identifies whether or not the command is reexecuted if the command properties are invalid. Read/write. #	Boolean
Force no parameter rebinding when executing a command	Identifies whether the command parameters are rebound every time the command is executed. Read/write. #	Boolean
Force SQL Server Firehose Mode cursor	Identifies whether or not a forward-only, read-only cursor is always created. Read/write. #	Boolean
Generate a Rowset that can be marshaled	Identifies whether the ODBC driver generates a rowset that can be marshaled across process boundaries. Read/write.	Boolean
Hidden Columns	Indicates the number of hidden columns in the rowset added by the provider to uniquely identify rows.	Long
Hold Rows	Indicates whether the rowset allows the consumer to retrieve more rows or change the next fetch position while holding previously fetched rows with pending changes. Read/write.	Boolean
Immobile Rows	Indicates whether the rowset will reorder inserted or updated rows. Read/write.	Boolean
Include SQL_FLOAT, SQL_DOUBLE, and SQL_REAL in QBU where clauses	When using a query-based update, setting this to True will include REAL, FLOAT, and DOUBLE numeric types in the WHERE clause; otherwise, they will be omitted. Read/write.	Boolean

Table continues on the following page

511

Property Name	Description	Data Type
Initial Fetch Size	Identifies the initial size of the cache into which records are fetched. Read/write.	Long
Jet OLEDB:Bulk Transaction	Determines whether bulk operations are transacted.	DBPROPVAL_BT
Jet OLEDB:Enable Fat Cursors	Indicates whether Jet caches multiple rows for remote row sources.	Boolean
Jet OLEDB:Fat Cursor Cache Size	The number of rows that should be cached if the dynamic property Jet OLEDB:Enable Fat Cursors is set to True.	Long
Jet OLEDB:Inconsistent	Indicates whether inconsistent updates are allowed on queries.	Boolean
Jet OLEDB:Locking Granularity	Identifies the lock mode used to open a table. This applies only if Jet OLEDB:Database Locking Mode is set to DBPROPVAL_DL_ALCATRAZ.	DBPROPVAL_LG
Jet OLEDB:ODBC Pass-Through Statement	Identifies the statement used for a SQL pass-through statement. Read/write.	String
Jet OLEDB:Partial Bulk Ops	Indicates whether bulk operations will complete if some of the values fail.	Boolean
Jet OLEDB:Pass Through Query Bulk-Op	Indicates whether the pass-through query is a bulk operation.	Boolean
Jet OLEDB:Pass Through Query Connect String	Identifies the connect string for an ODBC pass-through query. Read/write.	String
Jet OLEDB:Stored Query	Indicates whether the command should be interpreted as a stored query.	Boolean
Jet OLEDB:Validate Rules On Set	Indicates whether Jet validation rules are applied when the value in a column is set (True) or when the changes are committed (False).	Boolean
Keep Identity	Indicates whether IDENTITY columns should keep the values if supplied by the client during an INSERT.	Boolean
Keep Nulls	Indicates whether Null values supplied by the client should be kept if DEFAULT values exist on the columns.	Boolean

Table continues on the following page

Property Name	Description	Data Type
Literal Bookmarks	Indicates whether bookmarks can be compared literally (as a series of bytes). Read/write.	Boolean
Literal Row Identity	Indicates whether the consumer can perform a binary comparison of two row handles to determine if they point to the same row. Read-only.	Boolean
Lock Mode	Identifies the level of locking performed by the rowset. Read/write.	DBPROPVAL_LM
Maintain Change Status	Indicates whether or not to maintain changes for pendingg rows.	Boolean
Maximum BLOB Length	Identifies the maximum length of a BLOB field. Read-only.	Long
Maximum Open Rows	Specifies the maximum number of rows that can be active at the same time. Read/write.	Long
Maximum Pending Rows	Specifies the maximum number of rows that can have pending changes at the same time. Read/write.	Long
Maximum Rows	Specifies the maximum number of rows that can be returned in the rowset. This is 0 if there is no limit. Read/write.	Long
Memory Usage	Specifies the amount of memory that can be used by the rowset. If set to 0, the amount is unlimited. If between 1 and 99, it specifies a percentage of the available virtual memory. If 100 or greater, it specifies the number of kilobytes. Read/write.	Long
Notification Granularity	Identifies when the consumer is notified for methods that operate on multiple rows. Read/write.	DBPROPVAL_NT
Notification Phases	Identifies the notification phases supported by the provider. Read-only.	DBPROPVAL_NP
Objects Transacted	Indicates whether any object created on the specified column is transacted. Read/write.	Boolean
ODBC Concurrency Type	Identifies the ODBC concurrency type. Read-only.	Integer
ODBC Cursor Type	Identifies the ODBC cursor type. Read-only.	Integer

Table continues on the following page

Property Name	Description	Data Type
Others' Changes Visible	Indicates whether the rowset can see updates and deletes made by someone other than the consumer of the rowset. Read/write.	Boolean
Others' Inserts Visible	Indicates whether the rowset can see rows inserted by someone other than the consumer of the rowset. Read/write.	Boolean
Own Changes Visible	Indicates whether the rowset can see its own updates and deletes. Read/write.	Boolean
Own Inserts Visible	Indicates whether the rowset can see its own inserts. Read/write.	Boolean
Position on the last row after insert	Identifies whether or not the cursor is placed on the last row after an insert. Read-only.	Boolean
Preserve on Abort	Indicates whether, after aborting a transaction, the rowset remains active. Read/write.	Boolean
Preserve on Commit	Indicates whether, after committing a transaction, the rowset remains active. Read/write.	Boolean
Query Based Updates/ Deletes/Inserts	Identifies whether queries are used for updates, deletes, and inserts. Read/write.	Boolean
Quick Restart	Indicates whether `RestartPosition` is relatively quick to execute. Read/write.	Boolean
Query Restriction	Indicates the restriction to use for a query.	String
Reentrant Events	Indicates whether the provider supports reentrancy during callbacks. Read-only.	Boolean
Remove Deleted Rows	Indicates whether the provider removes rows it detects as having been deleted from the rowset. Read/write.	Boolean
Report Multiple Changes	Indicates whether an update or delete can affect multiple rows, and the provider can detect that multiple rows have been updated or deleted. Read-only.	Boolean
Reshape Name	Indicates the name of the recordset that can be used in reshaping commands.	String
Resync Command	The command string that the `Resync` method will use to refresh data in the Unique Table.	String

Table continues on the following page

Property Name	Description	Data Type
Return PROPVARIANTs in variant binding	Indicates whether to return `PROPVARIANTS` when binding to variant columns.	`Boolean`
Return Pending	Inserts Indicates whether methods that fetch rows can return pending insert rows. Read-only.	`Boolean`
Row Delete Notification	Indicates whether deleting a row is cancelable. Read-only.	`DBPROPVAL_NP`
Row First Change Notification	Indicates whether changing the first row is cancelable. Read-only.	`DBPROPVAL_NP`
Row Insert Notification	Indicates whether inserting a new row is cancelable. Read-only.	`DBPROPVAL_NP`
Row Privileges	Indicates whether access rights are restricted on a row-by-row basis. Read-only.	`Boolean`
Row Resynchronization Notification	Indicates whether resynchronizing a row is cancelable. Read-only.	`DBPROPVAL_NP`
Row Threading Model	Identifies the threading models supported by the rowset. Read/write.	`DBPROPVAL_RT`
Row Undo Change Notification	Indicates whether undoing a change is cancelable. Read-only.	`DBPROPVAL_NP`
Row Undo Delete Notification	Indicates whether undoing a delete is cancelable. Read-only.	`DBPROPVAL_NP`
Row Undo Insert Notification	Indicates whether undoing an insert is cancelable. Read-only.	`DBPROPVAL_NP`
Row Update Notification	Indicates whether updating a row is cancelable. Read-only.	`DBPROPVAL_NP`
Rowset Fetch Position Change Notification	Indicates whether changing the fetch position is cancelable. Read-only.	`DBPROPVAL_NP`
Rowset Release Notification	Indicates whether releasing a rowset is cancelable. Read-only.	`DBPROPVAL_NP`
Scroll Backward	Indicates whether the rowset can scroll backward. Read/write.	`Boolean`
Server Cursor	Indicates whether the cursor underlying the rowset (if any) must be materialized on the server. Read/write.	`Boolean`

Table continues on the following page

Property Name	Description	Data Type
Server Data on	Insert Indicates whether, at the time an insert is transmitted to the server, the provider retrieves data from the server to update the local row cache. Read/write.	Boolean
Skip Deleted Bookmarks	Indicates whether the rowset allows positioning to continue if a bookmark row was deleted. Read/write.	Boolean
SQL Content Query Locale String	The locale string to use for queries.	String
Strong Row Identity	Indicates whether the handles of newly inserted rows can be compared. Read-only.	Boolean
Unique Catalog	Specifies the catalog or database name containing the table named in the Unique Table property.	String
Unique Rows	Indicates whether each row is uniquely identified by its column values. Read/write.	Boolean
Unique Schema	Specifies the schema, or owner of the table named in the Unique Table property.	String
Unique Table	Specifies the name of the base table upon which edits are allowed. This is required when updateable recordsets are created from one-to-many JOIN statements.	String
Updatability	Identifies the supported methods for updating a rowset. Read/write.	DBPROPVAL_UP
Update Criteria	Specifies which fields can be used to detect conflicts during optimistic updates. Read/write.	ADCPROP_ UPDATE CRITERIA_ENUM
Update Operation	For chaptered recordsets, identifies the operation to be performed with a re-query. Read/write.	String
Update Resync	Specifies whether an implicit Resync method is called directly after an UpdateBatch method.	CEResyncEnum
Use Bookmarks	Indicates whether the rowset supports bookmarks. Read/write.	Boolean

The Field Object's Properties

The field properties names are different from the other properties because they are less readable and appear more like the schema column names.

Property Name	Description	Data Type
BASECATALOGNAME	The name of the catalog. Read-only.	String
BASECOLUMNNAME	The name of the column. Read-only.	String
BASESCHEMANAME	The name of the schema. Read-only.	String
BASETABLEINSTANCE	The SQL Server 2000 instance of the base table.	Integer
BASETABLENAME	The table name. Read-only.	String
CALCULATIONINFO	This is only available on client cursors.	Binary
CLSID	The class ID of the field.	GUID
COLLATINGSEQUENCE	The locale ID of the sort sequence.	Long
COMPFLAGS	Compatibility flags for SL Variants.	Integer
COMPUTEMODE	Indicates the mode of recalculation for computed fields.	DBCOMPUTEMODE
DATETIMEPRECISION	The number of digits in the fraction seconds portion if a datetime column. Read-only.	Long
DEFAULTVALUE	The default value of the field.	Variant
DOMAINCATALOG	The name of the catalog containing this column's domain.	String
DOMAINNAME	The name of the domain of which this column is a member.	String
DOMAINSCHEMA	The name of the schema containing this column's domain.	String
HASDEFAULT	Indicates whether the field has a default value.	Boolean
ISAUTOINCREMENT	Identifies whether the column is an auto-increment column, such as an Access Autonumber or a SQL Server IDENTITY column. Read-only.	Boolean
ISCASESENSITIVE	Identifies whether the contents of the column are case sensitive. Useful when searching. Read-only.	Boolean

Table continues on the following page

Property Name	Description	Data Type
ISSEARCHABLE	Identifies the searchability of the column. Read-only.	DB_SEARCHABLE
ISUNIQUE	Indicates whether the field uniquely identifies the row.	Boolean
KEYCOLUMN	Identifies whether the column is a key column used to uniquely identify the row. Read-only.	Boolean
OCTETLENGTH	The maximum column length in bytes for character or binary data columns. Read-only.	Long
OPTIMIZE	Identifies whether the column is indexed locally. This is available only on client cursors. Read/write.	Boolean
RELATIONCONDITIONS	Identifies the relationship between fields. This is available only on client cursors. #	Binary
SORTID	The Sort Order ID for the collation of the column.	Integer

The Command Object's Properties

Property Name	Description	Data Type
Access Order	Indicates the order in which columns must be accessed on the rowset. Read/write.	DBPROPVAL_AO
Base Path	The path where XPATH mapping schema and template files are stored. The default is the current directory. Read/write.	String
Blocking Storage Objects	Indicates whether storage objects might prevent use of other methods on the rowset. Read/write.	Boolean
Bookmark Information	Identifies additional information about bookmarks over the rowset. Read-only.	DBPROPVAL_BI
Bookmark Type	Identifies the bookmark type supported by the rowset. Read/write.	DBPROPVAL_BMK
Bookmarkable	Indicates whether bookmarks are supported. Read-only.	Boolean

Table continues on the following page

Property Name	Description	Data Type
Change Inserted Rows	Indicates whether the consumer can delete or update newly inserted rows. An inserted row is assumed to be one that has been transmitted to the data source, as opposed to a pending insert row. Read/write.	Boolean
Column Privileges	Indicates whether access rights are restricted on a column-by-column basis. Read-only.	Boolean
Column Set Notification	Indicates whether changing a column set is cancelable. Read-only.	DBPROPVAL_NP
Command Time Out	The number of seconds to wait before a command times out. A value of 0 indicates an infinite timeout. Read/write.	Long
Content type	For URL access to SQL Server 2000, specifies the Content-Type of the returned document.	String
Cursor Auto Fetch	Indicates whether a cursor is automatically fetched. Corresponds to the `adExecuteNoRecords` option for the `Execute` method.	Boolean
Defer Column	Indicates whether the data in a column is not fetched until specifically requested. Read/write.	Boolean
Defer Prepare	Indicates whether command parsing is deferred until the statement is prepared.	Boolean
Delay Storage Object Updates	Indicates whether, when in delayed update mode, storage objects are also used in delayed update mode. Read/write.	Boolean
Determine Key Columns For Rowset	Indicates whether or not key column is automatically identified, thus avoiding update errors due to changed values (see MSKB 270636)	Boolean
Fastload Options	Indicates the options to use when in Fastload mode.	String
Fetch Backward	Indicates whether a rowset can fetch backward. Read/write.	Boolean
Hidden Columns	Indicates the number of hidden columns in the rowset added by the provider to uniquely identify rows.	Long

Table continues on the following page

Property Name	Description	Data Type
Hold Rows	Indicates whether the rowset allows the consumer to retrieve more rows or change the next fetch position while holding previously fetched rows with pending changes. Read/write.	Boolean
Immobile Rows	Indicates whether the rowset will reorder inserted or updated rows. Read/write.	Boolean
Keep Identity	Indicates whether IDENTITY columns should keep the values if supplied by the client during an INSERT.	Boolean
Keep Nulls	Indicates whether Null values supplied by the client should be kept if DEFAULT values exist on the columns.	Boolean
Literal Bookmarks	Indicates whether bookmarks can be compared literally as a series of bytes. Read/write.	Boolean
Literal Row	Identity Indicates whether the consumer can perform a binary comparison of two row handles to determine if they point to the same row. Read-only.	Boolean
Lock Mode	Identifies the level of locking performed by the rowset. Read/write.	DBPROPVAL_LM
Mapping Schema	The name of the XPATH mapping schema to be used. The path is taken from the Base Path dynamic property.	String
Maximum BLOB Length	Identifies the maximum length of a BLOB field. Read-only.	Long
Maximum Open Rows	Specifies the maximum number of rows that can be active at the same time. Read/write.	Long
Maximum Pending Rows	Specifies the maximum number of rows that can have pending changes at the same time. Read/write.	Long
Maximum Rows	Specifies the maximum number of rows that can be returned in the rowset. This is 0 if there is no limit. Read/write.	Long
Notification Granularity	Identifies when the consumer is notified for methods that operate on multiple rows. Read/write.	DBPROPVAL_NT

Table continues on the following page

Property Name	Description	Data Type
Notification Phases	Identifies the notification phases supported by the provider. Read-only.	`DBPROPVAL_NP`
Objects Transacted	Indicates whether any object created on the specified column is transacted. Read/write.	`Boolean`
Others' Changes Visible	Indicates whether the rowset can see updates and deletes made by someone other that the consumer of the rowset. Read/write.	`Boolean`
Others' Inserts Visible	Indicates whether the rowset can see rows inserted by someone other than the consumer of the rowset. Read/write.	`Boolean`
Output Encoding	Specifies the encoding to use in the stream returned by the command. The default is UTF8. Read/write.	`String`
Output Stream	Identifies the `Stream` object (or object supporting the `IStream` interface) into which the results of the command should be stored.	`Stream`
Own Changes Visible	Indicates whether the rowset can see its own updates and deletes. Read/write.	`Boolean`
Own Inserts Visible	Indicates whether the rowset can see its own inserts. Read/write.	`Boolean`
Preserve on Abort	Indicates whether, after aborting a transaction, the rowset remains active. Read/write.	`Boolean`
Preserve on Commit	Indicates whether, after committing a transaction, the rowset remains active. Read/write.	`Boolean`
Quick Restart	Indicates whether `RestartPosition` is relatively quick to execute. Read/write.	`Boolean`
Reentrant Events	Indicates whether the provider supports reentrancy during callbacks. Read-only.	`Boolean`
Remove Deleted Rows	Indicates whether the provider removes rows it detects as having been deleted from the rowset. Read/write.	`Boolean`
Report Multiple Changes	Indicates whether an update or delete can affect multiple rows and the provider can detect that multiple rows have been updated or deleted. Read-only.	`Boolean`

Table continues on the following page

Property Name	Description	Data Type
Return Pending Inserts	Indicates whether methods that fetch rows can return pending insert rows. Read-only.	`Boolean`
Row Delete Notification	Indicates whether deleting a row is cancelable. Read-only.	`DBPROPVAL_NP`
Row Insert Notification	Indicates whether inserting a new row is cancelable. Read-only.	`DBPROPVAL_NP`
Row Privileges	Indicates whether access rights are restricted on a row-by-row basis. Read-only.	`Boolean`
Row Resynchronization Notification	Indicates whether resynchronizing a row is cancelable. Read-only.	`DBPROPVAL_NP`
Row Threading Model	Identifies the threading models supported by the rowset. Read/write.	`DBPROPVAL_RT`
Row Undo Change Notification	Indicates whether undoing a change is cancelable. Read-only.	`DBPROPVAL_NP`
Row Undo Delete Notification	Indicates whether undoing a delete is cancelable. Read-only.	`DBPROPVAL_NP`
Row Undo Insert Notification	Indicates whether undoing an insert is cancelable. Read-only.	`DBPROPVAL_NP`
Row Update Notification	Indicates whether updating a row is cancelable. Read-only.	`DBPROPVAL_NP`
Rowset Fetch Position Change Notification	Indicates whether changing the fetch position is cancelable. Read-only.	`DBPROPVAL_NP`
Rowset Release Notification	Indicates whether releasing a rowset is cancelable. Read-only.	`DBPROPVAL_NP`
Scroll Backward	Indicates whether the rowset can scroll backward. Read/write.	`Boolean`
Server Cursor	Indicates whether the cursor underlying the rowset (if any) must be materialized on the server. Read/write.	`Boolean`
Server Data on Insert	Indicates whether, at the time an insert is transmitted to the server, the provider retrieves data from the server to update the local row cache. Read/write.	`Boolean`
Skip Deleted Bookmarks	Indicates whether the rowset allows positioning to continue if a bookmark row was deleted. Read/write.	`Boolean`

Table continues on the following page

Property Name	Description	Data Type
SS Stream Flags	SQL Server flags for the TDS Stream. #	Integer
Strong Row Identity	Indicates whether the handles of newly inserted rows can be compared. Read-only.	Boolean
Unique Rows	Indicates whether each row is uniquely identified by its column values. Read/write.	Boolean
Updatability	Identifies the supported methods for updating a rowset. Read/write.	DBPROPVAL_UP
Use Bookmarks	Indicates whether the rowset supports bookmarks. Read/write.	Boolean
XML root	The tag name in which to wrap the resulting XML.	String
XSL	Specifies an XSL file or URL used to transform the XML. Read/write.	String

D

Schemas

Two terms are important to understand when dealing with schemas:

❑ A **Catalog** is like a normal paper catalog, but contains a list of schemas. It always contains a schema named INFORMATION_SCHEMA, which is the information schema. When dealing with Microsoft SQL Server and Access, a catalog is a database.

❑ A **Schema** is a collection of database objects owned by (or have been created by) a particular user. Microsoft Access does not have an equivalent to a schema, so all database objects in Access appear in a single schema.

This appendix details the schema objects that you can access by using the OpenSchema method of the Connection object.

The following table shows the main providers and the list of schemas supported by them:

Schema	ODBC Access 97	ODBC Access 2000	ODBC SQL 6.5	ODBC SQL 7/2000	OLE DB Access 97	OLE DB Access 2000	OLE DB SQL 6.5	OLE DB SQL 7/2000	OLAP
adSchemaActions									✓
adSchemaAsserts									
adSchemaCatalogs	✓	✓	✓	✓			✓	✓	✓

Table continues on the following page

Schema	ODBC Access 97	ODBC Access 2000	ODBC SQL 6.5	ODBC SQL 7/2000	OLE DB Access 97	OLE DB Access 2000	OLE DB SQL 6.5	OLE DB SQL 7/2000	OLAP
adSchemaCharacterSets									
adSchemaCheckConstraints					✓	✓			
adSchemaCollations									
adSchemaColumnPrivileges				✓	✓		✓	✓	
adSchemaColumns	✓	✓	✓	✓	✓	✓	✓	✓	✓
adSchemaColumnsDomainUsage									
adSchemaCommands									
adSchemaConstraintColumnUsage					✓	✓			
adSchemaConstraintTableUsage									
adSchemaCubes	✓								
adSchemaDBInfoKeywords	✓	✓	✓	✓	✓	✓	✓	✓	✓
adSchemaDBInfoLiterals	✓	✓	✓	✓	✓	✓	✓	✓	✓
adSchemaDimensions									✓
adSchemaForeignKeys			✓	✓	✓	✓	✓	✓	
adSchemaFunctions									✓
adSchemaHierarchies									✓
adSchemaIndexes	✓	✓	✓	✓	✓	✓	✓	✓	
adSchemaKeyColumnUsage					✓	✓			
adSchemaLevels									✓
adSchemaMeasures									✓
adSchemaMembers									✓
adSchemaPrimaryKeys			✓	✓	✓	✓	✓	✓	
adSchemaProcedureColumns	✓	✓							

Table continues on the following page

Schema	ODBC Access 97	ODBC Access 2000	ODBC SQL 6.5	ODBC SQL 7/2000	OLE DB Access 97	OLE DB Access 2000	OLE DB SQL 6.5	OLE DB SQL 7/2000	OLAP
adSchemaProcedureParameters	✓	✓	✓	✓			✓	✓	
adSchemaProcedures	✓	✓	✓	✓	✓	✓	✓	✓	
adSchemaProperties									✓
adSchemaProviderTypes	✓	✓	✓	✓	✓	✓	✓	✓	✓
adSchemaReferentialContraints					✓	✓			
adSchemaSchemata			✓	✓			✓	✓	
adSchemaSets									✓
adSchemaSQLLanguages									
adSchemaStatistics					✓	✓	✓	✓	
adSchemaTableConstraints					✓	✓	✓	✓	
adSchemaTablePrivileges							✓	✓	
adSchemaTables	✓	✓	✓	✓	✓	✓	✓	✓	✓
adSchemaTranslations									
adSchemaTrustees									
adSchemaUsagePrivileges									
adSchemaViewColumnUsage									
adSchemaViews					✓	✓			
adSchemaViewTableUsage									

Schema Usage

Using schemas is quite easy; all you must do is use the OpenSchema method of the Connection object. For example, to list all of the tables on a particular connection:

```
Set objRec = objConn.OpenSchema (adSchemaTables)
While Not objRec.EOF
  Print objRec("TABLE_NAME")
  objRec.MoveNext
Wend
```

This simply opens a recordset on the tables schema and loops through it, printing each table name. You can use the TABLE_TYPE column to check for system tables:

```
Set objRec = objConn.OpenSchema (adSchemaTables)
While Not objRec.EOF
    If objRec("TABLE_TYPE") <> "SYSTEM TABLE" Then
        Print objRec("TABLE_NAME")
    End If
    objRec.MoveNext
Wend
```

You can use the Restrictions argument of OpenSchema to return only certain rows. This argument accepts an array that matches the column names. For example, to find only the system tables:

```
Set objRec = objConn.OpenSchema (adSchemaTables, _
                  Array (Empty, Empty, Empty, "SYSTEM_TABLE"))
```

Because the type is the fourth column in the recordset, you must specify empty values for the columns you wish to skip.

For multidimensional providers using adSchemaMembers, the restrictions can either be the columns in the members schema, or one of the MDTREEOP constants, as defined in Appendix L.

When connecting to Microsoft Access, you should be aware of some interesting things. If you wish to see the queries, you might have to use both adSchemaProcedures and adSchemaViews depending upon the query type. Normal select queries appear as Views, whereas action queries (Update, Delete, etc.) and CrossTab queries appear as procedures. This is only for the native Jet provider. For the ODBC provider, Select and CrossTab queries appear as tables with a table type set to VIEW.

adSchemaActions

This identifies the actions linked to data in the cube.

Column Name	Type	Description
CATALOG_NAME	String	The catalog name
SCHEMA_NAME	String	Schema name, or Null if the provider does not support schemas
CUBE_NAME	String	The name of the cube
ACTION_NAME	String	The name of the action
COORDINATE	String	A string identifying the "coordinate" of the action
COORDINATE_TYPE	Integer	Indicates what the "coordinate" column contains.

Table continues on the following page

Column Name	Type	Description
CAPTION	String	The friendly name of the action
DESCRIPTION	String	A description of the action
CONTENT	String	The string containing the action
APPLICATION	String	The application name

adSchemaAsserts

This identifies the assertions defined in the catalog.

Column Name	Type	Description
CONSTRAINT_CATALOG	String	Catalog name, or Null if the provider does not support catalogs
CONSTRAINT_SCHEMA	String	Schema name, or Null if the provider does not support schemas
CONSTRAINT_NAME	String	Constraint name
IS_DEFERRABLE	Boolean	True if the assertion is deferrable, False otherwise
INITIALLY_DEFERRED	Boolean	True if the assertion is initially deferred, False otherwise
DESCRIPTION	String	Description of the assertion

adSchemaCatalogs

This defines the physical attributes of a database's catalogs. In SQL Server, the catalogs are the databases within the Server. In Access, the catalogs contain the current database.

Column Name	Type	Description
CATALOG_NAME	String	Catalog name
DESCRIPTION	String	Catalog description

adSchemaCharacterSets

This identifies the character sets supported by the catalog.

Column Name	Type	Description
CHARACTER_SET_CATALOG	String	Catalog name, or Null if the provider does not support catalogs
CHARACTER_SET_SCHEMA	String	Schema name, or Null if the provider does not support schemas
CHARACTER_SET_NAME	String	Character set name
FORM_OF_USE	String	Name of form-of-use of the character set
NUMBER_OF_CHARACTERS	Big Integer	Number of characters in the character repertoire
DEFAULT_COLLATE_CATALOG	String	Catalog name containing the default collation, or Null if the provider does not support catalogs or different collations
DEFAULT_COLLATE_SCHEMA	String	Schema name containing the default collation, or Null if the provider does not support schemas or different collations
DEFAULT_COLLATE_NAME	String	Default collation name, or Null if the provider does not support different collations

adSchemaCheckConstraints

This identifies the check constraints available in the catalog. Check constraints identify the valid values allowed for columns.

Column Name	Type	Description
CONSTRAINT_CATALOG	String	Catalog name, or Null if the provider does not support catalogs
CONSTRAINT_SCHEMA	String	Schema name, or Null if the provider does not support schemas
CONSTRAINT_NAME	String	Constraint name
CHECK_CLAUSE	String	The WHERE clause specified in the CHECK constraint
DESCRIPTION	String	Check constraint description

adSchemaCollations

Collations identify how the catalog sorts data.

Column Name	Type	Description
COLLATION_CATALOG	String	Catalog name, or Null if the provider does not support catalogs
COLLATION_SCHEMA	String	Schema name, or Null if the provider does not support schemas
COLLATION_NAME	String	Collation name
CHARACTER_SET_CATALOG	String	Catalog name containing the character set on which the collation is defined, or Null if the provider does not support catalogs or different character sets
CHARACTER_SET_SCHEMA	String	Schema name containing the character set on which the collation is defined, or Null if the provider does not support schemas or different character sets
CHARACTER_SET_NAME	String	Character set name on which the collation is defined, or Null if the provider does not support different character sets
PAD_ATTRIBUTE	String	"NO PAD" if the collation being described has the NO PAD attribute, "PAD SPACE" if the collation being described has the PAD SPACE attribute (identifies whether variable length character columns are padded with spaces)

adSchemaColumnPrivileges

This identifies the privileges on table columns for a given user.

Column Name	Type	Description
GRANTOR	String	User who granted the privileges on the table in TABLE_NAME
GRANTEE	String	User name (or "PUBLIC") to whom the privilege has been granted
TABLE_CATALOG	String	Catalog name in which the table is defined, or Null if the provider does not support catalogs

Table continues on the following page

Column Name	Type	Description
TABLE_SCHEMA	String	Schema name in which the table is defined, or Null if the provider does not support schemas
TABLE_NAME	String	Table name
COLUMN_NAME	String	Column name
COLUMN_GUID	GUID	Column GUID
COLUMN_PROPID	Long	Column property ID
PRIVILEGE_TYPE	String	Privilege type (can be one of the following: SELECT, DELETE, INSERT, UPDATE, REFERENCES)
IS_GRANTABLE	Boolean	True if the privilege being described was granted with the WITH GRANT OPTION clause, False if the privilege being described was not granted with the WITH GRANT OPTION clause

adSchemaColumns

This identifies the columns of tables.

Column Name	Type	Description
TABLE_CATALOG	String	This is the catalog name, or Null if the provider does not support catalogs.
TABLE_SCHEMA	Long	This is the schema name, or Null if the provider does not support schemas.
TABLE_NAME	String	This is the table name. This column cannot contain a Null.
COLUMN_NAME	String	This is the name of the column, or Null if this cannot be determined.
COLUMN_GUID	GUID	This is the column GUID, or Null for providers that do not use GUIDs to identify columns.
COLUMN_PROPID	Long	This is the column property ID, or it is Null for providers that do not associate PROPIDs with columns.
ORDINAL_POSITION	Long	This is the ordinal of the column, or it is Null if no stable ordinal value exists for the column. Columns are numbered starting from one.

Table continues on the following page

Column Name	Type	Description
COLUMN_HASDEFAULT	Boolean	This indicates whether the column has a default value. It is True if the column has a default value, or False if the column does not have a default value or it is unknown whether the column has a default value.
COLUMN_DEFAULT	String	This is the column's default value.
COLUMN_FLAGS	Long	This is a bitmask that describes column characteristics. The DBCOLUMNFLAGS enumerated type specifies the bits in the bitmask. The values for DBCOLUMNFLAGS appear in Appendix B. This column cannot contain a Null value.
IS_NULLABLE	Boolean	This indicates whether the column can contain null values. It is True if the column might be Nullable, or False if the column is known not to be Nullable.
DATA_TYPE	Integer	This indicates the column's data type. If the column's data type varies from row to row, this must be a Variant. This column cannot contain Null. For a list of valid Types, see DataTypeEnum in Appendix B.
TYPE_GUID	GUID	This is the GUID of the column's data type. Providers that do not use GUIDs to identify data types should return Null in this column.
CHARACTER_MAXIMUM _LENGTH	Long	This is the maximum possible length of a value in the column. See. CHARACTER_OCTET_LENGTH for details.
CHARACTER_OCTET _LENGTH	Long	This indicates the column's maximum length in octets (bytes) if the column type is character or binary. A value of zero means the column has no maximum length. The value is Null for all other column types.
NUMERIC_PRECISION	Integer	If the column's data type is numeric, this is the column's maximum precision. The precision of columns with a data type of Decimal or Numeric depends on the definition of the column. If the column's data type is not numeric, this is Null.

Table continues on the following page

Column Name	Type	Description
NUMERIC_SCALE	Integer	If the column's Type is Decimal or Numeric, this is the number of digits to the right of the decimal point. Otherwise, this is Null.
DATETIME_PRECISION	Long	This is the datetime precision (number of digits in the fractional seconds portion) of the column if the column is a datetime or interval type. If the column's data type is not datetime, this is Null.
CHARACTER_SET_CATALOG	String	This is the catalog name in which the character set is defined, or Null if the provider does not support catalogs or different character sets.
CHARACTER_SET_SCHEMA	String	This is the schema name in which the character set is defined, or Null if the provider does not support schemas or different character sets.
CHARACTER_SET_NAME	String	This is the character set name, or Null if the provider does not support different character sets.
COLLATION_CATALOG	String	This is the catalog name in which the collation is defined, or Null if the provider does not support catalogs or different collations.
COLLATION_SCHEMA	String	This is the Schema name in which the collation is defined, or Null if the provider does not support schemas or different collations.
COLLATION_NAME	String	This is the collation name, or Null if the provider does not support different collations.
DOMAIN_CATALOG	String	This is the catalog name in which the domain is defined, or Null if the provider does not support catalogs or domains.
DOMAIN_SCHEMA	String	This is the unqualified schema name in which the domain is defined, or Null if the provider does not support schemas or domains.
DOMAIN_NAME	String	This is the domain name, or Null if the provider does not support domains.
DESCRIPTION	String	This is the description of the column, or Null if there is no description associated with the column.

Table continues on the following page

Column Name	Type	Description
SS_DATA_TYPE	Integer	This is the SQL Server data type.
COLUMN_LCID	Integer	This is the locale ID of the column.
COLUMN_COMPFLAGS	Integer	This is the column comparison flags.
COLUMN_SORTID	Integer	This is the column sort order.
COLUMN_TDS COLLATION	Integer	This is the SQL Server collation.

CHARACTER_MAXIMUM_LENGTH varies depending upon the column's data type. For character, binary, or bit columns, this is one of the following:

❑ The maximum length of the column in characters, bytes, or bits, respectively, if one is defined (e.g., a CHAR(5) column in a SQL table has a maximum length of five)

❑ The maximum length of the data type in characters, bytes, or bits, respectively, if the column does not have a defined length

❑ Zero if neither the column nor the data type has a defined maximum length

It will be Null for all other types of columns.

adSchemaColumnsDomainUsage

This identifies the columns that use domains for integrity checking.

Column Name	Type	Description
DOMAIN_CATALOG	String	Catalog name, or Null if the provider does not support catalogs
DOMAIN_SCHEMA	String	Schema name, or Null if the provider does not support schemas
DOMAIN_NAME	String	View name
TABLE_CATALOG	String	Catalog name in which the table is defined, or Null if the provider does not support catalogs
TABLE_SCHEMA	String	Unqualified schema name in which the table is defined, or Null if the provider does not support schemas
TABLE_NAME	String	Table name

Table continues on the following page

Column Name	Type	Description
COLUMN_NAME	String	Column name–together with the COLUMN_GUID and COLUMN_PROPID columns, forms the column ID (One or more of these columns will be Null depending on which elements of the DBID structure the provider uses)
COLUMN_GUID	GUID	Column GUID
COLUMN_PROPID	Long	Column property ID

adSchemaConstraintColumnUsage

This identifies the columns used for referential integrity constraints, unique constraints, check constraints, and assertions.

Column Name	Type	Description
TABLE_CATALOG	String	Catalog name in which the table is defined, or Null if the provider does not support catalogs.
TABLE_SCHEMA	String	Schema name in which the table is defined, or Null if the provider does not support schemas
TABLE_NAME	String	Table name
COLUMN_NAME	String	Column name
COLUMN_GUID	GUID	Column GUID
COLUMN_PROPID	Long	Column property ID
CONSTRAINT_CATALOG	String	Catalog name, or Null if the provider does not support catalogs
CONSTRAINT_SCHEMA	String	Schema name, or Null if the provider does not support schemas
CONSTRAINT_NAME	String	Constraint name

adSchemaConstraintTableUsage

This identifies the tables used for referential integrity constraints, unique constraints, check constraints, and assertions.

Column Name	Type	Description
TABLE_CATALOG	String	Catalog name in which the table is defined, or Null if the provider does not support catalogs
TABLE_SCHEMA	String	Schema name in which the table is defined, or Null if the provider does not support schemas
TABLE_NAME	String	Table name
CONSTRAINT_CATALOG	String	Catalog name, or Null if the provider does not support catalogs
CONSTRAINT_SCHEMA	String	Schema name, or Null if the provider does not support schemas
CONSTRAINT_NAME	String	Constraint name

adSchemaCubes

This identifies the cubes in an OLAP catalog.

Column Name	Type	Description
CATALOG_NAME	String	Catalog name in which the table is defined, or Null if the provider does not support catalogs
SCHEMA_NAME	String	Schema name in which the table is defined, or Null if the provider does not support schemas
CUBE_NAME	String	The name of the cube
CUBE_TYPE	String	Either CUBE to indicate a regular cube, or VIRTUAL CUBE to indicate a virtual cube
CUBE_GUID	String	The GUID of the cube, or Null if no GUID exists
CREATED_ON	Date	Date and time cube was created
LAST_SCHEMA_UPDATE	Date	Date and time when schema was last updated
SCHEMA_UPDATED_BY	String	User ID of person who last updated the schema
LAST_DATA_UPDATE	Date	Date and time when data was last updated
DATA_UPDATED_BY	String	User ID of person who last updated the data
DESCRIPTION	String	The cube description

adSchemaDBInfoKeywords

This identifies a list of provider-specific keywords.

Column Name	Type	Description
KEYWORD	String	The keyword supported by the provider

adSchemaDBInfoLiterals

This identifies a list of provider-specific literals used in text commands.

Column Name	Type	Description
LiteralName	String	The literal name
LiteralValue	String	The literal value
InvalidChars	String	Characters that are invalid as part of a literal
InvalidStartingChars	String	Characters that cannot start the literal
Literal	Integer	The literal type (can be one of the DBLITERAL constants described in Appendix B)
Supported	Boolean	True if the provider supports the literal
Maxlen	Integer	Maximum length of the literal name

adSchemaDimensions

This identifies the dimensions in an OLAP catalog.

Column Name	Type	Description
CATALOG_NAME	String	Catalog name in which the table is defined, or Null if the provider does not support catalogs
SCHEMA_NAME	String	Schema name in which the table is defined, or Null if the provider does not support schemas
CUBE_NAME	String	The name of the cube to which this dimension belongs
DIMENSION_NAME	String	The name of the dimension
DIMENSION_UNIQUE_NAME	String	The fully qualified name of the dimension

Table continues on the following page

Column Name	Type	Description
DIMENSION_UNIQUE_NAME	String	The fully qualified name of the dimension
DIMENSION_GUID	GUID	The GUID of the dimension, or Null if no GUID exists
DIMENSION_CAPTION	String	The name of the dimension
DIMENSION_ORDINAL	Long	The number of the ordinal (zero based)
DIMENSION_TYPE	Integer	The type of the dimension—can be one of these: MD_DIMTYPE_MEASURE indicates a measure dimension MD_DIMTYPE_TIME indicates a time dimension MD_DIMTYPE_OTHER indicates neither a measure nor a time dimension MD_DIMTYPE_UNKNOWN indicates that the type is unknown
DIMENSION_CARDINALITY	Long	The number of members in the dimension (this figure's accuracy not guaranteed)
DEFAULT_HIERARCHY	String	The default hierarchy for this dimension, or Null if no default exists
DESCRIPTION	String	The description of the hierarchy
IS_VIRTUAL	Boolean	True if the dimension is virtual, False otherwise

adSchemaForeignKeys

This identifies the foreign key columns, as used in referential integrity checks.

Column Name	Type	Description
PK_TABLE_CATALOG	String	Catalog name in which the primary key table is defined, or Null if the provider does not support catalogs
PK_TABLE_SCHEMA	String	Schema name in which the primary key table is defined, or Null if the provider does not support schemas
PK_TABLE_NAME	String	Primary key table name
PK_COLUMN_NAME	String	Primary key column name
PK_TABLE_CATALOG	String	Catalog name in which the primary key table is defined, or Null if the provider does not support catalogs

Table continues on the following page

Column Name	Type	Description
PK_TABLE_SCHEMA	String	Schema name in which the primary key table is defined, or Null if the provider does not support schemas
PK_TABLE_NAME	String	Primary key table name
PK_COLUMN_NAME	String	Primary key column name
PK_COLUMN_GUID	GUID	Primary key column GUID
PK_COLUMN_PROPID	Long	Primary key column property ID
FK_TABLE_CATALOG	String	Catalog name in which the foreign key table is defined, or Null if the provider does not support catalogs
FK_TABLE_SCHEMA	String	Schema name in which the foreign key table is defined, or Null if the provider does not support schemas
FK_TABLE_NAME	String	Foreign key table name
FK_COLUMN_NAME	String	Foreign key column name
FK_COLUMN_GUID	GUID	Foreign key column GUID
FK_COLUMN_PROPID	Long	Foreign key column property ID
ORDINAL	Long	The order of the column in the key (For example, a table might contain several foreign key references to another table. The ordinal starts over for each reference: two references to a three-column key would return 1, 2, 3, 1, 2, 3)
UPDATE_RULE	String	The action if an UPDATE rule was specified (This will be Null only if the provider cannot determine the UPDATE_RULE. In most cases, this implies a default of NO ACTION)
DELETE_RULE	String	The action if a DELETE rule was specified (This will be Null if the provider cannot determine the DELETE_RULE. In most cases, this implies a default of NO ACTION)
FK_NAME	String	Foreign key name, or Null if the provider does not support named foreign key constraints
PK_NAME	String	Primary key name, or Null if the provider does not support named primary key constraints
DEFERRABILITY	Integer	Deferability of the foreign key (can be one of the DBPROPVAL_DF types, as shown in Appendix B)

For UPDATE_RULE and DELETE_RULE, the value will be one of the following:

❏ CASCADE–A referential action of CASCADE was specified.

❏ SET NULL–A referential action of SET NULL was specified.

❏ SET DEFAULT–A referential action of SET DEFAULT was specified.

❏ NO ACTION–A referential action of NO ACTION was specified.

adSchemaFunctions

This identifies all of the supported functions of the OLAP provider.

Column Name	Type	Description
FUNCTION_NAME	String	The name of the function
DESCRIPTION	String	The description of the function
PARAM_LIST	String	A comma-delimited list of parameters, in Visual Basic style (like Age As Integer)
RETURN_TYPE	Integer	The data type of the function return value
ORIGIN	Integer	The origin of the function (provider-supplied function or user-defined function)
INTERFACE_NAME	String	The name of the interface for a user-defined function, or the group name for an MDX function
LIBRARY_NAME	String	The name of the type library for user-defined functions, or NULL for MDX functions
DLL_NAME	String	The name of the .dll or .exe implementing the function, or NULL for MDX functions
HELP_FILE	String	The name of the help file documenting this function, or NULL for MDX functions
HELP_CONTEXT	Integer	The Help Context ID in the help file for this function
OBJECT	String	The object to which this function applies (such as a level or dimension)

adSchemaHierarchies

This identifies the hierarchies in an OLAP catalog.

Column Name	Type	Description
CATALOG_NAME	String	Catalog name in which the table is defined, or Null if the provider does not support catalogs
SCHEMA_NAME	String	Schema name in which the table is defined, or Null if the provider does not support schemas
CUBE_NAME	String	The name of the cube to which this hierarchy belongs
DIMENSION_UNIQUE_NAME	String	The fully qualified name of the dimension to which this hierarchy belongs
HIERARCHY_NAME	String	The name of the hierarchy
HIERARCHY_UNIQUE_NAME	String	The fully qualified name of the hierarchy
HIERARCHY_GUID	GUID	The GUID of the hierarchy, or Null if no GUID exists
HIERARCHY_CAPTION	String	The name of the hierarchy
DIMENSION_TYPE	Integer	The type of the dimension–can be one of these: MD_DIMTYPE_MEASURE indicates a measure dimension MD_DIMTYPE_TIME indicates a time dimension MD_DIMTYPE_OTHER indicates neither a measure nor a time dimension MD_DIMTYPE_UNKNOWN indicates that the type is unknown
HIERARCHY_CARDINALITY	Long	The number of members in the hierarchy (this figure's accuracy not guaranteed)
DEFAULT_MEMBER	String	The default level for this hierarchy, or Null if no default exists
ALL_MEMBER	String	The name of the default member if the first level is All, or Null if the first level is not All
DESCRIPTION	String	The description of the hierarchy

adSchemaIndexes

This identifies the list of indexes in the catalog.

Column Name	Type	Description
TABLE_CATALOG	String	Catalog name, or Null if the provider does not support catalogs
TABLE_SCHEMA	String	Unqualified schema name, or Null if the provider does not support schemas
TABLE_NAME	String	Table name
INDEX_CATALOG	String	Catalog name, or Null if the provider does not support catalogs
INDEX_SCHEMA	String	Schema name, or Null if the provider does not support schemas
INDEX_NAME	String	Index name
PRIMARY_KEY	Boolean	Whether the index represents the primary key on the table, or Null if this is not known
UNIQUE	Boolean	Whether index keys must be unique (True if the index keys must be unique, False if duplicate keys are allowed)
CLUSTERED	Boolean	Whether an index is clustered
TYPE	Integer	The type of the index (can be one of the DBPROPVAL_IT constants as shown in Appendix B)
FILL_FACTOR	Long	For a B+ tree index, represents the storage utilization factor of page nodes during the creation of the index
INITIAL_SIZE	Long	The total amount of bytes allocated to this structure at creation time
NULLS	Long	Whether Null keys are allowed (can be one of the DBPROVAL_IN constants as shown in Appendix B)
SORT_BOOKMARKS	Boolean	How the index treats repeated keys (True if the index sorts repeated keys by bookmark, False if it doesn't)
AUTO_UPDATE	Boolean	Whether the index is maintained automatically when changes are made to the corresponding base table (True if the index is automatically maintained, False if it isn't)

Table continues on the following page

Column Name	Type	Description
NULL_COLLATION	Long	How Nulls are collated in the index (can be one of the DBPROPVAL_NC constants as shown in Appendix B)
ORDINAL_POSITION	Long	Ordinal position of the column in the index, starting with one
COLUMN_NAME	String	Column name
COLUMN_GUID	GUID	Column GUID
COLUMN_PROPID	Long	Column property ID
COLLATION	Integer	Identifies the sort order (can be one of the DB_COLLATION constants as shown in Appendix B)
CARDINALITY	Unsigned Big Integer	Number of unique values in the index
PAGES	Long	Number of pages used to store the index
FILTER_CONDITION	String	The WHERE clause identifying the filtering restriction
INTEGRATED	Boolean	Whether the index is integrated, that is, all base table columns are available from the index (True if the index is integrated, False if it isn't, always True for clustered indexes)

adSchemaKeyColumnUsage

This identifies the key columns and table names in the catalog.

Column Name	Type	Description
CONSTRAINT_CATALOG	String	Catalog name, or Null if the provider does not support catalogs
CONSTRAINT_SCHEMA	String	Schema name, or Null if the provider does not support schemas
CONSTRAINT_NAME	String	Constraint name
TABLE_CATALOG	String	Catalog name in which the table containing the key column is defined, or Null if the provider does not support catalogs

Table continues on the following page

Column Name	Type	Description
TABLE_SCHEMA	String	Schema name in which the table containing the key column is defined, or Null if the provider does not support schemas
TABLE_NAME	String	Table name containing the key column
COLUMN_NAME	String	Name of the column participating in the unique, primary, or foreign key
COLUMN_GUID	GUID	Column GUID
COLUMN_PROPID	Long	Column property ID
ORDINAL_POSITION	Long	Ordinal position of the column in the constraint being described

adSchemaLevels

This identifies the levels in an OLAP catalog.

Column Name	Type	Description
CATALOG_NAME	String	Catalog name, or Null if the provider does not support catalogs
SCHEMA_NAME	String	Schema name, or Null if the provider does not support schemas
CUBE_NAME	String	The cube name to which the level belongs
DIMENSION_UNIQUE_NAME	String	The unique name of the dimension to which the level belongs
HIERARCHY_UNIQUE_NAME	String	The unique name of the hierarchy to which the level belongs
LEVEL_NAME	String	The level name
LEVEL_UNIQUE_NAME	String	The unique level name
LEVEL_GUID	String	The GUID of the level, or Null if no GUID exists
LEVEL_CAPTION	String	The Caption of the level
LEVEL_NUMBER	String	The index number of the level

Table continues on the following page

Column Name	Type	Description
LEVEL_CARDINALITY	Long	The number of members in the level (figure's accuracy not guaranteed)
LEVEL_TYPE	Integer	The Type of the level (can be one of the MDLEVEL_TYPE constants, as described in Appendix L)
DESCRIPTION	String	The description of the level

adSchemaMeasures

This identifies the measures in an OLAP catalog.

Column Name	Type	Description
CATALOG_NAME	String	Catalog name, or Null if the provider does not support catalogs
SCHEMA_NAME	String	Schema name, or Null if the provider does not support schemas
CUBE_NAME	String	The cube name to which the measure belongs
MEASURE_NAME	String	The name of the measure
MEASURE_UNIQUE_NAME	String	The unique name of the measure
MEASURE_CAPTION	String	The caption of the measure
MEASURE_GUID	GUID	The GUID of the measure, or Null if no GUID exists
MEASURE_AGGEGATOR	Long	The type of aggregation for the measure (can be one of the MDMEASURE_AGGR constants, as described in Appendix L)
DATA_TYPE	Integer	The data type that most closely matches the OLAP Provider type
NUMERIC_PRECISION	Integer	The numeric precision of the data type
NUMERIC_SCALE	Integer	The numeric scale of the data type
MEASURE_UNITS	String	The unit of measurement for the measure
DESCRIPTION	String	Description of the measure
EXPRESSION	String	The expression upon which the measure is based

adSchemaMembers

This identifies the members in an OLAP catalog.

Column Name	Type	Description
CATALOG_NAME	String	Catalog name, or Null if the provider does not support catalogs
SCHEMA_NAME	String	Schema name, or Null if the provider does not support schemas
CUBE_NAME	String	The cube name to which the member belongs
DIMENSION_UNIQUE_NAME	String	The unique name of the dimension to which the member belongs
HIERARCHY_UNIQUE_NAME	String	The unique name of the hierarchy to which the member belongs
LEVEL_UNIQUE_NAME	String	The unique name of the level to which the member belongs
LEVEL_NUMBER	Long	The position of the member
MEMBER_ORDINAL	Long	The ordinal of the member, indicating the sorting rank
MEMBER_NAME	String	The name of the member
MEMBER_UNIQUE_NAME	String	The unique name of the member
MEMBER_TYPE	Integer	The type of the member (can be one of the MemberTypeEnum constants, as detailed in Appendix L)
MEMBER_GUID	GUID	The GUID of the member, or Null if no GUID exists
MEMBER_CAPTION	String	The caption of the member
CHILDREN_CARDINALITY	Long	The number of children that the member contains (number's accuracy not guaranteed)
PARENT_LEVEL	Long	The position, or level number, of the member's parent
PARENT_UNIQUE_NAME	String	The unique name of the member's parent
PARENT_COUNT	Long	The number of parents this member has
DESCRIPTION	String	The description of the member

adSchemaPrimaryKeys

This identifies the primary keys and table name in the catalog.

Column Name	Type	Description
TABLE_CATALOG	String	Catalog name in which the table is defined, or Null if the provider does not support catalogs
TABLE_SCHEMA	String	Schema name in which the table is defined, or Null if the provider does not support schemas
TABLE_NAME	String	Table name
COLUMN_NAME	String	Primary key column name
COLUMN_GUID	GUID	Primary key column GUID
COLUMN_PROPID	Long	Primary key column property ID
ORDINAL	Long	The order of the column names (and GUIDs and property IDs) in the key
PK_NAME	String	Primary key name, or Null if the provider does not support primary key constraints.

adSchemaProcedureColumns

This identifies the columns used in procedures.

Column Name	Type	Description
PROCEDURE_CATALOG	String	Catalog name, or Null if the provider does not support catalogs
PROCEDURE_SCHEMA	String	Schema name, or Null if the provider does not support schemas
PROCEDURE_NAME	String	Table name
COLUMN_NAME	String	The name of the column, or Null if this cannot be determined (might not be unique)
COLUMN_GUID	GUID	Column GUID
COLUMN_PROPID	Long	Column property ID
ROWSET_NUMBER	Long	Number of the rowset containing the column (greater than one only if the procedure returns multiple rowsets)

Table continues on the following page

Column Name	Type	Description
ORDINAL_POSITION	Long	The ordinal of the column, or Null if there is no stable ordinal value for the column (Columns are numbered starting from one.)
IS_NULLABLE	Boolean	True if the column might be Nullable, False if the column is known not to be Nullable
DATA_TYPE	Integer	The indicator of the column's data type (can be one of the types listed under DataTypeEnum in Appendix B)
TYPE_GUID	GUID	The GUID of the column's data type
CHARACTER_MAXIMUM_LENGTH	Long	The maximum possible length of a value in the column (See CHARACTER_OCTET_LENGTH, following.)
CHARACTER_OCTET_LENGTH	Long	Maximum length in octets (bytes) of the column if the column type is character or binary (A value of zero means the column has no maximum length. All other column types are Null.)
NUMERIC_PRECISION	Integer	If the column's data type is numeric, this is the maximum precision of the column. If the column's data type is not numeric, this is Null.
NUMERIC_SCALE	Integer	If the column's type is DBTYPE_DECIMAL or DBTYPE_NUMERIC, this is the number of digits to the right of the decimal point. Otherwise, this is Null.
DESCRIPTION	String	This is the column's description.

CHARACTER_MAXIMUM_LENGTH varies depending upon the column's data type. For character, binary, or bit columns, this is one of the following:

❑ The maximum length of the column in characters, bytes, or bits, respectively, if one is defined (e.g., a CHAR(5) column in an SQL table has a maximum length of five)

❑ The maximum length of the data type in characters, bytes, or bits, respectively, if the column does not have a defined length

❑ Zero if neither the column nor the data type has a defined maximum length

It will be Null for all other types of columns.

adSchemaProcedureParameters

This identifies the parameters of stored procedures.

Column Name	Type	Description
PROCEDURE_CATALOG	String	This is either the catalog name, or it is Null if the provider does not support catalogs.
PROCEDURE_SCHEMA	String	This is either the schema name, or it is Null if the provider does not support catalogs.
PROCEDURE_NAME	String	This is procedure name.
PARAMETER_NAME	String	This is either the parameter name, or it is Null if the parameter is not named.
ORDINAL_POSITION	Integer	If the parameter is an input, input/output, or output parameter, this is the one-based ordinal position of the parameter in the procedure call. If the parameter is the return value, this is zero.
PARAMETER_TYPE	Integer	This is the type (direction) of the parameter, which will be one of the DBPARAMTYPE constants shown in Appendix B. If the provider cannot determine the parameter type, this is Null.
PARAMETER_HASDEFAULT	Boolean	This indicates whether the parameter has a default value. It is True if the parameter has a default value, or False if it doesn't or if the provider doesn't know whether it has a default value.
PARAMETER_DEFAULT	String	This is the default value of parameter. A default value of Null is valid.
IS_NULLABLE	Boolean	This indicates whether the parameter can contain null values. It is True if the parameter might be Nullable, or False if the parameter is not Nullable.
DATA_TYPE	Integer	This identifies the parameter's data type. For a list of valid types, see DataTypeEnum in Appendix B.

Table continues on the following page

Column Name	Type	Description
CHARACTER_MAXIMUM_LENGTH	Long	This is the maximum possible length of a value in the parameter.
CHARACTER_OCTET_LENGTH	Long	This is the maximum length in octets (bytes) of the parameter if the type of the parameter is character or binary. A value of zero means the parameter has no maximum length. All other parameter types are Null.
NUMERIC_PRECISION	Integer	If the column's data type is numeric, this is the maximum precision of the column. If the column's data type is nonnumeric, this is Null.
NUMERIC_SCALE	Integer	If the column's type is DBTYPE_DECIMAL or DBTYPE_NUMERIC, this is the number of digits to the right of the decimal point. Otherwise, this is Null.
DESCRIPTION	String	This contains the parameter's description.
TYPE_NAME	String	This is the provider-specific data type name.
LOCAL_TYPE_NAME	String	This is either the localized version of TYPE_NAME, or it is Null if the data provider does not support a localized name.
SS_DATA_TYPE	Integer	This identifies the SQL Server data type.

CHARACTER_MAXIMUM_LENGTH varies depending upon the column's data type. For character, binary, or bit columns, this is one of the following:

❑ The maximum length of the column in characters, bytes, or bits, respectively, if one is defined (e.g., a CHAR(5) column in an SQL table has a maximum length of five)

❑ The maximum length of the data type in characters, bytes, or bits, respectively, if the column does not have a defined length

❑ Zero if neither the column nor the data type has a defined maximum length.

It will be Null for all other types of columns.

adSchemaProcedures

This identifies the stored procedures or queries.

Column Name	Type	Description
PROCEDURE_CATALOG	String	Catalog name, or Null if the provider does not support catalogs
PROCEDURE_SCHEMA	String	Schema name, or Null if the provider does not support schemas
PROCEDURE_NAME	String	Procedure name
PROCEDURE_TYPE	Integer	Identifies whether there will be a return value or not (will be one of the DB_PT constants defined in Appendix B)
PROCEDURE_DEFINITION	String	Procedure definition
DESCRIPTION	String	Procedures description
DATE_CREATED	Date/Time	Date when the procedure was created, or Null if the provider does not have this information
DATE_MODIFIED	Date/Time	Date when the procedure definition was last modified, or Null if the provider does not have this information

adSchemaProperties

This identifies the properties for each level of a dimension.

Column Name	Type	Description
CATALOG_NAME	String	The name of the catalog to which the property belongs
SCHEMA_NAME	String	The name of the schema to which the property belongs
CUBE_NAME	String	The name of the cube to which the property belongs
DIMENSION_UNIQUE_NAME	String	The unique name of the dimension
HIERARCHY_UNIQUE_NAME	String	The unique name of the hierarchy

Table continues on the following page

Column Name	Type	Description
LEVEL_UNIQUE_NAME	String	The unique name of the level
MEMBER_UNIQUE_NAME	String	The unique name of the member
PROPERTY_TYPE	Integer	The type of the property—can be one of these: MDPROP_MEMBER indicates that the property relates to a member MDPROP_CELL indicates that the property relates to a cell
PROPERTY_NAME	String	The name of the property
PROPERTY_CAPTION	String	The caption of the property
DATA_TYPE	Long	The data type of the property (can be one of the types listed under DataTypeEnum in Appendix B)
CHARACTER_MAXIMUM_LENGTH	Long	The maximum possible length of data in the property, or 0 to indicate no defined maximum
CHARACTER_OCTET_LENGTH	Long	The maximum length in bytes of the property for character and binary data types, or 0 to indicate no defined maximum
NUMERIC_PRECISION	Integer	The numeric precision of the data type
NUMERIC_SCALE	Integer	The numeric scale of the data type
DESCRIPTION	String	The description of the property

adSchemaProviderSpecific

The contents returned by this setting are dependent upon the provider. Consult the provider-specific information for details regarding them.

adSchemaProviderTypes

This identifies the data types supported by the provider.

Column Name	Type	Description
TYPE_NAME	String	This is the provider-specific data type name.
DATA_TYPE	Integer	This is the indicator of the data type.
COLUMN_SIZE	Long	The length of a nonnumeric column or parameter refers to either the maximum or the defined length for this type set by the provider. For character data, this is the maximum or defined length in characters. For datetime data types, this is the length of the String representation (assuming the maximum allowed precision of the fractional seconds component). If the data type is numeric, this is the upper bound on the maximum precision of the data type.
LITERAL_PREFIX	String	This is the character or characters used to prefix a literal of this type in a text command.
LITERAL_SUFFIX	String	This is the character or characters used to suffix a literal of this type in a text command.
CREATE_PARAMS	String	The creation parameters are specified by the consumer when creating a column of this data type. For example, the SQL data type DECIMAL needs a precision and a scale. In this case, the creation parameters might be the string precision, scale. In a text command to create a DECIMAL column with a precision of 10 and a scale of 2, the value of the TYPE_NAME column might be DECIMAL(), and the complete type specification would be DECIMAL(10,2).
IS_NULLABLE	Boolean	This indicates whether the data type can contain null values. It is True if the data type is Nullable, False if the data type is not Nullable, and Null if it is not known whether the data type is Nullable.
CASE_SENSITIVE	Boolean	This indicates whether the data type is case sensitive for its contents. It is True if the data type is a character type and is case sensitive, or False if the data type is not a character type or is not case sensitive.

Table continues on the following page

Column Name	Type	Description
SEARCHABLE	Long	This identifies whether the column can be used in WHERE clauses. It will be one of the DB_SEARCHABLE constants in Appendix B.
UNSIGNED_ATTRIBUTE	Boolean	This indicates whether the data type contains unsigned data. It is True if the data type is unsigned, False if the data type is signed, or Null if not applicable to data type.
FIXED_PREC_SCALE	Boolean	This indicates whether the data type contains fixed precision data. It is True if the data type has a fixed precision and scale, or False if the data type does not have a fixed precision and scale.
AUTO_UNIQUE_VALUE	Boolean	This indicates whether the data type contains auto-incrementing data. It is True if values of this type can be auto-incrementing, or False if values of this type cannot be auto-incrementing.
LOCAL_TYPE_NAME	String	This is the localized version of TYPE_NAME, or Null if a localized name is not supported by the data provider.
MINIMUM_SCALE	Integer	This is the minimum number of digits allowed to the right of the decimal point for decimal and numeric data types. Otherwise, this is Null.
MAXIMUM_SCALE	Integer	This is the maximum number of digits allowed to the right of the decimal point for a decimal and numeric data types. Otherwise, this is Null.
GUID	GUID	This is the GUID of the type. All types supported by a provider are described in a type library, so each type has a corresponding GUID.
TYPELIB	String	This identifies the type library containing the description of this type.
VERSION	String	This is the version of the type definition. Providers may wish to version type definitions. Different providers may use different version schemes, such as a timestamp or number (integer or float), or Null if not supported.

Table continues on the following page

Column Name	Type	Description
IS_LONG	Boolean	This indicates whether the data type contains long data. It is True if the data type is a BLOB that contains very long data, or False if the data type is a BLOB that does not contain very long data or is not a BLOB. The definition of very long data is provider-specific.
BEST_MATCH	Boolean	This indicates whether the data type is the best match for the required data type. It is True if the data type is the best match between all data types in the data source and the OLEDB data type indicated by the value in the DATA_TYPE column, or it is False if the data type is not the best match.
IS_FIXEDLENGTH	Boolean	This indicates whether the data type contains fixed-length data. It is True if columns of this type created by the DDL will be of fixed length. It is False if columns of this type created by the DDL will be of variable length. If the field is Null, it is not known whether the provider will map this field with a fixed or variable length.

adSchemaReferentialConstraints

This identifies the referential integrity constraints for the catalog.

Column Name	Type	Description
CONSTRAINT_CATALOG	String	Catalog name, or Null if the provider does not support catalogs
CONSTRAINT_SCHEMA	String	Schema name, or Null if the provider does not support schemas
CONSTRAINT_NAME	String	Constraint name
UNIQUE_CONSTRAINT_CATALOG	String	Catalog name in which the unique or primary key constraint is defined, or Null if the provider does not support catalogs

Table continues on the following page

Column Name	Type	Description
UNIQUE_CONSTRAINT_SCHEMA	String	Unqualified schema name in which the unique or primary key constraint is defined, or Null if the provider does not support schemas
UNIQUE_CONSTRAINT_NAME	String	Unique or primary key constraint name
MATCH_OPTION	String	The type of match that was specified
UPDATE_RULE	String	The action if an UPDATE rule was specified (This will be Null only if the provider cannot determine the UPDATE_RULE. In most cases, this implies a default of NO ACTION.)
DELETE_RULE	String	The action if a DELETE rule was specified (This will be Null if the provider cannot determine the DELETE_RULE. In most cases, this implies a default of NO ACTION.)
DESCRIPTION	String	Human-readable description of the constraint

For MATCH_OPTION, the values will be one of:

❑   NONE–No match type was specified.

❑   PARTIAL–A match type of PARTIAL was specified.

❑   FULL–A match type of FULL was specified.

For UPDATE_RULE and DELETE_RULE, the value will be one of the following:

❑   CASCADE–A referential action of CASCADE was specified.

❑   SET NULL–A referential action of SET NULL was specified.

❑   SET DEFAULT–A referential action of SET DEFAULT was specified.

❑   NO ACTION–A referential action of NO ACTION was specified.

adSchemaSchemata

This identifies the schemas owned by a particular user.

Column Name	Type	Description
CATALOG_NAME	String	Catalog name, or Null if the provider does not support catalogs
SCHEMA_NAME	String	Unqualified schema name
SCHEMA_OWNER	String	User who owns the schemas
DEFAULT_CHARACTER_SET_CATALOG	String	Catalog name of the default character set for columns and domains in the schemas, or Null if the provider does not support catalogs or different character sets
DEFAULT_CHARACTER_SET_SCHEMA	String	Unqualified schema name of the default character set for columns and domains in the schemas, or Null if the provider does not support different character sets
DEFAULT_CHARACTER_SET_NAME	String	Default character set name, or Null if the provider does not support different character sets

adSchemaSets

This identifies the named sets in the schema or catalog.

Column Name	Type	Description
CATALOG_NAME	String	Catalog name, or Null if the provider does not support catalogs
SCHEMA_NAME	String	Schema name, or Null if the provider does not support schemas
CUBE_NAME	String	Name of the cube to which the set belongs
SET_NAME	String	The name of the set, as specified by the CREATE SET statement
SCOPE	Integer	Can be one of: MDSET_SCOPE _GLOBAL for global scope MDSET_SCOPE_SESSION for session only scope
DESCRIPTION	String	The description of the set

adSchemaSQLLanguages

This identifies the conformance levels and other options supported by the catalog.

Column Name	Type	Description
SQL_LANGUAGE_SOURCE	String	Should be ISO 9075 for standard SQL
SQL_LANGUAGE_YEAR	String	Should be 1992 for ANSI SQL92-compliant SQL
SQL_LANGUAGE_CONFORMANCE	String	The language conformance level
SQL_LANGUAGE_INTEGRITY	String	Yes if the optional integrity feature is supported, or No if the optional integrity feature is not supported
SQL_LANGUAGE_IMPLEMENTATION	String	Null for ISO 9075 implementation
SQL_LANGUAGE_BINDING_STYLE	String	DIRECT for C/C++ callable direct execution of SQL
SQL_LANGUAGE_PROGRAMMING_LANGUAGE	String	Null.

SQL_LANGUAGE_CONFORMANCE will be one of the following values:

❑ ENTRY–for entry level conformance

❑ INTERMEDIATE–for intermediate conformance

❑ FULL–for full conformance

adSchemaStatistics

This identifies the catalog statistics.

Column Name	Type	Description
TABLE_CATALOG	String	Catalog name, or Null if the provider does not support catalogs
TABLE_SCHEMA	String	Schema name, or Null if the provider does not support schemas
TABLE_NAME	String	Table name
CARDINALITY	Unsigned Big Integer	Cardinality (number of rows) of the table

adSchemaTableConstraints

This identifies the referential table constraints.

Column Name	Type	Description
CONSTRAINT_CATALOG	String	Catalog name, or Null if the provider does not support catalogs
CONSTRAINT_SCHEMA	String	Schema name, or Null if the provider does not support schemas
CONSTRAINT_NAME	String	Constraint name
TABLE_CATALOG	String	Catalog name in which the table is defined, or Null if the provider does not support catalogs
TABLE_SCHEMA	String	Unqualified schema name in which the table is defined, or Null if the provider does not support schemas
TABLE_NAME	String	Table name
CONSTRAINT_TYPE	String	The constraint type
IS_DEFERRABLE	Boolean	True if the table constraint is deferrable, or False if the table constraint is not deferrable
INITIALLY_DEFERRED	Boolean	True if the table constraint is initially deferred, or False if the table constraint is initially immediate
DESCRIPTION	String	Column description

CONSTRAINT_TYPE will be one of the following values:

❑   UNIQUE–for a unique constraint

❑   PRIMARY KEY–for a primary key constraint

❑   FOREIGN KEY–for a foreign key constraint

❑   CHECK–for a check constraint

adSchemaTablePrivileges

This identifies the user privileges of tables.

Column Name	Type	Description
GRANTOR	String	User who granted the privileges on the table in TABLE_NAME
GRANTEE	String	User name (or PUBLIC) to whom the privilege has been granted
TABLE_CATALOG	String	Catalog name in which the table is defined, or Null if the provider does not support catalogs
TABLE_SCHEMA	String	Unqualified schema name in which the table is defined, or Null if the provider does not support schemas
TABLE_NAME	String	Table name
PRIVILEGE_TYPE	String	Privilege type
IS_GRANTABLE	Boolean	False if the privilege being described was granted with the WITH GRANT OPTION clause, or True if the privilege being described was not granted with the WITH GRANT OPTION clause

PRIVILEGE_TYPE will be one of the following values:

❑ SELECT–for SELECT privileges

❑ DELETE–for DELETE privileges

❑ INSERT–for INSERT privileges

❑ UPDATE–for UPDATE privileges

❑ REFERENCES–for REFERENCE privileges

adSchemaTables

This identifies the tables in a catalog.

Column Name	Type	Description
TABLE_CATALOG	String	Catalog name, or Null if the provider does not support catalogs
TABLE_SCHEMA	String	Schema name, or Null if the provider does not support schemas
TABLE_NAME	String	Table name (cannot contain a Null)

Table continues on the following page

Column Name	Type	Description
TABLE_TYPE	String	Table type (cannot contain a Null)
TABLE_GUID	GUID	GUID that uniquely identifies the table (Providers that do not use GUIDs to identify tables should return Null in this column.)
DESCRIPTION	String	Human-readable description of the table, or Null if there is no description associated with the column
TABLE_PROPID	Long	Property ID of the table (Providers that do not use PROPIDs to identify columns should return Null in this column.)
DATE_CREATED	Date/Time	Date when the table was created, or Null if the provider does not have this information
DATE_MODIFIED	Date/Time	Date when the table definition was last modified, or Null if the provider does not have this information

TABLE_TYPE will be a provider-specific value or one of the following:

❑ ALIAS—the table is an alias.

❑ TABLE—the table is a normal table.

❑ SYNONYM—the table is a synonym.

❑ SYSTEM TABLE—the table is a system table.

❑ VIEW—the table is a view.

❑ GLOBAL TEMPORARY—the table is a global, temporary table.

❑ LOCAL TEMPORARY—the table is a local, temporary table.

Provider-specific values should be defined in the provider documentation. For example, Access returns PASS-THROUGH for linked tables.

adSchemaTranslations

This identifies character translations that the catalog supports.

Column Name	Type	Description
TRANSLATION_CATALOG	String	Catalog name, or Null if the provider does not support catalogs
TRANSLATION_SCHEMA	String	Schema name, or Null if the provider does not support schemas
TRANSLATION_NAME	String	Translation name
SOURCE_CHARACTER_SET_CATALOG	String	Catalog name containing the source character set on which the translation is defined, or Null if the provider does not support catalogs
SOURCE_CHARACTER_SET_SCHEMA	String	Unqualified schema name containing the source character set on which the translation is defined, or Null if the provider does not support schemas
SOURCE_CHARACTER_SET_NAME	String	Source character set name on which the translation is defined
TARGET_CHARACTER_SET_CATALOG	String	Catalog name containing the target character set on which the translation is defined, or Null if the provider does not support catalogs
TARGET_CHARACTER_SET_SCHEMA	String	Unqualified schema name containing the target character set on which the translation is defined, or Null if the provider does not support schemas
TARGET_CHARACTER_SET_NAME	String	Target character set name on which the translation is defined

adSchemaUsagePrivileges

This identifies the usage privileges that are available to a user.

Column Name	Type	Description
GRANTOR	String	User who granted the privileges on the object in OBJECT_NAME
GRANTEE	String	User name (or PUBLIC) to whom the privilege has been granted

Table continues on the following page

Column Name	Type	Description
OBJECT_CATALOG	String	Catalog name in which the object is defined, or Null if the provider does not support catalogs
OBJECT_SCHEMA	String	Unqualified schema name in which the object is defined, or Null if the provider does not support schemas
OBJECT_NAME	String	Object name
OBJECT_TYPE	String	Object type.
PRIVILEGE_TYPE	String	Privilege type
IS_GRANTABLE	Boolean	True if the privilege being described was granted with the WITH GRANT OPTION clause, or False if the privilege being described was not granted with the WITH GRANT OPTION clause

OBJECT_TYPE will be one of the following values:

❑   DOMAIN–the object is a domain.

❑   CHARACTER SET–the object is a character set.

❑   COLLATION–the object is a collation.

❑   TRANSLATION–the object is a translation.

adSchemaViewColumnUsage

This identifies the columns used in views.

Column Name	Type	Description
VIEW_CATALOG	String	Catalog name, or Null if the provider does not support catalogs
VIEW_SCHEMA	String	Schema name, or Null if the provider does not support schemas
VIEW_NAME	String	View name
TABLE_CATALOG	String	Catalog name in which the table is defined, or Null if the provider does not support catalogs
TABLE_SCHEMA	String	Schema name in which the table is defined, or Null if the provider does not support schemas

Table continues on the following page

Column Name	Type	Description
TABLE_NAME	String	Table name
COLUMN_NAME	String	Column name
COLUMN_GUID	GUID	Column GUID
COLUMN_PROPID	Long	Column property ID

adSchemaViews

This identifies the views in the catalog.

Column Name	Type	Description
TABLE_CATALOG	String	Catalog name, or Null if the provider does not support catalogs
TABLE_SCHEMA	String	Schema name, or Null if the provider does not support schemas
TABLE_NAME	String	View name
VIEW_DEFINITION	String	View definition (a query expression)
CHECK_OPTION	Boolean	True if local update checking only, or False for cascaded update checking (same as no CHECK OPTION specified on view definition)
IS_UPDATABLE	Boolean	True if the view is updateable, or False if the view is not updateable
DESCRIPTION	String	View description
DATE_CREATED	Date/Time	Date when the view was created, or Null if the provider does not have this information
DATE_MODIFIED	Date/Time	Date when the view definition was last modified, or Null if the provider does not have this information

adSchemaViewTableUsage

This identifies the tables used in views.

Column Name	Type	Description
VIEW_CATALOG	String	Catalog name, or Null if the provider does not support catalogs
VIEW_SCHEMA	String	Schema name, or Null if the provider does not support schemas
VIEW_NAME	String	View name
TABLE_CATALOG	String	Catalog name in which the table is defined, or Null if the provider does not support catalogs
TABLE_SCHEMA	String	Schema name in which the table is defined, or Null if the provider does not support schemas
TABLE_NAME	String	Table name

ADO Data Types

You might find the large array of data types supported by ADO confusing, especially because your language or database might not support them all. This appendix details how the DataTypeEnum constants listed in Appendix B map to SQL and Access data types and the data types used in Visual Basic and Visual C++.

ODBC to Access 97

Database Type	ADO Type
Text	adVarChar
Memo	adLongVarChar
Number (Byte)	adUnsignedTinyInt
Number (Integer)	adSmallInt
Number (Long Integer)	adInteger
Number (Single)	adSingle
Number (Double)	adDouble
Number (Replication ID)	adGUID
Date/Time	adDBTimeStamp
Currency	adCurrency
Long Integer	adInteger
Yes/No	adBoolean
OLE Object	adLongVarBinary
Hyperlink	adLongVarChar

ODBC to Access 2000

Database Type	ADO Type
Text	adVarWChar
Memo	adLongVarWChar
Number (Byte)	adUnsignedTinyInt
Number (Integer)	adSmallInt
Number (Long Integer)	adInteger
Number (Single)	adSingle
Number (Double)	adDouble
Number (Replication ID)	adGUID
Number (Decimal)	adNumeric
Date/Time	adDBTimeStamp
Currency	adCurrency
AutoNumber	adInteger
Yes/No	adBoolean
OLE Object	adLongVarBinary
Hyperlink	adLongVarWChar

ODBC to SQL 6.5

Database Type	ADO Type
binary	adBinary
bit	adBoolean
char	adChar
datetime	adDBTimeStamp
decimal	adNumeric
float	adDouble
image	adLongVarBinary
int	adInteger

Table continues on the following page

Database Type	ADO Type
money	adCurrency
numeric	adNumeric
real	adSingle
smalldatetime	adDBTimeStamp
smallint	adSmallInt
smallmoney	adCurrency
sysname	adVarChar
text	adLongVarChar
timestamp	adBinary
tinyint	adUnsignedTinyInt
varbinary	adVarBinary
varchar	adVarChar

ODBC to SQL 7.0/2000

Database Type	ADO Type
binary	adBinary
bit	adBoolean
har	adChar
datetime	adDBTimeStamp
decimal	adNumeric
float	adDouble
image	adLongVarBinary
int	adInteger
money	adCurrency
nchar	adWChar
ntext	adLongVarWChar
numeric	adNumeric

Table continues on the following page

Database Type	ADO Type
nvarchar	adVarWChar
real	adSingle
smalldatetime	adDBTimeStamp
smallint	adSmallInt
smallmoney	adCurrency
text	adLongVarChar
timestamp	adBinary
tinyint	adUnsignedTinyInt
uniqueidentifier	adGUID
varbinary	adVarBinary
varchar	adVarChar

Native Jet Provider to Access 97

Database Type	ADO Type
Text	AdVarWChar
Memo	AdLongVarWChar
Number (Byte)	AdUnsignedTinyInt
Number (Integer)	AdSmallInt
Number (Long Integer)	AdInteger
Number (Single)	AdSingle
Number (Double)	AdDouble
Number (Replication ID)	adGUID
Date/Time	adDate
Currency	adCurrency
Long Integer	adInteger
Yes/No	adBoolean
OLE Object	adLongVarBinary
Hyperlink	adLongVarWChar

Native Jet Provider to Access 2000

Database Type	ADO Type
Text	adVarWChar
Memo	adLongVarWChar
Number (Byte)	adUnsignedTinyInt
Number (Integer)	adSmallInt
Number (Long Integer)	adInteger
Number (Single)	adSingle
Number (Double)	adDouble
Number (Replication ID)	adGUID
Number (Decimal)	adNumeric
Date/Time	adDate
Currency	adCurrency
AutoNumber	adInteger
Yes/No	adBoolean
OLE Object	adLongVarBinary
Hyperlink	adLongVarWChar

Native SQL Provider to SQL Server 6.5

Database Type	ADO Type
binary	adBinary
bit	adBoolean
char	adChar
datetime	adDBTimeStamp
decimal	adNumeric
float	adDouble
image	adLongVarBinary
int	adInteger

Table continues on the following page

Database Type	ADO Type
money	adCurrency
numeric	adNumeric
real	adSingle
smalldatetime	adDBTimeStamp
smallint	adSmallInt
smallmoney	adCurrency
sysname	adVarChar
text	adLongVarChar
timestamp	adBinary
tinyint	adUnsignedTinyInt
varbinary	adVarBinary
varchar	adVarChar

Native SQL Provider to SQL Server 7.0/2000

Database Type	ADO Type
binary	adBinary
bit	adBoolean
char	adChar
datetime	adDBTimeStamp
decimal	adNumeric
float	adDouble
image	adLongVarBinary
int	adInteger
money	adCurrency
nchar	adWChar
ntext	adLongVarWChar
numeric	adNumeric

Table continues on the following page

Database Type	ADO Type
nvarchar	adVarWChar
real	adSingle
smalldatetime	adDBTimeStamp
smallint	adSmallInt
smallmoney	adCurrency
text	adLongVarChar
timestamp	adBinary
tinyint	adUnsignedTinyInt
uniqueidentifier	adGUID
varbinary	adVarBinary
varchar	adVarChar

Language Types

The following table lists the data types you should use in your programming language.

A blank value indicates that the language does not natively support the data type, although there may be support in other libraries, or other data types might be used instead.

Constant	Visual Basic	Visual C++
adBinary	Variant	
adBoolean	Boolean	bool
adChar	String	char[]
adCurrency	Currency	
adDate	Date	
adDBTimeStamp	Variant	
adDouble	Double	double
adGUID		char[]
adInteger	Long	int

Table continues on the following page

Constant	Visual Basic	Visual C++
adLongVarBinary	Variant	
adLongVarChar	String	
adNumeric		
adSingle	Single	float
adSmallInt	Integer	short
adUnsignedTinyInt	Byte	char
adVarBinary		char[]
adVarChar	String	char[]
adVarWChar	String	char[]

RDS Object Summary

The Remote Data Service (RDS) provides a set of objects that you can use to allow a client machine to access data remotely over HTTP protocol. This section lists the properties, methods, and events for two RDS controls; the **RDS/ADC Data Source Object** (DSO) and the **Tabular Data Control** (TDC). It also lists the properties, methods, events, and constants for the `DataSpace` and `DataFactory` objects used by the RDS/ADC control.

> **All properties are read/write unless otherwise stated.**

The RDS Advanced Data Control (RDS/ADC)

The RDS/ADC Data Control is used on the client to provide read/write access to a data store or custom business object on the server. To instantiate the control in a Web page, an `<OBJECT>` tag is used:

```
<OBJECT CLASSID="clsid:BD96C556-65A3-11D0-983A-00C04FC29E33"
        ID="dsoBookList" HEIGHT=0 WIDTH=0>
  <PARAM NAME="Server" VALUE="http://www.yourserver.com">
  <PARAM NAME="Connect" VALUE="DSN=yourdsn;UID=anon;PWD=">
  <PARAM NAME="SQL" VALUE="SELECT * FROM BookList">
</OBJECT>
```

The `<PARAM>` elements are used to set the properties of the control at design time. They can be changed at run time by using script code. The following tables list the properties, methods, and events for the control.

Properties of the RDS/ADC	Return Type	Description
Connect	String	The data store connection string or DSN.
ExecuteOptions	Integer	Specifies if the control will execute asynchronously (can be one of the adcExecuteOptionEnum constants, as detailed in Appendix G)
FetchOptions	Integer	Specifies if the data will be fetched asynchronously (can be one of the adcFetchOptionEnum constants, as detailed in Appendix G)
FilterColumn	String	Name of the column to filter on
FilterCriterion	String	The criterion for the filter (can be <, <=, >, >=, =, or <>)
FilterValue	String	The value to filter on (The column used as the source of the filter values is defined in FilterColumn)
Handler	String	Specifies the server-side security handler to use with the control if not the default
InternetTimeout	Long	Indicates the timeout (in milliseconds) for the HTTP connection
ReadyState	Integer	Indicates the state of the control as data is received (can be one of the adcReadyStateEnum constants, as detailed in Appendix G [read-only])
Recordset	Object	Provides a reference to the ADO Recordset object in use by the control (read-only)
Server	String	Specifies the communication protocol and the address of the server to execute the query on.
SortColumn	String	Name of the column to sort on
SortDirection	Boolean	The sort direction for the column (Default, True, is ascending order. Use False for descending order.)
SourceRecordset	Object	Can be used to bind the control to a different Recordset object at run time (write-only)
SQL	String	The SQL statement used to extract the data from the data store
URL	String	URL to the path of the file

Table continues on the following page

Methods of the RDS/ADC	Description
Cancel	Cancels an asynchronous action such as fetching data
CancelUpdate	Cancels all changes made to the source recordset
CreateRecordSet	Creates and returns an empty, disconnected recordset on the client
MoveFirst	Moves to the first record in a displayed recordset
MoveLast	Moves to the last record in a displayed recordset
MoveNext	Moves to the next record in a displayed recordset
MovePrevious	Moves to the previous record in a displayed recordset
Refresh	Refreshes the client-side recordset from the data source
Reset	Updates the local recordset to reflect current filter and sort criteria
SubmitChanges	Sends changes to the client-side recordset back to the data store

Methods Syntax

```
datacontrol.Cancel
datacontrol.CancelUpdate
(Set) object = datacontrol.CreateRecordSet(varColumnInfos As Variant)
datacontrol.Recordset.MoveFirst
datacontrol.Recordset.MoveLast
datacontrol.Recordset.MoveNext
datacontrol.Recordset.MovePrevious
datacontrol.Refresh
datacontrol.Reset(refilter As Integer)
datacontrol.SubmitChanges
```

Events of the RDS/ADC	Description
onerror	Occurs if an error prevents the data being fetched from the server, or prevents a user action from being carried out
onreadystatechange	Occurs when the value of the ReadyState property changes

Events Syntax

```
onError(StatusCode, Description, Source, CancelDisplay)
onReadyStateChange()
```

The TDC

The TDC uses a formatted text file that is downloaded to the client and exposed there as an ADO recordset. The control cannot be used to update the server data store. To instantiate the control in a Web page, an <OBJECT> tag is used:

```
<OBJECT CLASSID="clsid:333C7BC4-460F-11D0-BC04-0080C7055A83"
        ID="dsoBookList" WIDTH=0 HEIGHT=0>
  <PARAM NAME="DataURL" VALUE="/data/booklist.txt">
  <PARAM NAME="FieldDelim" VALUE=";">
  <PARAM NAME="UseHeader" VALUE="true">
  <PARAM NAME="Sort" VALUE="tCategory; -dReleasedate">
  <PARAM NAME="Filter" VALUE="tCode=16-1*" >
  <PARAM NAME="EscapeChar" VALUE="\">
</OBJECT>
```

The <PARAM> elements are used to set the properties of the control at design time. They can be changed at run time using script code. The following tables list the properties, methods, and events for the control.

Properties of the TDC	Return Type	Description
AppendData	Boolean	If True, this specifies that the Reset method will attempt to append returned data to the existing recordset rather than replacing the recordset. Default is False.
CaseSensitive	Boolean	This specifies whether string comparisons will be case sensitive. Default is True.
CharSet	String	This specifies the character set for the data. Default is windows-1252 (Western).
DataURL	String	This is the URL or location of the source text data file.
EscapeChar	String	This single character string is used to avoid the meaning of the other special characters specified by the FieldDelim, RowDelim, and TextQualifier properties.
FieldDelim	String	This specifies the character in the file that delimits each column (field). Default is a comma. Only a single character may be used.
Filter	String	This specifies the complete filter that will be applied to the data, such as "Name=Jonson." An asterisk acts as a wildcard for any set of characters.
FilterColumn	String	This specifies the name of the column to filter on. It is not supported in all versions of the TDC.

Table continues on the following page

Properties of the TDC	Return Type	Description
FilterCriterion	String	This is the criterion for the filter. It can be <, <=, >, >=, =, or <>. It is not supported in all versions of the TDC.
FilterValue	String	The value to filter on (The column used as the source of the filter values is defined in FilterColumn. This is not supported in all versions of the TDC.)
Language	String	This specifies the language of the data file. Default is en-us (U.S. English).
ReadyState	Integer	This indicates the state of the control as data is received. It can be one of the adcReadyStateEnum constants, as detailed in Appendix G. It is read-only.
RowDelim	String	This specifies the character in the file that delimits each row (record). Default is a carriage return. Only a single character may be used.
Sort	String	This specifies the sort order for the data as a comma-delimited list of column names. For descending order, prefix column name with a minus sign (-).
SortAscending	Boolean	This is the sort direction for the column. The default is ascending order (True). Use False for descending order. This is not supported in all versions of the TDC.
SortColumn	String	This is the name of the column to sort on. It is not supported in all versions of the TDC.
TextQualifier	String	This is the character in the data file used to enclose field values. Default is the double-quote (") character.
UseHeader	Boolean	If True, this specifies that the data file's first line is a set of column (field) names and (optionally) the field data type definitions.

Methods of the TDC	Description
Reset	Updates the local recordset to reflect current filter and sort criteria

Events of the TDC	Description
onreadystatechange	Occurs when the value of the ReadyState property changes

The RDS DataSpace Object

The `DataSpace` object is responsible for caching the recordset on the client and connecting it to a data source control. To instantiate the object in a Web page, an `<OBJECT>` tag is used:

```
<OBJECT ID="dspDataSpace"
        CLASSID="CLSID:BD96C556-65A3-11D0-983A-00C04FC29E36">
</OBJECT>
```

A `DataSpace` object is also created automatically when a data source object (such as the RDS/ADC) is instantiated. The `DataSpace` object exposes one property and one method:

Properties of the RDS DataSpace Object	Return Type	Description
InternetTimeout	Long	Indicates the timeout (in milliseconds) for the HTTP connection

Methods of the RDS DataSpace Object	Description
CreateObject	Creates a data factory or custom object of type specified by a class string, at a location specified by the connection (address) parameter

Methods Syntax

```
variant = dataspace.CreateObject(bstrProgId As String,
                                 bstrConnection As String)
```

For a connection over HTTP, the connection parameter is the URL of the server. Over DCOM, the UNC machine name is used. When the `CreateObject` method is used to create in-process objects, the connection should be a `Null` string.

The RDS DataFactory Object

The `DataFactory` object handles transport of the data from server to client and vice versa. It creates a stub and proxy that can communicate over HTTP. To instantiate the object, the `CreateObject` method of an existing `DataSpace` control is used. The class string for the `DataFactory` object is `RDSServer.DataFactory`, and the address of the server on which the object is to be created, must also be provided:

```
<OBJECT ID="dspDataSpace"
        CLASSID="CLSID:BD96C556-65A3-11D0-983A-00C04FC29E36">
</OBJECT>
...
```

```
<SCRIPT LANGUAGE="JavaScript">
  <myDataFactory = dspDataSpace.CreateObject("RDSServer.DataFactory",
"http://servername.com");
</SCRIPT>
```

A `DataFactory` object is also created automatically when a data source object (such as the RDS/ADC) is instantiated. The `DataFactory` object provides four methods:

Methods of the RDS DataFactory Object	Return Type	Description
ConvertToString	String	Converts a recordset into a MIME64-encoded string
CreateRecordSet	Object	Creates and returns an empty recordset
Query	Object	Executes a valid SQL string query over a specified connection and returns an ADO recordset object
SubmitChanges		Marshals the records and submits them to the server for updating the source data store

Methods Syntax

```
string = datafactory.ConvertToString(recordset As Object)
(Set) recordset = datafactory.CreateRecordSet(varColumnInfos
                                                 As Variant)
(Set) recordset = datafactory.Query(bstrConnection As String,
                                      bstrQuery As String)
datafactory.SubmitChanges(bstrConnection As String,
                            pRecordset As Object)
```

RDS Constants

RDS Constants

adcExecuteOptionEnum

Name	Value	Description
adcExecAsync	2	The next Refresh of the recordset is executed asynchronously.
adcExecSync	1	The next Refresh of the recordset is executed synchronously.

adcFetchOptionEnum

Name	Value	Description
adcFetchAsync	3	Records are fetched in the background, and control is returned to the application immediately. Attempts to access a record not yet read will cause control to return immediately, and the record nearest to the sought record will be returned. This indicates that the end of the recordset has been reached, even though there may be more records.

Table continues on the following page

Name	Value	Description
adcFetchBackground	2	The first batch of records is read, and control returns to the application. Access to records not in the first batch will cause a wait until the requested record is fetched.
adcFetchUpFront	1	The complete recordset is fetched before control is returned to the application.

adcReadyStateEnum

Name	Value	Description
adcReadyStateComplete	4	All rows have been fetched.
adcReadyStateInteractive	3	Rows are still being fetched, although some rows are available.
adcReadyStateLoaded	2	The recordset is not available for use because the rows are still being loaded.

ADCPROP_UPDATECRITERIA_ENUM

Name	Value	Description
adCriteriaAllCols	1	Collisions should be detected if any column is changed.
adCriteriaKey	0	Collisions should be detected if the key column is changed.
adCriteriaTimeStamp	3	Collisions should be detected if a row has been accessed.
adCriteriaUpdCols	2	Collisions should be detected if columns being updated are changed.

ADOX Object Summary

This appendix contains details of the Microsoft ActiveX Data Objects Extensions for DDL and Security Library.

The ADOX Objects

Name	Description
Catalog	Acts as a parent for the Tables, Groups, Users, Procedures, and Views collections
Column	An individual Column in a Table, Index, or Key
Columns	Contains one or more Column objects
Group	An individual Group account describing data store permissions and containing a Users collection describing the members of the group
Groups	Contains one or more Group objects
Index	An individual index on a Table (Each Index contains a Columns collection describing the columns that compose the index.)
Indexes	Contains one or more Index objects
Key	An individual Key representing a primary or foreign key for a table and containing a Columns collection to describe the columns that the Key comprises
Keys	Contains one or more Key objects

Table continues on the following page

Name	Description
Procedure	Describes a stored procedure and contains an ADO `Command` object to obtain the details of the procedure
Procedures	Contains one or more `Procedure` objects
Properties	Contains one or more `Property` objects
Property	Describes an individual property of a particular object
Table	Describes an individual data store table and contains `Columns`, `Indexes`, `Keys`, and `Properties` collections
Tables	Contains one or more `Table` objects
User	An individual `User` account describing an authorized user of the data store and containing a `Groups` collection to indicate the groups to which the user belongs
Users	Contains one or more `User` objects
View	Describes a virtual table or a filtered set of records from the data store and contains an ADO `Command` object to obtain the exact details of the view
Views	Contains one or more `View` objects

The Catalog Object

Methods of the Catalog Object	Return Type	Description
Create	Variant	Creates a new catalog, using its argument as a connection string for the catalog
GetObjectOwner	String	Obtains the name of the user or group that owns a particular catalog object
SetObjectOwner		Sets the owner for a particular catalog object

Properties of the Catalog Object	Return Type	Description
ActiveConnection	Object	Sets or returns the ADO `Connection` object or string to which the catalog belongs

Collections of the Catalog Object	Return Type	Description
Groups	Groups	Contains one or more Group objects (read-only).
Procedures	Procedures	Contains one or more Procedure objects (read-only).
Tables	Tables	Contains one or more Table objects (read-only).
Users	Users	Contains one or more User objects (read-only).
Views	Views	Contains one or more View objects (read-only).

The Column Object

Properties of the Column Object	Return Type	Description
Attributes	ColumnAttributesEnum	Describes the characteristics of the column
DefinedSize	Long	Indicates the maximum size for a column
Name	String	The name of the column
NumericScale	Byte	The numeric scale of the column (read-only for existing columns)
ParentCatalog	Catalog	Indicates the Catalog to which the column's parent object belongs
Precision	Integer	The maximum precision of data in the column (read-only for existing columns)
RelatedColumn	String	Indicates (for key columns) the name of the related column in the related table (read-only for existing columns)
SortOrder	SortOrderEnum	Indicates the order in which the column is sorted (applies only to columns in an Index)
Type	DataTypeEnum	Identifies the data type of the column (read-only once the column is appended to a collection)

Collections of the Column Object	Return Type	Description
Properties	Properties	Contains one or more provider specific column properties (read-only)

The Columns Collection

Methods of the Columns Collection	Return Type	Description
Append		Appends a Column object to the Columns collection
Delete		Deletes a Column object from the Columns collection
Refresh		Updates the Column objects in the Columns collection

Properties of the Columns Collection	Return Type	Description
Count	Integer	Indicates the number of Column objects in the Columns collection (read-only)
Item	Column	Allows indexing into the Columns collection to reference a specific Column object (read-only)

The Group Object

Methods of the Group Object	Return Type	Description
GetPermissions	RightsEnum	Obtains the permissions on a catalog object for the Group
SetPermissions		Sets the permissions on a catalog object for the Group

Properties of the Group Object	Return Type	Description
Name	String	The name of the group

Collections of the Group Object	Return Type	Description
Users	Users	Contains the User objects that belong to this group (read-only)
Properties	Properties	Contains a Property object for each provider-specific property (read-only)

The Groups Collection

Methods of the Groups Collection	Return Type	Description
Append		Appends a Group object to the Groups collection
Delete		Deletes a Group object from the Groups collection
Refresh		Updates the Group objects in the Groups collection

Properties of the Groups Collection	Return Type	Description
Count	Integer	Indicates the number of Group objects in the Groups collection (read-only)
Item	Column	Allows indexing into the Groups collection to reference a specific Group object (read-only)

The Index Object

Properties of the Index Object	Return Type	Description
Clustered	Boolean	Indicates whether or not the Index is clustered (read-only on Index objects already appended to a collection)
IndexNulls	AllowNullsEnum	Indicates whether or not index entries are created for records that have Null values (read-only on Index objects already appended to a collection)
Name	String	The name of the Index
PrimaryKey	Boolean	Indicates whether or not the index is the primary key (read-only on Index objects already appended to a collection)
Unique	Boolean	Indicates whether or not the keys in the Index must be unique (read-only on Index objects already appended to a collection)

Collections of the Index Object	Return Type	Description
Columns	Columns	Contains one or more Column objects, which make up the Index object (read-only)
Properties	Properties	Contains provider specific properties for the Index object (read-only)

The Indexes Collection

Methods of the Indexes Collection	Return Type	Description
Append		Appends an Index object to the Indexes collection
Delete		Deletes an Index object from the Indexes collection
Refresh		Updates the Index objects in the Indexes collection

Properties of the Indexes Collection	Return Type	Description
Count	Integer	Indicates the number of Index objects in the Indexes collection (read-only)
Item	Column	Allows indexing into the Indexes collection to reference a specific Index object (read-only)

The Key Object

Properties of the Key Object	Return Type	Description
DeleteRule	RuleEnum	Indicates what happens to the key values when a primary key is deleted (read-only on Key objects already appended to a collection)
Name	String	The name of the Key
RelatedTable	String	For foreign keys, indicates the name of the foreign table.
Type	KeyTypeEnum	Specifies the type of the Key (read-only on Key objects already appended to a collection)
UpdateRule	RuleEnum	Indicates what happens to the key values when a primary key is updated (read-only on Key objects already appended to a collection)

Collections of the Key Object	Return Type	Description
Columns	Columns	Contains one or more Column objects that make up the Key (read-only)

The Keys Collection

Methods of the Keys Collection	Return Type	Description
Append		Appends a Key object to the Keys collection
Delete		Deletes a Key object from the Keys collection
Refresh		Updates the Key objects in the Keys collection

Properties of the Keys Collection	Return Type	Description
Count	Integer	Indicates the number of Key objects in the Keys collection (read-only)
Item	Column	Allows indexing into the Keys collection to reference a specific Key object (read-only)

The Procedure Object

Properties of the Procedure Object	Return Type	Description
Command	Object	Specifies an ADO Command object containing the details of the procedure
DateCreated	Variant	The date the Procedure was created (read-only)
DateModified	Variant	The date the Procedure was last modified (read-only)
Name	String	The name of the Procedure (read-only)

The Procedures Collection

Methods of the Procedures Collection	Return Type	Description
Append		Appends a Procedure object to the Procedures collection
Delete		Deletes a Procedure object from the Procedures collection
Refresh		Updates the Procedure objects in the Procedures collection

Properties of the Procedures Collection	Return Type	Description
Count	Integer	Indicates the number of Procedure objects in the Procedures collection (read-only)
Item	Column	Allows indexing into the Procedures collection to reference a specific Procedure object (read-only)

The Properties Collection

Methods of the Properties Collection	Return Type	Description
Refresh		Updates the Property objects in the Properties collection

Properties of the Properties Collection	Return Type	Description
Count	Integer	Indicates the number of Property objects in the Properties collection(read-only)
Item	Column	Allows indexing into the Properties collection to reference a specific Property object (read-only)

The Property Object

Properties of the Property Object	Return Type	Description
Attributes	Integer	Indicates one or more characteristics of the Property
Name	String	The Property Name (read-only)
Type	DataTypeEnum	The data type of the Property (read-only)
Value	Variant	The value assigned to the Property

The Table Object

Properties of the Table Object	Return Type	Description
DateCreated	Variant	The date the Table was created (read-only)
DateModified	Variant	The date the Table was last modified (read-only)
Name	String	The name of the Table
ParentCatalog	Catalog	The Catalog to which the Table belongs
Type	String	Indicates whether the Table is a permanent, temporary, or system table (read-only)

Collections of the Table Object	Return Type	Description
Columns	Columns	One or more Column objects that make up the Table (read-only)
Indexes	Indexes	Zero or more Index objects that belong to the Table (read-only)
Keys	Keys	Zero or more Key objects that the Table contains (read-only)
Properties	Properties	One or more Property objects describing provider specific properties (read-only)

The Tables Collection

Methods of the Tables Collection	Return Type	Description
Append		Appends a Table object to the Tables collection
Delete		Deletes a Table object from the Tables collection
Refresh		Updates the Table objects in the Tables collection

Properties of the Tables Collection	Return Type	Description
Count	Integer	Indicates the number of Table objects in the Tables collection (read-only)
Item	Column	Allows indexing into the Tables collection to reference a specific Table object (read-only)

The User Object

Methods of the User Object	Return Type	Description
ChangePassword		Changes the password for a User
GetPermissions	RightsEnum	Gets the permissions on a Catalog object for a User
SetPermissions		Sets the permissions on a Catalog object for a User

Properties of the User Object	Return Type	Description
Name	String	The user name

Collections of the User Object	Return Type	Description
Groups	Groups	One or more Group objects, to which the user belongs (read-only)
Properties	Properties	Contains a Property object for each provider-specific property (read-only)

The Users Collection

Methods of the Users Collection	Return Type	Description
Append		Appends a User object to the Users collection
Delete		Deletes a User object from the Users collection
Refresh		Updates the User objects in the Users collection

Properties of the Users Collection	Return Type	Description
Count	Integer	Indicates the number of User objects in the Users collection (read-only)
Item	Column	Allows indexing into the Users collection to reference a specific User object (read-only)

The View Object

Properties of the View Object	Return Type	Description
Command	Object	Specifies an ADO Command object containing the details of the View
DateCreated	Variant	The date the View was created (read-only)
DateModified	Variant	The date the View was last modified (read-only)
Name	String	The name of the View (read-only)

The Views Collection

Methods of the Views Collection	Return Type	Description
Append		Appends a View object to the Views collection
Delete		Deletes a View object from the Views collection
Refresh		Updates the View objects in the Views collection

Properties of the Views Collection	Return Type	Description
Count	Integer	Indicates the number of View objects in the Views collection (read-only)
Item	Column	Allows indexing into the Views collection to reference a specific View object (read-only)

Method Calls

The Catalog Object

```
Variant = Catalog.Create(ConnectString As String)
String = Catalog.GetObjectOwner(ObjectName As String, _
            ObjectType As ObjectTypeEnum, [ObjectTypeId As Variant])
Catalog.SetObjectOwner(ObjectName As String, _
            ObjectType As ObjectTypeEnum, UserName As String, _
            [ObjectTypeId As Variant])
```

The Columns Collection

```
Columns.Append(Item As Variant, [Type As DataTypeEnum], _
            [DefinedSize As Integer])
Columns.Delete(Item As Variant)
Columns.Refresh
```

The Group Object

```
RightsEnum = Group.GetPermissions(Name As Variant, _
            ObjectType As ObjectTypeEnum, [ObjectTypeId As Variant])
Group.SetPermissions(Name As Variant, ObjectType As ObjectTypeEnum, _
            Action As ActionEnum, Rights As RightsEnum, _
            [Inherit As InheritTypeEnum], [ObjectTypeId As Variant])
```

The Groups Collection

```
Groups.Append(Item As Variant)
Groups.Delete(Item As Variant)
Groups.Refresh
```

The Indexes Collection

```
Indexes.Append(Item As Variant, [Columns As Variant])
Indexes.Delete(Item As Variant)
Indexes.Refresh
```

The Keys Collection

```
Keys.Append(Item As Variant, [Type As KeyTypeEnum], _
            [Column As Variant], [RelatedTable As String], _
            [RelatedColumn As String])
Keys.Delete(Item As Variant)
Keys.Refresh
```

The Procedures Collection

```
Procedures.Append(Name As String, Command As Object)
Procedures.Delete(Item As Variant)
Procedures.Refresh
```

The Properties Collection

```
Properties.Refresh
```

The Tables Collection

```
Tables.Append(Item As Variant)
Tables.Delete(Item As Variant)
Tables.Refresh
```

The User Object

```
User.ChangePassword(OldPassword As String, NewPassord As String)
RightsEnum = User.GetPermissions(Name As Variant, _
                ObjectType As ObjectTypeEnum, [ObjectTypeId As Variant])
User.SetPermissions(Name As Variant, ObjectType As ObjectTypeEnum, _
                Action As ActionEnum, Rights As RightsEnum, _
                [Inherit As InheritTypeEnum], [ObjectTypeId As Variant])
```

The Users Collection

```
Users.Append(Item As Variant, [Password As String])
Users.Delete(Item As Variant)
Users.Refresh
```

The Views Collection

```
Views.Append(Name As String, Command As Object)
Views.Delete(Item As Variant)
Views.Refresh
```

ADOX Constants

ActionEnum

Constant Name	Value	Description
adAccessDeny	3	Deny the specific permissions to the Group or User.
adAccessGrant	1	Grant the specific permissions to the Group or User. Other permissions may remain in effect.
adAccessRevoke	4	Revoke any specific access rights to the Group or User.
adAccessSet	2	Set the exact permissions for the Group or User. Other permissions will not remain in effect.

AllowNullsEnum

Constant Name	Value	Description
adIndexNullsAllow	0	Key columns with Null values have index values.
adIndexNullsDisallow	1	Do not allow index entries if the key columns are Null.
adIndexNullsIgnore	2	Null values in key columns are ignored, and an index entry is not created.
adIndexNullsIgnoreAny	4	Null values in any part of the key (for multiple columns) are ignored, and an index entry is not created.

ColumnAttributesEnum

Constant Name	Value	Description
adColFixed	1	The column is of a fixed length.
adColNullable	2	The column may contain Null values.

DataTypeEnum

The ADOX data type constants are the same as the ADO data type constants. See the listing for DataTypeEnum in Appendix B.

InheritTypeEnum

Constant Name	Value	Description
adInheritBoth	3	Permissions for the object are inherited by both objects and other containers.
adInheritContainers	2	Permissions for the object are inherited by other containers.
adInheritNone	0	No permissions are inherited.
adInheritNoPropogate	4	The adInheritObjects and adInheritContainers permissions are not propagated to child objects.
adInheritObjects	1	Permissions are only inherited by objects that are not containers.

KeyTypeEnum

Constant Name	Value	Description
adKeyForeign	2	The key is a foreign key.
adKeyPrimary	1	The key is a primary key.
adKeyUnique	3	The key is unique.

ObjectTypeEnum

Constant Name	Value	Description
adPermObjColumn	2	The object is a column.
adPermObjDatabase	3	The object is a database.
adPermObjProcedure	4	The object is a procedure.
adPermObjProviderSpecific	-1	The object is of a provider-specific type.
adPermObjTable	1	The object is a table.
adPermObjView	5	The object is a view.

RightsEnum

Constant Name	Value	Description
adRightCreate	16384	The User or Group has permission to create the object.
adRightDelete	65536	The User or Group has permission to delete the object.
adRightDrop	256	The User or Group has permission to drop the object.
adRightExclusive	512	The User or Group has permission to obtain exclusive access to the object.
adRightExecute	536870912	The User or Group has permission to execute the object.
adRightFull	268435456	The User or Group has full permissions on the object.
adRightInsert	32768	The User or Group has permission to insert the object.
adRightMaximumAllowed	33554432	The User or Group has the maximum number of permissions allowed by the provider.
adRightNone	0	The User or Group has no permissions on the object.
adRightRead	-2147483648	The User or Group has permission to read the object.

Table continues on the following page

Constant Name	Value	Description
adRightReadDesign	1024	The User or Group has permission to read the design of the object.
adRightReadPermissions	131072	The User or Group has permission to read the permissions of the object.
adRightReference	8192	The User or Group has permission to reference the object.
adRightUpdate	1073741824	The User or Group has permission to update the object.
adRightWithGrant	4096	The User or Group has permission to grant permissions to other Users or Groups.
adRightWriteDesign	2048	The User or Group has permission to change the design of the object.
adRightWriteOwner	524288	The User or Group has permission to change the owner of the object.
adRightWritePermissions	262144	The User or Group has permission to change the permissions of the object.

RuleEnum

Constant Name	Value	Description
adRICascade	1	Updates and deletes are cascaded.
adRINone	0	Updates and deletes are not cascaded.
adRISetDefault	3	Set the foreign key to its default value for updates and deletes.
adRISetNull	2	Set the foreign key to Null for updates and deletes.

SortOrderEnum

Constant Name	Value	Description
adSortAscending	1	The key column is in ascending order.
adSortDescending	2	The key column is in descending order.

DBPROPVAL_IN

Constant Name	Value	Description
DBPROPVAL_IN_DISALLOWNULL	1	Keys containing Null values are not allowed. This generates an error if an attempt is made to insert a key that contains Null.
DBPROPVAL_IN_IGNORENULL	2	Keys containing Null values are allowed, but are ignored and not added to the index. No error is generated.
DBPROPVAL_IN_IGNOREANYNULL	4	Keys consisting of multi-columns will allow a Null in any column, but the key is ignored and not added to the index. No error is generated.

DBPROPVAL_IT

Constant Name	Value	Description
DBPROPVAL_IT_BTREE	1	The index is a B+ tree.
DBPROPVAL_IT_CONTENT	3	The index is a content index.
DBPROPVAL_IT_HASH	2	The index is a hash file using linear or extensible hashing.
DBPROPVAL_IT_OTHER	4	The index is some other type of index.

DBPROPVAL_NC

Constant Name	Value	Description
DBPROPVAL_NC_END	1	Null values are collated at the end of the list, irrespective of the collation order.
DBPROPVAL_NC_HIGH	2	Null values are collated at the high end of the list.
DBPROPVAL_NC_LOW	4	Null values are collated at the low end of the list.
DBPROPVAL_NC_START	8	Null values are collated at the start of the list, irrespective of the collation order.

ADOX Properties Collection

Property Support

The following table shows a list of all OLE DB properties and indicates which are supported by Microsoft Access and Microsoft SQL Server. The property support is the same whether using the OLE DB Provider for ODBC or the native OLE DB Providers. Because this list contains dynamic properties, not every property may show up under all circumstances. Other providers may also implement properties not listed in this table.

A checkmark indicates that the property is supported, and a blank space indicates that it is not supported.

Property Name	Object	Jet	SQL
Auto-Update	Index	✓	
Autoincrement	Column	✓	✓
Clustered	Index	✓	✓
Column Level Collation Name	Column		✓
Default	Column	✓	✓
Description	Column	✓	
Fill Factor	Index	✓	✓
Fixed Length	Column	✓	✓
Increment	Column	✓	

Table continues on the following page

Property Name	Object	Jet	SQL
Index Type	Index	✓	
Initial Size	Index	✓	
Jet OLEDB:Allow Zero Length	Column	✓	
Jet OLEDB:AutoGenerate	Column	✓	
Jet OLEDB:Cache Link Name/Password	Table	✓	
Jet OLEDB:Column Validation Rule	Column	✓	
Jet OLEDB:Column Validation Text	Column	✓	
Jet OLEDB:Compressed UNICODE Strings	Column	✓	
Jet OLEDB:Create Link	Table	✓	
Jet OLEDB:Exclusive Link	Table	✓	
Jet OLEDB:Hyperlink	Column	✓	
Jet OLEDB:IISAM Not Last Column	Column	✓	
Jet OLEDB:Link Datasource	Table	✓	
Jet OLEDB:Link Provider String	Table	✓	
Jet OLEDB:One BLOB per Page	Column	✓	
Jet OLEDB:Remote Table Name	Table	✓	
Jet OLEDB:Table Hidden In Access	Table	✓	
Jet OLEDB:Table Validation Rule	Table	✓	
Jet OLEDB:Table Validation Text	Table	✓	
Null Collation	Index	✓	
Null Keys	Index	✓	
Nullable	Column	✓	✓
Primary Key	Column		✓
Primary Key	Index	✓	✓
Seed	Column	✓	
Sort Bookmarks	Index	✓	
Temporary Index	Index	✓	
Temporary Table	Table	✓	✓
Unique	Column		✓
Unique	Index	✓	✓

The Column Object's Properties

Name	Description	Data Type
Autoincrement	Indicates whether the column is auto-incrementing	`Boolean`
Column Level Collation Name	The collation name in use for the column	`String`
Default	Specifies the default value for the column if no explicit value is supplied	`Variant`
Description	The column description	`String`
Fixed Length	Indicates whether the column holds fixed-length data	`Boolean`
Increment	The value by which auto-increment columns are increased	`Long`
Jet OLEDB:Allow Zero Length	Indicates whether zero-length strings can be inserted into the field	`Boolean`
Jet OLEDB:Autogenerate	Indicates whether, for a GUID data type, a GUID should be automatically created.	`Boolean`
Jet OLEDB:Column Validation Rule	The validation rule to apply to column values before allowing the column to be set	`String`
Jet OLEDB:Column Validation Text	Errors string to display if changes to a row do not meet the column validation rule	`String`
Jet OLEDB:Compressed UNICODE Strings	Indicates whether Jet should compress UNICODE strings (applicable to only Jet 4.0 databases)	`Boolean`
Jet OLEDB:Hyperlink	Indicates whether the column is a hyperlink	`Boolean`
Jet OLEDB:IISAM Not Last Column	When creating columns (or a table) for installable IISAMs, indicates whether this is the last column	`Boolean`
Jet OLEDB:One BLOB Per Page	Indicates whether BLOB columns can share data pages	`Boolean`
Nullable	Indicates whether the column can contain `Null` values	`Boolean`
Primary Key	Indicates whether the column is part of the primary key	`Boolean`
Seed	The initial seed value of an auto-increment column	`Long`
Unique	Indicates whether the column allows unique values.	`Boolean`

The Index Object's Properties

Property Name	Description	Data Type
Auto-Update	Indicates whether the index is maintained automatically when changes are made to rows	`Boolean`
Clustered	Indicates whether the index is clustered	`Boolean`
Fill Factor	Identifies the fill-factor of the index (This is the storage use of page-nodes during index creation. It is always 100 for the Jet provider.)	`Long`
Index Type	The type of the index	`DBPROPVAL_IT`
Initial Size	The total number of bytes allocated to the index when first created	`Long`
`Null` Collation	Specifies how `Null` values are collated in the index	`DBPROPVAL_NC`
`Null` Keys	Specifies whether key values containing `Nulls` are allowed	`DBPROPVAL_IN`
Primary Key	Indicates whether the index represents the primary key on the table	`Boolean`
Sort Bookmarks	Indicates whether repeated keys are sorted by bookmarks	`Boolean`
Temporary Index	Indicates whether the index is temporary	`Boolean`
Unique	Indicates whether index keys must be unique	`Boolean`

The Table Object's Properties

Property	Name Description	Data Type
Jet OLEDB:Cache Link Name/Password	Indicates whether the authentication information for a linked table should be cached locally in the Jet database	Boolean
Jet OLEDB:Create Link	Indicates whether a link is created to a remote data source when creating a new table	Boolean
Jet OLEDB:Exclusive Link	Indicates whether the remote data source is opened exclusively when creating a link	Boolean
Jet OLEDB:Link Datasource	The name of the remote data source to link to	String
Jet OLEDB:Link Provider String	The connection string to the remote provider	String
Jet OLEDB:Remote Table Name	The name of the remote table in a link	String
Jet OLEDB:Table Hidden In Access	Indicates whether the table is shown in the Access user interface	Boolean
Jet OLEDB:Table Validation Rule	The validation rule to apply to row values before committing changes to the row	String
Jet OLEDB:Table Validation Text	Errors string to display if changes to a row do not meet the table validation rule	String
Temporary Table	Indicates whether the table is temporary	Boolean

ADOMD Object Summary

This appendix contains details of the Microsoft ActiveX Data Objects (Multidimensional) Library.

The ADOMD Objects

Name	Description
Axes	Contains an `Axis` object for each axis in the `Cellset`
Axis	An `Axis` of a `Cellset` containing members of one or more dimensions
Catalog	Contains the multidimensional schema information
Cell	The data at an intersection of `Axis` coordinates
Cellset	The results of a multidimensional query
CubeDef	A `Cube` from a multidimensional schema containing related `Dimension` objects
CubeDefs	One or more `CubeDef` objects contained within a `Catalog`
Dimension	A dimension of a multidimensional cube containing one or more `Hierarchy` objects
Dimensions	One or more `Dimension` objects making up the dimensions of a `CubeDef`
Hierarchies	One or more `Hierarchy` objects representing the ways a `Dimension` can be aggregated
Hierarchy	Indicates one way in which aggregation of a `Dimension` can take place

Table continues on the following page

Name	Description
Level	Contains the members that make up the Hierarchy
Levels	Contains one or more Level objects contained within the Hierarchy
Member	An individual member of the Members collection
Members	A collection of Member objects for the level
Position	A position in the Cellset
Positions	A collection of Position objects in the Cellset

The Axes Collection

Methods of the Axes Collection	Return Type	Description
Refresh		Refreshes the collection with details from the provider

Properties of the Axes Collection	Return Type	Description
Count	Long	The number of Axis objects in the collection (read-only)
Item	Axis	The default property, allowing indexing into the collection (read-only)

The Axis Object

Properties of the Axis Object	Return Type	Description
DimensionCount	Long	The number of Dimensions on this Axis (read-only)
Name	String	The name of the Axis (read-only)

Collections of the Axis Object	Return Type	Description
Positions	Positions	A collection of Position objects in the Axis (read-only)
Properties	Properties	A collection of provider-specific properties for the Axis (read-only)

The Catalog Object

Properties of the Catalog Object	Return Type	Description
ActiveConnection	Object	The ADO Connection object or string indicating the data provider to which the catalog is attached
Name	String	The name of the Catalog (read-only)

Collections of the Catalog Object	Return Type	Description
CubeDefs	CubeDefs	A collection of CubeDef objects available in the catalog (read-only)

The Cell Object

Properties of the Cell Object	Return Type	Description
FormattedValue	String	The formatted value of the cell
Ordinal	Long	The unique number identifying a cell (read-only)
Value	Variant	The value of the cell

Collections of the Cell Object	Return Type	Description
Positions	Positions	A collection of Position objects available for the cell (read-only)
Properties	Properties	A collection of provider-specific properties for the cell (read-only)

The Cellset Object

Methods of the Cellset Object	Return Type	Description
Close		Closes the `Cellset`
Open		Opens the `Cellset`

Properties of the Cellset Object	Return Type	Description
ActiveConnection	Object	The ADO `Connection` object or string indicating the data provider to which the catalog is attached
FilterAxis	Axis	Indicates the filtering information for the `Cellset` (read-only)
Item	Cell	The default property, which allows indexing into the `Cellset` (read-only)
Source	Variant	The multidimensional query used to generate the `Cellset`
State	Long	Indicates whether the `Cellset` is open or closed (read-only)

Collections of the Cellset Object	Return Type	Description
Axes	Axes	A collection of `Axis` objects in the `Cellset` (read-only)
Properties	Properties	A collection of provider-specific properties for the `Cellset` (read-only)

The CubeDef Object

Methods of the CubeDef Object	Return Type	Description
GetSchemaObject	Object	Returns an object from the schema, given the objects name

Properties of the CubeDef Object	Return Type	Description
Description	String	Text describing the cube (read-only)
Name	String	The name of the cube (read-only)

Collections of the CubeDef Object	Return Type	Description
Dimensions	Dimensions	A collection of Dimensions available in the cube (read-only)
Properties	Properties	A collection of provider-specific properties for the CubeDef (read-only)

The CubeDefs Collection

Methods of the CubeDefs Collection	Return Type	Description
Refresh		Refreshes the CubeDef objects from the provider

Properties of the CubeDefs Collection	Return Type	Description
Count	Long	Indicates the number of CubeDef objects in the collection (read-only)
Item	CubeDef	The default property, which allows indexing into the collection (read-only)

The Dimension Object

Properties of the Dimension Object	Return Type	Description
Description	String	A description of the dimension (read-only)
Name	String	The name of the dimension (read-only)
UniqueName	String	The unique name of the dimension (read-only)

Collections of the Dimension Object	Return Type	Description
Hierarchies	Hierarchies	A collection of hierarchies available in the dimension (read-only)
Properties	Properties	A collection of provider-specific properties for the dimension (read-only)

The Dimensions Collection

Methods of the Dimensions Collection	Return Type	Description
Refresh		Refreshes the Dimensions collection from the provider

Properties of the Dimensions Collection	Return Type	Description
Count	Long	The number of Dimension objects in the collection (read-only)
Item	Dimension	The default property, which allows indexing into the collection (read-only)

The Hierarchies Collection

Methods of the Hierarchies Collection	Return Type	Description
Refresh		Refreshes the Hierarchies collection from the provider

Properties of the Hierarchies Collection	Return Type	Description
Count	Long	The number of Hierarchy objects in the collection (read-only)
Item	Hierarchy	The default property, which allows indexing into the collection (read-only)

The Hierarchy Object

Properties of the Hierarchy Object	Return Type	Description
Description	String	The description of the hierarchy (read-only)

Properties of the Hierarchy Object	Return Type	Description
Name	String	The name of the hierarchy (read-only)
UniqueName	String	The unique name of the hierarchy (read-only)

Collections of the Hierarchy Object	Return Type	Description
Levels	Levels	A collection of levels in the hierarchy (read-only)
Properties	Properties	A collection of provider specific properties for the hierarchy (read-only)

The Level Object

Properties of the Level Object	Return Type	Description
Caption	String	The caption of the level (read-only)
Depth	Integer	How deep in the hierarchy this level is (read-only)
Description	String	The description of the level (read-only)
Name	String	The name of the level (read-only)
UniqueName	String	The unique name of the level (read-only)

Collections of the Level Object	Return Type	Description
Members	Members	A collection of Member objects available in this level (read-only)
Properties	Properties	A collection of provider-specific properties for the level (read-only)

The Levels Collection

Methods of the Levels Collection	Return Type	Description
Refresh		Refreshes the Levels collection from the provider

Properties of the Levels Collection	Return Type	Description
Count	Long	The number of Level objects in the collection (read-only)
Item	Level	The default property, which allows indexing into the collection (read-only)

The Member Object

Properties of the Member Object	Return Type	Description
Caption	String	The caption of the member (read-only)
ChildCount	Long	The number of children belonging to this member (read-only)
Description	String	A description of the member (read-only)
DrilledDown	Boolean	Indicates whether or not this is a leaf node (contains no children) (read-only)
LevelDepth	Long	How deep in the collection this member is (read-only)
LevelName	String	The name of the Level to which this member belongs (read-only)
Name	String	The name of the member (read-only)
Parent	Member	The Member object that is the parent of this member (read-only)
ParentSameAsPrev	Boolean	Indicates whether the Parent member is the same as the Parent member of the previous member in the collection (read-only)
TypeMember	TypeEnum	The type of the member (read-only)
UniqueName	String	The unique name of the member (read-only)

Collections of the Member Object	Return Type	Description
Children	Members	A collection of Member objects that are children of this member (read-only)
Properties	Properties	A collection of provider-specific properties for the member (read-only)

The Members Collection

Methods of the Members Collection	Return Type	Description
Refresh		Refreshes the `Members` collection from the provider

Properties of the Members Collection	Return Type	Description
Count	Long	The number of `Member` objects in the collection (read-only)
Item	Member	The default property, which allows indexing into the collection (read-only)

The Position Object

Properties of the Position Object	Return Type	Description
Ordinal	Long	A unique identifier indicating the location of the position in the collection (read-only)

Collections of the Position Object	Return Type	Description
Members	Members	A collection of `Member` objects in this position (read-only)

The Positions Collection

Methods of the Positions Collection	Return Type	Description
Refresh		Refreshes the `Positions` collection from the provider

Properties of the Positions Collection	Return Type	Description
Count	Long	The number of `Position` objects in the collection (read-only)
Item	Position	The default property, which allows indexing into the collection (read-only)

ADOMD Method Calls

The Axes Collection

```
Axes.Refresh
```

The Cellset Object

```
Cellset.Close
Cellset.Open([DataSource As Variant],
          [ActiveConnection As Variant])
```

The CubeDef Object

```
Set Object = CubeDef.GetSchemaObject(eObjType As
          SchemaObjectTypeEnum, bsUniqueName As String)
```

The CubeDefs Collection

```
CubeDefs.Refresh
```

The Dimensions Collection

```
Dimensions.Refresh
```

The Hierarchies Collection

```
Hierarchies.Refresh
```

The Levels Collection

```
Levels.Refresh
```

The Members Collection

```
Members.Refresh
```

The Positions Collection

```
Positions.Refresh
```

ADOMD Constants

MemberTypeEnum

Constant Name	Value	Description
adMemberAll	2	The member is the All member, at the top of the members hierarchy.
adMemberFormula	4	The member identifies a formula.
adMemberMeasure	3	The member identifies a measure.
adMemberRegular	1	The member identifies a regular member.
adMemberUnknown	0	The type of member is unknown.

SchemaObjectTypeEnum

Constant Name	Value	Description
adObjectTypeDimension	1	Return a Dimension object from the CubeDef.
adObjectTypeHierarchy	2	Return a Hierarchy object from the CubeDef.
adObjectTypeLevel	3	Return a Level object from the CubeDef.
adObjectTypeMember	4	Return a Member object from the CubeDef.

MD_DIMTYPE

Constant Name	Value	Description
MD_DIMTYPE_UNKNOWN	0	The dimension type is unknown.
MD_DIMTYPE_TIME	1	The dimension is a time dimension.
MD_DIMTYPE_MEASURE	2	The dimension is a measure dimension.
MD_DIMTYPE_OTHER	3	The dimension is neither a time nor a measure dimension.

MDLEVEL_TYPE

Constant Name	Value	Description
MDLEVEL_TYPE_REGULAR	0	The level is a regular level.
MDLEVEL_TYPE_ALL	1	The level identifies the top of the hierarchy, or All level.
MDLEVEL_TYPE_CALCULATED	2	The level is a calculated level.
MDLEVEL_TYPE_TIME	4	The level is a time level.
MDLEVEL_TYPE_TIME_YEARS	20	The level is a time level, based on years.
MDLEVEL_TYPE_TIME_HALF_YEAR	36	The level is a time level, based on half-years.
MDLEVEL_TYPE_TIME_QUARTERS	68	The level is a time level, based on quarters.
MDLEVEL_TYPE_TIME_MONTHS	132	The level is a time level, based on months.
MDLEVEL_TYPE_TIME_WEEKS	260	The level is a time level, based on weeks.
MDLEVEL_TYPE_TIME_DAYS	516	The level is a time level, based on days.
MDLEVEL_TYPE_TIME_HOURS	772	The level is a time level, based on hours.
MDLEVEL_TYPE_TIME_MINUTES	1028	The level is a time level, based on minutes.
MDLEVEL_TYPE_TIME_SECONDS	2052	The level is a time level, based on seconds.
MDLEVEL_TYPE_TIME_UNDEFINED	4100	The level type is not defined.
MDLEVEL_TYPE_UNKNOWN	0	The level type is unknown.

MDMEASURE_AGGR

Constant Name	Value	Description
MDMEASURE_AGGR_SUM	1	The aggregate function is SUM.
MDMEASURE_AGGR_COUNT	2	The aggregate function is COUNT.
MDMEASURE_AGGR_MIN	3	The aggregate function is MIN.
MDMEASURE_AGGR_MAX	4	The aggregate function is MAX.
MDMEASURE_AGGR_AVG	5	The aggregate function is AVG.
MDMEASURE_AGGR_VAR	6	The aggregate function is VAR.
MDMEASURE_AGGR_STD	7	The aggregate function is one of SUM, COUNT, MIN, MAX, AVG, VAR, STDEV.
MDMEASURE_AGGR_CALCULATED	127	The aggregate function is derived from formula that is not a standard one.
MDMEASURE_AGGR_UNKNOWN	0	The aggregate function is not known.

MDMEMBER_TYPE

Constant Name	Value	Description
MDMEMBER_TYPE_ALL	1	The member identifies the top of the hierarchy, or All members.
MDMEMBER_TYPE_REGULAR	2	The member is a regular member.
MDMEMBER_TYPE_MEASURE	3	The member is a measure.
MDMEMBER_TYPE_FORMULA	4	The member is a calculated formula.
MDMEMBER_TYPE_UNKNOWN	0	The member type is unknown.

MDPROPVAL_AU

Constant Name	Value	Description
MDPROPVAL_AU_UNSUPPORTED	0	Updating of aggregated cells is not supported.
MDPROPVAL_AU_UNCHANGED	1	Aggregated cells can be changed, but the cells that make up the aggregation remain unchanged.
MDPROPVAL_AU_UNKNOWN	2	Aggregated cells can be changed, but the cells that make up the aggregation remain undefined.

MDPROPVAL_FS

Constant Name	Value	Description
MDPROPVAL_FS_FULL_SUPPORT	1	The provider supports flattening.
MDPROPVAL_FS_GENERATED_COLUMN	2	The provider supports flattening by using dummy names.
MDPROPVAL_FS_GENERATED_DIMENSION	3	The provider supports flattening by generating one column per dimension.
MDPROPVAL_FS_NO_SUPPORT	4	The provider does not support flattening.

MDPROPVAL_MC

Constant Name	Value	Description
MDPROPVAL_MC_SINGLECASE	1	The provider supports simple case statements.
MDPROPVAL_MC_SEARCHEDCASE	2	The provider supports searched case statements.

MDPROPVAL_MD

Constant Name	Value	Description
MDPROPVAL_MD_BEFORE	2	The BEFORE flag is supported.
MDPROPVAL_MD_AFTER	4	The AFTER flag is supported.
MDPROPVAL_MD_SELF	1	The SELF flag is supported.

MDPROPVAL_MF

Constant Name	Value	Description
MDPROPVAL_MF_WITH_CALCMEMBERS	1	Calculated members are supported by use of the WITH clause.
MDPROPVAL_MF_WITH_NAMEDSETS	2	Named sets are supported by use of the WITH clause.
MDPROPVAL_MF_CREATE_CALCMEMBERS	4	Named calculated members are supported by use of the CREATE clause.
MDPROPVAL_MF_CREATE_NAMEDSETS	8	Named sets are supported by use of the CREATE clause.
MDPROPVAL_MF_SCOPE_SESSION	16	The scope value of SESSION is supported during the creation of named sets and calculated members.
MDPROPVAL_MF_SCOPE_GLOBAL	32	The scope value of GLOBAL is supported during the creation of named sets and calculated members.

MDPROPVAL_MJC

Constant Name	Value	Description
MDPROPVAL_MJC_IMPLICITCUBE	4	An empty FROM clause is supported, and the cube is implicitly resolved.
MDPROPVAL_MJC_SINGLECUBE	1	Only one cube is supported in the FROM clause.
MDPROPVAL_MJC_MULTICUBES	2	More than one cube is supported in the FROM clause.

MDPROPVAL_MMF

Constant Name	Value	Description
MDPROPVAL_MMF_COUSIN	1	The COUSIN function is supported.
MDPROPVAL_MMF_PARALLELPERIOD	2	The PARALLELPERIOD function is supported.
MDPROPVAL_MMF_OPENINGPERIOD	4	The OPENINGPERIOD function is supported.
MDPROPVAL_MMF_CLOSINGPERIOD	8	The CLOSINGPERIOD function is supported.

MDPROPVAL_MNF

Constant Name	Value	Description
MDPROPVAL_MNF_MEDIAN	1	The MEDIAN function is supported.
MDPROPVAL_MNF_VAR	2	The VAR function is supported.
MDPROPVAL_MNF_STDDEV	4	The STDDEV function is supported.
MDPROPVAL_MNF_RANK	8	The RANK function is supported.
MDPROPVAL_MNF_AGGREGATE	16	The AGGREGATE function is supported.
MDPROPVAL_MNF_COVARIANCE	32	The COVARIANCE function is supported.
MDPROPVAL_MNF_CORRELATION	64	The CORRELATION function is supported.
MDPROPVAL_MNF_LINREGSLOPE	128	The LINREGSLOPE function is supported.
MDPROPVAL_MNF_LINREGVARIANCE	256	The LINREGVARIANCE function is supported.
MDPROPVAL_MNF_LINREGR2	512	The LINREGR2 function is supported.
MDPROPVAL_MNF_LINREGPOINT	1024	The LINREGPOINT function is supported.
MDPROPVAL_MNF_LINREGINTERCEPT	2048	The LINREGINTERCEPT function is supported.

MDPROPVAL_MOQ

Constant Name	Value	Description
MDPROPVAL_MOQ_DATASOURCE_CUBE	1	Cubes can be qualified by the data source name.
MDPROPVAL_MOQ_CATALOG_CUBE	2	Cubes can be qualified by the catalog name.
MDPROPVAL_MOQ_SCHEMA_CUBE	4	Cubes can be qualified by the schema name.
MDPROPVAL_MOQ_CUBE_DIM	8	Dimensions can be qualified by the cube name.
MDPROPVAL_MOQ_DIM_HIER	16	Hierarchies can be qualified by the dimension name.
MDPROPVAL_MOQ_DIMHIER_LEVEL	32	Levels can be qualified by the schema name, and/or the hierarchy name.
MDPROPVAL_MOQ_LEVEL_MEMBER	64	Members can be qualified by a level name.
MDPROPVAL_MOQ_MEMBER_MEMBER	128	Members can be qualified by their ancestor names.

MDPROPVAL_MS

Constant Name	Value	Description
MDPROPVAL_MS_SINGLETUPLE	2	Only one tuple is supported in the WHERE clause.
MDPROPVAL_MS_MULTIPLETUPLES	1	Multiple tuples are supported in the WHERE clause.

MDPROPVAL_MSC

Constant Name	Value	Description
MDPROPVAL_MSC_LESSTHAN	1	The provider supports the less than operator.
MDPROPVAL_MSC_GREATERTHAN	2	The provider supports the greater than operator.
MDPROPVAL_MSC_LESSTHANEQUAL	4	The provider supports the less than or equal to operator.
MDPROPVAL_MSC_GREATERTHANEQUAL	8	The provider supports the greater than or equal to operator.

MDPROPVAL_MSF

Constant Name	Value	Description
MDPROPVAL_MSF_TOPPERCENT	1	The TOPPERCENT function is supported.
MDPROPVAL_MSF_BOTTOMPERCENT	2	The BOTTOMPERCENT function is supported.
MDPROPVAL_MSF_TOPSUM	4	The TOPSUM function is supported.
MDPROPVAL_MSF_BOTTOMSUM	8	The BOTTOMSUM function is supported.
MDPROPVAL_MSF_DRILLDOWNLEVEL	2048	The DRILLDOWNLEVEL function is supported.
MDPROPVAL_MSF_DRILLDOWNMEMBER	1024	The DRILLDOWNMEMBER function is supported.
MDPROPVAL_MSF_DRILLDOWNMEMBERTOP	4096	The DRILLDOWNMEMBERTOP function is supported.
MDPROPVAL_MSF_DRILLDOWNMEMBERBOTTOM	8192	The DRILLDOWNMEMBERBOTTOM function is supported.
MDPROPVAL_MSF_DRILLDOWNLEVELTOP	16384	The DRILLDOWNLEVELTOP function is supported.
MDPROPVAL_MSF_DRILLDOWNLEVELBOTTOM	32768	The DRILLDOWNLEVELBOTTOM function is supported.

Table continues on the following page

Constant Name	Value	Description
MDPROPVAL_MSF_DRILLUPMEMBER	65536	The DRILLUPMEMBER function is supported.
MDPROPVAL_MSF_DRILLUPLEVEL	131072	The DRILLUPLEVEL function is supported.
MDPROPVAL_MSF_PERIODSTODATE	16	The PERIODSTODATE function is supported.
MDPROPVAL_MSF_LASTPERIODS	32	The LASTPERIODS function is supported.
MDPROPVAL_MSF_YTD	64	The YTD function is supported.
MDPROPVAL_MSF_QTD	128	The QTD function is supported.
MDPROPVAL_MSF_MTD	256	The MTD function is supported.
MDPROPVAL_MSF_WTD	512	The WTD function is supported.

MDPROPVAL_NL

Constant Name	Value	Description
MDPROPVAL_NL_NAMEDLEVELS	1	The provider supports named levels.
MDPROPVAL_NL_NUMBEREDLEVELS	2	The provider supports numbered levels.
MDPROPVAL_NL_SCHEMAONLY	4	The provider supports 'dummy' levels, for display only.

MDPROPVAL_RR

Constant Name	Value	Description
MDPROPVAL_RR_NORANGEROWSET	1	The provider does not support range rowsets.
MDPROPVAL_RR_READONLY	2	The provider supports read-only range rowsets.
MDPROPVAL_RR_UPDATE	4	The provider supports updateable range rowsets.

MDTREEOP

Constant Name	Value	Description
MDTREEOP_ANCESTORS	32	Show only members that are ancestors of the selected member.
MDTREEOP_CHILDREN	1	Show only members that are children of the selected member.
MDTREEOP_SIBLINGS	2	Show only members that are siblings of the selected member.
MDTREEOP_PARENT	4	Show only members that are parents of the selected member.
MDTREEOP_SELF	8	Show the selected member in the list.
MDTREEOP_DESCENDANTS	16	Show only members that are descendants of the selected member.

ADOMD Properties Collection

The following table shows a list of all OLE DB properties for the Microsoft OLAP Provider.

Descriptions marked with a hash mark (#) indicate undocumented properties where I've taken a guess at the description.

The Connection Object's Properties

Property Name	Description	Type
Active Sessions	The maximum number of sessions allowable (Zero indicates no limit.)	Long
Asynchable Abort	Whether transactions can be aborted asynchronously (read-only)	Boolean
Asynchable Commit	Whether transactions can be committed asynchronously (read-only)	Boolean
Asynchronous Initialization	Indicates the asynchronous initialization setting (This can be only DBPROPVAL_ASYNCH_INITIALIZE from the ADO constants.)	Long
Auto Synch Period	Identifies the time (in milliseconds) of the synchronization between the client and the server (The default value is 10,000 [10 seconds].)	Long

Table continues on the following page

Property Name	Description	Type
Autocommit Isolation Levels	Indicates the transaction isolation level when in auto-commit mode (This can be one of the DBPROPVAL_TI constants from ADO.)	Long
Cache Policy	Reserved for future use	Long
Catalog Location	The position of the catalog name in a table name in a text command (The value can be one of the DBPROPVAL_CL constants from ADO.)	Long
Catalog Term	The name the data source uses for a catalog, such as "catalog" or "database" (read/write)	String
Catalog Usage	Specifies how catalog names can be used in text commands (This can be zero or more of DBPROPVAL_CU constants from ADO.)	Long
Client Cache Size	The amount of memory used by the cache on the client (A value of 0 means there is no limit on the client memory that can be used. A value of 1–99 indicates the percentage of virtual memory to use for the cache. A value above 100 indicates the amount in Kb that can be used by the cache.)	Long
Column Definition	Defines the valid clauses for the definition of a column (This can be one of the DBPROPVAL_CD constants from ADO.)	Long
CompareCase NotSensitive StringFlags	Identifies the type of comparison to perform for case-insensitive strings	Long
CompareCase Sensitive StringFlags	Identifies the type of comparison to perform for case-sensitive strings	Long
Connect Timeout	The amount of time, in seconds, to wait for the initialization to complete (read/write)	Long
Connection Status	The status of the current connection (This can be one of the DBPROPVAL_CS constants from ADO.)	Long
CREATE CUBE	The statement used to create a cube	String

Table continues on the following page

Property Name	Description	Type
Current Catalog	The name of the current catalog	String
Data Source	The name of the data source to connect to	String
Data Source Name	The name of the data source	String
Data Source Object Threading Model	Specifies the threading models supported by the data source object	Long
Data Source Type	The type of data source	Long
DBMS Name	The name of the product accessed by the provider	String
DBMS Version	The version of the product accessed by the provider	String
Default Isolation Mode	Identifies whether the isolation mode is "isolated," or identifies the mode requested by the rowset properties (Isolated mode will be used if this value starts with Y, T, or a number other than 0.)	String
Default MDX Visual Mode	The default visibility mode of columns	Integer
Distinct Measures By Key	The key used to obtain distinct measures #	String
Do Not Apply Commands	The supplied commands do not apply to this OLAP Provider #	String
Execution Location	Identifies whether the query is resolved—values can be: 0—for automatic selection (default) 1—for automatic selection 2—to execute the query on the client 3—to execute the query on the server	Long
Extended Properties	Contains provider-specific, extended connection information	String
Flattening Support	Indicates the level of support by the provider for flattening	MDPROPVAL_FS
GROUP BY Support	The relationship between the columns in a GROUP BY clause and the nonaggregated columns in the select list (This can be one of the DBPROPVAL_GB constants from ADO.)	Long

Table continues on the following page

Property Name	Description	Type
Heterogeneous Table Support	Specifies whether the provider can join tables from different catalogs or providers (This can be one of the DBPROPVAL_HT constants from ADO.)	Long
Identifier Case Sensitivity	How identifiers treat case sensitivity (This can be one of the DBPROPVAL_IC constants from ADO.)	Long
Initial Catalog	The name of the initial, or default, catalog to use when connecting to the data source (If the provider supports changing the catalog for an initialized data source, a different catalog name can be specified in the Current Catalog property.)	String
INSERTINTO	The statement used for inserting data into a local cube	String
Integrated Security	Contains the name of the authentication service used by the server to identify the user	String
Isolation Levels	Identifies the supported transaction isolation levels (This can be one of the DBPROPVAL_TI constants from ADO.)	Long
Isolation Retention	Identifies the supported transaction isolation retention levels (This can be one of the DBPROPVAL_TR constants from ADO.)	Long
Large Level Threshold	Defines the number of levels a Dimension can have before it is deemed to be a "large" dimension (A large level Dimension will have the levels sent from the server in increments rather than all at once.)	Long
Locale Identifier	The locale ID of preference for the consumer	Long
Location	The location of the data source to connect to (Typically, this will be the server name.)	String
Maximum Index Size	The maximum number of bytes allowed in the combined columns of an index (This is 0 if there is no specified limit or the limit is unknown.)	Long

Table continues on the following page

Property Name	Description	Type
Maximum Row Size	The maximum length of a single row in a table (This is 0 if there is no specified limit or the limit is unknown.)	Long
Maximum Row Size Includes BLOB	Identifies whether Maximum Row Size includes the length for BLOB data	Boolean
Maximum Tables in SELECT	The maximum number of tables allowed in the FROM clause of a SELECT statement (This is 0 if there is no specified limit or the limit is unknown.)	Long
MDX Calculated Members Extensions	Defines any supported extensions for calculated members #	Integer
MDX Calculated Members Mode	Reserved for future use	Integer
MDX DDL Extensions	Defines any DDL extensions supported by the provider	Long
MDX Unique Name Style	The style used for unique names— will be one of: 0—same as value 2, but included for compatibility with previous versions (default) 1—to use the key path algorithm [dimension].&[Key1].&[Key2] 2—to use the name path algorithm [dimension].[n1].[n2] (included for compatibility with SQL Server 7.0) 3—for names that are stable over time (included for compatibility with SQL Server 2000)	Integer
MDX USE Extensions	Defines the USE extensions supported by the provider, allowing creation of user-defined functions	Long
Mining Location	The location where data mining takes place #	String
Mode	Specifies the access permissions (This can be one of the DB_MODE constants from ADO.)	Long
Multiple Results	Identifies whether the provider supports multiple results objects and what restrictions it places on those objects	Long

Table continues on the following page

Property Name	Description	Type
Multiple Storage Objects	Identifies whether the provider supports multiple open storage objects simultaneously	Boolean
Multi-Table Update	Identifies whether the provider can update rowsets derived from multiple tables	Boolean
NULL Collation Order	Identifies where Nulls are sorted in a list	Long
NULL Concatenation Behavior	How the data source handles concatenation of Null-valued character data type columns with non-Null valued character data type columns	Long
Number of axes in the dataset	Maximum number of axes that the provider supports	Long
OLE DB for OLAP Version	The version of OLAP in use by the provider	String
OLE DB Services	Specifies the OLE DB services to enable	Long
OLE DB Version	Specifies the version of OLE DB supported by the provider	String
OLE Object Support	Specifies the way in which the provider supports access to BLOBs and OLE objects stored in columns	Long
ORDER BY Columns in Select List	Identifies whether columns in an ORDER BY clause must be in the SELECT list	Boolean
Output Parameter Availability	Identifies the time at which output parameter values become available. Can be one of the DBPROPVAL_AO constants in ADO	Long
Pass By Ref Accessors	Whether the provider supports the DBACCESSOR_PASSBYREF flag	Boolean
Password	The password to be used to connect to the data source	String
Perf Cell count	PerfMon cell count #	Integer
Perf Net count	PerfMon network count #	Integer
Perf Net Time	PerfMon network time #	Double
Perf Query count	PerfMon query count #	Integer
Perf Query time	PerfMon query time #	Double

Table continues on the following page

Property Name	Description	Type
Persist Security Info	Indicates whether the consumer requires that the data source object persist sensitive authentication information, such as a password, in encrypted form	Boolean
Persistent ID Type	Specifies the type of DBID that the provider uses when persisting DBIDs for tables, indexes, and columns (This can be one of the DBPROPVAL_PT constants in ADO.)	Long
Prepare Abort Behavior	Identifies how aborting a transaction affects prepared commands (This can be one of the DBPROPVAL_CB constants in ADO.)	Long
Prepare Commit Behavior	Identifies how committing a transaction affects prepared commands (This can be one of the DBPROPVAL_CB constants in ADO.)	Long
Procedure Term	Specifies the data source provider's name for a procedure, such as "database procedure" or "stored procedure"	String
Prompt	Specifies whether to prompt the user during initialization	Integer
Provider Friendly Name	The friendly name of the provider	String
Provider Name	The filename of the provider	String
Provider Version	The version of the provider	String
Provider's ability to qualify a cube name	Identifies how object names in a schema can be qualified in an MDX expression	MDPROPVAL_ MOQ
Quoted Identifier Sensitivity	Identifies how quoted identifiers treat case (This can be one of the DBPROPVAL_IC constants from ADO)	Long
Read-Only Session	Reserved for future use	String
Read-Only Data Source	Indicates whether the data source is read-only	Boolean
Reset Datasource	Specifies the data source state to reset (This can be one of the DBPROPVAL_RD constants from ADO.)	Long
Roles	The security roles for the current user [#]	String
Rowset Conversions on Command	Indicates whether callers can inquire about rowset conversions	Boolean

Table continues on the following page

Property Name	Description	Type
Schema Usage	Identifies how schema names can be used in commands (This can be one of the DBPROPVAL_SU constants from ADO.)	Long
Secured Cell Value	Indicates the return value resulting from the call to a secured cell—will be one of: 1—if the string #N/A is returned 2—if an error is returned 3—if Null is returned 4—if 0 is returned 5—if the string #SEC is returned	Integer
Server Name	The name of the server	String
SOURCE_DSN	The connection string for the source data store	String
SOURCE_DSN_ SUFFIX	The suffix to append to the SOURCE_DSN property for a local cube	String
SQL Compatibility	Identifies the level of compatibility for SQL	Long
SQL Support	Identifies the level of support for SQL (This can be one of the DBPROPVAL_SQL constants from ADO.)	Long
SSPI	Determines the security package that will be used for the session	String
Structured Storage	Identifies what interfaces the rowset supports on storage objects (This can be one of the DBPROPVAL_SS constants from ADO.)	Long
Subquery Support	Identifies the predicates in text commands that support subqueries (This can be one of the DBPROPVAL_SQ constants from ADO.)	Long
Support for cell updates	Indicates whether the provider supports updating of the cells	MDPROPVAL_ PR
Support for creation of named sets and calculated members	Indicates the level of support for named sets and calculated members	MDPROPVAL_ MF
Support for MDX case statements	The level of support for case statements	MDPROPVAL_ MC
Support for named levels	The level of support for named and/or numbered Levels	MDPROPVAL_ NL

Table continues on the following page

Property Name	Description	Type
Support for outer reference in an MDX statement	The level of support for outer references	MDPROPVAL_ MO
Support for query joining multiple cubes	The level of support for joining multiple cubes	MDPROPVAL_ MJC
Support for querying by property values in an MDX statement	Indicates whether the provider supports the query of property statements	Boolean
Support for string comparison operators other than equals and not-equals operators	The level of support for complex string comparison operators	MDPROPVAL_ MSC
Support for updating aggregated cells	The level of support for updating aggregated cells	MDPROPVAL_ AU
Support for various <desc_flag> values in the DESCENDANTS function	The level of support for flags when describing descendants	MDPROPVAL_ MD
Support for various member functions	The level of support for functions that act on members	MDPROPVAL_ MMF
Support for various numeric functions	The level of support for numeric functions	MDPROPVAL_ MNF
Support for various set functions	The level of support for set functions	MDPROPVAL_ MSF
Table Term	The name the data source uses for a table, such as "table" or "file"	String
The capabilities of the WHERE clause of an MDX statement	The WHERE clause support for tuples	MDPROPVAL_ MS
Transaction DDL	Indicates whether DDL statements are supported in transactions (This can be one of the DBPROPVAL_TC constants from ADO.)	Long

Table continues on the following page

Property Name	Description	Type
USEEXISTING FILE	When using CREATE CUBE or INSERT INTO, indicates whether an existing local cube file is overwritten (If the value starts with Y, T or a number other than 0, the existing file is used. If the value starts with any other character, the existing cube file is overwritten.)	String
User ID	The User ID to be used when connecting to the data source	String
User Name	The User Name used in a particular database	String
Visual Totals Mode	Determines whether aggregate values reflect the entire aggregation or only those for a given cellset	Long
Window Handle	The window handle to be used if the data source object needs to prompt for additional information	Long
Writeback Timeout	The maximum amount of time (in seconds) to wait while committing changes back to the server	Long

The CubeDef Object's Properties

Property Name	Description	Type
CATALOG_NAME	The name of the catalog to which the cube belongs	String
CREATED_ON	The date the cube was created	Date/Time
CUBE_GUID	The GUID of the cube	GUID
CUBE_NAME	The cube name	String
CUBE_TYPE	Will be CUBE for a standard cube or VIRTUAL CUBE for a virtual cube	String
DATA_UPDATED_BY	The ID of the person who last update data in the cube	String
DESCRIPTION	The cube description	String
LAST_DATA_UPDATE	The date the cube data was last updated	Date/Time

Table continues on the following page

Property Name	Description	Type
LAST_SCHEMA_UPDATE	The date the cube schema was last updated	Date/Time
SCHEMA_NAME	The name of the schema to which this cube belongs	String
SCHEMA_UPDATED_BY	The ID of the person who last updated the schema	String

The Dimension Object's Properties

Property Name	Description	Type
CATALOG_NAME	The name of the Catalog to which this Dimension belongs	String
CUBE_NAME	The name of the Cube to which this Dimension belongs	String
DEFAULT_HIERARCHY	The unique name of the default Hierarchy for this Dimension	String
DESCRIPTION	The description of the Dimension	String
DIMENSION_CAPTION	The caption of the Dimension	String
DIMENSION_CARDINALITY	The number of members in the Dimension (This figure's accuracy is not guaranteed.)	Long
DIMENSION_GUID	The GUID of the Dimension, or Null if no GUID exists	GUID
DIMENSION_IS_VISIBLE	Indicates whether the Dimension is visible	Boolean
DIMENSION_MASTER_UNIQUE_NAME	The master unique name of the Dimension	String
DIMENSION_NAME	The name of the Dimension	String
DIMENSION_ORDINAL	The number or the ordinal of the Dimension (zero-based)	Long
DIMENSION_TYPE	The type of the Dimension	MD_DIMTYPE
DIMENSION_UNIQUE_NAME	The unique name of the Dimension	String
DIMENSION_UNIQUE_SETTINGS	The unique settings for the Dimension	Integer

Table continues on the following page

Property Name	Description	Type
IS_READWRITE	Indicates whether the Dimension is writeable	Boolean
IS_VIRTUAL	Indicates whether or not the Dimension is a virtual dimension	Boolean
SCHEMA_NAME	The schema name to which this Dimension belongs	String

The Hierarchy Object's Properties

Property Name	Description	Type
ALL_MEMBER	The name of the default member if the first level is All, or Null if the first level is not All	String
CATALOG_NAME	Catalog name in which the table is defined, or Null if the provider does not support catalogs	String
CUBE_NAME	The name of the Cube to which this Hierarchy belongs	String
DEFAULT_MEMBER	The default Level for this Hierarchy, or Null if no default exists	String
DESCRIPTION	The description of the Hierarchy	String
DIMENSION_IS_SHARED	Indicates whether the dimension is shared	Boolean
DIMENSION_IS_VISIBLE	Indicates whether the dimension is visible	Boolean
DIMENSION_MASTER_UNIQUE_NAME	The master unique name of the dimension	String
DIMENSION_TYPE	The type of the dimension	MD_DIMTYPE
DIMENSION_UNIQUE_NAME	The fully qualified name of the Dimension to which this Hierarchy belongs	String
HIERARCHY_GUID	The GUID of the Hierarchy, or Null if no GUID exists	GUID
DIMENSION_UNIQUE_SETTINGS	The unique settings for the dimension	Integer

Table continues on the following page

Property Name	Description	Type
HIERARCHY_CAPTION	The caption of the Hierarchy	String
HIERARCHY_ CARDINALITY	The number of members in the Hierarchy (This figure's accuracy is not guaranteed.)	Long
HIERARCHY_NAME	The name of the Hierarchy	String
HIERARCHY_ORDINAL	The ordinal of the hierarchy	Integer
HIERARCHY_UNIQUE_ NAME	The fully qualified name of the Hierarchy	String
IS_READWRITE	Indicates whether the hierarchy is writeable	Boolean
SCHEMA_NAME	Schema name in which the table is defined, or Null if the provider does not support schemas	String
STRUCTURE	The hierarchy structure in use for the dimension	Integer

The Level Object's Properties

Property Name	Description	Type
CATALOG_NAME	Catalog name, or Null if the provider does not support catalogs	String
CUBE_NAME	The Cube name to which the level belongs	String
CUSTOM_ROLLUP_ SETTINGS	The custom settings in use for ROLLUPs	Integer
DESCRIPTION	The description of the level	String
DIMENSION_ UNIQUE_NAME	The unique name of the Dimension to which the level belongs	String
HIERARCHY_ UNIQUE_NAME	The unique name of the Hierarchy to which the level belongs	String
LEVEL_CAPTION	The Caption of the level	String
LEVEL_CARDINALITY	The number of members in the level (This figure's accuracy is not guaranteed.)	Long
LEVEL_DBTYPE	The database type of the level	Integer
LEVEL_GUID	The GUID of the level, or Null if no GUID exists	GUID

Table continues on the following page

Property Name	Description	Type
LEVEL_IS_VISIBLE	Indicates whether the level is visible	Boolean
LEVEL_KEY_SQL_ COLUMN_NAME	The SQL column key name details of the level	String
LEVEL_MASTER_ UNIQUE_NAME	The master unique name for the level	String
LEVEL_NAME	The level name	String
LEVEL_NAME_SQL_ COLUMN_NAME	The SQL column name from which the level is derived	String
LEVEL_NUMBER	The index number of the level	Long
LEVEL_ORDERING_ PROPERTY	The ordering details for the level	String
LEVEL_TYPE	The Type of the level	MDLEVEL_ TYPE
LEVEL_UNIQUE_NAME	The unique level name	String
LEVEL_UNIQUE_NAME_ SQL_COLUMN_NAME	The SQL column name for the unique level name	String
LEVEL_UNIQUE_ SETTINGS	The unique settings for the level	Integer
SCHEMA_NAME	Schema name, or Null if the provider does not support schemas	String

The Member Object's Properties

Property Name	Description	Type
EXPRESSION	The expression that underlies a calculated measure	String

JRO Object Summary

This appendix contains details of the Microsoft Jet Replication Objects 2.6 Library.

JRO Objects

Name	Description
Filter	A Filter that limits replication
Filters	A collection of Filter objects
JetEngine	The Jet database engine
Replica	A copy of a replicated database

The Filter Object

Properties of the Filter Object	Return Type	Description
FilterCriteria	String	The filter criteria, which allow a record to be replicated (read-only)
FilterType	Filter TypeEnum	The type of the filter (This can be one of the FilterTypeEnum constants, as discussed in Appendix O. [read-only].)
TableName	String	The table to which the filter applies (read-only)

The Filters Collection

Methods of the Filters Collection	Return Type	Description
Append		Adds a new `Filter` object to the collection
Delete		Removes a `Filter` object from the collection
Refresh		Refreshes the collection from the design master

Properties of the Filters Collection	Return Type	Description
Count	Integer	The number of `Filter` objects in the collection (read-only)
Item	Filter	The default property, which allows indexing into the collection (read-only)

The JetEngine Object

Methods of the JetEngine Object	Return Type	Description
CompactDatabase		Compacts the requested database
RefreshCache		Forces the memory cache to write changes to the MDB file, and then refreshes the memory with data from the MDB file

The Replica Object

Methods of the Replica Object	Return Type	Description
CreateReplica		Creates a new replica of the current, replicable database
GetObject Replicability	Boolean	Identifies whether or not an object is local or replicable
MakeReplicable		Make a database replicable
PopulatePartial		Populates a partial replica with data from the full replica

Table continues on the following page

Methods of the Replica Object	Return Type	Description
SetObject Replicability		Sets whether an object is local or replicable
Synchronize		Synchronizes two replicable databases

Properties of the Replica Object	Return Type	Description
Active Connection	Object	An ADO Connection object or string to which the replica belongs
Conflict Function	String	The name of the custom function to use for conflict resolution
Conflict Tables	Recordset	A recordset that contains the tables and conflict tables for each table that had conflicts (read-only)
DesignMasterId	Variant	The unique identifier of the design master in a replica set
Priority	Integer	The relative priority of the replica, for use during conflict resolution (read-only)
ReplicaId	Variant	The unique ID of the replica database in the replica set (read-only)
ReplicaType	ReplicaTypeEnum	The type of replica (This can be one of the ReplicaTypeEnum constants, as discussed in Appendix O [read-only].)
RetentionPeriod	Integer	How many days replication histories are kept
Visibility	VisibilityEnum	Indicates whether the replica is global, local, or anonymous (This can be one of the VisibilityEnum constants, as discussed in Appendix O [read-only].)

Collections of the Replica Object	Return Type	Description
Filters	Filters	A collection of Filter objects, which specify the criteria that records must match to be replicated (read-only)

Method Calls

Filters

```
Filters.Append(TableName As String, FilterType As FilterTypeEnum, _
            FilterCriteria As String)
Filters.Delete(Index As Variant)
Filters.Refresh
```

JetEngine

```
JetEngine.CompactDatabase(SourceConnection As String, _
                        Destconnection As String)
JetEngine.RefreshCache(Connection As   )
```

Replica

```
Replica.CreateReplica(replicaName As String, _
                    description As String, _
                    [ReplicaType As ReplicaTypeEnum], _
                    [Visibility As VisibilityEnum], _
                    [Priority As Integer], _
                    [updatability As UpdatabilityEnum])
Boolean = Replica.GetObjectReplicability(objectName As String, _
                                    objectType As String)
Replica.MakeReplicable([connectionString As String], _
                    [columnTracking As Boolean])
Replica.PopulatePartial(FullReplica As String)
Replica.SetObjectReplicability(objectName As String, _
                            objectType As String, _
                            replicability As Boolean)
Replica.Synchronize(target As String, syncType As SyncTypeEnum,_
                [syncMode As SyncModeEnum])
```

JRO Constants

FilterTypeEnum

Name	Value	Description
jrFilterTypeRelationship	2	The filter is based upon a relationship.
jrFilterTypeTable	1	The filter is based upon a table (default).

ReplicaTypeEnum

Name	Value	Description
jrRepTypeDesignMaster	1	The replica is the design master.
jrRepTypeFull	2	The replica is a full replica.
jrRepTypeNotReplicable	0	The database is not replicable (default).
jrRepTypePartial	3	The replica is a partial replica.

SyncModeEnum

Name	Value	Description
jrSyncModeDirect	2	Use direct synchronization.
jrSyncModeIndirect	1	Use indirect synchronization.
jrSyncModeInternet	3	Use Internet based synchronization.

SyncTypeEnum

Name	Value	Description
jrSyncTypeExport	1	Export changes to the target database.
jrSyncTypeImpExp	3	Import and export changes to and from the target database.
jrSyncTypeImport	2	Import databases from the target database.

UpdatabilityEnum

Name	Value	Description
jrRepUpdFull	0	The replica can be updated.
jrRepUpdReadOnly	2	The replica is read-only.

VisibilityEnum

Name	Value	Description
jrRepVisibilityAnon	4	The replica is anonymous.
jrRepVisibilityGlobal	1	The replica is global.
jrRepVisibilityLocal	2	The replica is local.

ADO Error Codes

Standard Errors

The following table lists the standard errors than might be returned from ADO operations.

Constant name	Number	Description
adErrBoundToCommand	3707	The application cannot change the ActiveConnection property of a Recordset object with a Command object as its source.
adErrCannotComplete	3732	The server cannot complete the operation.
adErrCantChangeConnection	3748	The connection was refused because the requested connection has different characteristics from the one in use.
adErrCantChangeProvider	3220	The supplied provider is different from the one in use.
adErrCantConvertValue	3724	Data cannot be converted for reasons other than an overflow or sign mismatch (such as truncation).
adErrCantCreate	3725	The data value cannot be set, either because the type was not known or because the provider has run out of resources.

Table continues on the following page

Constant name	Number	Description
adErrCatalogNotSet	3747	The requested operation requires a valid `ParentCatalog`.
adErrColumnNotOnThisRow	3726	The Record does not contain the requested field.
adErrDataConversion	3421	The application is using a value of the wrong type for the current operation.
adErrDataOverflow	3721	The data value is too large for the supplied field.
adErrDelResOutOfScope	3738	The URL is outside the current Record's scope.
adErrDenyNotSupported	3750	Sharing restrictions are not supported by the provider.
adErrDenyTypeNotSuported	3751	The requested sharing restriction is not supported by the provider.
adErrFeatureNotAvailable	3251	The operation requested by the application is not supported by the provider.
adErrFieldsUpdateFailed	3749	An update to the `Fields` collection failed, or a Record or Recordset `Update` method call failed, due to a problem in one of the fields. The `Status` property will identify the reason.
adErrIllegalOperation	3219	The operation requested by the application is not allowed in this context.
adErrIntegrityViolation	3719	A data change caused a data integrity conflict.
adErrInTransaction	3246	The application cannot explicitly close a `Connection` object while in the middle of a transaction.
adErrInvalidArgument	3001	The application is using arguments that are of the wrong type, are out of acceptable range, or are in conflict with one another.
adErrInvalidConnection	3709	The application requested an operation on an object with a reference to a closed or invalid `Connection` object.
adErrInvalidParamInfo	3708	The application has improperly defined a `Parameter` object.
adErrInvalidTransaction	3714	The coordinating transaction is invalid, or has not started.

Table continues on the following page

Constant name	Number	Description
`adErrInvalidURL`	3729	The supplied URL is invalid, and contains invalid characters.
`adErrItemNotFound`	3265	ADO could not find the object in the collection corresponding to the name or ordinal reference requested by the application.
`adErrNoCurrentRecord`	3021	Either BOF or EOF is True, or the current record has been deleted; the operation requested by the application requires a current record.
`adErrNotReentrant`	3710	Cannot perform this operation while an event is being processed.
`adErrObjectClosed`	3704	The operation requested by the application is not allowed if the object is closed.
`adErrObjectInCollection`	3367	Can't append. The object is already in the collection.
`adErrObjectNotSet`	3420	The object referenced by the application no longer points to a valid object.
`adErrObjectOpen`	3705	The operation requested by the application is not allowed if the object is open.
`adErrOpeningFile`	3002	The requested file could not be opened.
`adOperationCancelled`	3712	The user cancelled the operation, with a CancelBatch or CancelUpdate method call.
`adErrOutOfSpace`	3734	The provider cannot obtain enough space to complete the operation.
`adErrPermissionDenied`	3720	The field cannot be written to because of insufficient permissions.
`adErrPropConflicting`	3742	The action cannot be completed due to conflicting properties.
`adErrPropInvalidColumn`	3739	The property references an invalid column.
`adErrPropInvalidOption`	3740	The property option supplied is invalid.
`adErrPropInvalidValue`	3741	The property value supplied is invalid.
`adErrPropNotAllSettable`	3743	The property values supplied cannot all be set.
`adErrPropNotSet`	3744	The property is not set.
`adErrPropNotSettable`	3745	The property is read-only.

Table continues on the following page

Constant name	Number	Description
adErrPropNotSupported	3746	The provider does not support this property.
adErrProviderFailed	3000	The provider failed to perform the operation.
adErrProviderNotFound	3706	ADO could not find the specified provider.
adErrReadFile	3003	The supplied file could not be read.
adErrResourceExists	3731	The copy operation cannot complete, because a resource exists at the target location. To overwrite specify adCopyOverwrite.
adErrResourceLocked	3730	The requested resource is locked by another process.
adErrResourceOutOfScope	3735	Either the source or destination URL is outside the scope of the current Record.
adErrSchemaViolation	3722	The data values violate the schema (such as the data type or field constraint).
adErrSignMismatch	3723	Conversion failed due to the provider using an unsigned field, and the supplied value being signed.
adErrStillConnecting	3713	The provider is still connecting (during an asynchronous open).
adErrStillExecuting	3711	The provider is still executing a previous command (during an asynchronous fetch).
adErrTreePermission Denied	3728	Insufficient privileges to access the tree or subtree.
adErrUnavailable	3736	The operation failed and the status is unavailable.
adErrUnsafeOperation	3716	You cannot access data on another domain due to a safety setting on this computer.
adErrURLDoesNotExist	3727	The source URL or the parent of the destination does not exist.
adErrURLNamedRow DoesNotExist	3737	The Record named by this URL does not exist.
adErrVolumeNotFound	3733	The storage device in the URL cannot be located.
adErrWriteFile	3004	The write to a file failed.
adWrnSecurityDialog	3717	For internal use only. Included for completeness.
adWrnSecurityDialogHeader	3718	For internal use only. Included for completeness.

Extended Errors

The following table lists the extended ADO errors and their descriptions:

Error Number	Description
-2147483647	Not implemented.
-2147483646	Ran out of memory.
-2147483645	One or more arguments are invalid.
-2147483644	No such interface supported.
-2147483643	Invalid pointer.
-2147483642	Invalid handle.
-2147483641	Operation aborted.
-2147483640	Unspecified error.
-2147483639	General access denied error.
-2147483638	The data necessary to complete this operation is not yet available.
-2147467263	Not implemented.
-2147467262	No such interface supported.
-2147467261	Invalid pointer.
-2147467260	Operation aborted.
-2147467259	Unspecified error.
-2147467258	Thread local storage failure.
-2147467257	Get shared memory allocator failure.
-2147467256	Get memory allocator failure.
-2147467255	Unable to initialize class cache.
-2147467254	Unable to initialize RPC services.
-2147467253	Cannot set thread local storage channel control.
-2147467252	Could not allocate thread local storage channel control.
-2147467251	The user supplied memory allocator is unacceptable.
-2147467250	The OLE service mutex already exists.
-2147467249	The OLE service file mapping already exists.
-2147467248	Unable to map view of file for OLE service.

Table continues on the following page

Error Number	Description
-2147467247	Failure attempting to launch OLE service.
-2147467246	There was an attempt to call `CoInitialize` a second time while single threaded.
-2147467245	A Remote activation was necessary but was not allowed.
-2147467244	A Remote activation was necessary but the server name provided was invalid.
-2147467243	The class is configured to run as a security ID different from the caller.
-2147467242	Use of OLE1 services requiring DDE windows is disabled.
-2147467241	A RunAs specification must be <domain name>\<user name> or simply <user name>.
-2147467240	The server process could not be started. The pathname may be incorrect.
-2147467239	The server process could not be started as the configured identity. The pathname may be incorrect or unavailable.
-2147467238	The server process could not be started because the configured identity is incorrect. Check the username and password.
-2147467237	The client is not allowed to launch this server.
-2147467236	The service providing this server could not be started.
-2147467235	This computer was unable to communicate with the computer providing the server.
-2147467234	The server did not respond after being launched.
-2147467233	The registration information for this server is inconsistent or incomplete.
-2147467232	The registration information for this interface is inconsistent or incomplete.
-2147467231	The operation attempted is not supported.
-2147418113	Catastrophic failure.
-2147024891	General access denied error.
-2147024890	Invalid handle.
-2147024882	Ran out of memory.
-2147024809	One or more arguments are invalid.

OLE DB Errors

Listed below are the OLE DB errors. Although they might not be relevant for some ADO work, they are included for completeness:

Error Number	Description
-2147217920	Invalid accessor.
-2147217919	Creating another row would have exceeded the total number of active rows supported by the rowset.
-2147217918	Unable to write with a read-only accessor.
-2147217917	Given values violate the database schema.
-2147217916	Invalid row handle.
-2147217915	An object was open.
-2147217914	Invalid chapter.
-2147217913	A literal value in the command could not be converted to the correct type due to a reason other than data overflow.
-2147217912	Invalid binding info.
-2147217911	Permission denied.
-2147217910	Specified column does not contain bookmarks or chapters.
-2147217909	Some cost limits were rejected.
-2147217908	No command has been set for the command object.
-2147217907	Unable to find a query plan within the given cost limit.
-2147217906	Invalid bookmark.
-2147217905	Invalid lock mode.
-2147217904	No value given for one or more required parameters.
-2147217903	Invalid column ID.
-2147217902	Invalid ratio.
-2147217901	Invalid value.
-2147217900	The command contained one or more errors.
-2147217899	The executing command cannot be cancelled.
-2147217898	The provider does not support the specified dialect.

Table continues on the following page

Error Number	Description
-2147217897	A data source with the specified name already exists.
-2147217896	The rowset was built over a live data feed and cannot be restarted.
-2147217895	No key matching the described characteristics could be found within the current range.
-2147217894	Ownership of this tree has been given to the provider.
-2147217893	The provider is unable to determine identity for newly inserted rows.
-2147217892	No non-zero weights specified for any goals supported, so goal was rejected; current goal was not changed.
-2147217891	Requested conversion is not supported.
-2147217890	lRowsOffset would position you past either end of the rowset, regardless of the cRows value specified; cRowsObtained is 0.
-2147217889	Information was requested for a query, and the query was not set.
-2147217888	Provider called a method from IRowsetNotify in the consumer and the method has not yet returned.
-2147217887	Errors occurred.
-2147217886	A non-Null controlling IUnknown was specified and the object being created does not support aggregation.
-2147217885	A given HROW referred to a hard- or soft-deleted row.
-2147217884	The rowset does not support fetching backwards.
-2147217883	All HROWs must be released before new ones can be obtained.
-2147217882	One of the specified storage flags was not supported.
-2147217881	Invalid comparison operator.
-2147217880	The specified status flag was neither DBCOLUMNSTATUS_OK nor DBCOLUMNSTATUS_ISNULL.
-2147217879	The rowset cannot scroll backwards.
-2147217878	Invalid region handle.
-2147217877	The specified set of rows was not contiguous to or overlapping the rows in the specified watch region.
-2147217876	A transition from ALL* to MOVE* or EXTEND* was specified.
-2147217875	The specified region is not a proper subregion of the region identified by the given watch region handle.

Table continues on the following page

Error Number	Description
-2147217874	The provider does not support multi-statement commands.
-2147217873	A specified value violated the integrity constraints for a column or table.
-2147217872	The given type name was unrecognized.
-2147217871	Execution aborted because a resource limit has been reached; no results have been returned.
-2147217870	Cannot clone a Command object whose command tree contains a rowset or rowsets.
-2147217869	Cannot represent the current tree as text.
-2147217868	The specified index already exists.
-2147217867	The specified index does not exist.
-2147217866	The specified index was in use.
-2147217865	The specified table does not exist.
-2147217864	The rowset was using optimistic concurrency and the value of a column has been changed since it was last read.
-2147217863	Errors were detected during the copy.
-2147217862	A specified precision was invalid.
-2147217861	A specified scale was invalid.
-2147217860	Invalid table ID.
-2147217859	A specified type was invalid.
-2147217858	A column ID occurred more than once in the specification.
-2147217857	The specified table already exists.
-2147217856	The specified table was in use.
-2147217855	The specified locale ID was not supported.
-2147217854	The specified record number is invalid.
-2147217853	Although the bookmark was validly formed, no row could be found to match it.
-2147217852	The value of a property was invalid.
-2147217851	The rowset was not chaptered.
-2147217850	Invalid accessor.

Table continues on the following page

Error Number	Description
-2147217849	Invalid storage flags.
-2147217848	By-ref accessors are not supported by this provider.
-2147217847	Null accessors are not supported by this provider.
-2147217846	The command was not prepared.
-2147217845	The specified accessor was not a parameter accessor.
-2147217844	The given accessor was write-only.
-2147217843	Authentication failed.
-2147217842	The change was canceled during notification; no columns are changed.
-2147217841	The rowset was single-chaptered and the chapter was not released.
-2147217840	Invalid source handle.
-2147217839	The provider cannot derive parameter info and SetParameterInfo has not been called.
-2147217838	The data source object is already initialized.
-2147217837	The provider does not support this method.
-2147217836	The number of rows with pending changes has exceeded the set limit.
-2147217835	The specified column did not exist.
-2147217834	There are pending changes on a row with a reference count of zero.
-2147217833	A literal value in the command overflowed the range of the type of the associated column.
-2147217832	The supplied HRESULT was invalid.
-2147217831	The supplied LookupID was invalid.
-2147217830	The supplied DynamicErrorID was invalid.
-2147217829	Unable to get visible data for a newly inserted row that has not yet been updated.
-2147217828	Invalid conversion flag.
-2147217827	The given parameter name was unrecognized.
-2147217826	Multiple storage objects cannot be opened simultaneously.
-2147217825	Cannot open requested filter.
-2147217824	Cannot open requested order.
-2147217823	Invalid tuple.

Table continues on the following page

Error Number	Description
-2147217822	Invalid coordinate.
-2147217821	Invalid axis for this dataset.
-2147217820	One or more cell ordinals are invalid.
-2147217819	Invalid columnID.
-2147217817	Command does not have a DBID.
-2147217816	DBID already exists.
-2147217815	Maximum number of sessions supported by the provider already created. Consumer must release one or more currently held sessions before obtaining a new session object.
-2147217814	Invalid trustee value.
-2147217813	Trustee is not for the current data source.
-2147217812	Trustee does not support memberships/collections.
-2147217811	Object is invalid or unknown to the provider.
-2147217810	No owner exists for the object.
-2147217809	Invalid access entry list.
-2147217808	Trustee supplied as owner is invalid or unknown to the provider.
-2147217807	Invalid permission in the access entry list.
-2147217806	Invalid index ID.
-2147217805	Initialization string does not conform to specification.
-2147217804	OLE DB root enumerator did not return any providers that matched any requested SOURCES_TYPE.
-2147217803	Initialization string specifies a provider that does not match the currently active provider.
-2147217802	Invalid DBID.
-2147217801	ConstraintType is invalid or not supported by the provider.
-2147217800	ConstraintType is not DBCONSTRAINTTYPE_FOREIGNKEY and cForeignKeyColumns is not zero.
-2147217799	Deferability is invalid or the value is not supported by the provider.
-2147217798	MatchType is invalid or the value is not supported by the provider.
-2147217782	UpdateRule or DeleteRule is invalid or the value is not supported by the provider.

Table continues on the following page

Error Number	Description
-2147217781	pConstraintID does not exist in the data source.
-2147217780	Invalid dwFlags.
-2147217779	rguidColumnType points to a GUID that does not match the object type of this column, or this column was not set.
-2147217778	URL is out of scope.
-2147217776	Provider cannot drop the object.
-2147217775	No source row.
-2147217774	OLE DB object represented by this URL is locked by one or more other processes.
-2147217773	Client requested an object type that is valid only for a collection.
-2147217772	Caller requested write access to a read-only object.
-2147217771	Provider does not support asynchronous binding.
-2147217770	Provider cannot connect to server for this object.
-2147217769	Attempt to bind to the object timed out.
-2147217768	Provider cannot create an object at this URL because an object named by this URL already exists.
-2147217767	Constraint already exists.
-2147217766	Provider cannot create an object at this URL because the server is out of physical storage.
-2147217765	Unsafe operation was attempted in safe mode. Provider denied this operation.
265920	Fetching requested number of rows would have exceeded total number of active rows supported by the rowset.
265921	One or more column types are incompatible; conversion errors will occur during copying.
265922	Parameter type information has been overridden by caller.
265923	Skipped bookmark for deleted or non-member row.
265924	Errors found in validating tree.
265925	There are no more rowsets.
265926	Reached start or end of rowset or chapter.
265927	The provider re-executed the command.

Table continues on the following page

Error Number	Description
265928	Variable data buffer full.
265929	There are no more results.
265930	Server cannot release or downgrade a lock until the end of the transaction.
265931	Specified weight was not supported or exceeded the supported limit and was set to 0 or the supported limit.
265932	Consumer is uninterested in receiving further notification calls for this operation.
265933	Input dialect was ignored and text was returned in different dialect.
265934	Consumer is uninterested in receiving further notification calls for this phase.
265935	Consumer is uninterested in receiving further notification calls for this reason.
265936	Operation is being processed asynchronously.
265937	In order to reposition to the start of the rowset, the provider had to re-execute the query; either the order of the columns changed or columns were added to or removed from the rowset.
265938	The method had some errors; errors have been returned in the error array.
265939	Invalid row handle.
265940	A given HROW referred to a hard-deleted row.
265941	The provider was unable to keep track of all the changes; the client must re-fetch the data associated with the watch region using another method.
265942	Execution stopped because a resource limit has been reached; results obtained so far have been returned but execution cannot be resumed.
265943	Method requested a singleton result but multiple rows are selected by the command or rowset. First row is returned.
265944	A lock was upgraded from the value specified.
265945	One or more properties were changed as allowed by provider.
265946	Errors occurred.
265947	A specified parameter was invalid.
265948	Updating this row caused more than one row to be updated in the data source.
265949	Row has no row-specific columns.

Index

(continued)

(continued)

(continued)

S

T

X

forums.apress.com

JOIN THE APRESS FORUMS AND BE PART OF OUR COMMUNITY. You'll find discussions that cover topics of interest to IT professionals, programmers, and enthusiasts just like you. If you post a query to one of our forums, you can expect that some of the best minds in the business—especially Apress authors, who all write with *The Expert's Voice*™—will chime in to help you. Why not aim to become one of our most valuable participants (MVPs) and win cool stuff? Here's a sampling of what you'll find:

DATABASES
Data drives everything.
Share information, exchange ideas, and discuss any database programming or administration issues.

PROGRAMMING/BUSINESS
Unfortunately, it is.
Talk about the Apress line of books that cover software methodology, best practices, and how programmers interact with the "suits."

INTERNET TECHNOLOGIES AND NETWORKING
Try living without plumbing (and eventually IPv6).
Talk about networking topics including protocols, design, administration, wireless, wired, storage, backup, certifications, trends, and new technologies.

WEB DEVELOPMENT/DESIGN
Ugly doesn't cut it anymore, and CGI is absurd.
Help is in sight for your site. Find design solutions for your projects and get ideas for building an interactive Web site.

JAVA
We've come a long way from the old Oak tree.
Hang out and discuss Java in whatever flavor you choose: J2SE, J2EE, J2ME, Jakarta, and so on.

SECURITY
Lots of bad guys out there—the good guys need help.
Discuss computer and network security issues here. Just don't let anyone else know the answers!

MAC OS X
All about the Zen of OS X.
OS X is both the present and the future for Mac apps. Make suggestions, offer up ideas, or boast about your new hardware.

TECHNOLOGY IN ACTION
Cool things. Fun things.
It's after hours. It's time to play. Whether you're into LEGO® MINDSTORMS™ or turning an old PC into a DVR, this is where technology turns into fun.

OPEN SOURCE
Source code is good; understanding (open) source is better.
Discuss open source technologies and related topics such as PHP, MySQL, Linux, Perl, Apache, Python, and more.

WINDOWS
No defenestration here.
Ask questions about all aspects of Windows programming, get help on Microsoft technologies covered in Apress books, or provide feedback on any Apress Windows book.

HOW TO PARTICIPATE:
Go to the Apress Forums site at **http://forums.apress.com/**.
Click the New User link.

ASP Today

ASPToday is a unique solutions library for professional ASP Developers, giving quick and convenient access to a constantly growing library of **over 1000 practical and relevant articles and case studies**. We aim to publish a completely original professionally written and reviewed article every working day of the year. Consequently our resource is completely without parallel in the industry. Thousands of web developers use and recommend this site for real solutions, keeping up to date with new technologies, or simply increasing their knowledge.

Exciting Site Features!

Find it FAST!
Powerful full-text search engine so you can find exactly the solution you need.

Printer-friendly!
Print articles for a bound archive and quick desk reference.

Working Sample Code Solutions!
Many articles include complete downloadable sample code ready to adapt for your own projects.

ASPToday covers a broad range of topics including:

► ASP.NET 1.x and 2.0
► ADO.NET and SQL
► XML
► Web Services
► E-Commerce

► Security
► Site Design
► Site Admin
► SMTP and Mail
► Classic ASP and ADO

and much, much more…

To receive a FREE two-month subscription to ASPToday, visit **www.asptoday.com/subscribe.aspx** and answer the question about this book!